E.X.O.™

The Legend of Wale Williams

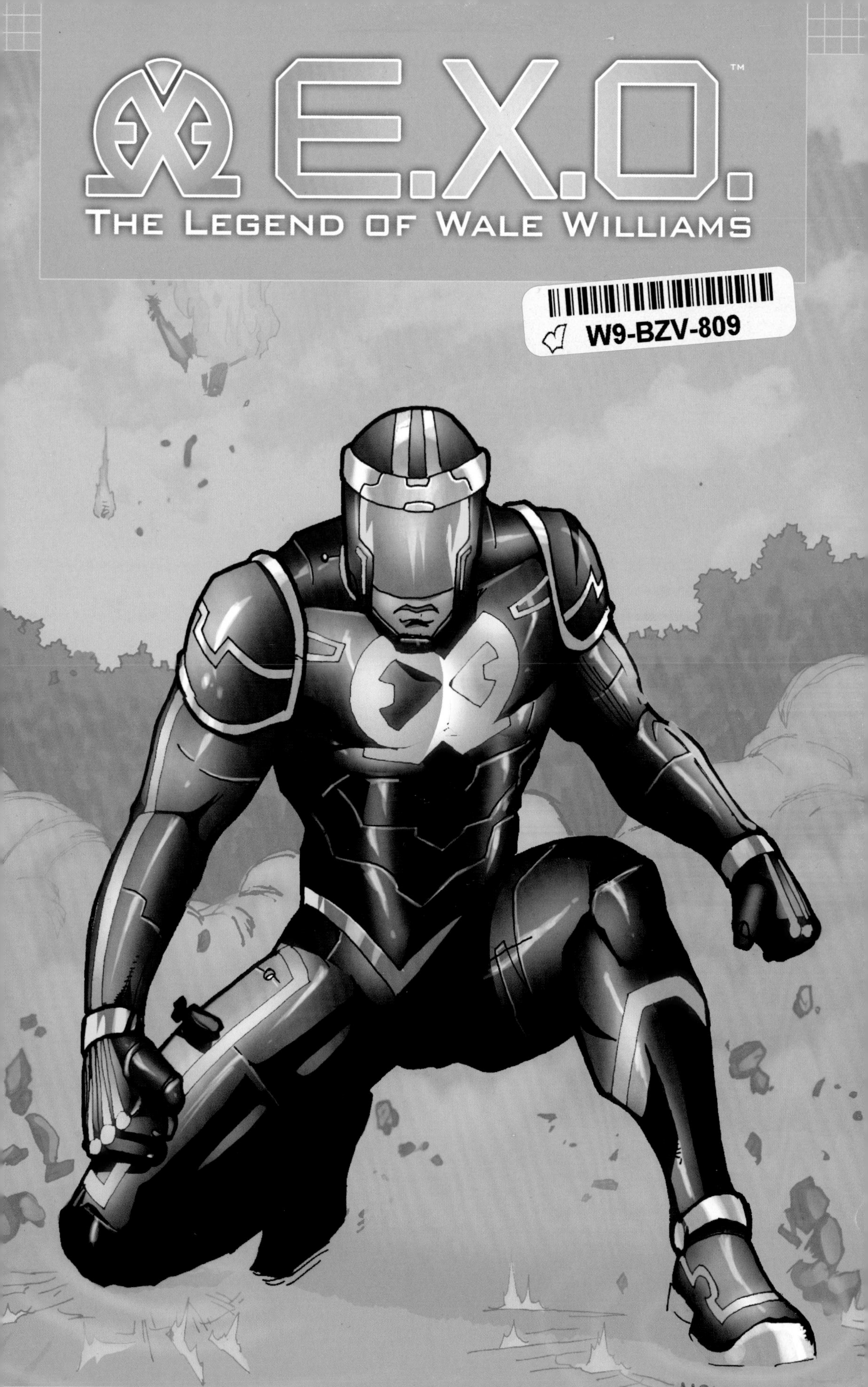

E.X.O.™

THE LEGEND OF WALE WILLIAMS

VOLUME ONE

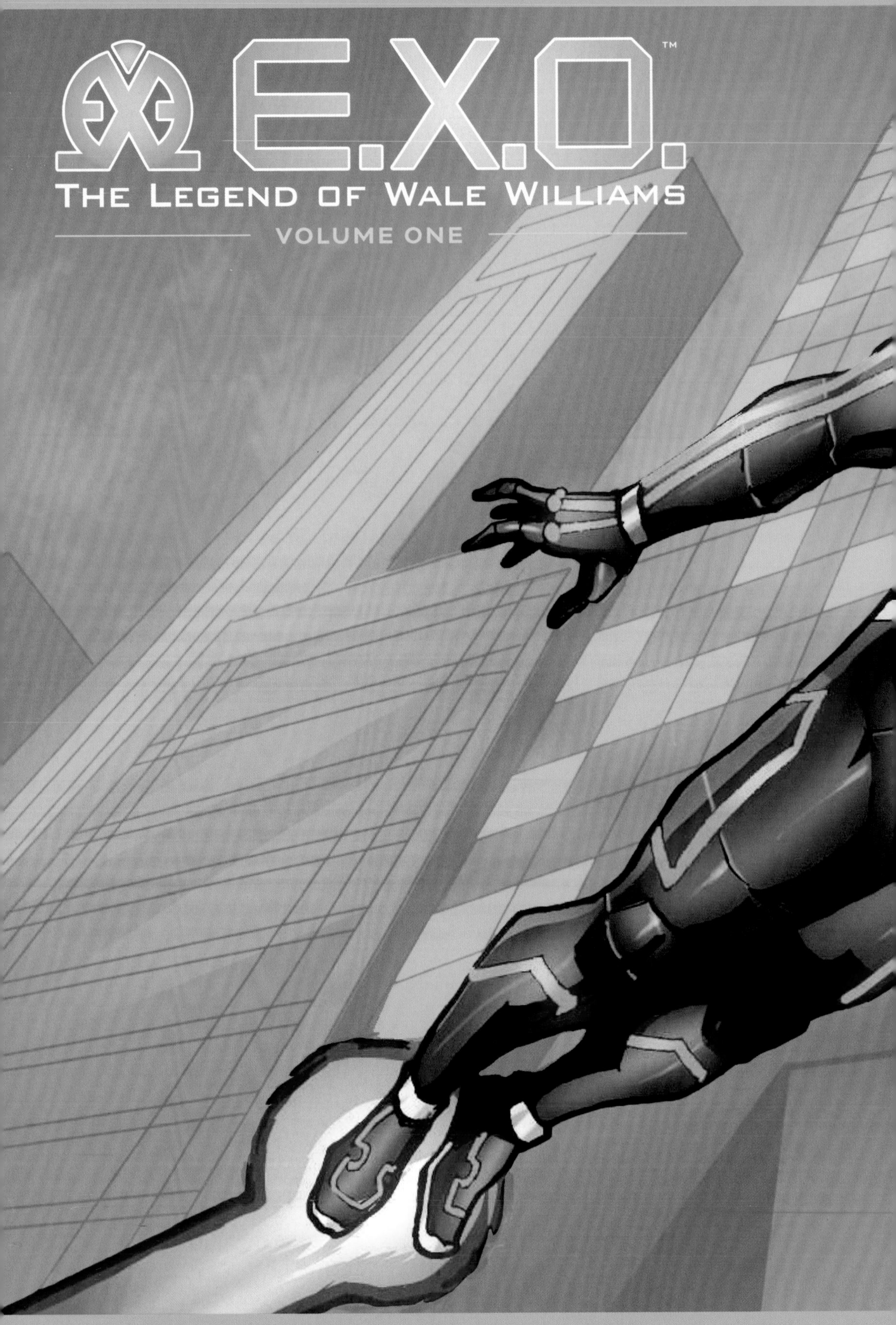

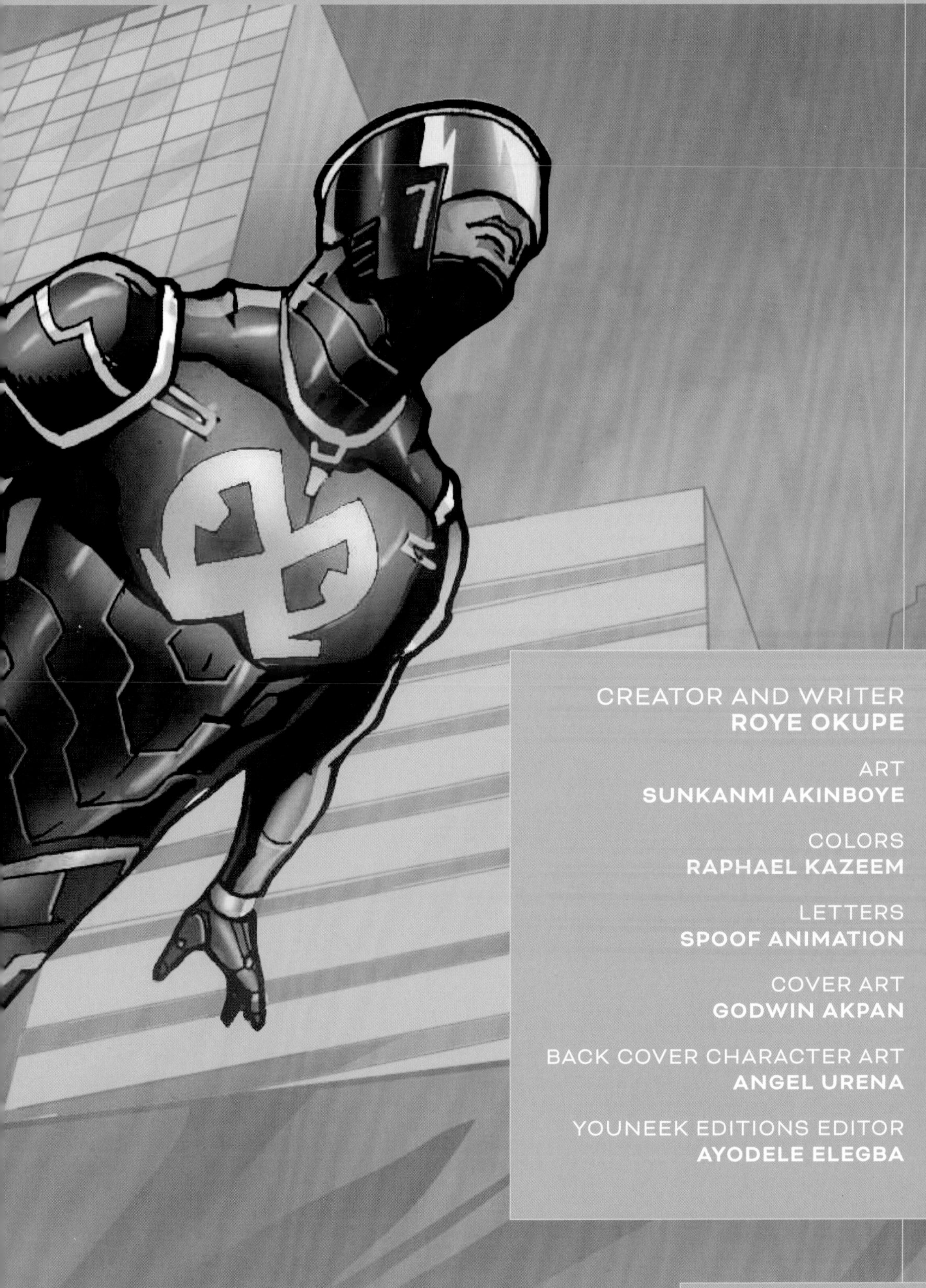

CREATOR AND WRITER
ROYE OKUPE

ART
SUNKANMI AKINBOYE

COLORS
RAPHAEL KAZEEM

LETTERS
SPOOF ANIMATION

COVER ART
GODWIN AKPAN

BACK COVER CHARACTER ART
ANGEL URENA

YOUNEEK EDITIONS EDITOR
AYODELE ELEGBA

YOUNEEK STUDIOS

DARK HORSE BOOKS

PUBLISHER
MIKE RICHARDSON

SENIOR EDITOR
PHILIP R. SIMON

ASSOCIATE EDITOR
JUDY KHUU

ASSISTANT EDITOR
ROSE WEITZ

DESIGNER
KATHLEEN BARNETT

DIGITAL ART TECHNICIAN
ADAM PRUETT

E.X.O.: THE LEGEND OF WALE WILLIAMS VOLUME 1

This volume features all story pages from E.X.O.: *The Legend of Wale Williams* Volumes 1 and 2 (published by YouNeek Studios in 2016) with completely remastered and re-lettered story pages, and also collects the one-shot story "Malika: Creed & Fury," originally published by YouNeek Studios for Free Comic Book Day 2018.

Published by Dark Horse Books
A division of Dark Horse Comics LLC
10956 SE Main Street Milwaukie, OR 97222
DarkHorse.com

To find a comics shop in your area, visit comicshoplocator.com

Library of Congress Cataloging-in-Publication Data

Names: Okupe, Roye, writer. | Akinboye, Sunkanmi, artist. | Kazeem, Raphael, colourist. | Spoof Animation, letterer.
Title: E.X.O. : the legend of Wale Williams / writer, Roye Okupe ; artist, Sunkanmi Akinboye ; colors, Raphael Kazeem ; letters, Spoof Animation.
Description: Milwaukie, OR : Dark Horse Books, 2021. | Summary: "A superhero story about redemption, set in a futuristic 2025 Africa! Wale Wiliams, an impetuous young man who inherits a suit with super powers after his father goes missing is tricked into returning home to Lagoon City, Nigeria following a five year absence. Wale embarks on a journey to investigate his father's mysterious disappearance. As he comes to understand the suit's powers, Wale realizes he must restore hope to his city by preventing catastrophic attacks from the sociopathic Oniku, the leader of an extremist group called the CREED."
Identifiers: LCCN 2021013841 | ISBN 9781506723020 (trade paperback)
Subjects: LCSH: Superheroes--Comic books, strips, etc. | Nigeria--Comic books, strips, etc. | Graphic novels.
Classification: LCC PN6790.N563 O584 2021 | DDC 741.5/9669--dc23
LC record available at https://lccn.loc.gov/2021013841

First edition: October 2021

eBook ISBN 978-1-50672-312-9
Trade Paperback ISBN 978-1-50672-302-0

10 9 8 7 6 5 4 3 2 1

Printed in China

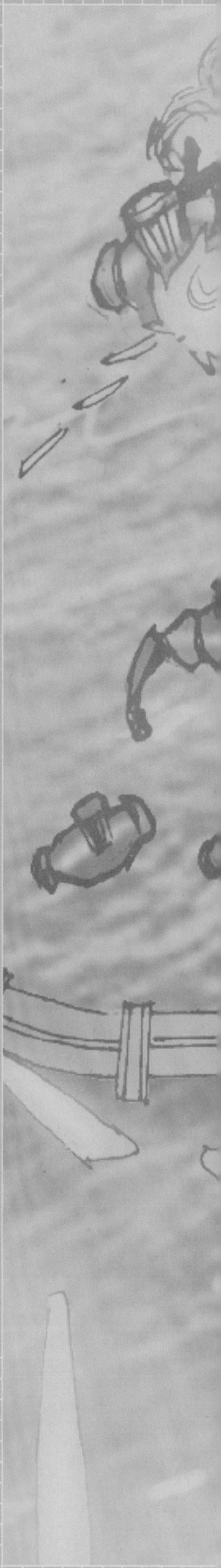

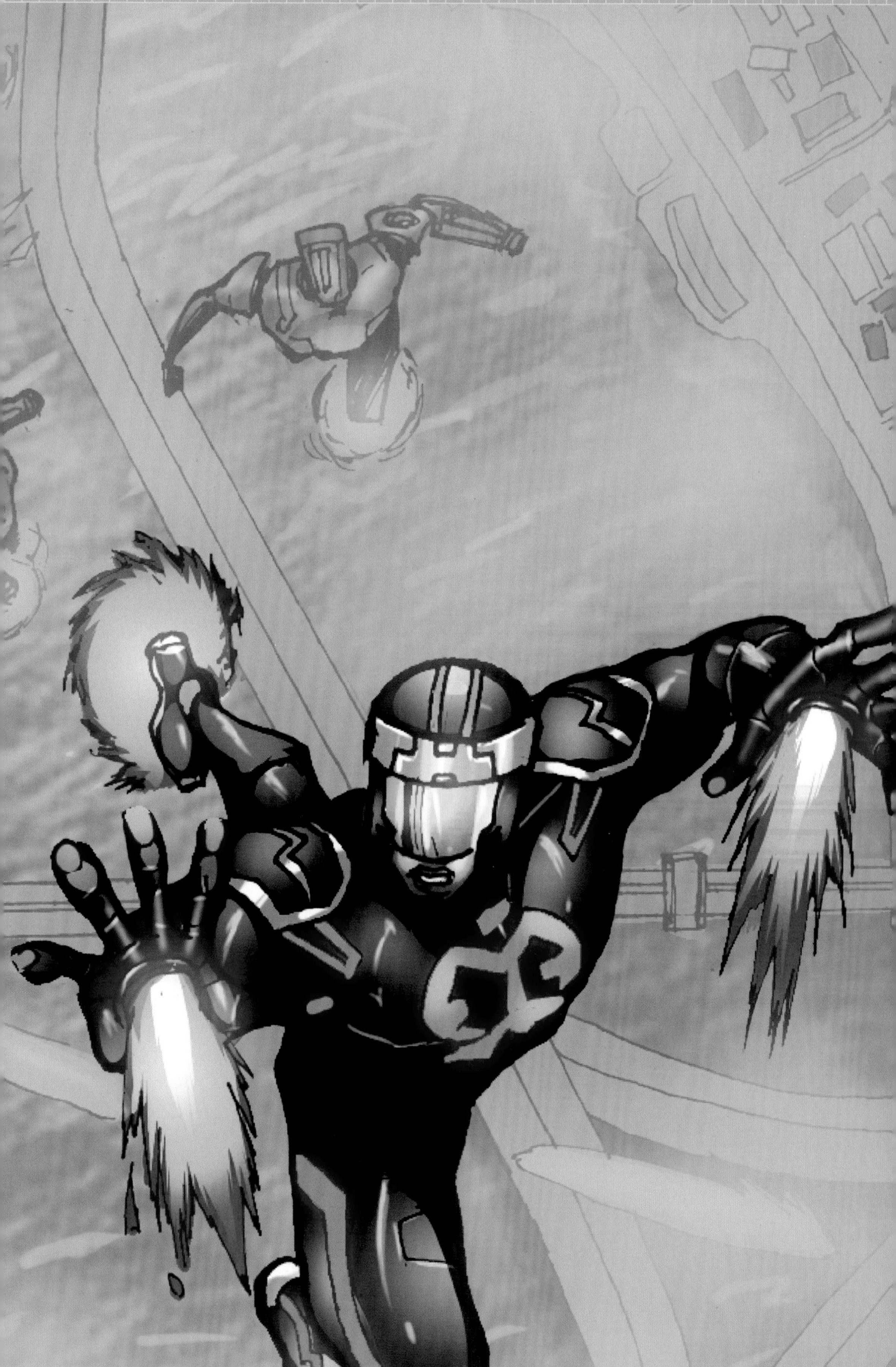

Arise, O Compatriots,
Nigeria's call obey
To serve our Fatherland
With love and strength and faith.
The labour of our heroes past,
    shall never be in vain
To serve with heart and might,
One Nation bound in freedom,
    peace, and unity.
—NATIONAL ANTHEM OF NIGERIA

CHAPTER ONE

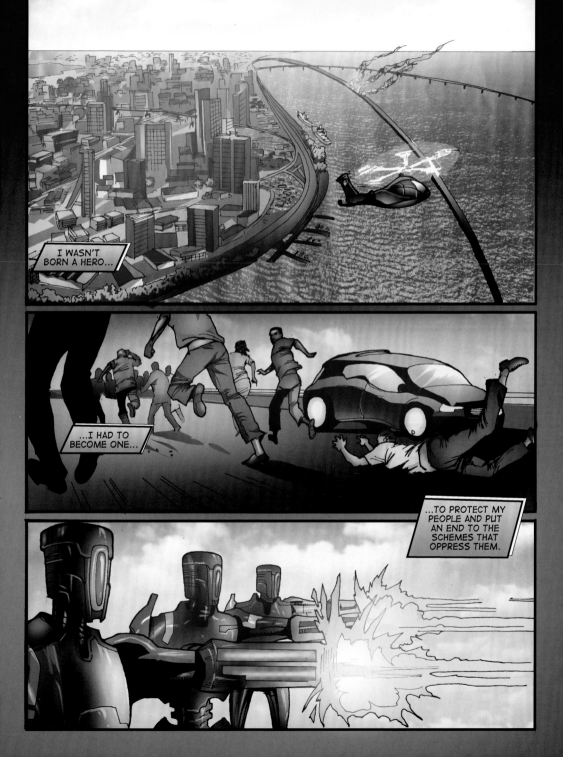

LAGOON CITY,
LAGOS, NIGERIA, 2025.

I WASN'T
BORN A HERO...

...I HAD TO
BECOME ONE...

...TO PROTECT MY
PEOPLE AND PUT
AN END TO THE
SCHEMES THAT
OPPRESS THEM.

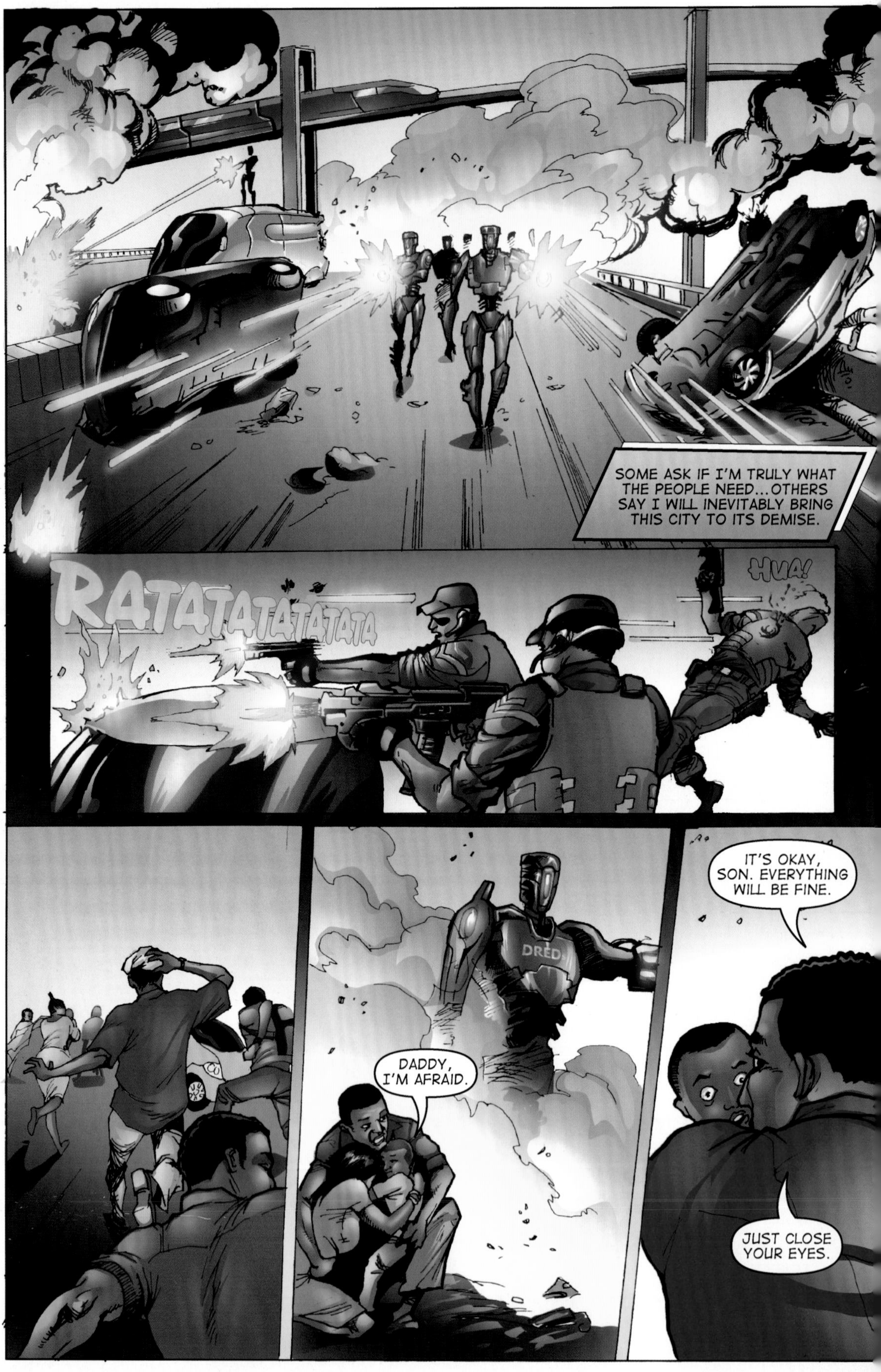
SOME ASK IF I'M TRULY WHAT THE PEOPLE NEED...OTHERS SAY I WILL INEVITABLY BRING THIS CITY TO ITS DEMISE.
RATATATATATATA
HUA!
DRED
DADDY, I'M AFRAID.
IT'S OKAY, SON. EVERYTHING WILL BE FINE.
JUST CLOSE YOUR EYES.

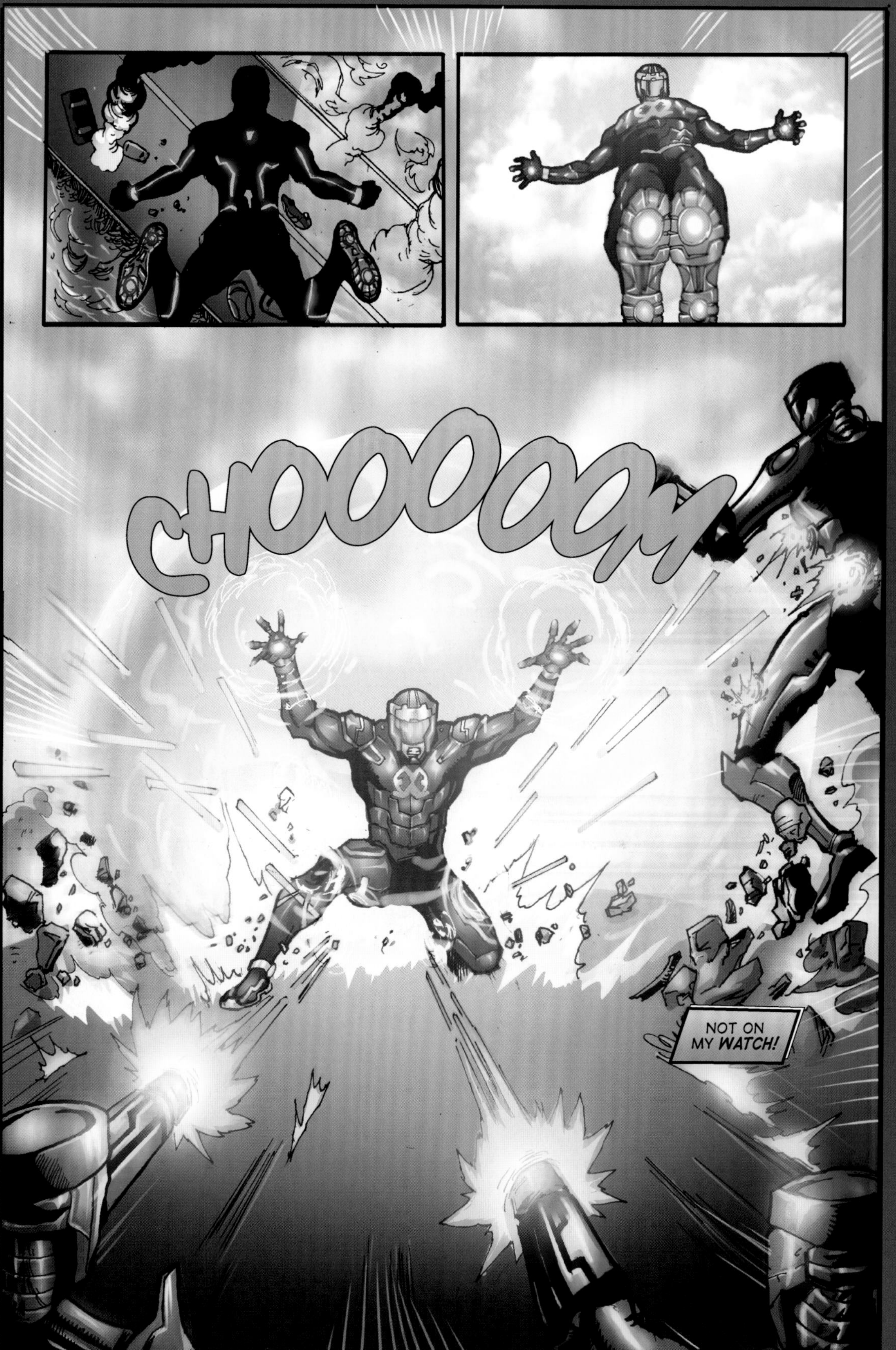
CHOOOOOM
NOT ON MY WATCH!

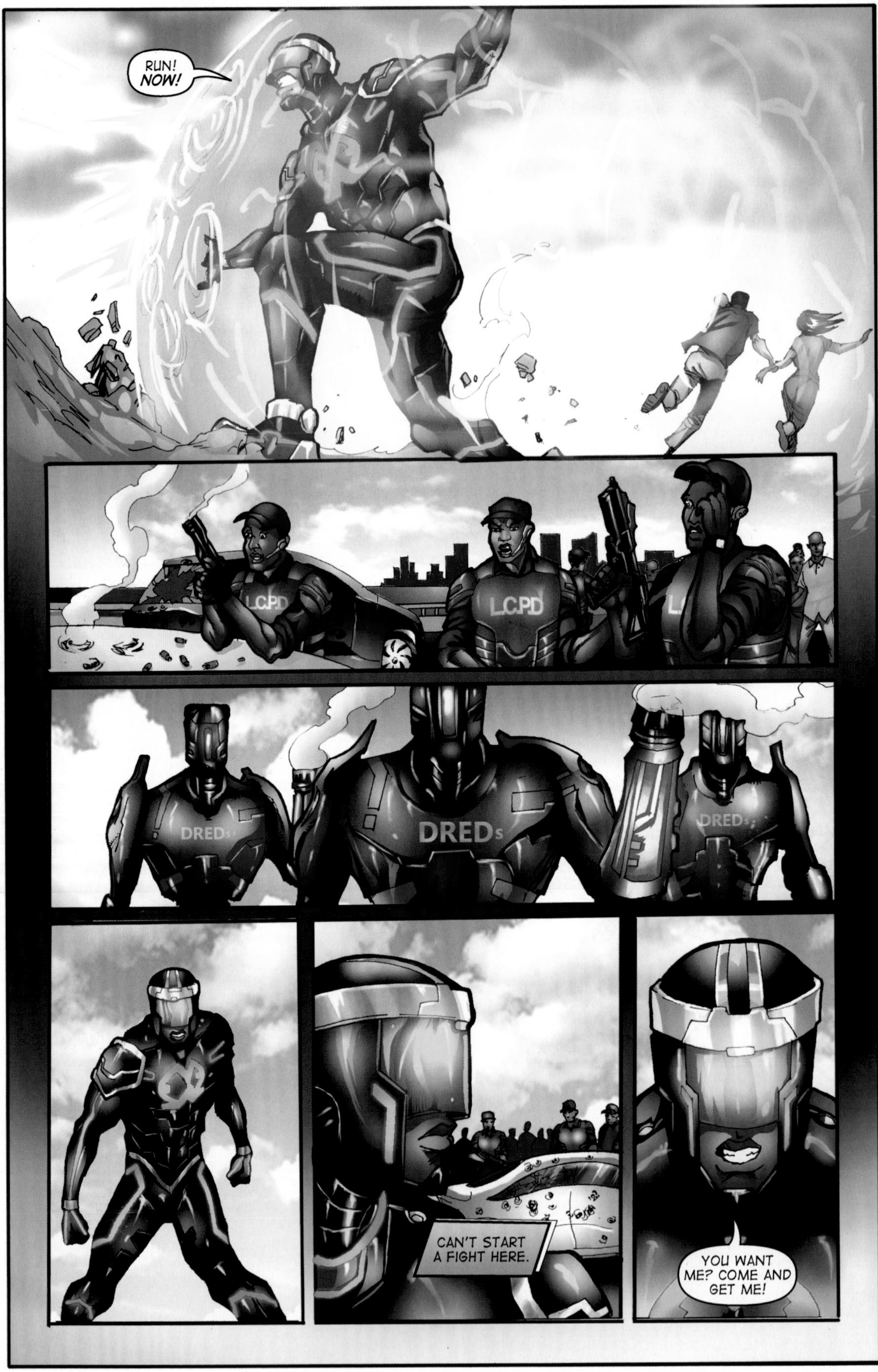
RUN! NOW!
L.C.P.D
L.C.P.D
DREDs
DREDs
DREDs
CAN'T START A FIGHT HERE.
YOU WANT ME? COME AND GET ME!

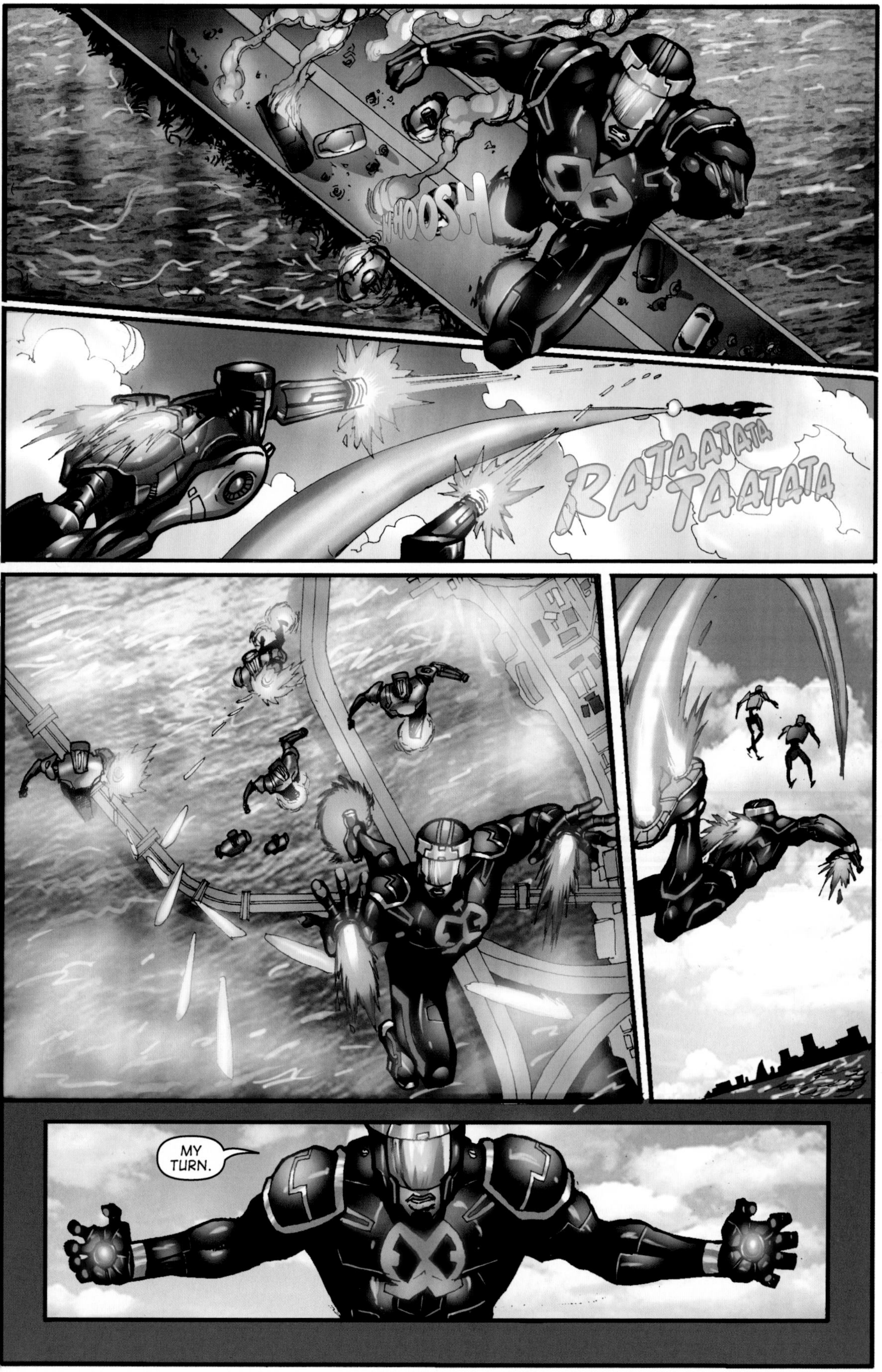
WHOOSH
RATAATATA
TAATATA
MY TURN.

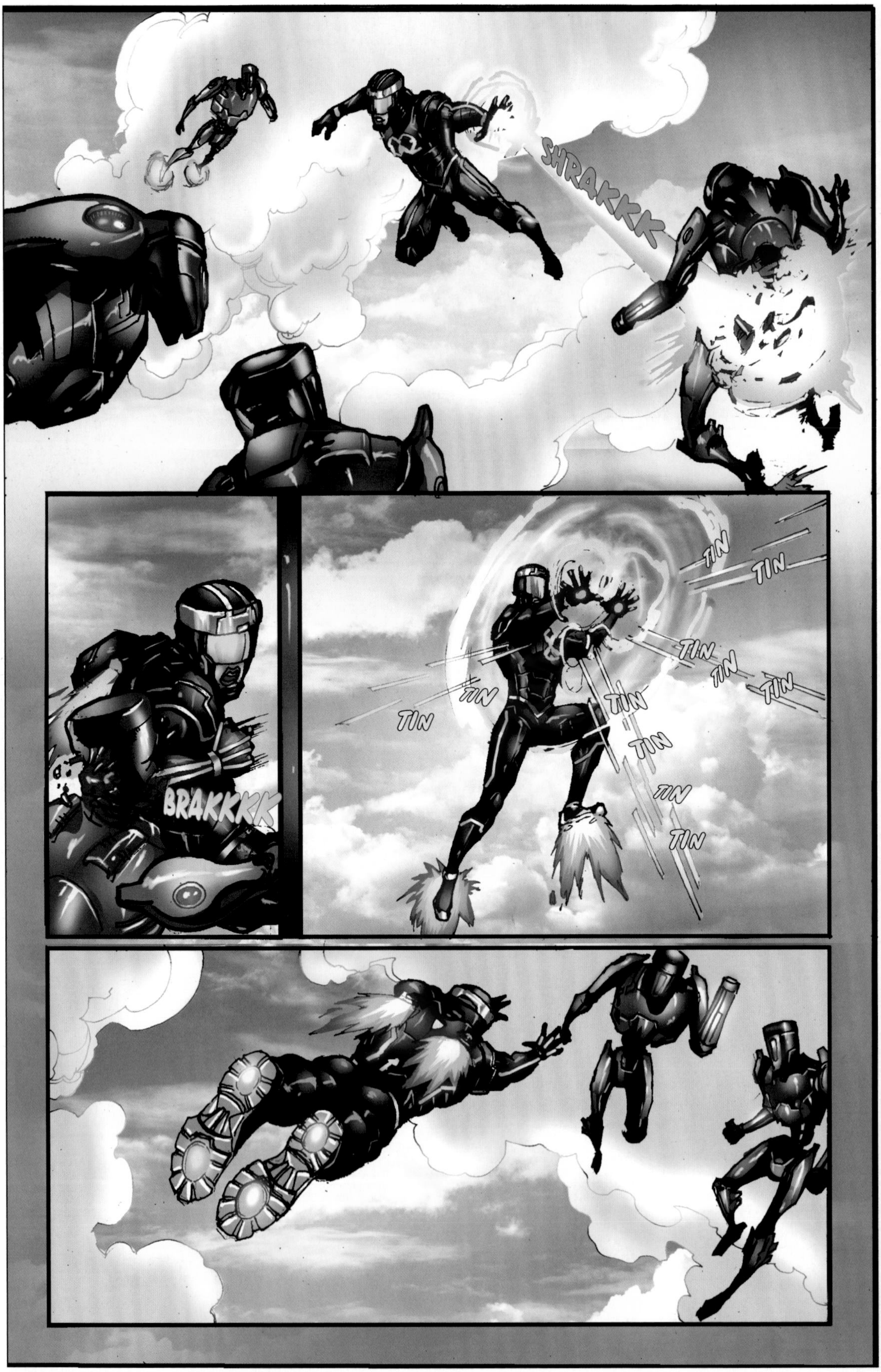
SHRAKKK
BRAKKKK
TIN
TIN
TIN
TIN
TIN
TIN
TIN
TIN
TIN
TIN
TIN

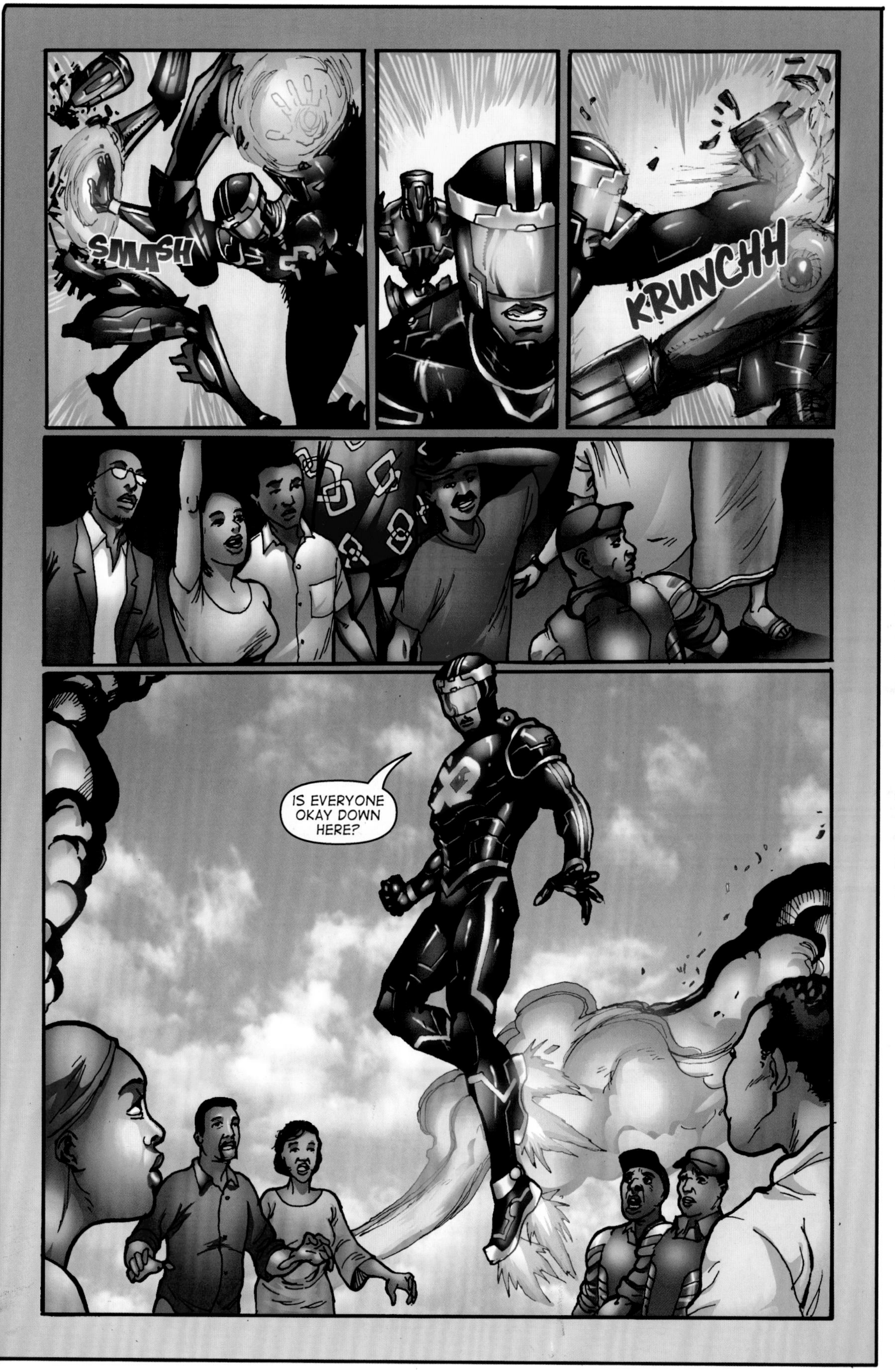
SMASH
KRUNCHH
IS EVERYONE OKAY DOWN HERE?

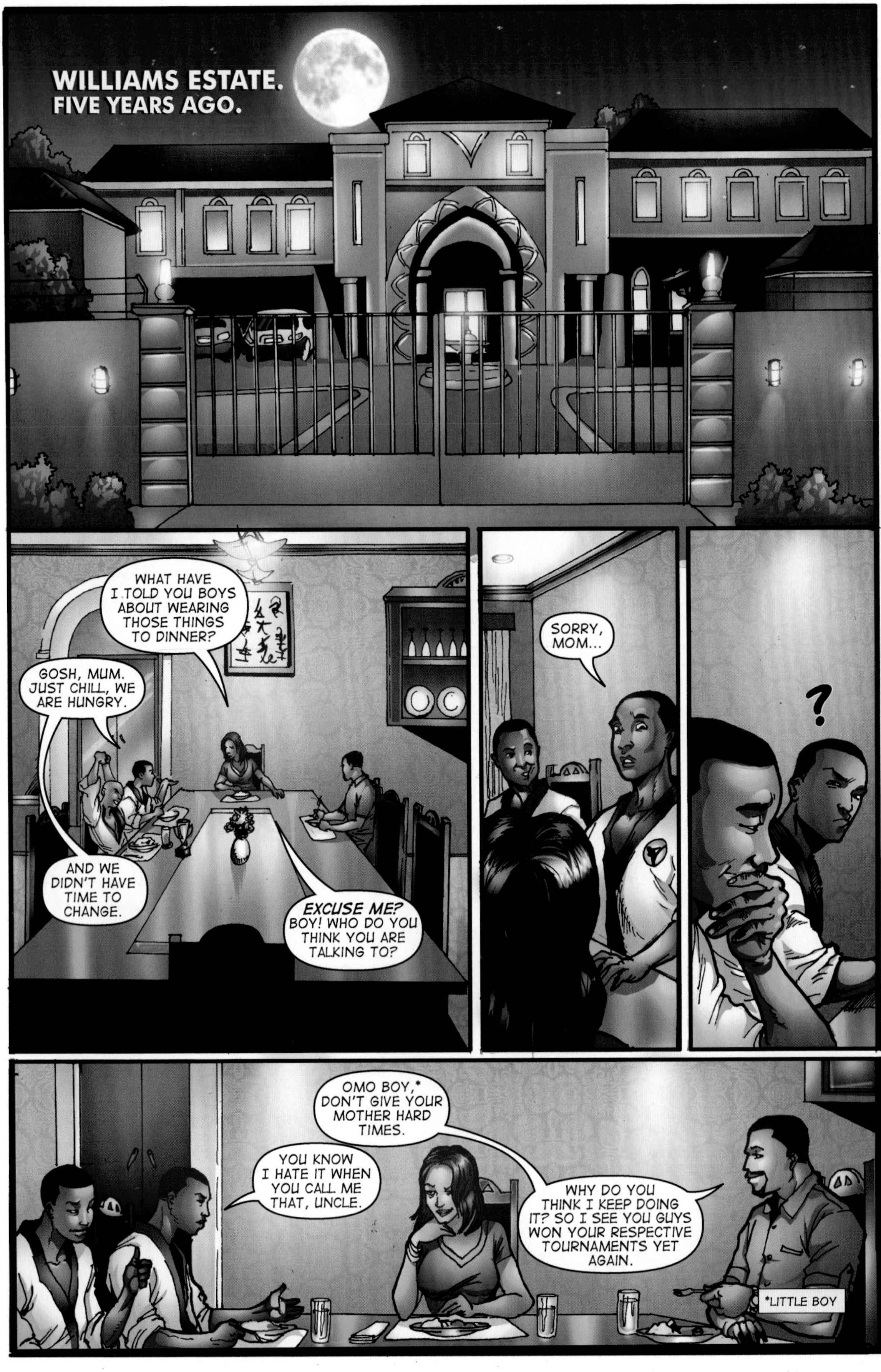
WILLIAMS ESTATE.
FIVE YEARS AGO.
WHAT HAVE I TOLD YOU BOYS ABOUT WEARING THOSE THINGS TO DINNER?
GOSH, MUM. JUST CHILL, WE ARE HUNGRY.
AND WE DIDN'T HAVE TIME TO CHANGE.
EXCUSE ME? BOY! WHO DO YOU THINK YOU ARE TALKING TO?
SORRY, MOM...
?
OMO BOY,* DON'T GIVE YOUR MOTHER HARD TIMES.
YOU KNOW I HATE IT WHEN YOU CALL ME THAT, UNCLE.
WHY DO YOU THINK I KEEP DOING IT? SO I SEE YOU GUYS WON YOUR RESPECTIVE TOURNAMENTS YET AGAIN.
*LITTLE BOY

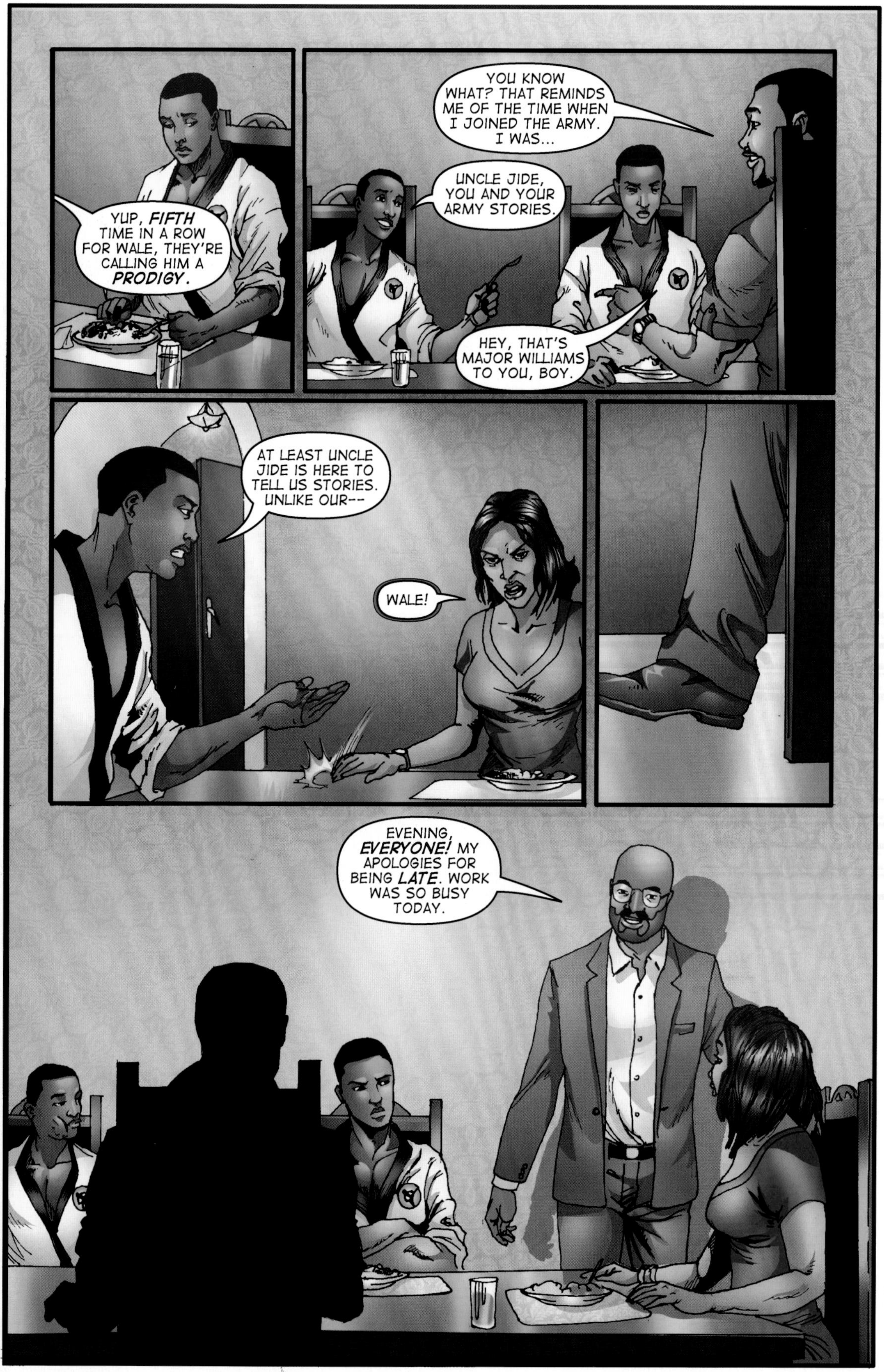

YUP, FIFTH TIME IN A ROW FOR WALE, THEY'RE CALLING HIM A PRODIGY.
YOU KNOW WHAT? THAT REMINDS ME OF THE TIME WHEN I JOINED THE ARMY. I WAS...
UNCLE JIDE, YOU AND YOUR ARMY STORIES.
HEY, THAT'S MAJOR WILLIAMS TO YOU, BOY.
AT LEAST UNCLE JIDE IS HERE TO TELL US STORIES. UNLIKE OUR--
WALE!
EVENING, EVERYONE! MY APOLOGIES FOR BEING LATE. WORK WAS SO BUSY TODAY.

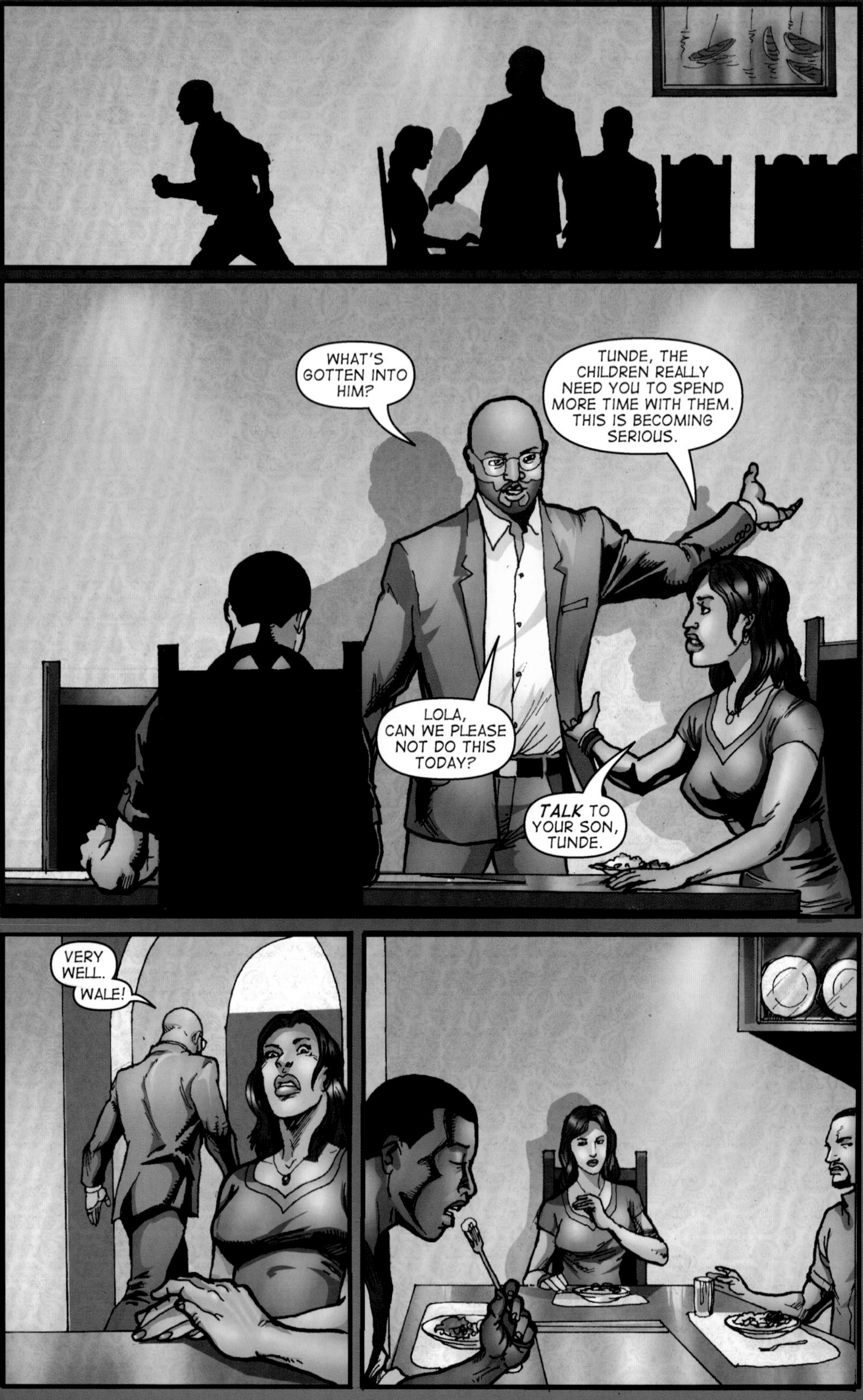
WHAT'S GOTTEN INTO HIM?
TUNDE, THE CHILDREN REALLY NEED YOU TO SPEND MORE TIME WITH THEM. THIS IS BECOMING SERIOUS.
LOLA, CAN WE PLEASE NOT DO THIS TODAY?
TALK TO YOUR SON, TUNDE.
VERY WELL.
WALE!

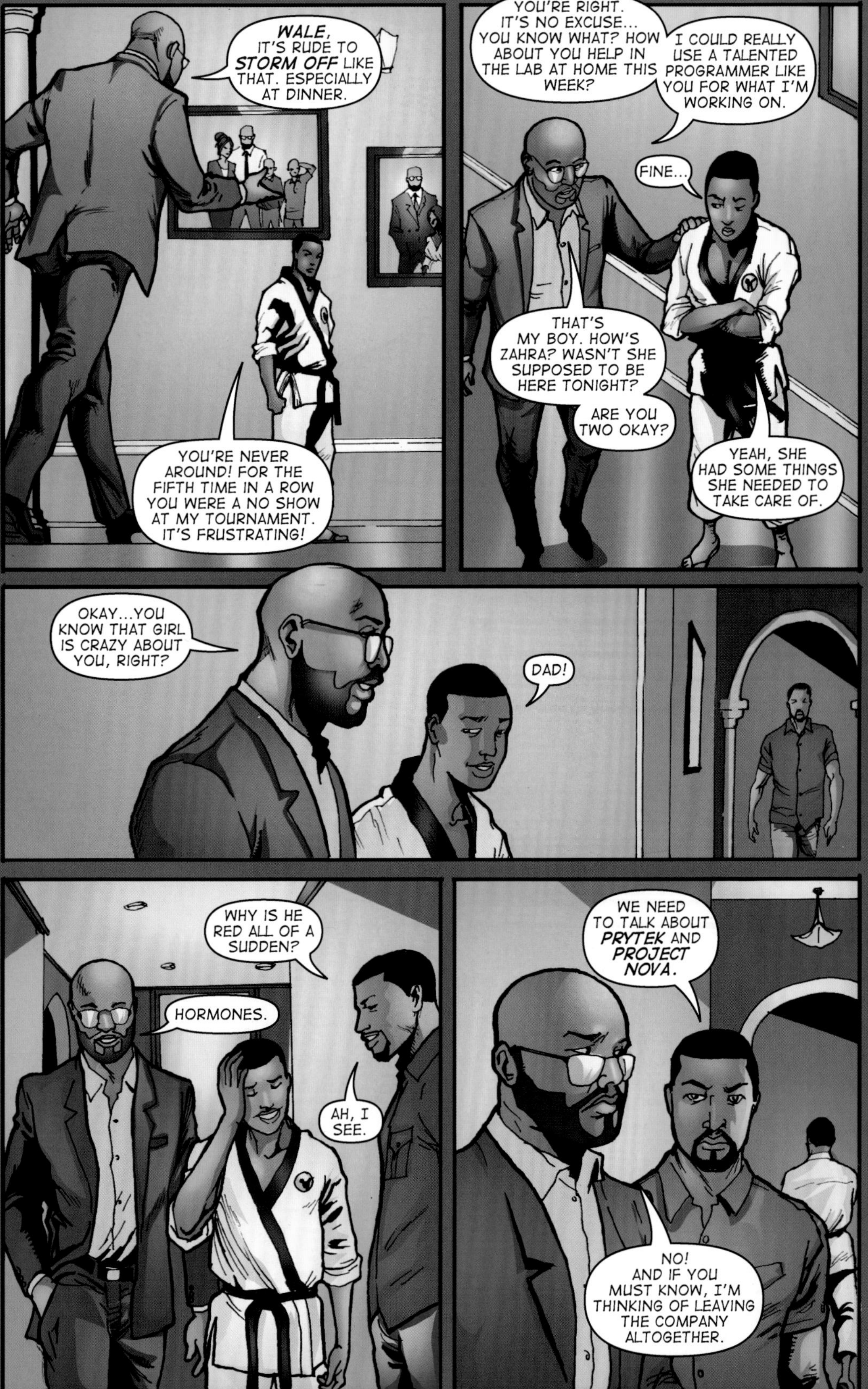
WALE, IT'S RUDE TO STORM OFF LIKE THAT. ESPECIALLY AT DINNER.
YOU'RE NEVER AROUND! FOR THE FIFTH TIME IN A ROW YOU WERE A NO SHOW AT MY TOURNAMENT. IT'S FRUSTRATING!
YOU'RE RIGHT. IT'S NO EXCUSE... YOU KNOW WHAT? HOW ABOUT YOU HELP IN THE LAB AT HOME THIS WEEK?
I COULD REALLY USE A TALENTED PROGRAMMER LIKE YOU FOR WHAT I'M WORKING ON.
FINE...
THAT'S MY BOY. HOW'S ZAHRA? WASN'T SHE SUPPOSED TO BE HERE TONIGHT?
ARE YOU TWO OKAY?
YEAH, SHE HAD SOME THINGS SHE NEEDED TO TAKE CARE OF.
OKAY...YOU KNOW THAT GIRL IS CRAZY ABOUT YOU, RIGHT?
DAD!
WHY IS HE RED ALL OF A SUDDEN?
HORMONES.
AH, I SEE.
WE NEED TO TALK ABOUT PRYTEK AND PROJECT NOVA.
NO! AND IF YOU MUST KNOW, I'M THINKING OF LEAVING THE COMPANY ALTOGETHER.

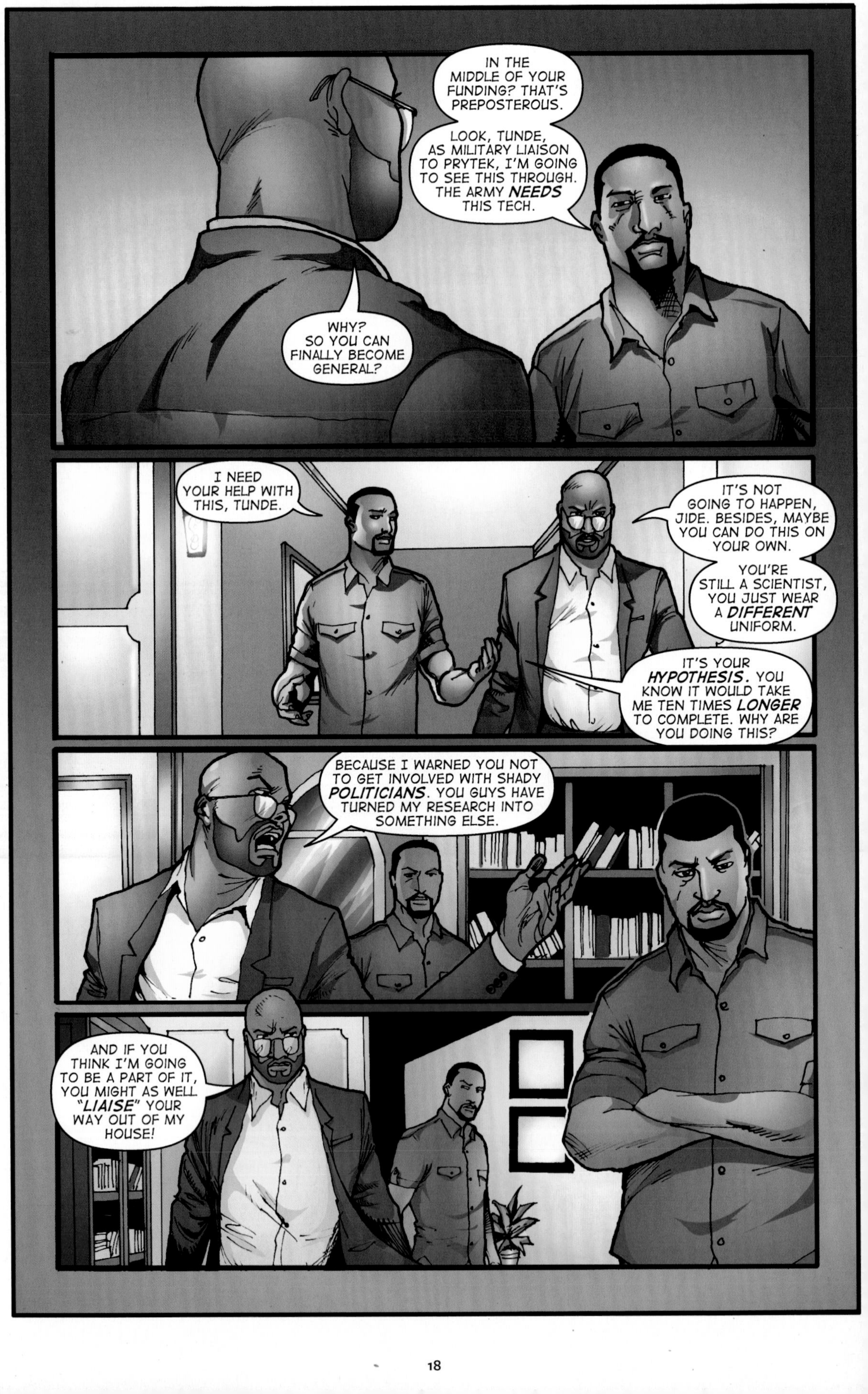
IN THE MIDDLE OF YOUR FUNDING? THAT'S PREPOSTEROUS.
LOOK, TUNDE, AS MILITARY LIAISON TO PRYTEK, I'M GOING TO SEE THIS THROUGH. THE ARMY ***NEEDS*** THIS TECH.
WHY? SO YOU CAN FINALLY BECOME GENERAL?
I NEED YOUR HELP WITH THIS, TUNDE.
IT'S NOT GOING TO HAPPEN, JIDE. BESIDES, MAYBE YOU CAN DO THIS ON YOUR OWN.
YOU'RE STILL A SCIENTIST, YOU JUST WEAR A ***DIFFERENT*** UNIFORM.
IT'S YOUR ***HYPOTHESIS.*** YOU KNOW IT WOULD TAKE ME TEN TIMES ***LONGER*** TO COMPLETE. WHY ARE YOU DOING THIS?
BECAUSE I WARNED YOU NOT TO GET INVOLVED WITH SHADY ***POLITICIANS***. YOU GUYS HAVE TURNED MY RESEARCH INTO SOMETHING ELSE.
AND IF YOU THINK I'M GOING TO BE A PART OF IT, YOU MIGHT AS WELL "***LIAISE***" YOUR WAY OUT OF MY HOUSE!

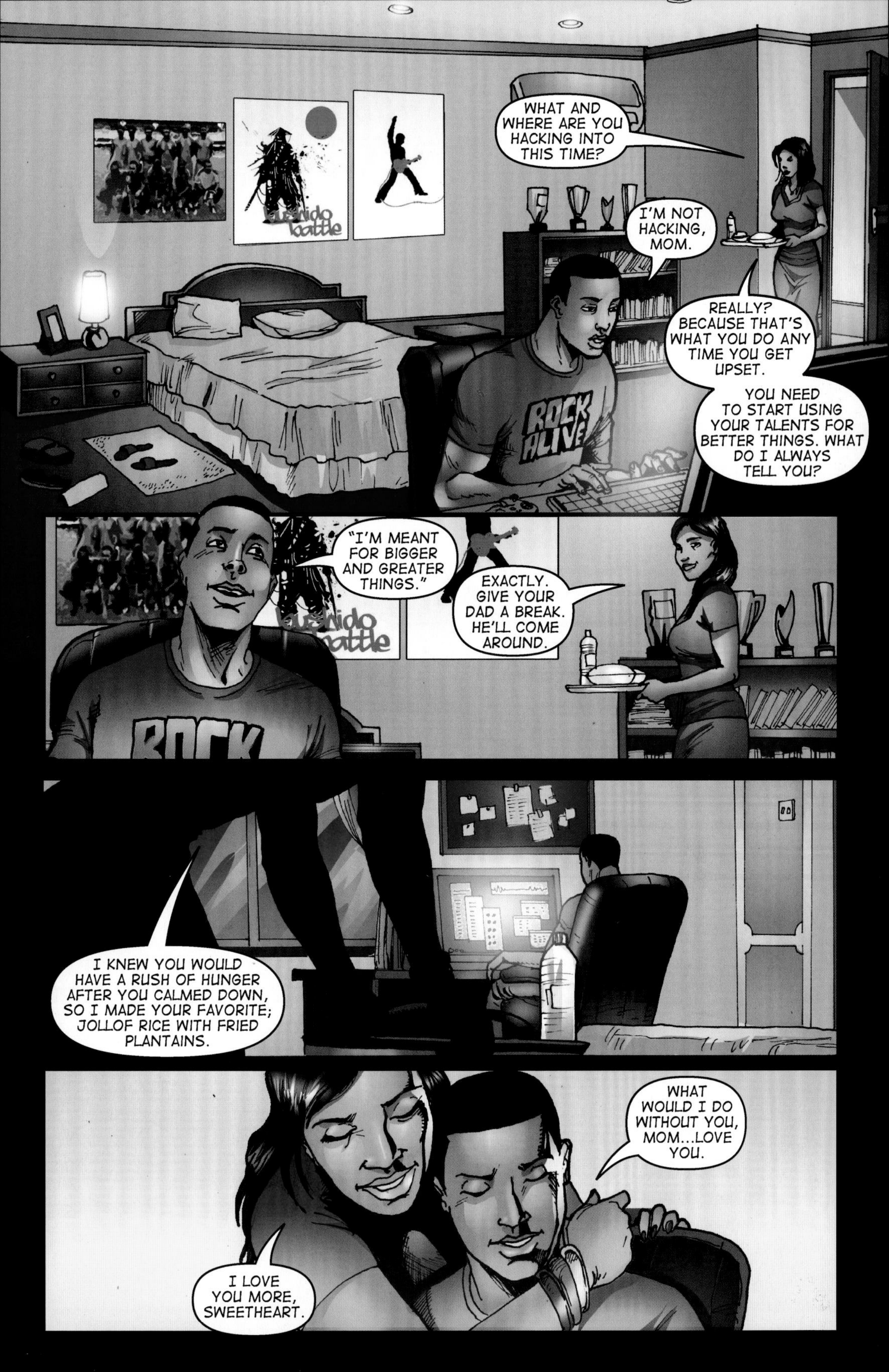
bushido battle
WHAT AND WHERE ARE YOU HACKING INTO THIS TIME?
I'M NOT HACKING, MOM.
REALLY? BECAUSE THAT'S WHAT YOU DO ANY TIME YOU GET UPSET.
YOU NEED TO START USING YOUR TALENTS FOR BETTER THINGS. WHAT DO I ALWAYS TELL YOU?
ROCK ALIVE
"I'M MEANT FOR BIGGER AND GREATER THINGS."
EXACTLY. GIVE YOUR DAD A BREAK. HE'LL COME AROUND.
I KNEW YOU WOULD HAVE A RUSH OF HUNGER AFTER YOU CALMED DOWN, SO I MADE YOUR FAVORITE; JOLLOF RICE WITH FRIED PLANTAINS.
WHAT WOULD I DO WITHOUT YOU, MOM...LOVE YOU.
I LOVE YOU MORE, SWEETHEART.

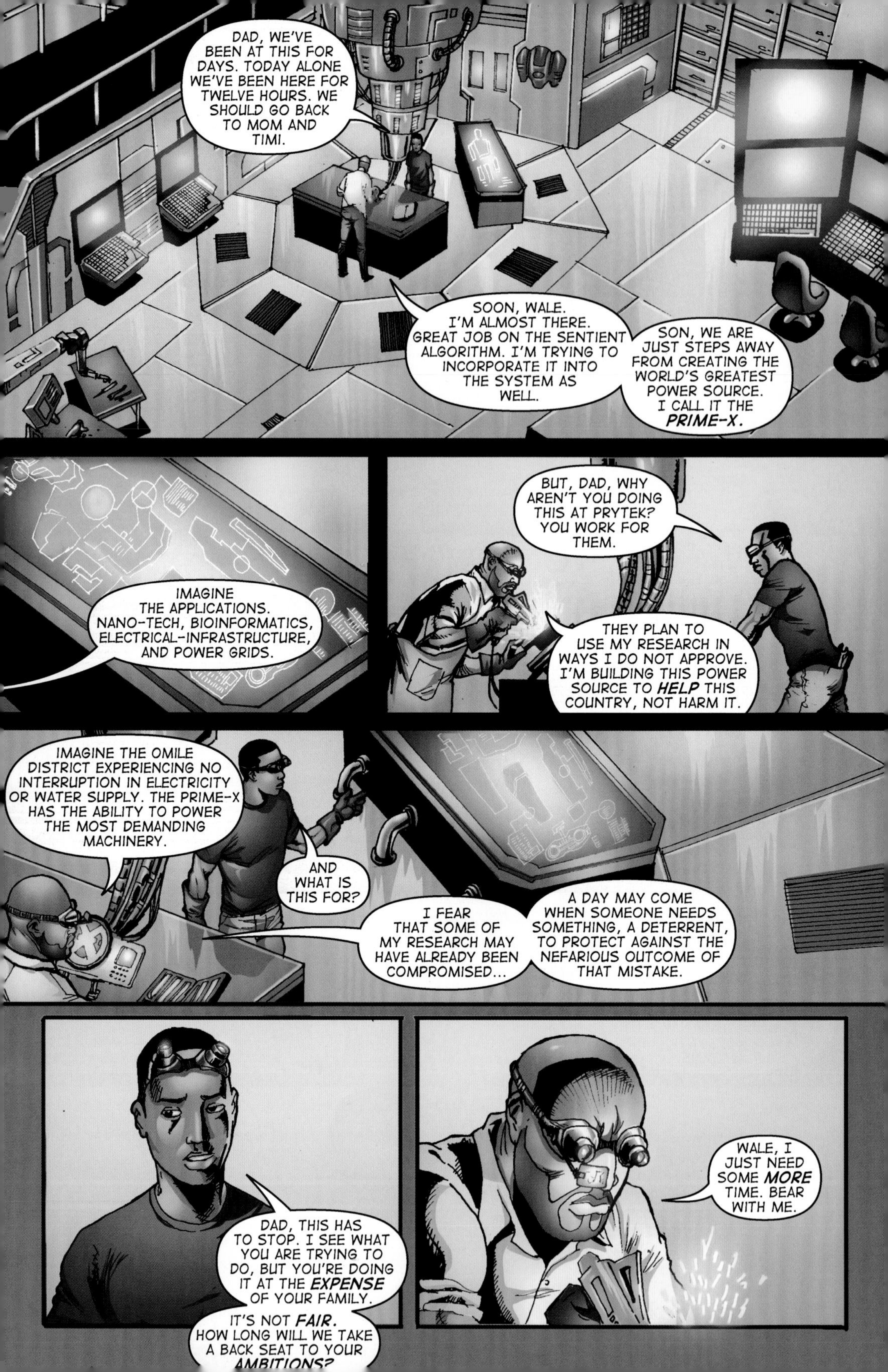
DAD, WE'VE BEEN AT THIS FOR DAYS. TODAY ALONE WE'VE BEEN HERE FOR TWELVE HOURS. WE SHOULD GO BACK TO MOM AND TIMI.
SOON, WALE. I'M ALMOST THERE. GREAT JOB ON THE SENTIENT ALGORITHM. I'M TRYING TO INCORPORATE IT INTO THE SYSTEM AS WELL.
SON, WE ARE JUST STEPS AWAY FROM CREATING THE WORLD'S GREATEST POWER SOURCE. I CALL IT THE *PRIME-X*.
IMAGINE THE APPLICATIONS. NANO-TECH, BIOINFORMATICS, ELECTRICAL-INFRASTRUCTURE, AND POWER GRIDS.
BUT, DAD, WHY AREN'T YOU DOING THIS AT PRYTEK? YOU WORK FOR THEM.
THEY PLAN TO USE MY RESEARCH IN WAYS I DO NOT APPROVE. I'M BUILDING THIS POWER SOURCE TO *HELP* THIS COUNTRY, NOT HARM IT.
IMAGINE THE OMILE DISTRICT EXPERIENCING NO INTERRUPTION IN ELECTRICITY OR WATER SUPPLY. THE PRIME-X HAS THE ABILITY TO POWER THE MOST DEMANDING MACHINERY.
AND WHAT IS THIS FOR?
I FEAR THAT SOME OF MY RESEARCH MAY HAVE ALREADY BEEN COMPROMISED...
A DAY MAY COME WHEN SOMEONE NEEDS SOMETHING, A DETERRENT, TO PROTECT AGAINST THE NEFARIOUS OUTCOME OF THAT MISTAKE.
DAD, THIS HAS TO STOP. I SEE WHAT YOU ARE TRYING TO DO, BUT YOU'RE DOING IT AT THE *EXPENSE* OF YOUR FAMILY.
IT'S NOT *FAIR*. HOW LONG WILL WE TAKE A BACK SEAT TO YOUR *AMBITIONS?*
WALE, I JUST NEED SOME *MORE* TIME. BEAR WITH ME.

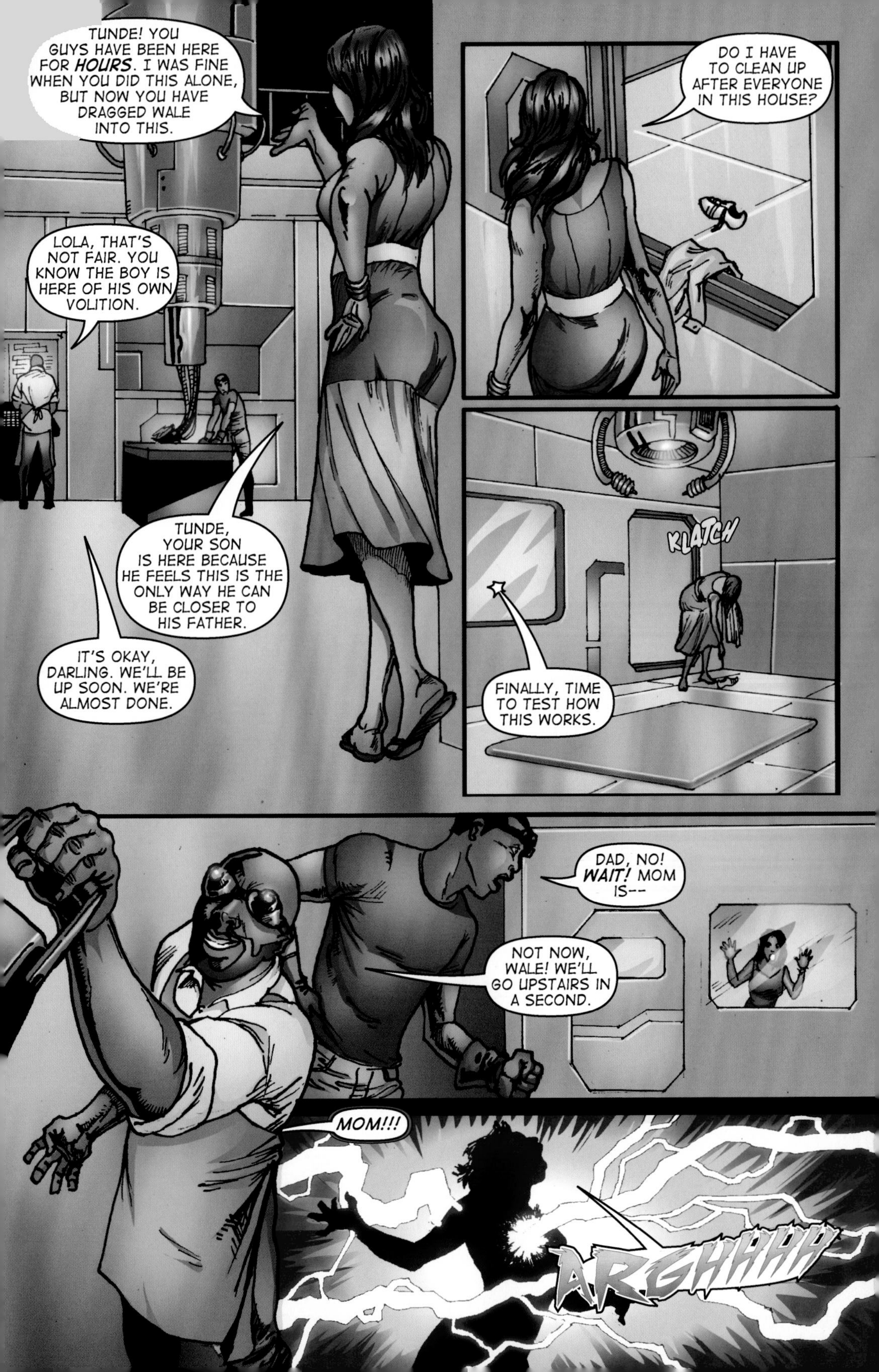
TUNDE! YOU GUYS HAVE BEEN HERE FOR ***HOURS***. I WAS FINE WHEN YOU DID THIS ALONE, BUT NOW YOU HAVE DRAGGED WALE INTO THIS.
LOLA, THAT'S NOT FAIR. YOU KNOW THE BOY IS HERE OF HIS OWN VOLITION.
TUNDE, YOUR SON IS HERE BECAUSE HE FEELS THIS IS THE ONLY WAY HE CAN BE CLOSER TO HIS FATHER.
IT'S OKAY, DARLING. WE'LL BE UP SOON. WE'RE ALMOST DONE.
DO I HAVE TO CLEAN UP AFTER EVERYONE IN THIS HOUSE?
KLATCH
FINALLY, TIME TO TEST HOW THIS WORKS.
DAD, NO! ***WAIT!*** MOM IS--
NOT NOW, WALE! WE'LL GO UPSTAIRS IN A SECOND.
MOM!!!
ARGHHHH

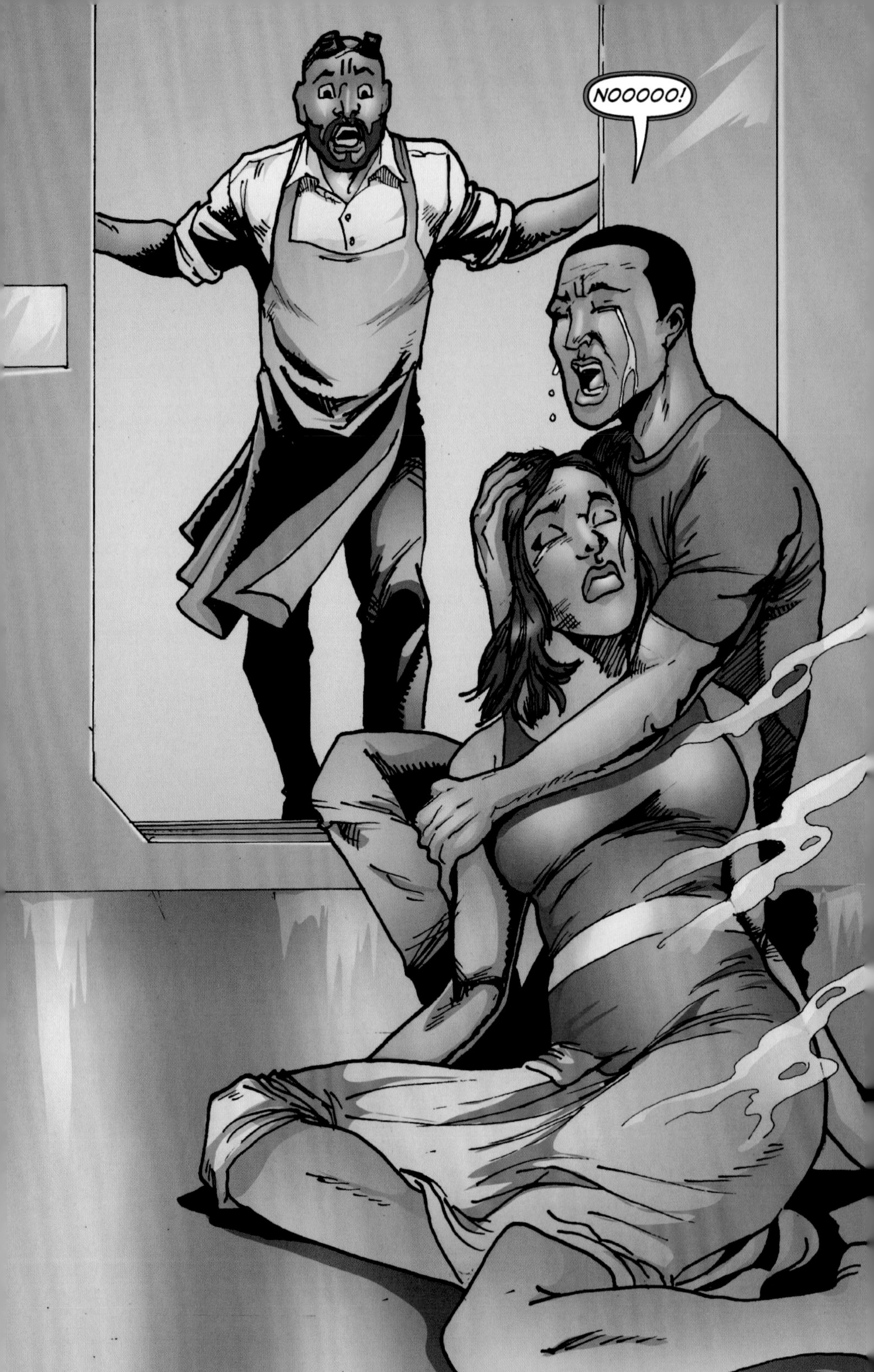
NOOOOO!

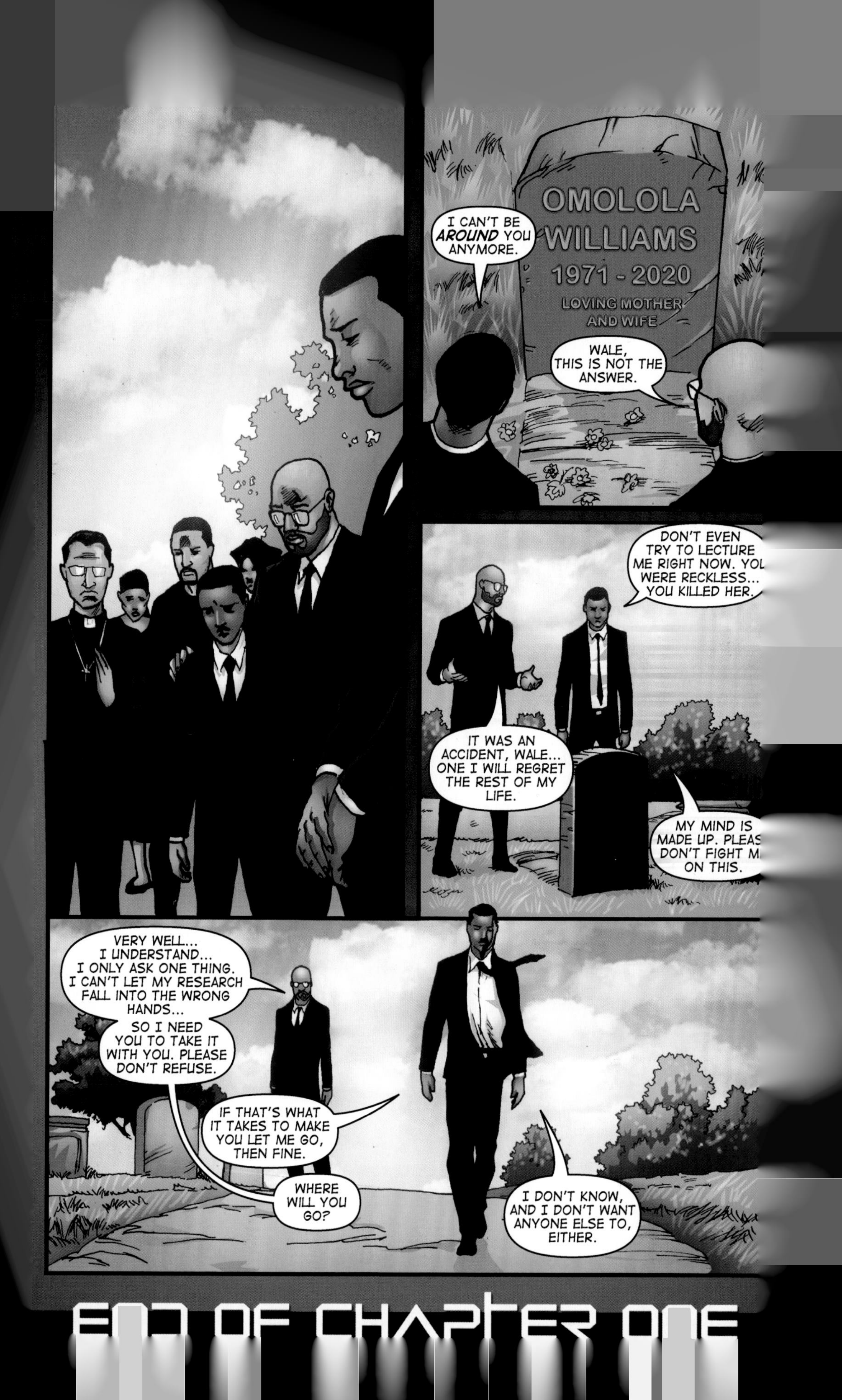
OMOLOLA WILLIAMS
1971 - 2020
LOVING MOTHER AND WIFE
I CAN'T BE *AROUND* YOU ANYMORE.
WALE, THIS IS NOT THE ANSWER.
DON'T EVEN TRY TO LECTURE ME RIGHT NOW. YOU WERE RECKLESS... YOU KILLED HER.
IT WAS AN ACCIDENT, WALE... ONE I WILL REGRET THE REST OF MY LIFE.
MY MIND IS MADE UP. PLEASE DON'T FIGHT ME ON THIS.
VERY WELL... I UNDERSTAND... I ONLY ASK ONE THING. I CAN'T LET MY RESEARCH FALL INTO THE WRONG HANDS...
SO I NEED YOU TO TAKE IT WITH YOU. PLEASE DON'T REFUSE.
IF THAT'S WHAT IT TAKES TO MAKE YOU LET ME GO, THEN FINE.
WHERE WILL YOU GO?
I DON'T KNOW, AND I DON'T WANT ANYONE ELSE TO, EITHER.

END OF CHAPTER ONE

"I wasn't born a hero . . .
I had to become one."
—EXO

CHAPTER TWO   2025, BACK TO THE PRESENT

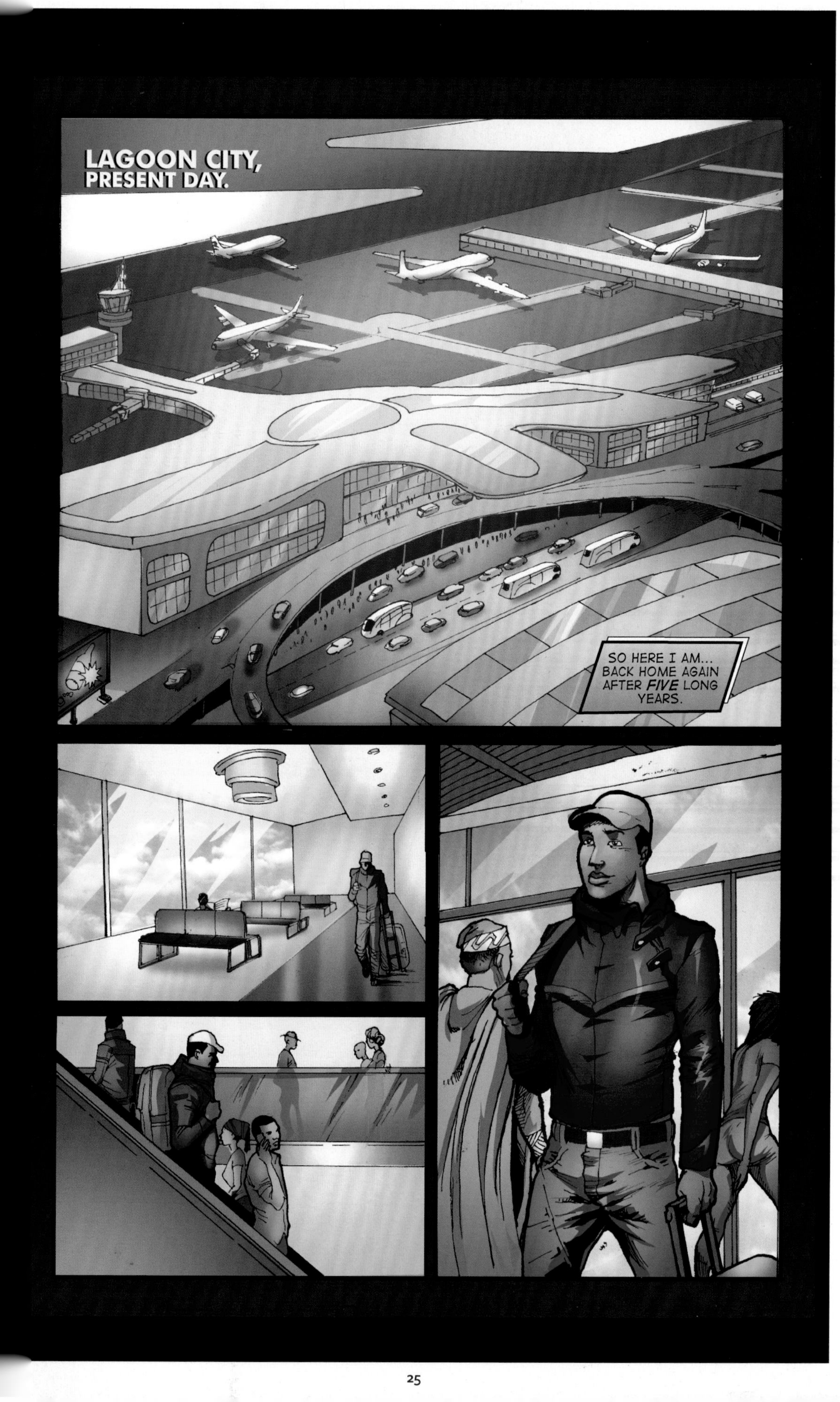
LAGOON CITY, PRESENT DAY.
SO HERE I AM... BACK HOME AGAIN AFTER FIVE LONG YEARS.

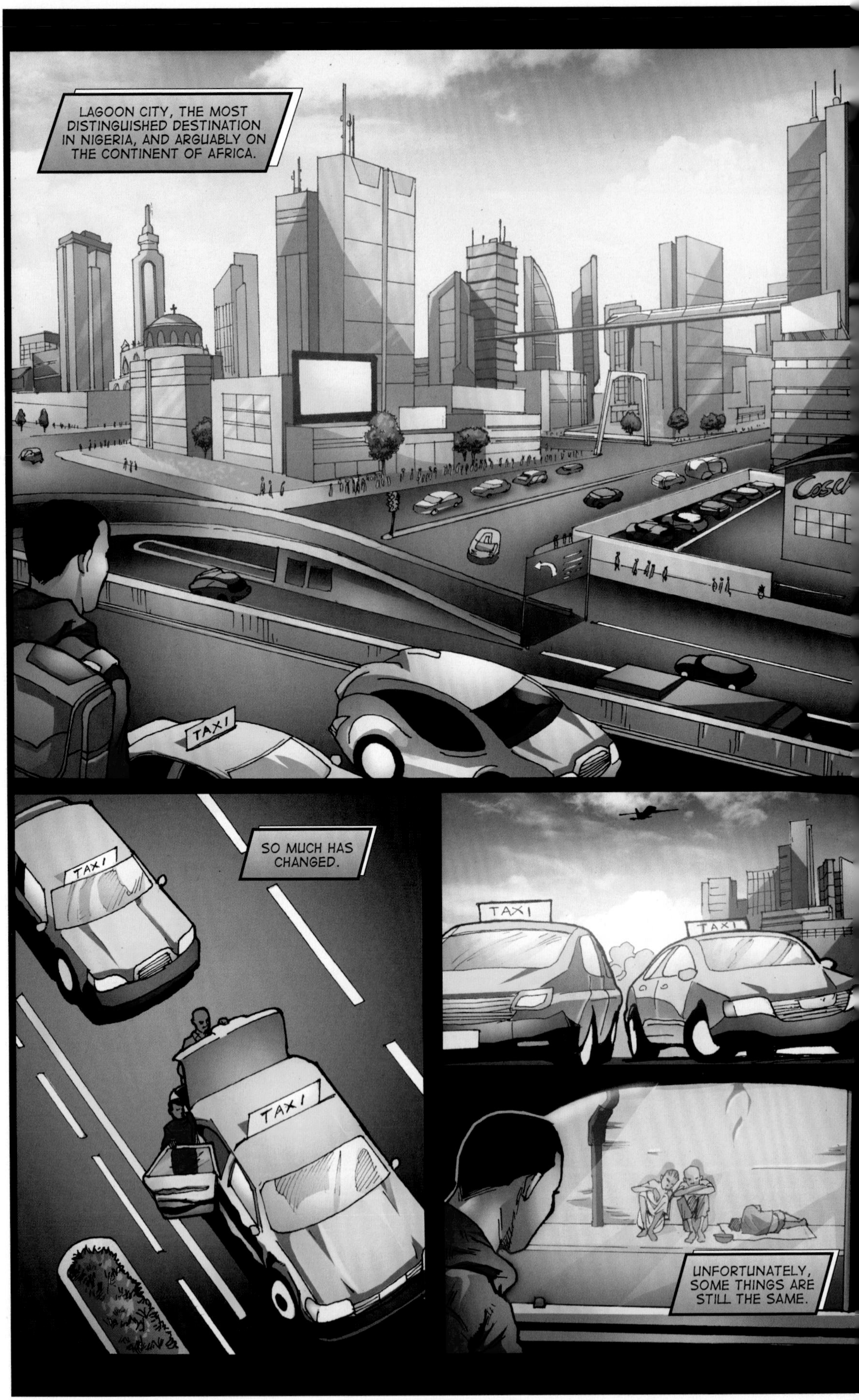
LAGOON CITY, THE MOST DISTINGUISHED DESTINATION IN NIGERIA, AND ARGUABLY ON THE CONTINENT OF AFRICA.
TAXI
SO MUCH HAS CHANGED.
TAXI
TAXI
TAXI
TAXI
UNFORTUNATELY, SOME THINGS ARE STILL THE SAME.

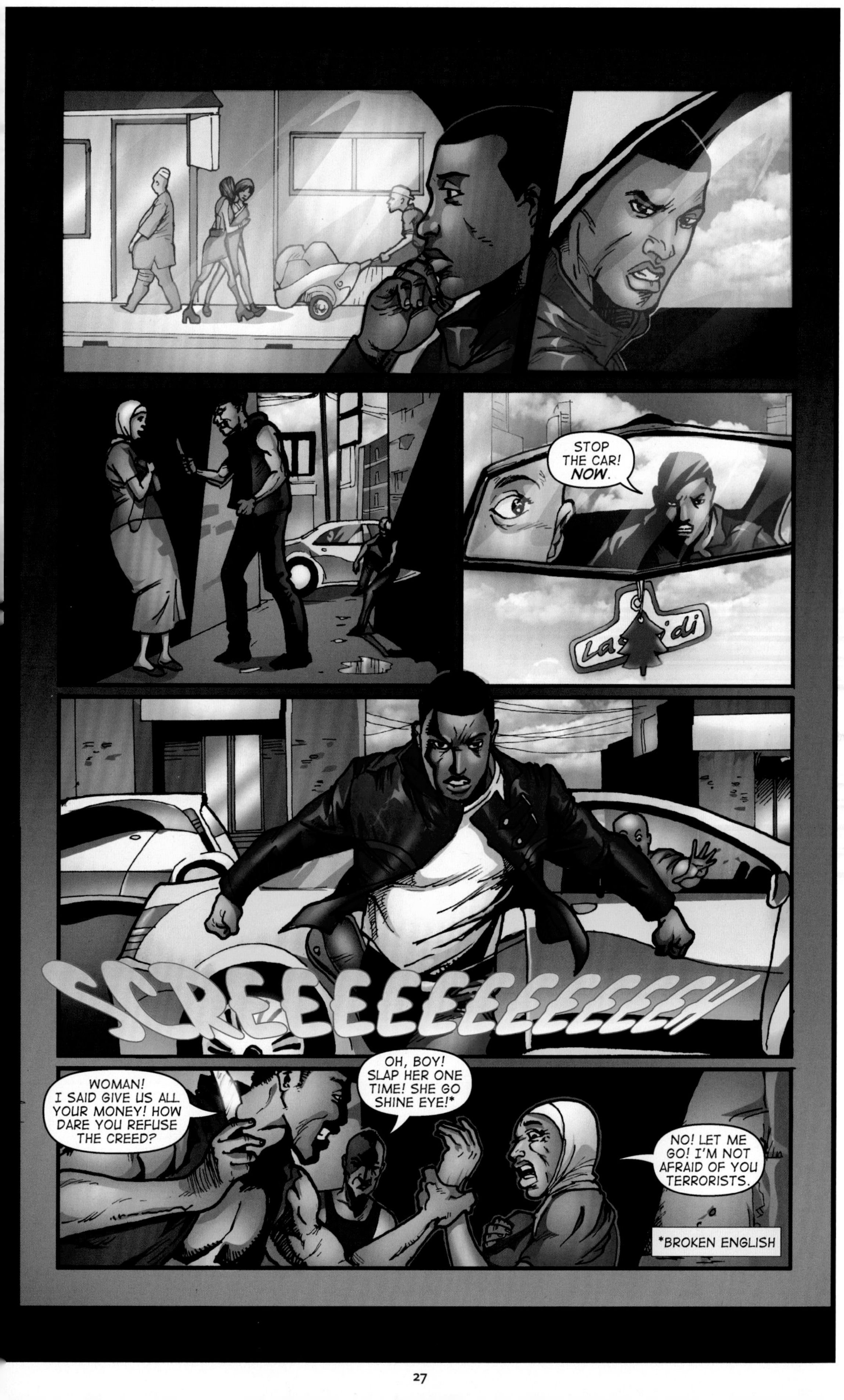
STOP THE CAR! NOW.
SCREEEEEEEEEEEEEH
WOMAN! I SAID GIVE US ALL YOUR MONEY! HOW DARE YOU REFUSE THE CREED?
OH, BOY! SLAP HER ONE TIME! SHE GO SHINE EYE!*
NO! LET ME GO! I'M NOT AFRAID OF YOU TERRORISTS.
*BROKEN ENGLISH

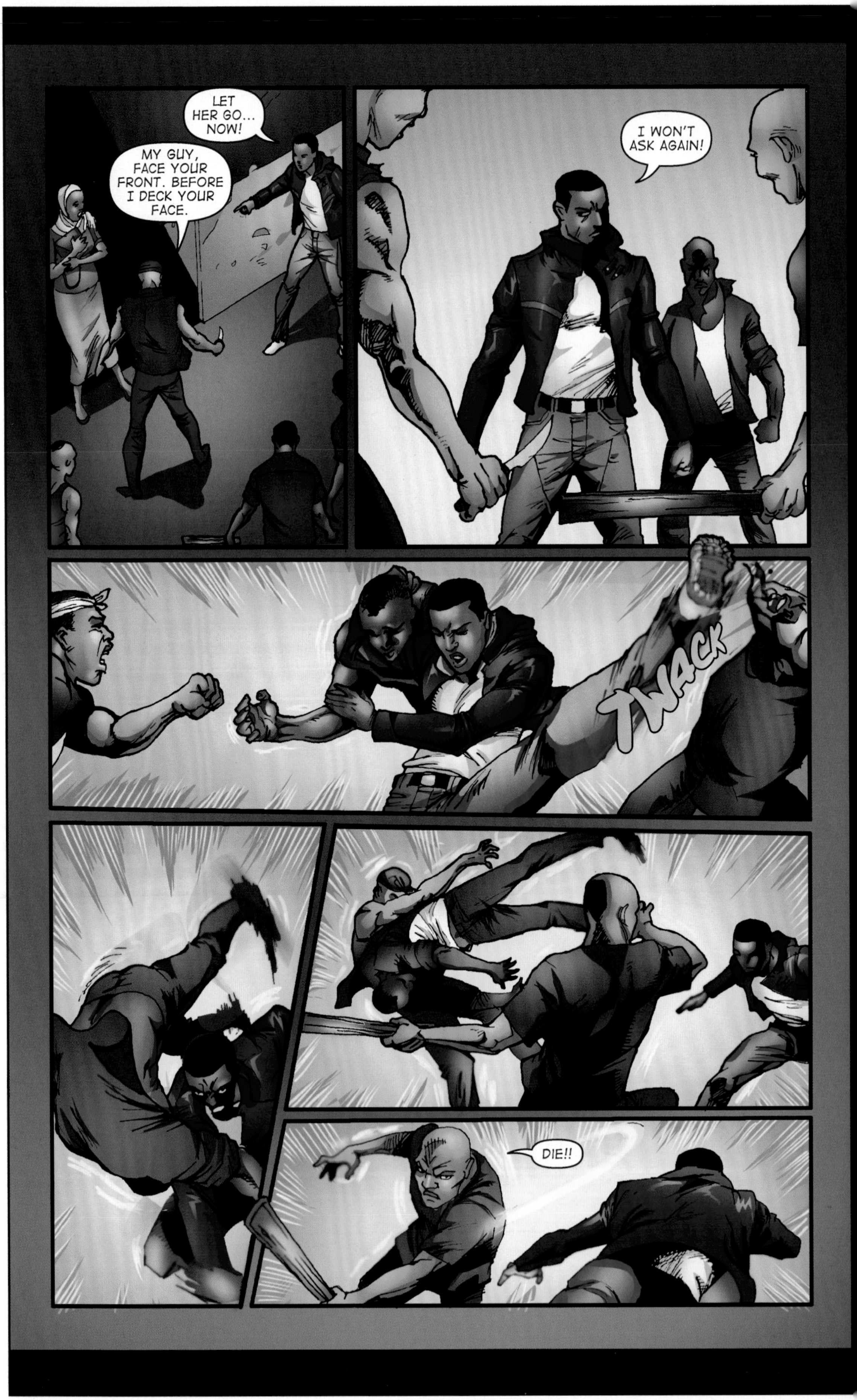
LET HER GO... NOW!
MY GUY, FACE YOUR FRONT. BEFORE I DECK YOUR FACE.
I WON'T ASK AGAIN!
TWACK
DIE!!

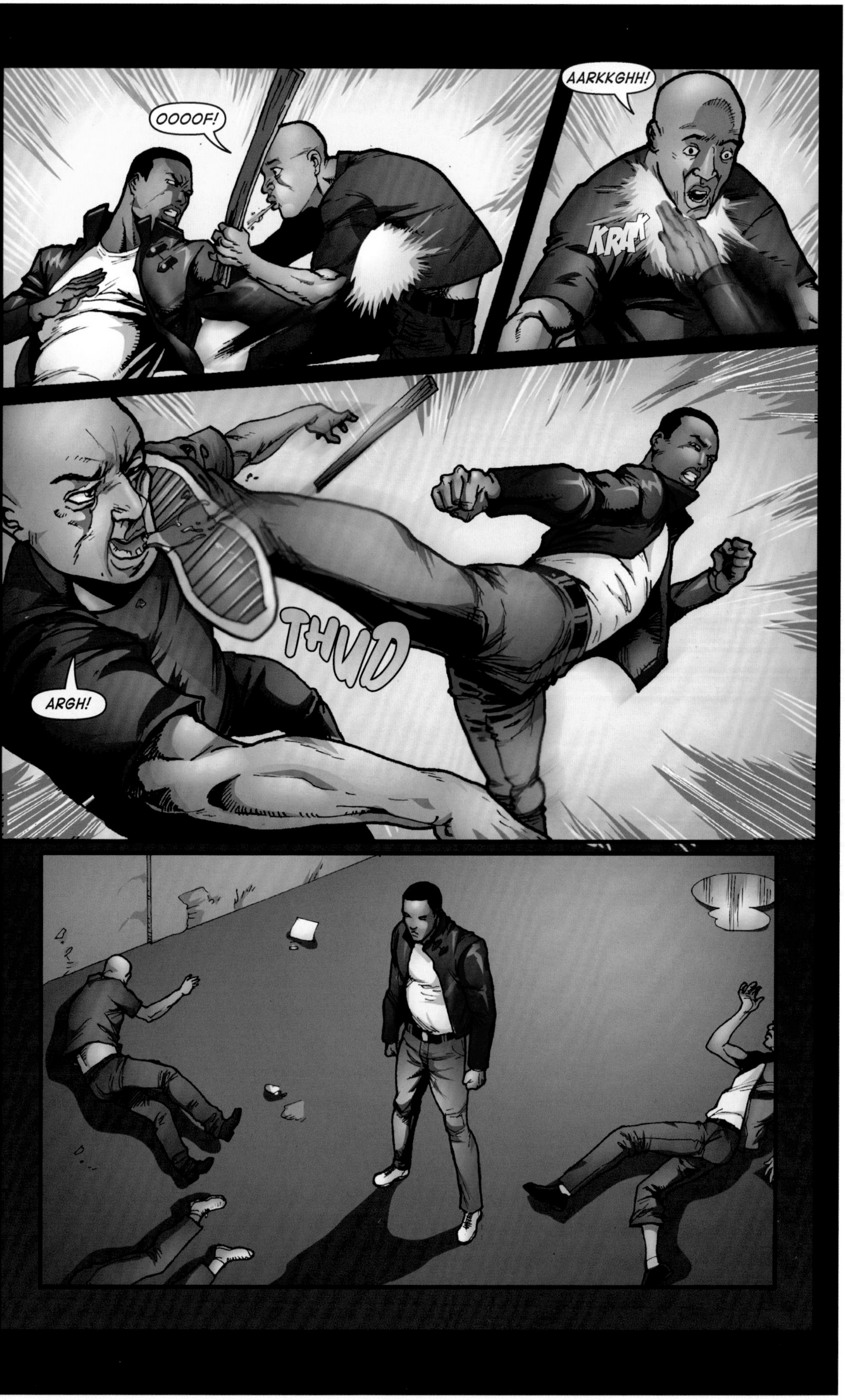
OOOOF!
AARKKGHH!
KRAK
THUD
ARGH!

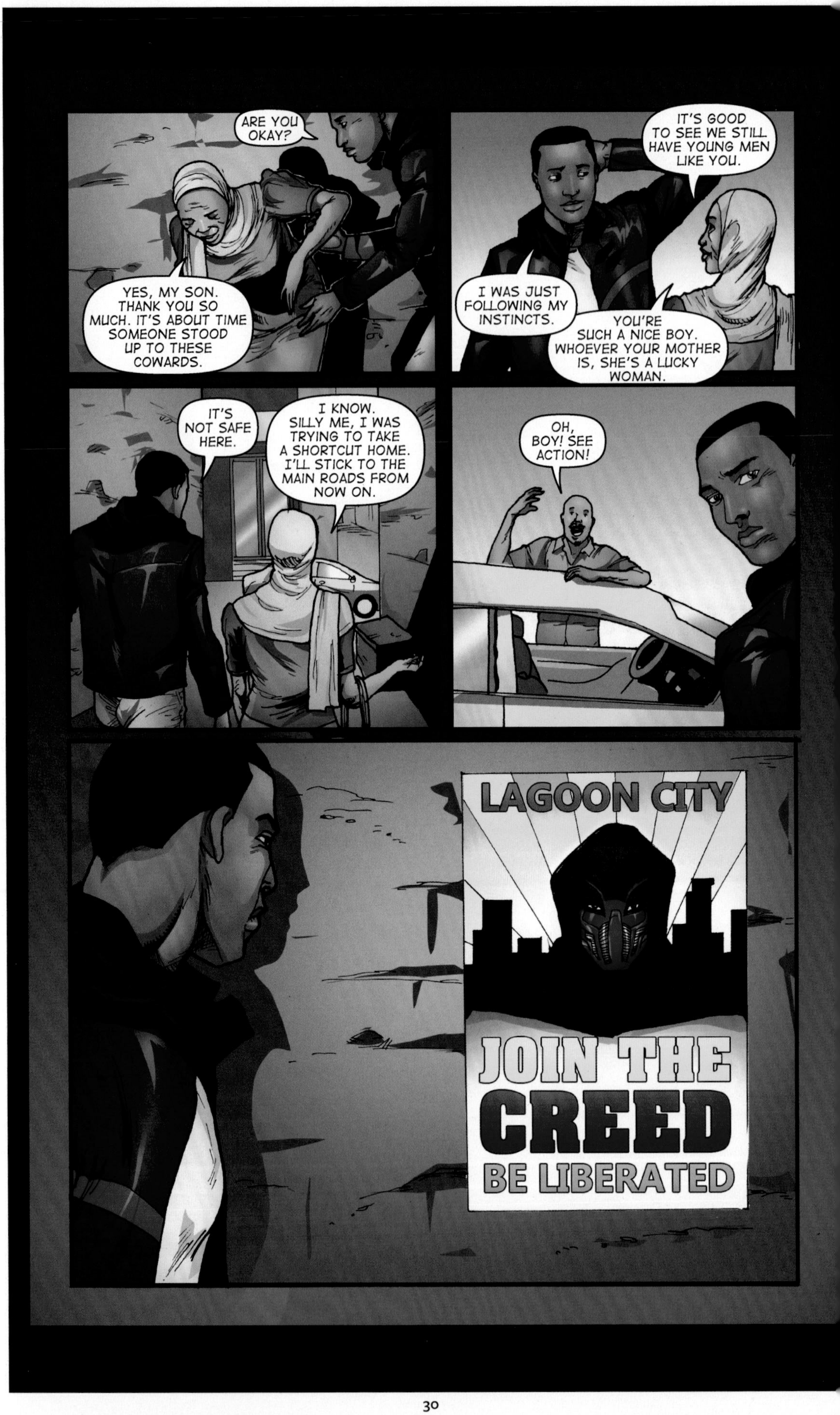
ARE YOU OKAY?
YES, MY SON. THANK YOU SO MUCH. IT'S ABOUT TIME SOMEONE STOOD UP TO THESE COWARDS.
IT'S GOOD TO SEE WE STILL HAVE YOUNG MEN LIKE YOU.
I WAS JUST FOLLOWING MY INSTINCTS.
YOU'RE SUCH A NICE BOY. WHOEVER YOUR MOTHER IS, SHE'S A LUCKY WOMAN.
IT'S NOT SAFE HERE.
I KNOW. SILLY ME, I WAS TRYING TO TAKE A SHORTCUT HOME. I'LL STICK TO THE MAIN ROADS FROM NOW ON.
OH, BOY! SEE ACTION!
LAGOON CITY
JOIN THE
CREED
BE LIBERATED

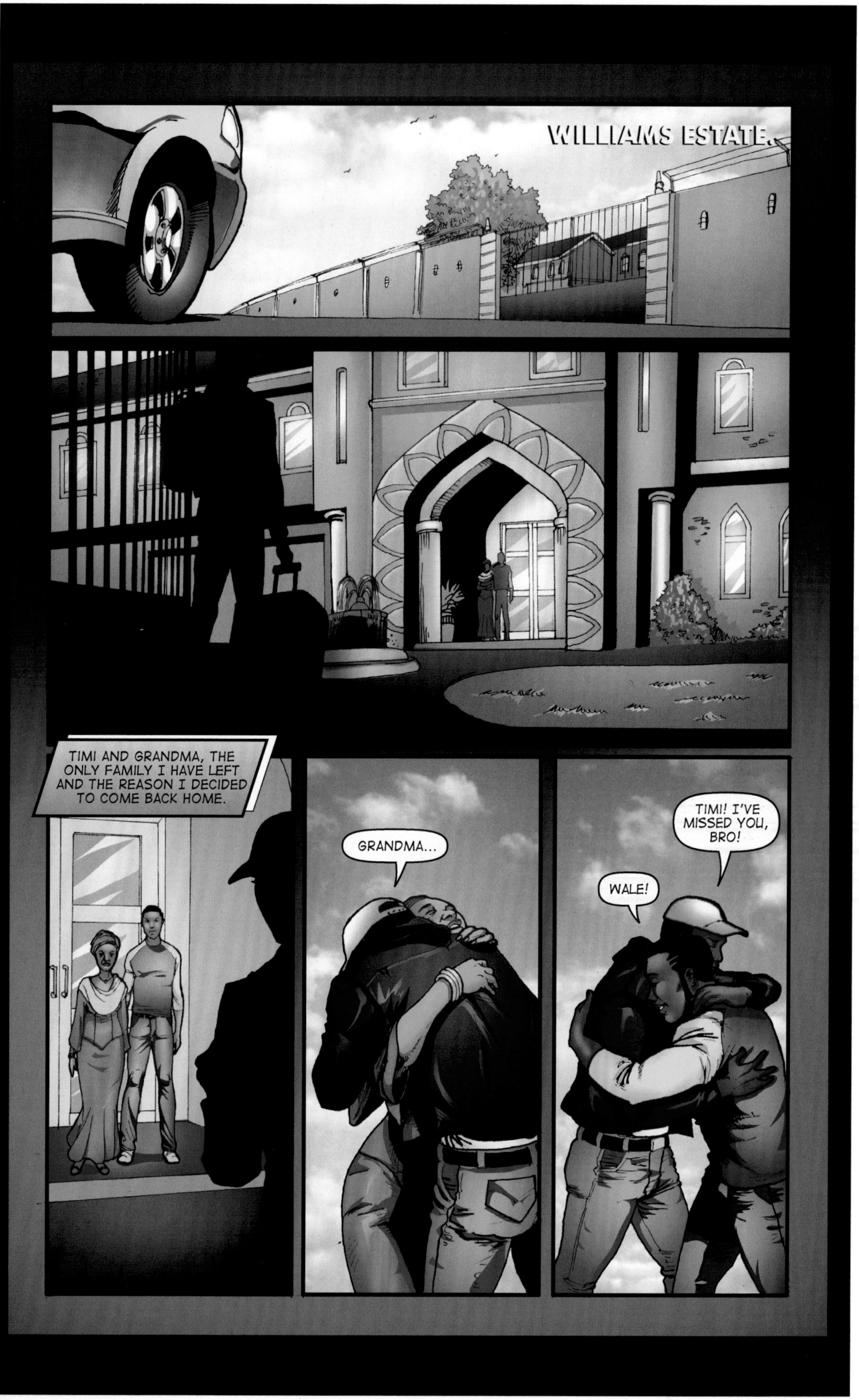
WILLIAMS ESTATE.
TIMI AND GRANDMA, THE ONLY FAMILY I HAVE LEFT AND THE REASON I DECIDED TO COME BACK HOME.
GRANDMA...
TIMI! I'VE MISSED YOU, BRO!
WALE!

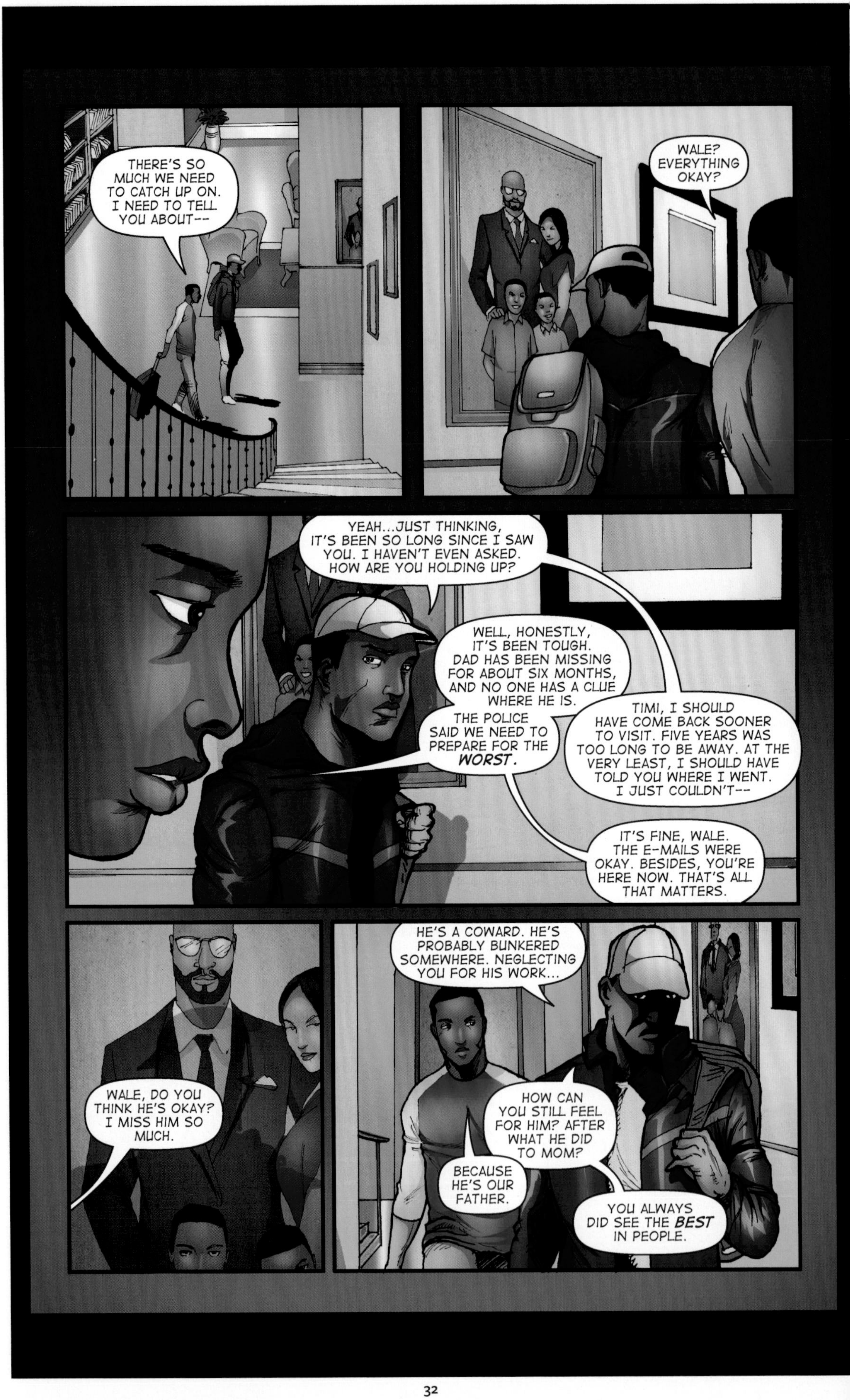
THERE'S SO MUCH WE NEED TO CATCH UP ON. I NEED TO TELL YOU ABOUT--
WALE? EVERYTHING OKAY?
YEAH...JUST THINKING, IT'S BEEN SO LONG SINCE I SAW YOU. I HAVEN'T EVEN ASKED. HOW ARE YOU HOLDING UP?
WELL, HONESTLY, IT'S BEEN TOUGH. DAD HAS BEEN MISSING FOR ABOUT SIX MONTHS, AND NO ONE HAS A CLUE WHERE HE IS.
THE POLICE SAID WE NEED TO PREPARE FOR THE WORST.
TIMI, I SHOULD HAVE COME BACK SOONER TO VISIT. FIVE YEARS WAS TOO LONG TO BE AWAY. AT THE VERY LEAST, I SHOULD HAVE TOLD YOU WHERE I WENT. I JUST COULDN'T--
IT'S FINE, WALE. THE E-MAILS WERE OKAY. BESIDES, YOU'RE HERE NOW. THAT'S ALL THAT MATTERS.
WALE, DO YOU THINK HE'S OKAY? I MISS HIM SO MUCH.
HE'S A COWARD. HE'S PROBABLY BUNKERED SOMEWHERE. NEGLECTING YOU FOR HIS WORK...
HOW CAN YOU STILL FEEL FOR HIM? AFTER WHAT HE DID TO MOM?
BECAUSE HE'S OUR FATHER.
YOU ALWAYS DID SEE THE BEST IN PEOPLE.

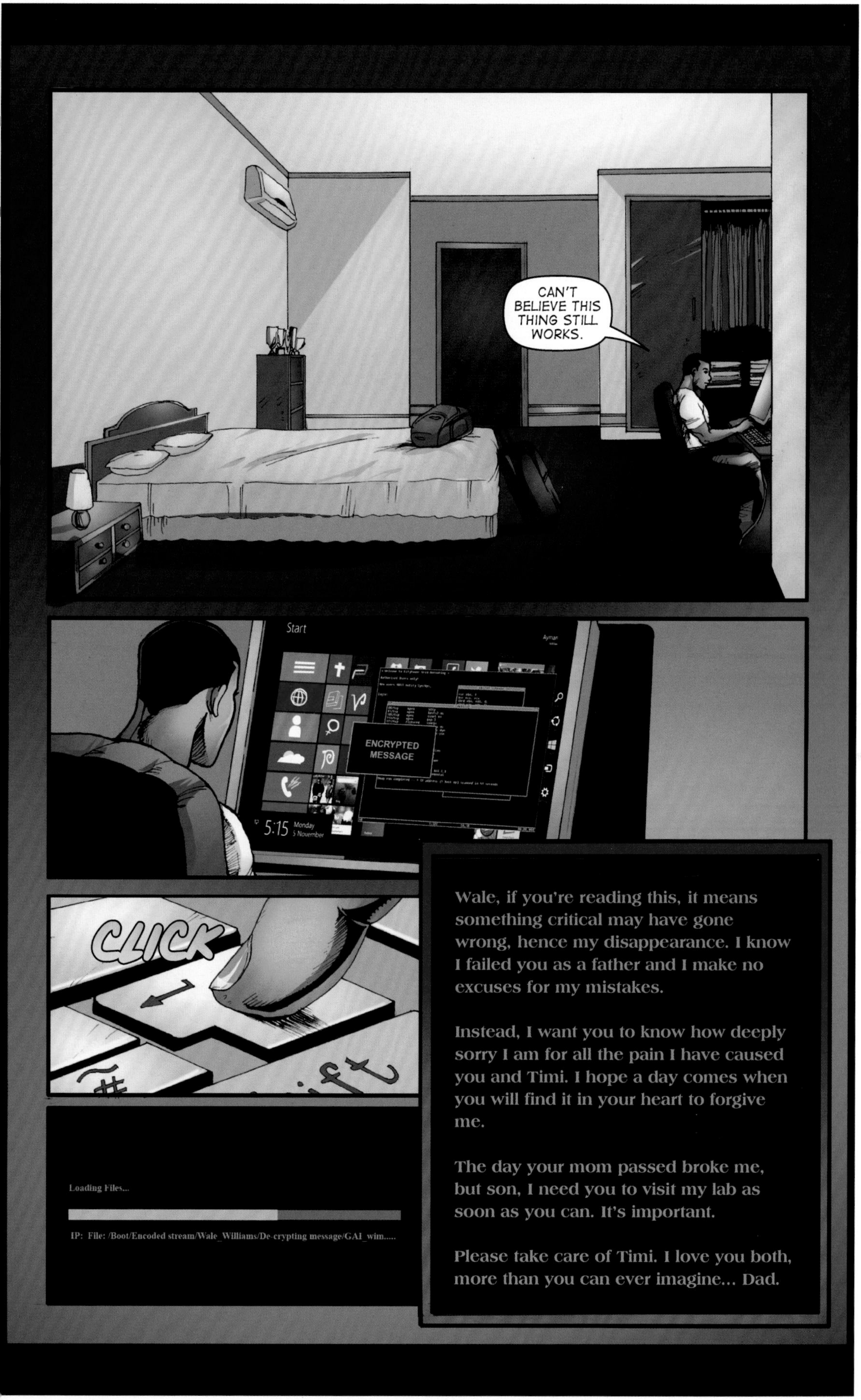
CAN'T BELIEVE THIS THING STILL WORKS.
Start
ENCRYPTED MESSAGE
5:15 Monday 5 November
CLICK
Loading Files...
IP: File: /Boot/Encoded stream/Wale_Williams/De-crypting message/GAI_wim.....
Wale, if you're reading this, it means something critical may have gone wrong, hence my disappearance. I know I failed you as a father and I make no excuses for my mistakes.
Instead, I want you to know how deeply sorry I am for all the pain I have caused you and Timi. I hope a day comes when you will find it in your heart to forgive me.
The day your mom passed broke me, but son, I need you to visit my lab as soon as you can. It's important.
Please take care of Timi. I love you both, more than you can ever imagine... Dad.

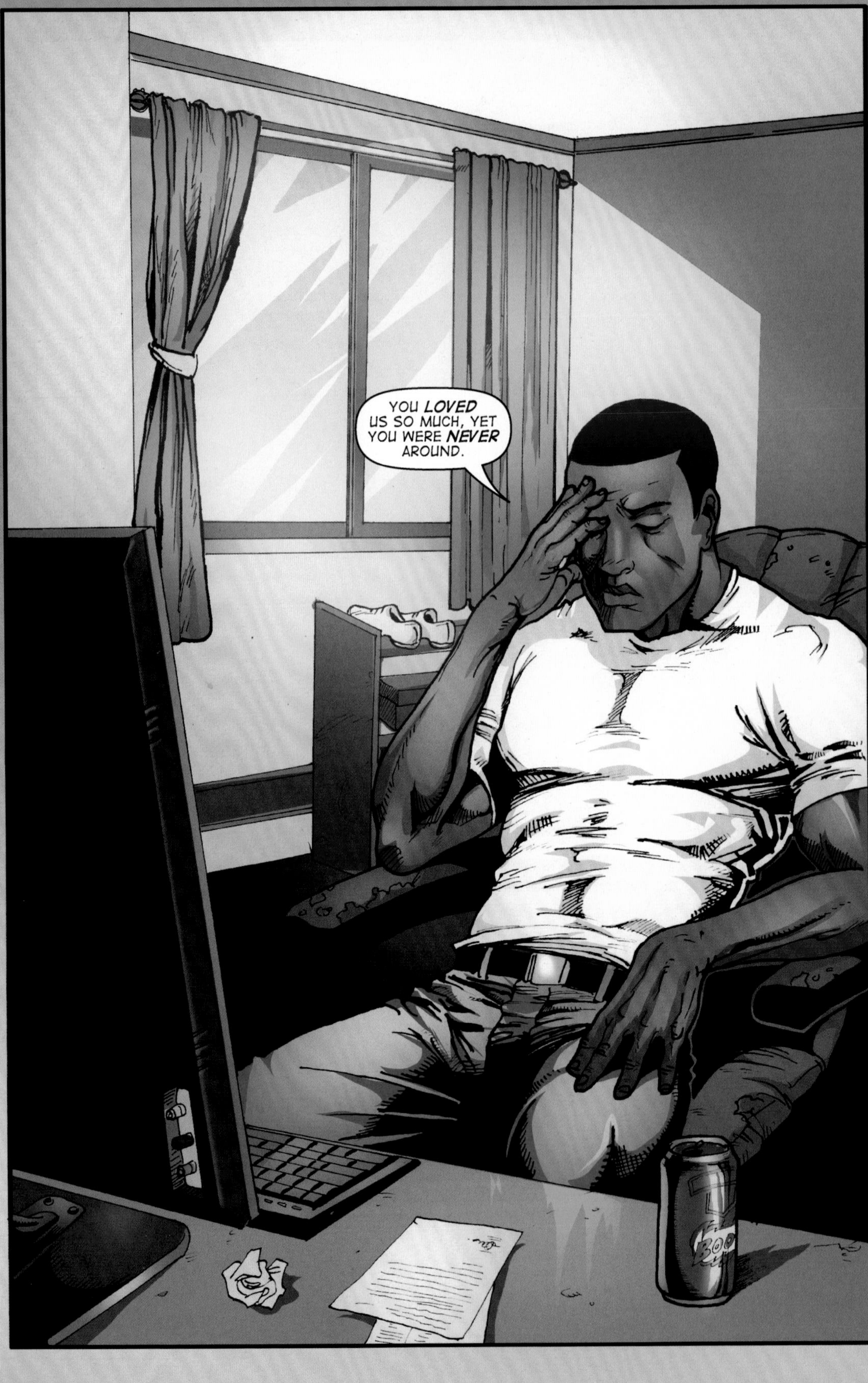
YOU *LOVED* US SO MUCH, YET YOU WERE *NEVER* AROUND.

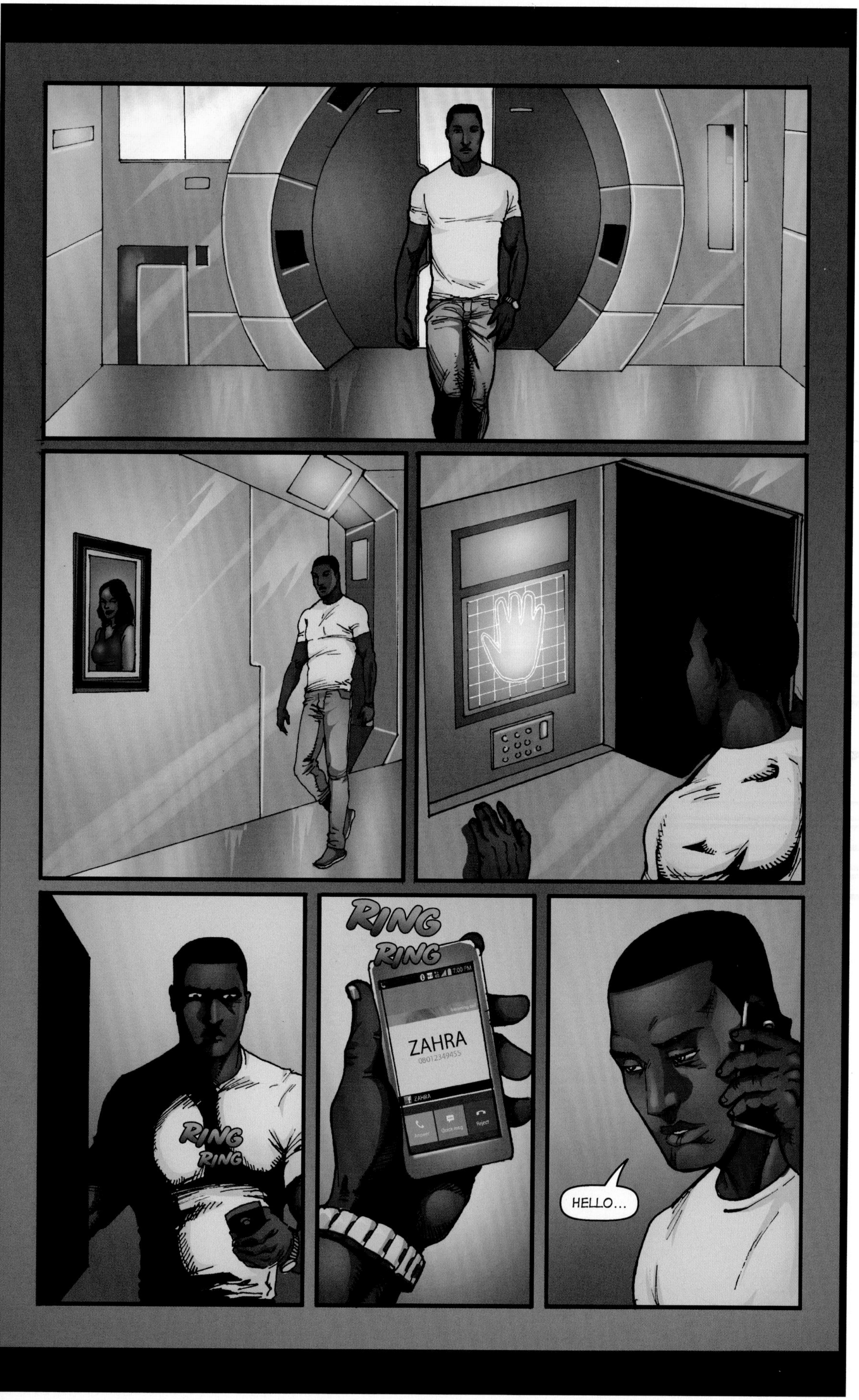
RING
RING
RING
RING
ZAHRA
08012349455
Answer
Quick msg
Reject
HELLO...

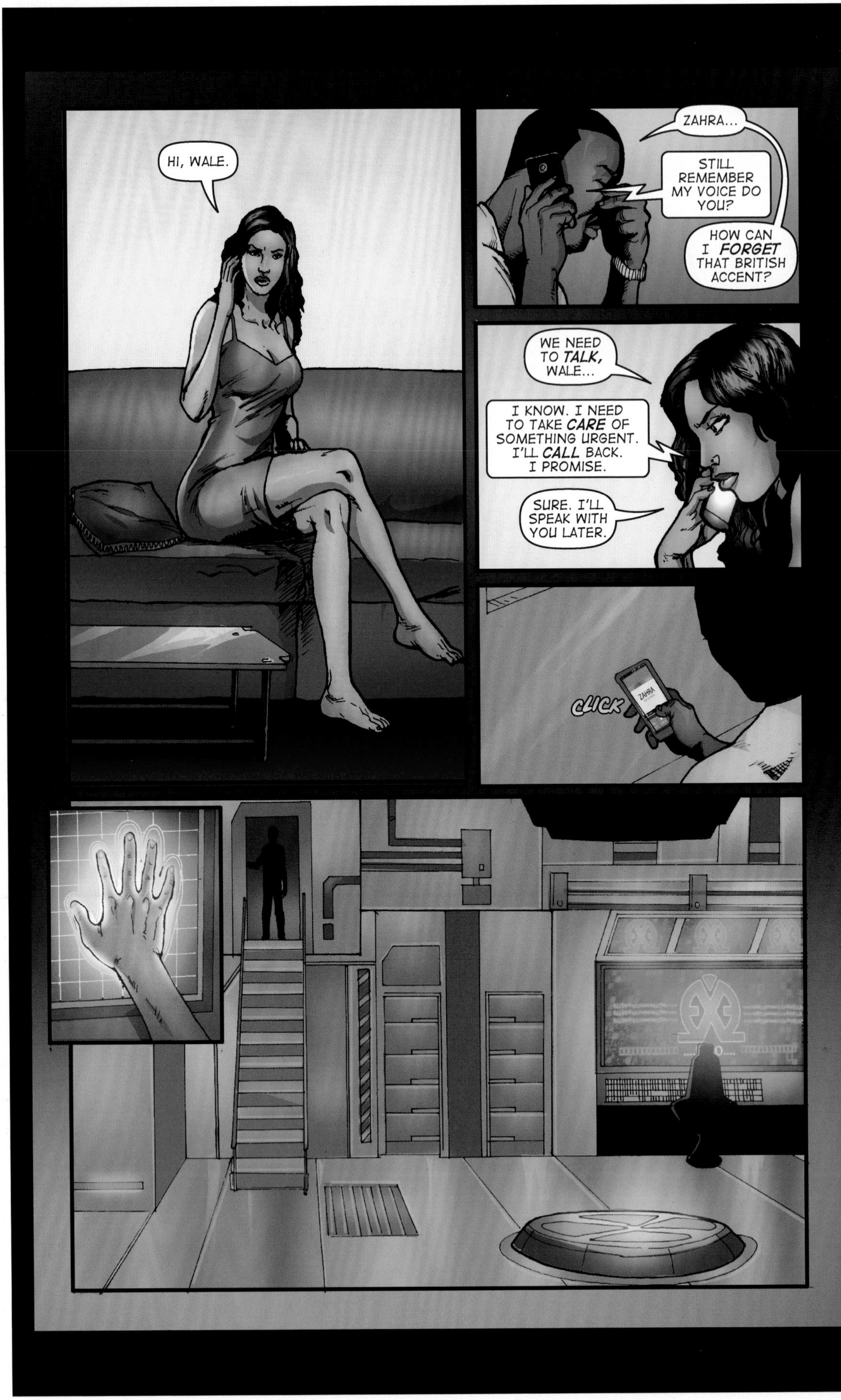
HI, WALE.
ZAHRA...
STILL REMEMBER MY VOICE DO YOU?
HOW CAN I FORGET THAT BRITISH ACCENT?
WE NEED TO TALK, WALE...
I KNOW. I NEED TO TAKE CARE OF SOMETHING URGENT. I'LL CALL BACK. I PROMISE.
SURE. I'LL SPEAK WITH YOU LATER.
CLICK
ZAHRA

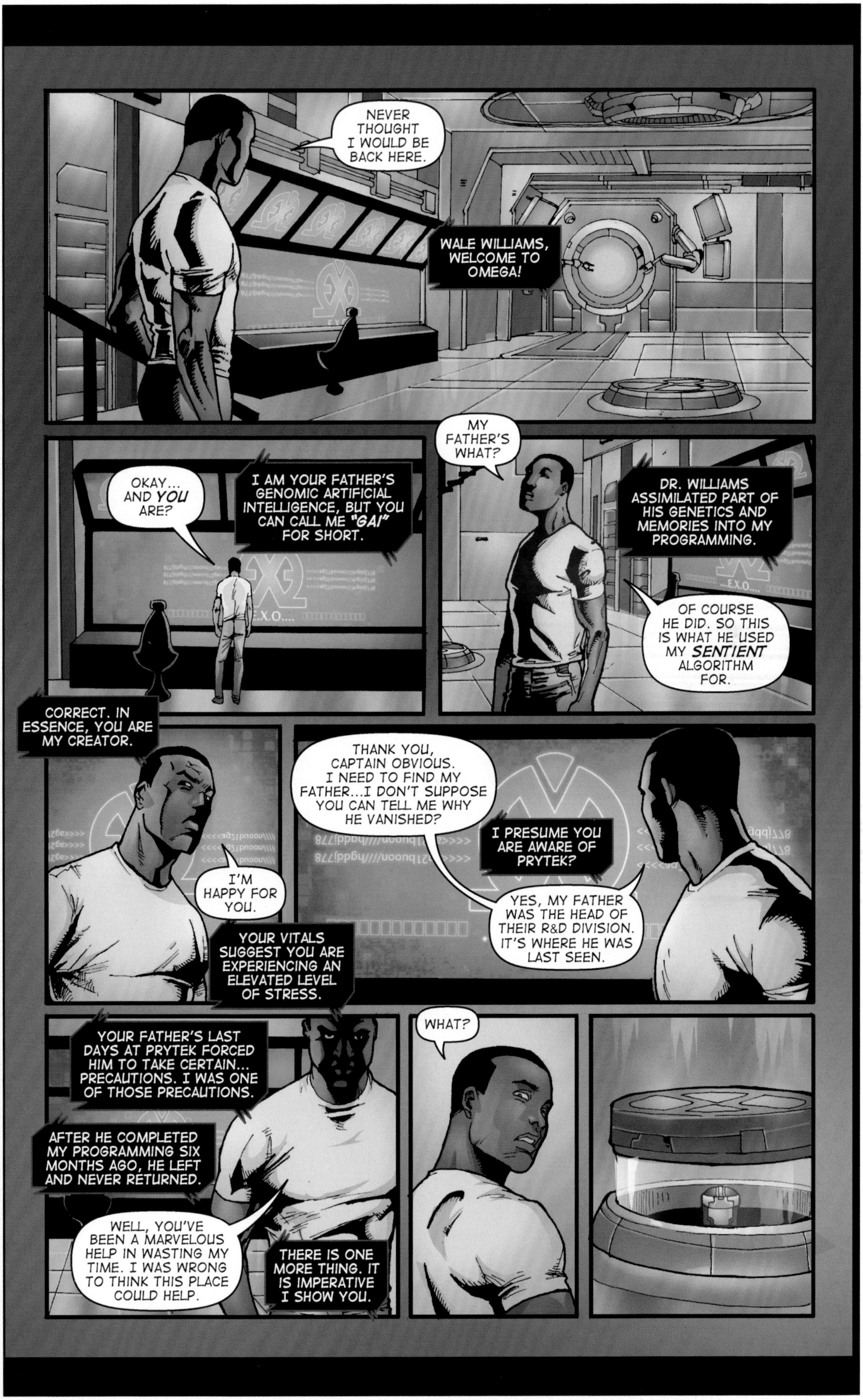
NEVER THOUGHT I WOULD BE BACK HERE.
WALE WILLIAMS, WELCOME TO OMEGA!
OKAY... AND YOU ARE?
I AM YOUR FATHER'S GENOMIC ARTIFICIAL INTELLIGENCE, BUT YOU CAN CALL ME "GAI" FOR SHORT.
MY FATHER'S WHAT?
DR. WILLIAMS ASSIMILATED PART OF HIS GENETICS AND MEMORIES INTO MY PROGRAMMING.
OF COURSE HE DID. SO THIS IS WHAT HE USED MY SENTIENT ALGORITHM FOR.
CORRECT. IN ESSENCE, YOU ARE MY CREATOR.
I'M HAPPY FOR YOU.
YOUR VITALS SUGGEST YOU ARE EXPERIENCING AN ELEVATED LEVEL OF STRESS.
THANK YOU, CAPTAIN OBVIOUS. I NEED TO FIND MY FATHER...I DON'T SUPPOSE YOU CAN TELL ME WHY HE VANISHED?
I PRESUME YOU ARE AWARE OF PRYTEK?
YES, MY FATHER WAS THE HEAD OF THEIR R&D DIVISION. IT'S WHERE HE WAS LAST SEEN.
YOUR FATHER'S LAST DAYS AT PRYTEK FORCED HIM TO TAKE CERTAIN... PRECAUTIONS. I WAS ONE OF THOSE PRECAUTIONS.
AFTER HE COMPLETED MY PROGRAMMING SIX MONTHS AGO, HE LEFT AND NEVER RETURNED.
WELL, YOU'VE BEEN A MARVELOUS HELP IN WASTING MY TIME. I WAS WRONG TO THINK THIS PLACE COULD HELP.
THERE IS ONE MORE THING. IT IS IMPERATIVE I SHOW YOU.
WHAT?

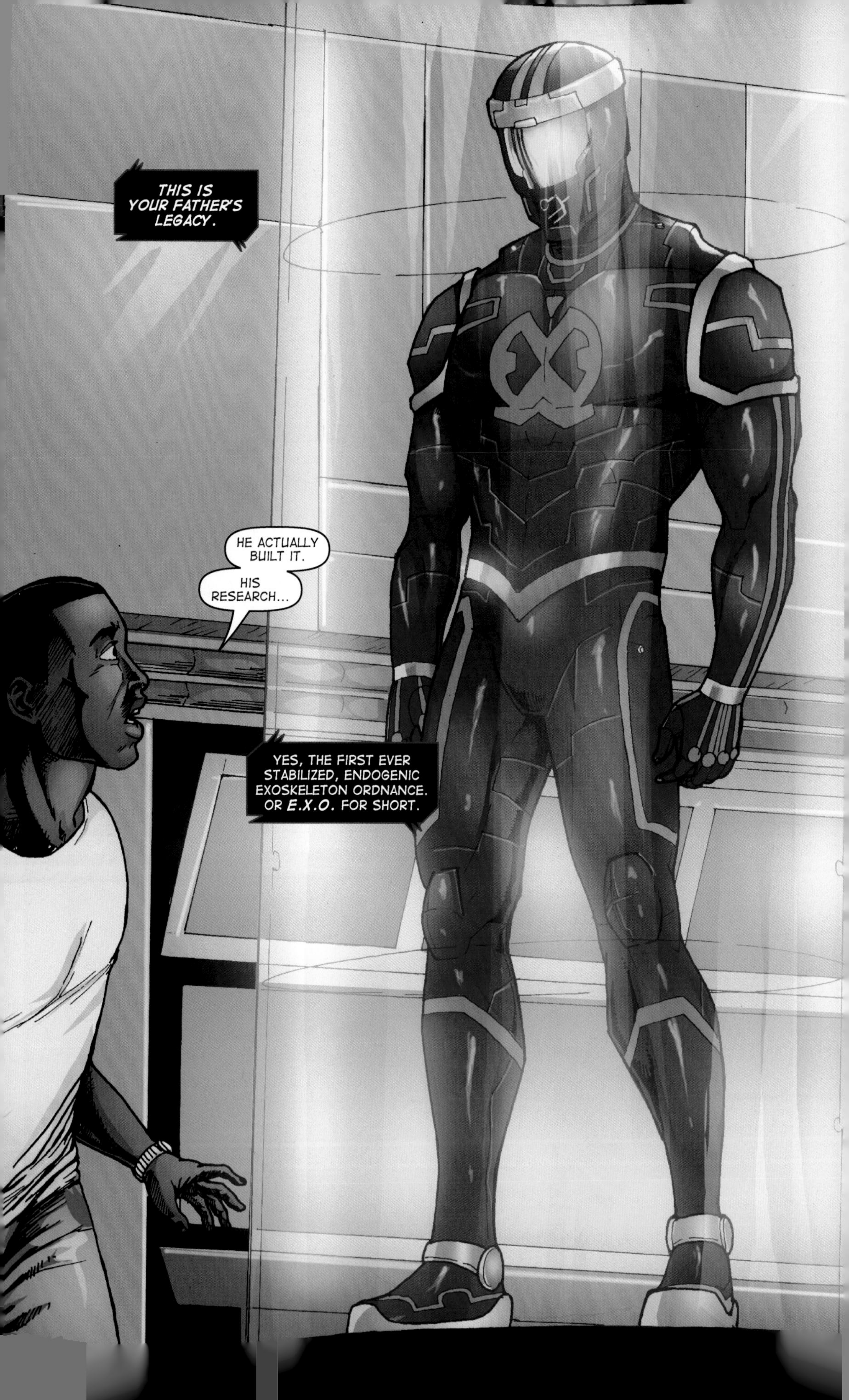
THIS IS YOUR FATHER'S LEGACY.
HE ACTUALLY BUILT IT.
HIS RESEARCH...
YES, THE FIRST EVER STABILIZED, ENDOGENIC EXOSKELETON ORDNANCE. OR E.X.O. FOR SHORT.

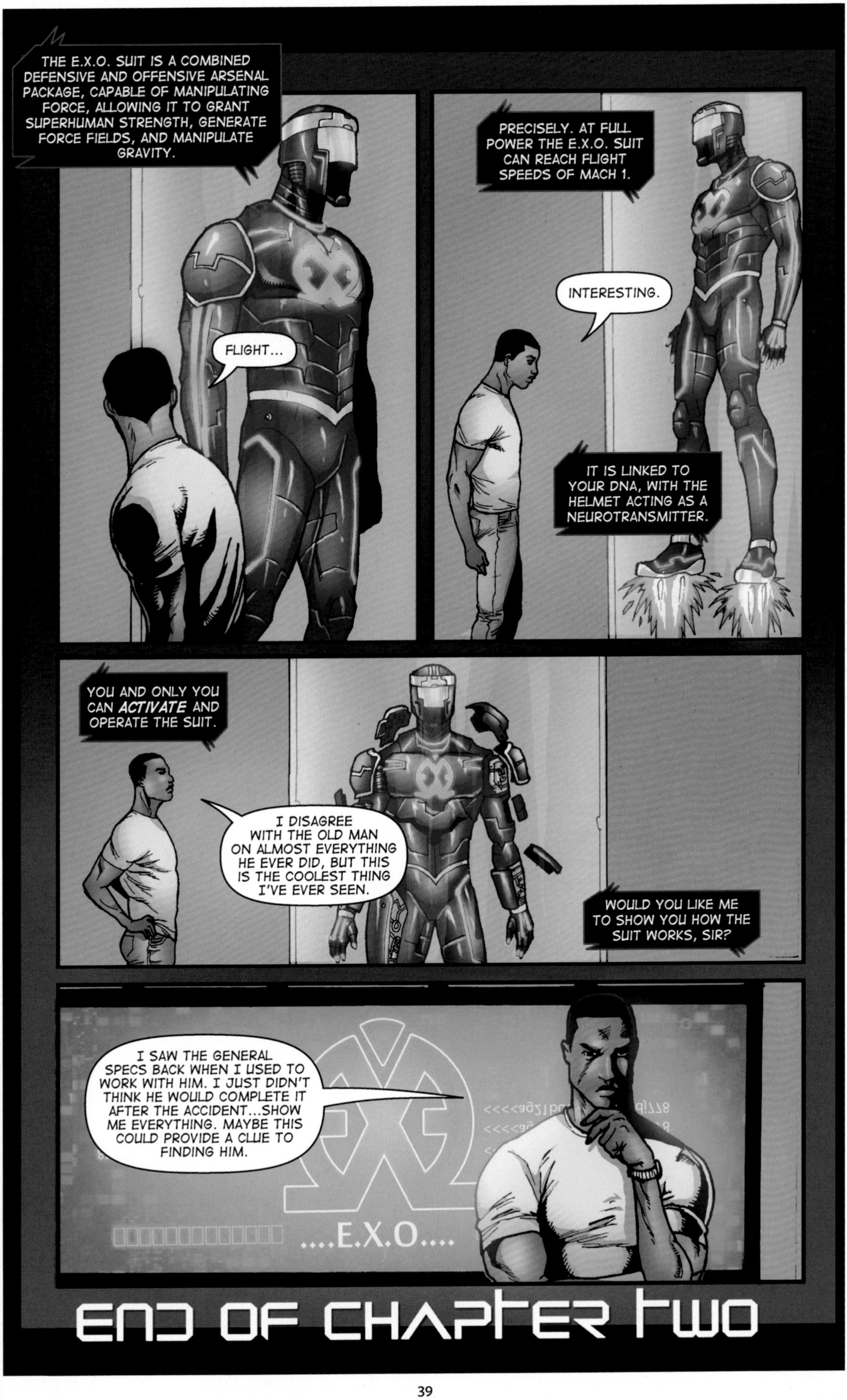
THE E.X.O. SUIT IS A COMBINED DEFENSIVE AND OFFENSIVE ARSENAL PACKAGE, CAPABLE OF MANIPULATING FORCE, ALLOWING IT TO GRANT SUPERHUMAN STRENGTH, GENERATE FORCE FIELDS, AND MANIPULATE GRAVITY.
FLIGHT...
PRECISELY. AT FULL POWER THE E.X.O. SUIT CAN REACH FLIGHT SPEEDS OF MACH 1.
INTERESTING.
IT IS LINKED TO YOUR DNA, WITH THE HELMET ACTING AS A NEUROTRANSMITTER.
YOU AND ONLY YOU CAN *ACTIVATE* AND OPERATE THE SUIT.
I DISAGREE WITH THE OLD MAN ON ALMOST EVERYTHING HE EVER DID, BUT THIS IS THE COOLEST THING I'VE EVER SEEN.
WOULD YOU LIKE ME TO SHOW YOU HOW THE SUIT WORKS, SIR?
I SAW THE GENERAL SPECS BACK WHEN I USED TO WORK WITH HIM. I JUST DIDN'T THINK HE WOULD COMPLETE IT AFTER THE ACCIDENT...SHOW ME EVERYTHING. MAYBE THIS COULD PROVIDE A CLUE TO FINDING HIM.
....E.X.O....
END OF CHAPTER TWO

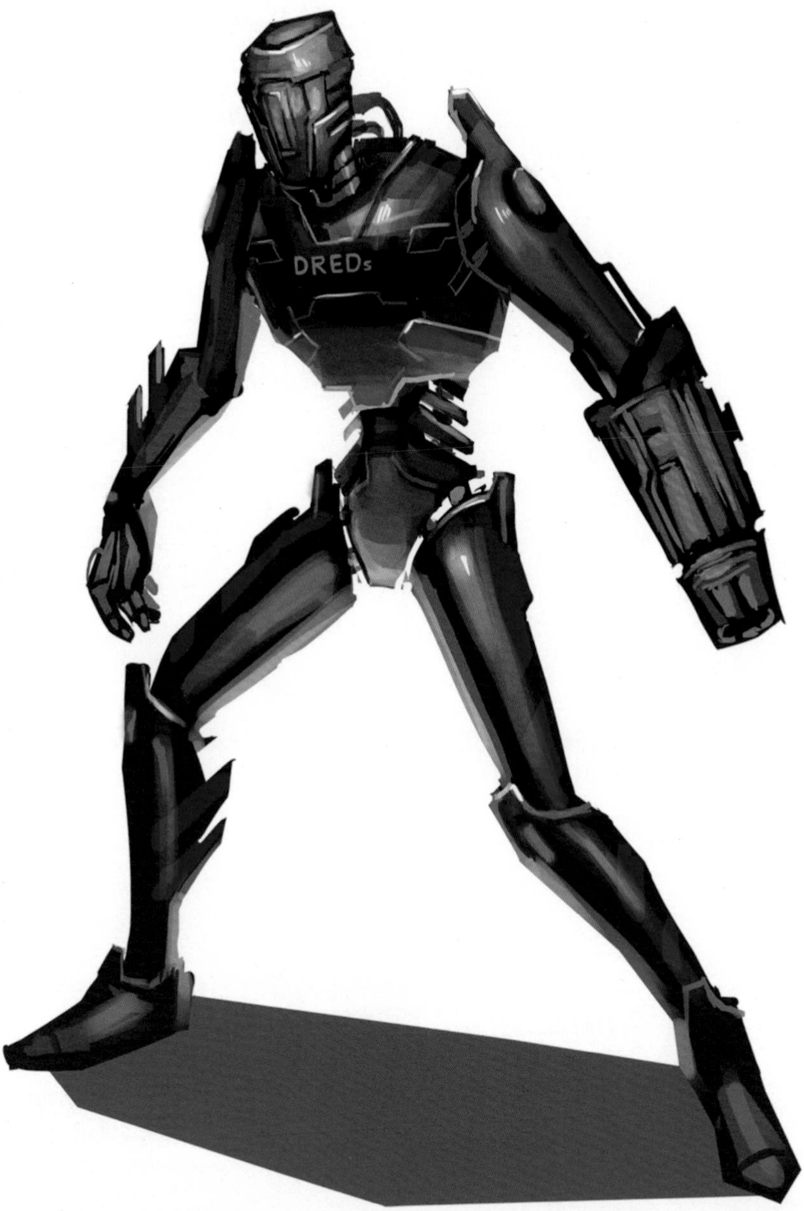
DREDs

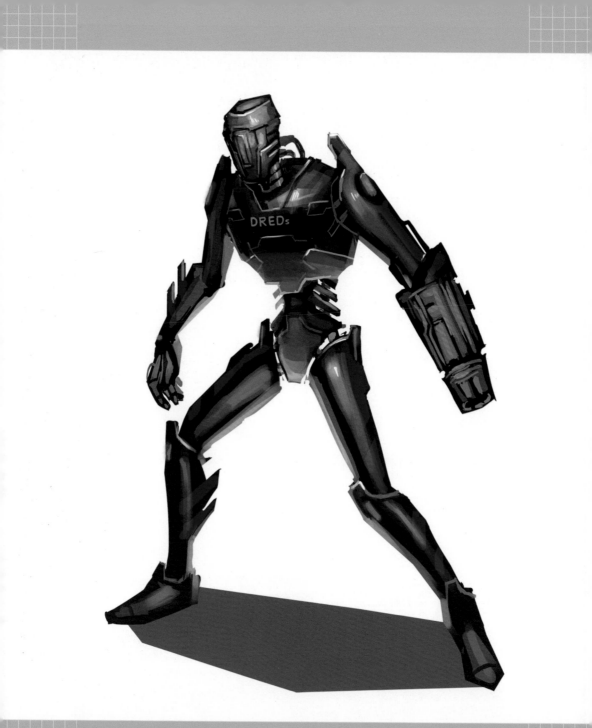

DREDs—Dominant Exoskeletal Drones

CHAPTER THREE

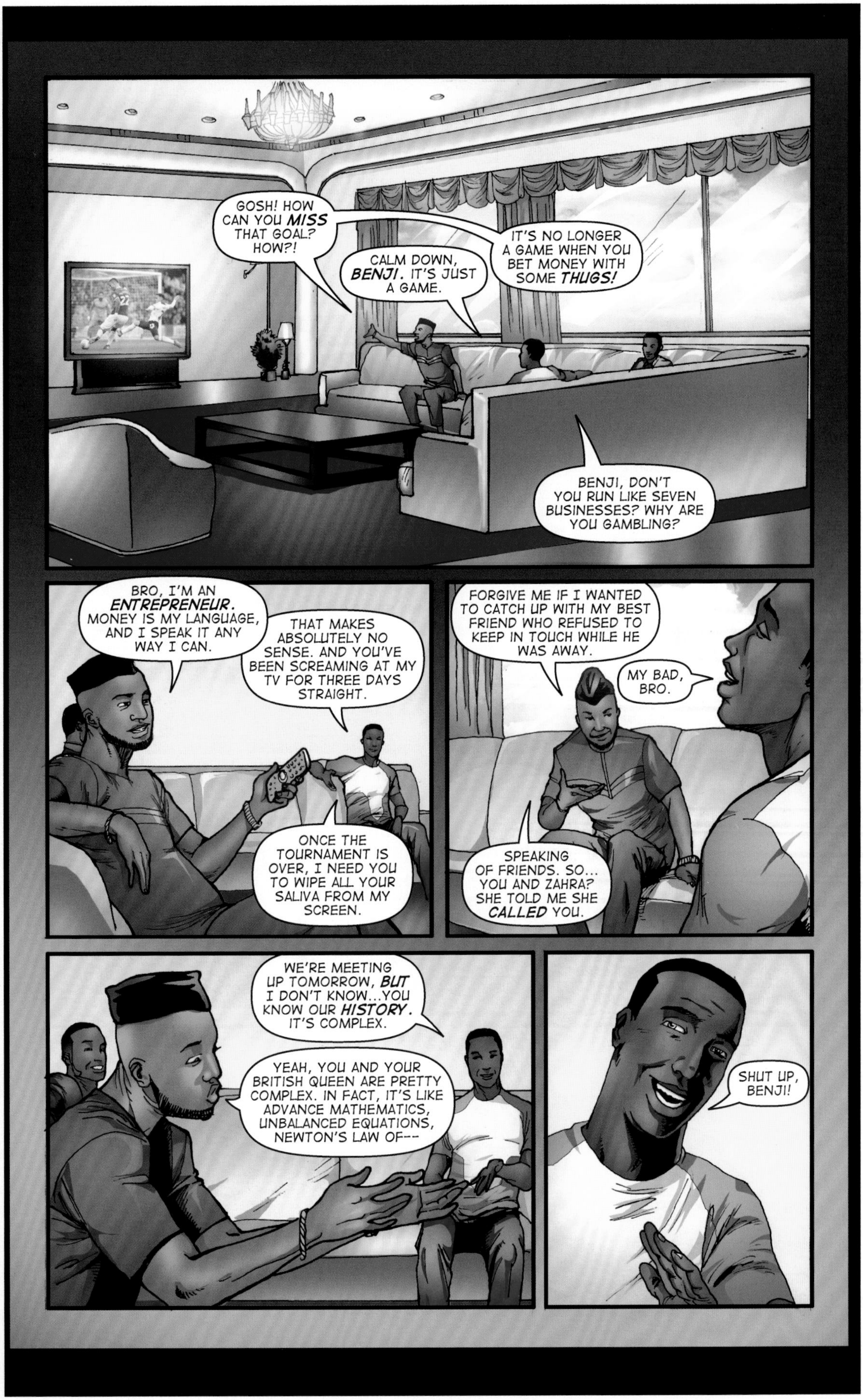
GOSH! HOW CAN YOU MISS THAT GOAL? HOW?!
IT'S NO LONGER A GAME WHEN YOU BET MONEY WITH SOME THUGS!
CALM DOWN, BENJI. IT'S JUST A GAME.
BENJI, DON'T YOU RUN LIKE SEVEN BUSINESSES? WHY ARE YOU GAMBLING?
BRO, I'M AN ENTREPRENEUR. MONEY IS MY LANGUAGE, AND I SPEAK IT ANY WAY I CAN.
THAT MAKES ABSOLUTELY NO SENSE. AND YOU'VE BEEN SCREAMING AT MY TV FOR THREE DAYS STRAIGHT.
ONCE THE TOURNAMENT IS OVER, I NEED YOU TO WIPE ALL YOUR SALIVA FROM MY SCREEN.
FORGIVE ME IF I WANTED TO CATCH UP WITH MY BEST FRIEND WHO REFUSED TO KEEP IN TOUCH WHILE HE WAS AWAY.
MY BAD, BRO.
SPEAKING OF FRIENDS. SO... YOU AND ZAHRA? SHE TOLD ME SHE CALLED YOU.
WE'RE MEETING UP TOMORROW, BUT I DON'T KNOW...YOU KNOW OUR HISTORY. IT'S COMPLEX.
YEAH, YOU AND YOUR BRITISH QUEEN ARE PRETTY COMPLEX. IN FACT, IT'S LIKE ADVANCE MATHEMATICS, UNBALANCED EQUATIONS, NEWTON'S LAW OF--
SHUT UP, BENJI!

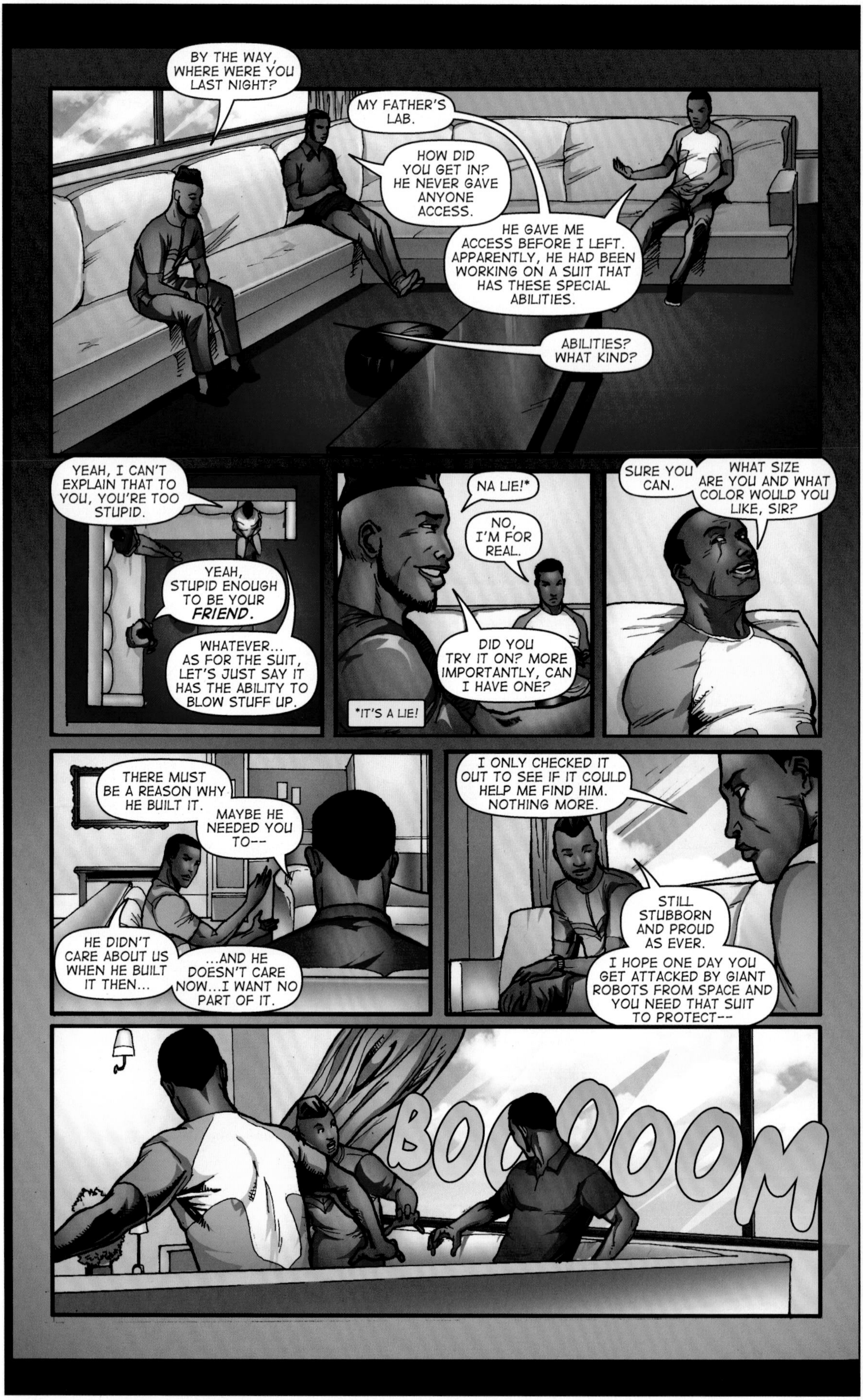
BY THE WAY, WHERE WERE YOU LAST NIGHT?
MY FATHER'S LAB.
HOW DID YOU GET IN? HE NEVER GAVE ANYONE ACCESS.
HE GAVE ME ACCESS BEFORE I LEFT. APPARENTLY, HE HAD BEEN WORKING ON A SUIT THAT HAS THESE SPECIAL ABILITIES.
ABILITIES? WHAT KIND?
YEAH, I CAN'T EXPLAIN THAT TO YOU, YOU'RE TOO STUPID.
YEAH, STUPID ENOUGH TO BE YOUR *FRIEND*.
WHATEVER... AS FOR THE SUIT, LET'S JUST SAY IT HAS THE ABILITY TO BLOW STUFF UP.
NA LIE!*
NO, I'M FOR REAL.
DID YOU TRY IT ON? MORE IMPORTANTLY, CAN I HAVE ONE?
*IT'S A LIE!
SURE YOU CAN.
WHAT SIZE ARE YOU AND WHAT COLOR WOULD YOU LIKE, SIR?
THERE MUST BE A REASON WHY HE BUILT IT.
MAYBE HE NEEDED YOU TO--
HE DIDN'T CARE ABOUT US WHEN HE BUILT IT THEN...
...AND HE DOESN'T CARE NOW...I WANT NO PART OF IT.
I ONLY CHECKED IT OUT TO SEE IF IT COULD HELP ME FIND HIM. NOTHING MORE.
STILL STUBBORN AND PROUD AS EVER.
I HOPE ONE DAY YOU GET ATTACKED BY GIANT ROBOTS FROM SPACE AND YOU NEED THAT SUIT TO PROTECT--
BOOOOOM

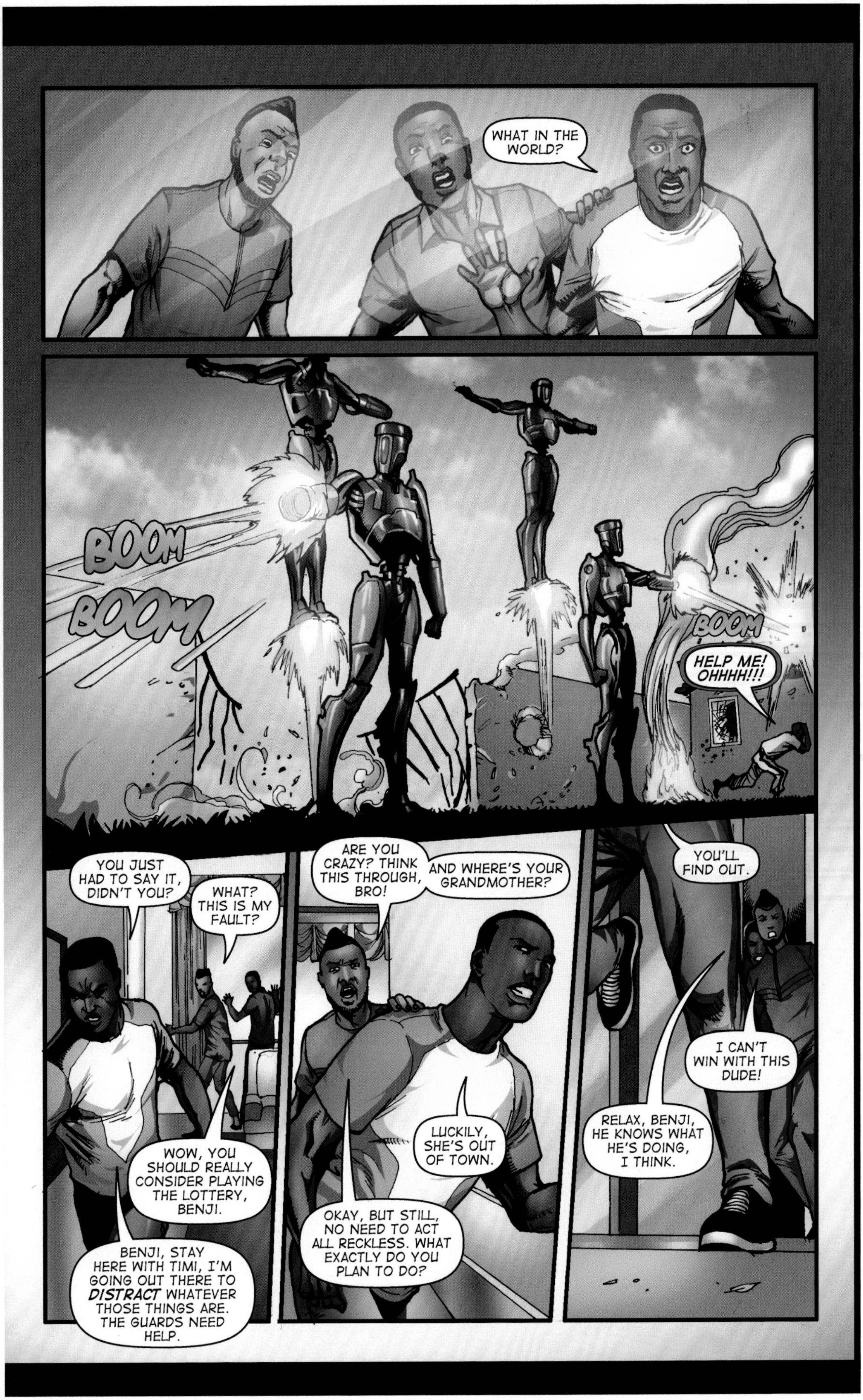
WHAT IN THE WORLD?
BOOM
BOOM
BOOM
HELP ME! OHHHH!!!
YOU JUST HAD TO SAY IT, DIDN'T YOU?
WHAT? THIS IS MY FAULT?
WOW, YOU SHOULD REALLY CONSIDER PLAYING THE LOTTERY, BENJI.
BENJI, STAY HERE WITH TIMI, I'M GOING OUT THERE TO *DISTRACT* WHATEVER THOSE THINGS ARE. THE GUARDS NEED HELP.
ARE YOU CRAZY? THINK THIS THROUGH, BRO!
AND WHERE'S YOUR GRANDMOTHER?
LUCKILY, SHE'S OUT OF TOWN.
OKAY, BUT STILL, NO NEED TO ACT ALL RECKLESS. WHAT EXACTLY DO YOU PLAN TO DO?
YOU'LL FIND OUT.
I CAN'T WIN WITH THIS DUDE!
RELAX, BENJI, HE KNOWS WHAT HE'S DOING, I THINK.

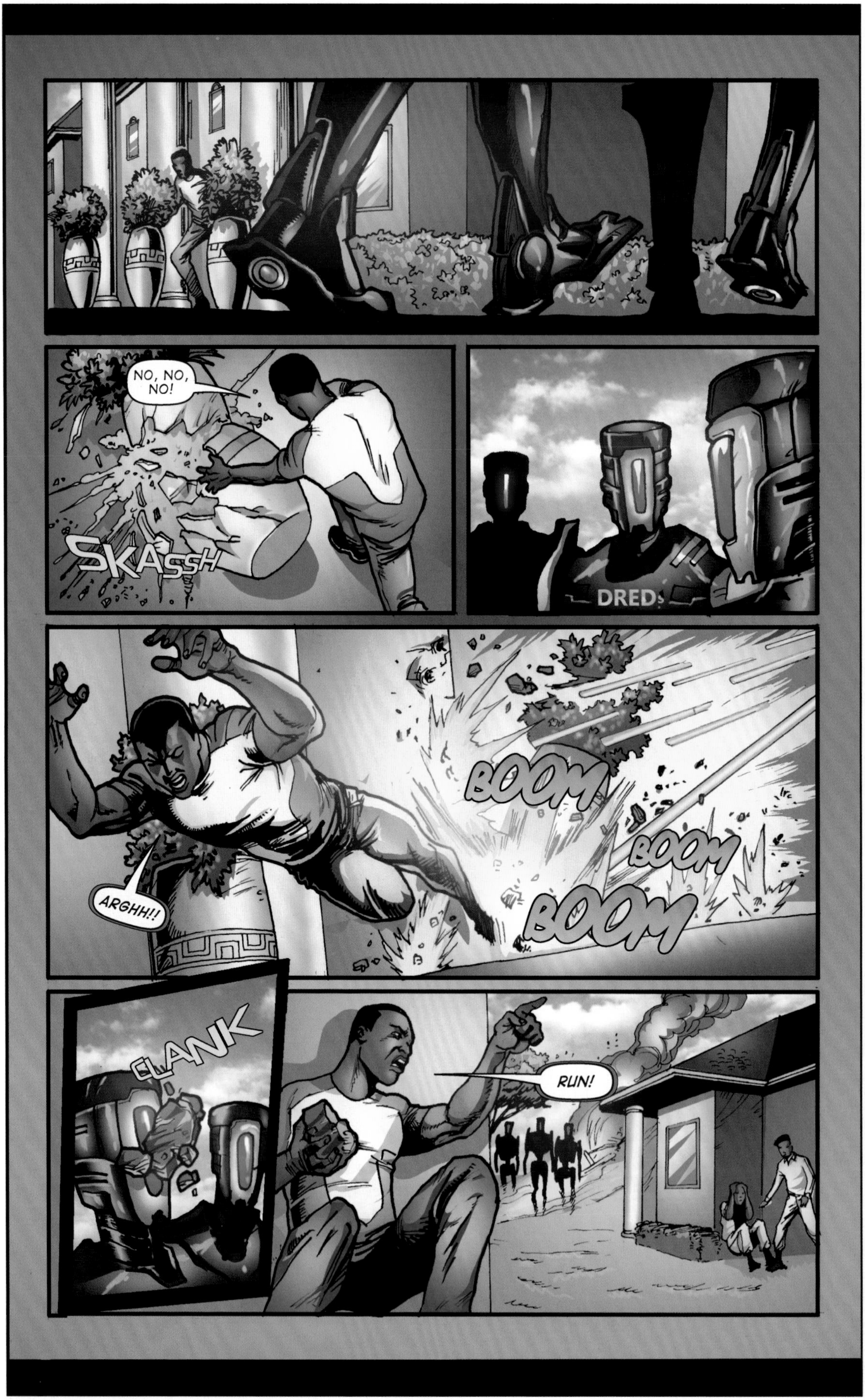
NO, NO, NO!
SKASSH
DREDs
BOOM
BOOM
BOOM
ARGHH!!
CLANK
RUN!

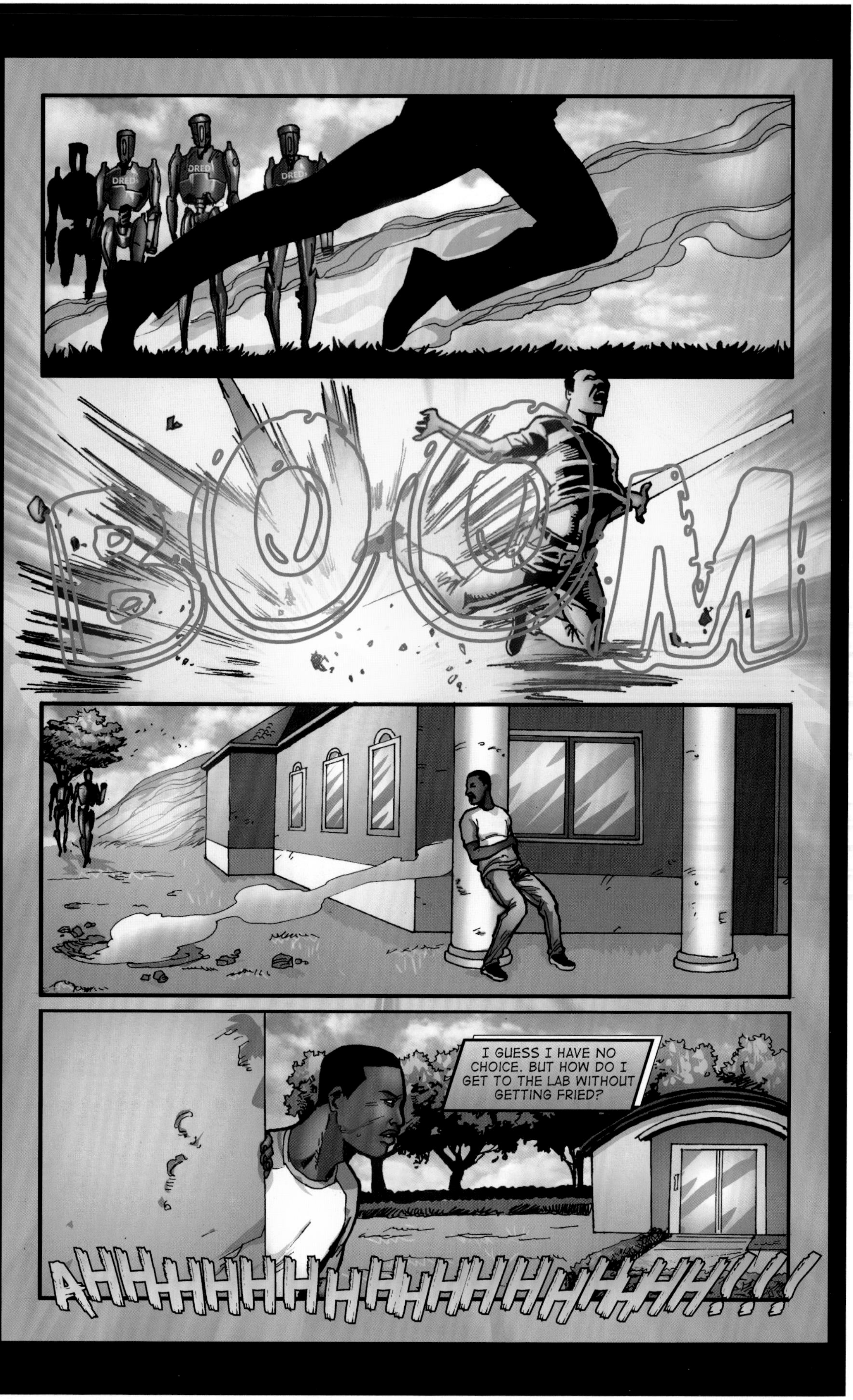
DRED
DRED
DRED
BOOM!
I GUESS I HAVE NO CHOICE. BUT HOW DO I GET TO THE LAB WITHOUT GETTING FRIED?
AHHHHHHHHHHHHHHHHHHH!!!

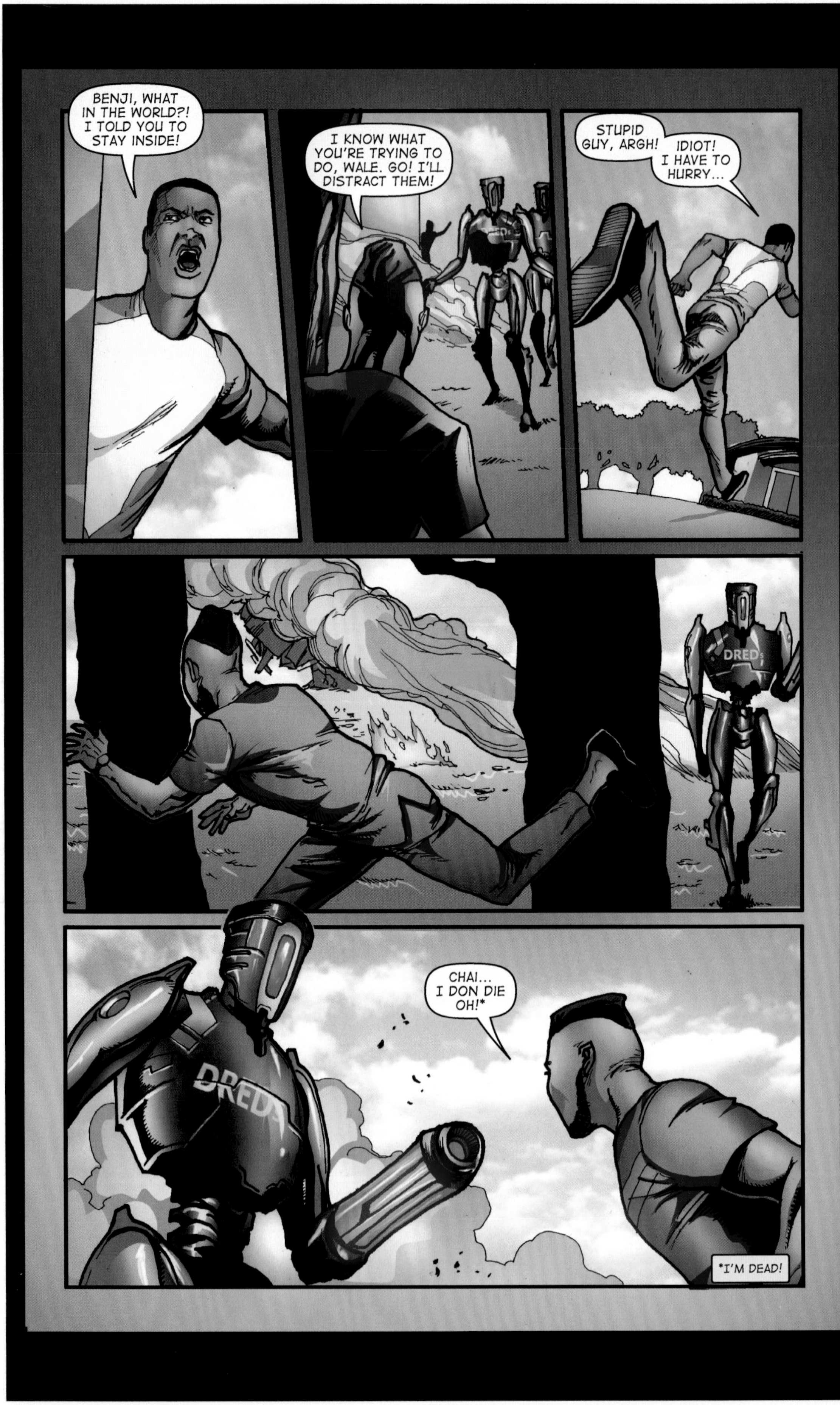

BENJI, WHAT IN THE WORLD?! I TOLD YOU TO STAY INSIDE!
I KNOW WHAT YOU'RE TRYING TO DO, WALE. GO! I'LL DISTRACT THEM!
STUPID GUY, ARGH!
IDIOT! I HAVE TO HURRY...
DREDs
DREDs
CHAI... I DON DIE OH!*
DREDs
*I'M DEAD!

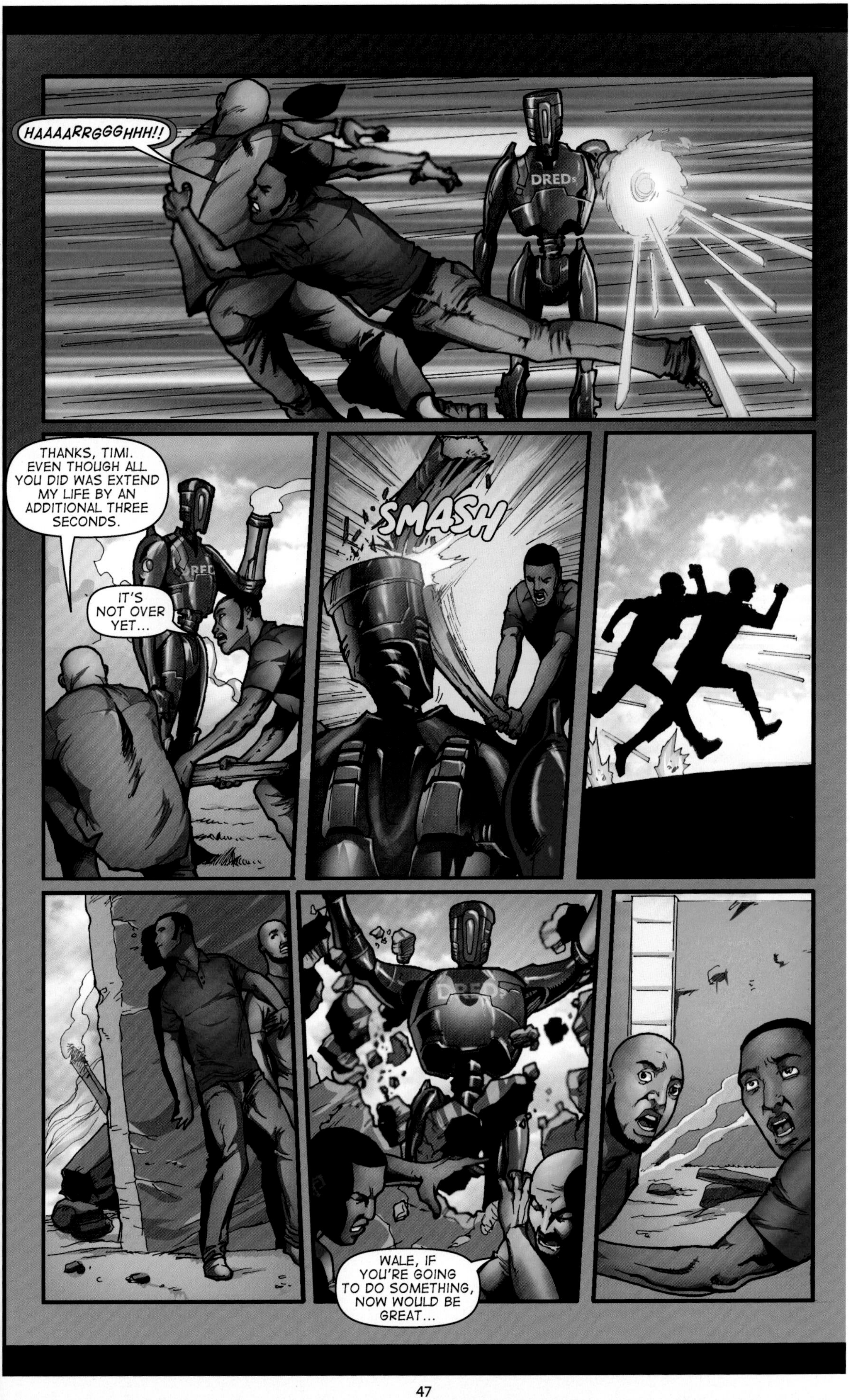
HAAAARRGGGHHH!!
DREDs
THANKS, TIMI. EVEN THOUGH ALL YOU DID WAS EXTEND MY LIFE BY AN ADDITIONAL THREE SECONDS.
IT'S NOT OVER YET...
SMASH
WALE, IF YOU'RE GOING TO DO SOMETHING, NOW WOULD BE GREAT...

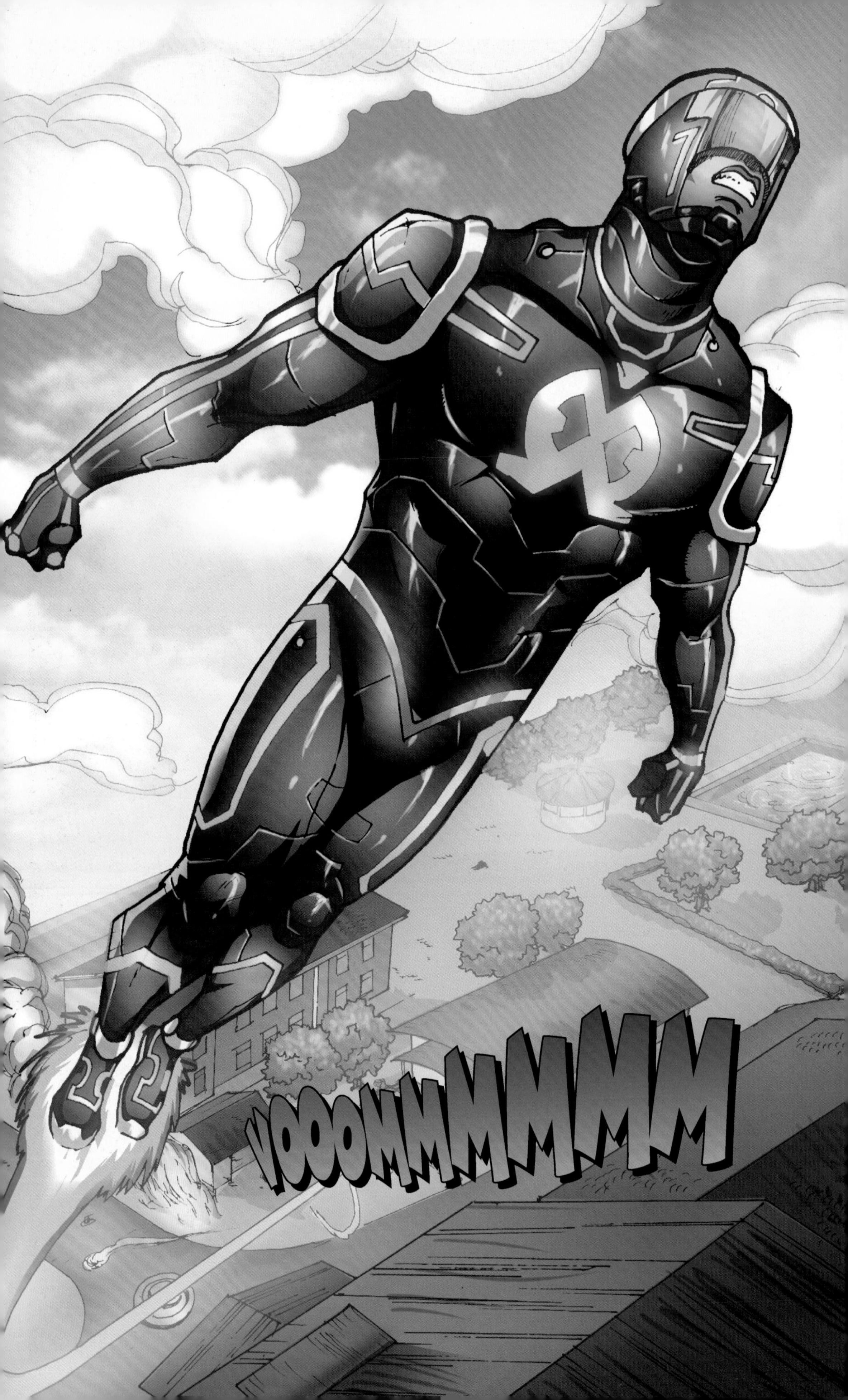
VOOOMMMMMMM

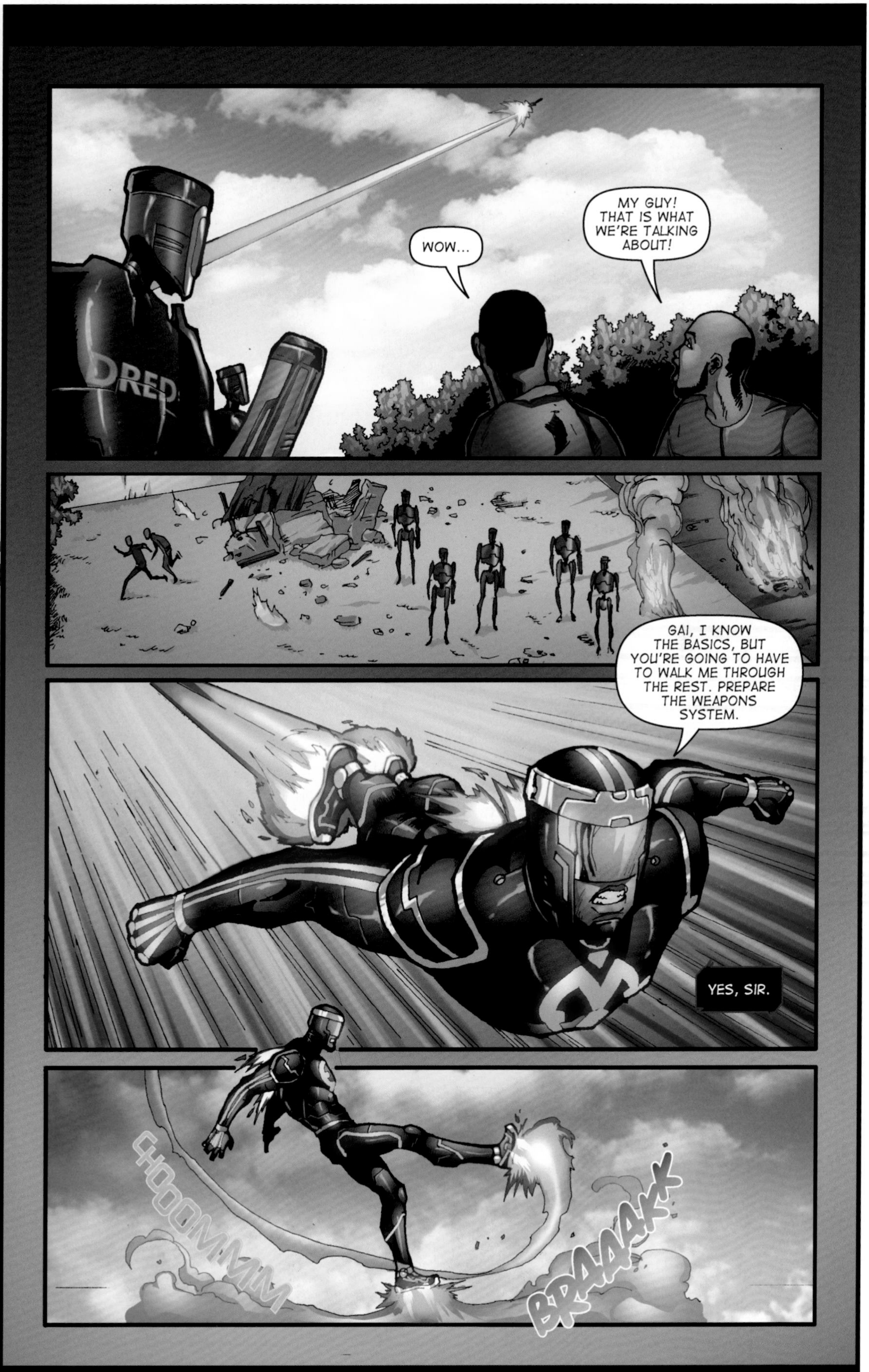
DRED
WOW...
MY GUY! THAT IS WHAT WE'RE TALKING ABOUT!
GAI, I KNOW THE BASICS, BUT YOU'RE GOING TO HAVE TO WALK ME THROUGH THE REST. PREPARE THE WEAPONS SYSTEM.
YES, SIR.
CHOOOMMM
BRAAAKK

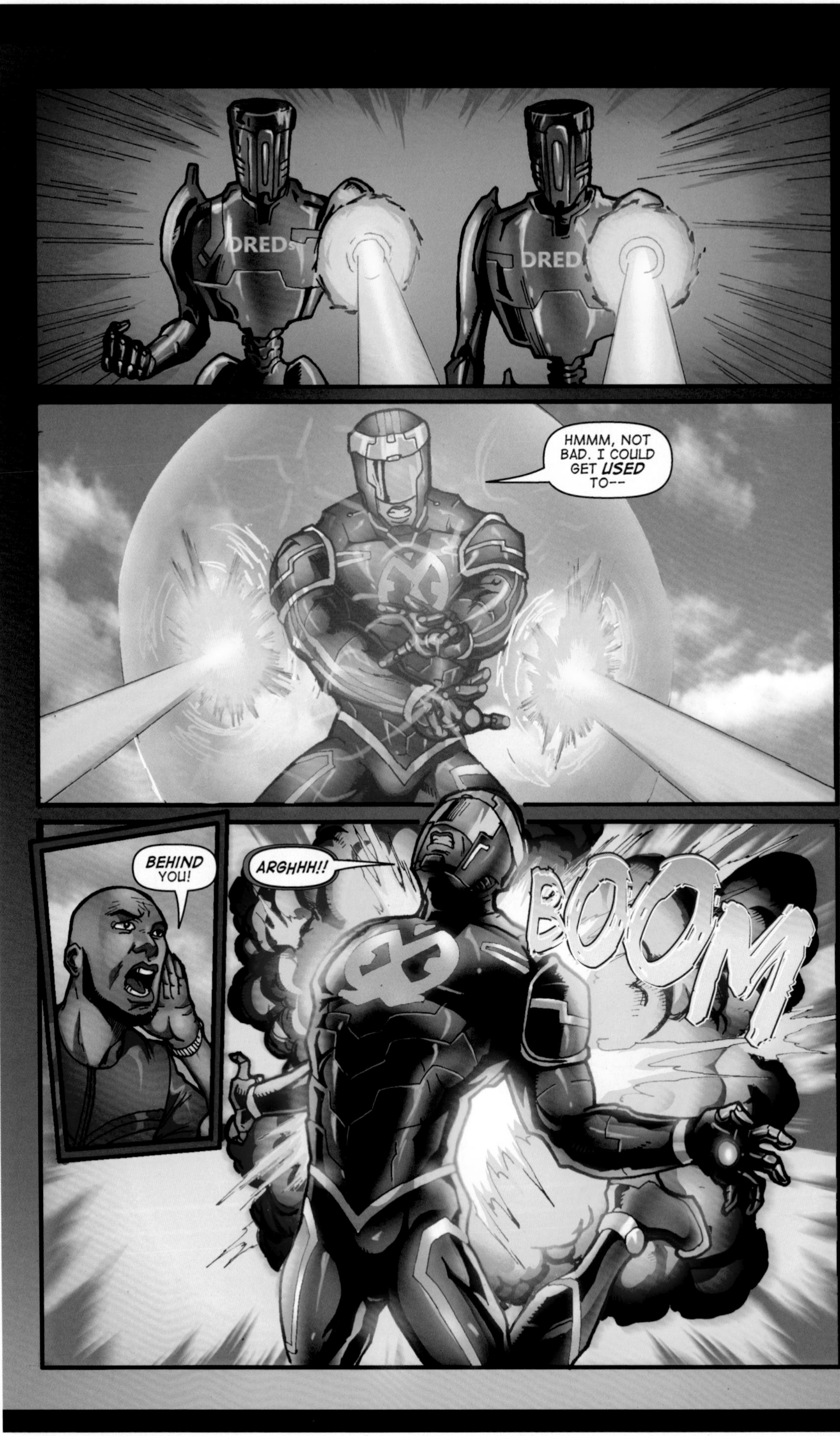
DREDs
DRED
HMMM, NOT BAD. I COULD GET *USED* TO--
BEHIND YOU!
ARGHHH!!
BOOM

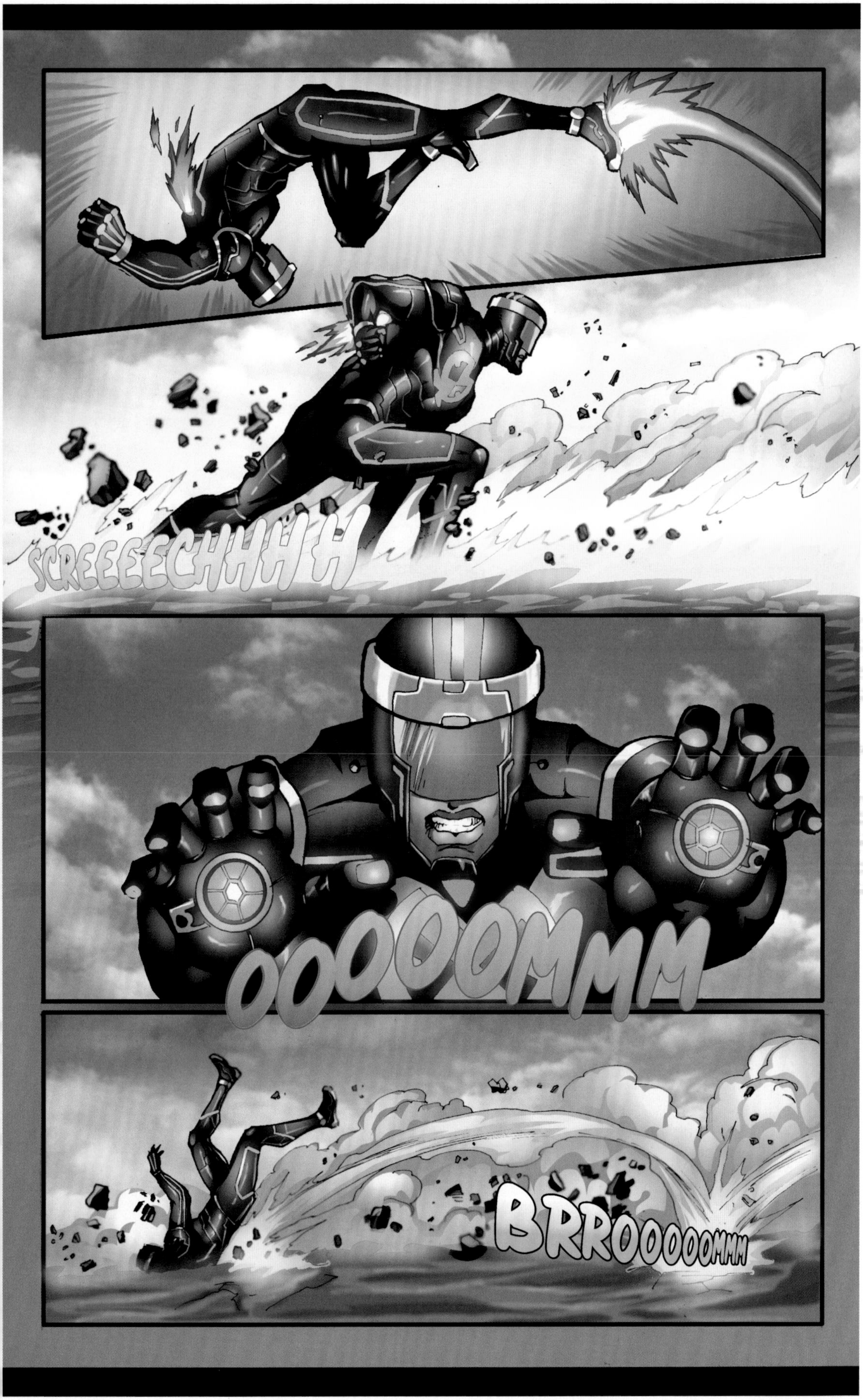
SCREEEEECHHHHH
OOOOOMMM
BRROOOOOMMM

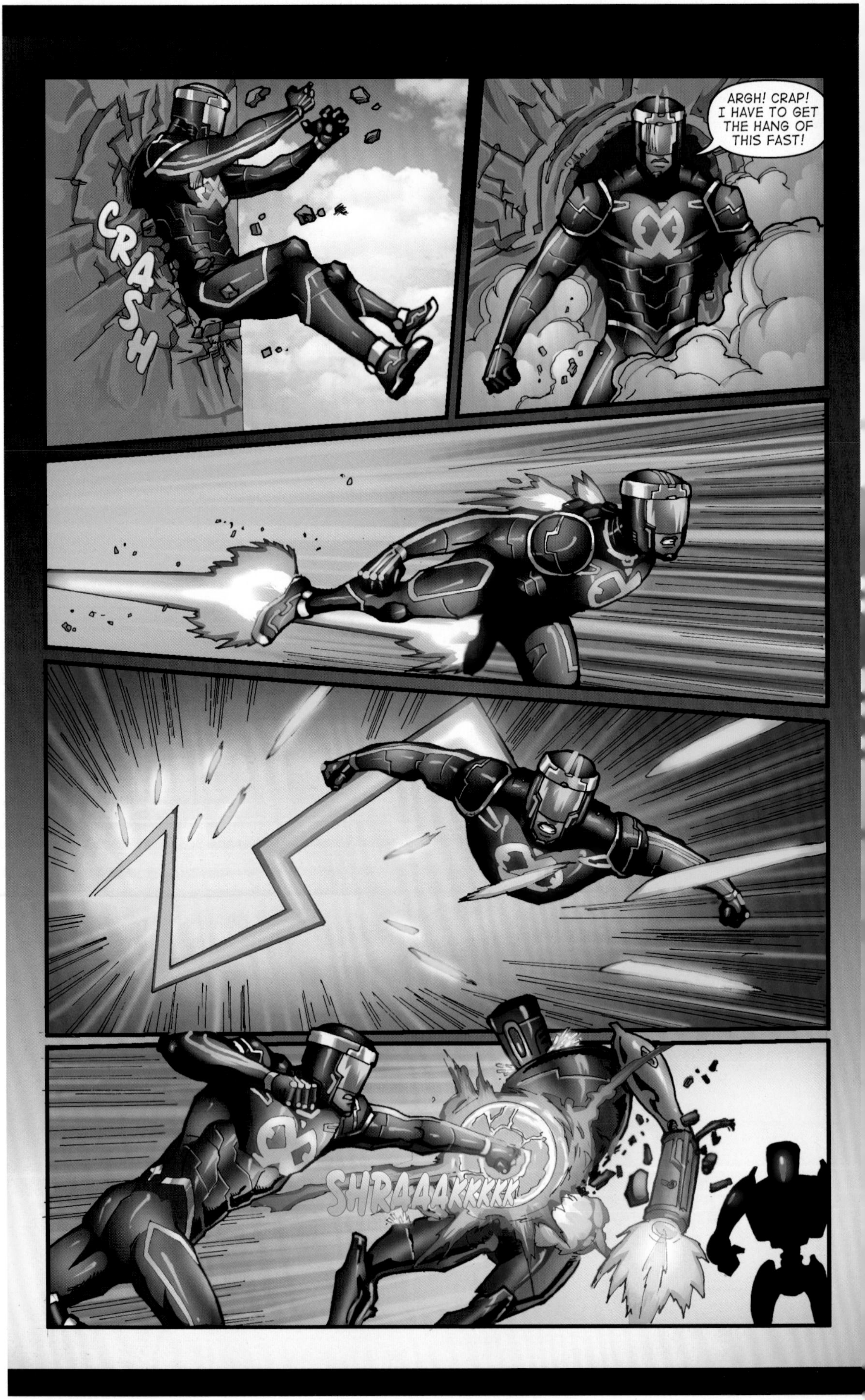
CRASH
ARGH! CRAP! I HAVE TO GET THE HANG OF THIS FAST!
SHRAAAKKKKK

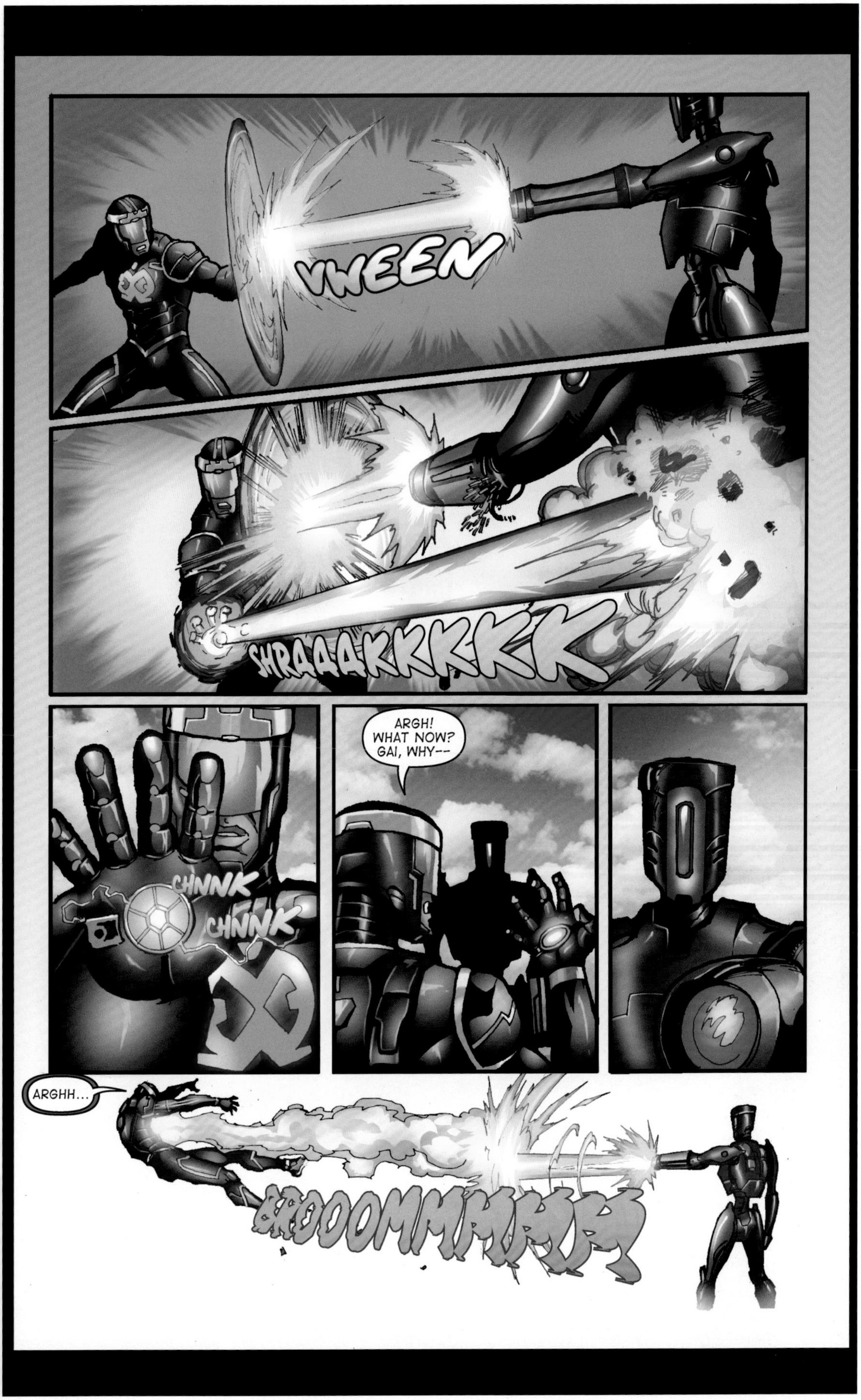
VWEEN
SHRAAAKKKKKK
CHNNK
CHNNK
ARGH! WHAT NOW? GAI, WHY--
ARGHH...
BROOOMMMMM

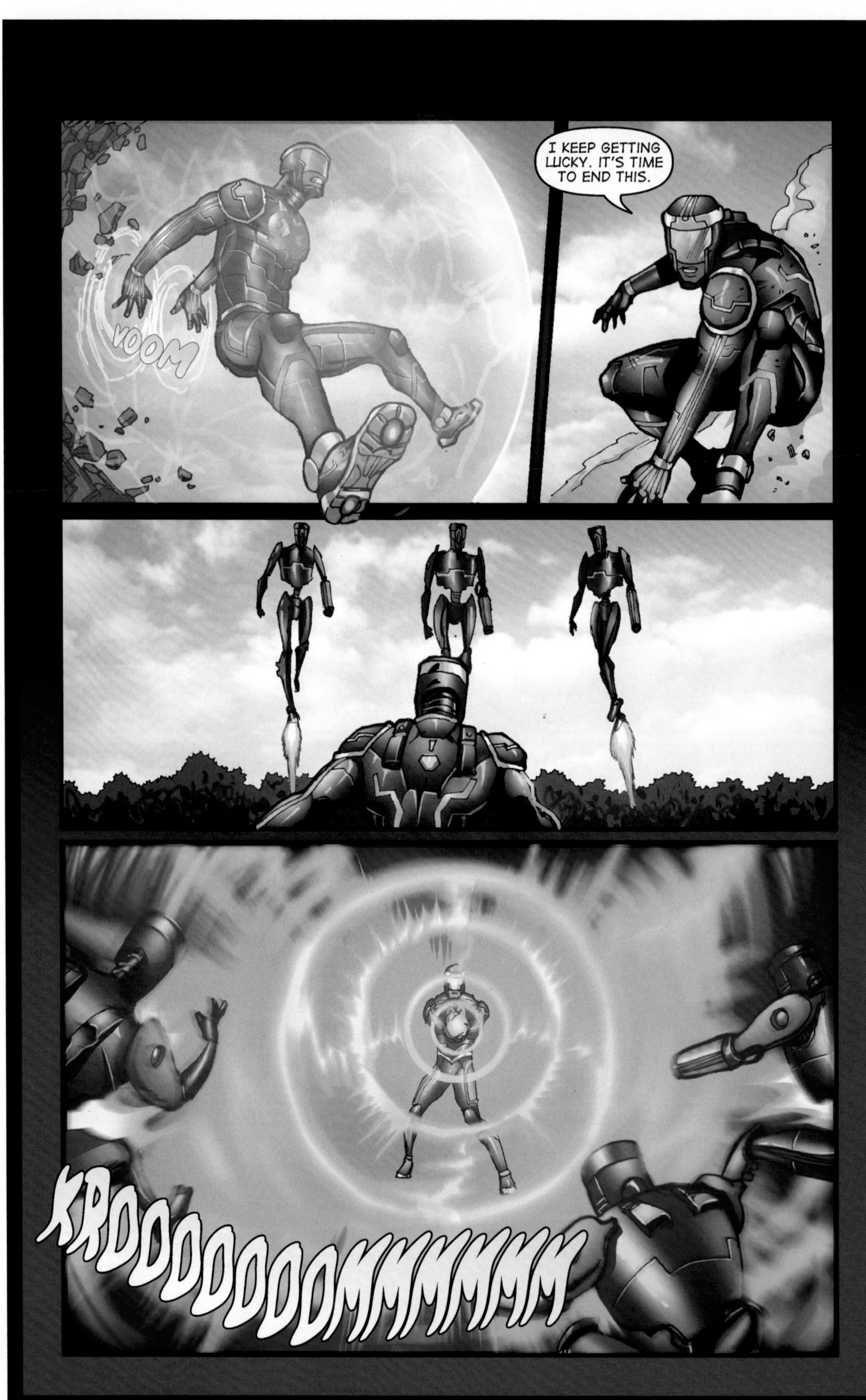
VOOM
I KEEP GETTING LUCKY. IT'S TIME TO END THIS.
KROOOOOOOMMMMMMM

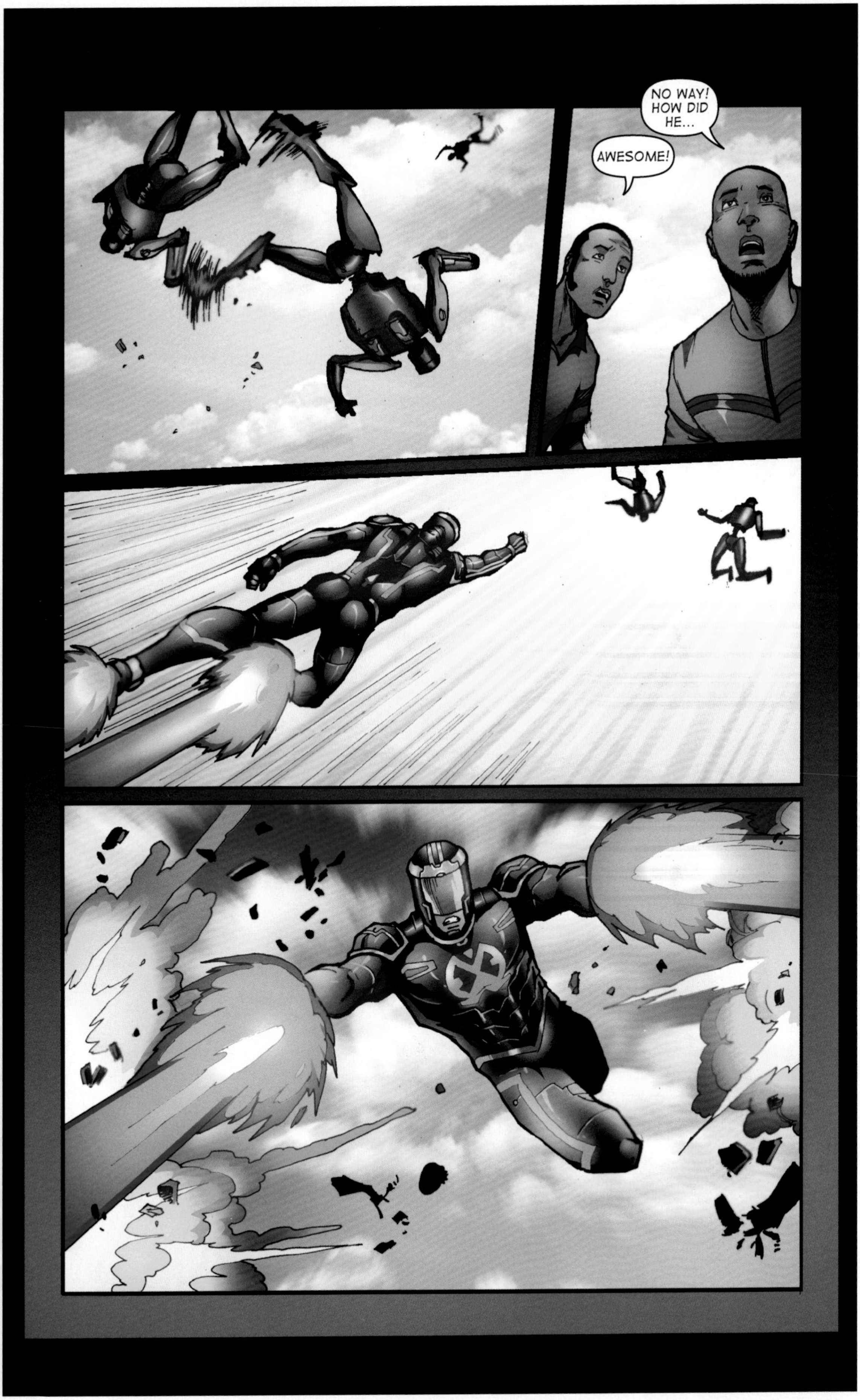
NO WAY! HOW DID HE...
AWESOME!

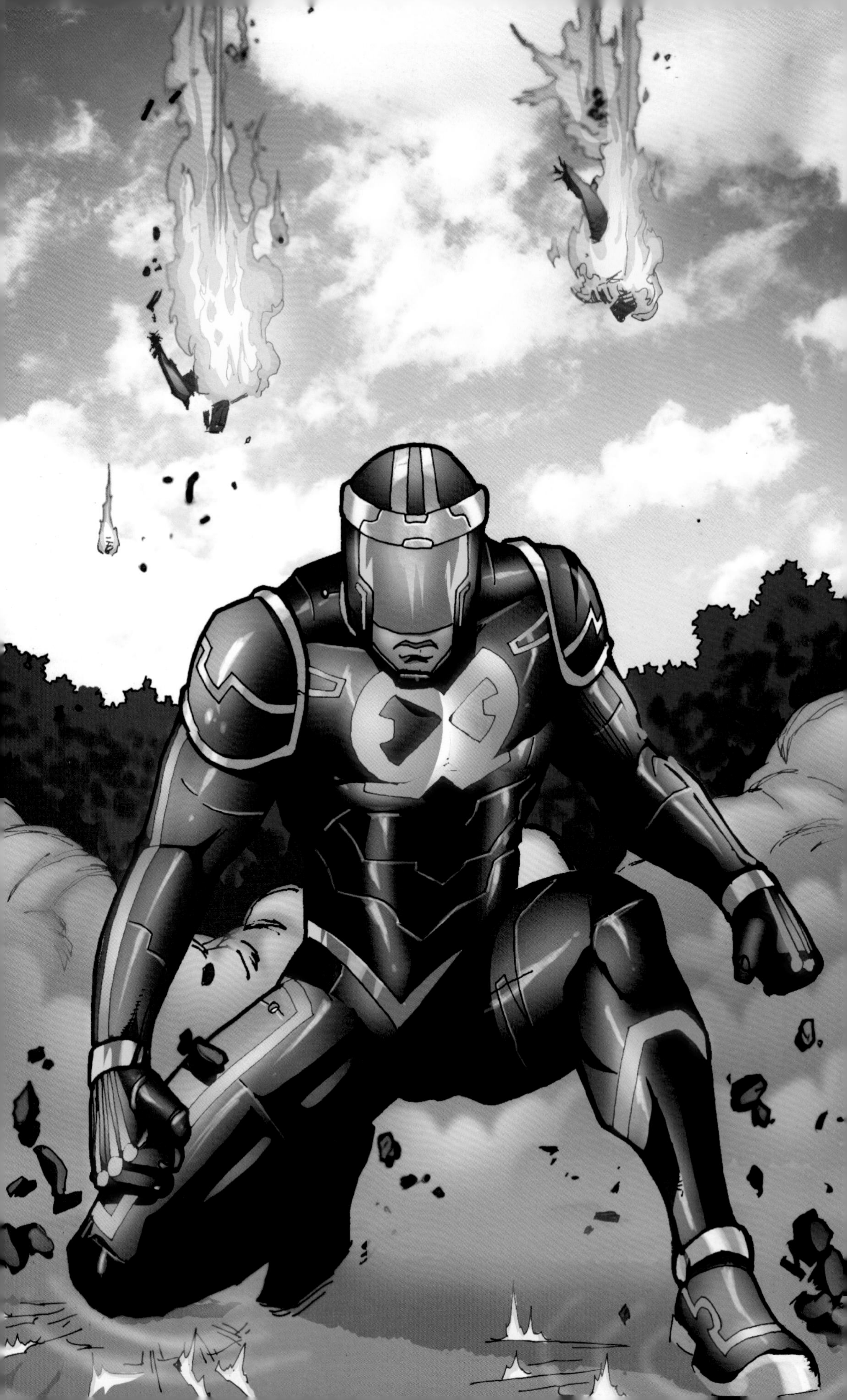

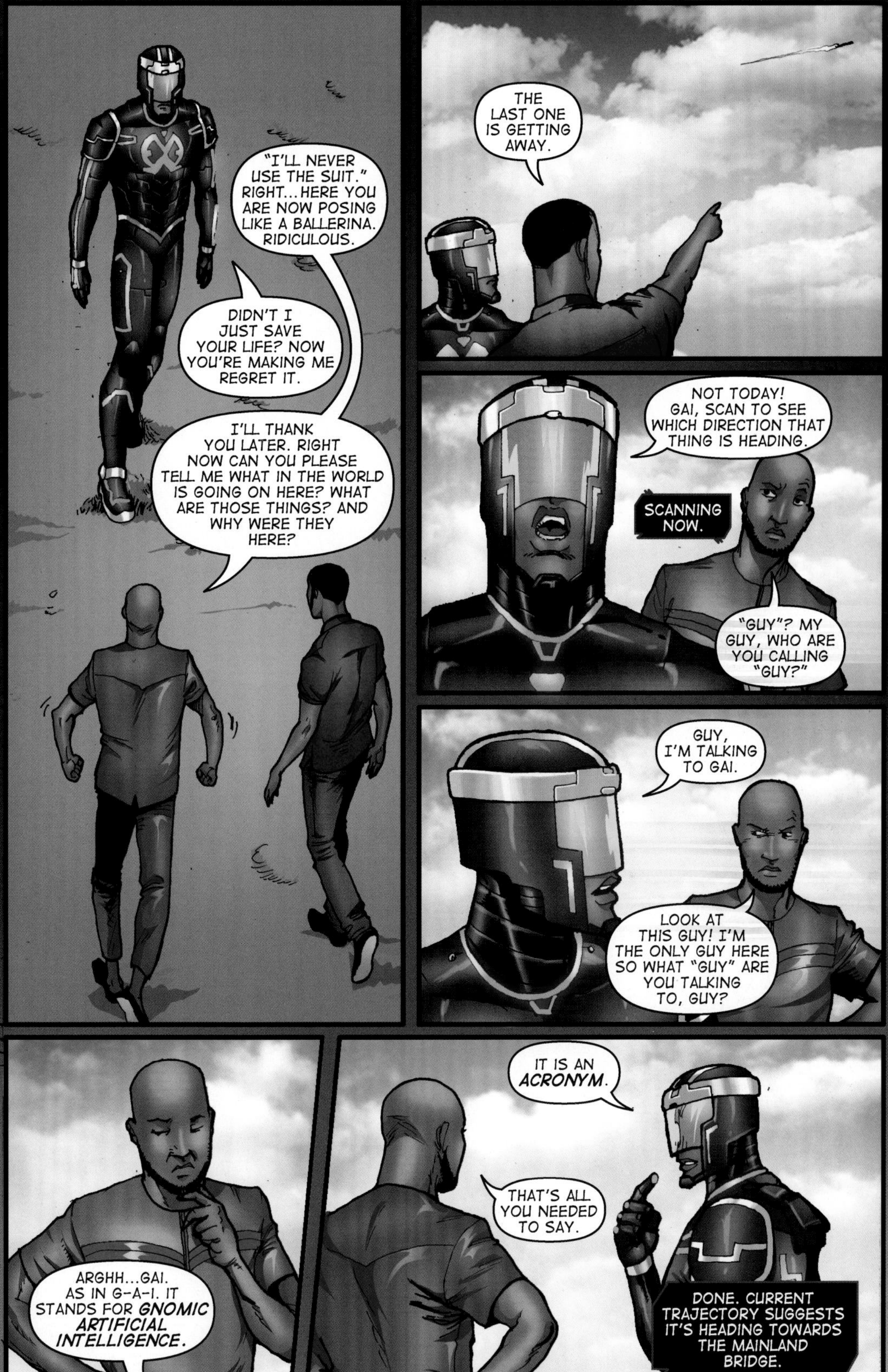
"I'LL NEVER USE THE SUIT." RIGHT... HERE YOU ARE NOW POSING LIKE A BALLERINA. RIDICULOUS.
DIDN'T I JUST SAVE YOUR LIFE? NOW YOU'RE MAKING ME REGRET IT.
I'LL THANK YOU LATER. RIGHT NOW CAN YOU PLEASE TELL ME WHAT IN THE WORLD IS GOING ON HERE? WHAT ARE THOSE THINGS? AND WHY WERE THEY HERE?
THE LAST ONE IS GETTING AWAY.
NOT TODAY! GAI, SCAN TO SEE WHICH DIRECTION THAT THING IS HEADING.
SCANNING NOW.
"GUY"? MY GUY, WHO ARE YOU CALLING "GUY?"
GUY, I'M TALKING TO GAI.
LOOK AT THIS GUY! I'M THE ONLY GUY HERE SO WHAT "GUY" ARE YOU TALKING TO, GUY?
ARGHH...GAI. AS IN G-A-I. IT STANDS FOR *GNOMIC ARTIFICIAL INTELLIGENCE*.
IT IS AN *ACRONYM*.
THAT'S ALL YOU NEEDED TO SAY.
DONE. CURRENT TRAJECTORY SUGGESTS IT'S HEADING TOWARDS THE MAINLAND BRIDGE.

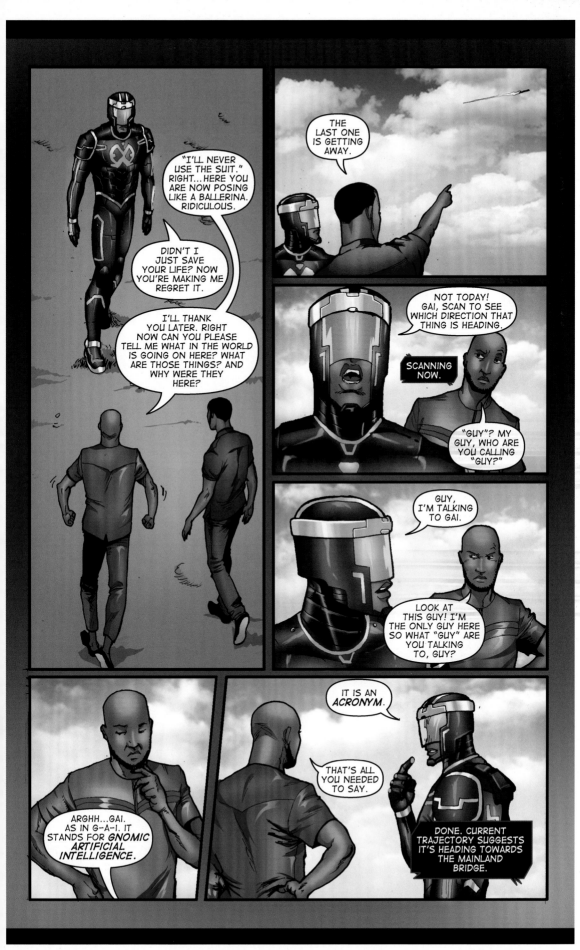

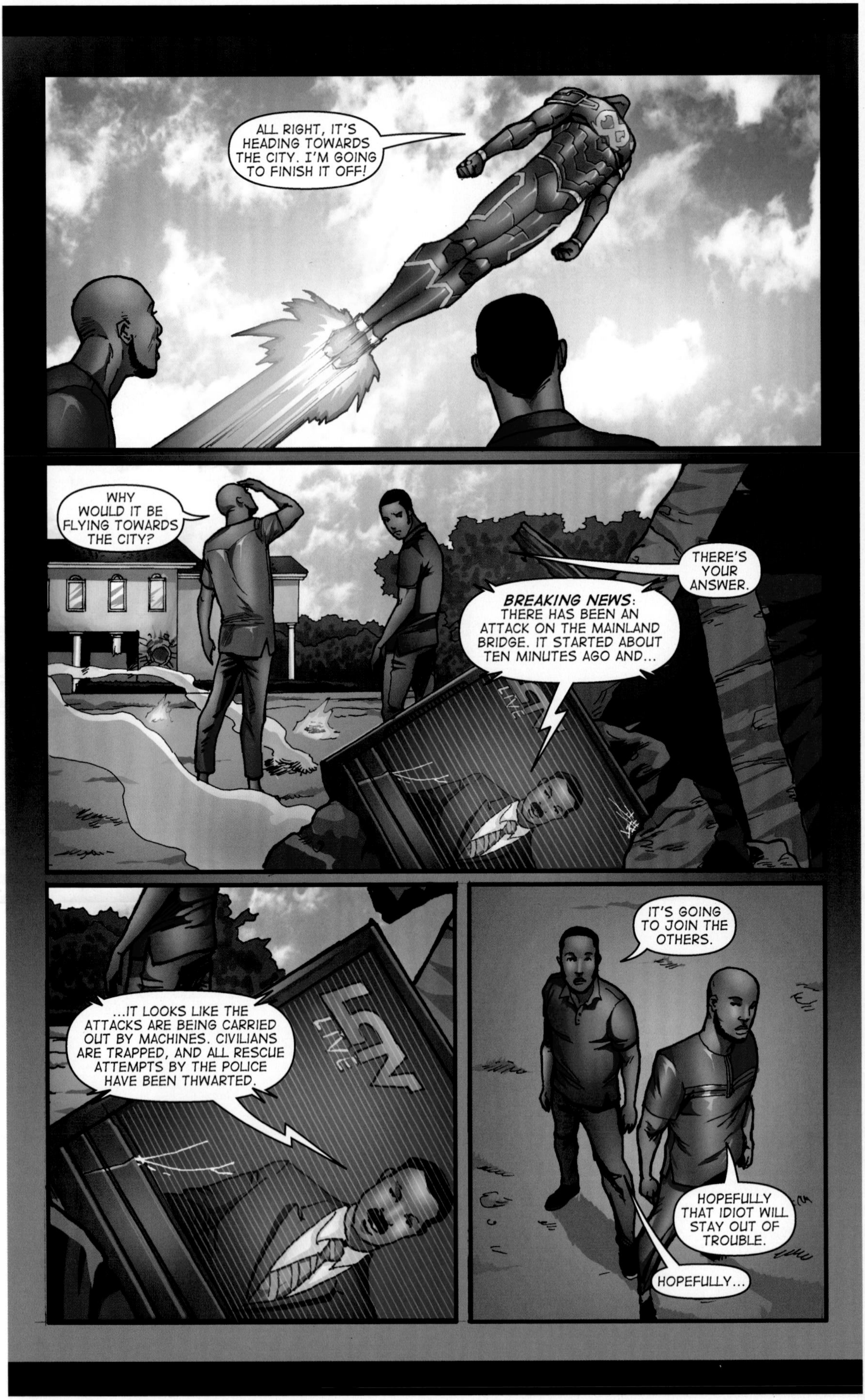
ALL RIGHT, IT'S HEADING TOWARDS THE CITY. I'M GOING TO FINISH IT OFF!
WHY WOULD IT BE FLYING TOWARDS THE CITY?
THERE'S YOUR ANSWER.
BREAKING NEWS: THERE HAS BEEN AN ATTACK ON THE MAINLAND BRIDGE. IT STARTED ABOUT TEN MINUTES AGO AND...
...IT LOOKS LIKE THE ATTACKS ARE BEING CARRIED OUT BY MACHINES. CIVILIANS ARE TRAPPED, AND ALL RESCUE ATTEMPTS BY THE POLICE HAVE BEEN THWARTED.
IT'S GOING TO JOIN THE OTHERS.
HOPEFULLY THAT IDIOT WILL STAY OUT OF TROUBLE.
HOPEFULLY...

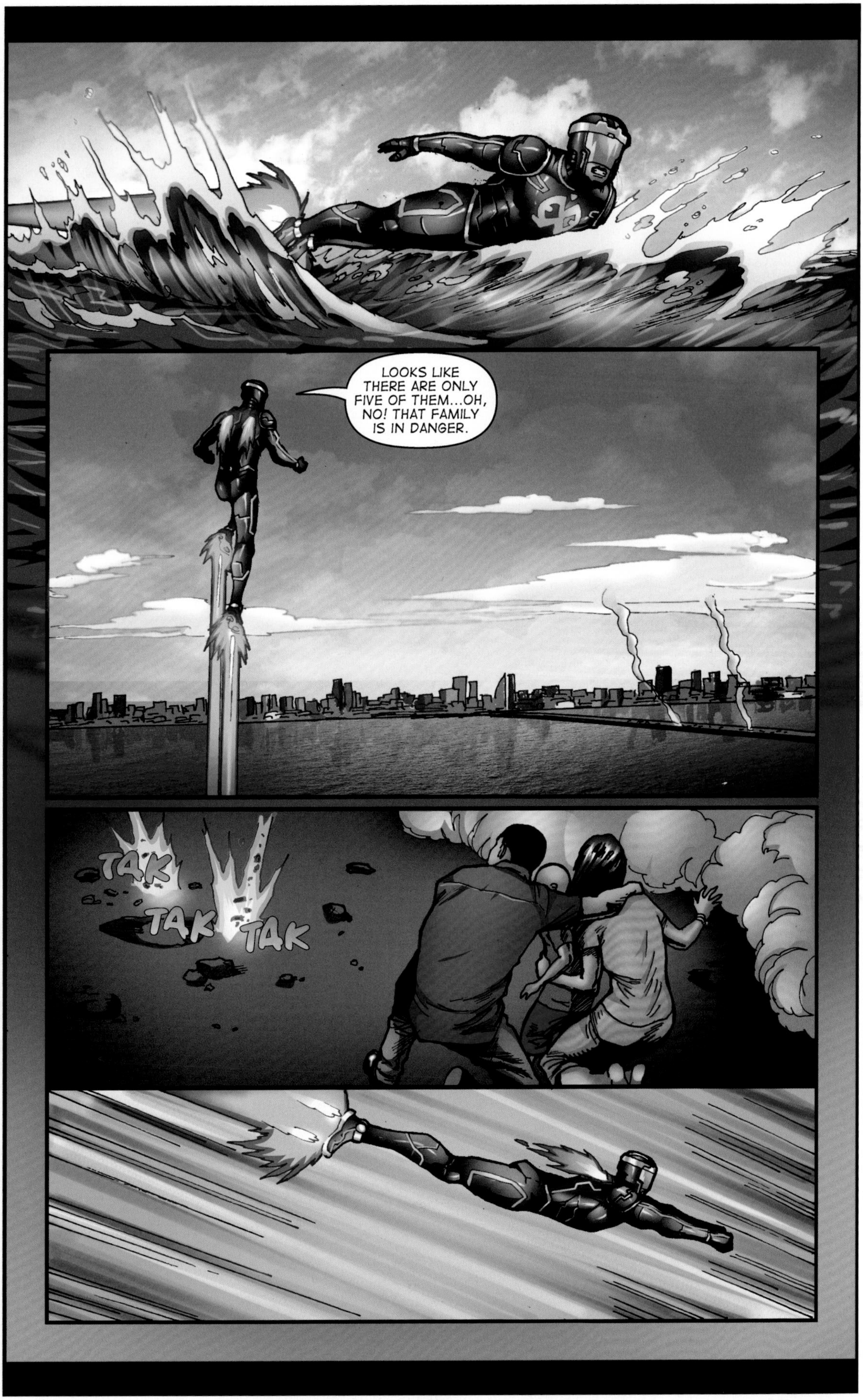
LOOKS LIKE THERE ARE ONLY FIVE OF THEM...OH, NO! THAT FAMILY IS IN DANGER.
TAK
TAK
TAK

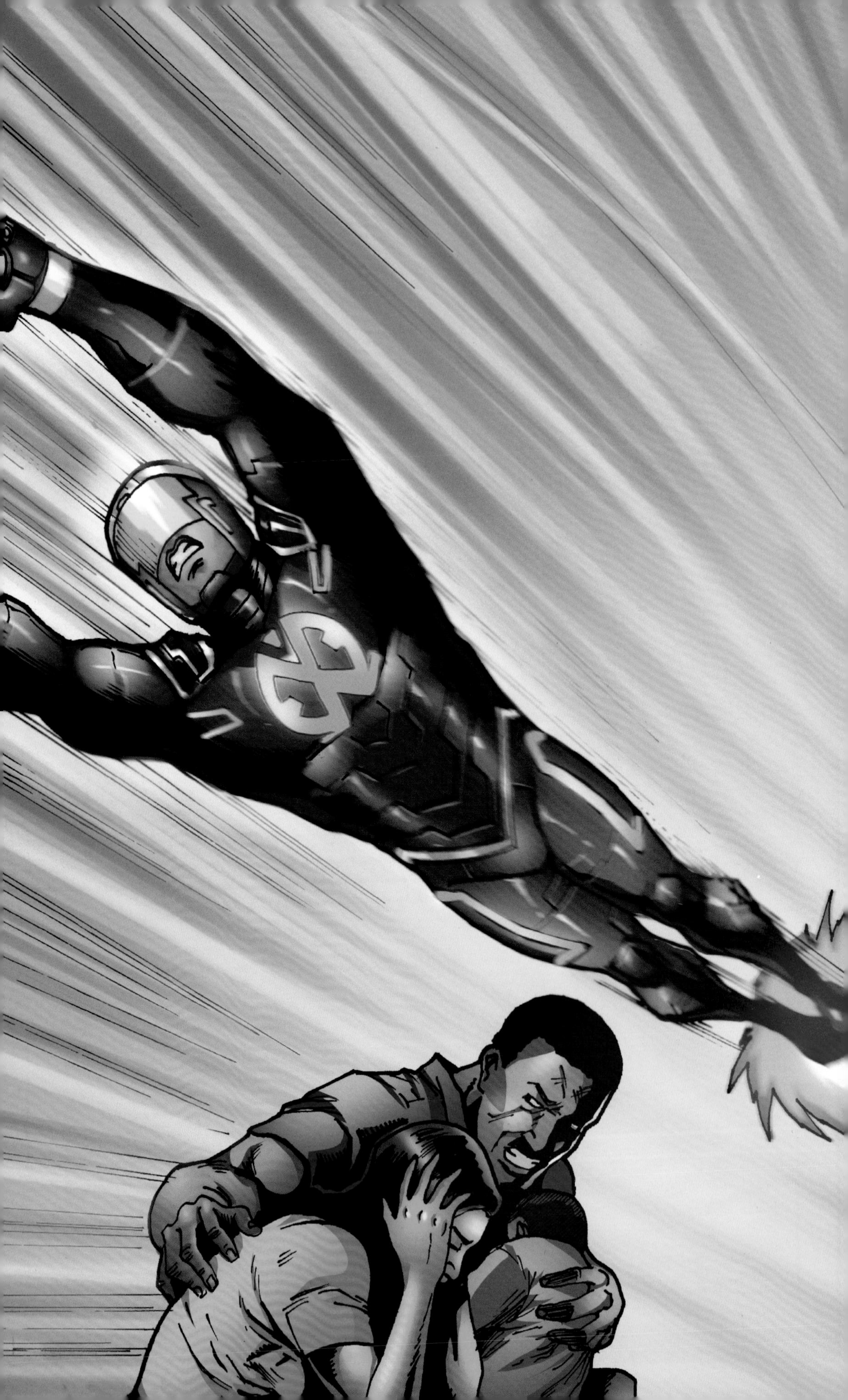

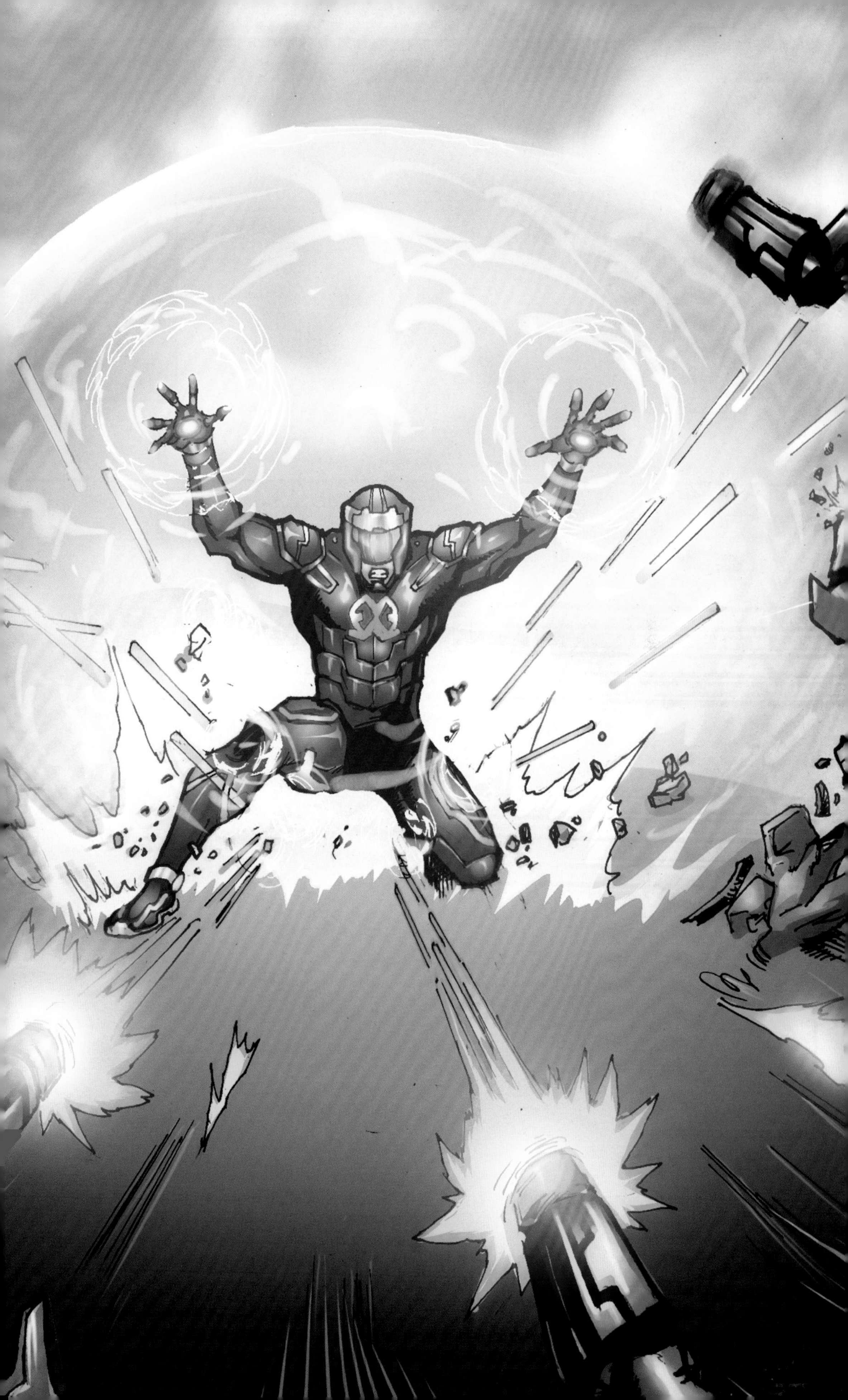

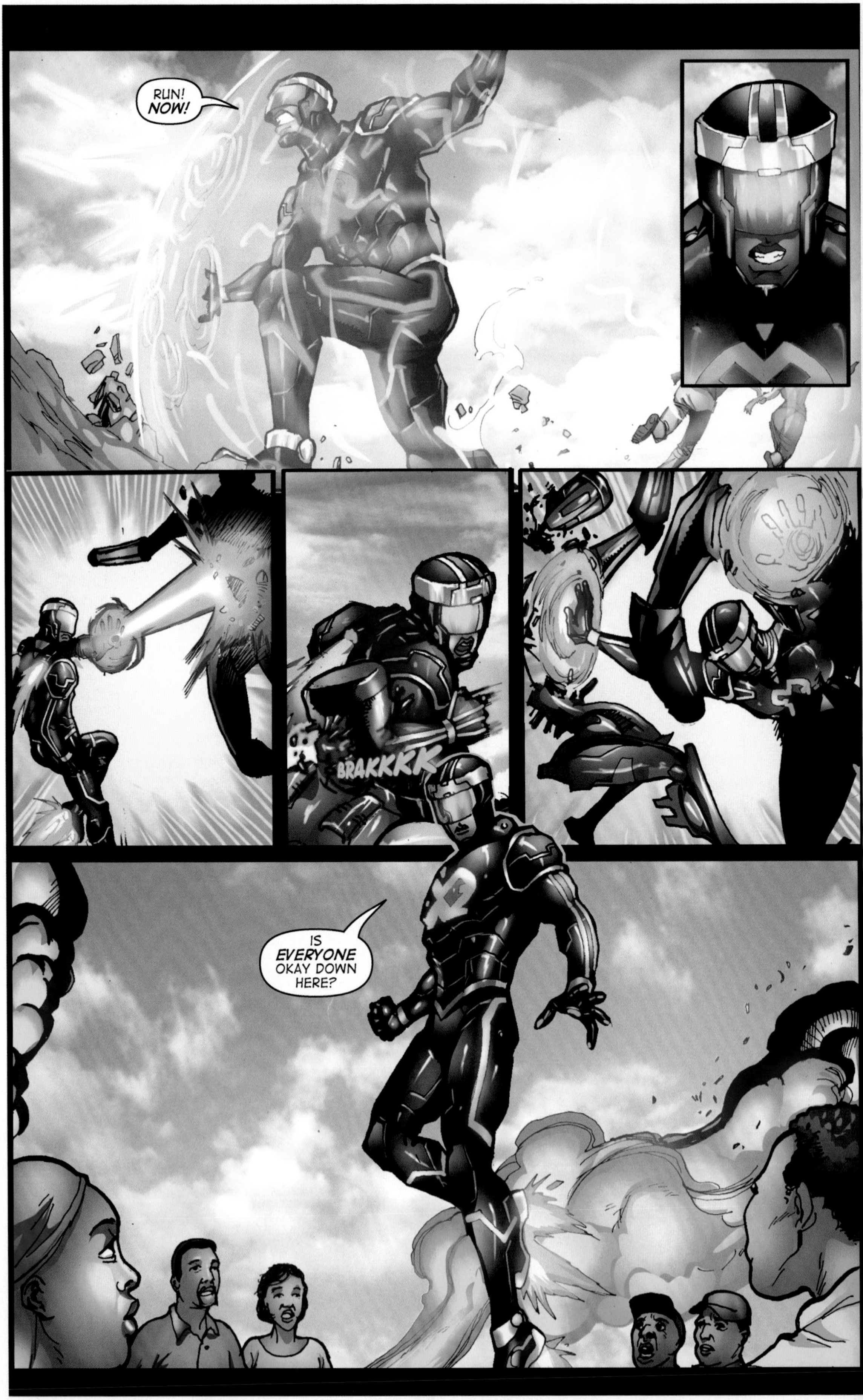
RUN! NOW!
BRAKKKK
IS EVERYONE OKAY DOWN HERE?

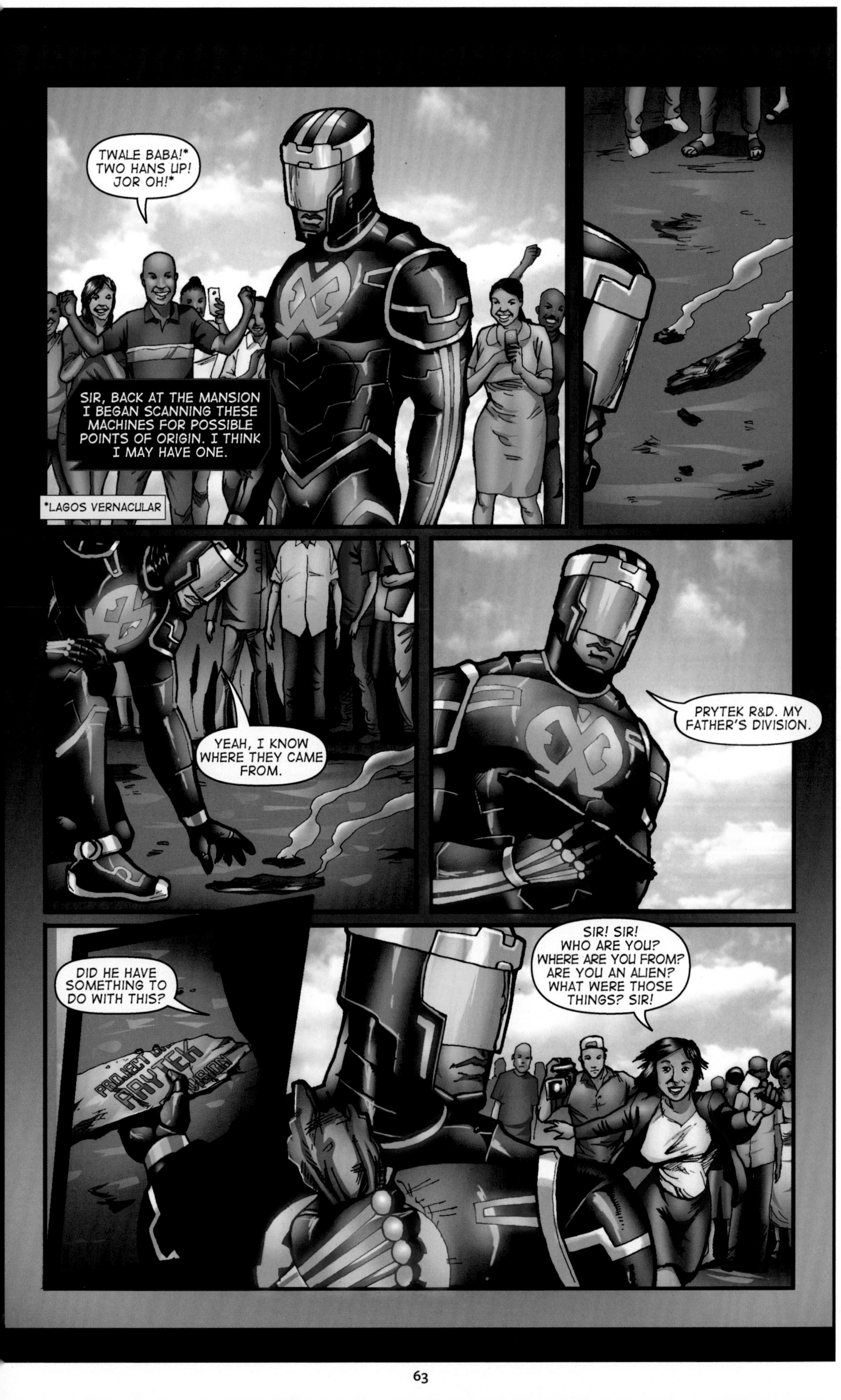
TWALE BABA!* TWO HANS UP! JOR OH!*
SIR, BACK AT THE MANSION I BEGAN SCANNING THESE MACHINES FOR POSSIBLE POINTS OF ORIGIN. I THINK I MAY HAVE ONE.
*LAGOS VERNACULAR
YEAH, I KNOW WHERE THEY CAME FROM.
PRYTEK R&D. MY FATHER'S DIVISION.
DID HE HAVE SOMETHING TO DO WITH THIS?
SIR! SIR! WHO ARE YOU? WHERE ARE YOU FROM? ARE YOU AN ALIEN? WHAT WERE THOSE THINGS? SIR!

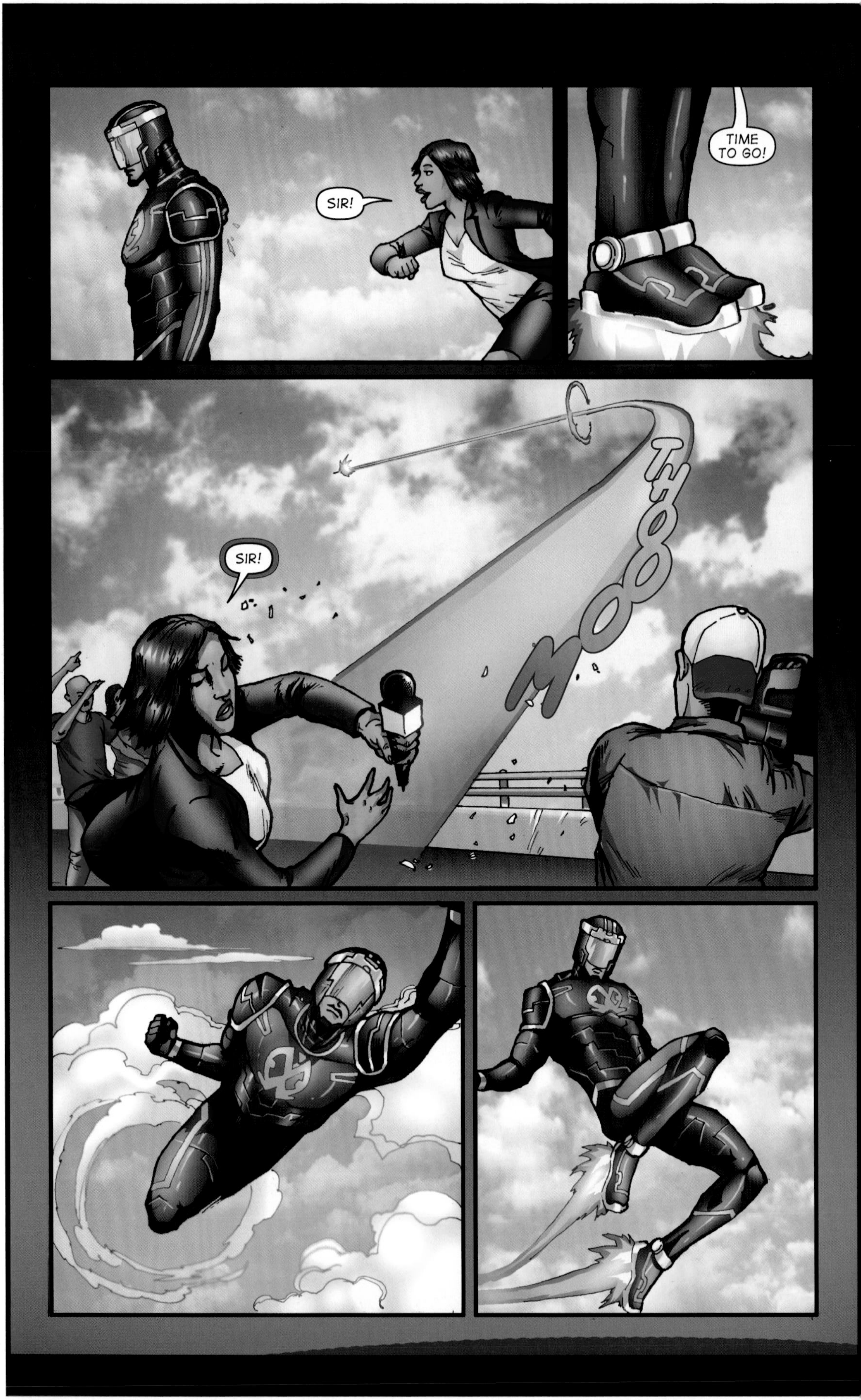
SIR!
TIME TO GO!
SIR!
THOOOOM

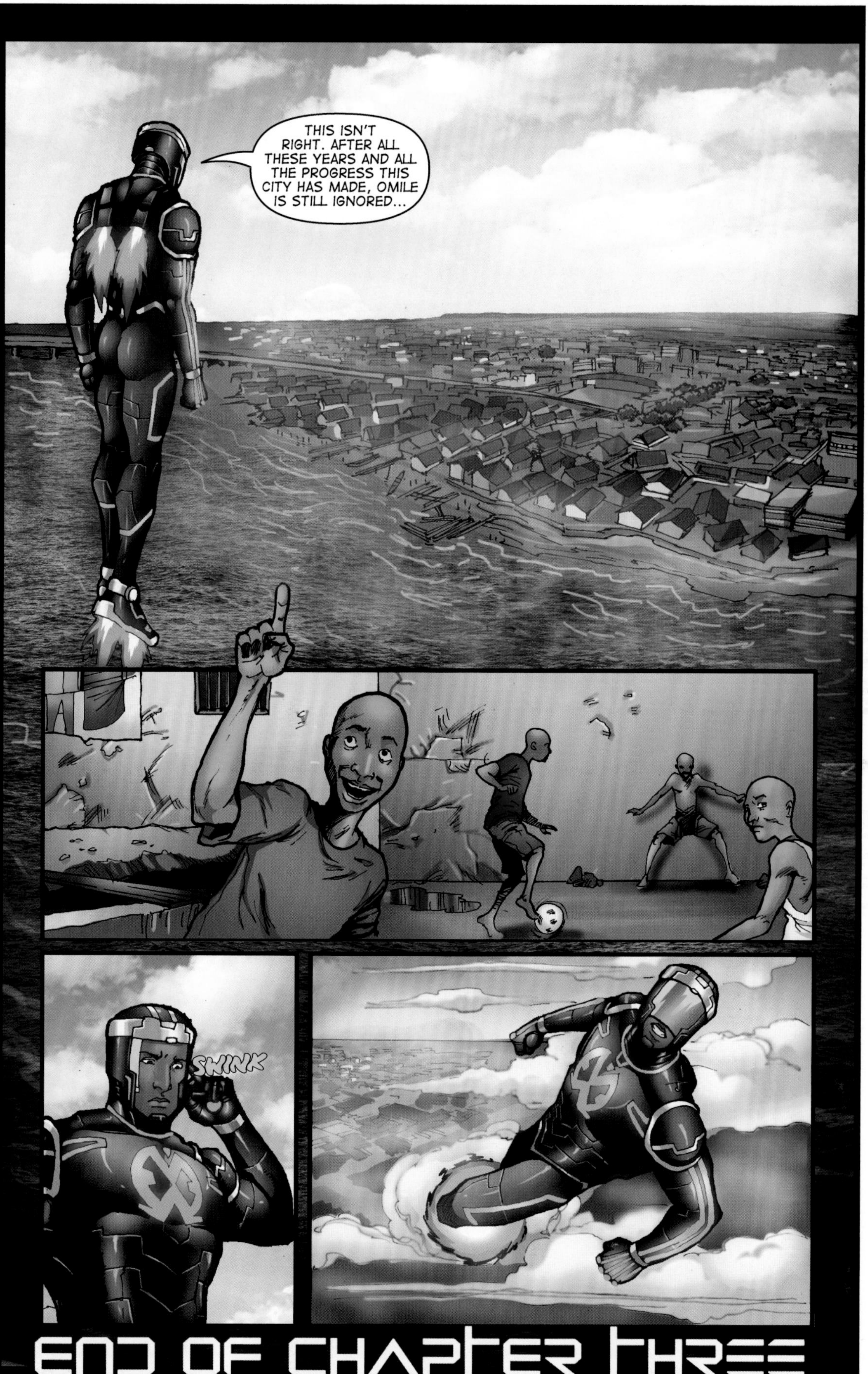
THIS ISN'T RIGHT. AFTER ALL THESE YEARS AND ALL THE PROGRESS THIS CITY HAS MADE, OMILE IS STILL IGNORED...
SWINK
END OF CHAPTER THREE

"Their corruption and
lack of discipline has given
birth to a frail nation."
—ONIKU

CHAPTER FOUR

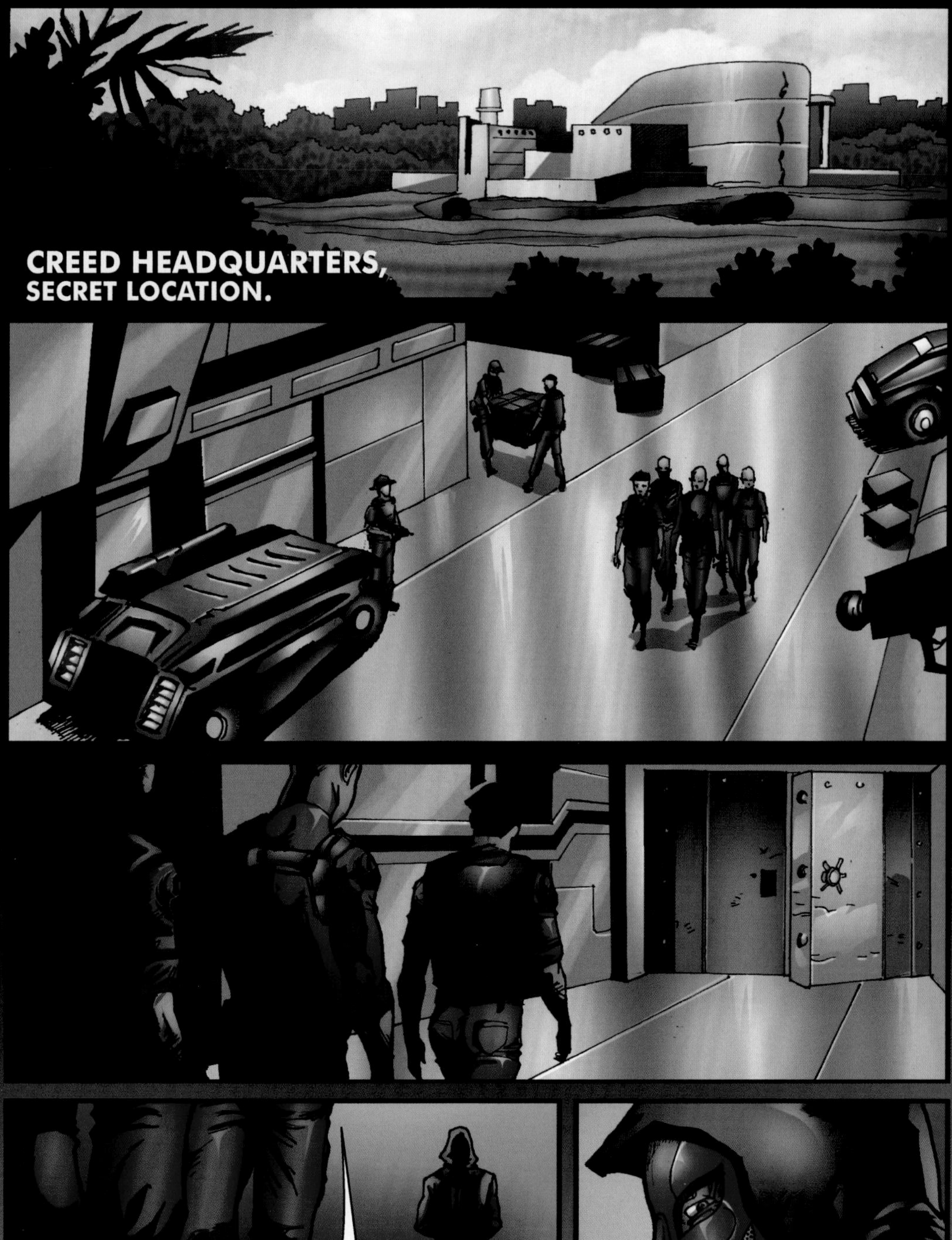
CREED HEADQUARTERS,
SECRET LOCATION.
GENERAL, WE WERE NOT ABLE TO GET PAST THE POLICE. THEY HAVE STATIONED MORE MEN AT THE BRIDGES.
IT'S MUCH MORE DIFFICULT TO GET INTO THE CITY. ONLY FIVE OF US WERE ABLE TO MAKE IT BACK.
FORGIVE ME, GENERAL.

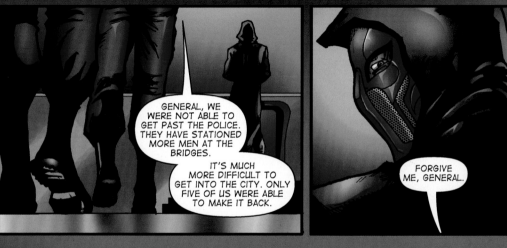

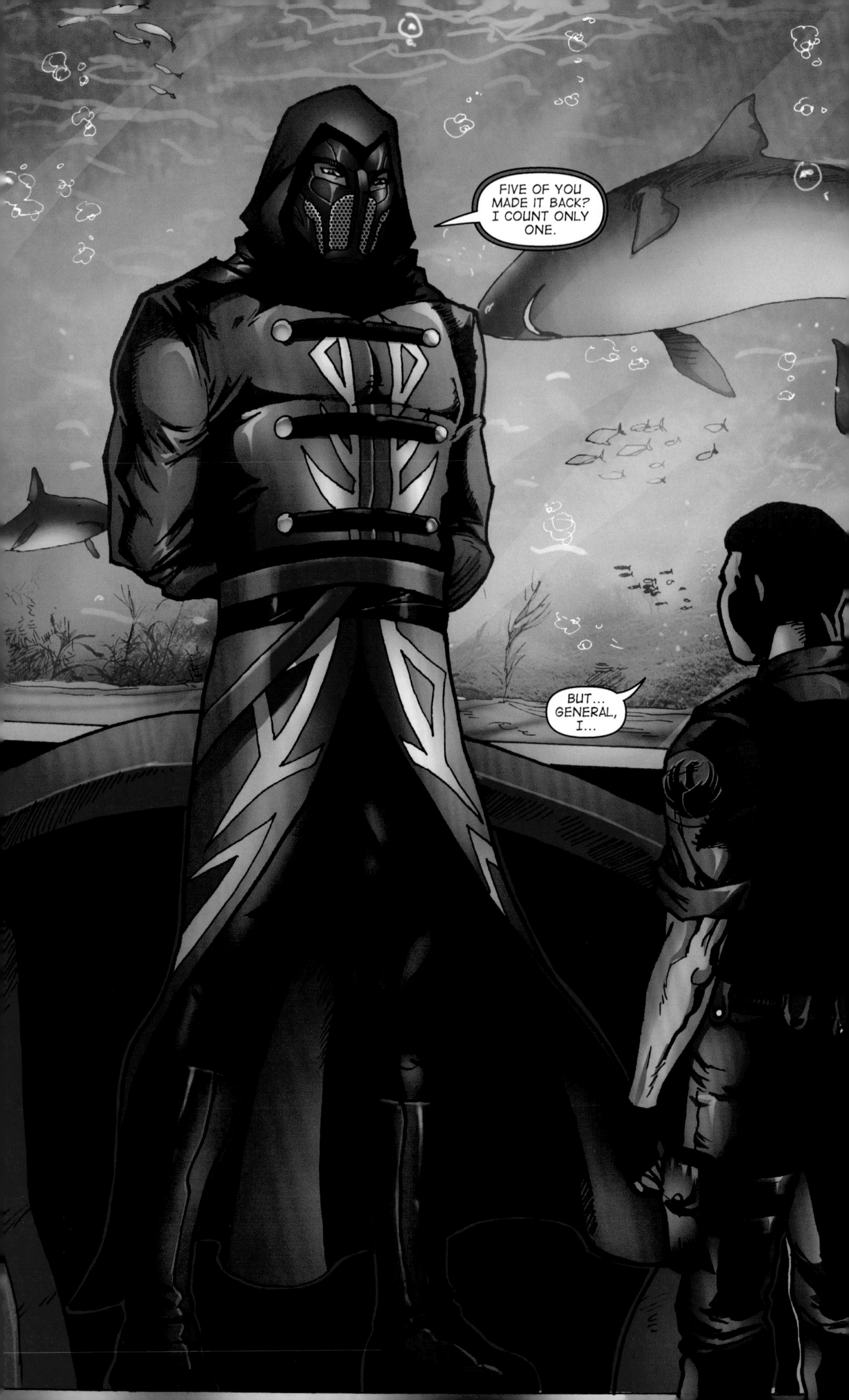
FIVE OF YOU MADE IT BACK? I COUNT ONLY ONE.
BUT... GENERAL, I...

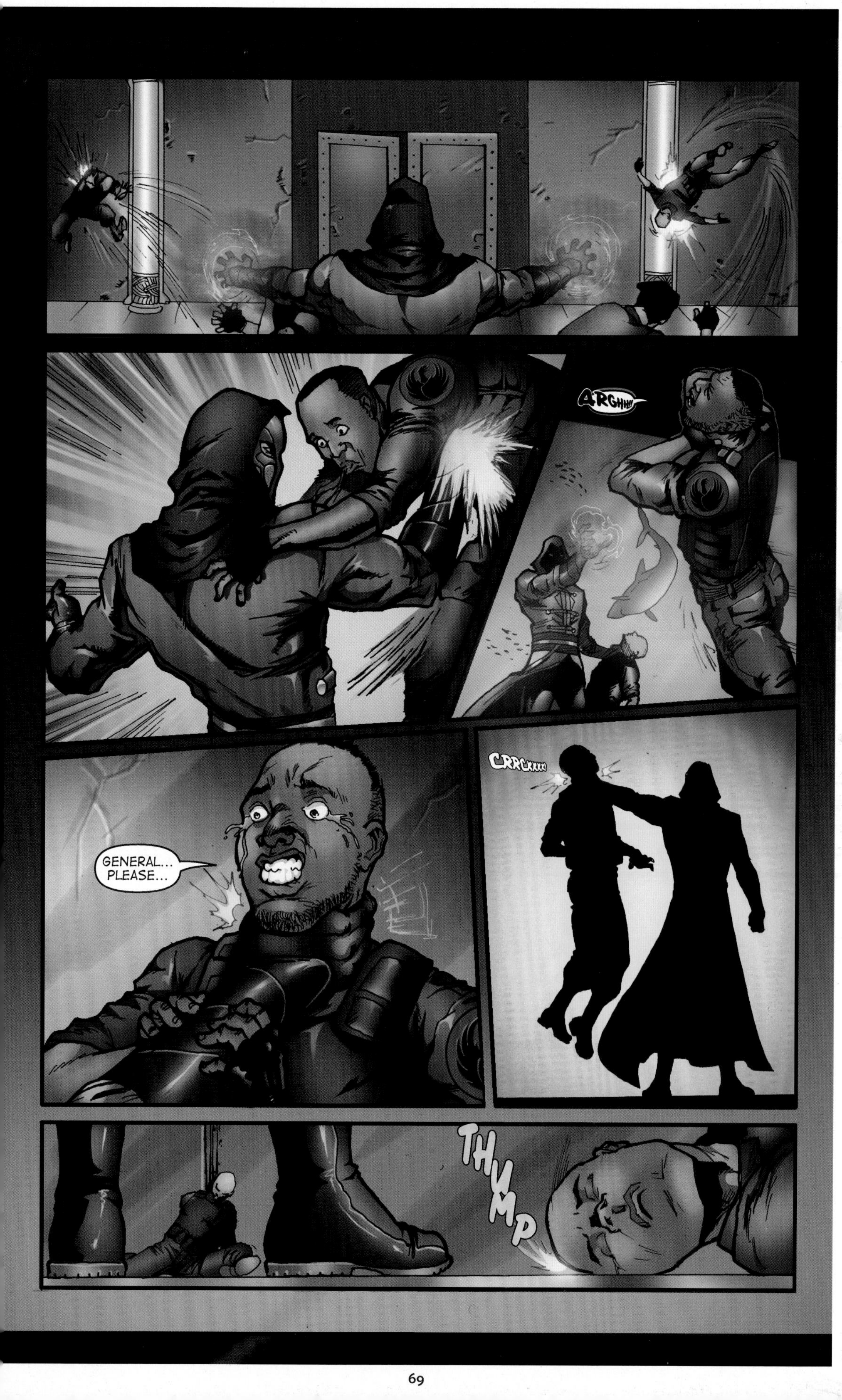
ARGH!!!
GENERAL... PLEASE...
CRRCKKKK!
THUMP

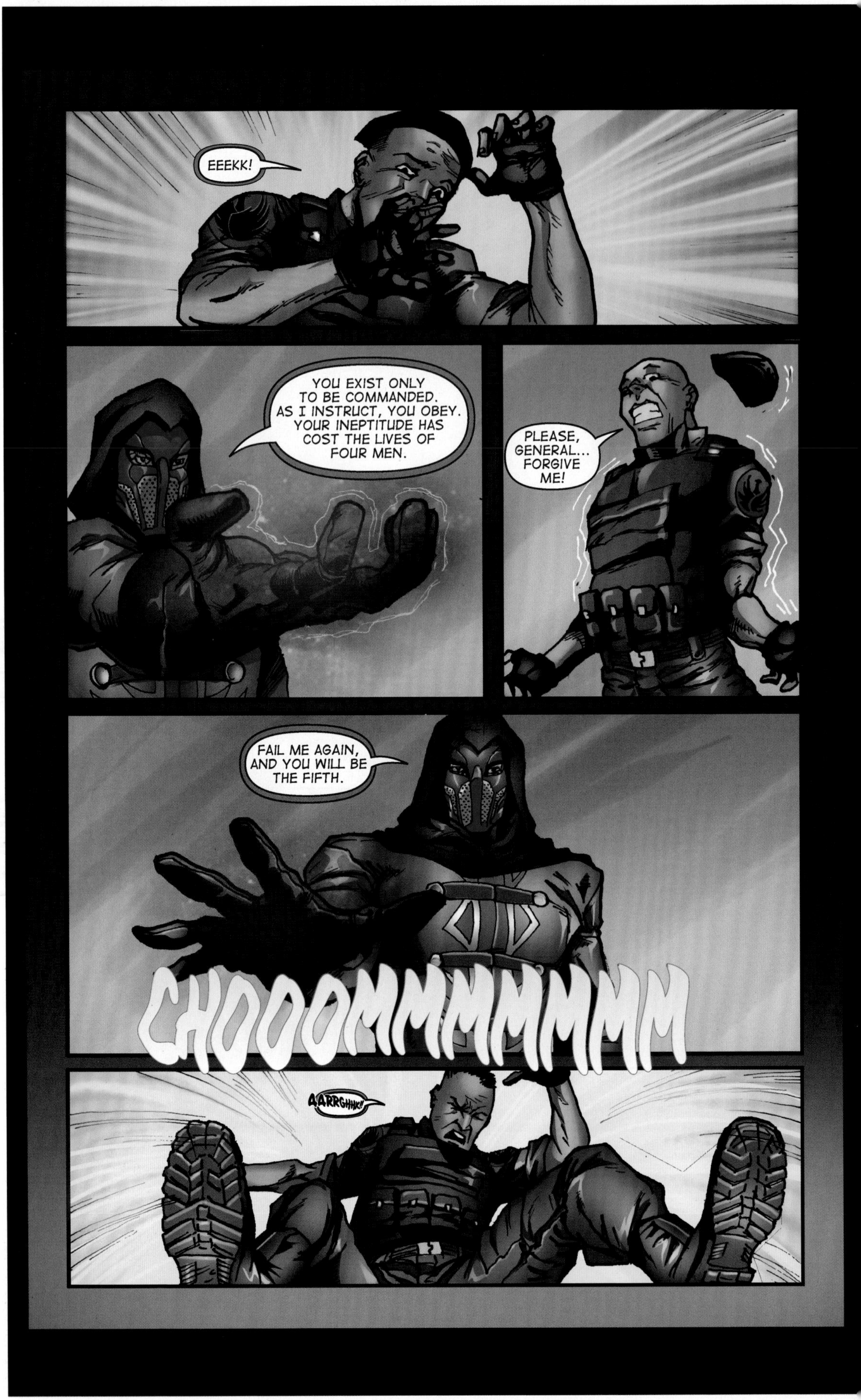
EEEKK!
YOU EXIST ONLY TO BE COMMANDED. AS I INSTRUCT, YOU OBEY. YOUR INEPTITUDE HAS COST THE LIVES OF FOUR MEN.
PLEASE, GENERAL... FORGIVE ME!
FAIL ME AGAIN, AND YOU WILL BE THE FIFTH.
CHOOOMMMMMMMM
AARRGHHK!!

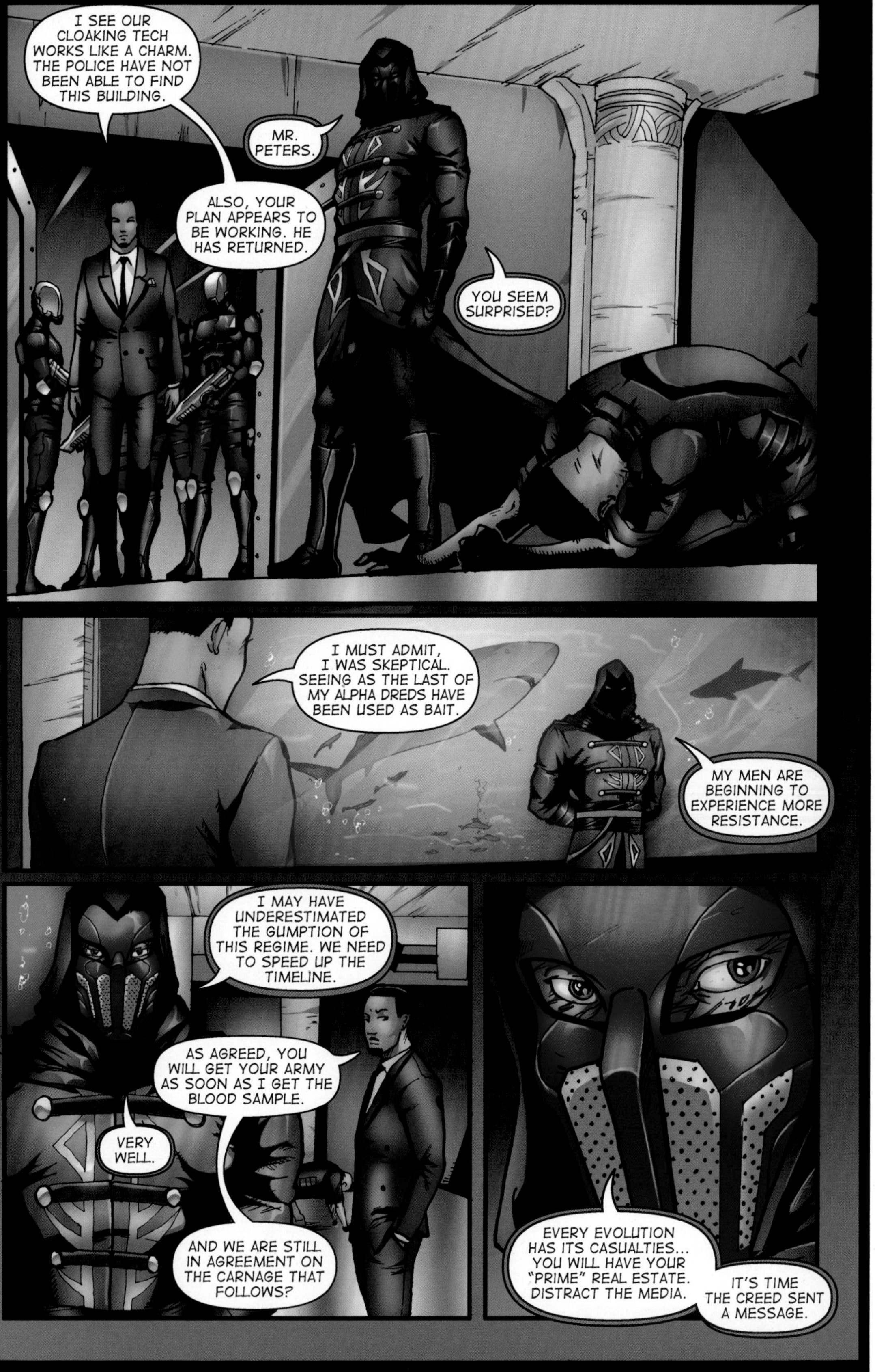
I SEE OUR CLOAKING TECH WORKS LIKE A CHARM. THE POLICE HAVE NOT BEEN ABLE TO FIND THIS BUILDING.
MR. PETERS.
ALSO, YOUR PLAN APPEARS TO BE WORKING. HE HAS RETURNED.
YOU SEEM SURPRISED?
I MUST ADMIT, I WAS SKEPTICAL. SEEING AS THE LAST OF MY ALPHA DREDS HAVE BEEN USED AS BAIT.
MY MEN ARE BEGINNING TO EXPERIENCE MORE RESISTANCE.
I MAY HAVE UNDERESTIMATED THE GUMPTION OF THIS REGIME. WE NEED TO SPEED UP THE TIMELINE.
AS AGREED, YOU WILL GET YOUR ARMY AS SOON AS I GET THE BLOOD SAMPLE.
VERY WELL.
AND WE ARE STILL IN AGREEMENT ON THE CARNAGE THAT FOLLOWS?
EVERY EVOLUTION HAS ITS CASUALTIES... YOU WILL HAVE YOUR "PRIME" REAL ESTATE. DISTRACT THE MEDIA.
IT'S TIME THE CREED SENT A MESSAGE.

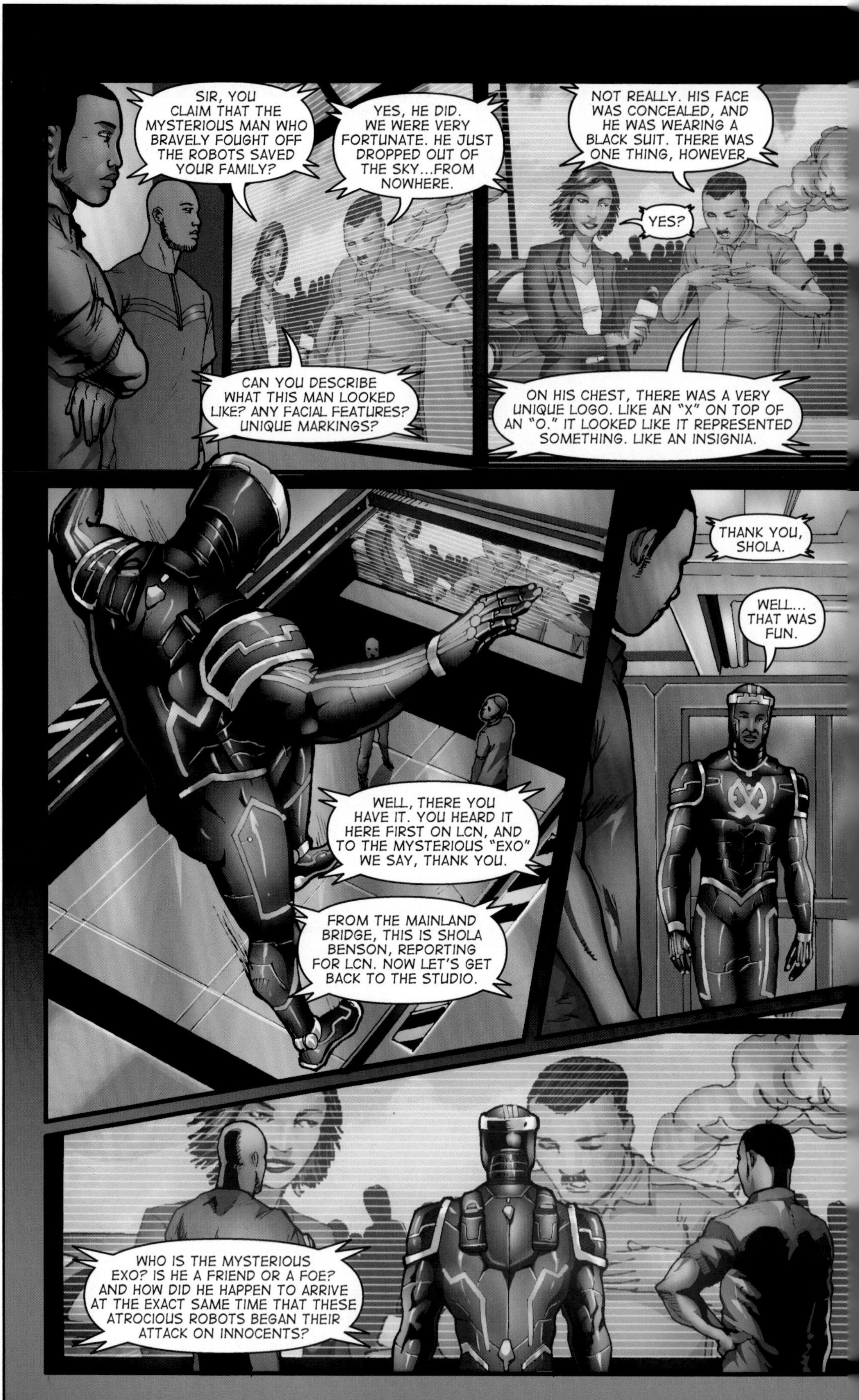
SIR, YOU CLAIM THAT THE MYSTERIOUS MAN WHO BRAVELY FOUGHT OFF THE ROBOTS SAVED YOUR FAMILY?
YES, HE DID. WE WERE VERY FORTUNATE. HE JUST DROPPED OUT OF THE SKY...FROM NOWHERE.
CAN YOU DESCRIBE WHAT THIS MAN LOOKED LIKE? ANY FACIAL FEATURES? UNIQUE MARKINGS?
NOT REALLY. HIS FACE WAS CONCEALED, AND HE WAS WEARING A BLACK SUIT. THERE WAS ONE THING, HOWEVER
YES?
ON HIS CHEST, THERE WAS A VERY UNIQUE LOGO. LIKE AN "X" ON TOP OF AN "O." IT LOOKED LIKE IT REPRESENTED SOMETHING. LIKE AN INSIGNIA.
WELL, THERE YOU HAVE IT. YOU HEARD IT HERE FIRST ON LCN, AND TO THE MYSTERIOUS "EXO" WE SAY, THANK YOU.
FROM THE MAINLAND BRIDGE, THIS IS SHOLA BENSON, REPORTING FOR LCN. NOW LET'S GET BACK TO THE STUDIO.
THANK YOU, SHOLA.
WELL... THAT WAS FUN.
WHO IS THE MYSTERIOUS EXO? IS HE A FRIEND OR A FOE? AND HOW DID HE HAPPEN TO ARRIVE AT THE EXACT SAME TIME THAT THESE ATROCIOUS ROBOTS BEGAN THEIR ATTACK ON INNOCENTS?

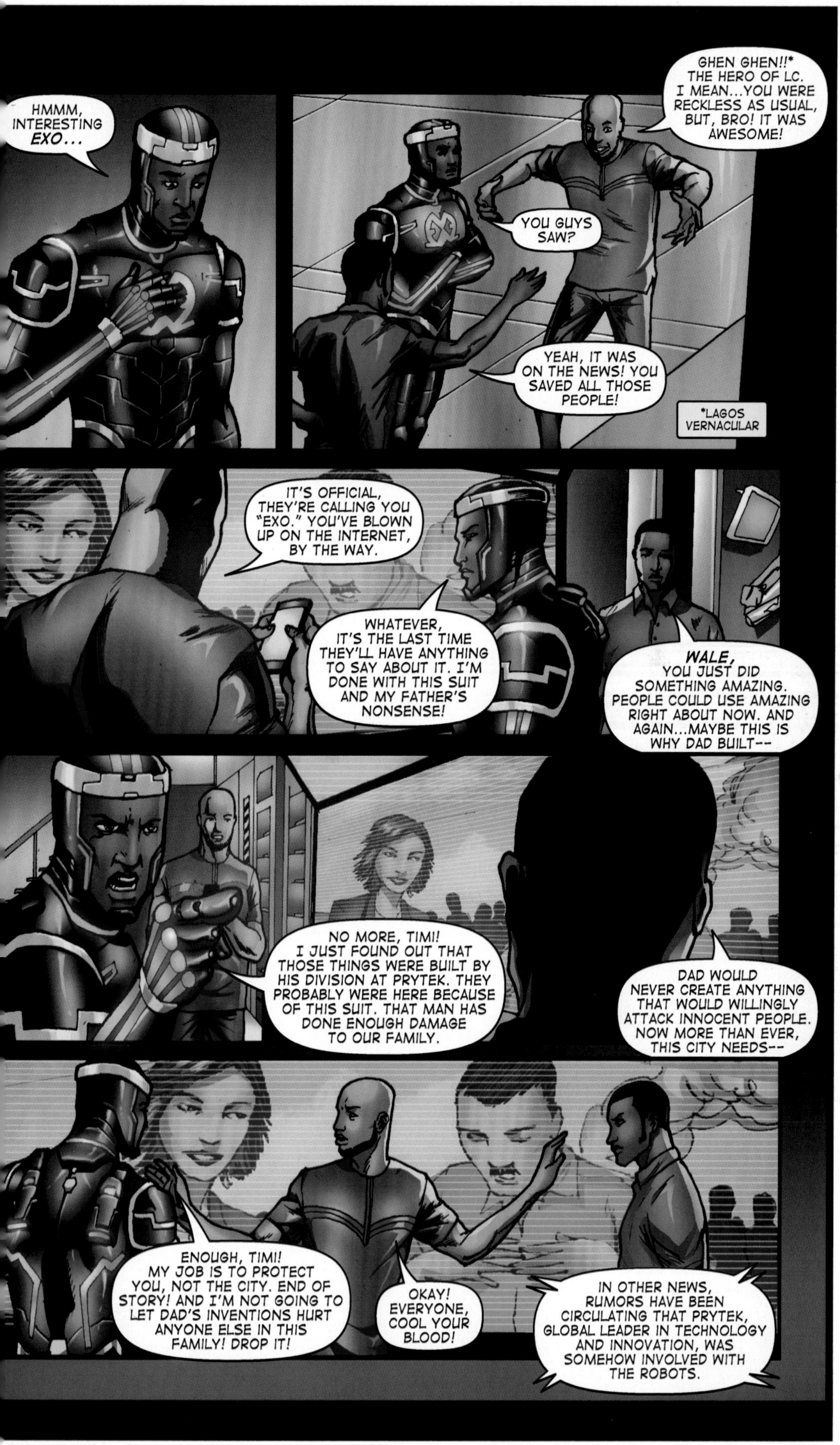
HMMM, INTERESTING *EXO...*
GHEN GHEN!!* THE HERO OF LC. I MEAN...YOU WERE RECKLESS AS USUAL, BUT, BRO! IT WAS AWESOME!
YOU GUYS SAW?
YEAH, IT WAS ON THE NEWS! YOU SAVED ALL THOSE PEOPLE!
*LAGOS VERNACULAR
IT'S OFFICIAL, THEY'RE CALLING YOU "EXO." YOU'VE BLOWN UP ON THE INTERNET, BY THE WAY.
WHATEVER, IT'S THE LAST TIME THEY'LL HAVE ANYTHING TO SAY ABOUT IT. I'M DONE WITH THIS SUIT AND MY FATHER'S NONSENSE!
WALE, YOU JUST DID SOMETHING AMAZING. PEOPLE COULD USE AMAZING RIGHT ABOUT NOW. AND AGAIN...MAYBE THIS IS WHY DAD BUILT--
NO MORE, TIMI! I JUST FOUND OUT THAT THOSE THINGS WERE BUILT BY HIS DIVISION AT PRYTEK. THEY PROBABLY WERE HERE BECAUSE OF THIS SUIT. THAT MAN HAS DONE ENOUGH DAMAGE TO OUR FAMILY.
DAD WOULD NEVER CREATE ANYTHING THAT WOULD WILLINGLY ATTACK INNOCENT PEOPLE. NOW MORE THAN EVER, THIS CITY NEEDS--
ENOUGH, TIMI! MY JOB IS TO PROTECT YOU, NOT THE CITY. END OF STORY! AND I'M NOT GOING TO LET DAD'S INVENTIONS HURT ANYONE ELSE IN THIS FAMILY! DROP IT!
OKAY! EVERYONE, COOL YOUR BLOOD!
IN OTHER NEWS, RUMORS HAVE BEEN CIRCULATING THAT PRYTEK, GLOBAL LEADER IN TECHNOLOGY AND INNOVATION, WAS SOMEHOW INVOLVED WITH THE ROBOTS.

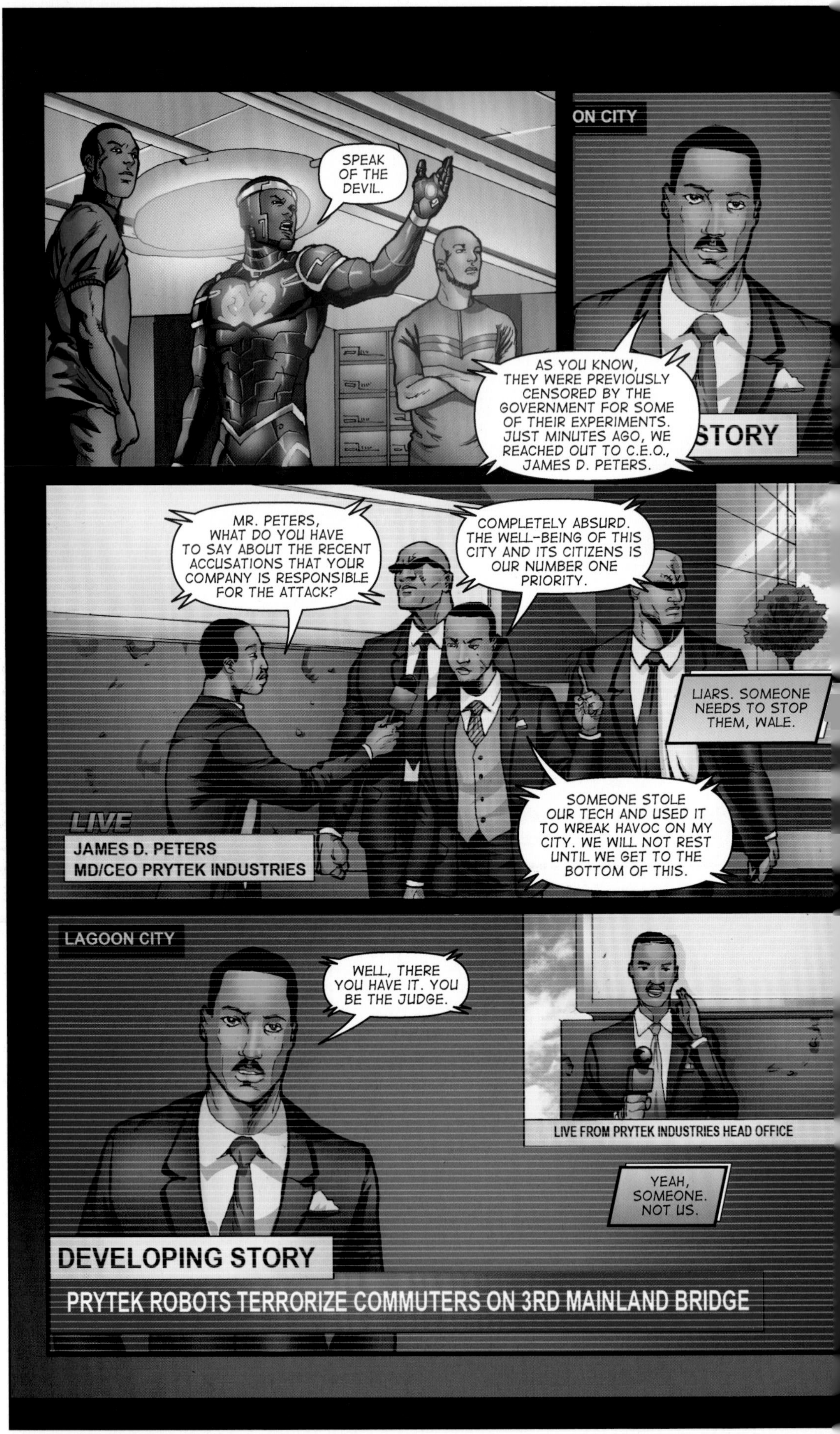
ON CITY
SPEAK OF THE DEVIL.
AS YOU KNOW, THEY WERE PREVIOUSLY CENSORED BY THE GOVERNMENT FOR SOME OF THEIR EXPERIMENTS. JUST MINUTES AGO, WE REACHED OUT TO C.E.O., JAMES D. PETERS.
STORY
MR. PETERS, WHAT DO YOU HAVE TO SAY ABOUT THE RECENT ACCUSATIONS THAT YOUR COMPANY IS RESPONSIBLE FOR THE ATTACK?
COMPLETELY ABSURD. THE WELL-BEING OF THIS CITY AND ITS CITIZENS IS OUR NUMBER ONE PRIORITY.
LIARS. SOMEONE NEEDS TO STOP THEM, WALE.
SOMEONE STOLE OUR TECH AND USED IT TO WREAK HAVOC ON MY CITY. WE WILL NOT REST UNTIL WE GET TO THE BOTTOM OF THIS.
LIVE
JAMES D. PETERS
MD/CEO PRYTEK INDUSTRIES
LAGOON CITY
WELL, THERE YOU HAVE IT. YOU BE THE JUDGE.
LIVE FROM PRYTEK INDUSTRIES HEAD OFFICE
YEAH, SOMEONE. NOT US.
DEVELOPING STORY
PRYTEK ROBOTS TERRORIZE COMMUTERS ON 3RD MAINLAND BRIDGE

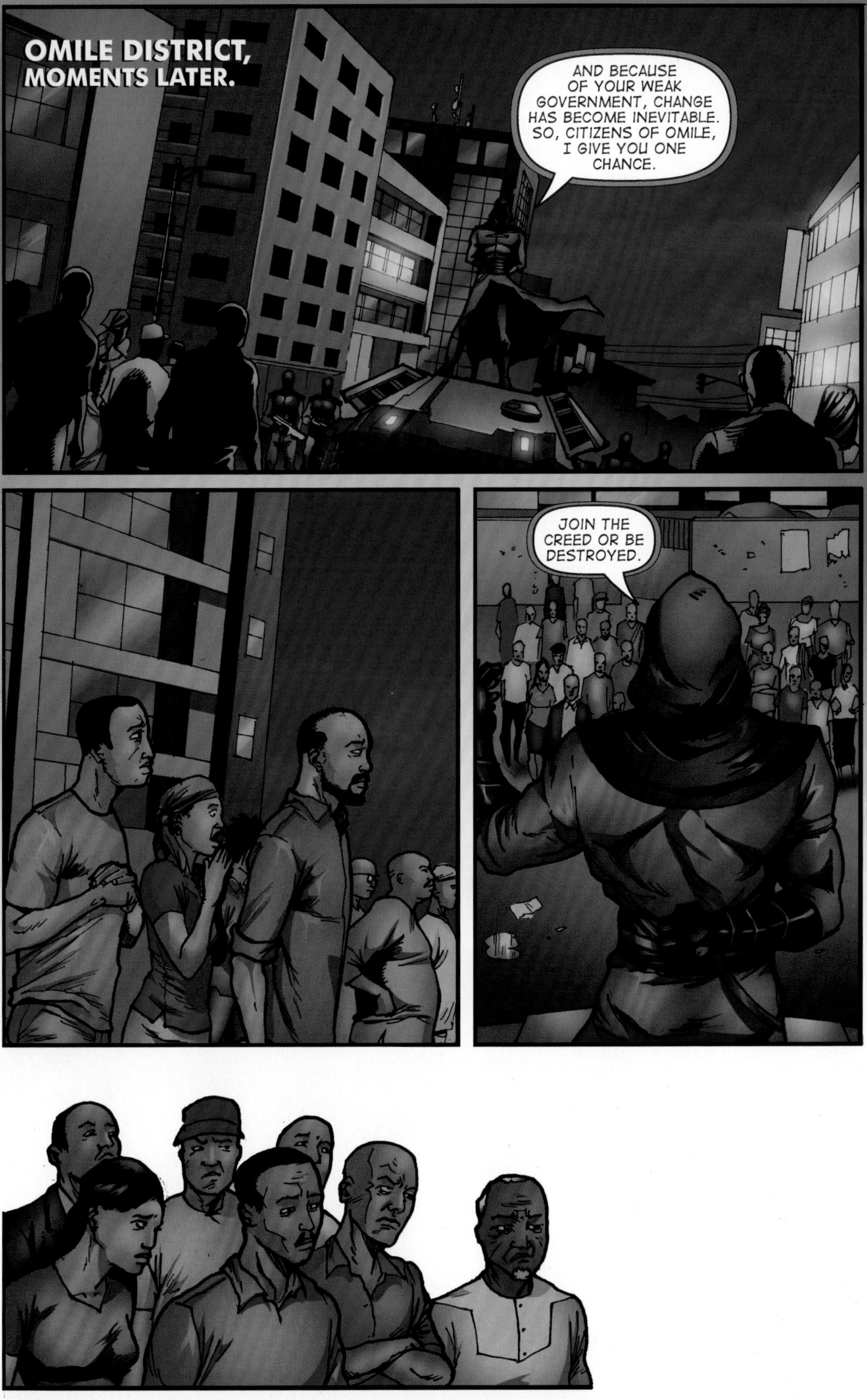
OMILE DISTRICT, MOMENTS LATER.
AND BECAUSE OF YOUR WEAK GOVERNMENT, CHANGE HAS BECOME INEVITABLE. SO, CITIZENS OF OMILE, I GIVE YOU ONE CHANCE.
JOIN THE CREED OR BE DESTROYED.

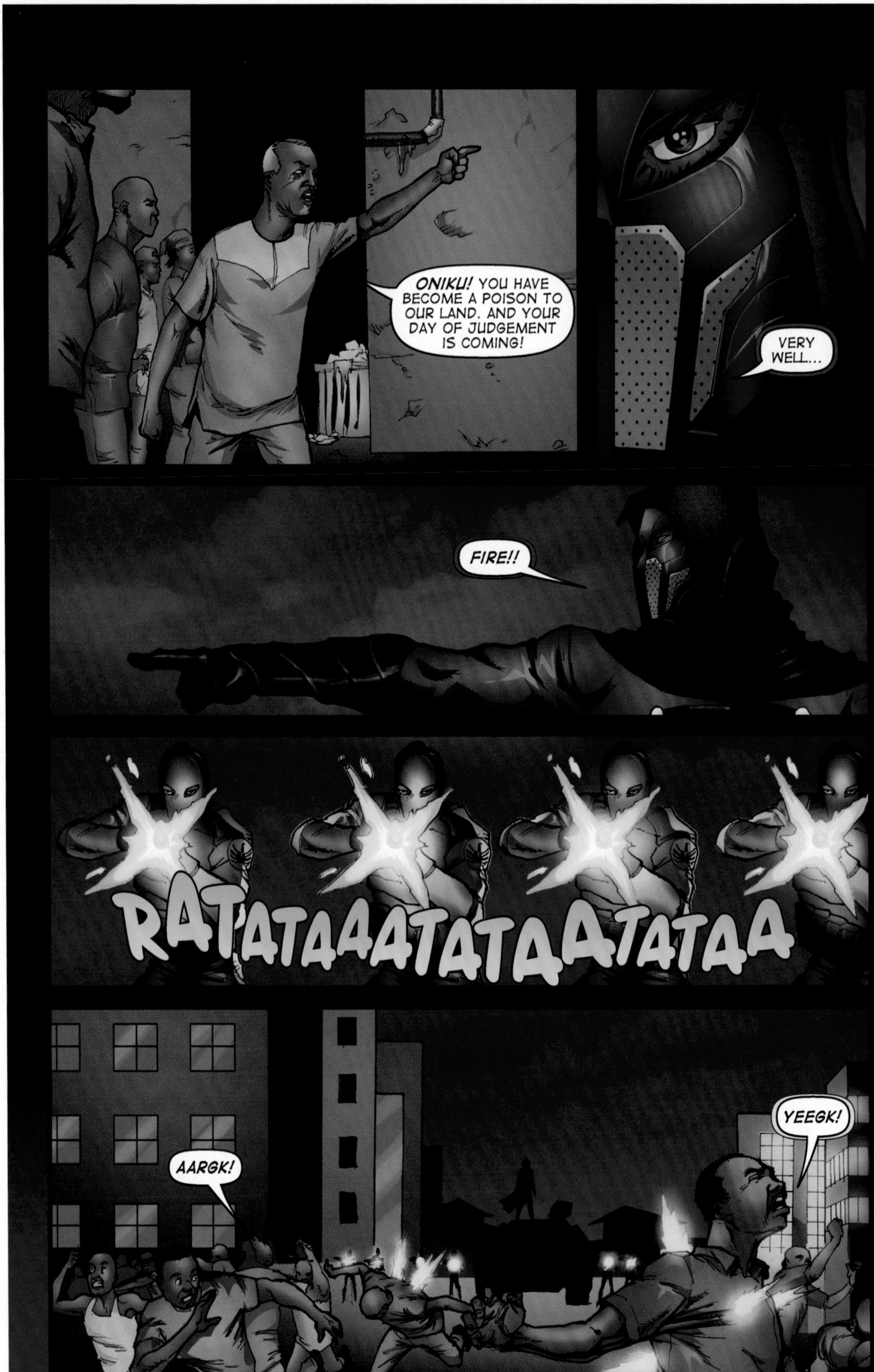
ONIKU! YOU HAVE BECOME A POISON TO OUR LAND. AND YOUR DAY OF JUDGEMENT IS COMING!
VERY WELL...
FIRE!!
RATATAAATATATAATATAA
AARGK!
YEEGK!

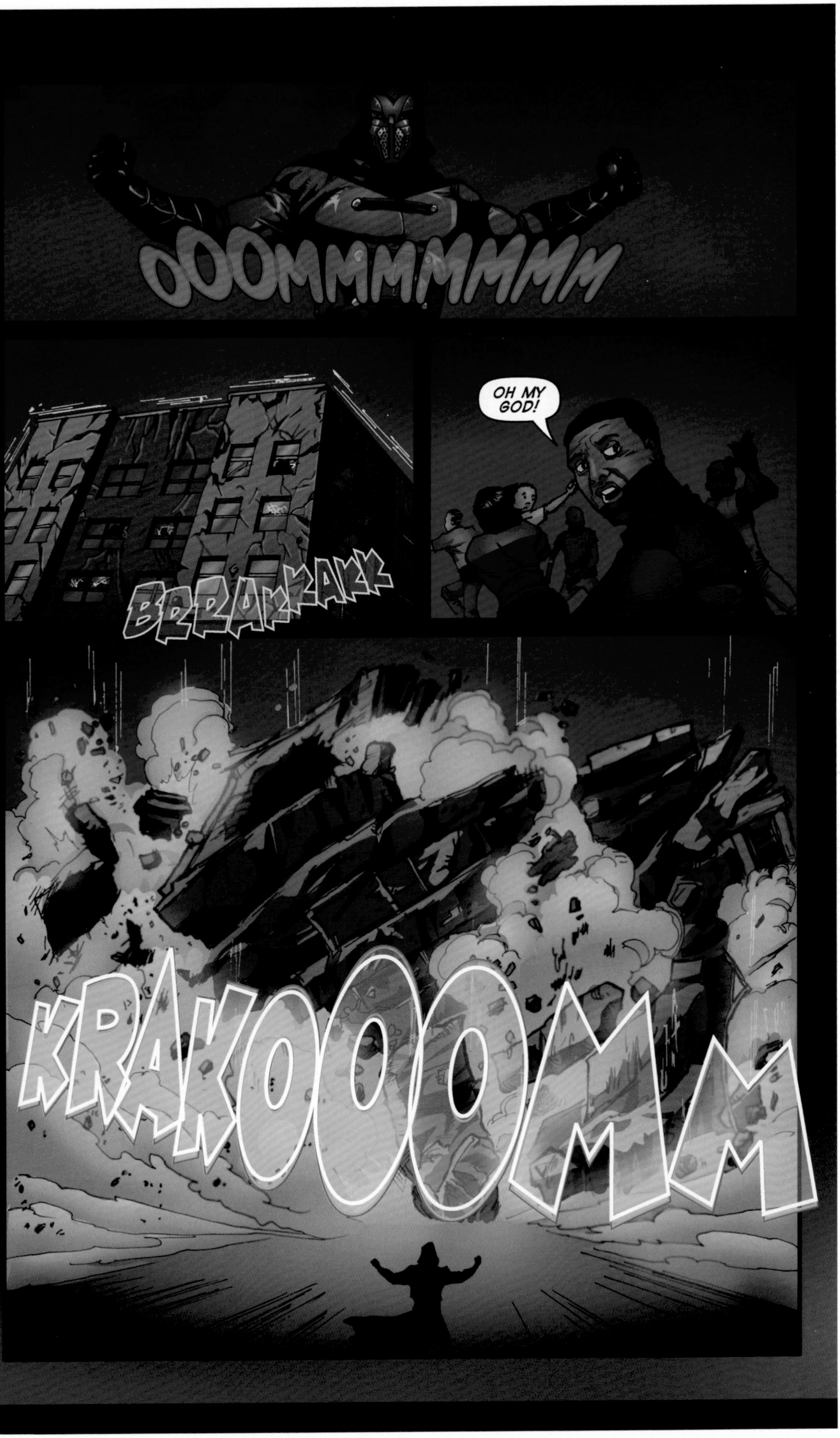
OOOMMMMMMMM
BRRAKKAKK
OH MY GOD!
KRAKOOOMM

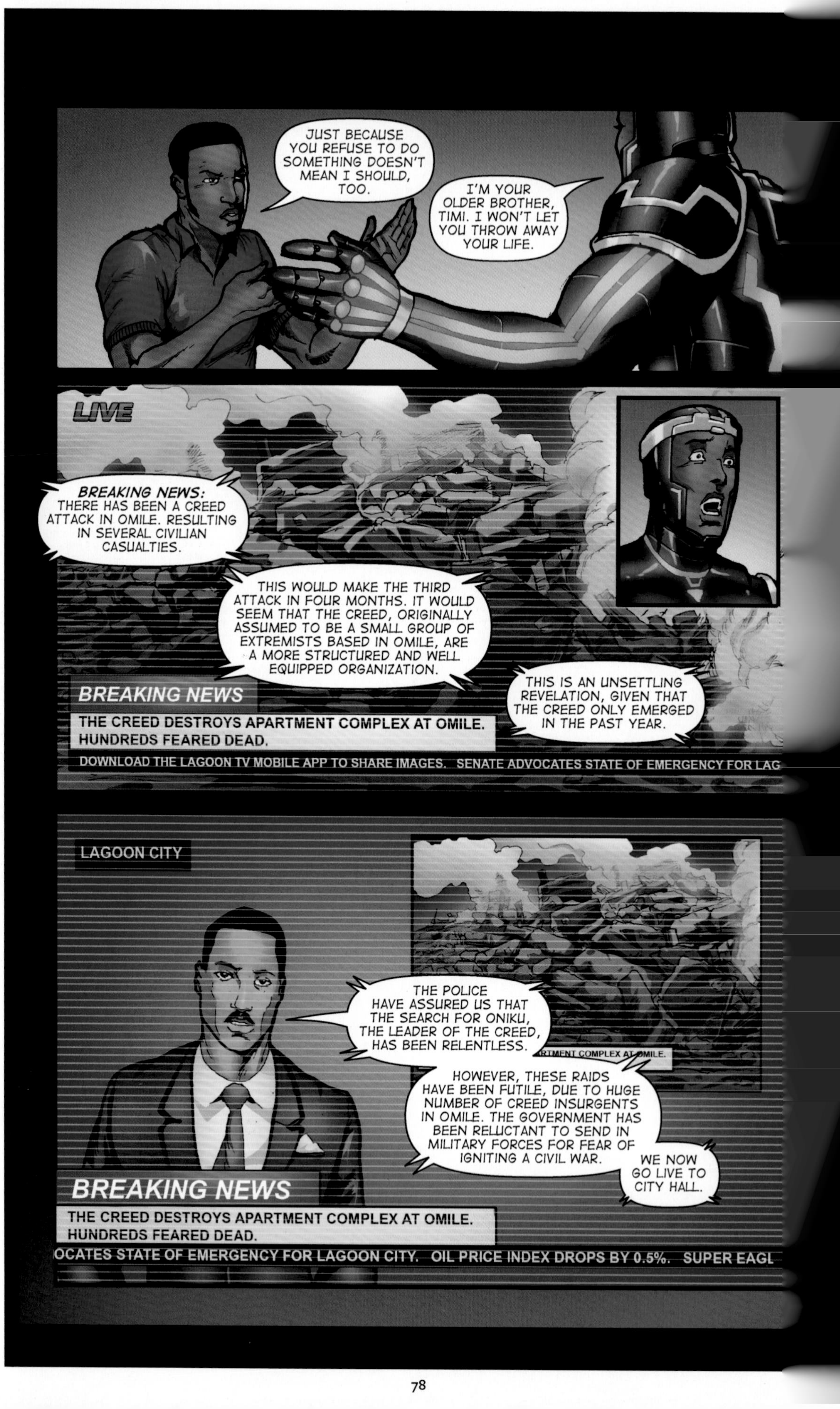
JUST BECAUSE YOU REFUSE TO DO SOMETHING DOESN'T MEAN I SHOULD, TOO.
I'M YOUR OLDER BROTHER, TIMI. I WON'T LET YOU THROW AWAY YOUR LIFE.
LIVE
BREAKING NEWS: THERE HAS BEEN A CREED ATTACK IN OMILE. RESULTING IN SEVERAL CIVILIAN CASUALTIES.
THIS WOULD MAKE THE THIRD ATTACK IN FOUR MONTHS. IT WOULD SEEM THAT THE CREED, ORIGINALLY ASSUMED TO BE A SMALL GROUP OF EXTREMISTS BASED IN OMILE, ARE A MORE STRUCTURED AND WELL EQUIPPED ORGANIZATION.
THIS IS AN UNSETTLING REVELATION, GIVEN THAT THE CREED ONLY EMERGED IN THE PAST YEAR.
BREAKING NEWS
THE CREED DESTROYS APARTMENT COMPLEX AT OMILE. HUNDREDS FEARED DEAD.
DOWNLOAD THE LAGOON TV MOBILE APP TO SHARE IMAGES. SENATE ADVOCATES STATE OF EMERGENCY FOR LAG
LAGOON CITY
THE POLICE HAVE ASSURED US THAT THE SEARCH FOR ONIKU, THE LEADER OF THE CREED, HAS BEEN RELENTLESS.
HOWEVER, THESE RAIDS HAVE BEEN FUTILE, DUE TO HUGE NUMBER OF CREED INSURGENTS IN OMILE. THE GOVERNMENT HAS BEEN RELUCTANT TO SEND IN MILITARY FORCES FOR FEAR OF IGNITING A CIVIL WAR.
WE NOW GO LIVE TO CITY HALL.
BREAKING NEWS
THE CREED DESTROYS APARTMENT COMPLEX AT OMILE. HUNDREDS FEARED DEAD.
OCATES STATE OF EMERGENCY FOR LAGOON CITY. OIL PRICE INDEX DROPS BY 0.5%. SUPER EAGL

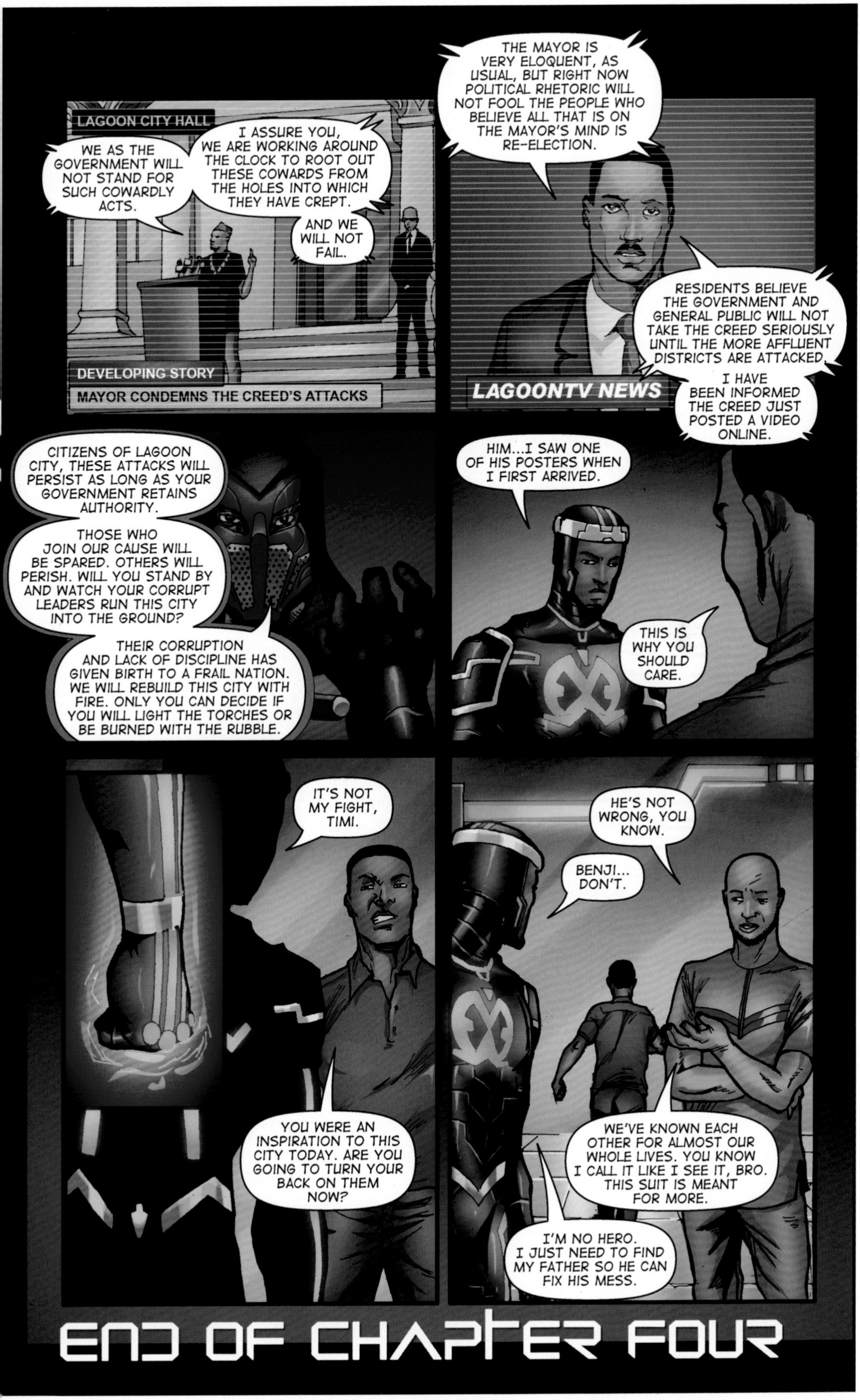
LAGOON CITY HALL
WE AS THE GOVERNMENT WILL NOT STAND FOR SUCH COWARDLY ACTS.
I ASSURE YOU, WE ARE WORKING AROUND THE CLOCK TO ROOT OUT THESE COWARDS FROM THE HOLES INTO WHICH THEY HAVE CREPT.
AND WE WILL NOT FAIL.
DEVELOPING STORY
MAYOR CONDEMNS THE CREED'S ATTACKS
THE MAYOR IS VERY ELOQUENT, AS USUAL, BUT RIGHT NOW POLITICAL RHETORIC WILL NOT FOOL THE PEOPLE WHO BELIEVE ALL THAT IS ON THE MAYOR'S MIND IS RE-ELECTION.
RESIDENTS BELIEVE THE GOVERNMENT AND GENERAL PUBLIC WILL NOT TAKE THE CREED SERIOUSLY UNTIL THE MORE AFFLUENT DISTRICTS ARE ATTACKED.
I HAVE BEEN INFORMED THE CREED JUST POSTED A VIDEO ONLINE.
LAGOONTV NEWS
CITIZENS OF LAGOON CITY, THESE ATTACKS WILL PERSIST AS LONG AS YOUR GOVERNMENT RETAINS AUTHORITY.
THOSE WHO JOIN OUR CAUSE WILL BE SPARED. OTHERS WILL PERISH. WILL YOU STAND BY AND WATCH YOUR CORRUPT LEADERS RUN THIS CITY INTO THE GROUND?
THEIR CORRUPTION AND LACK OF DISCIPLINE HAS GIVEN BIRTH TO A FRAIL NATION. WE WILL REBUILD THIS CITY WITH FIRE. ONLY YOU CAN DECIDE IF YOU WILL LIGHT THE TORCHES OR BE BURNED WITH THE RUBBLE.
HIM...I SAW ONE OF HIS POSTERS WHEN I FIRST ARRIVED.
THIS IS WHY YOU SHOULD CARE.
IT'S NOT MY FIGHT, TIMI.
YOU WERE AN INSPIRATION TO THIS CITY TODAY. ARE YOU GOING TO TURN YOUR BACK ON THEM NOW?
HE'S NOT WRONG, YOU KNOW.
BENJI... DON'T.
WE'VE KNOWN EACH OTHER FOR ALMOST OUR WHOLE LIVES. YOU KNOW I CALL IT LIKE I SEE IT, BRO. THIS SUIT IS MEANT FOR MORE.
I'M NO HERO. I JUST NEED TO FIND MY FATHER SO HE CAN FIX HIS MESS.
END OF CHAPTER FOUR

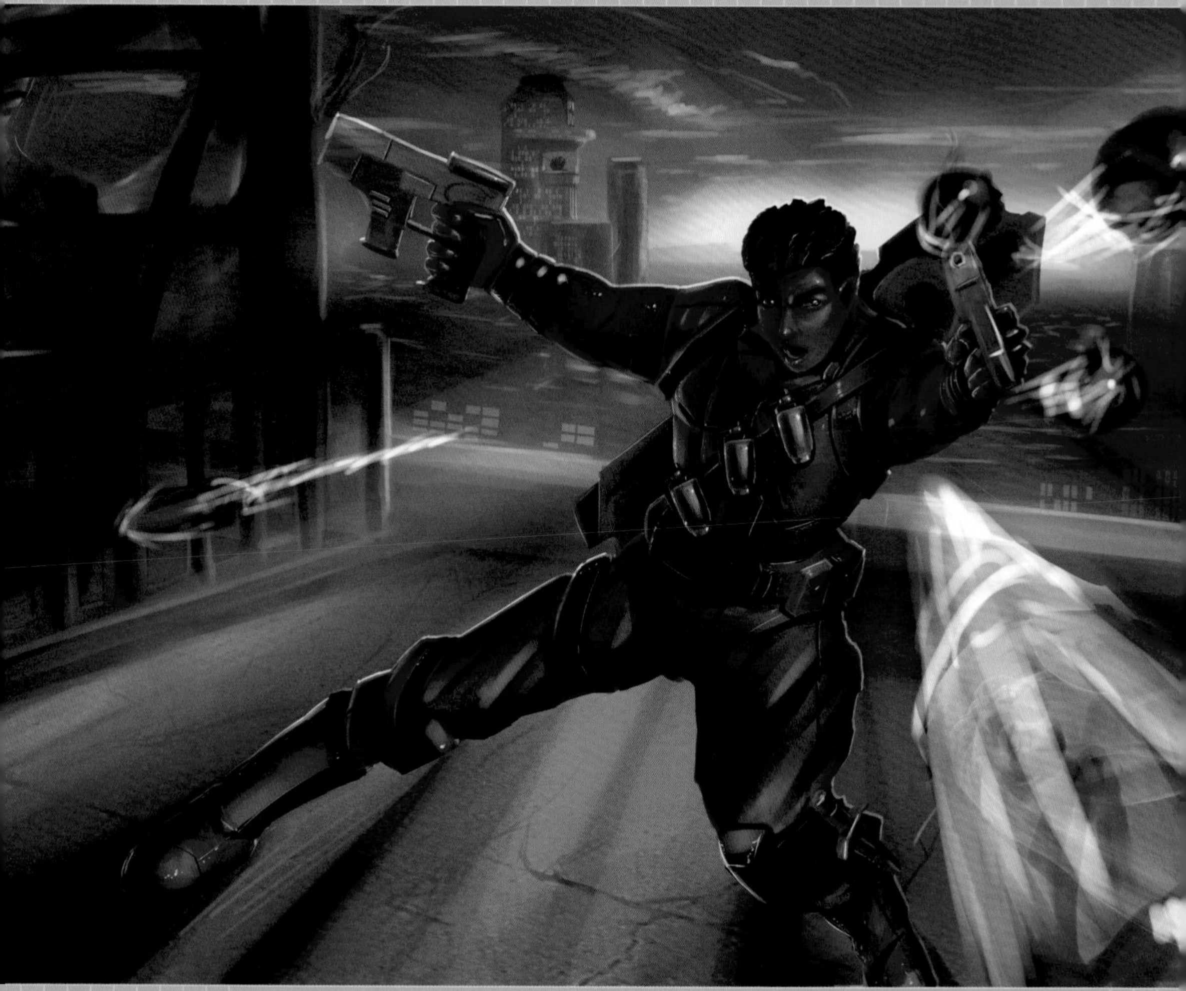

"The Creed is
all that matters.
It is all, and
I am none."
—TWOSHOTS

CHAPTER FIVE

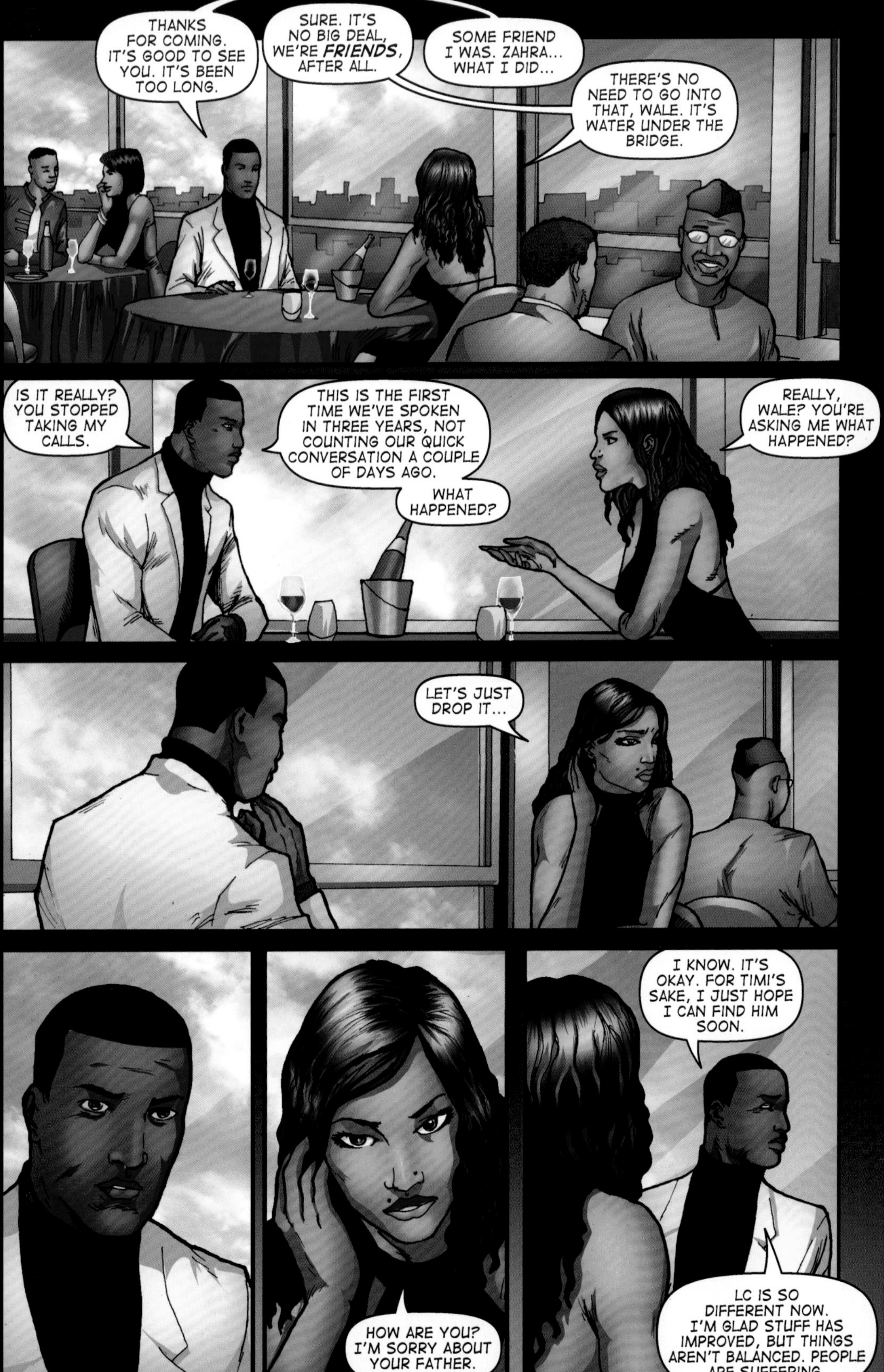
THANKS FOR COMING. IT'S GOOD TO SEE YOU. IT'S BEEN TOO LONG.
SURE. IT'S NO BIG DEAL, WE'RE FRIENDS, AFTER ALL.
SOME FRIEND I WAS. ZAHRA... WHAT I DID...
THERE'S NO NEED TO GO INTO THAT, WALE. IT'S WATER UNDER THE BRIDGE.
IS IT REALLY? YOU STOPPED TAKING MY CALLS.
THIS IS THE FIRST TIME WE'VE SPOKEN IN THREE YEARS, NOT COUNTING OUR QUICK CONVERSATION A COUPLE OF DAYS AGO.
WHAT HAPPENED?
REALLY, WALE? YOU'RE ASKING ME WHAT HAPPENED?
LET'S JUST DROP IT...
HOW ARE YOU? I'M SORRY ABOUT YOUR FATHER.
I KNOW. IT'S OKAY. FOR TIMI'S SAKE, I JUST HOPE I CAN FIND HIM SOON.
LC IS SO DIFFERENT NOW. I'M GLAD STUFF HAS IMPROVED, BUT THINGS AREN'T BALANCED. PEOPLE ARE SUFFERING.

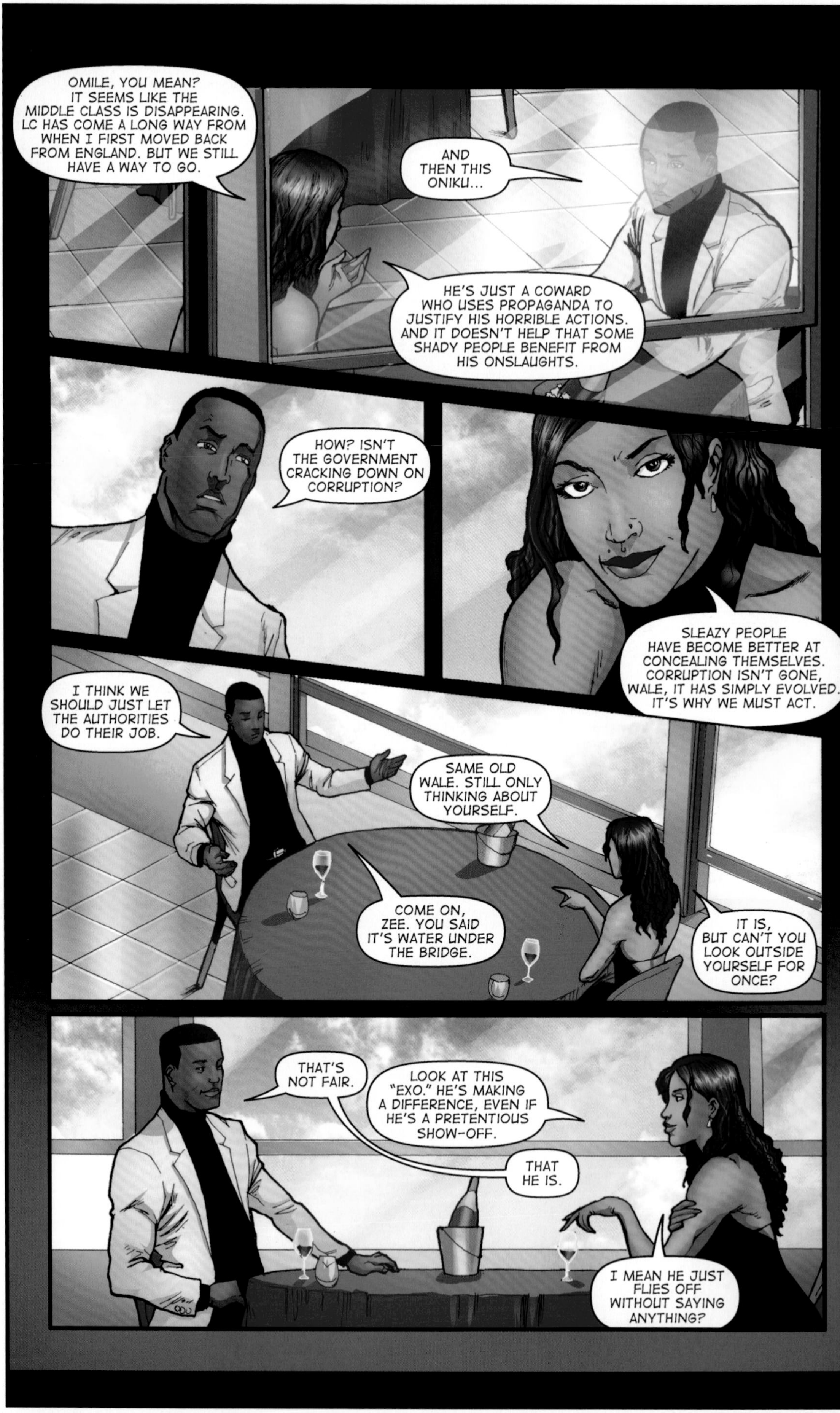
OMILE, YOU MEAN? IT SEEMS LIKE THE MIDDLE CLASS IS DISAPPEARING. LC HAS COME A LONG WAY FROM WHEN I FIRST MOVED BACK FROM ENGLAND. BUT WE STILL HAVE A WAY TO GO.
AND THEN THIS ONIKU...
HE'S JUST A COWARD WHO USES PROPAGANDA TO JUSTIFY HIS HORRIBLE ACTIONS. AND IT DOESN'T HELP THAT SOME SHADY PEOPLE BENEFIT FROM HIS ONSLAUGHTS.
HOW? ISN'T THE GOVERNMENT CRACKING DOWN ON CORRUPTION?
SLEAZY PEOPLE HAVE BECOME BETTER AT CONCEALING THEMSELVES. CORRUPTION ISN'T GONE, WALE, IT HAS SIMPLY EVOLVED. IT'S WHY WE MUST ACT.
I THINK WE SHOULD JUST LET THE AUTHORITIES DO THEIR JOB.
SAME OLD WALE. STILL ONLY THINKING ABOUT YOURSELF.
COME ON, ZEE. YOU SAID IT'S WATER UNDER THE BRIDGE.
IT IS, BUT CAN'T YOU LOOK OUTSIDE YOURSELF FOR ONCE?
THAT'S NOT FAIR.
LOOK AT THIS "EXO." HE'S MAKING A DIFFERENCE, EVEN IF HE'S A PRETENTIOUS SHOW-OFF.
THAT HE IS.
I MEAN HE JUST FLIES OFF WITHOUT SAYING ANYTHING?

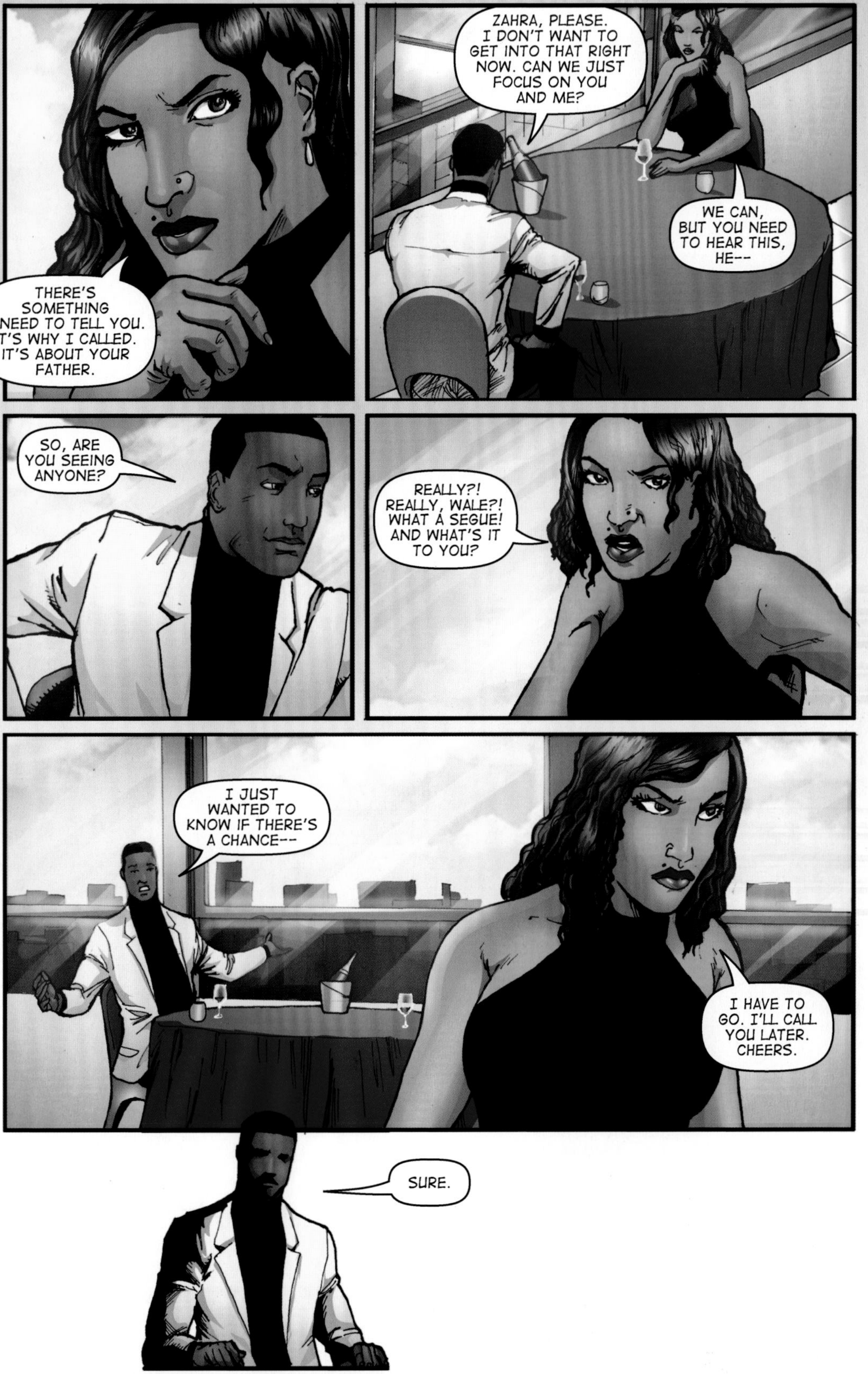
THERE'S SOMETHING I NEED TO TELL YOU. IT'S WHY I CALLED. IT'S ABOUT YOUR FATHER.
ZAHRA, PLEASE. I DON'T WANT TO GET INTO THAT RIGHT NOW. CAN WE JUST FOCUS ON YOU AND ME?
WE CAN, BUT YOU NEED TO HEAR THIS, HE--
SO, ARE YOU SEEING ANYONE?
REALLY?! REALLY, WALE?! WHAT A SEGUE! AND WHAT'S IT TO YOU?
I JUST WANTED TO KNOW IF THERE'S A CHANCE--
I HAVE TO GO. I'LL CALL YOU LATER. CHEERS.
SURE.

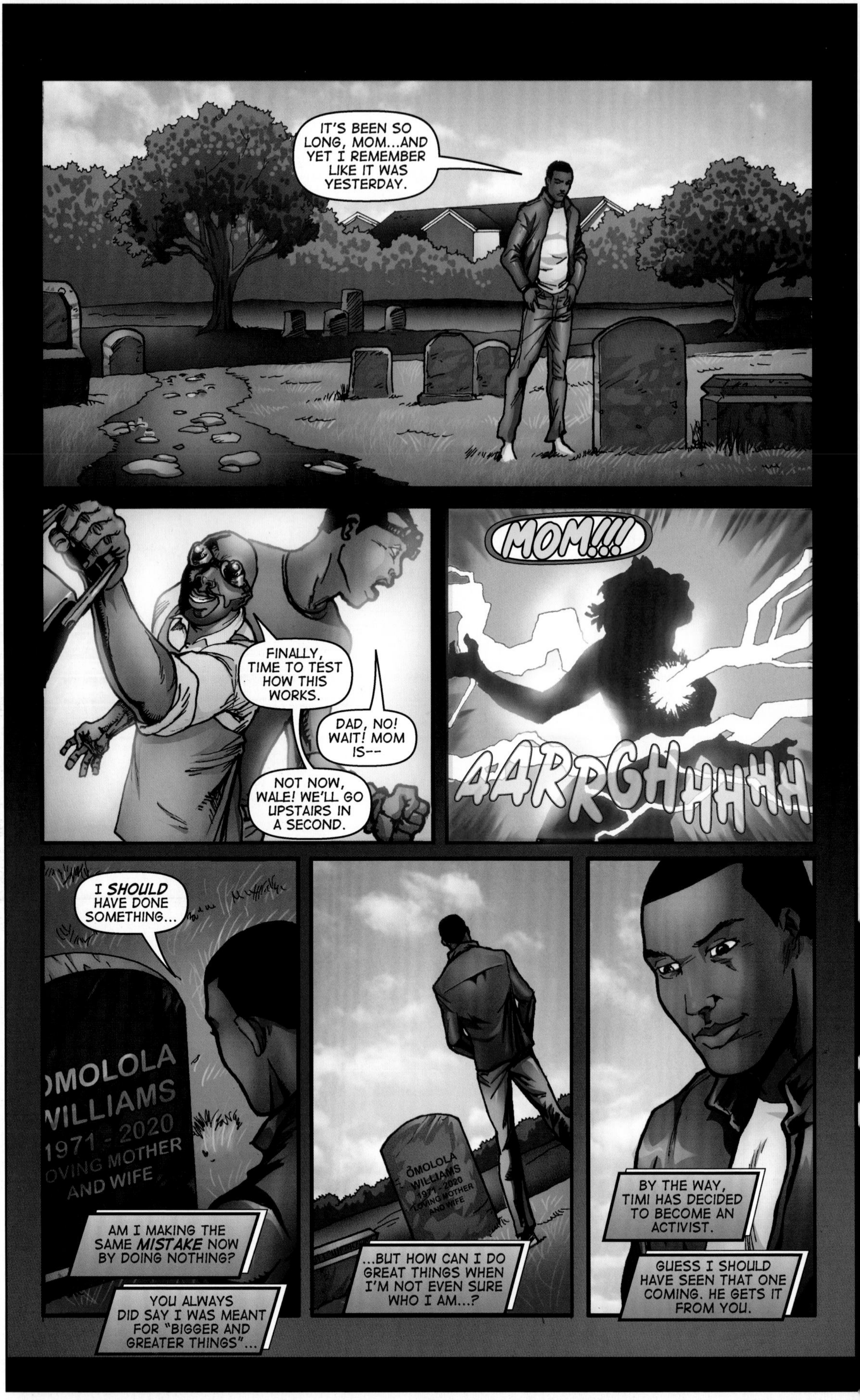
IT'S BEEN SO LONG, MOM...AND YET I REMEMBER LIKE IT WAS YESTERDAY.
FINALLY, TIME TO TEST HOW THIS WORKS.
DAD, NO! WAIT! MOM IS--
NOT NOW, WALE! WE'LL GO UPSTAIRS IN A SECOND.
MOM!!!
AARRGHHHHH
I SHOULD HAVE DONE SOMETHING...
OMOLOLA WILLIAMS 1971 - 2020 LOVING MOTHER AND WIFE
AM I MAKING THE SAME MISTAKE NOW BY DOING NOTHING?
YOU ALWAYS DID SAY I WAS MEANT FOR "BIGGER AND GREATER THINGS"...
...BUT HOW CAN I DO GREAT THINGS WHEN I'M NOT EVEN SURE WHO I AM...?
BY THE WAY, TIMI HAS DECIDED TO BECOME AN ACTIVIST.
GUESS I SHOULD HAVE SEEN THAT ONE COMING. HE GETS IT FROM YOU.

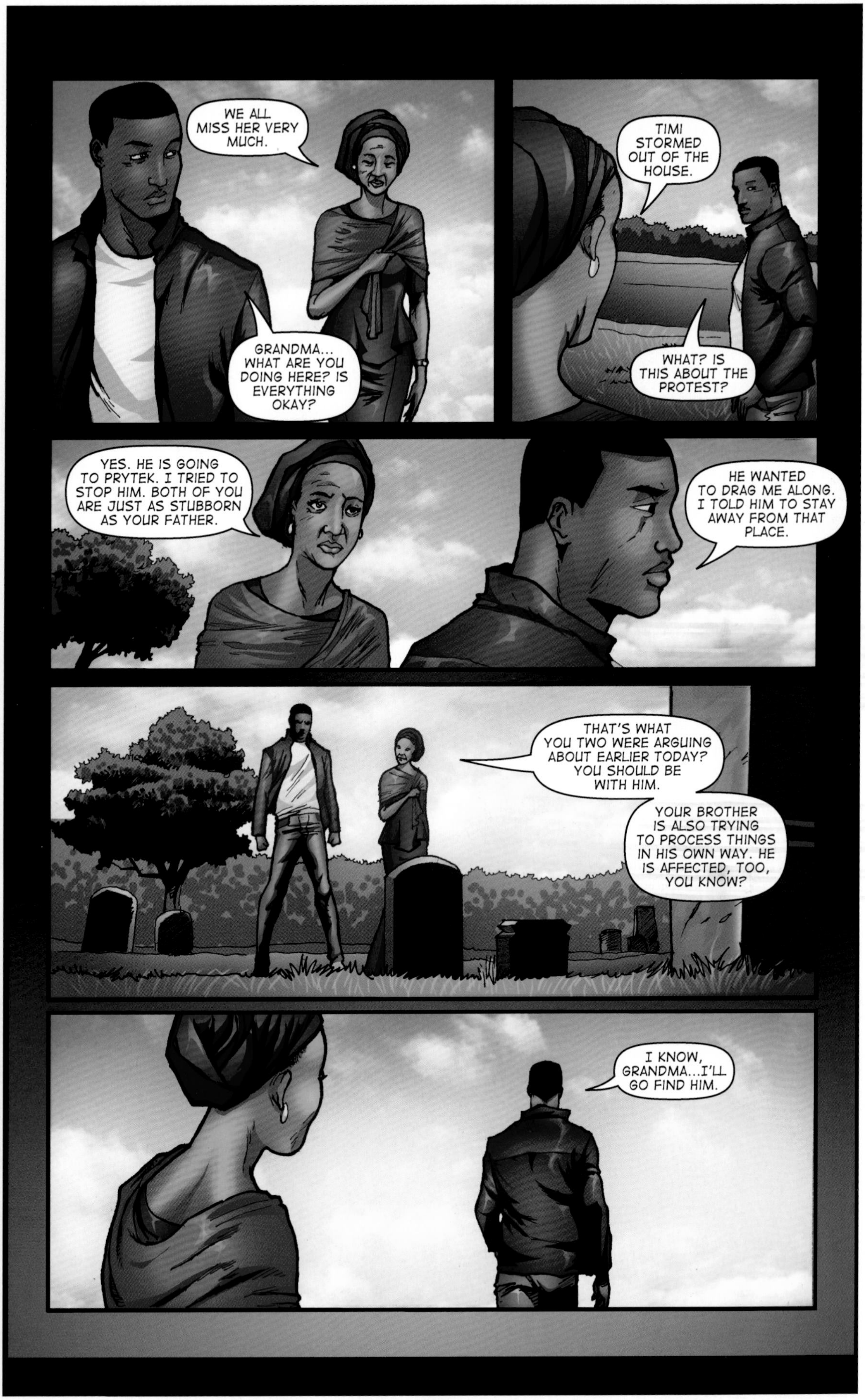
WE ALL MISS HER VERY MUCH.
GRANDMA... WHAT ARE YOU DOING HERE? IS EVERYTHING OKAY?
TIMI STORMED OUT OF THE HOUSE.
WHAT? IS THIS ABOUT THE PROTEST?
YES. HE IS GOING TO PRYTEK. I TRIED TO STOP HIM. BOTH OF YOU ARE JUST AS STUBBORN AS YOUR FATHER.
HE WANTED TO DRAG ME ALONG. I TOLD HIM TO STAY AWAY FROM THAT PLACE.
THAT'S WHAT YOU TWO WERE ARGUING ABOUT EARLIER TODAY? YOU SHOULD BE WITH HIM.
YOUR BROTHER IS ALSO TRYING TO PROCESS THINGS IN HIS OWN WAY. HE IS AFFECTED, TOO, YOU KNOW?
I KNOW, GRANDMA...I'LL GO FIND HIM.

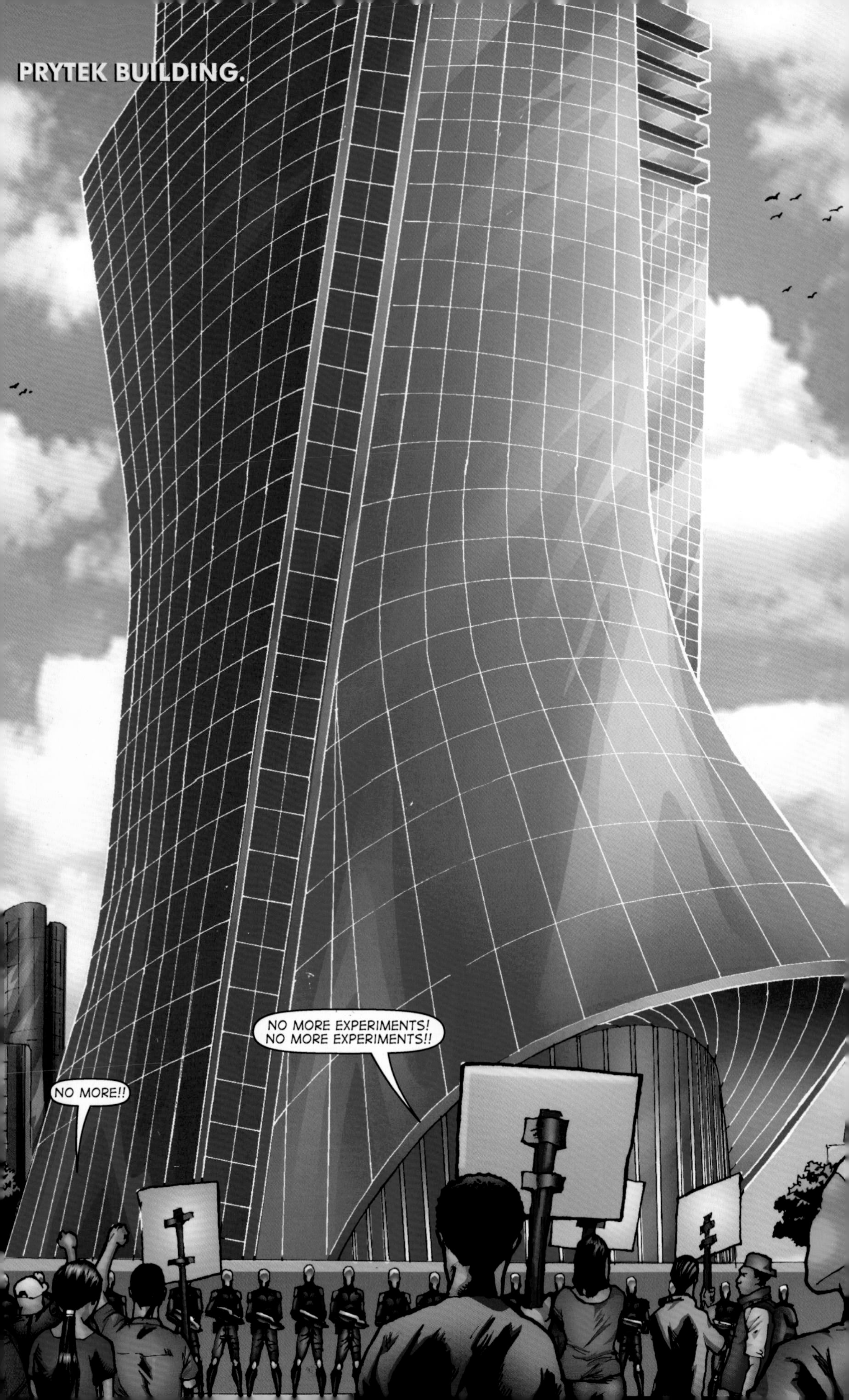

PRYTEK BUILDING.
NO MORE!!
NO MORE EXPERIMENTS! NO MORE EXPERIMENTS!!

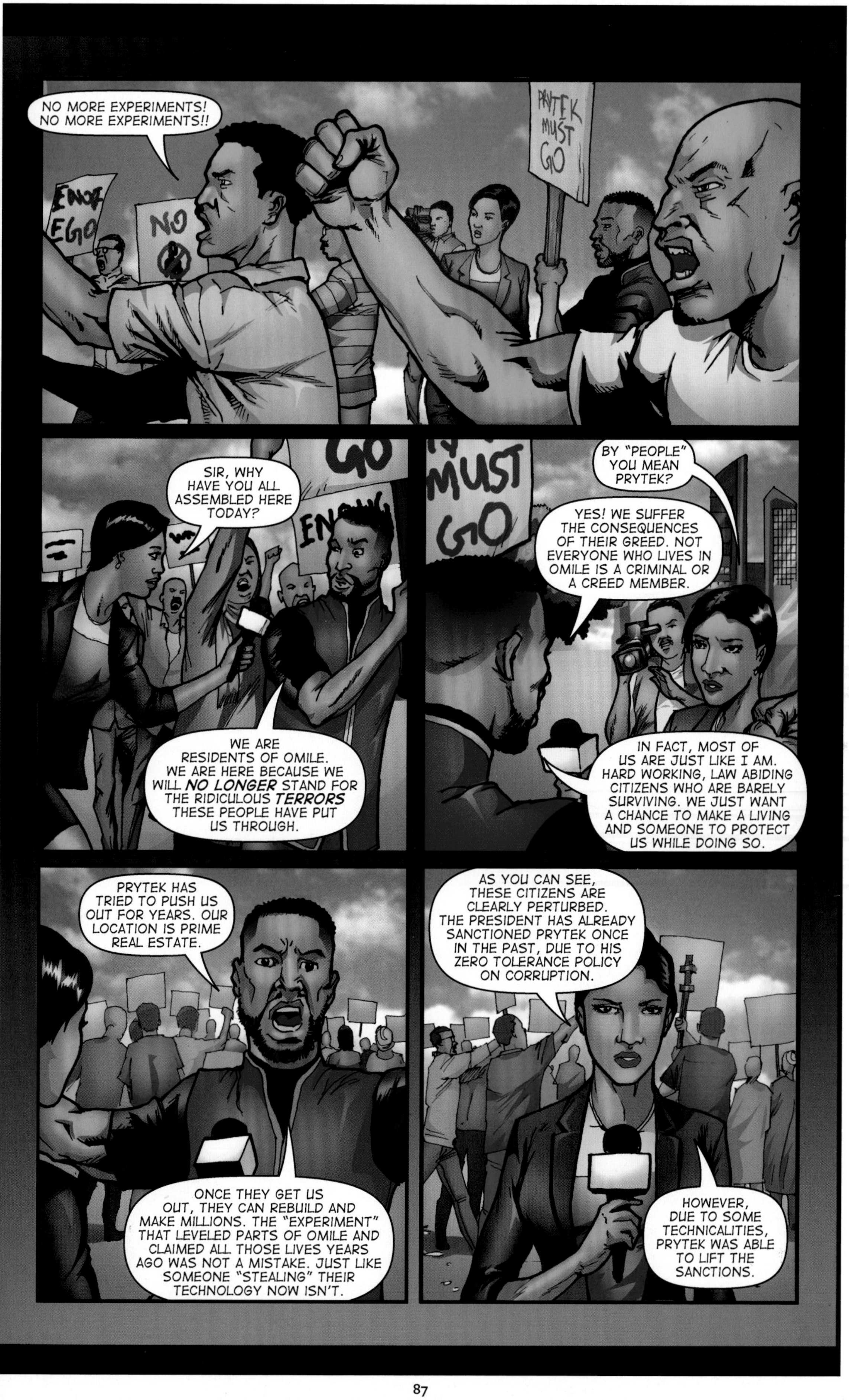

NO MORE EXPERIMENTS! NO MORE EXPERIMENTS!!
PRYTEK MUST GO
NO
SIR, WHY HAVE YOU ALL ASSEMBLED HERE TODAY?
WE ARE RESIDENTS OF OMILE. WE ARE HERE BECAUSE WE WILL NO LONGER STAND FOR THE RIDICULOUS TERRORS THESE PEOPLE HAVE PUT US THROUGH.
MUST GO
BY "PEOPLE" YOU MEAN PRYTEK?
YES! WE SUFFER THE CONSEQUENCES OF THEIR GREED. NOT EVERYONE WHO LIVES IN OMILE IS A CRIMINAL OR A CREED MEMBER.
IN FACT, MOST OF US ARE JUST LIKE I AM. HARD WORKING, LAW ABIDING CITIZENS WHO ARE BARELY SURVIVING. WE JUST WANT A CHANCE TO MAKE A LIVING AND SOMEONE TO PROTECT US WHILE DOING SO.
PRYTEK HAS TRIED TO PUSH US OUT FOR YEARS. OUR LOCATION IS PRIME REAL ESTATE.
ONCE THEY GET US OUT, THEY CAN REBUILD AND MAKE MILLIONS. THE "EXPERIMENT" THAT LEVELED PARTS OF OMILE AND CLAIMED ALL THOSE LIVES YEARS AGO WAS NOT A MISTAKE. JUST LIKE SOMEONE "STEALING" THEIR TECHNOLOGY NOW ISN'T.
AS YOU CAN SEE, THESE CITIZENS ARE CLEARLY PERTURBED. THE PRESIDENT HAS ALREADY SANCTIONED PRYTEK ONCE IN THE PAST, DUE TO HIS ZERO TOLERANCE POLICY ON CORRUPTION.
HOWEVER, DUE TO SOME TECHNICALITIES, PRYTEK WAS ABLE TO LIFT THE SANCTIONS.

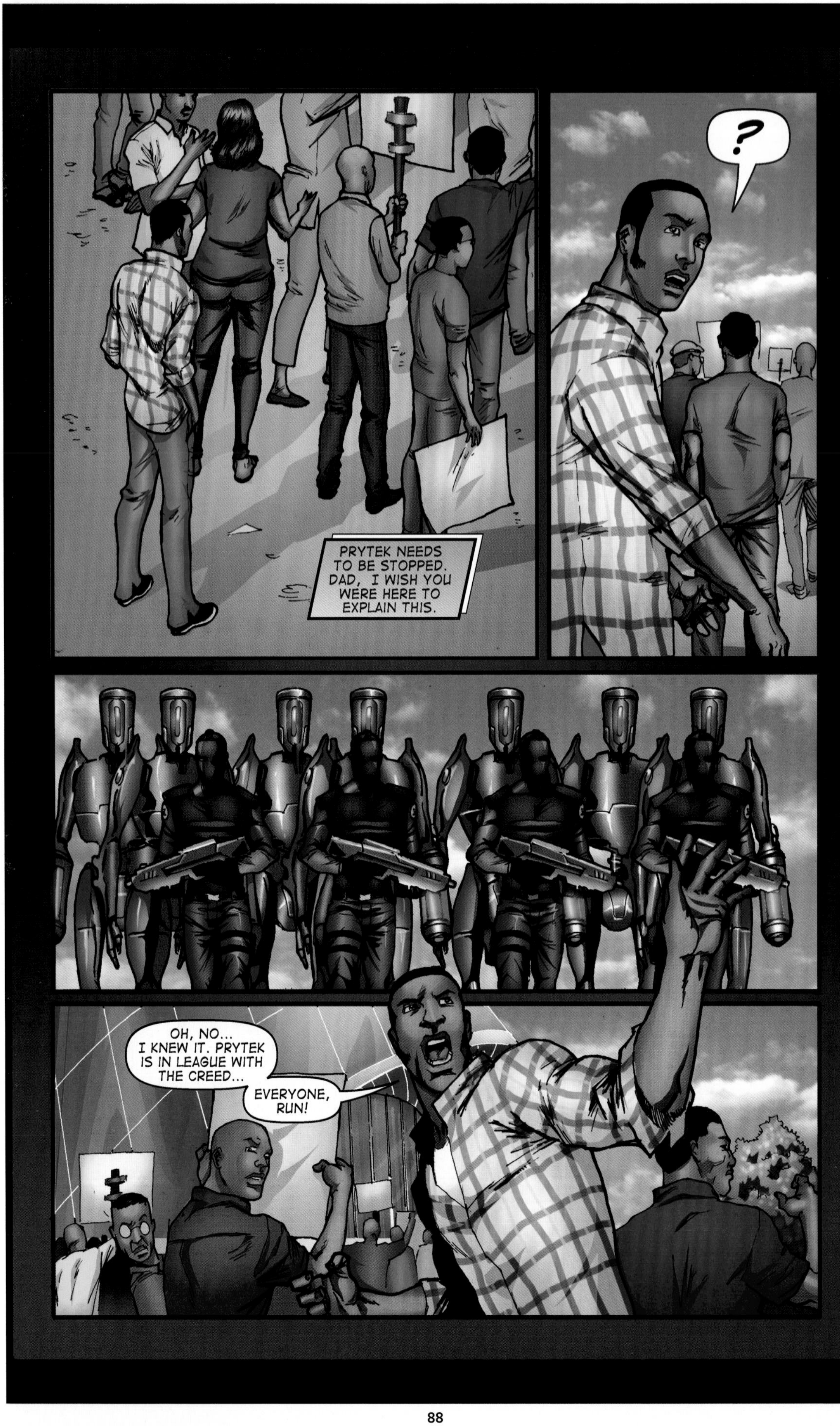
PRYTEK NEEDS TO BE STOPPED. DAD, I WISH YOU WERE HERE TO EXPLAIN THIS.
?
OH, NO... I KNEW IT. PRYTEK IS IN LEAGUE WITH THE CREED...
EVERYONE, RUN!

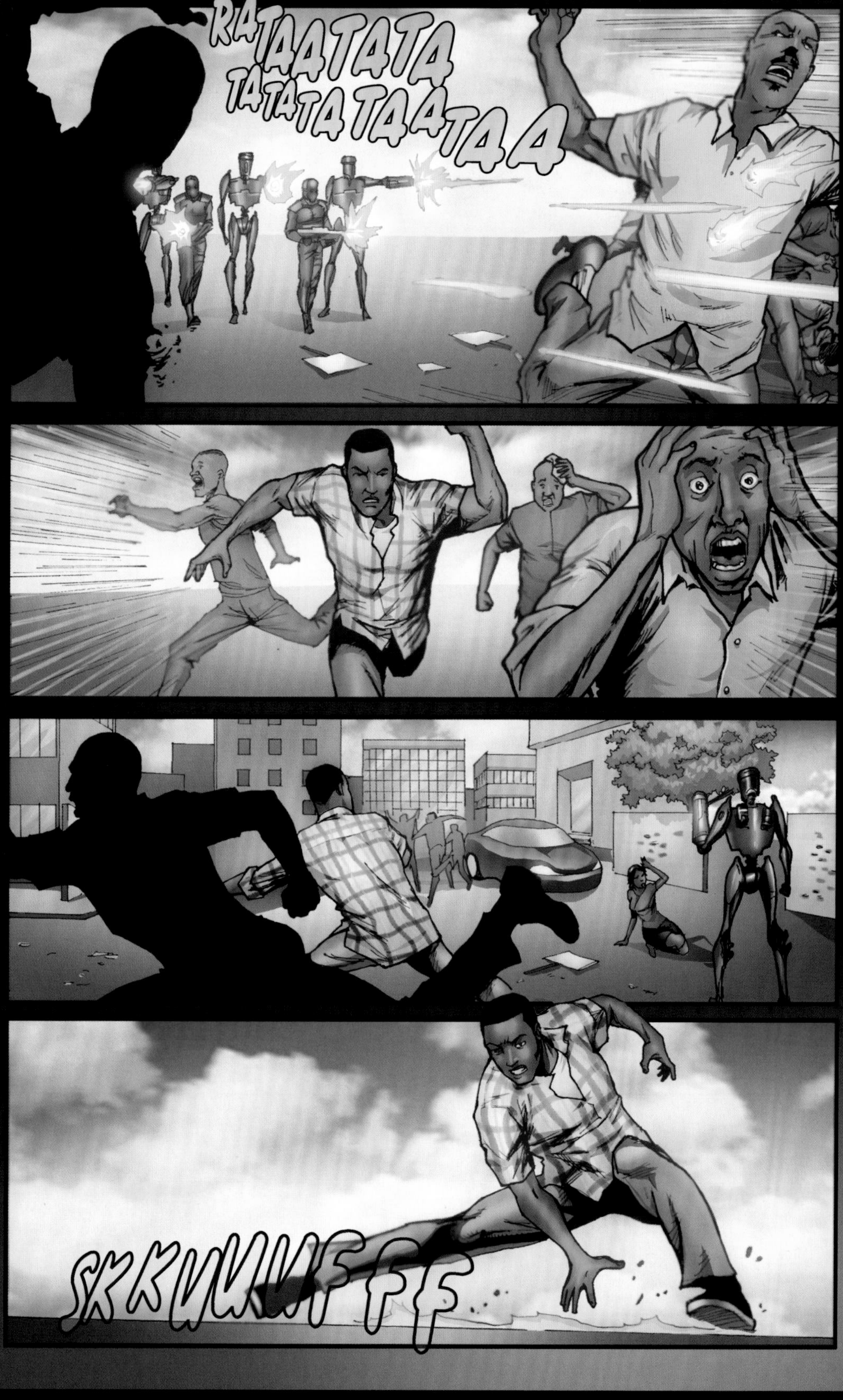
RATAATATA TATATATAATAA
SKKUUUFFF

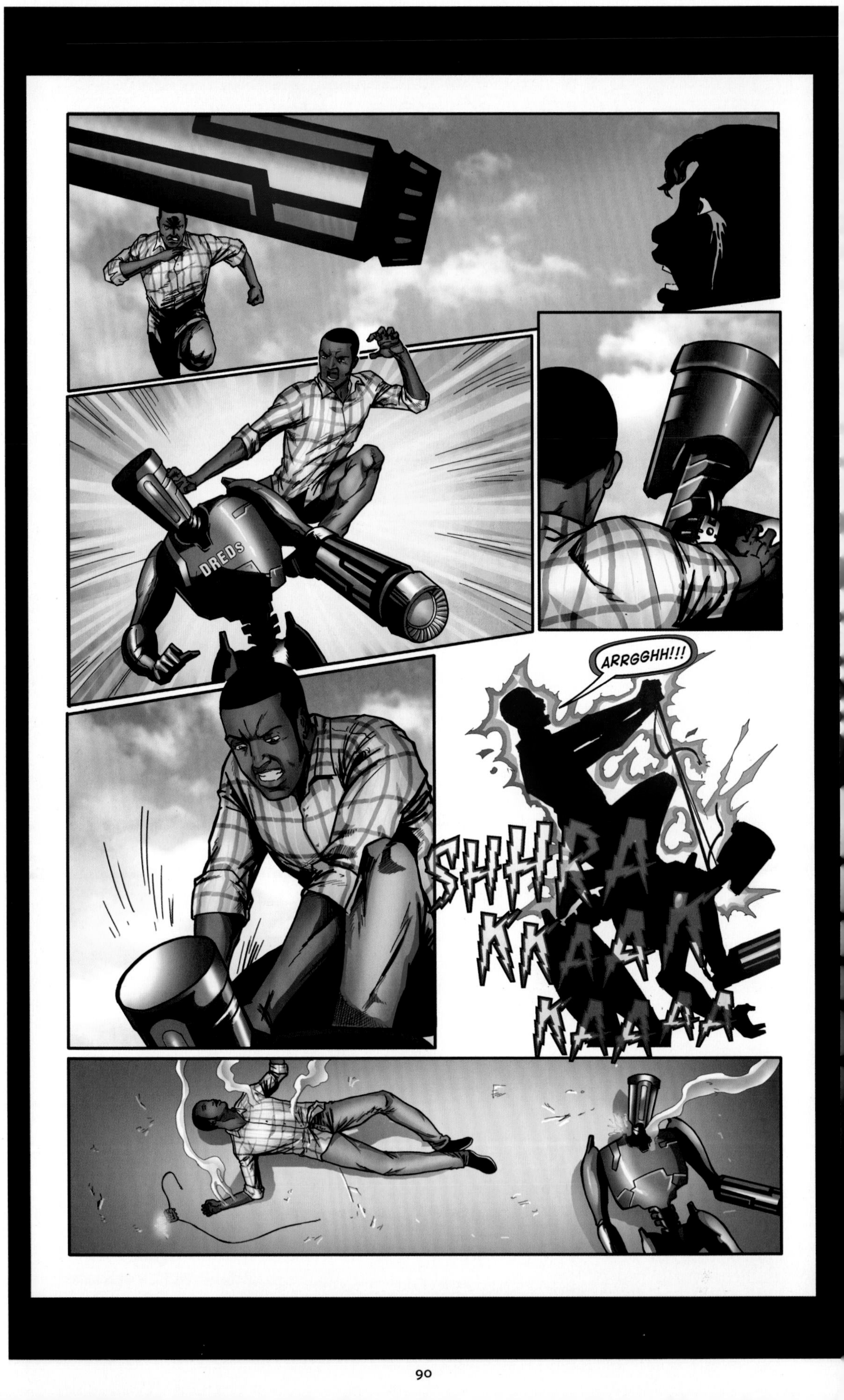
DREDS
ARRGGHH!!!
SHHRAK
KRAAK
KAAAA

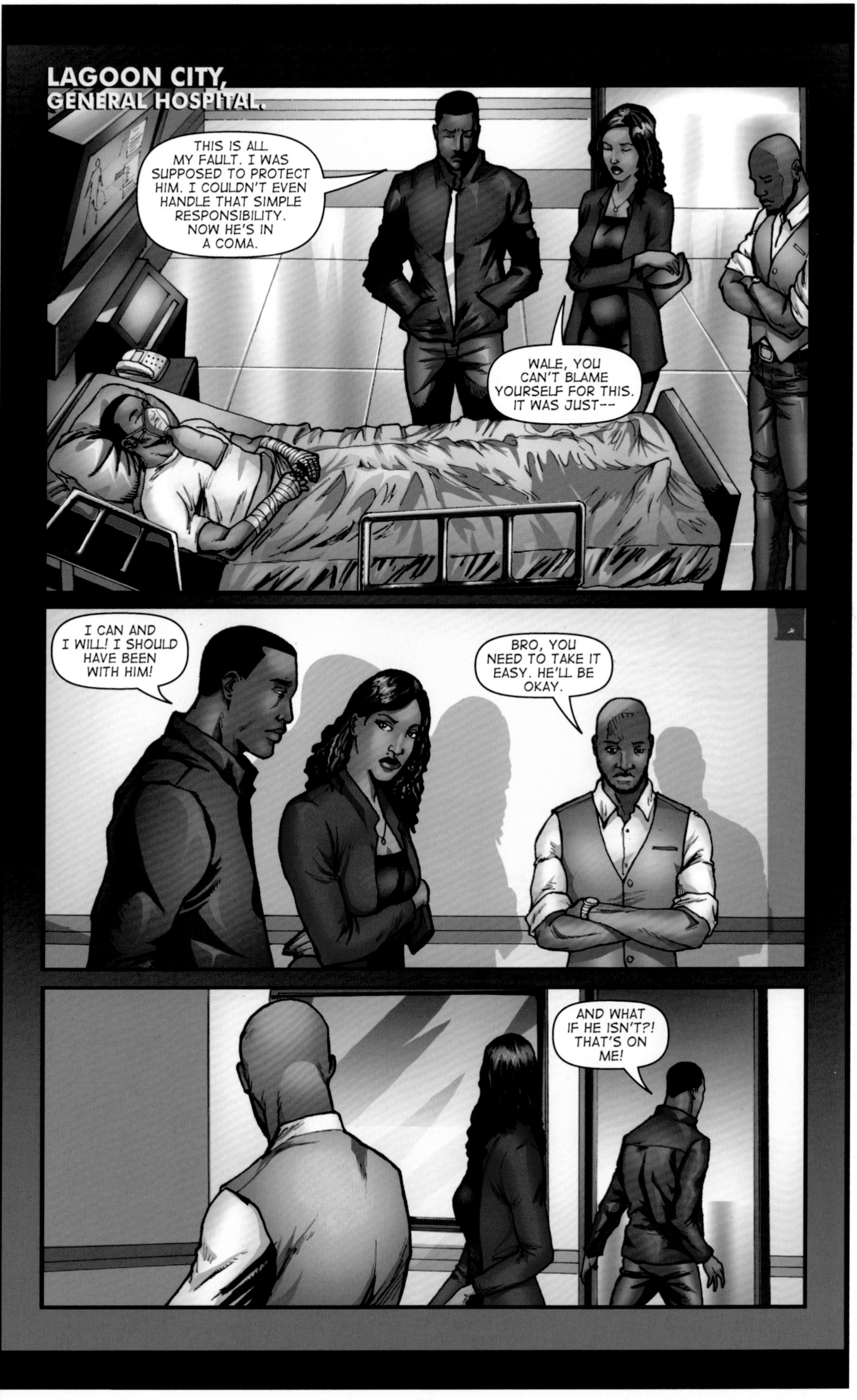
LAGOON CITY, GENERAL HOSPITAL.
THIS IS ALL MY FAULT. I WAS SUPPOSED TO PROTECT HIM. I COULDN'T EVEN HANDLE THAT SIMPLE RESPONSIBILITY. NOW HE'S IN A COMA.
WALE, YOU CAN'T BLAME YOURSELF FOR THIS. IT WAS JUST--
I CAN AND I WILL! I SHOULD HAVE BEEN WITH HIM!
BRO, YOU NEED TO TAKE IT EASY. HE'LL BE OKAY.
AND WHAT IF HE ISN'T?! THAT'S ON ME!

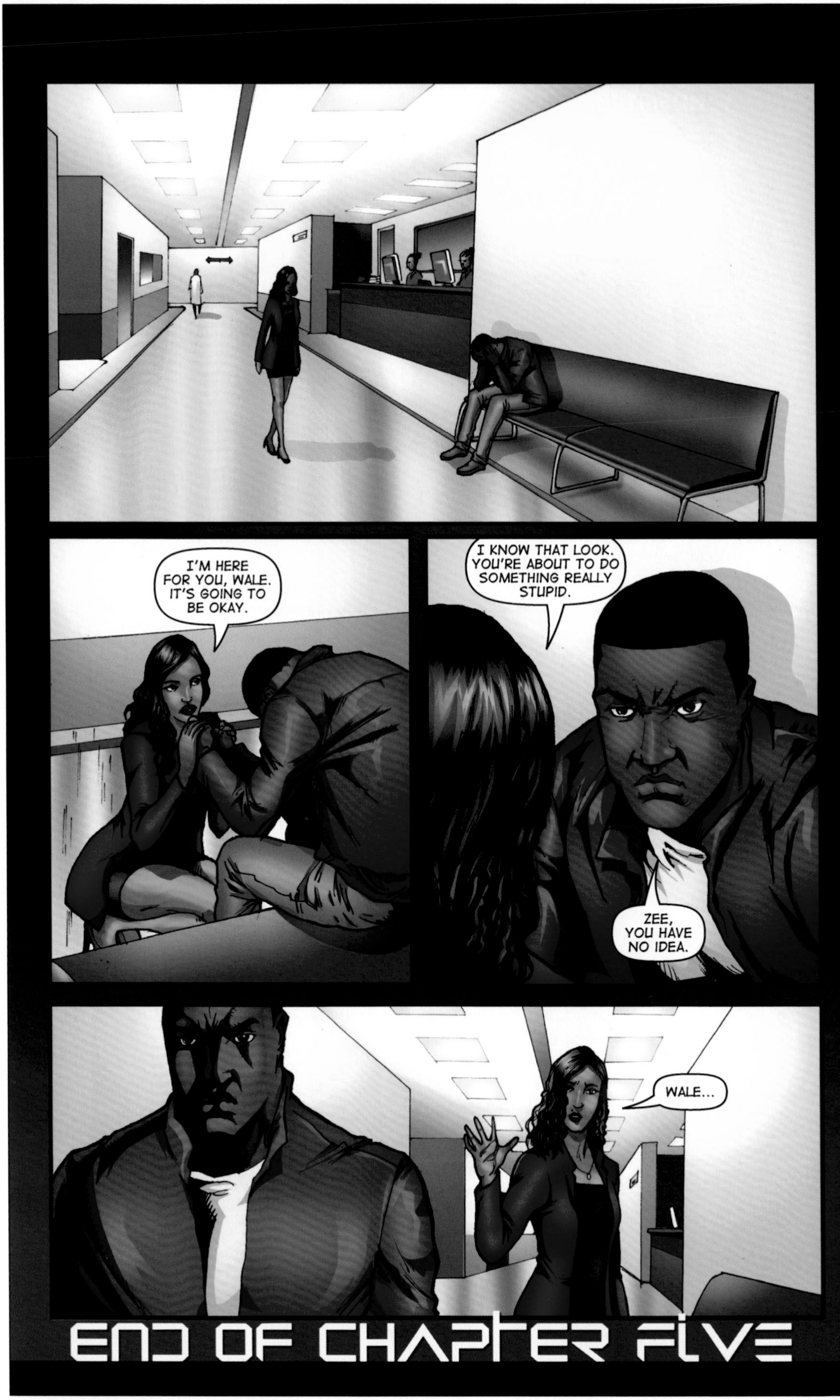
I'M HERE FOR YOU, WALE. IT'S GOING TO BE OKAY.
I KNOW THAT LOOK. YOU'RE ABOUT TO DO SOMETHING REALLY STUPID.
ZEE, YOU HAVE NO IDEA.
WALE...
END OF CHAPTER FIVE

"This time,
I won't
go easy."
—FURY

CHAPTER SIX

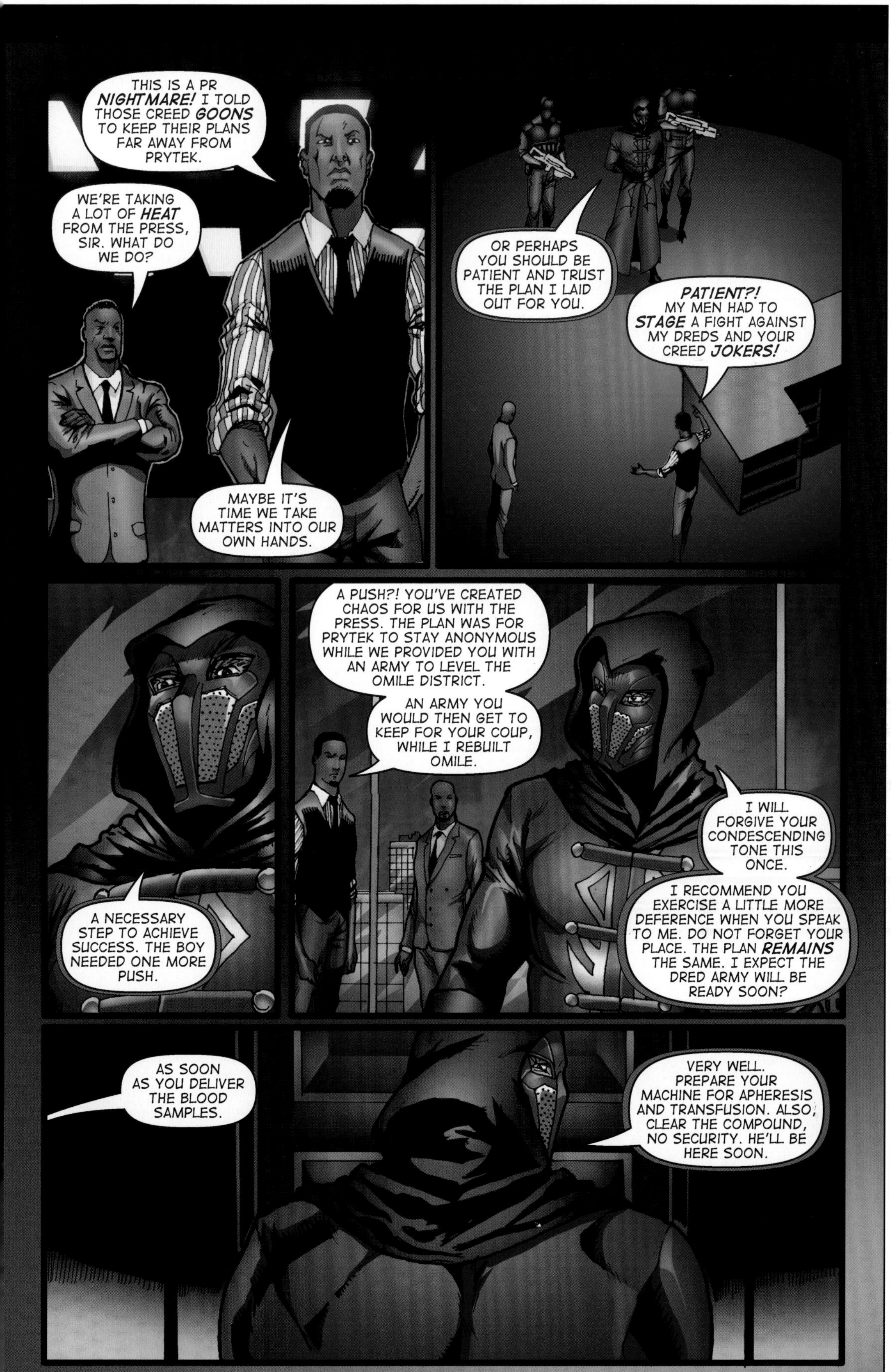
THIS IS A PR NIGHTMARE! I TOLD THOSE CREED GOONS TO KEEP THEIR PLANS FAR AWAY FROM PRYTEK.
WE'RE TAKING A LOT OF HEAT FROM THE PRESS, SIR. WHAT DO WE DO?
MAYBE IT'S TIME WE TAKE MATTERS INTO OUR OWN HANDS.
OR PERHAPS YOU SHOULD BE PATIENT AND TRUST THE PLAN I LAID OUT FOR YOU.
PATIENT?! MY MEN HAD TO STAGE A FIGHT AGAINST MY DREDS AND YOUR CREED JOKERS!
A NECESSARY STEP TO ACHIEVE SUCCESS. THE BOY NEEDED ONE MORE PUSH.
A PUSH?! YOU'VE CREATED CHAOS FOR US WITH THE PRESS. THE PLAN WAS FOR PRYTEK TO STAY ANONYMOUS WHILE WE PROVIDED YOU WITH AN ARMY TO LEVEL THE OMILE DISTRICT.
AN ARMY YOU WOULD THEN GET TO KEEP FOR YOUR COUP, WHILE I REBUILT OMILE.
I WILL FORGIVE YOUR CONDESCENDING TONE THIS ONCE.
I RECOMMEND YOU EXERCISE A LITTLE MORE DEFERENCE WHEN YOU SPEAK TO ME. DO NOT FORGET YOUR PLACE. THE PLAN REMAINS THE SAME. I EXPECT THE DRED ARMY WILL BE READY SOON?
AS SOON AS YOU DELIVER THE BLOOD SAMPLES.
VERY WELL. PREPARE YOUR MACHINE FOR APHERESIS AND TRANSFUSION. ALSO, CLEAR THE COMPOUND, NO SECURITY. HE'LL BE HERE SOON.

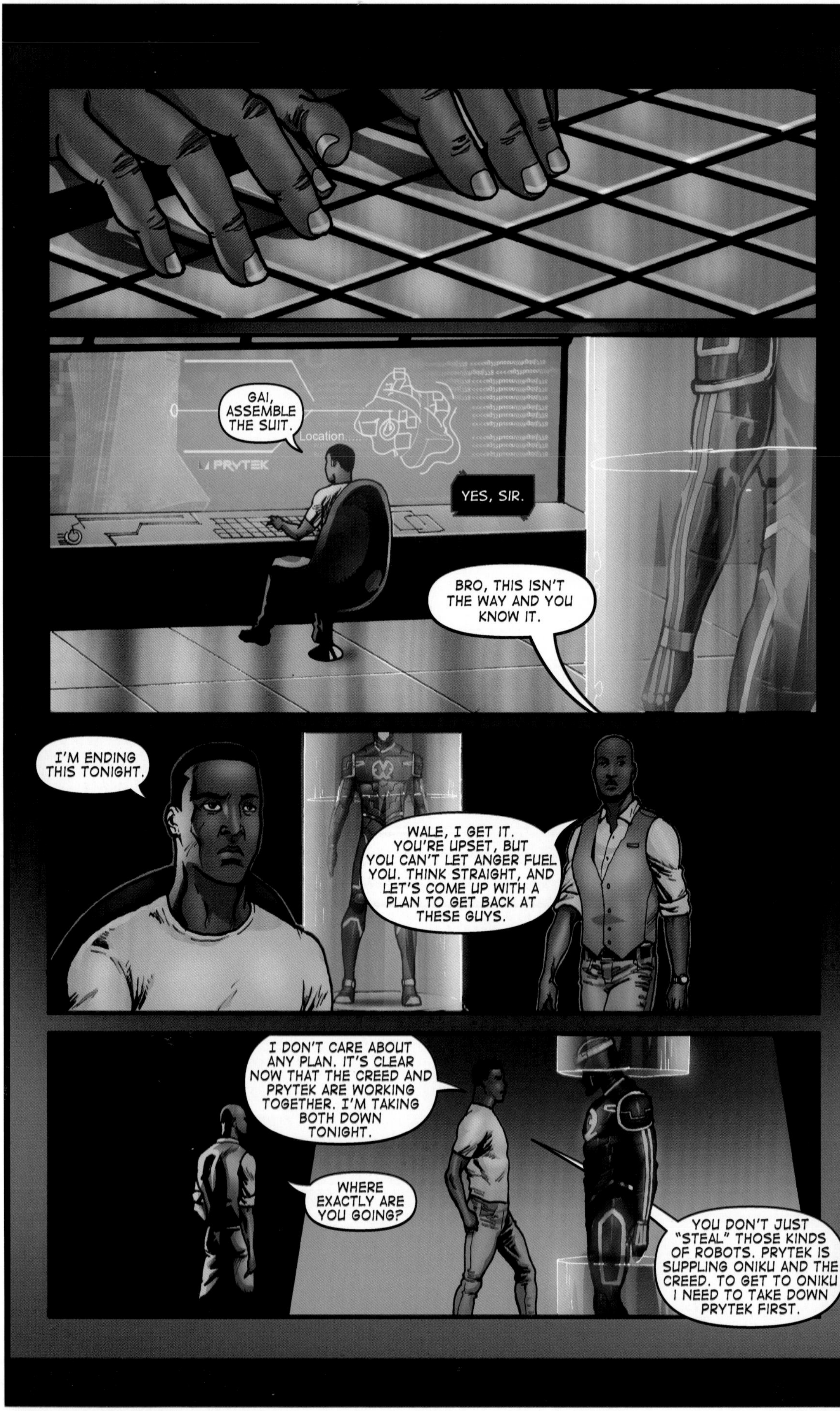
GAI, ASSEMBLE THE SUIT.
Location.....
PRYTEK
YES, SIR.
BRO, THIS ISN'T THE WAY AND YOU KNOW IT.
I'M ENDING THIS TONIGHT.
WALE, I GET IT. YOU'RE UPSET, BUT YOU CAN'T LET ANGER FUEL YOU. THINK STRAIGHT, AND LET'S COME UP WITH A PLAN TO GET BACK AT THESE GUYS.
I DON'T CARE ABOUT ANY PLAN. IT'S CLEAR NOW THAT THE CREED AND PRYTEK ARE WORKING TOGETHER. I'M TAKING BOTH DOWN TONIGHT.
WHERE EXACTLY ARE YOU GOING?
YOU DON'T JUST "STEAL" THOSE KINDS OF ROBOTS. PRYTEK IS SUPPLING ONIKU AND THE CREED. TO GET TO ONIKU I NEED TO TAKE DOWN PRYTEK FIRST.

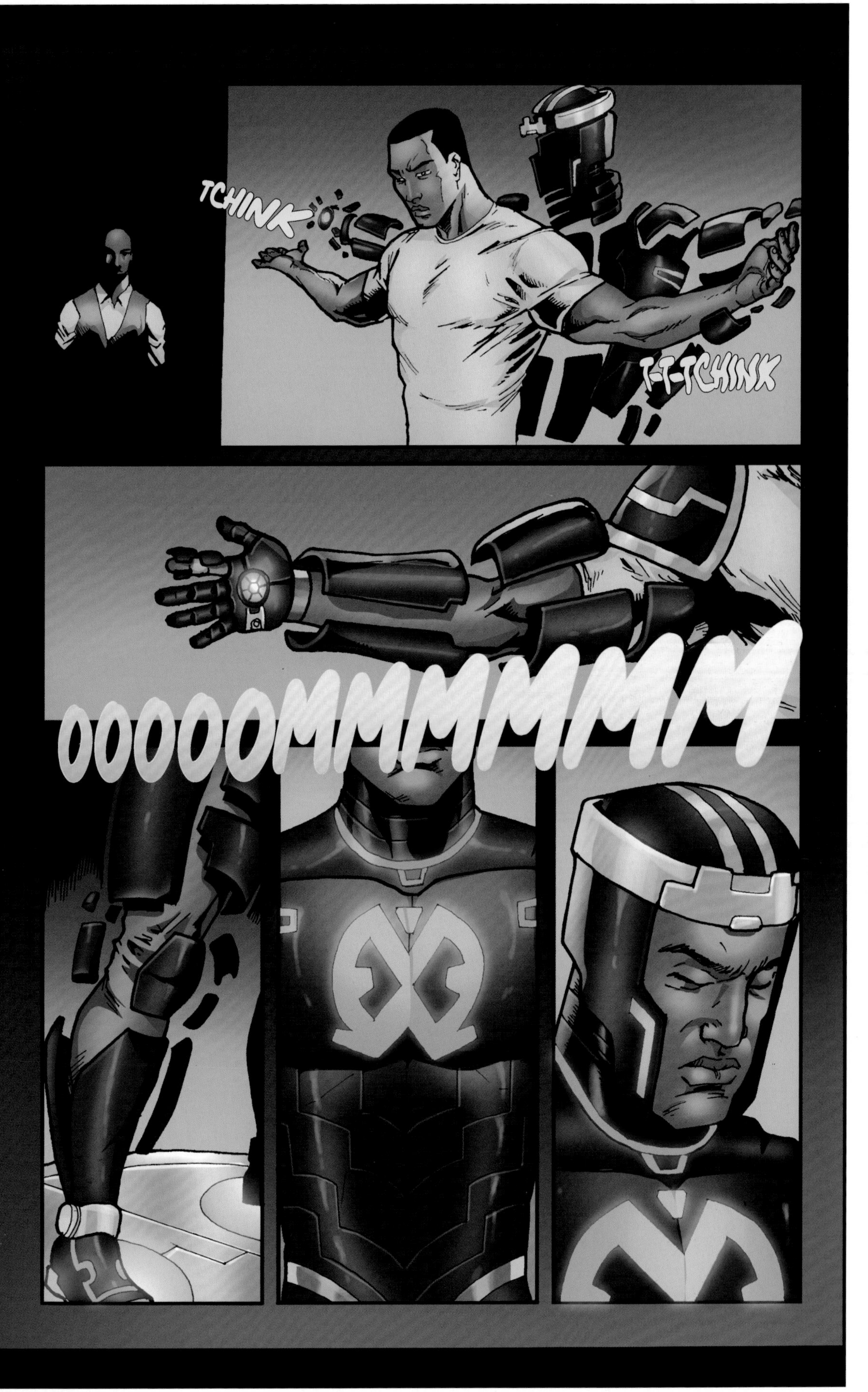
TCHINK
T-T-TCHINK
OOOOOMMMMMMM

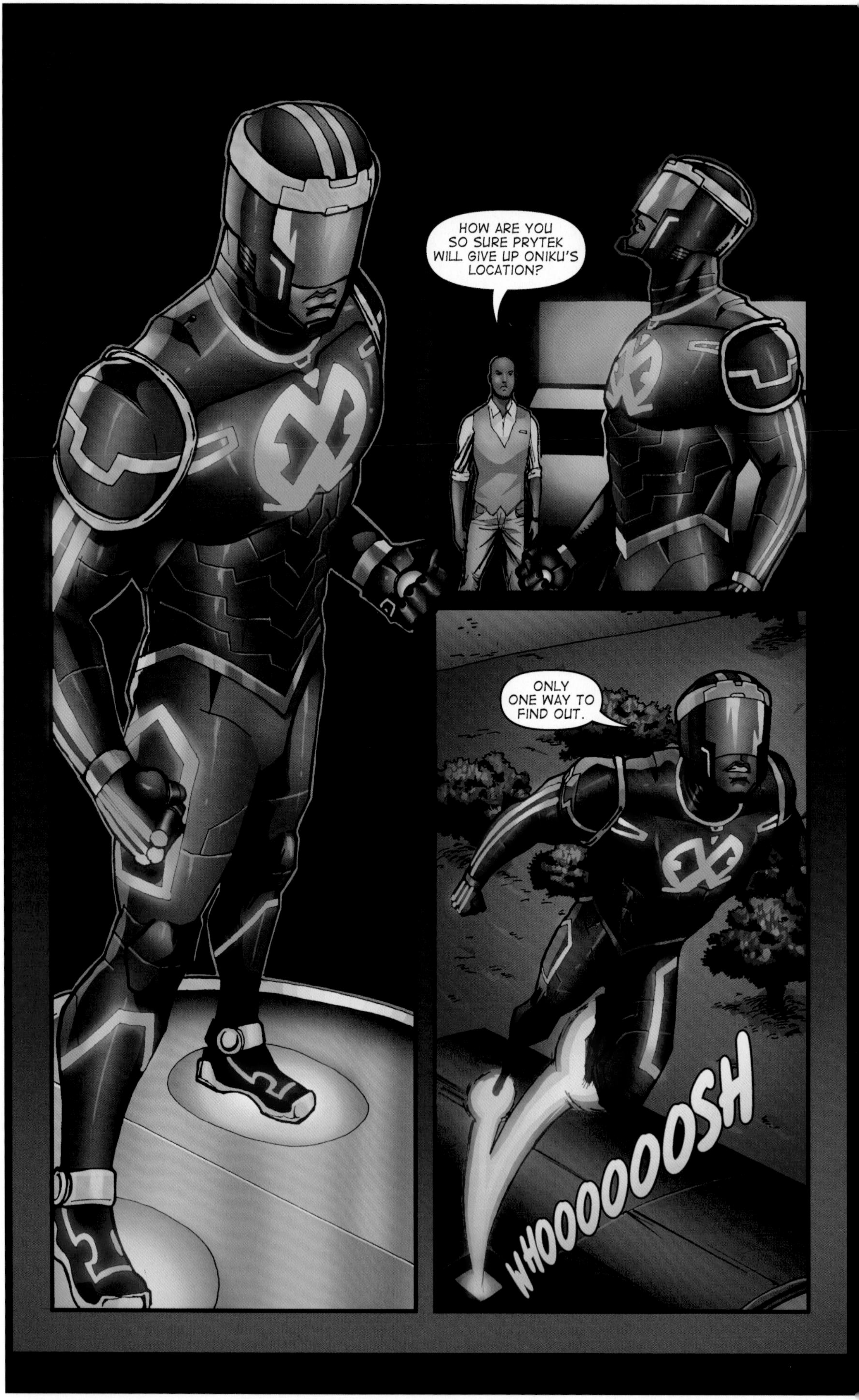
HOW ARE YOU SO SURE PRYTEK WILL GIVE UP ONIKU'S LOCATION?
ONLY ONE WAY TO FIND OUT.
WHOOOOOOOSH

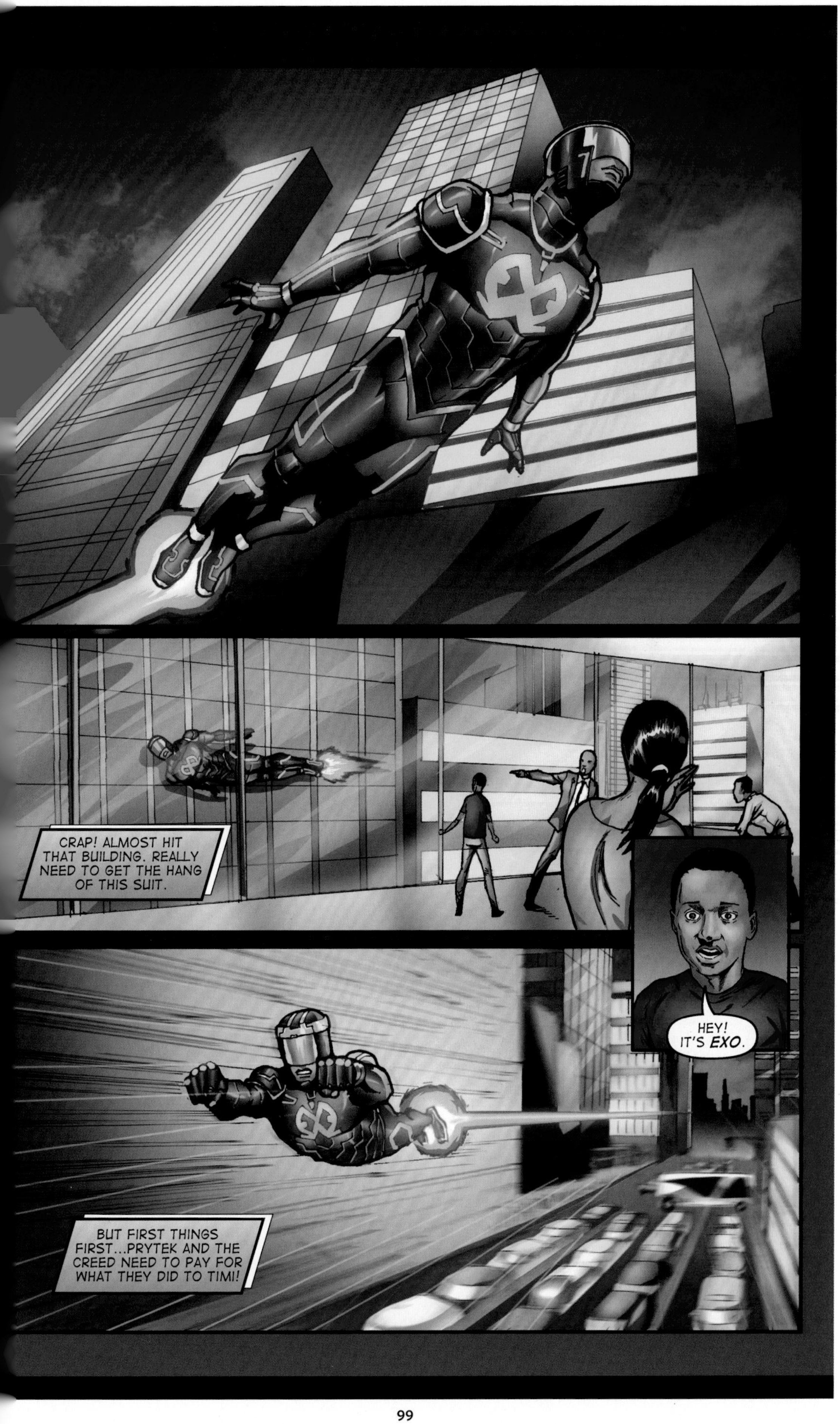
CRAP! ALMOST HIT THAT BUILDING. REALLY NEED TO GET THE HANG OF THIS SUIT.
HEY! IT'S EXO.
BUT FIRST THINGS FIRST...PRYTEK AND THE CREED NEED TO PAY FOR WHAT THEY DID TO TIMI!

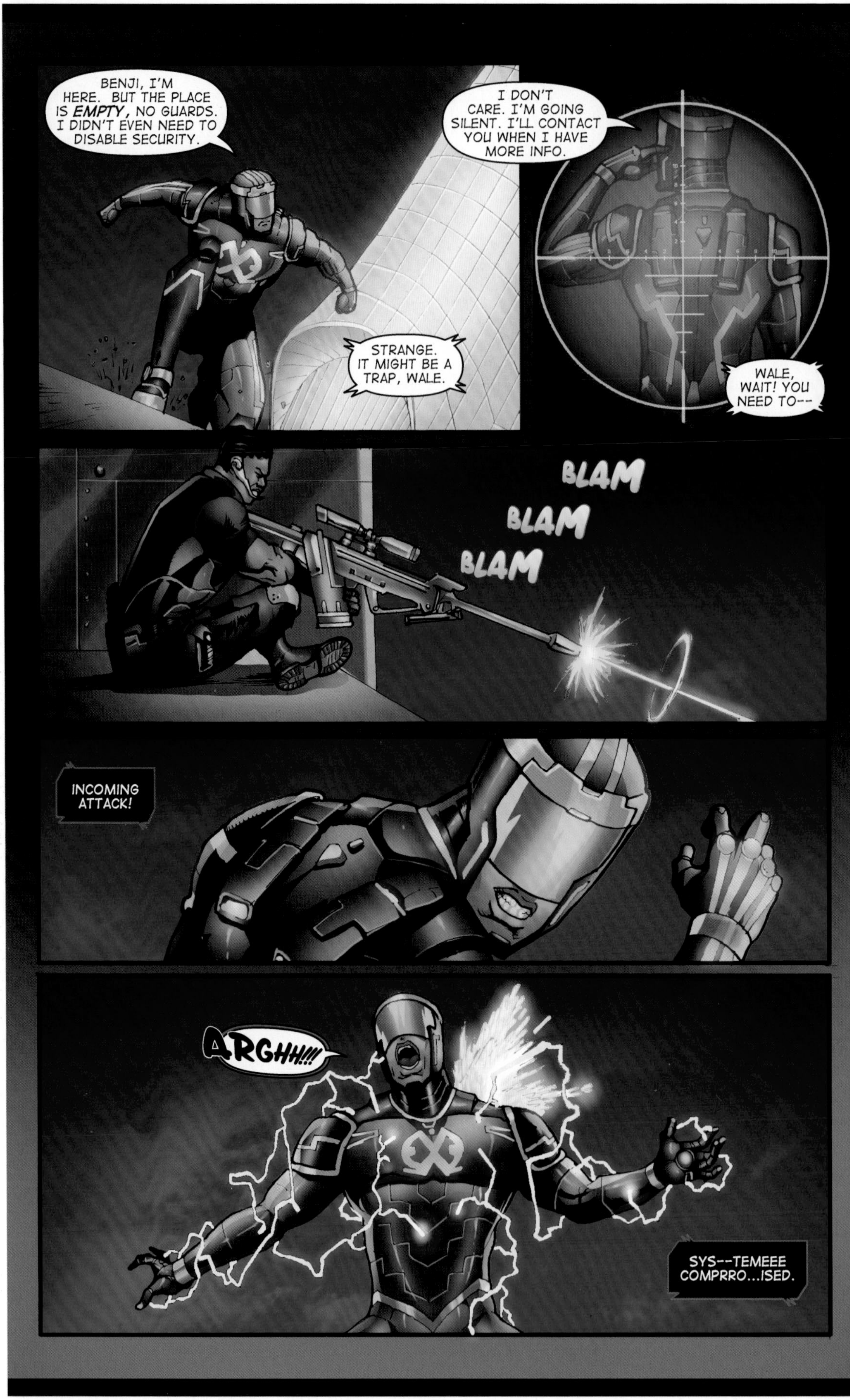
BENJI, I'M HERE. BUT THE PLACE IS *EMPTY*, NO GUARDS. I DIDN'T EVEN NEED TO DISABLE SECURITY.
STRANGE. IT MIGHT BE A TRAP, WALE.
I DON'T CARE. I'M GOING SILENT. I'LL CONTACT YOU WHEN I HAVE MORE INFO.
WALE, WAIT! YOU NEED TO--
BLAM
BLAM
BLAM
INCOMING ATTACK!
ARGHH!!!
SYS--TEMEEE COMPRRO...ISED.

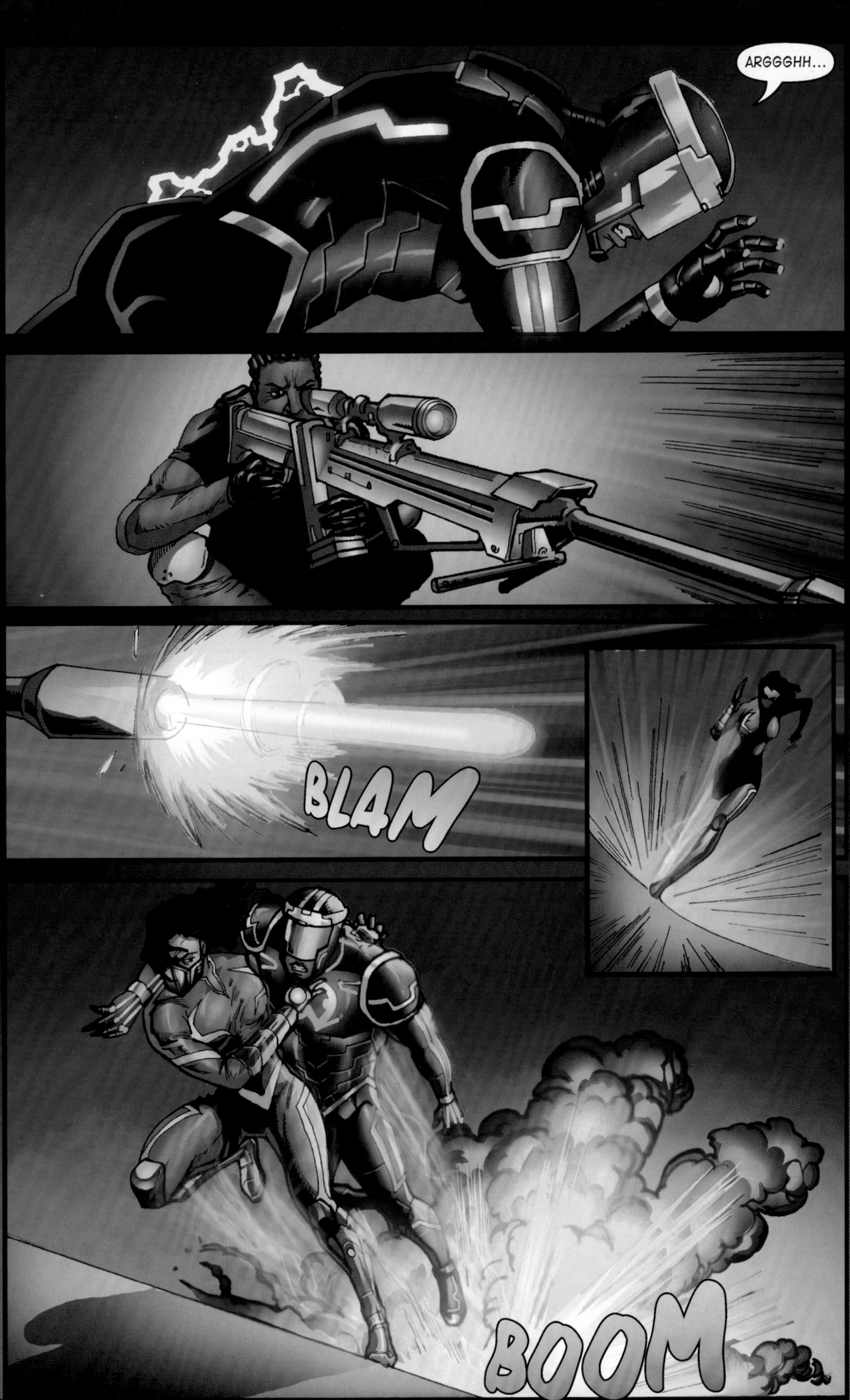
ARGGGHH...
BLAM
BOOM

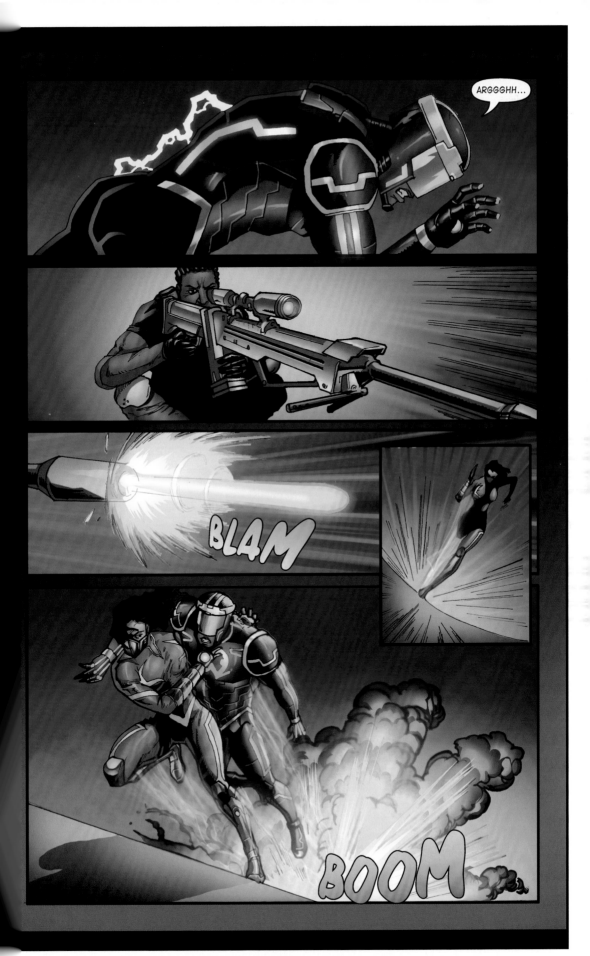

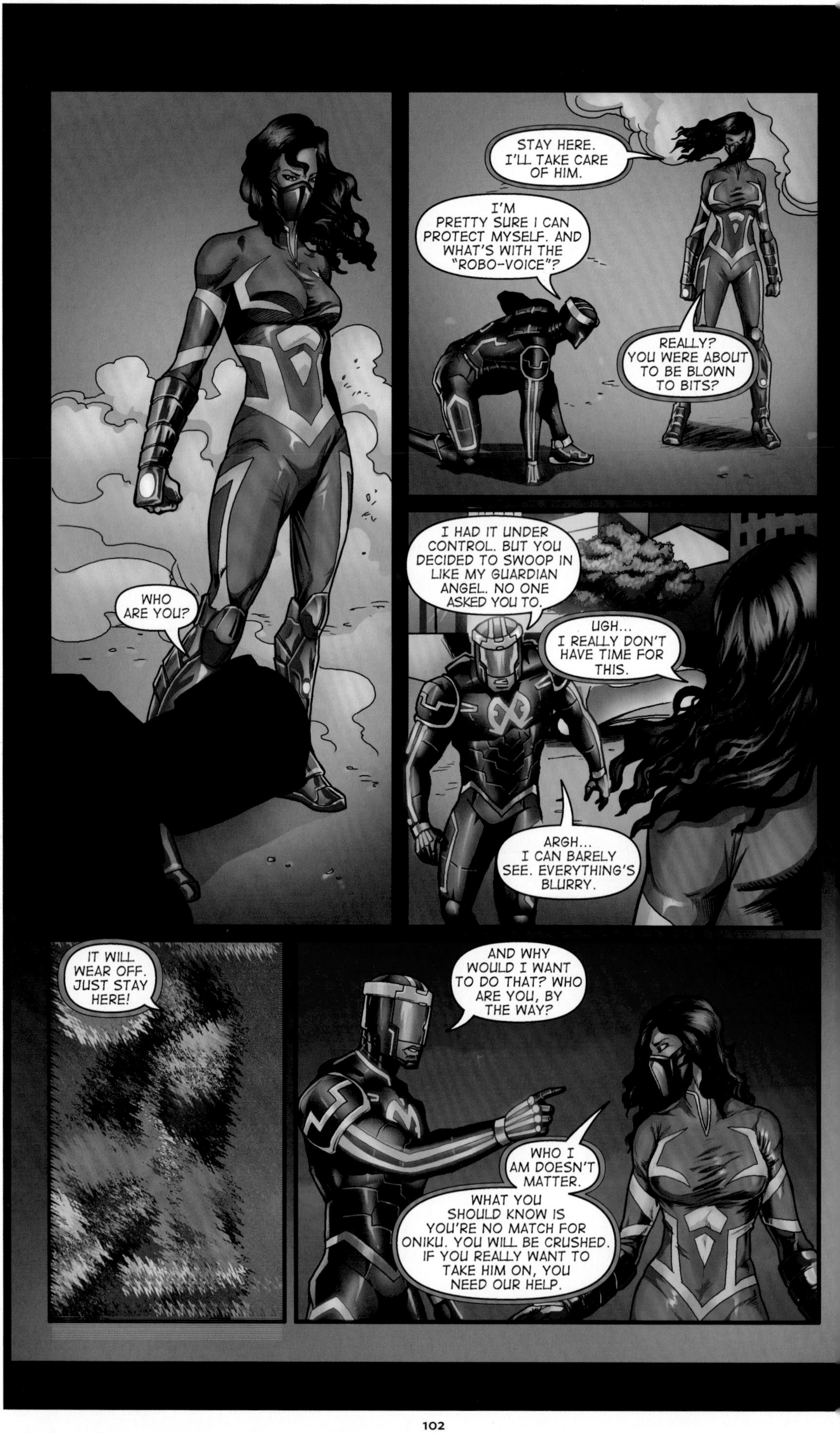
WHO ARE YOU?
STAY HERE. I'LL TAKE CARE OF HIM.
I'M PRETTY SURE I CAN PROTECT MYSELF. AND WHAT'S WITH THE "ROBO-VOICE"?
REALLY? YOU WERE ABOUT TO BE BLOWN TO BITS?
I HAD IT UNDER CONTROL. BUT YOU DECIDED TO SWOOP IN LIKE MY GUARDIAN ANGEL. NO ONE ASKED YOU TO.
UGH... I REALLY DON'T HAVE TIME FOR THIS.
ARGH... I CAN BARELY SEE. EVERYTHING'S BLURRY.
IT WILL WEAR OFF. JUST STAY HERE!
AND WHY WOULD I WANT TO DO THAT? WHO ARE YOU, BY THE WAY?
WHO I AM DOESN'T MATTER.
WHAT YOU SHOULD KNOW IS YOU'RE NO MATCH FOR ONIKU. YOU WILL BE CRUSHED. IF YOU REALLY WANT TO TAKE HIM ON, YOU NEED OUR HELP.

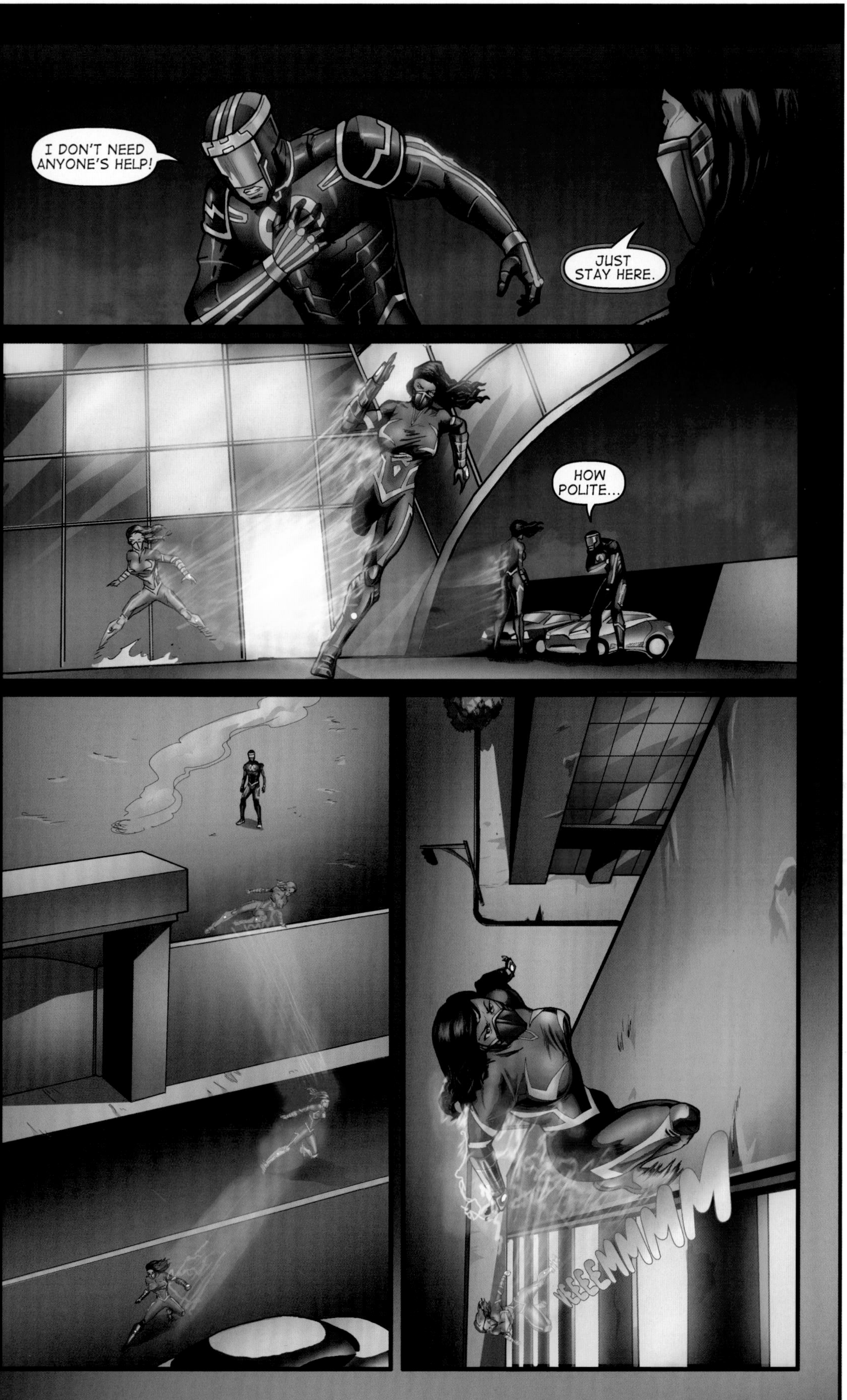

I DON'T NEED ANYONE'S HELP!
JUST STAY HERE.
HOW POLITE...
VREEEMMMMM

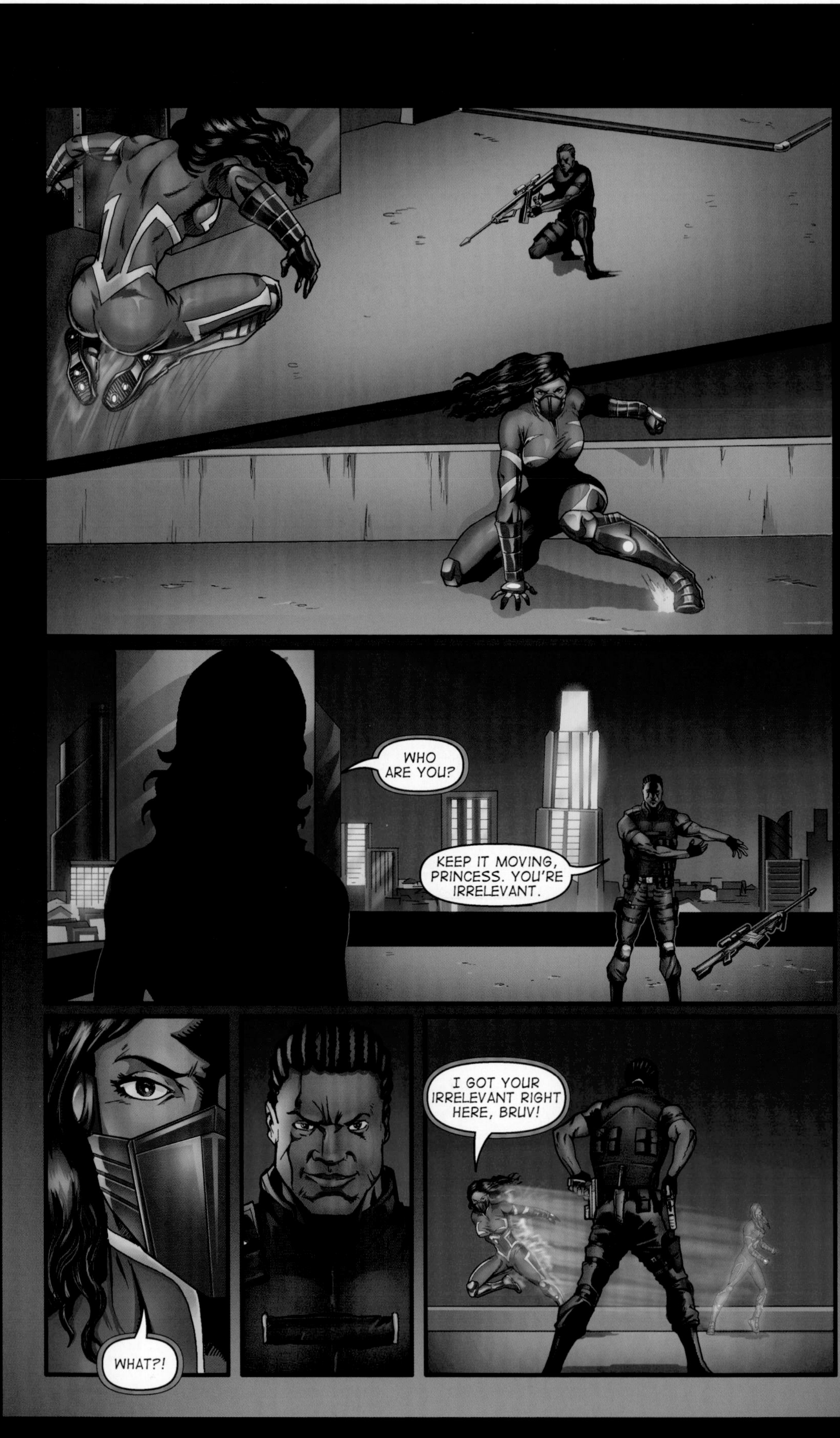
WHO ARE YOU?
KEEP IT MOVING, PRINCESS. YOU'RE IRRELEVANT.
WHAT?!
I GOT YOUR IRRELEVANT RIGHT HERE, BRUV!

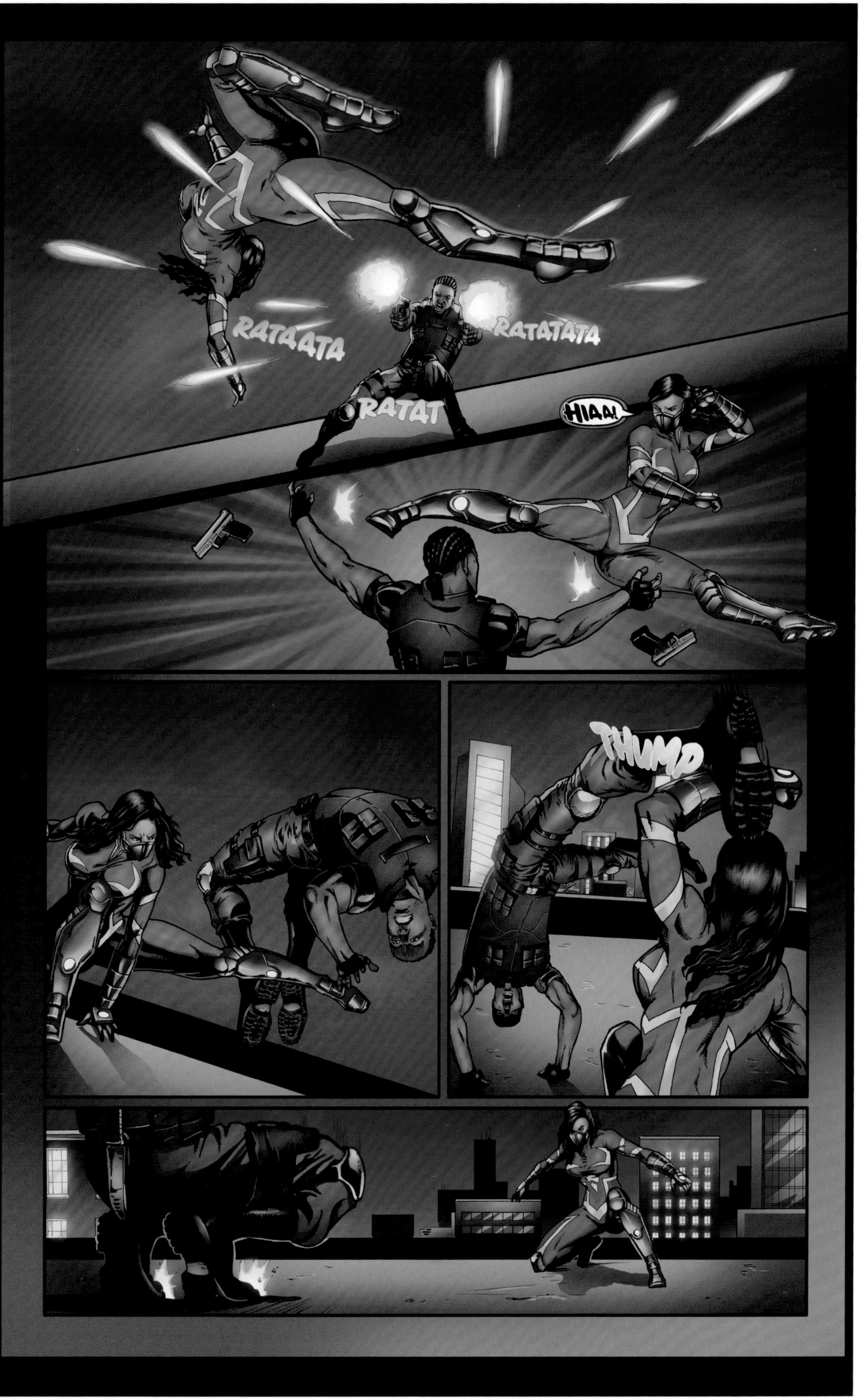
RATAATA
RATATATA
RATAT
HIAA!
THUMP

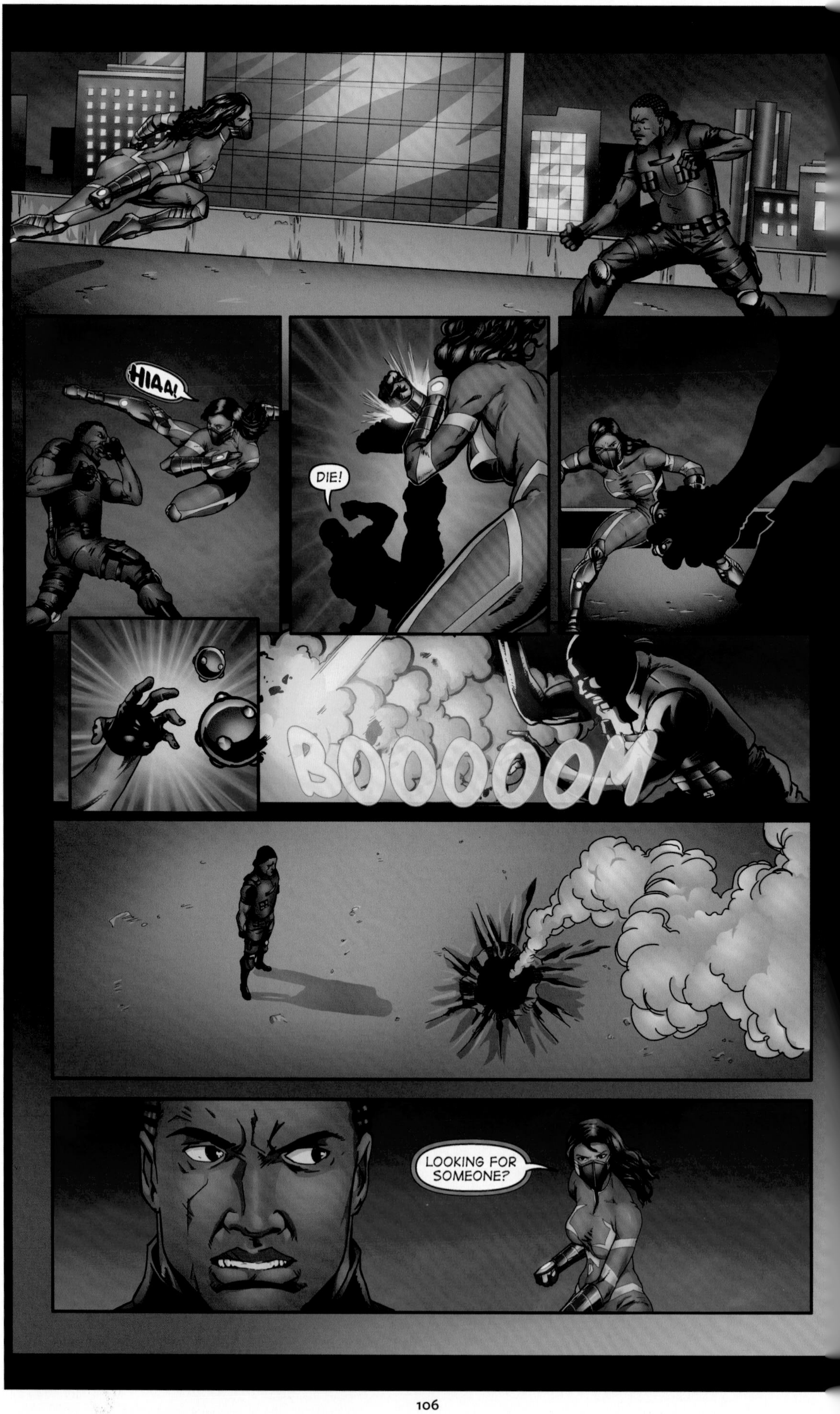
HIAA!
DIE!
BOOOOOM
LOOKING FOR SOMEONE?

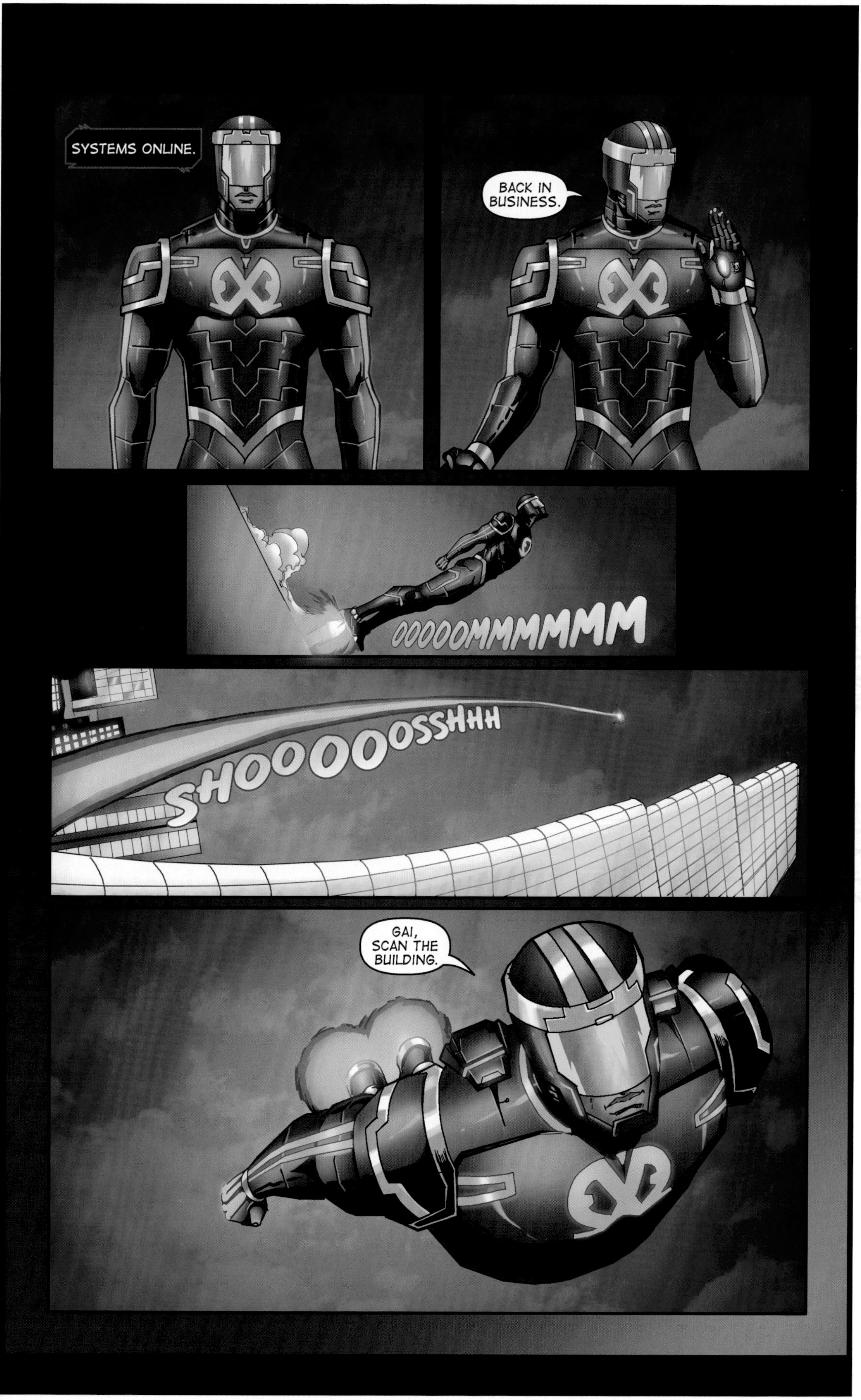
SYSTEMS ONLINE.
BACK IN BUSINESS.
OOOOOMMMMMM
SHOOOOOOSSHHH
GAI, SCAN THE BUILDING.

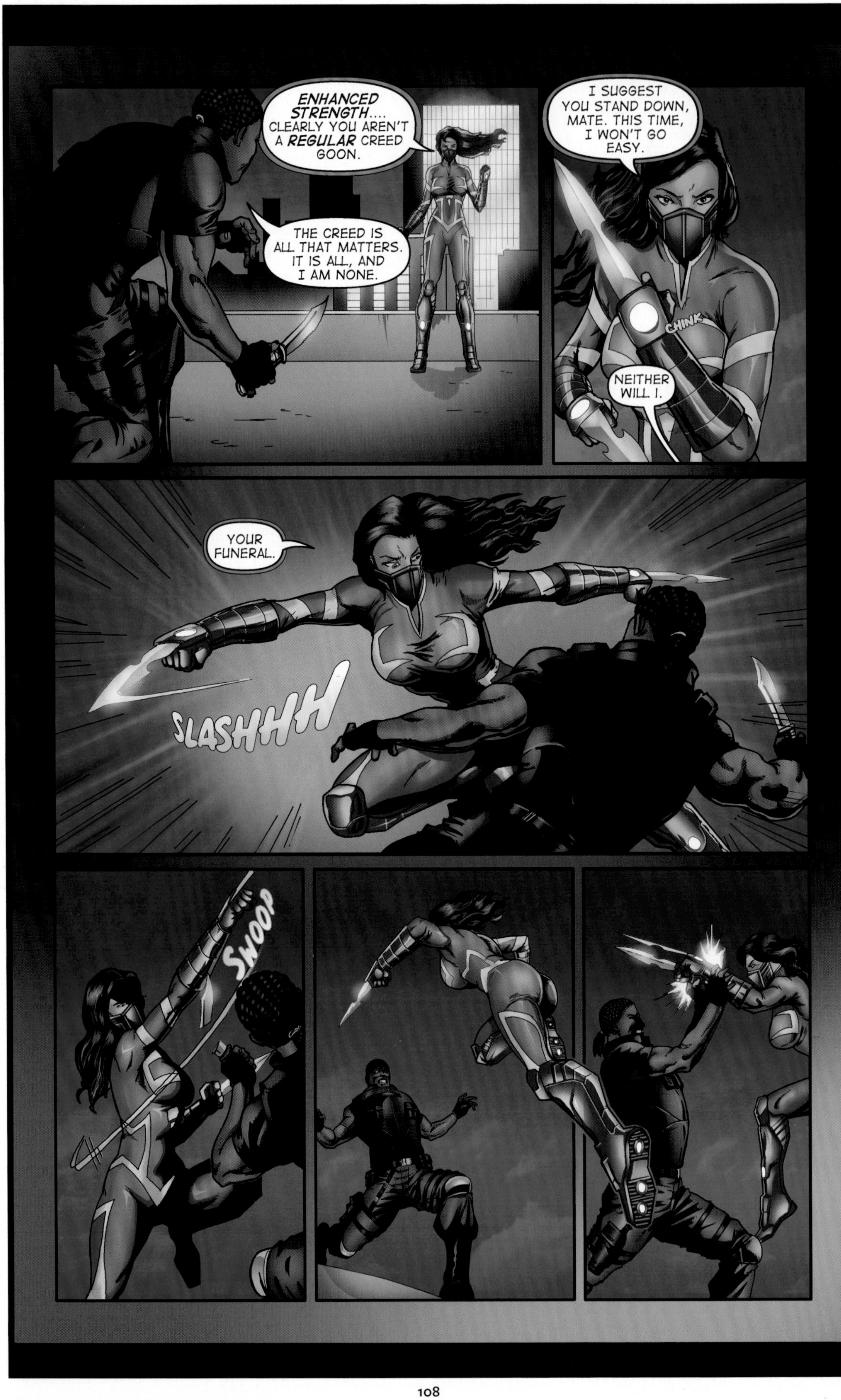
ENHANCED STRENGTH.... CLEARLY YOU AREN'T A REGULAR CREED GOON.
THE CREED IS ALL THAT MATTERS. IT IS ALL, AND I AM NONE.
I SUGGEST YOU STAND DOWN, MATE. THIS TIME, I WON'T GO EASY.
CHINK
NEITHER WILL I.
YOUR FUNERAL.
SLASHHH
SWOOP

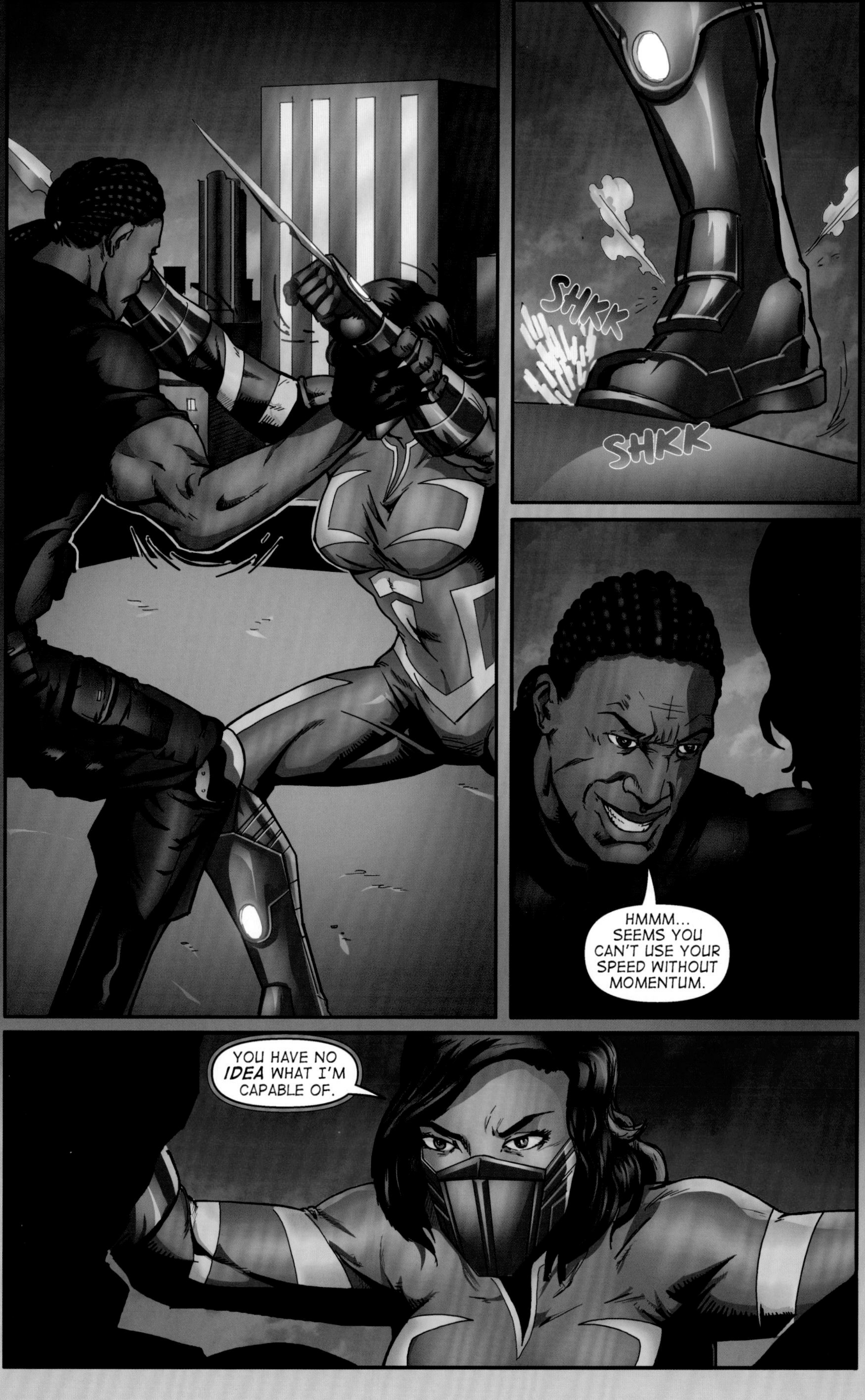
SHKK
SHKK
HMMM... SEEMS YOU CAN'T USE YOUR SPEED WITHOUT MOMENTUM.
YOU HAVE NO *IDEA* WHAT I'M CAPABLE OF.

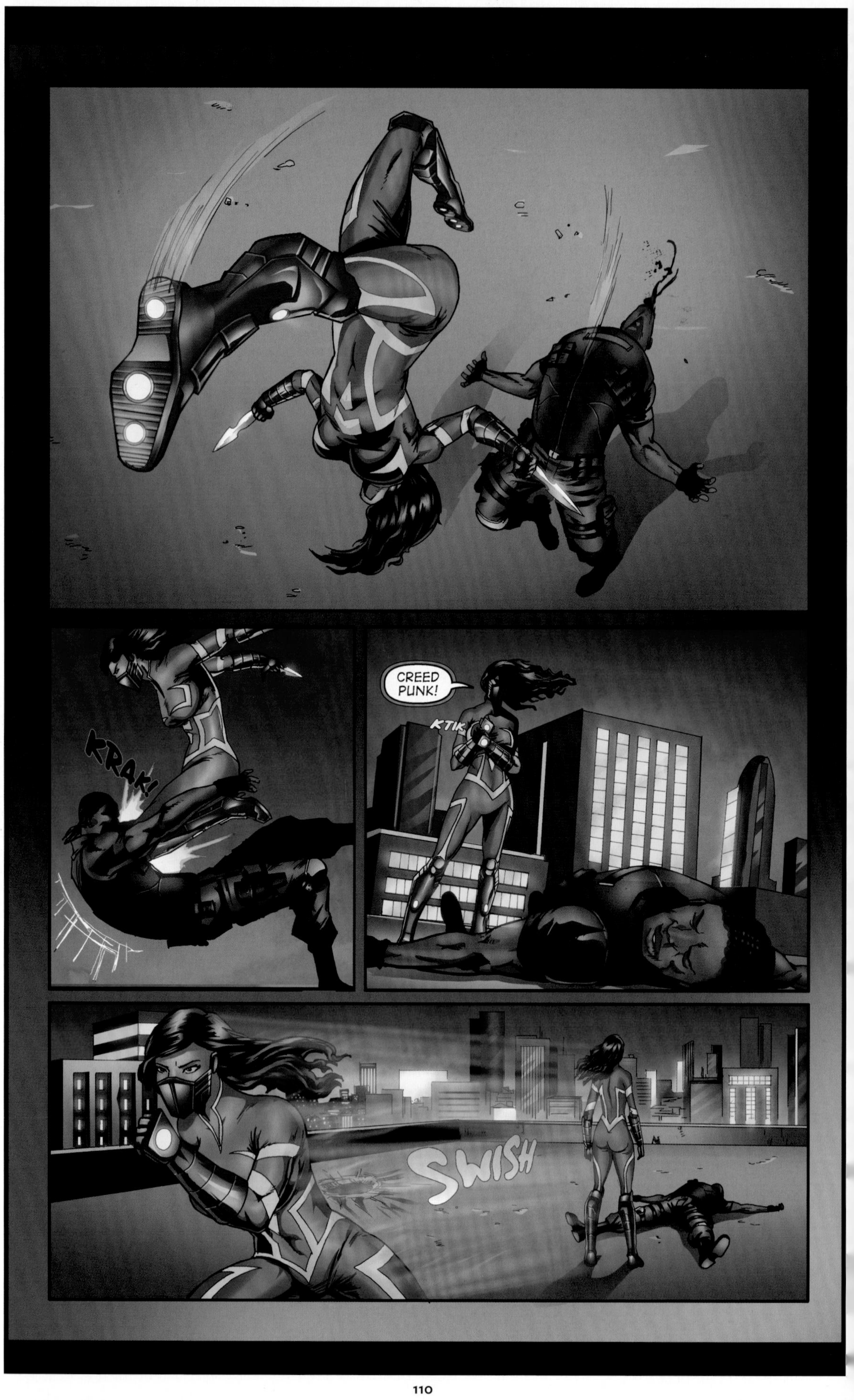
KRAK!
CREED PUNK!
KTIK
SWISH

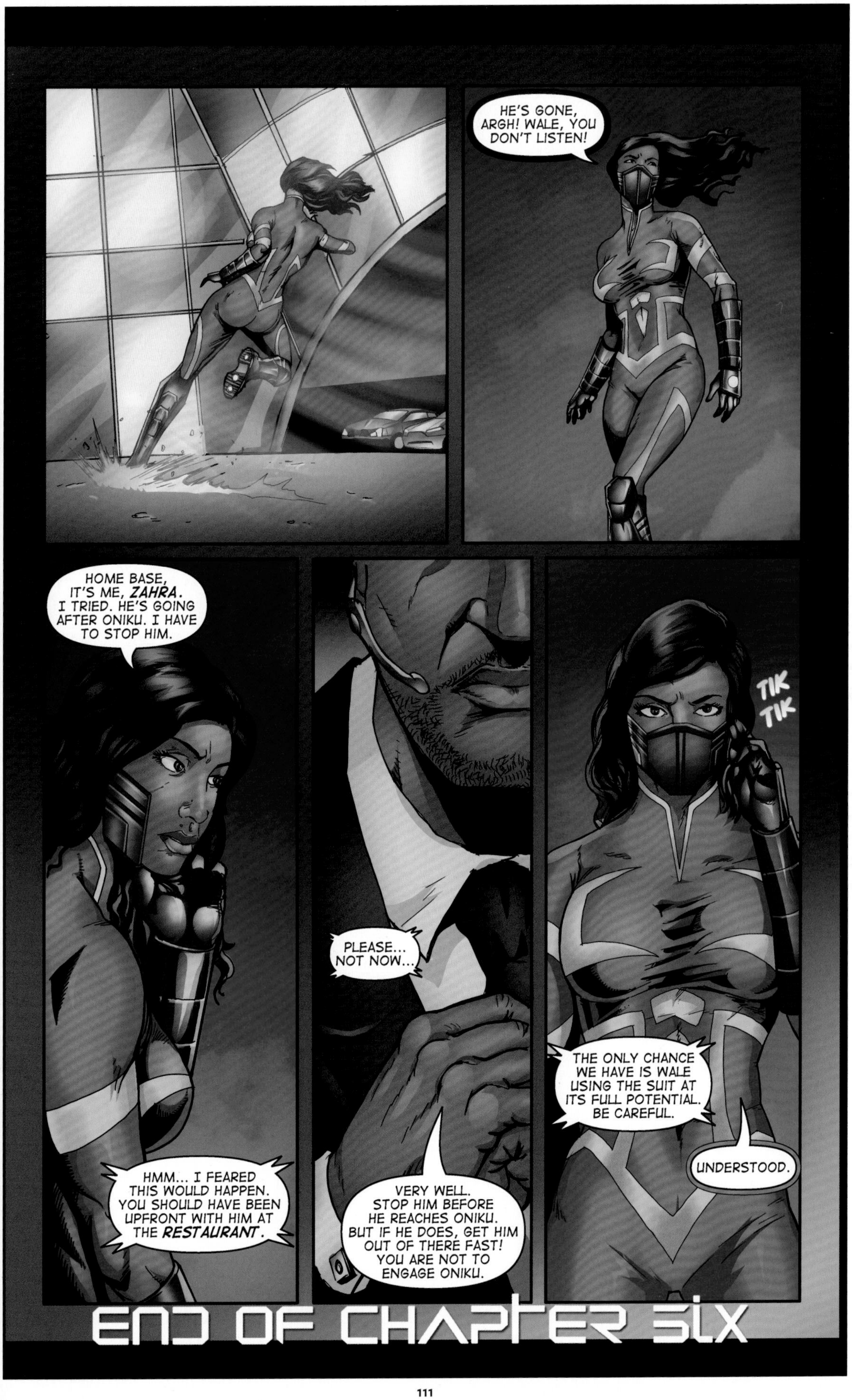
HE'S GONE, ARGH! WALE, YOU DON'T LISTEN!
HOME BASE, IT'S ME, ZAHRA. I TRIED. HE'S GOING AFTER ONIKU. I HAVE TO STOP HIM.
HMM... I FEARED THIS WOULD HAPPEN. YOU SHOULD HAVE BEEN UPFRONT WITH HIM AT THE RESTAURANT.
PLEASE... NOT NOW...
VERY WELL. STOP HIM BEFORE HE REACHES ONIKU. BUT IF HE DOES, GET HIM OUT OF THERE FAST! YOU ARE NOT TO ENGAGE ONIKU.
TIK TIK
THE ONLY CHANCE WE HAVE IS WALE USING THE SUIT AT ITS FULL POTENTIAL. BE CAREFUL.
UNDERSTOOD.
END OF CHAPTER SIX

"If you think I'm just going
to sit back while you kill
innocent people, you're out
of your mind!"

—EXO

CHAPTER SEVEN

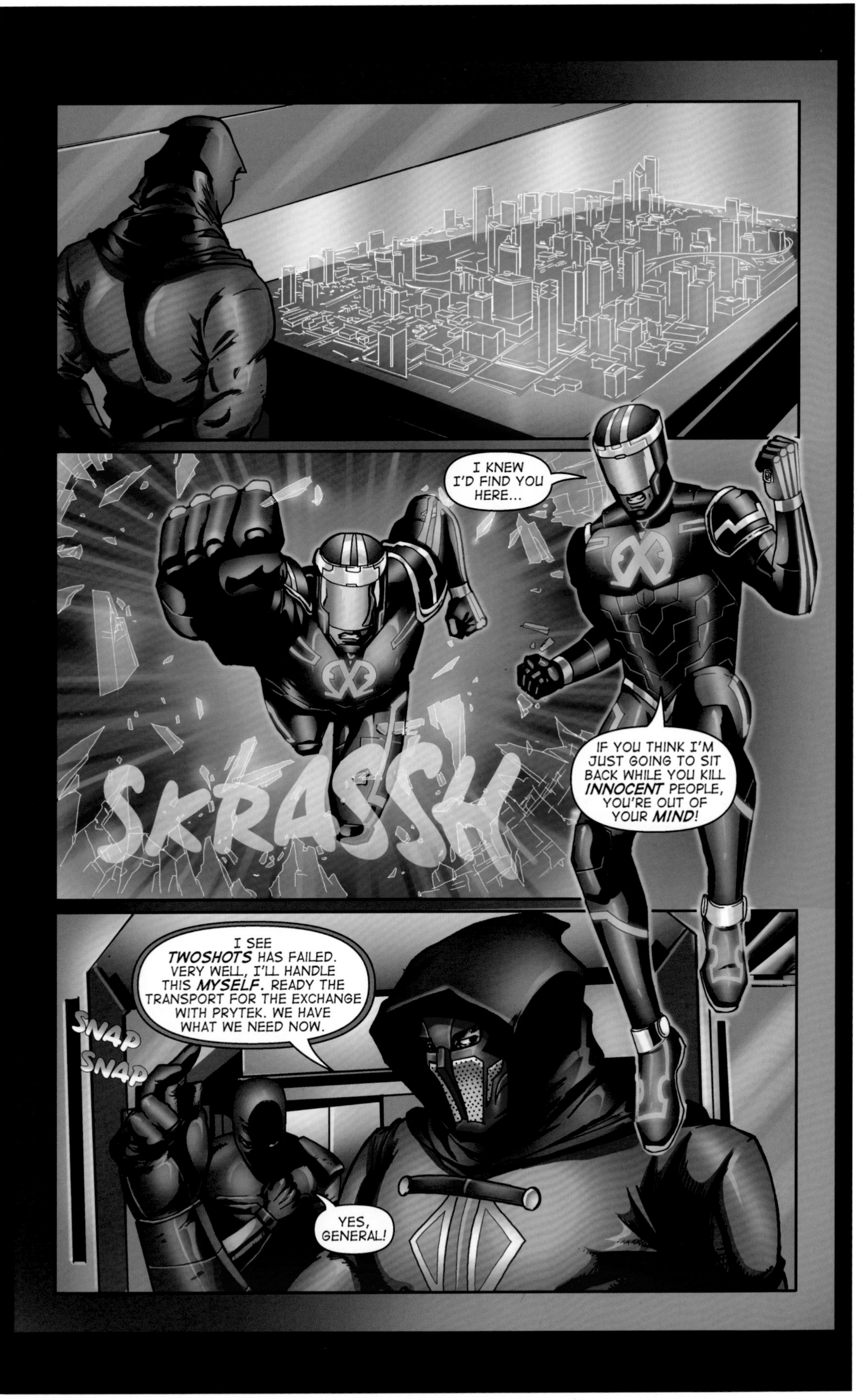

I KNEW I'D FIND YOU HERE...
SKRASSH
IF YOU THINK I'M JUST GOING TO SIT BACK WHILE YOU KILL *INNOCENT* PEOPLE, YOU'RE OUT OF YOUR *MIND*!
I SEE *TWOSHOTS* HAS FAILED. VERY WELL, I'LL HANDLE THIS *MYSELF*. READY THE TRANSPORT FOR THE EXCHANGE WITH PRYTEK. WE HAVE WHAT WE NEED NOW.
SNAP SNAP
YES, GENERAL!

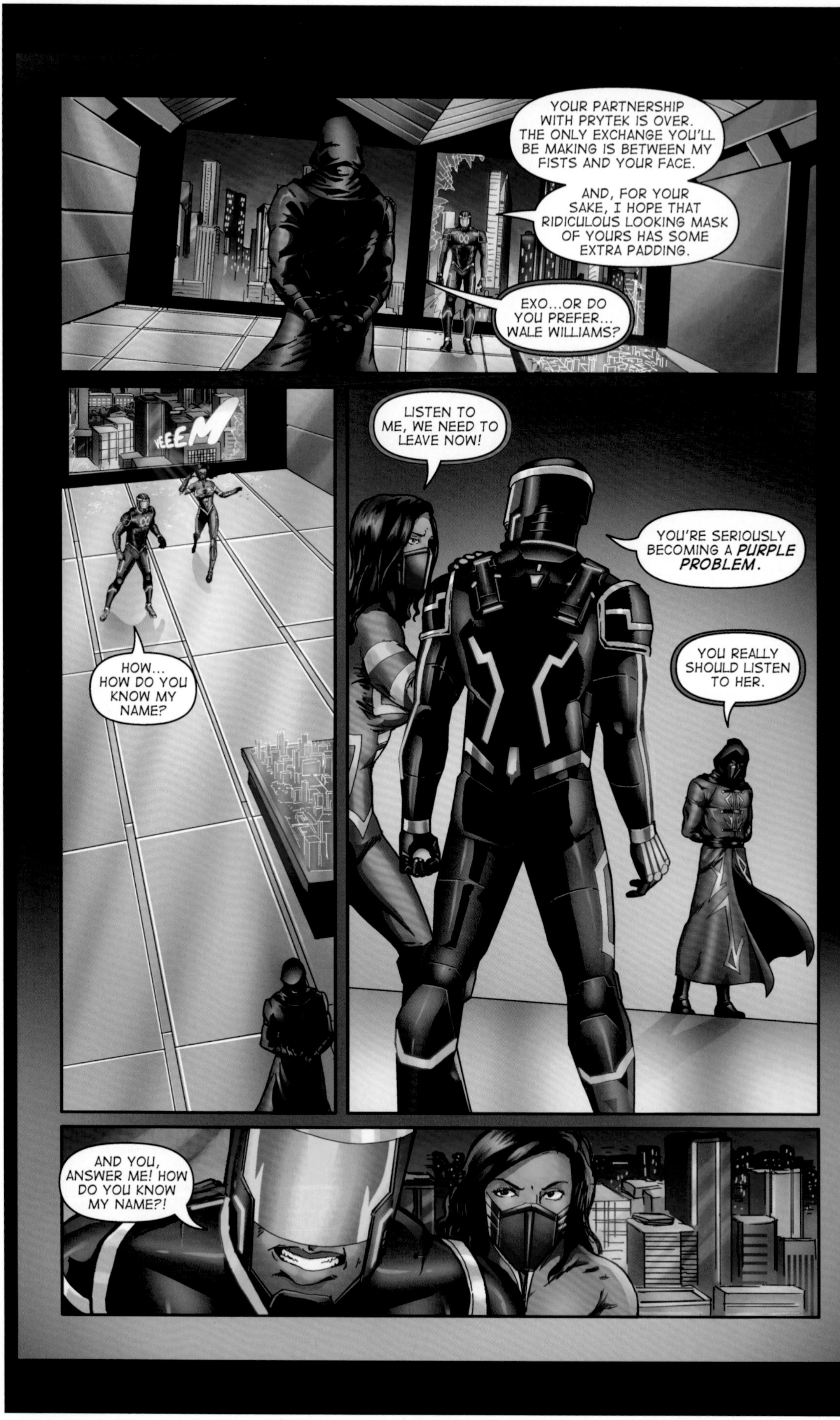
YOUR PARTNERSHIP WITH PRYTEK IS OVER. THE ONLY EXCHANGE YOU'LL BE MAKING IS BETWEEN MY FISTS AND YOUR FACE.
AND, FOR YOUR SAKE, I HOPE THAT RIDICULOUS LOOKING MASK OF YOURS HAS SOME EXTRA PADDING.
EXO...OR DO YOU PREFER... WALE WILLIAMS?
VEEEM
HOW... HOW DO YOU KNOW MY NAME?
LISTEN TO ME, WE NEED TO LEAVE NOW!
YOU'RE SERIOUSLY BECOMING A *PURPLE PROBLEM*.
YOU REALLY SHOULD LISTEN TO HER.
AND YOU, ANSWER ME! HOW DO YOU KNOW MY NAME?!

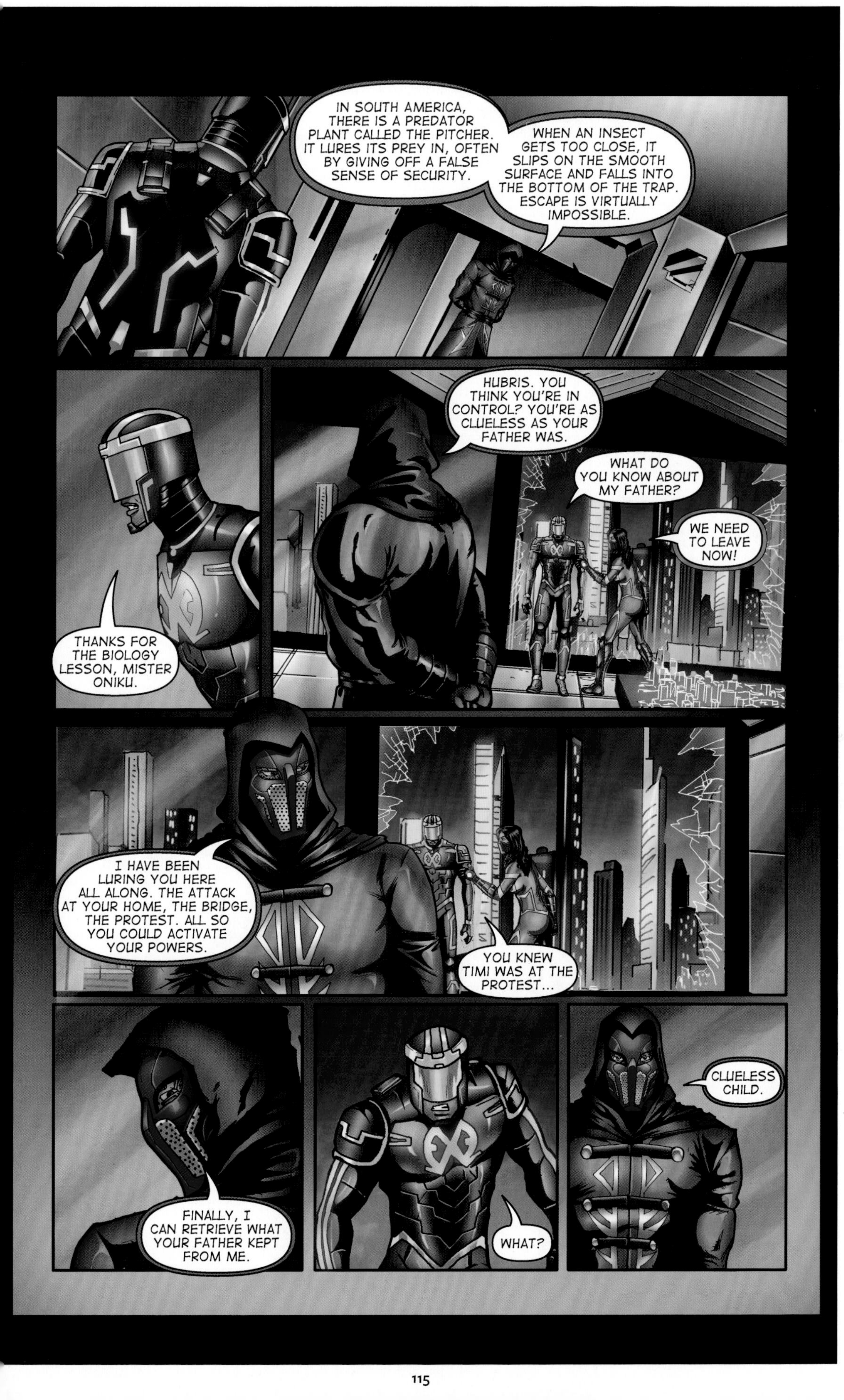
IN SOUTH AMERICA, THERE IS A PREDATOR PLANT CALLED THE PITCHER. IT LURES ITS PREY IN, OFTEN BY GIVING OFF A FALSE SENSE OF SECURITY.
WHEN AN INSECT GETS TOO CLOSE, IT SLIPS ON THE SMOOTH SURFACE AND FALLS INTO THE BOTTOM OF THE TRAP. ESCAPE IS VIRTUALLY IMPOSSIBLE.
THANKS FOR THE BIOLOGY LESSON, MISTER ONIKU.
HUBRIS. YOU THINK YOU'RE IN CONTROL? YOU'RE AS CLUELESS AS YOUR FATHER WAS.
WHAT DO YOU KNOW ABOUT MY FATHER?
WE NEED TO LEAVE NOW!
I HAVE BEEN LURING YOU HERE ALL ALONG. THE ATTACK AT YOUR HOME, THE BRIDGE, THE PROTEST. ALL SO YOU COULD ACTIVATE YOUR POWERS.
YOU KNEW TIMI WAS AT THE PROTEST...
FINALLY, I CAN RETRIEVE WHAT YOUR FATHER KEPT FROM ME.
WHAT?
CLUELESS CHILD.

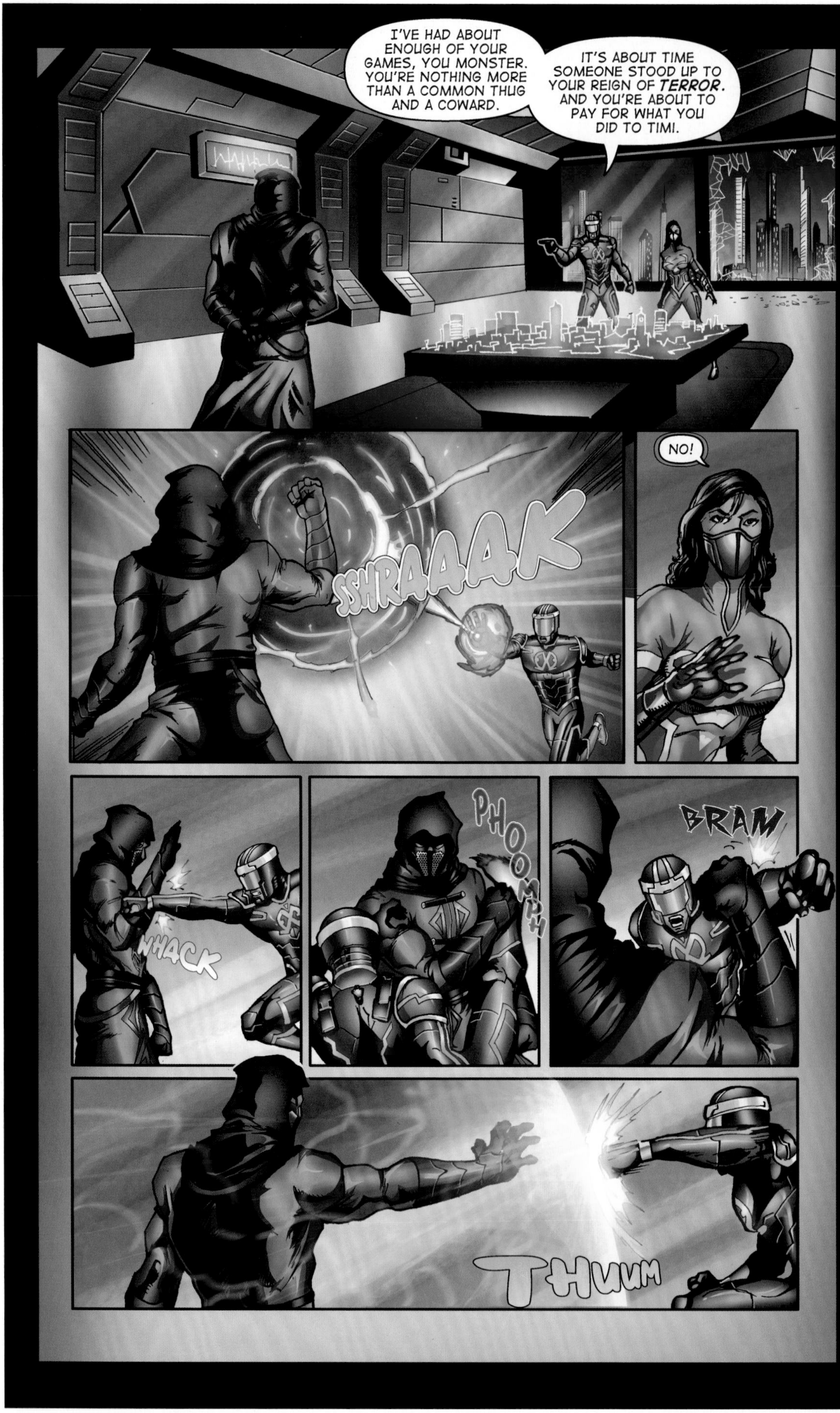
I'VE HAD ABOUT ENOUGH OF YOUR GAMES, YOU MONSTER. YOU'RE NOTHING MORE THAN A COMMON THUG AND A COWARD.
IT'S ABOUT TIME SOMEONE STOOD UP TO YOUR REIGN OF *TERROR*. AND YOU'RE ABOUT TO PAY FOR WHAT YOU DID TO TIMI.
SSHRAAAK
NO!
WHACK
PHOOOMPH
BRAM
THUUM

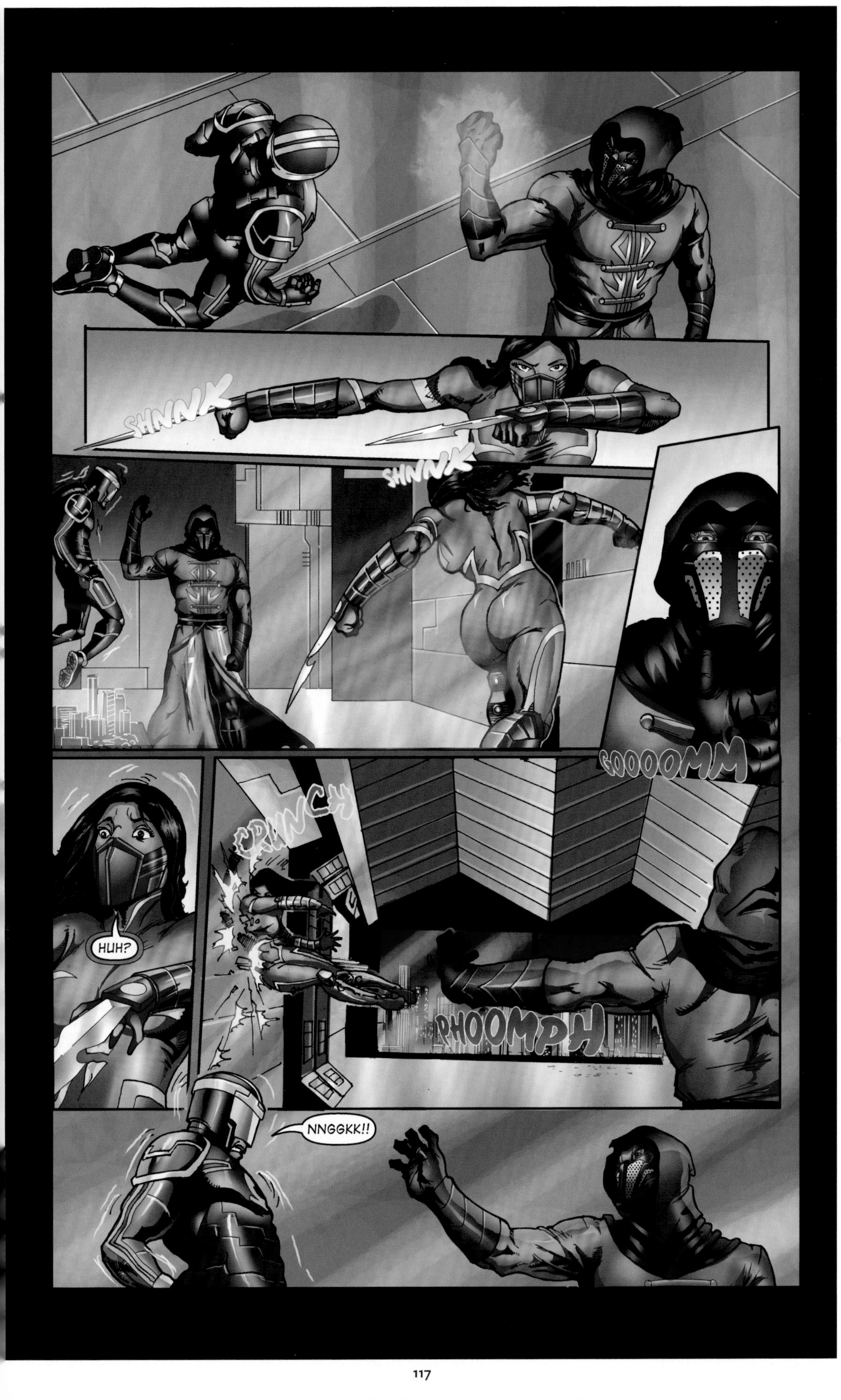
SHNNK
SHNNK
GOOOOMM
HUH?
CRUNCH
PHOOMPH
NNGGKK!!

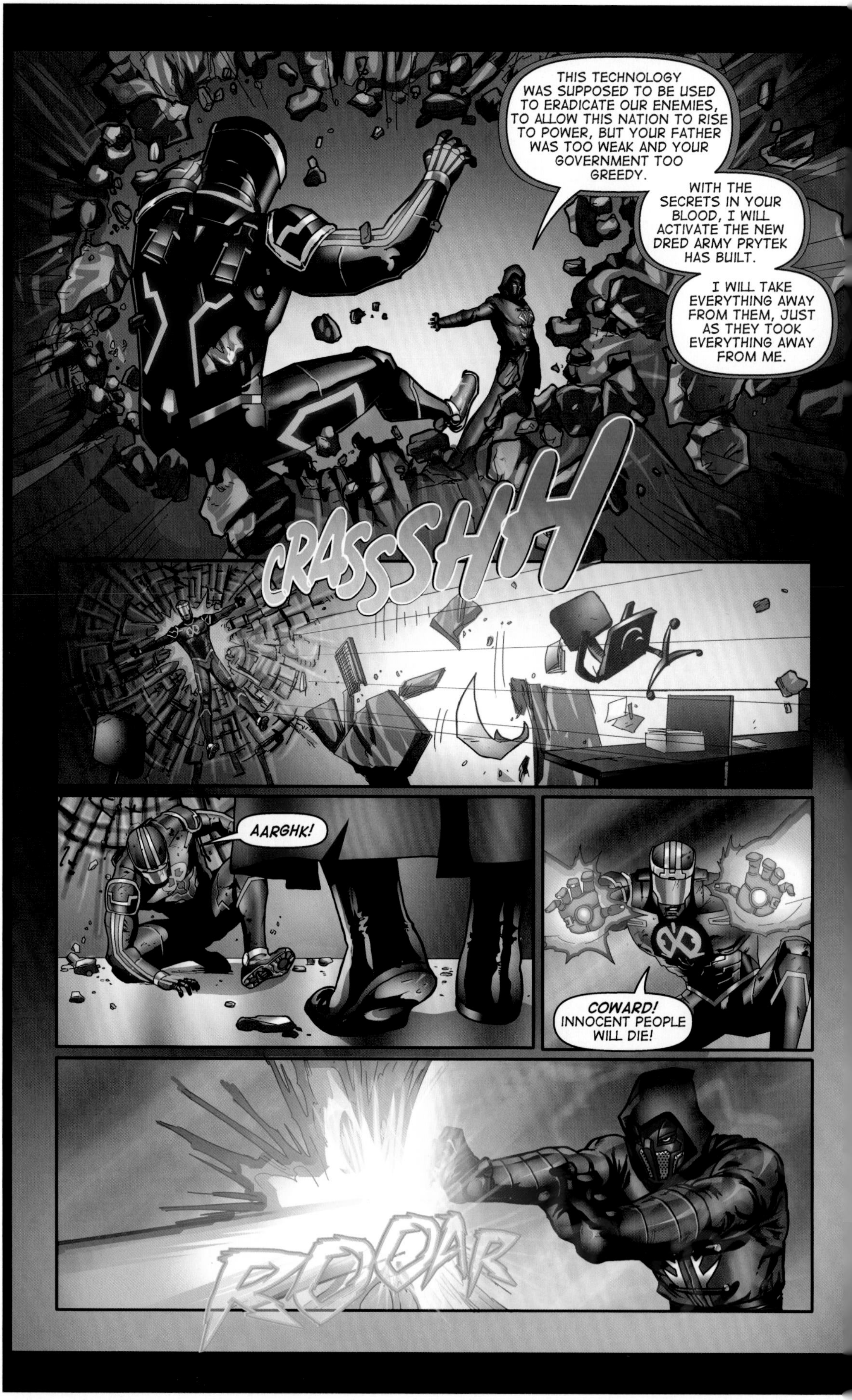
THIS TECHNOLOGY WAS SUPPOSED TO BE USED TO ERADICATE OUR ENEMIES, TO ALLOW THIS NATION TO RISE TO POWER, BUT YOUR FATHER WAS TOO WEAK AND YOUR GOVERNMENT TOO GREEDY.
WITH THE SECRETS IN YOUR BLOOD, I WILL ACTIVATE THE NEW DRED ARMY PRYTEK HAS BUILT.
I WILL TAKE EVERYTHING AWAY FROM THEM, JUST AS THEY TOOK EVERYTHING AWAY FROM ME.
CRASSSHH
AARGHK!
COWARD! INNOCENT PEOPLE WILL DIE!
ROOAR

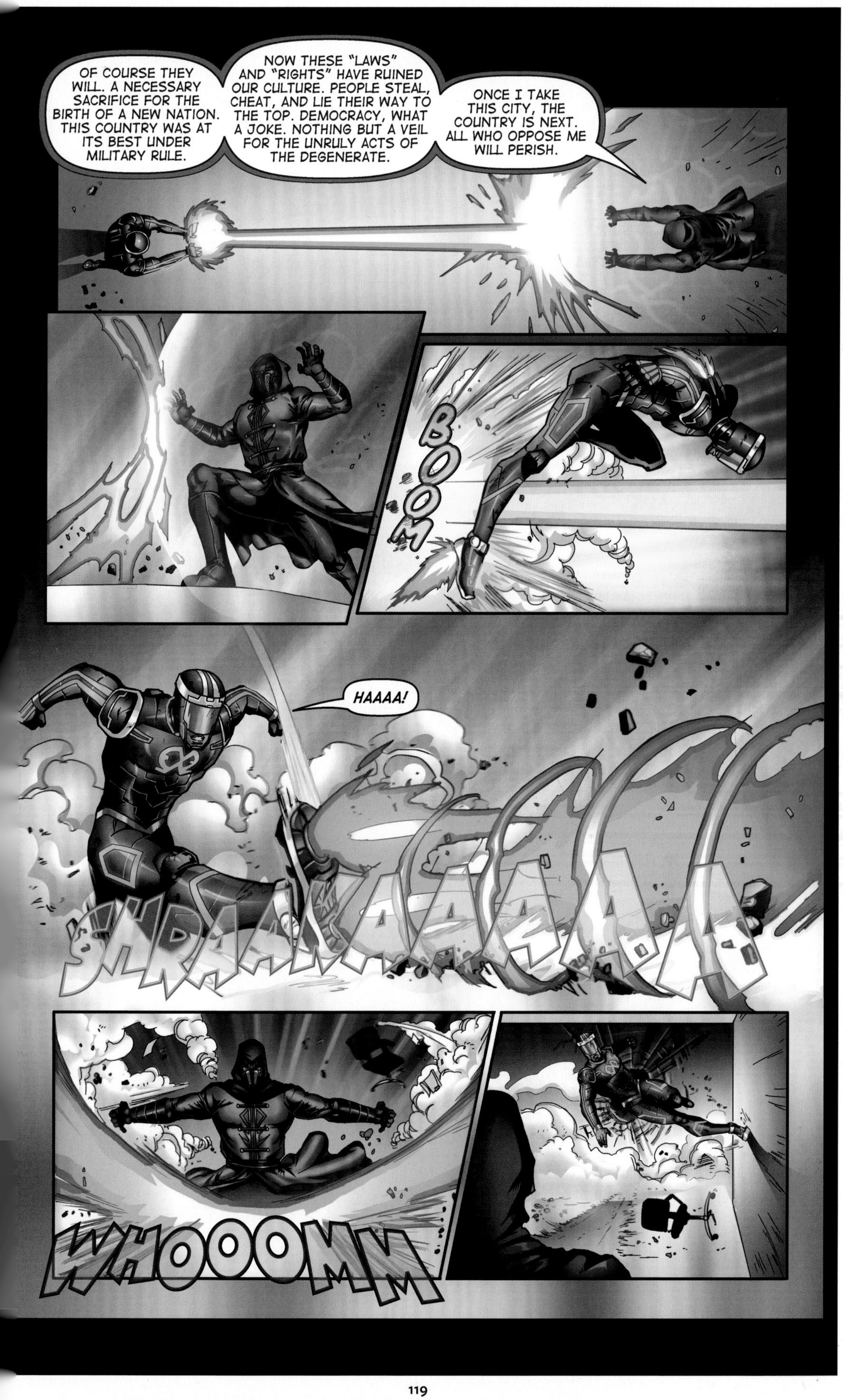
OF COURSE THEY WILL. A NECESSARY SACRIFICE FOR THE BIRTH OF A NEW NATION. THIS COUNTRY WAS AT ITS BEST UNDER MILITARY RULE.
NOW THESE "LAWS" AND "RIGHTS" HAVE RUINED OUR CULTURE. PEOPLE STEAL, CHEAT, AND LIE THEIR WAY TO THE TOP. DEMOCRACY, WHAT A JOKE. NOTHING BUT A VEIL FOR THE UNRULY ACTS OF THE DEGENERATE.
ONCE I TAKE THIS CITY, THE COUNTRY IS NEXT. ALL WHO OPPOSE ME WILL PERISH.
BOOOM
HAAAA!
SHRAAKAAAAAA
WHOOOMM

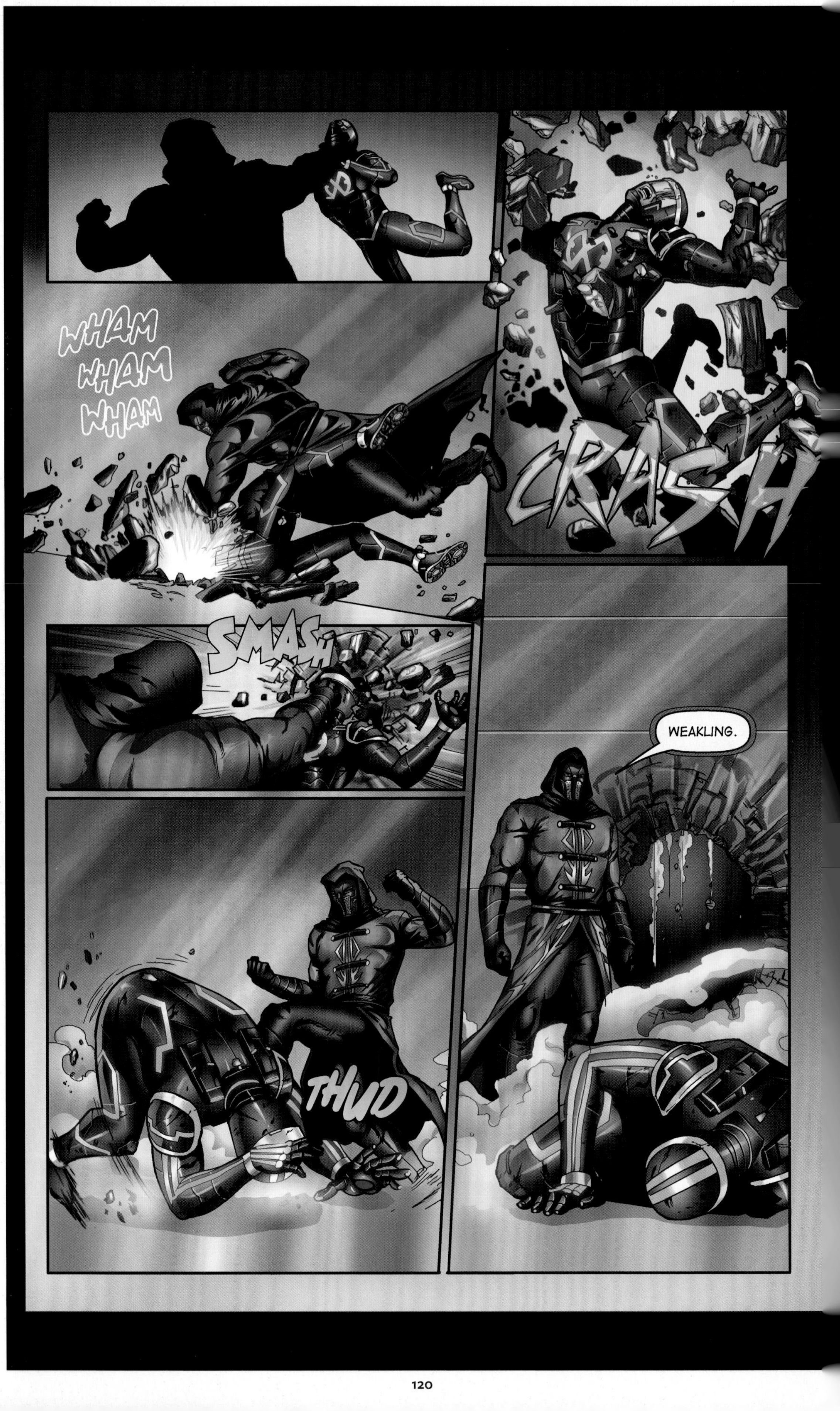
WHAM
WHAM
WHAM
CRASH
SMASH
WEAKLING.
THUD

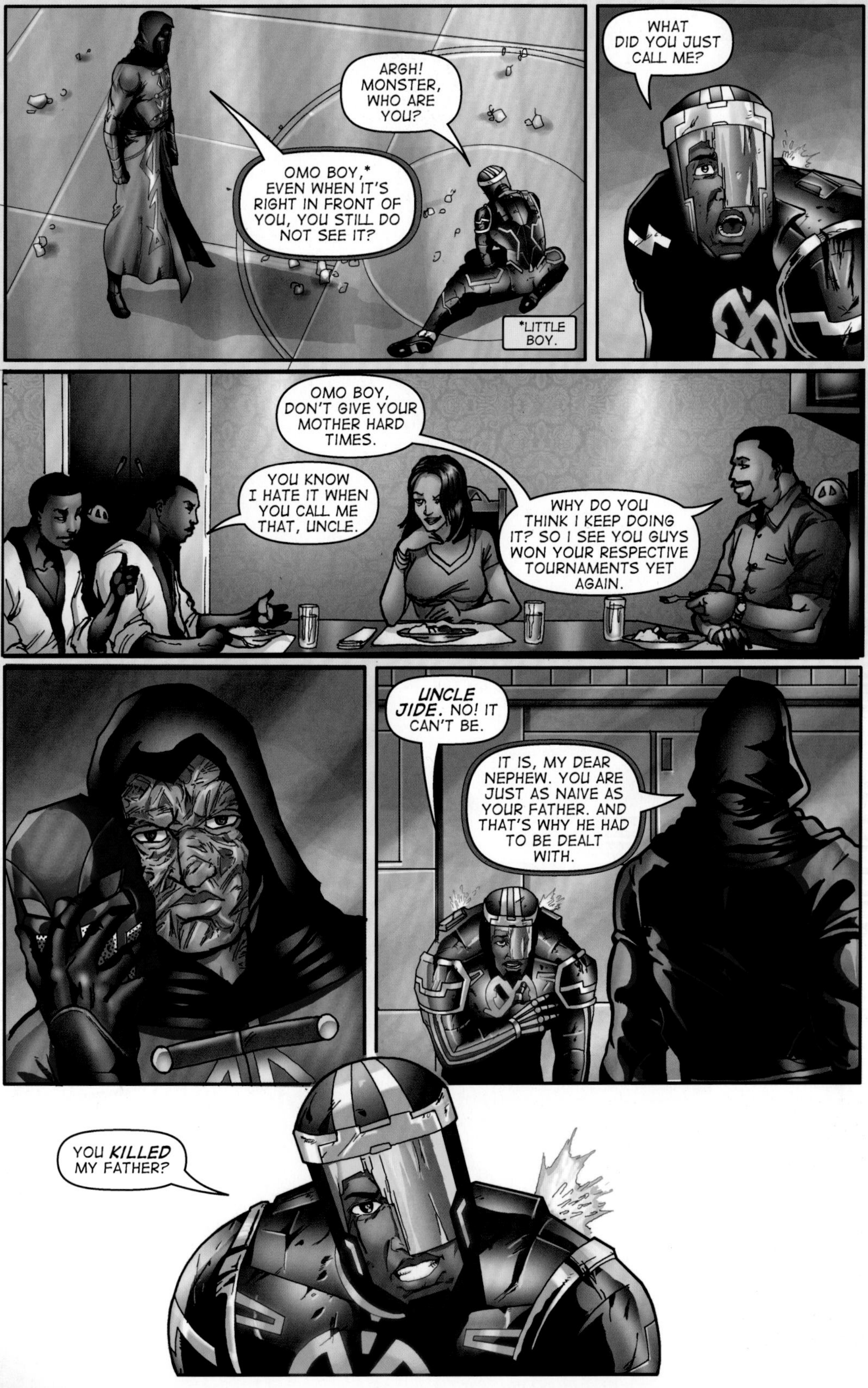
ARGH! MONSTER, WHO ARE YOU?
OMO BOY,* EVEN WHEN IT'S RIGHT IN FRONT OF YOU, YOU STILL DO NOT SEE IT?
*LITTLE BOY.
WHAT DID YOU JUST CALL ME?
OMO BOY, DON'T GIVE YOUR MOTHER HARD TIMES.
YOU KNOW I HATE IT WHEN YOU CALL ME THAT, UNCLE.
WHY DO YOU THINK I KEEP DOING IT? SO I SEE YOU GUYS WON YOUR RESPECTIVE TOURNAMENTS YET AGAIN.
UNCLE JIDE. NO! IT CAN'T BE.
IT IS, MY DEAR NEPHEW. YOU ARE JUST AS NAIVE AS YOUR FATHER. AND THAT'S WHY HE HAD TO BE DEALT WITH.
YOU KILLED MY FATHER?

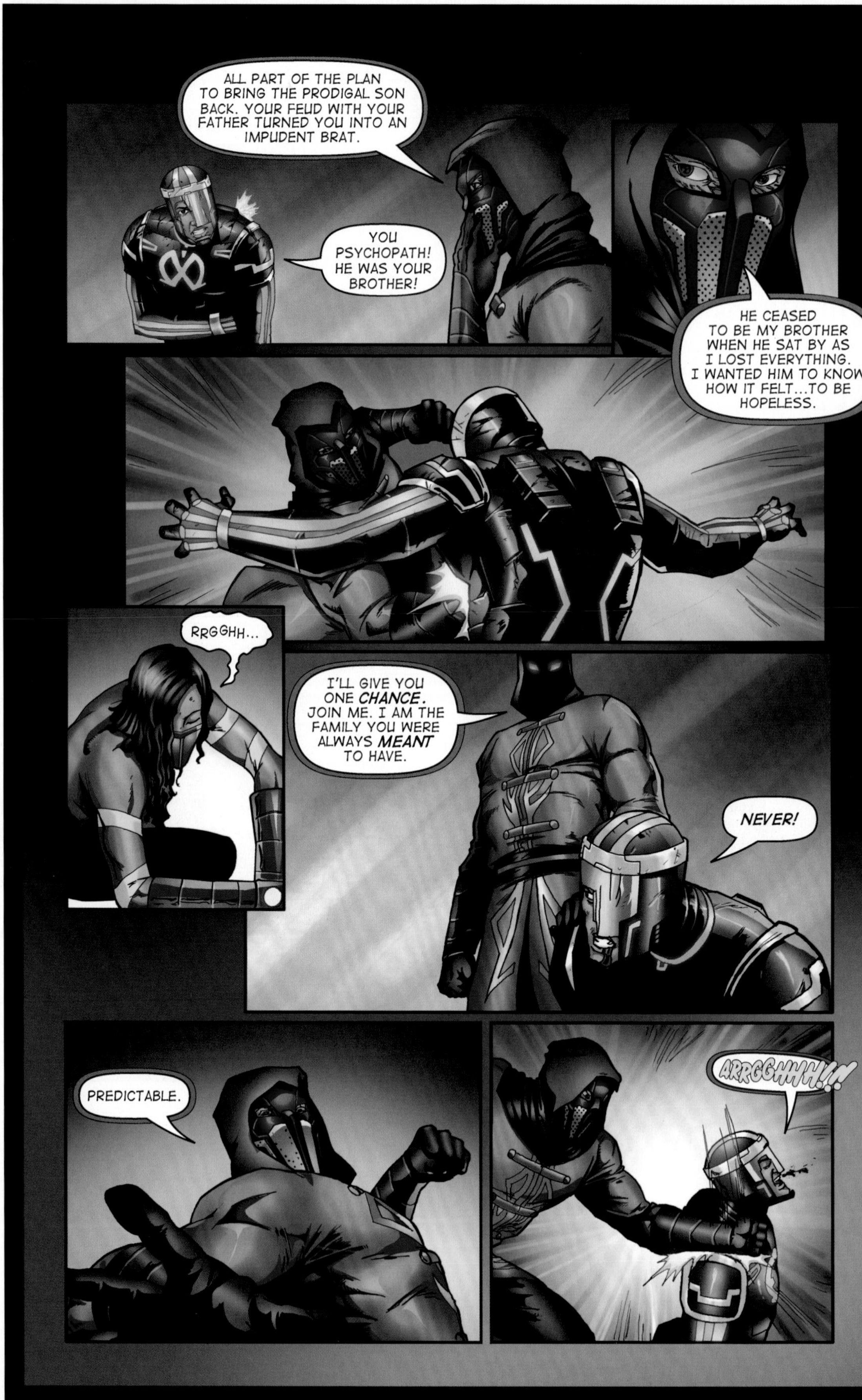
ALL PART OF THE PLAN TO BRING THE PRODIGAL SON BACK. YOUR FEUD WITH YOUR FATHER TURNED YOU INTO AN IMPUDENT BRAT.
YOU PSYCHOPATH! HE WAS YOUR BROTHER!
HE CEASED TO BE MY BROTHER WHEN HE SAT BY AS I LOST EVERYTHING. I WANTED HIM TO KNOW HOW IT FELT...TO BE HOPELESS.
RRGGHH...
I'LL GIVE YOU ONE CHANCE. JOIN ME. I AM THE FAMILY YOU WERE ALWAYS MEANT TO HAVE.
NEVER!
PREDICTABLE.
ARRGGHHH!!!

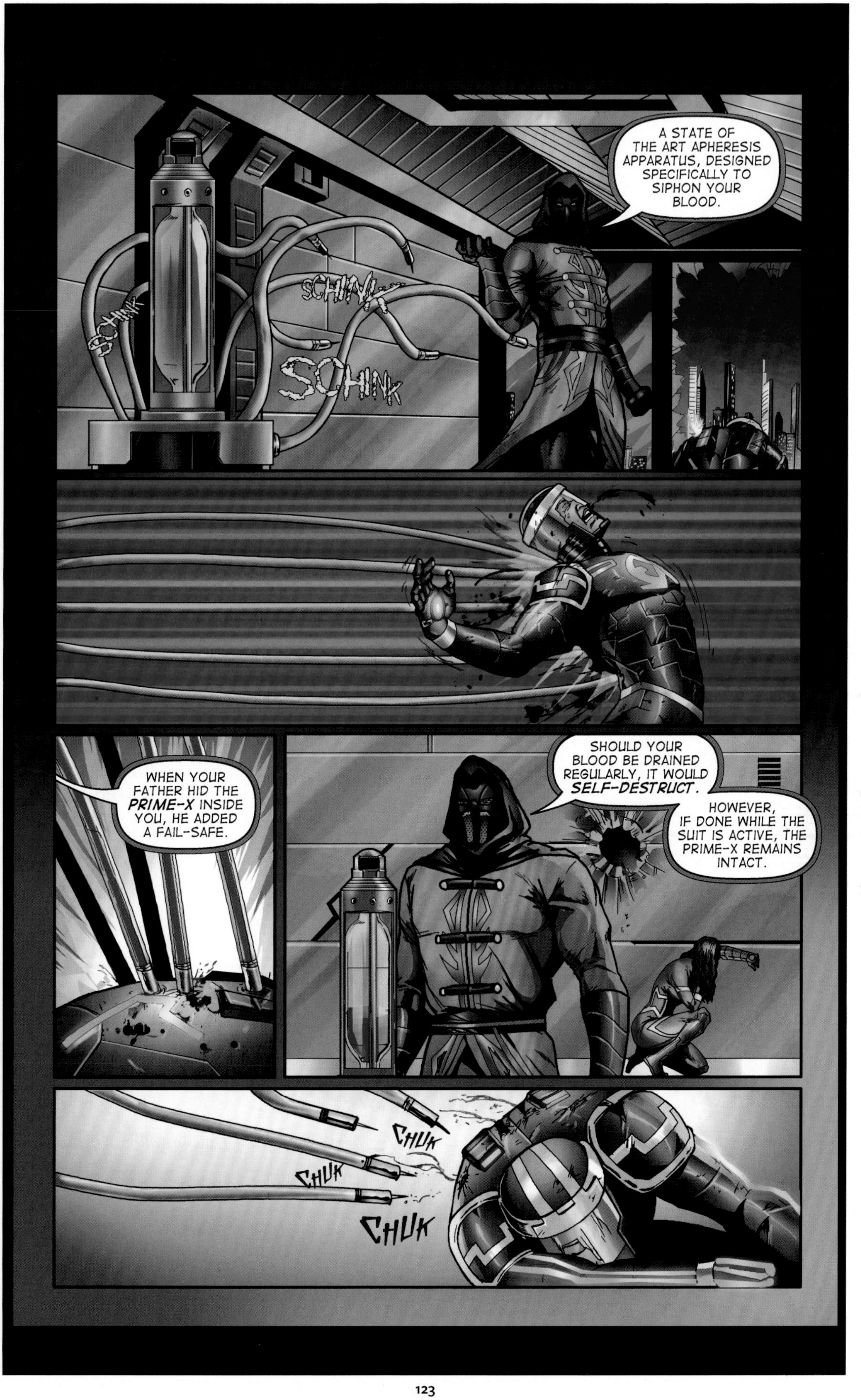
A STATE OF THE ART APHERESIS APPARATUS, DESIGNED SPECIFICALLY TO SIPHON YOUR BLOOD.
SCHINK
SCHINK
SCHINK
WHEN YOUR FATHER HID THE *PRIME-X* INSIDE YOU, HE ADDED A FAIL-SAFE.
SHOULD YOUR BLOOD BE DRAINED REGULARLY, IT WOULD *SELF-DESTRUCT*.
HOWEVER, IF DONE WHILE THE SUIT IS ACTIVE, THE PRIME-X REMAINS INTACT.
CHUK
CHUK
CHUK

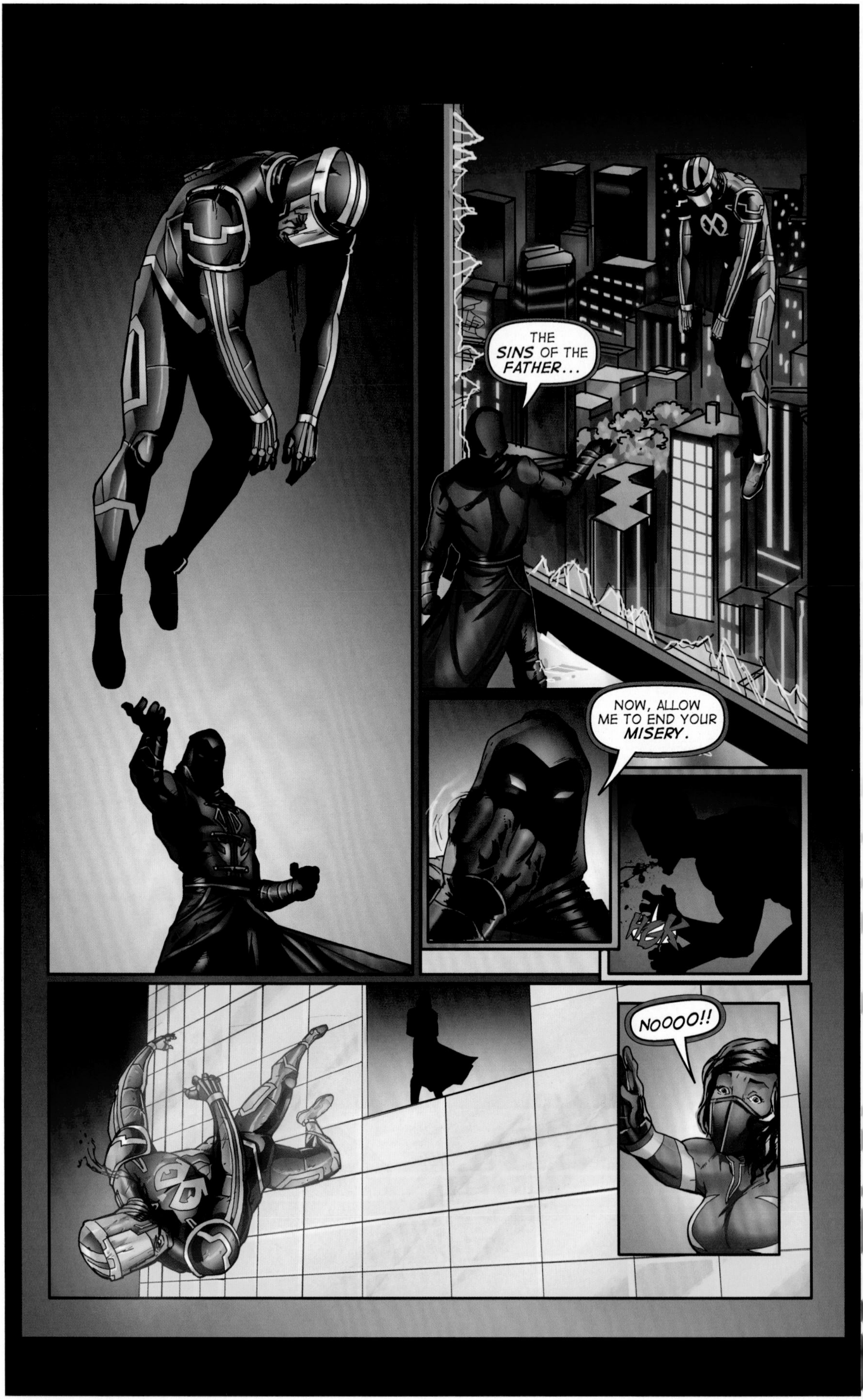
THE SINS OF THE FATHER...
NOW, ALLOW ME TO END YOUR MISERY.
HGK
NOOOO!!

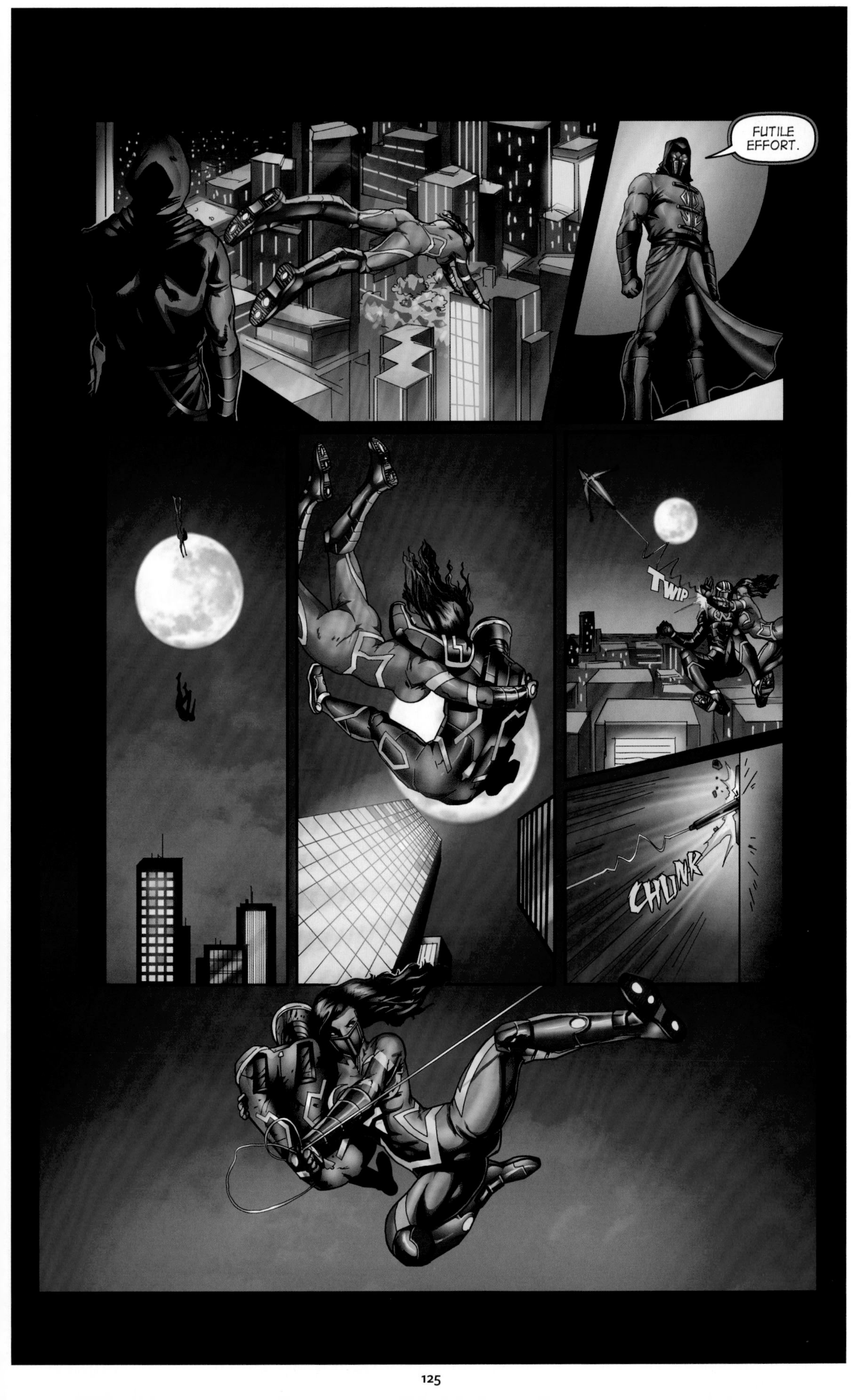
FUTILE EFFORT.
TWIP
CHUNK

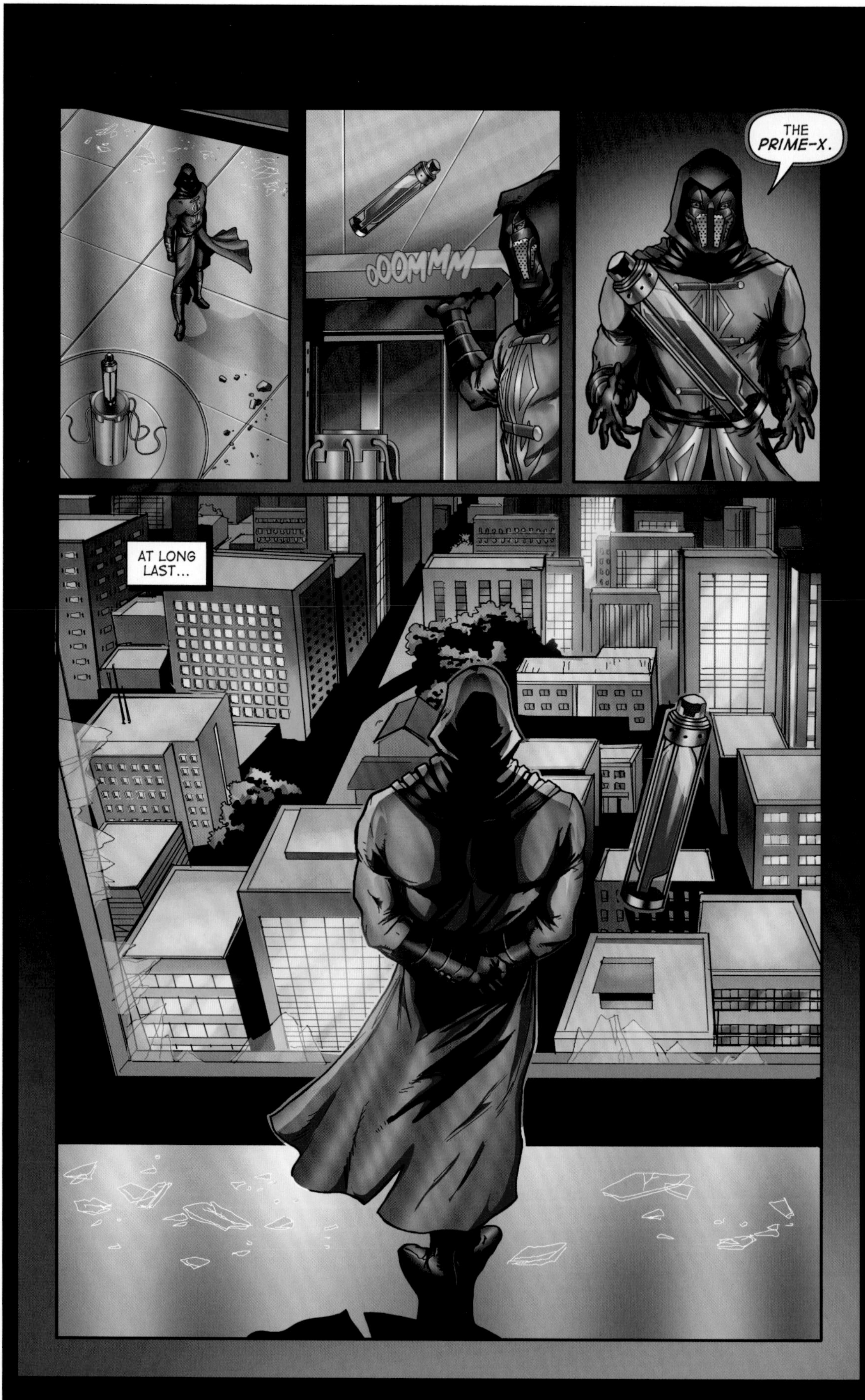
OOOMMM
THE PRIME-X.
AT LONG LAST...

PRYTEK R&D LAB.

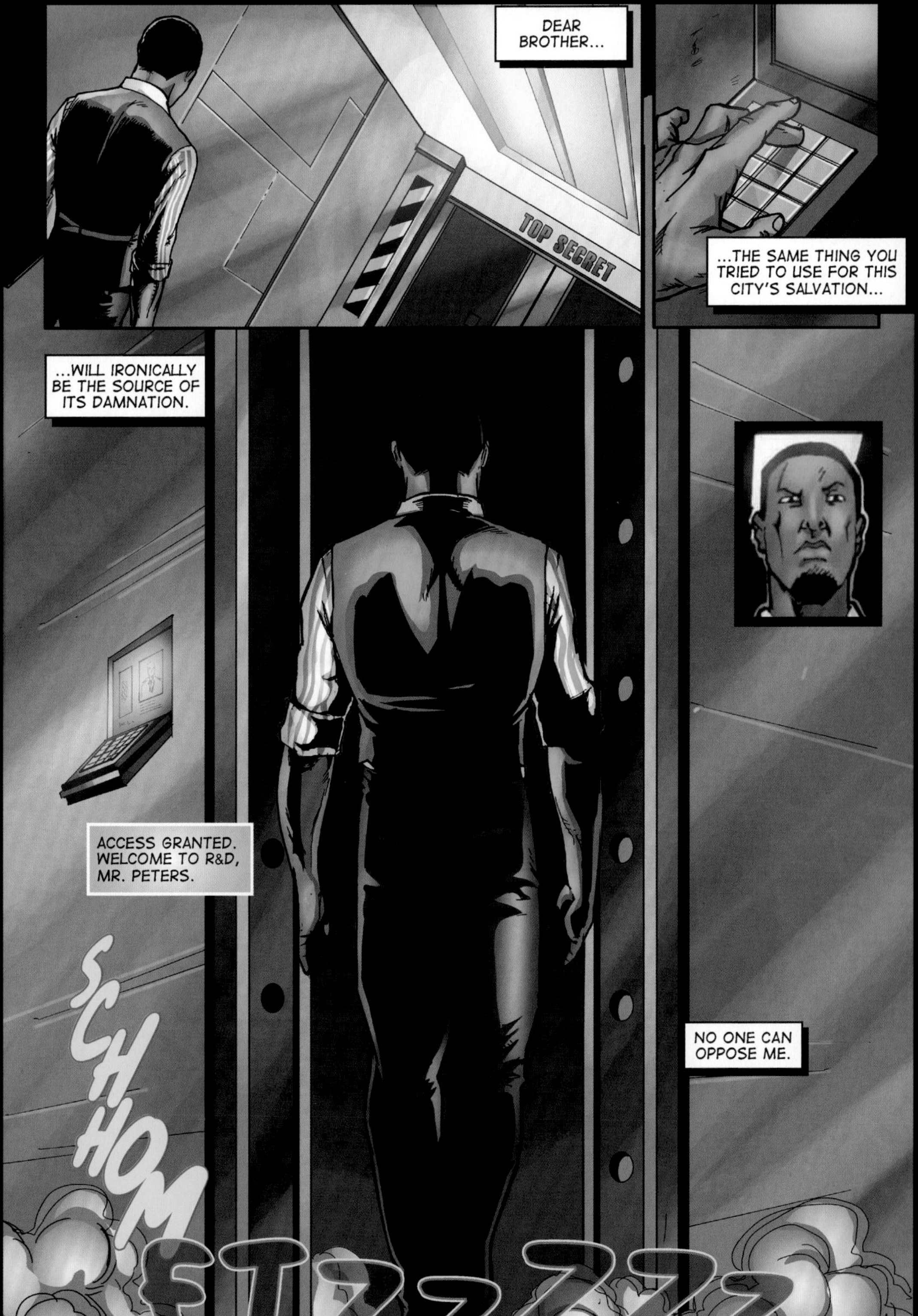
DEAR BROTHER...
TOP SECRET
...THE SAME THING YOU TRIED TO USE FOR THIS CITY'S SALVATION...
...WILL IRONICALLY BE THE SOURCE OF ITS DAMNATION.
ACCESS GRANTED. WELCOME TO R&D, MR. PETERS.
NO ONE CAN OPPOSE ME.
SCHHOM
FTZZZZZ

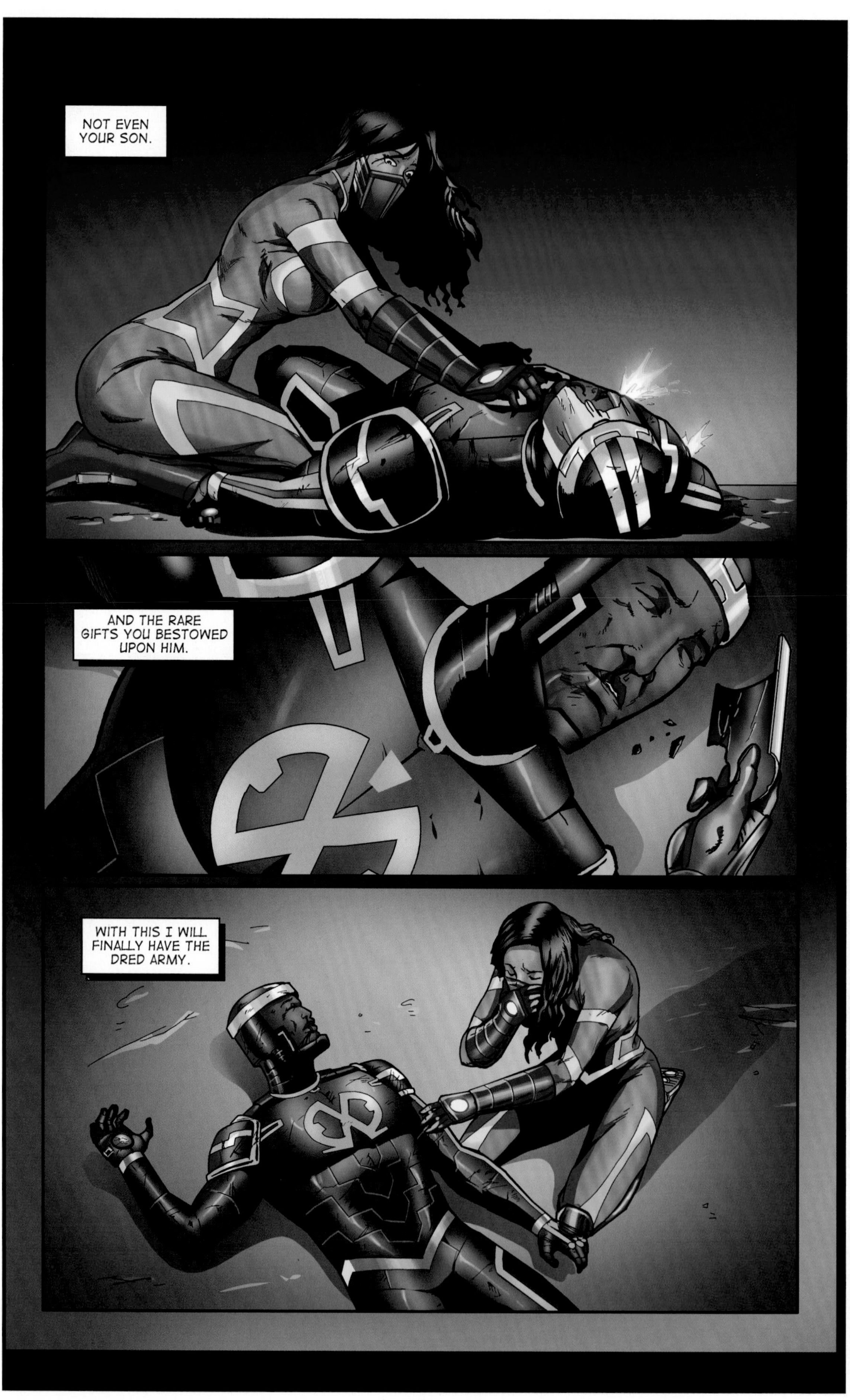
NOT EVEN YOUR SON.
AND THE RARE GIFTS YOU BESTOWED UPON HIM.
WITH THIS I WILL FINALLY HAVE THE DRED ARMY.

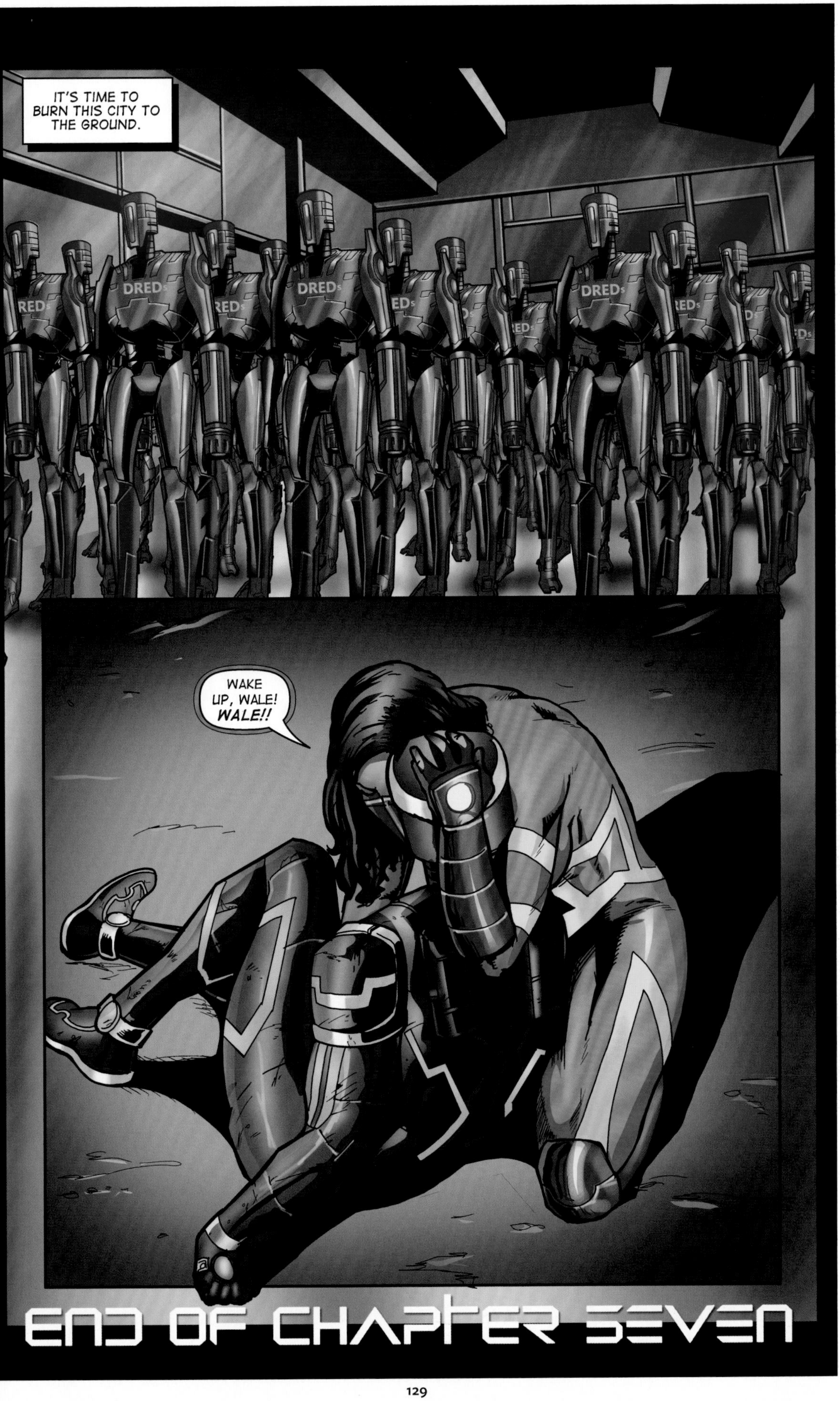
IT'S TIME TO BURN THIS CITY TO THE GROUND.
DREDs
WAKE UP, WALE! WALE!!
END OF CHAPTER SEVEN

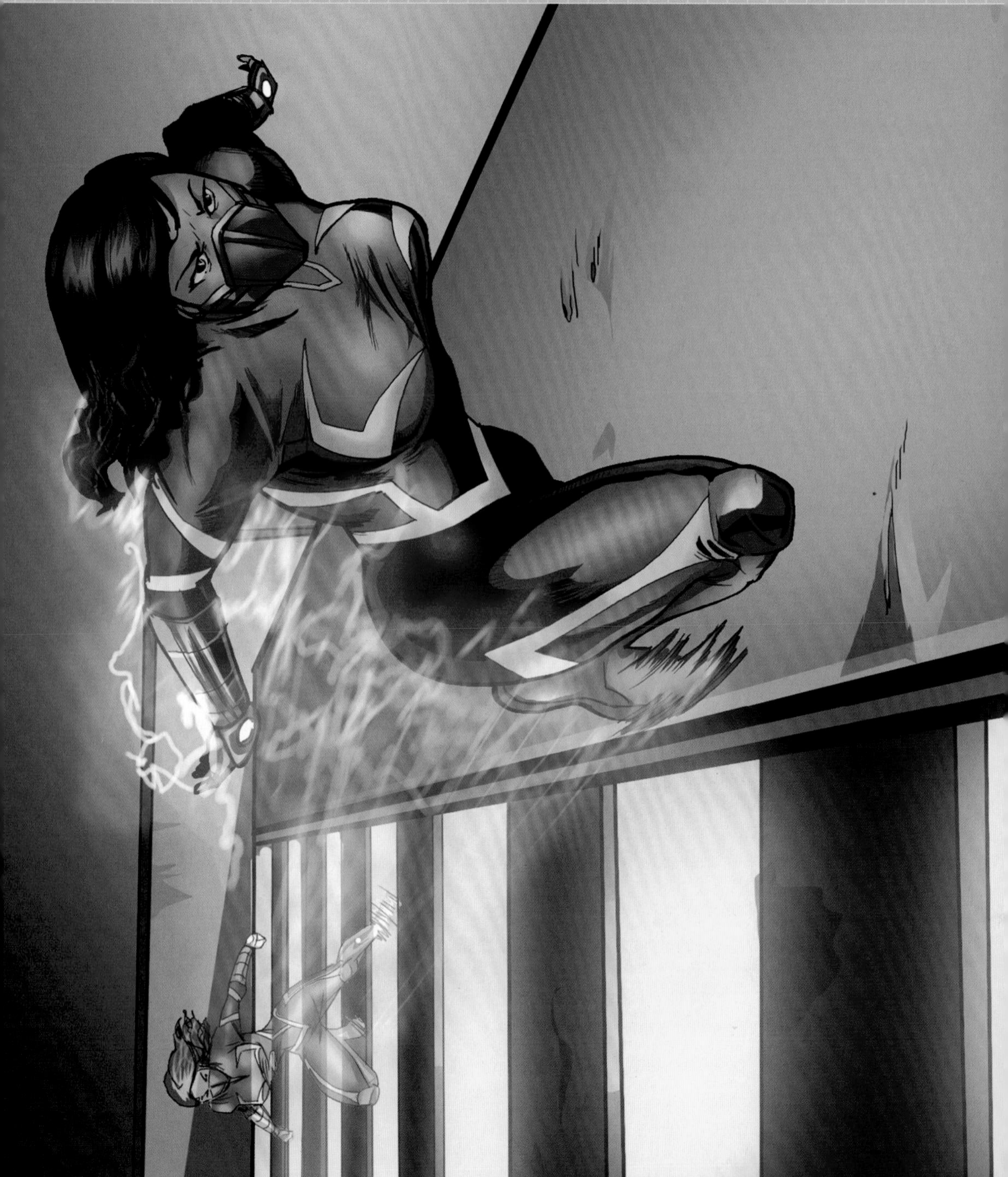

"This is the only way, and you know it."
—FURY

CHAPTER EIGHT

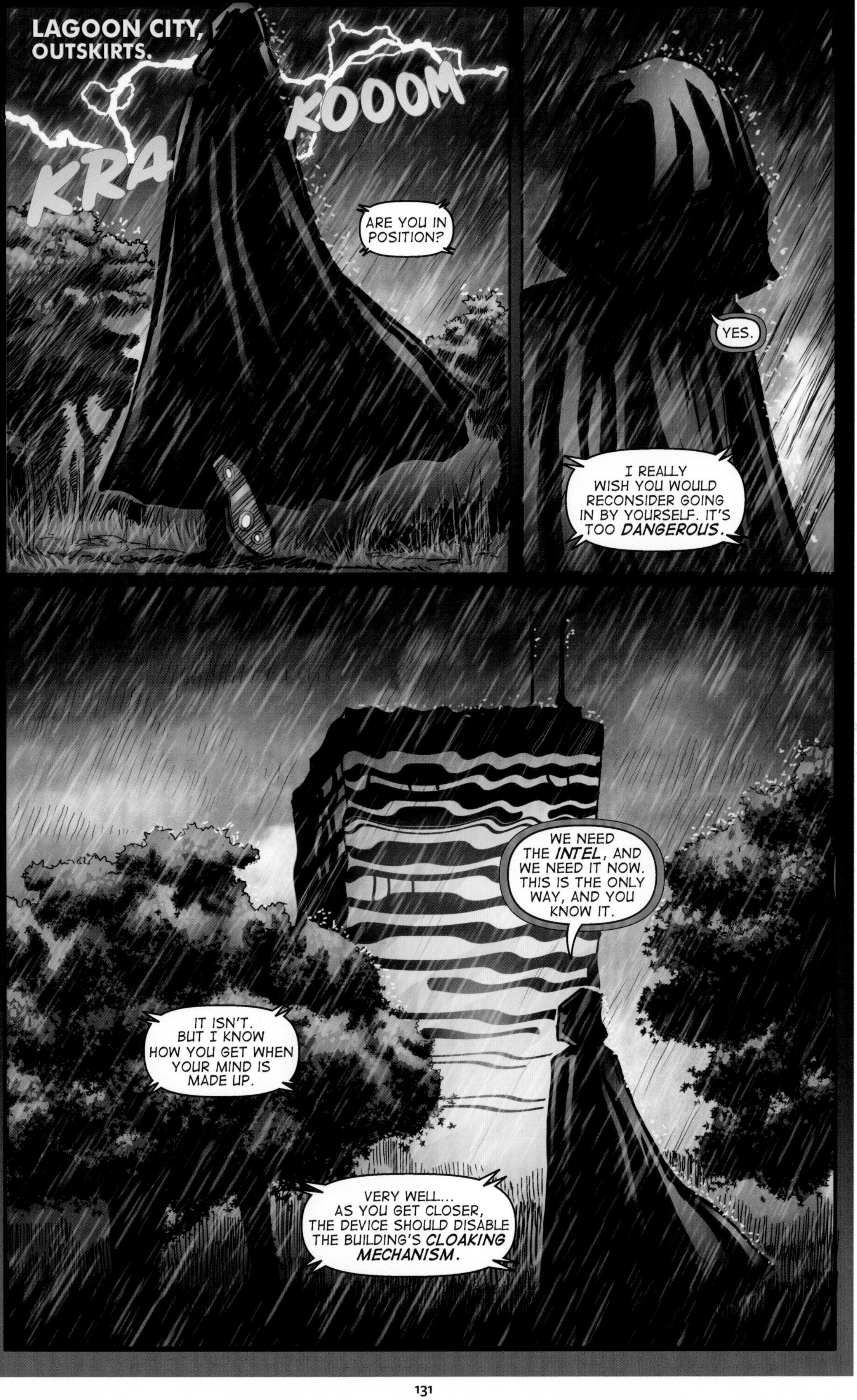
LAGOON CITY, OUTSKIRTS.
KRA KOOOM
ARE YOU IN POSITION?
YES.
I REALLY WISH YOU WOULD RECONSIDER GOING IN BY YOURSELF. IT'S TOO DANGEROUS.
WE NEED THE INTEL, AND WE NEED IT NOW. THIS IS THE ONLY WAY, AND YOU KNOW IT.
IT ISN'T. BUT I KNOW HOW YOU GET WHEN YOUR MIND IS MADE UP.
VERY WELL... AS YOU GET CLOSER, THE DEVICE SHOULD DISABLE THE BUILDING'S CLOAKING MECHANISM.

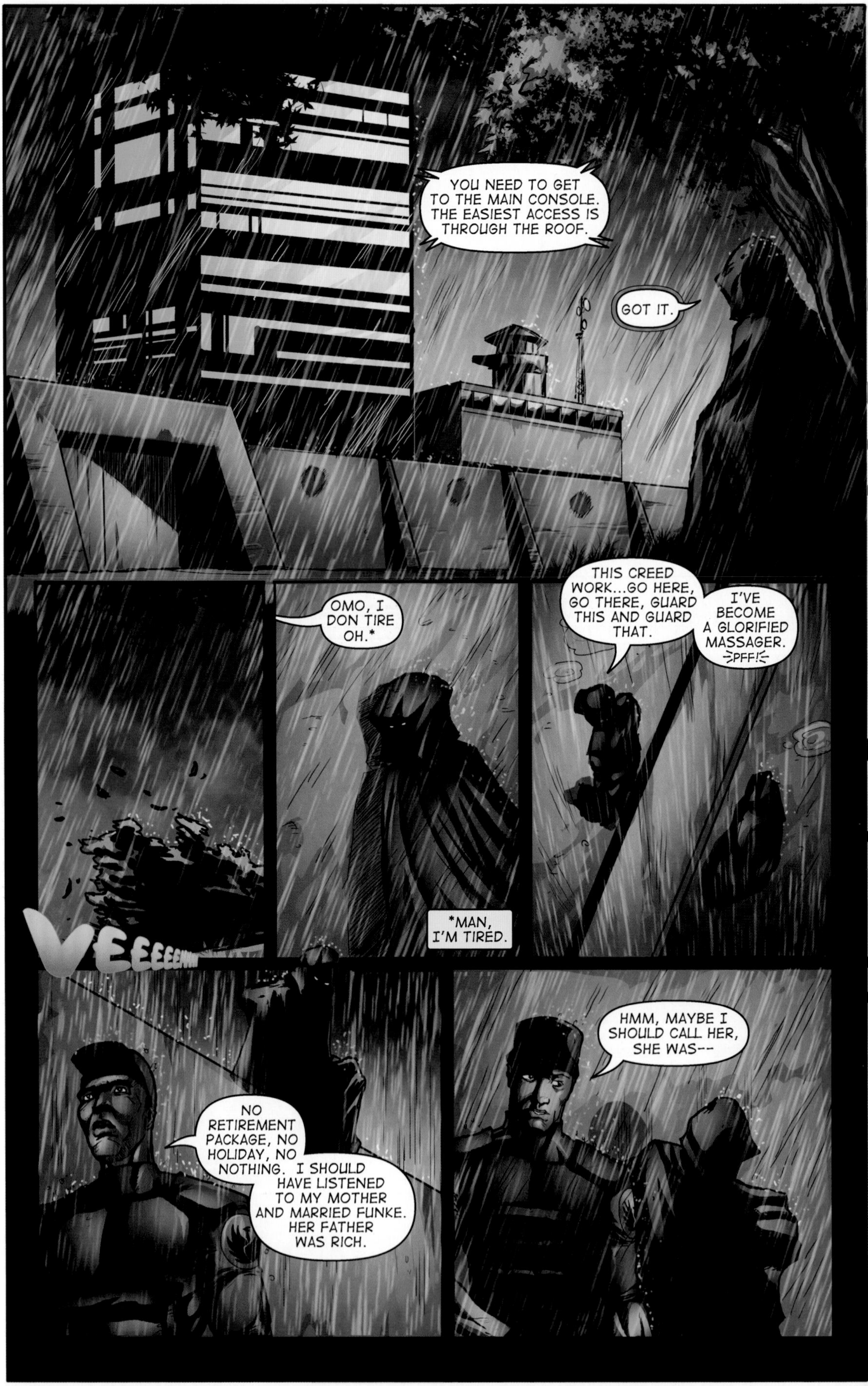
YOU NEED TO GET TO THE MAIN CONSOLE. THE EASIEST ACCESS IS THROUGH THE ROOF.
GOT IT.
OMO, I DON TIRE OH.*
*MAN, I'M TIRED.
THIS CREED WORK...GO HERE, GO THERE, GUARD THIS AND GUARD THAT.
I'VE BECOME A GLORIFIED MASSAGER.
PFF!
NO RETIREMENT PACKAGE, NO HOLIDAY, NO NOTHING. I SHOULD HAVE LISTENED TO MY MOTHER AND MARRIED FUNKE. HER FATHER WAS RICH.
HMM, MAYBE I SHOULD CALL HER, SHE WAS--

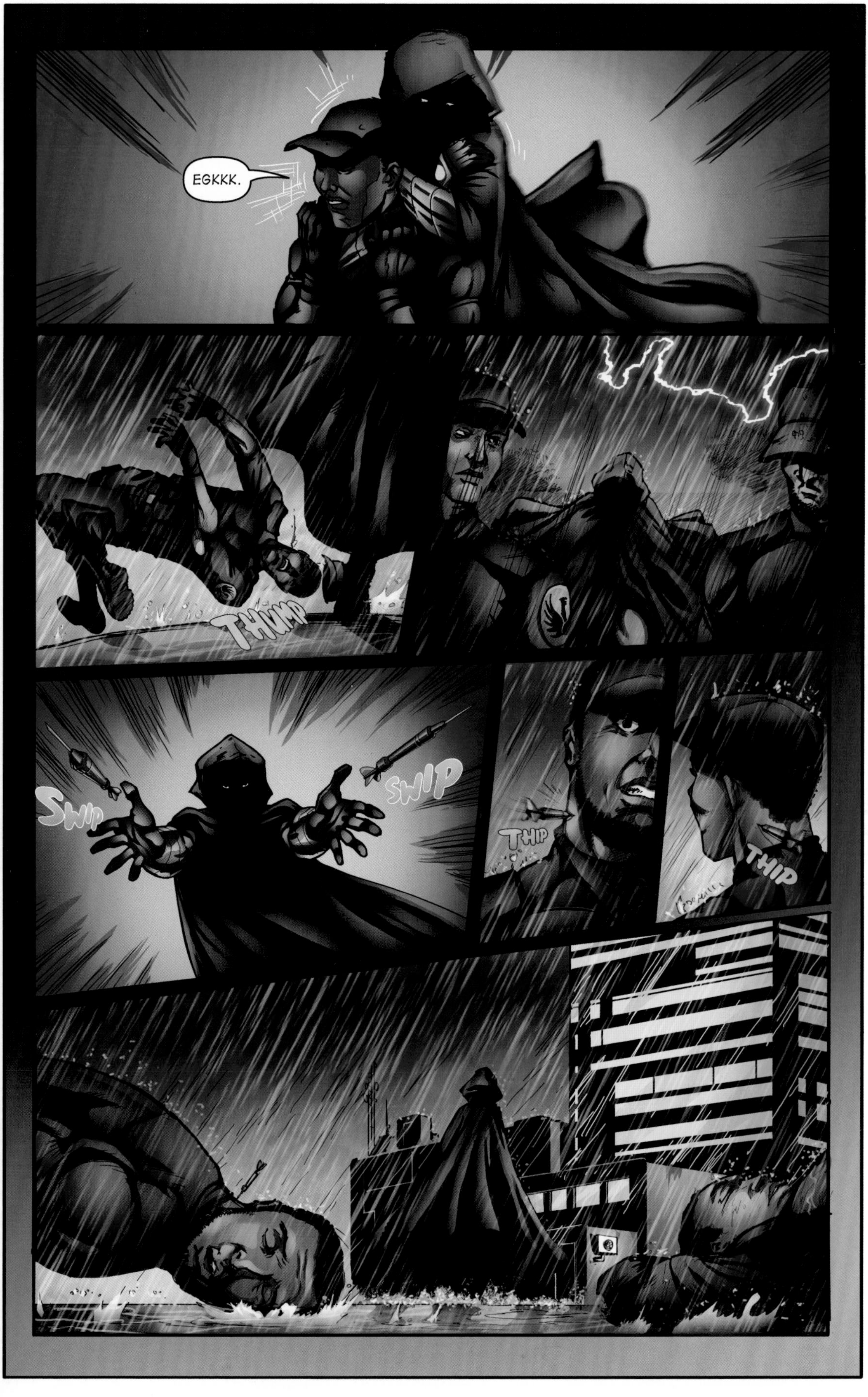

EGKKK.
THUMP
SWIP
SWIP
THIP
THIP

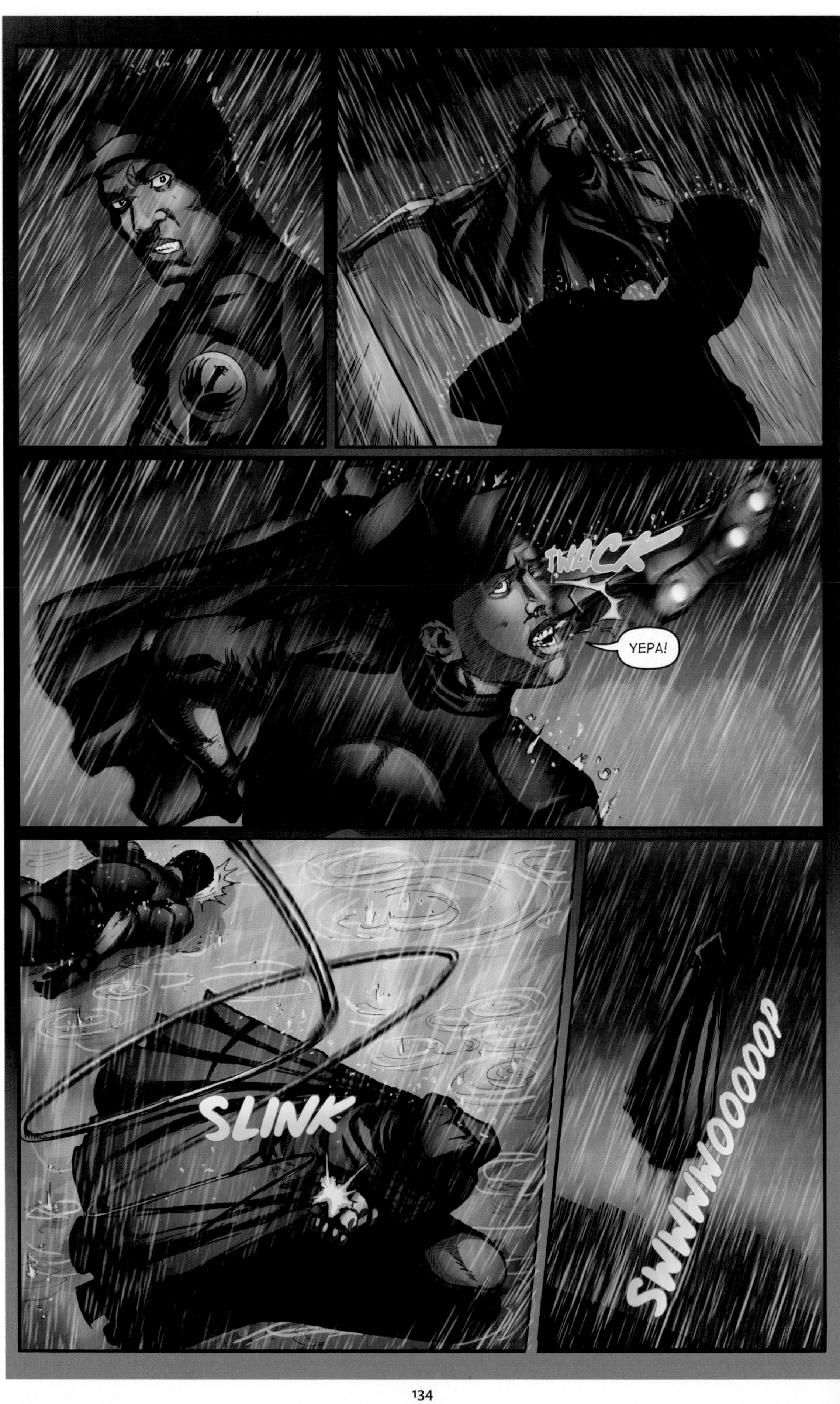
TWACK
YEPA!
SLINK
SWWWOOOOOP

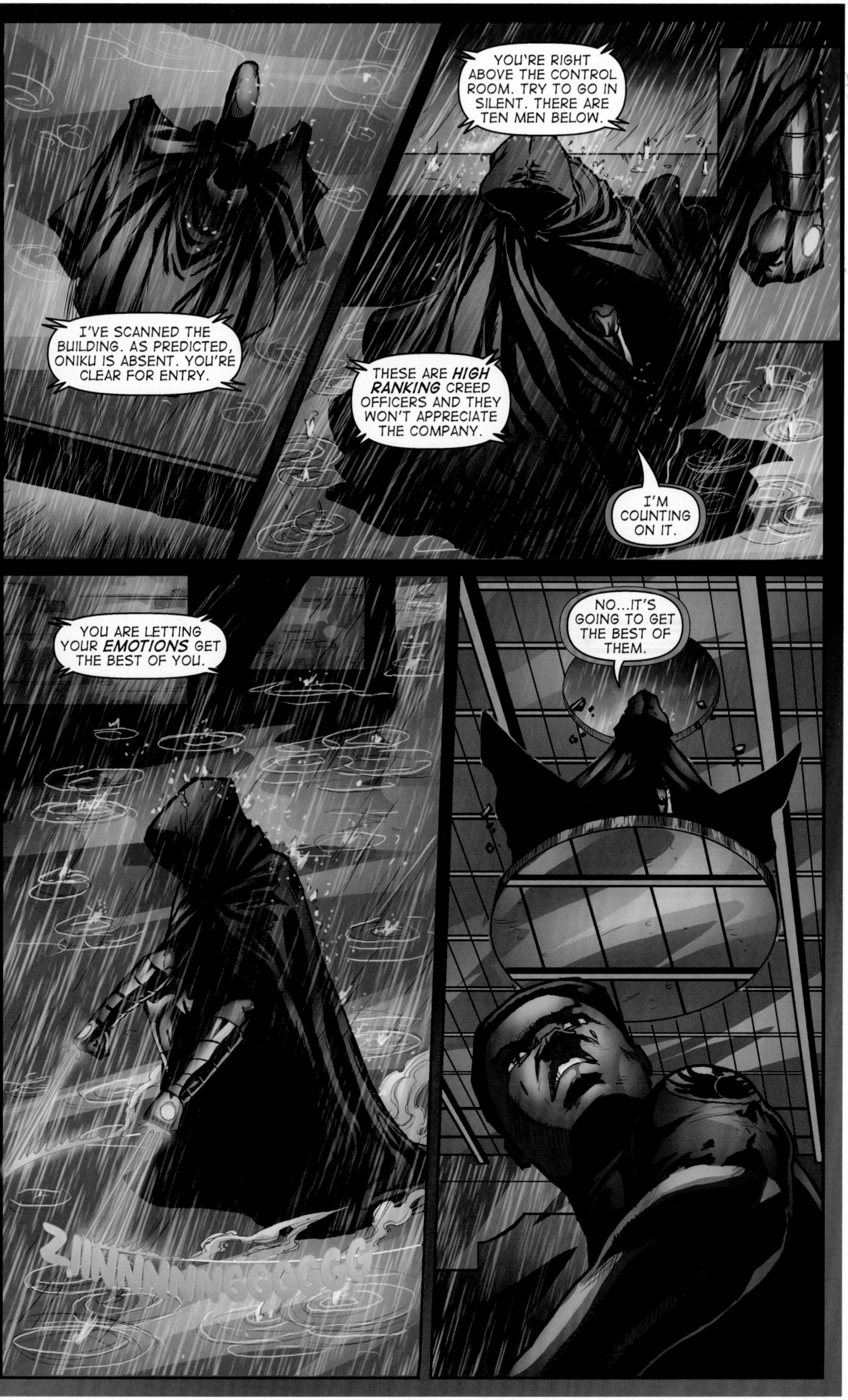
I'VE SCANNED THE BUILDING. AS PREDICTED, ONIKU IS ABSENT. YOU'RE CLEAR FOR ENTRY.
YOU'RE RIGHT ABOVE THE CONTROL ROOM. TRY TO GO IN SILENT. THERE ARE TEN MEN BELOW.
THESE ARE HIGH RANKING CREED OFFICERS AND THEY WON'T APPRECIATE THE COMPANY.
I'M COUNTING ON IT.
YOU ARE LETTING YOUR EMOTIONS GET THE BEST OF YOU.
ZIINNNNNNGGGGGG
NO...IT'S GOING TO GET THE BEST OF THEM.

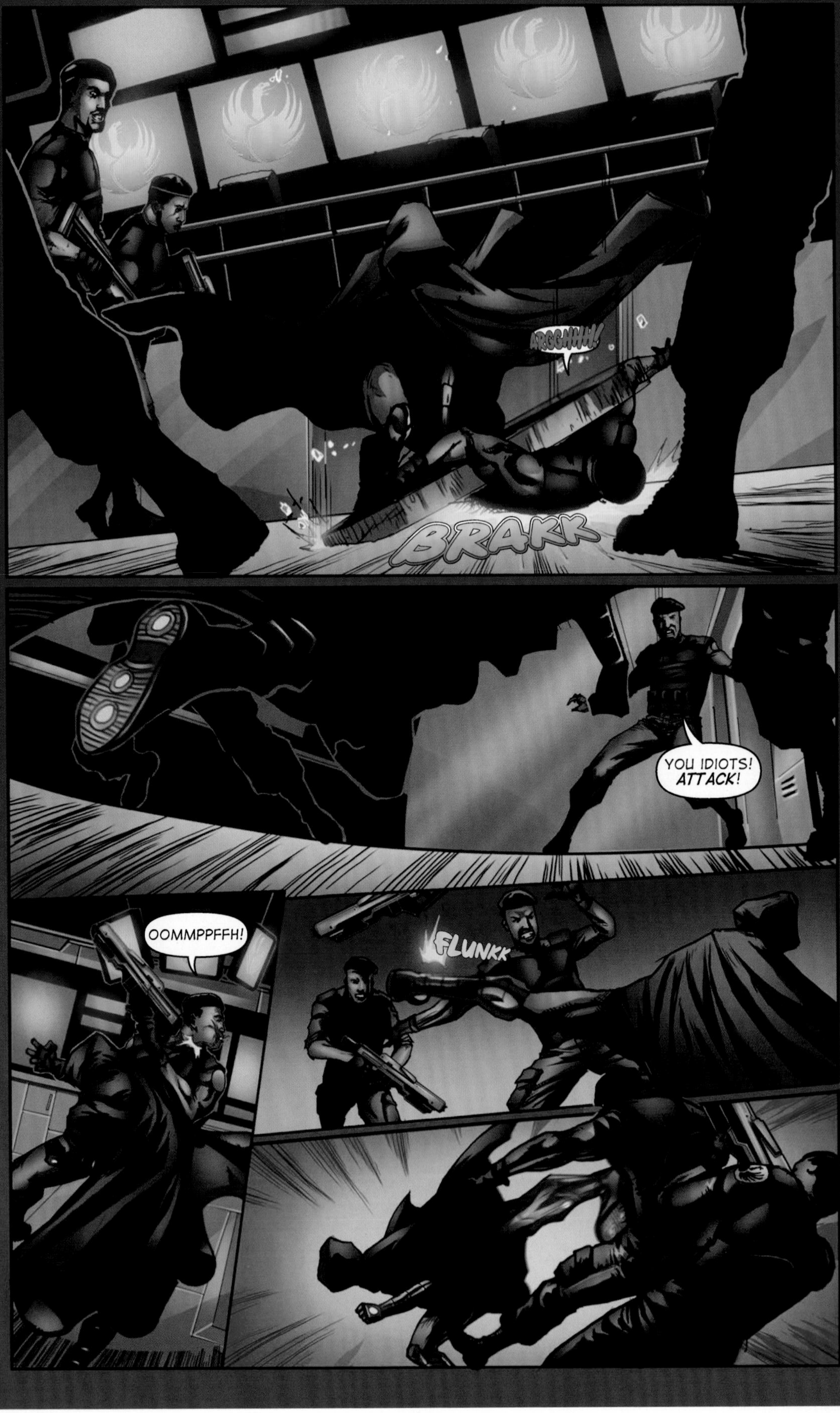
ARGGHHH!
BRAKK
YOU IDIOTS!
ATTACK!
OOMMPPFFH!
FLUNKK

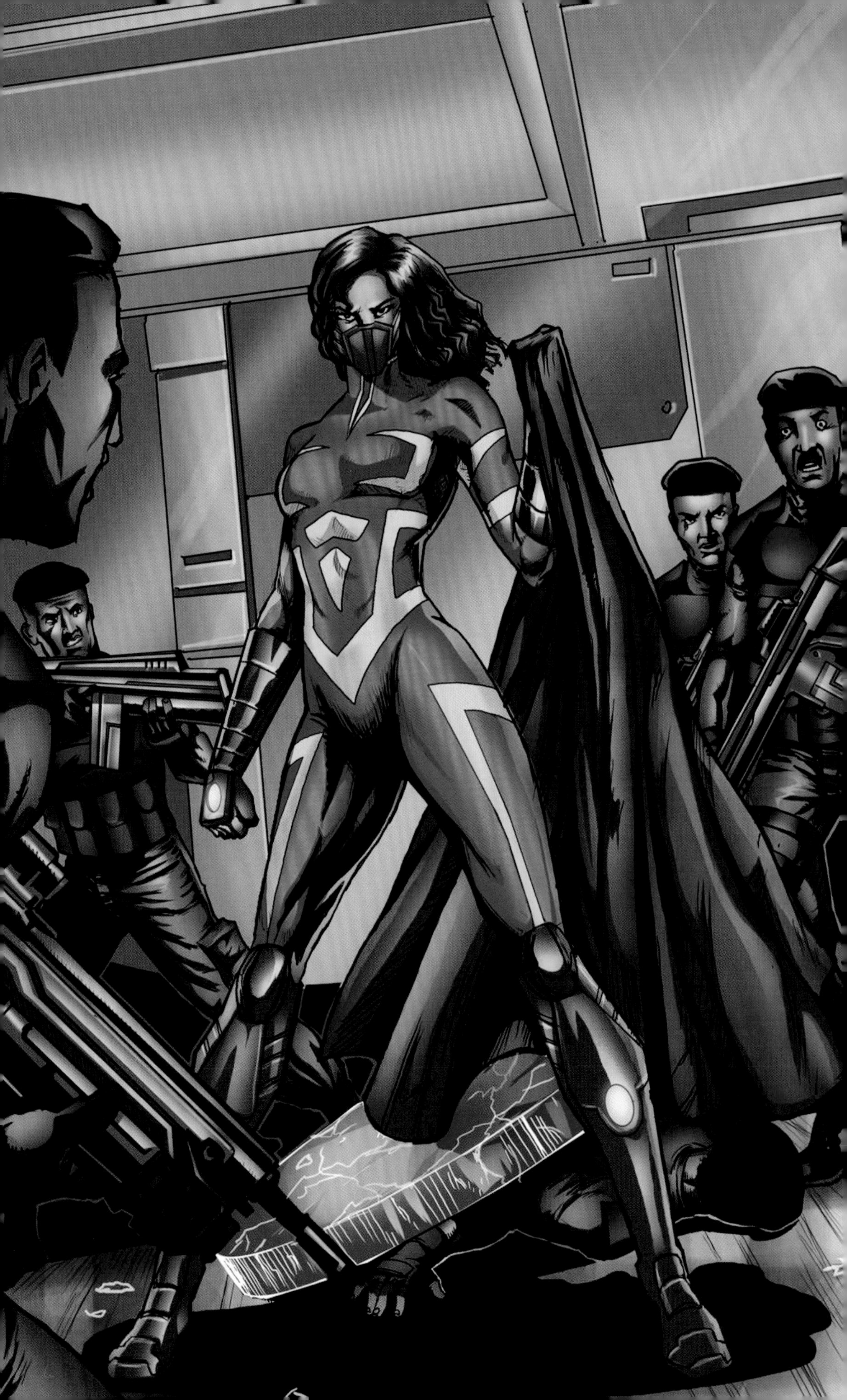

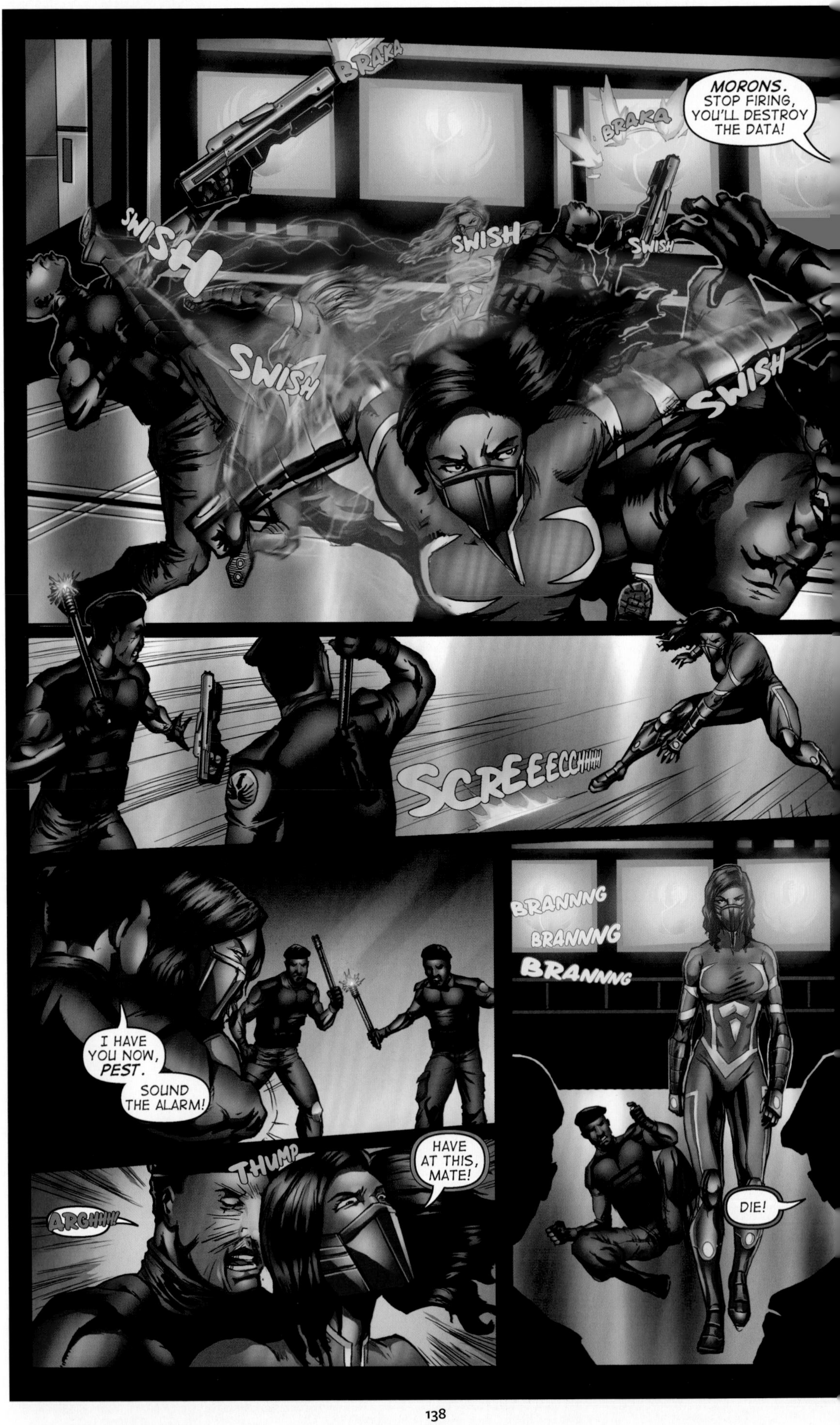
BRAKA
BRAKA
MORONS. STOP FIRING, YOU'LL DESTROY THE DATA!
SWISH
SWISH
SWISH
SWISH
SWISH
SCREEECCHHHH
I HAVE YOU NOW, PEST.
SOUND THE ALARM!
THUMP
HAVE AT THIS, MATE!
ARGHHH
BRANNNG
BRANNNG
BRANNNG
DIE!

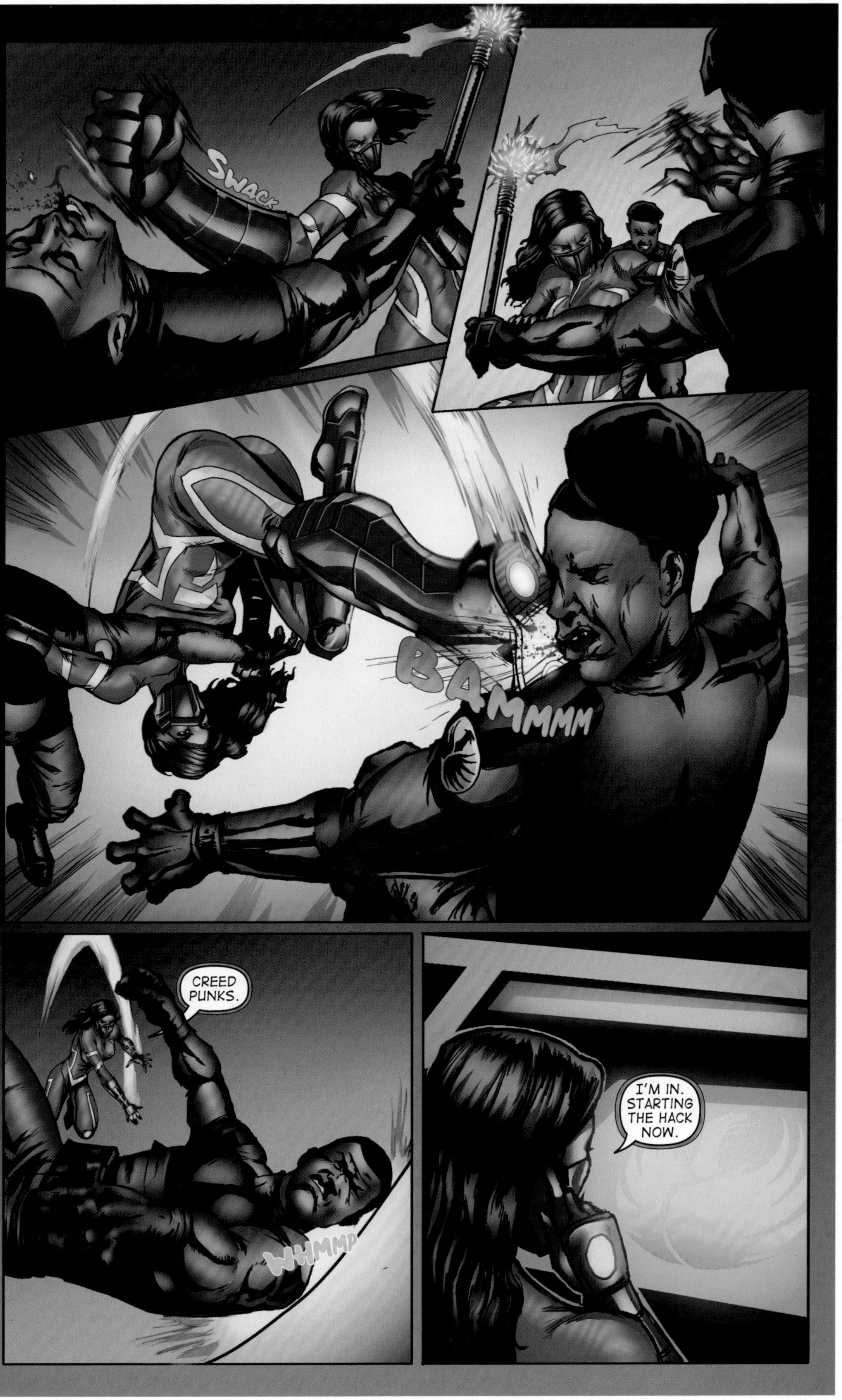
SWACK
BAMMMM
CREED PUNKS.
WHMMP
I'M IN. STARTING THE HACK NOW.

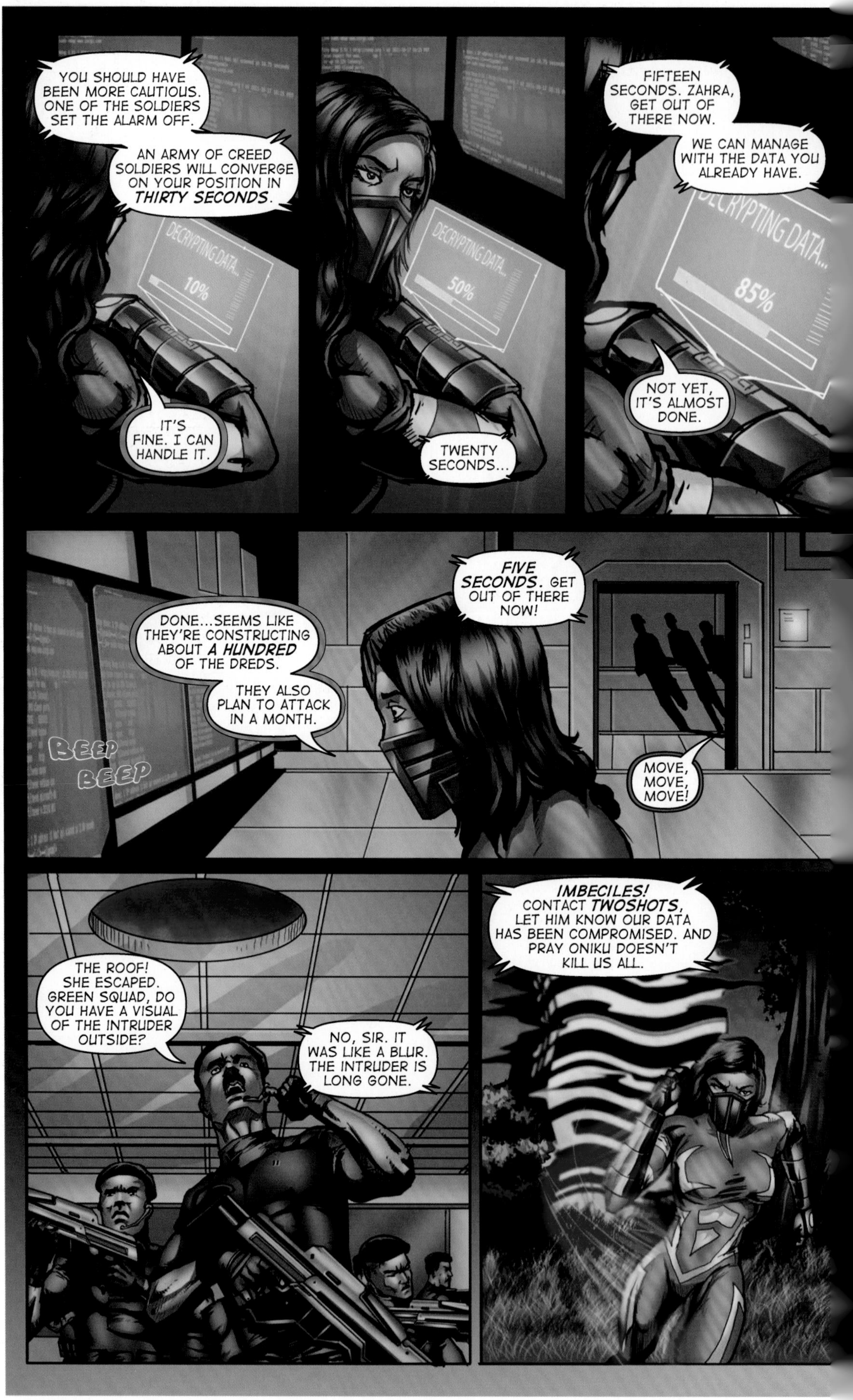

YOU SHOULD HAVE BEEN MORE CAUTIOUS. ONE OF THE SOLDIERS SET THE ALARM OFF.
AN ARMY OF CREED SOLDIERS WILL CONVERGE ON YOUR POSITION IN *THIRTY SECONDS*.
DECRYPTING DATA... 10%
IT'S FINE. I CAN HANDLE IT.
DECRYPTING DATA... 50%
TWENTY SECONDS...
FIFTEEN SECONDS. ZAHRA, GET OUT OF THERE NOW.
WE CAN MANAGE WITH THE DATA YOU ALREADY HAVE.
DECRYPTING DATA... 85%
NOT YET, IT'S ALMOST DONE.
FIVE SECONDS. GET OUT OF THERE NOW!
DONE...SEEMS LIKE THEY'RE CONSTRUCTING ABOUT *A HUNDRED* OF THE DREDS.
THEY ALSO PLAN TO ATTACK IN A MONTH.
BEEP BEEP
MOVE, MOVE, MOVE!
THE ROOF! SHE ESCAPED. GREEN SQUAD, DO YOU HAVE A VISUAL OF THE INTRUDER OUTSIDE?
NO, SIR. IT WAS LIKE A BLUR. THE INTRUDER IS LONG GONE.
IMBECILES! CONTACT ***TWOSHOTS***, LET HIM KNOW OUR DATA HAS BEEN COMPROMISED. AND PRAY ONIKU DOESN'T KILL US ALL.

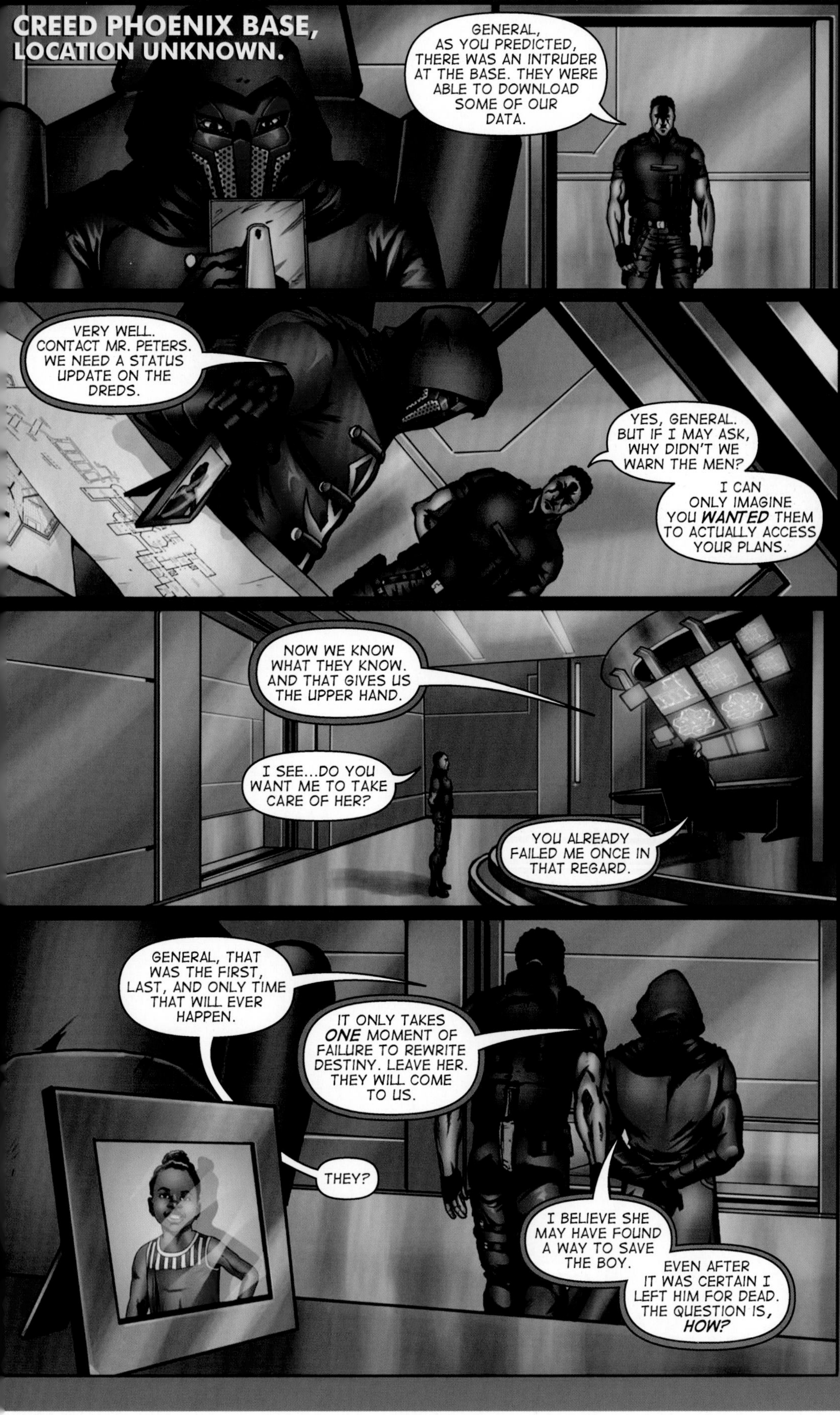
CREED PHOENIX BASE, LOCATION UNKNOWN.
GENERAL, AS YOU PREDICTED, THERE WAS AN INTRUDER AT THE BASE. THEY WERE ABLE TO DOWNLOAD SOME OF OUR DATA.
VERY WELL. CONTACT MR. PETERS. WE NEED A STATUS UPDATE ON THE DREDS.
YES, GENERAL. BUT IF I MAY ASK, WHY DIDN'T WE WARN THE MEN?
I CAN ONLY IMAGINE YOU WANTED THEM TO ACTUALLY ACCESS YOUR PLANS.
NOW WE KNOW WHAT THEY KNOW. AND THAT GIVES US THE UPPER HAND.
I SEE...DO YOU WANT ME TO TAKE CARE OF HER?
YOU ALREADY FAILED ME ONCE IN THAT REGARD.
GENERAL, THAT WAS THE FIRST, LAST, AND ONLY TIME THAT WILL EVER HAPPEN.
IT ONLY TAKES ONE MOMENT OF FAILURE TO REWRITE DESTINY. LEAVE HER. THEY WILL COME TO US.
THEY?
I BELIEVE SHE MAY HAVE FOUND A WAY TO SAVE THE BOY.
EVEN AFTER IT WAS CERTAIN I LEFT HIM FOR DEAD. THE QUESTION IS, HOW?

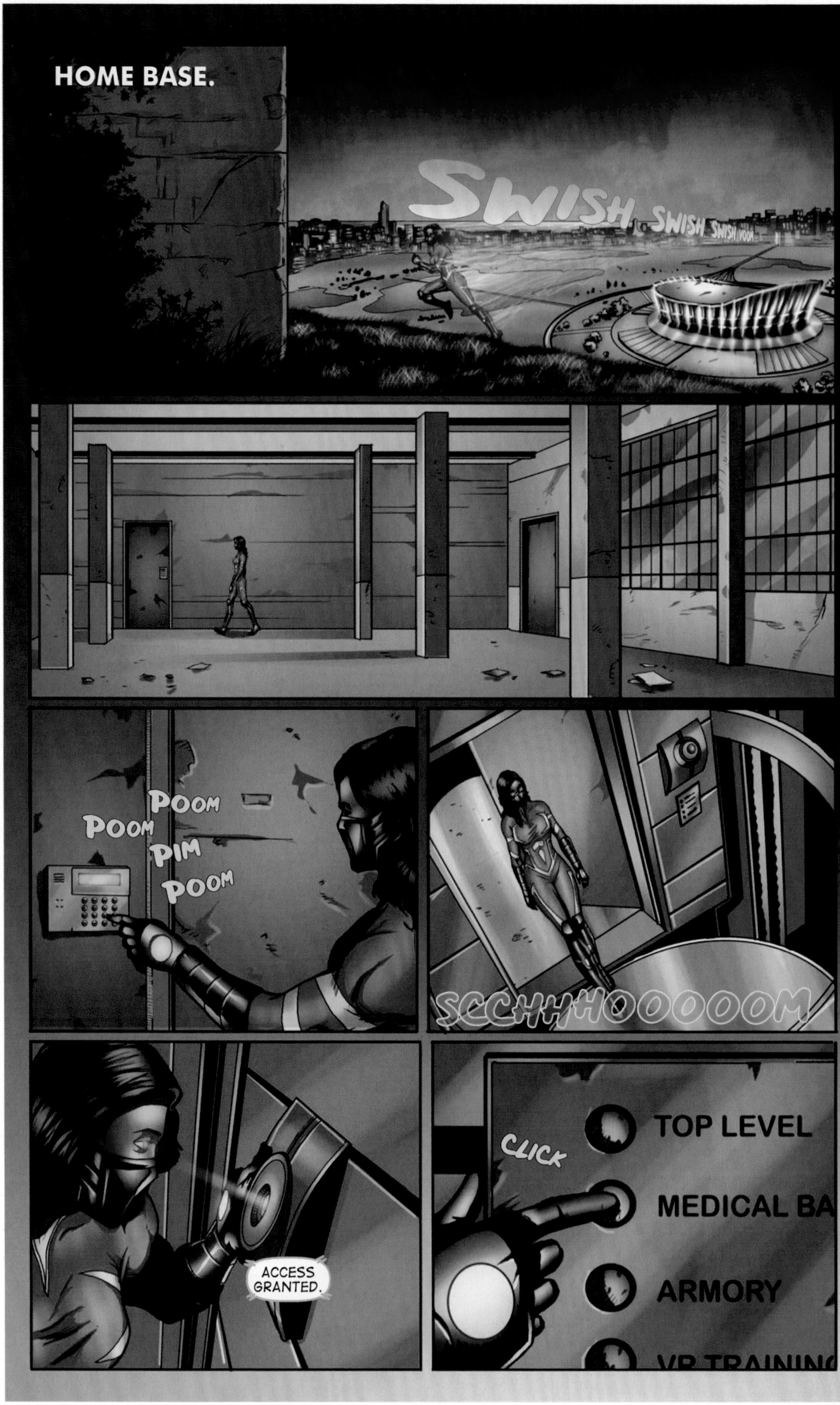
HOME BASE.
SWISH
SWISH
SWISH
VOOM
POOM
POOM
PIM
POOM
SCCHHHOOOOOOM
ACCESS GRANTED.
CLICK
TOP LEVEL
MEDICAL BA
ARMORY

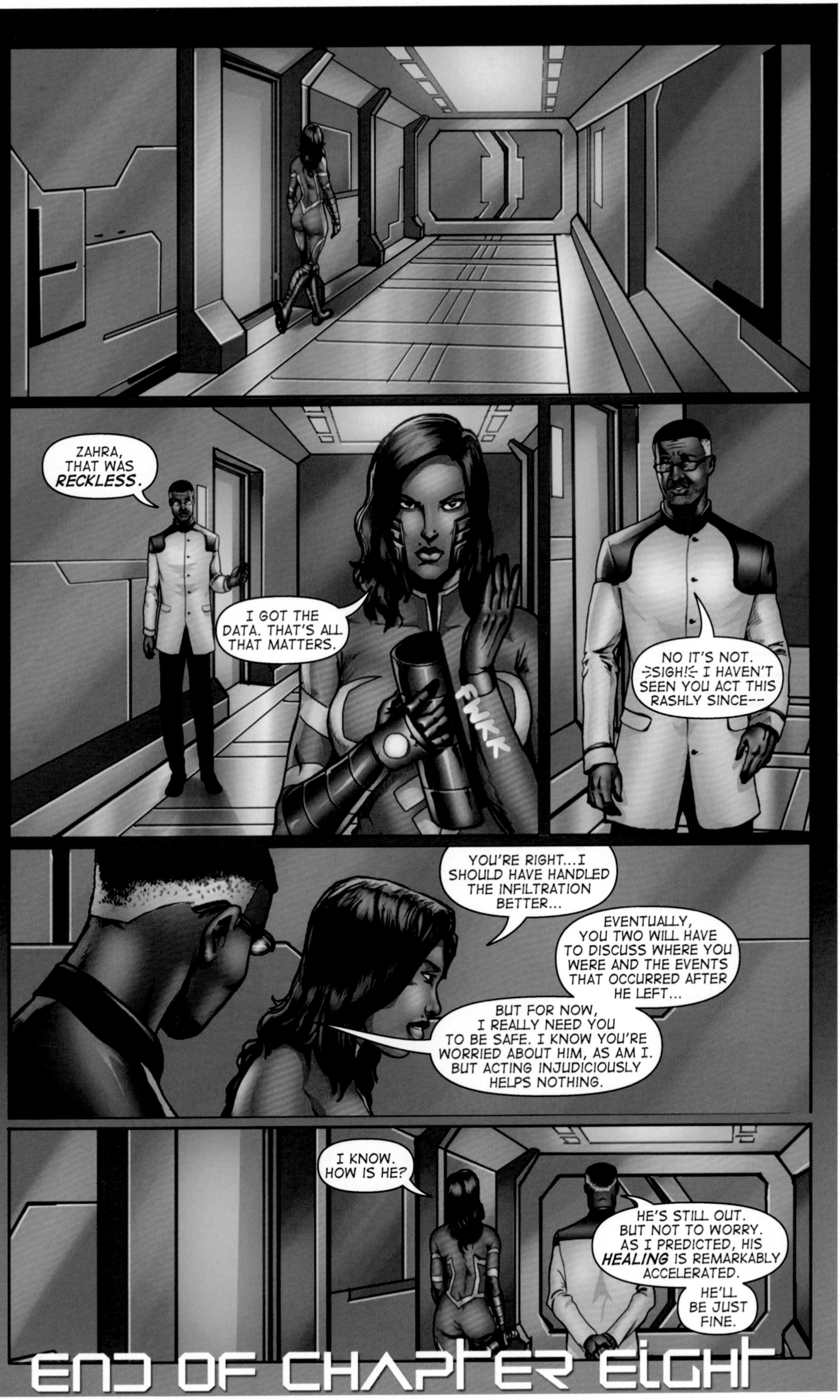
ZAHRA, THAT WAS *RECKLESS*.
I GOT THE DATA. THAT'S ALL THAT MATTERS.
FWKK
NO IT'S NOT. ⋺SIGH!⋲ I HAVEN'T SEEN YOU ACT THIS RASHLY SINCE--
YOU'RE RIGHT...I SHOULD HAVE HANDLED THE INFILTRATION BETTER...
EVENTUALLY, YOU TWO WILL HAVE TO DISCUSS WHERE YOU WERE AND THE EVENTS THAT OCCURRED AFTER HE LEFT...
BUT FOR NOW, I REALLY NEED YOU TO BE SAFE. I KNOW YOU'RE WORRIED ABOUT HIM, AS AM I. BUT ACTING INJUDICIOUSLY HELPS NOTHING.
I KNOW. HOW IS HE?
HE'S STILL OUT. BUT NOT TO WORRY. AS I PREDICTED, HIS *HEALING* IS REMARKABLY ACCELERATED.
HE'LL BE JUST FINE.
END OF CHAPTER EIGHT

FAN ART BY BABAJIDE BRIGGS ADEBIMPE

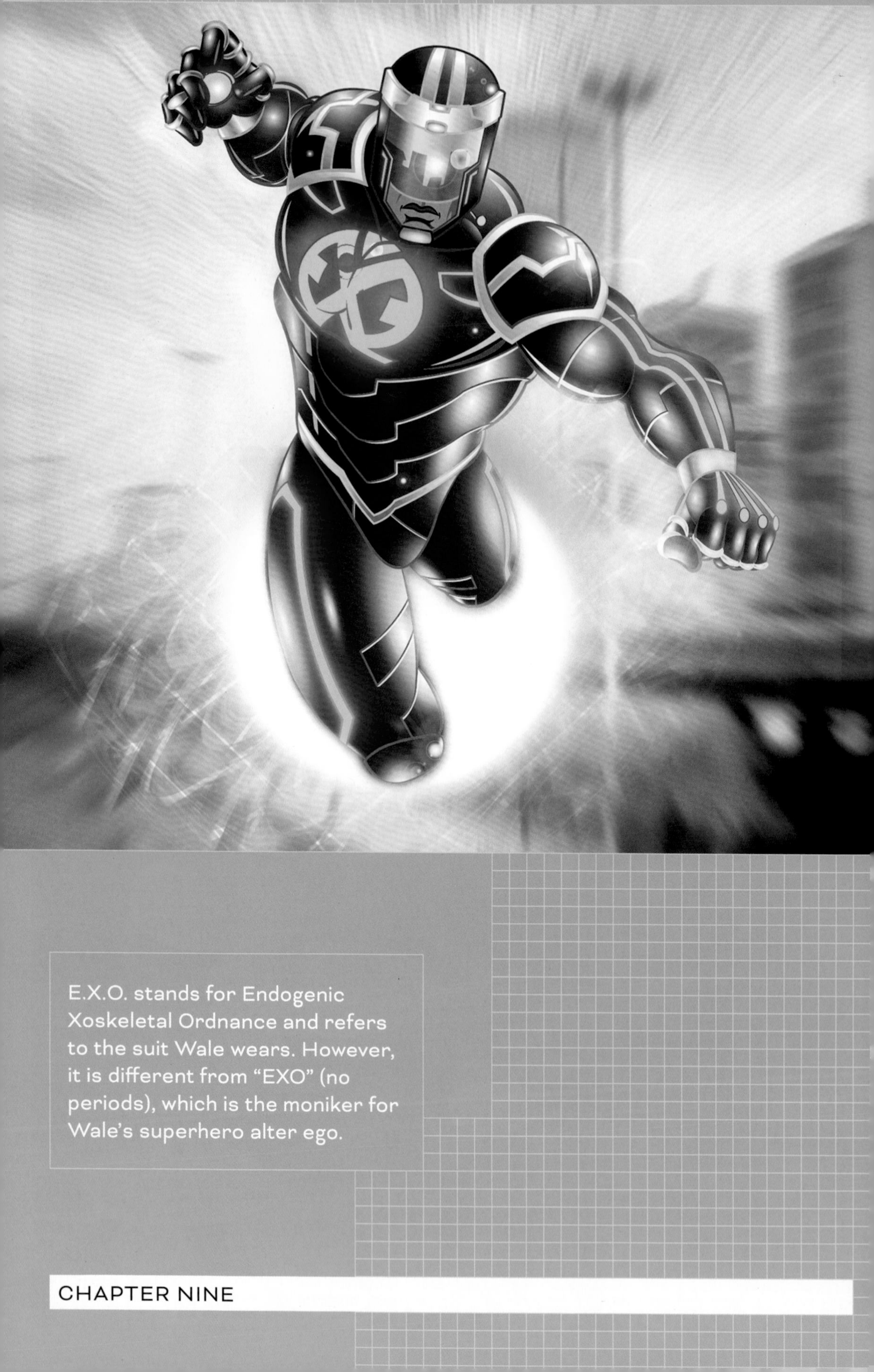

E.X.O. stands for Endogenic Xoskeletal Ordnance and refers to the suit Wale wears. However, it is different from "EXO" (no periods), which is the moniker for Wale's superhero alter ego.

CHAPTER NINE

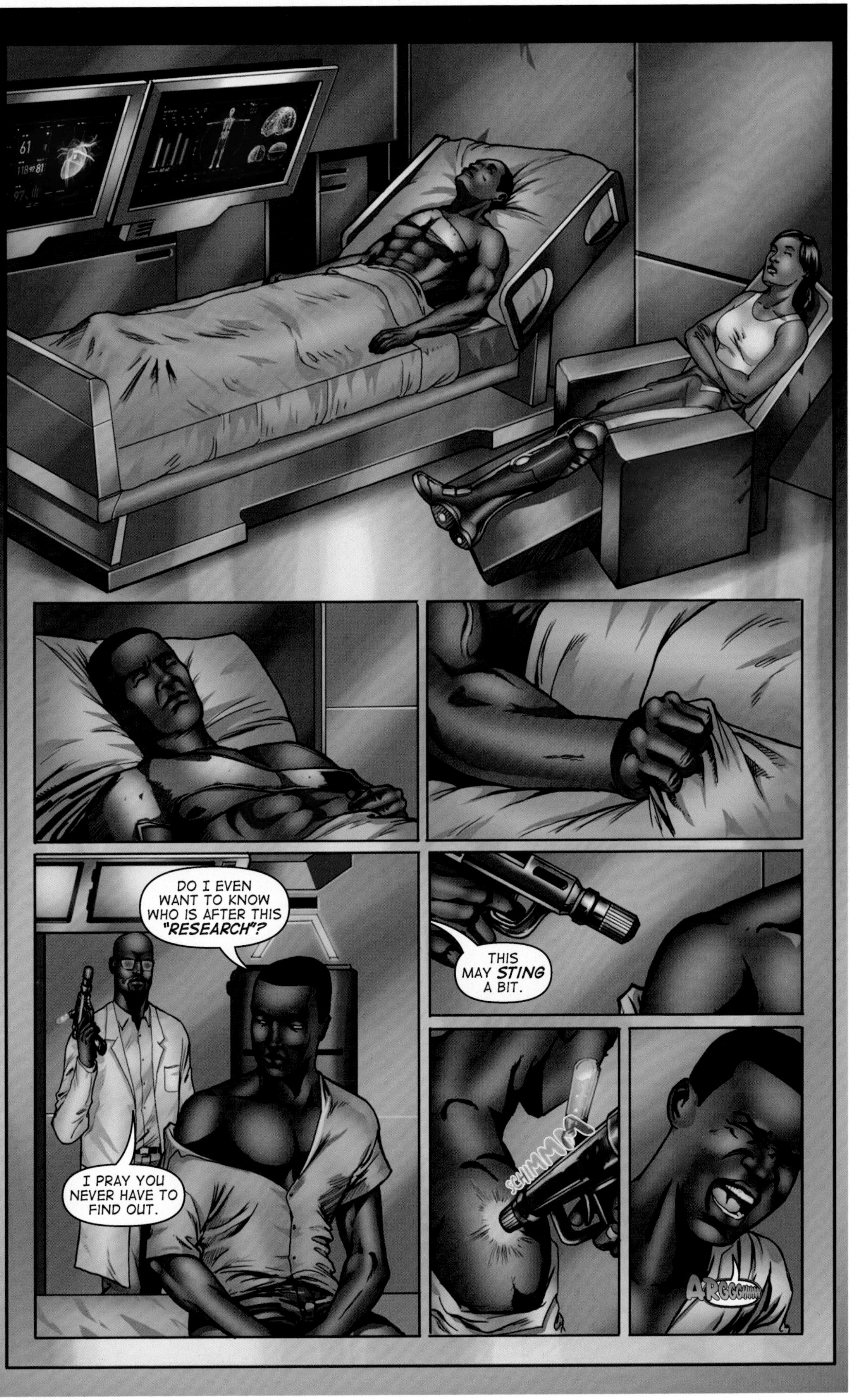

DO I EVEN WANT TO KNOW WHO IS AFTER THIS "RESEARCH"?
I PRAY YOU NEVER HAVE TO FIND OUT.
THIS MAY STING A BIT.
SCHIMMM
ARGGGHHHHH

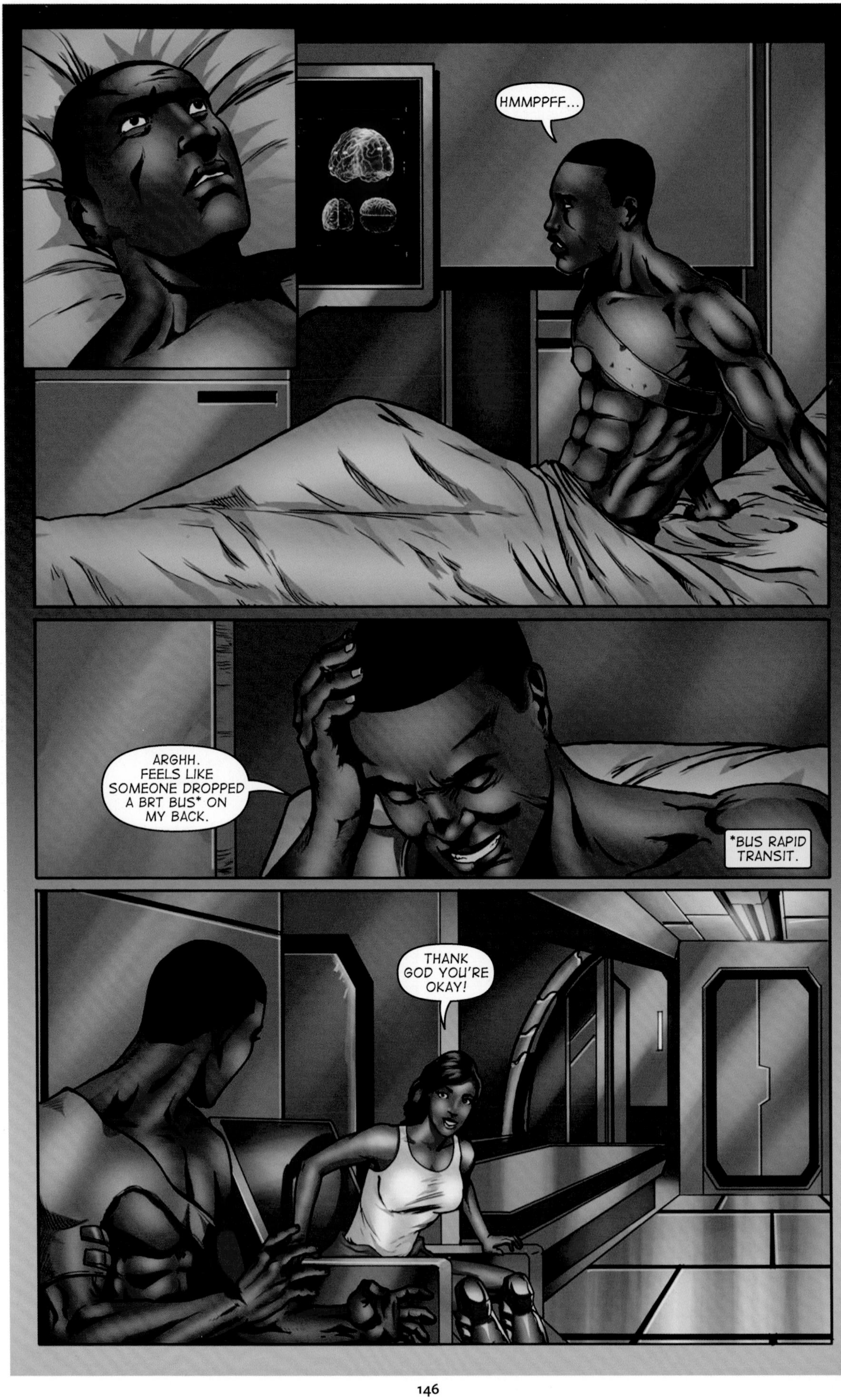
HMMPPFF...
ARGHH. FEELS LIKE SOMEONE DROPPED A BRT BUS* ON MY BACK.
*BUS RAPID TRANSIT.
THANK GOD YOU'RE OKAY!

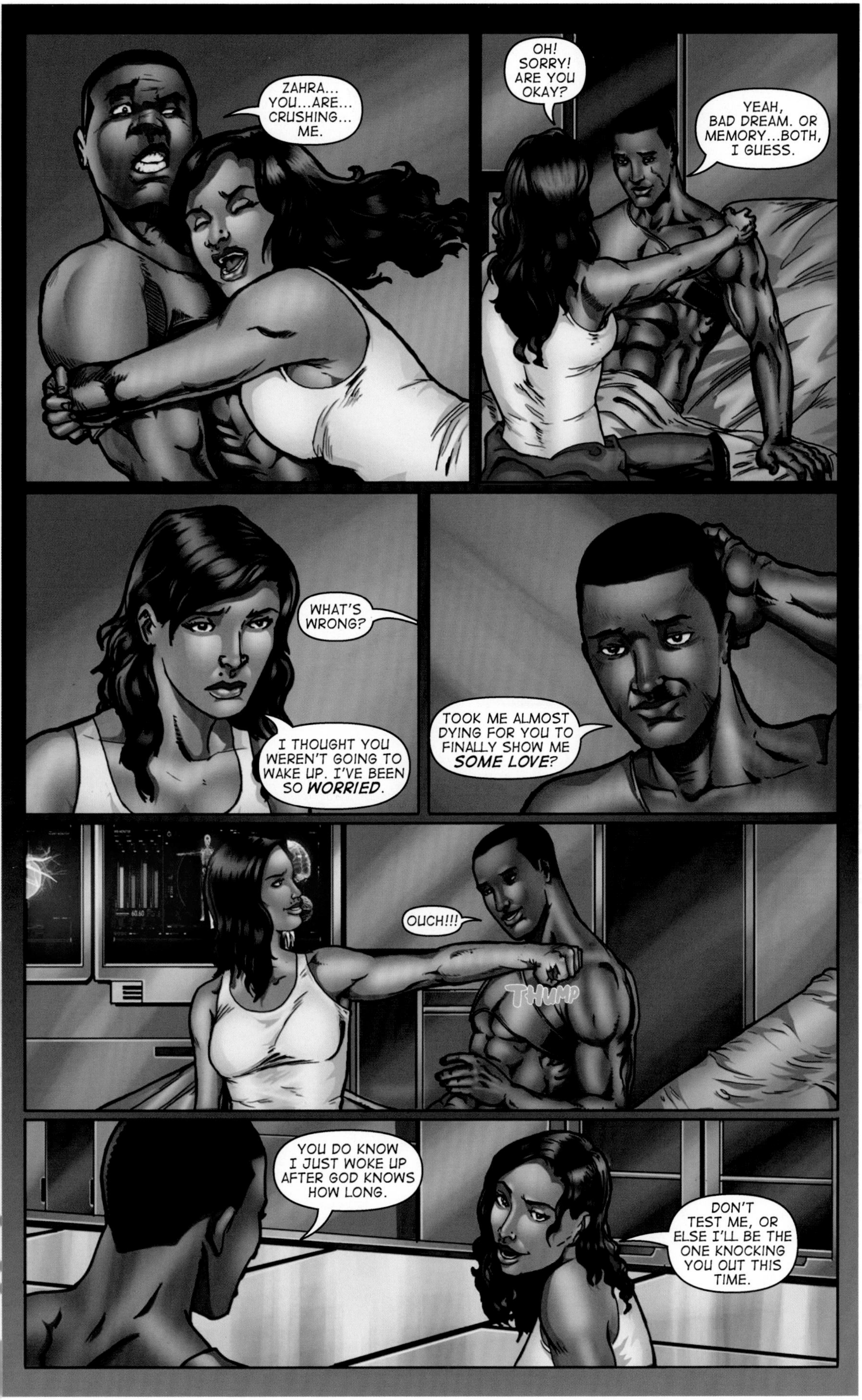
ZAHRA... YOU...ARE... CRUSHING... ME.
OH! SORRY! ARE YOU OKAY?
YEAH, BAD DREAM. OR MEMORY...BOTH, I GUESS.
WHAT'S WRONG?
I THOUGHT YOU WEREN'T GOING TO WAKE UP. I'VE BEEN SO **WORRIED**.
TOOK ME ALMOST DYING FOR YOU TO FINALLY SHOW ME **SOME LOVE**?
OUCH!!!
THUMP
YOU DO KNOW I JUST WOKE UP AFTER GOD KNOWS HOW LONG.
DON'T TEST ME, OR ELSE I'LL BE THE ONE KNOCKING YOU OUT THIS TIME.

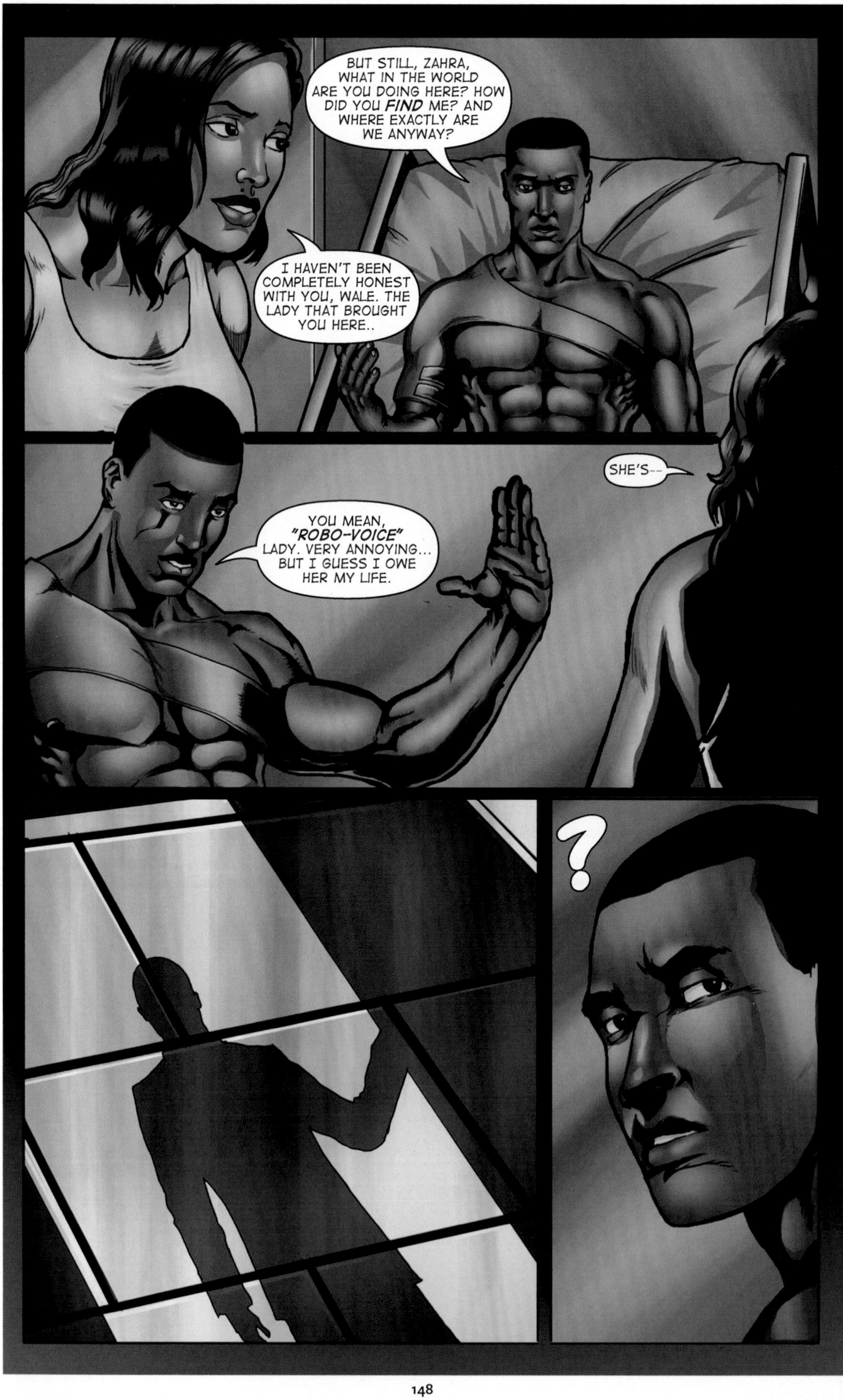
BUT STILL, ZAHRA, WHAT IN THE WORLD ARE YOU DOING HERE? HOW DID YOU *FIND* ME? AND WHERE EXACTLY ARE WE ANYWAY?
I HAVEN'T BEEN COMPLETELY HONEST WITH YOU, WALE. THE LADY THAT BROUGHT YOU HERE..
SHE'S--
YOU MEAN, *"ROBO-VOICE"* LADY. VERY ANNOYING... BUT I GUESS I OWE HER MY LIFE.
?

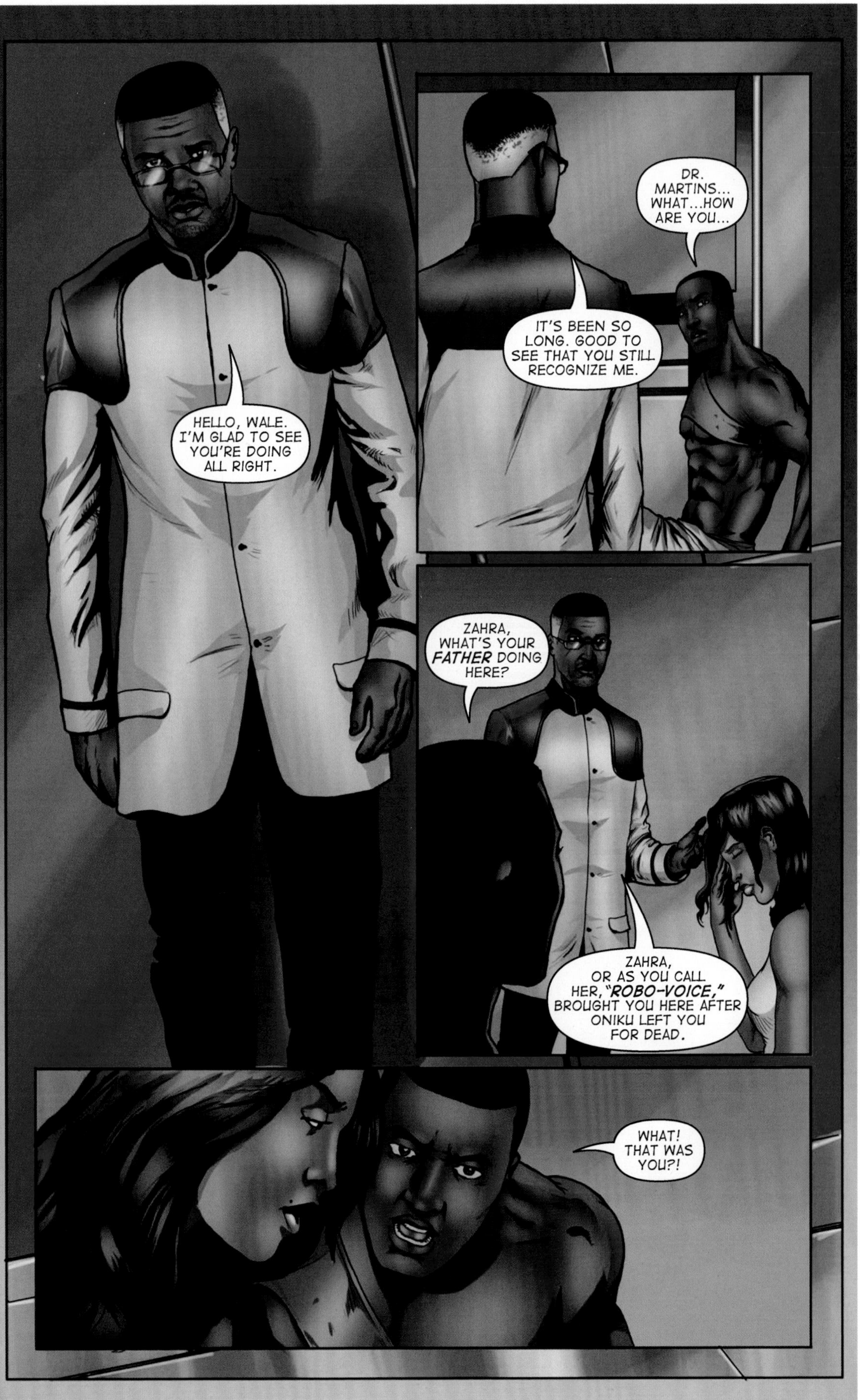
HELLO, WALE. I'M GLAD TO SEE YOU'RE DOING ALL RIGHT.
DR. MARTINS... WHAT...HOW ARE YOU...
IT'S BEEN SO LONG. GOOD TO SEE THAT YOU STILL RECOGNIZE ME.
ZAHRA, WHAT'S YOUR FATHER DOING HERE?
ZAHRA, OR AS YOU CALL HER, "ROBO-VOICE," BROUGHT YOU HERE AFTER ONIKU LEFT YOU FOR DEAD.
WHAT! THAT WAS YOU?!

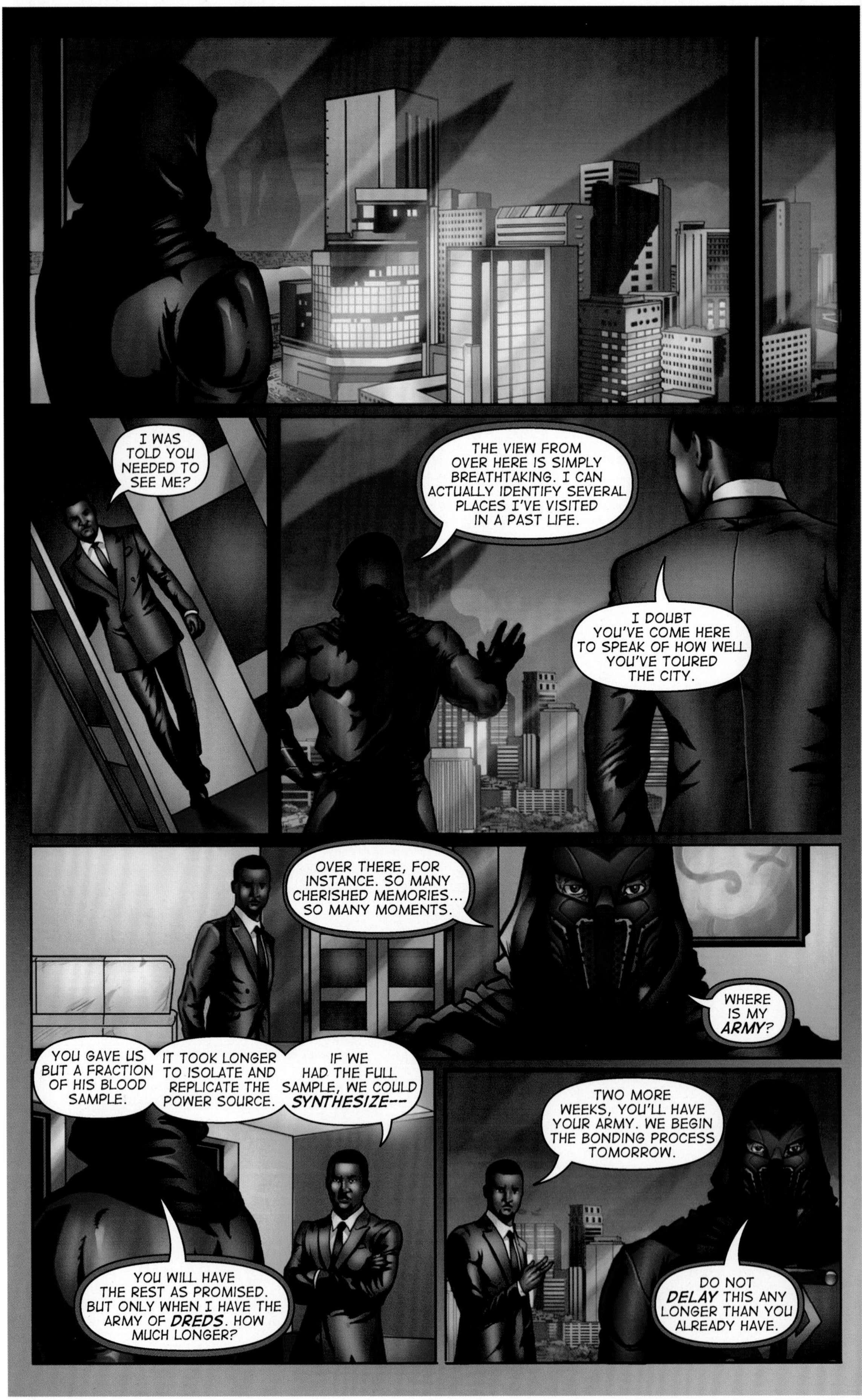
I WAS TOLD YOU NEEDED TO SEE ME?
THE VIEW FROM OVER HERE IS SIMPLY BREATHTAKING. I CAN ACTUALLY IDENTIFY SEVERAL PLACES I'VE VISITED IN A PAST LIFE.
I DOUBT YOU'VE COME HERE TO SPEAK OF HOW WELL YOU'VE TOURED THE CITY.
OVER THERE, FOR INSTANCE. SO MANY CHERISHED MEMORIES... SO MANY MOMENTS.
WHERE IS MY ARMY?
YOU GAVE US BUT A FRACTION OF HIS BLOOD SAMPLE.
IT TOOK LONGER TO ISOLATE AND REPLICATE THE POWER SOURCE.
IF WE HAD THE FULL SAMPLE, WE COULD SYNTHESIZE--
YOU WILL HAVE THE REST AS PROMISED. BUT ONLY WHEN I HAVE THE ARMY OF DREDS. HOW MUCH LONGER?
TWO MORE WEEKS, YOU'LL HAVE YOUR ARMY. WE BEGIN THE BONDING PROCESS TOMORROW.
DO NOT DELAY THIS ANY LONGER THAN YOU ALREADY HAVE.

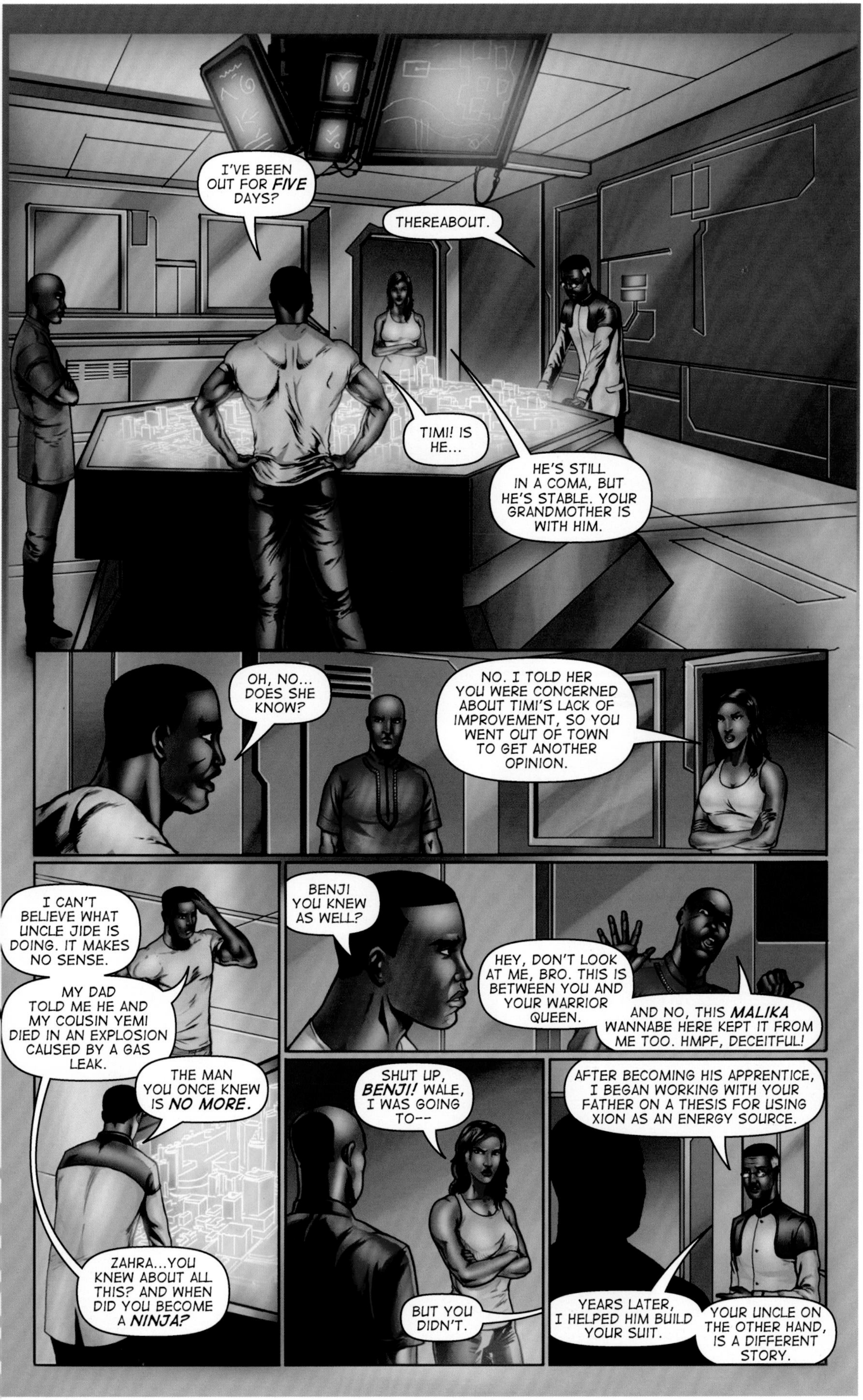
I'VE BEEN OUT FOR FIVE DAYS?
THEREABOUT.
TIMI! IS HE...
HE'S STILL IN A COMA, BUT HE'S STABLE. YOUR GRANDMOTHER IS WITH HIM.
OH, NO... DOES SHE KNOW?
NO. I TOLD HER YOU WERE CONCERNED ABOUT TIMI'S LACK OF IMPROVEMENT, SO YOU WENT OUT OF TOWN TO GET ANOTHER OPINION.
I CAN'T BELIEVE WHAT UNCLE JIDE IS DOING. IT MAKES NO SENSE.
MY DAD TOLD ME HE AND MY COUSIN YEMI DIED IN AN EXPLOSION CAUSED BY A GAS LEAK.
THE MAN YOU ONCE KNEW IS NO MORE.
ZAHRA...YOU KNEW ABOUT ALL THIS? AND WHEN DID YOU BECOME A NINJA?
BENJI YOU KNEW AS WELL?
HEY, DON'T LOOK AT ME, BRO. THIS IS BETWEEN YOU AND YOUR WARRIOR QUEEN.
AND NO, THIS MALIKA WANNABE HERE KEPT IT FROM ME TOO. HMPF, DECEITFUL!
SHUT UP, BENJI! WALE, I WAS GOING TO--
BUT YOU DIDN'T.
AFTER BECOMING HIS APPRENTICE, I BEGAN WORKING WITH YOUR FATHER ON A THESIS FOR USING XION AS AN ENERGY SOURCE.
YEARS LATER, I HELPED HIM BUILD YOUR SUIT.
YOUR UNCLE ON THE OTHER HAND, IS A DIFFERENT STORY.

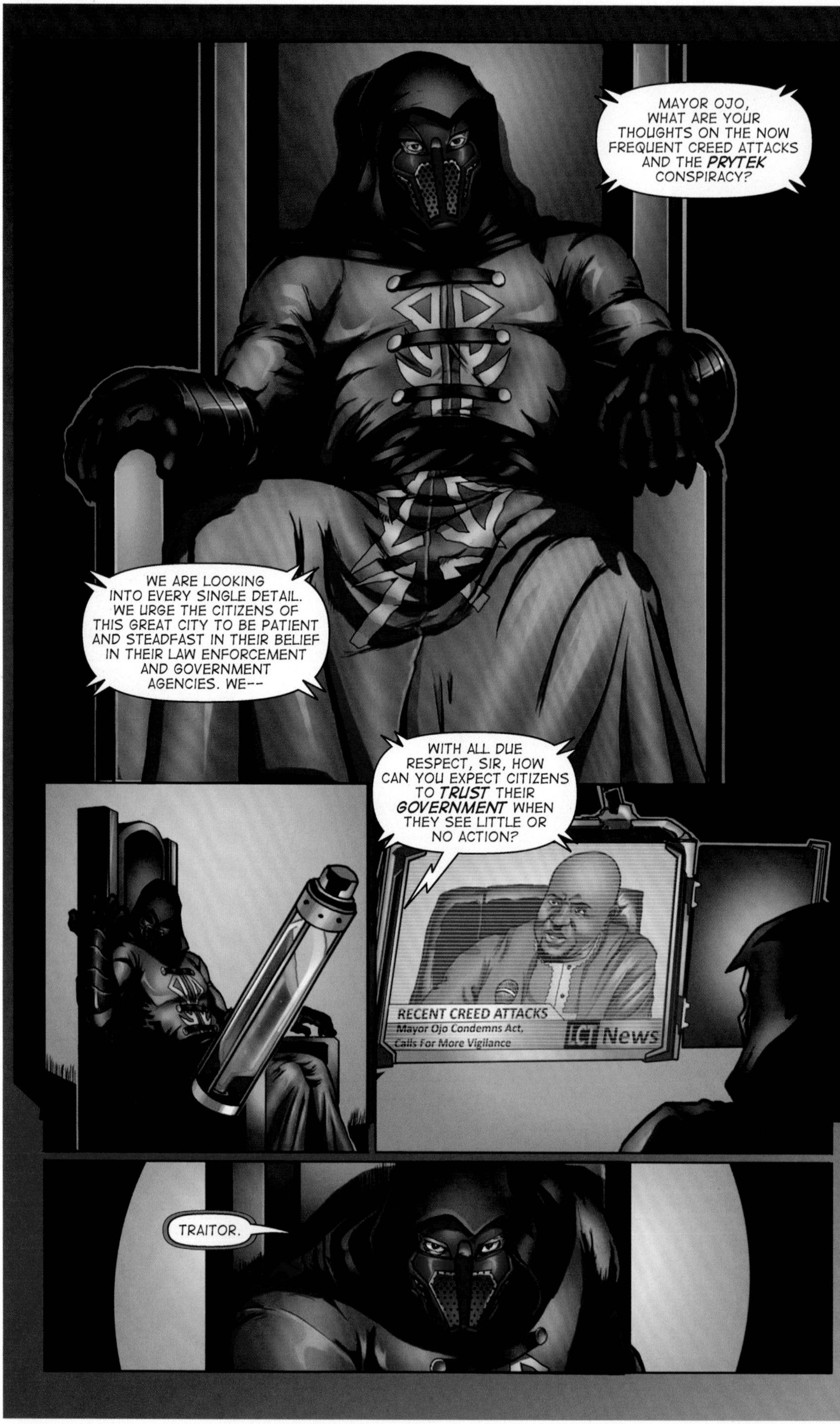
MAYOR OJO, WHAT ARE YOUR THOUGHTS ON THE NOW FREQUENT CREED ATTACKS AND THE PRYTEK CONSPIRACY?
WE ARE LOOKING INTO EVERY SINGLE DETAIL. WE URGE THE CITIZENS OF THIS GREAT CITY TO BE PATIENT AND STEADFAST IN THEIR BELIEF IN THEIR LAW ENFORCEMENT AND GOVERNMENT AGENCIES. WE--
WITH ALL DUE RESPECT, SIR, HOW CAN YOU EXPECT CITIZENS TO TRUST THEIR GOVERNMENT WHEN THEY SEE LITTLE OR NO ACTION?
RECENT CREED ATTACKS
Mayor Ojo Condemns Act. Calls For More Vigilance
CT News
TRAITOR.

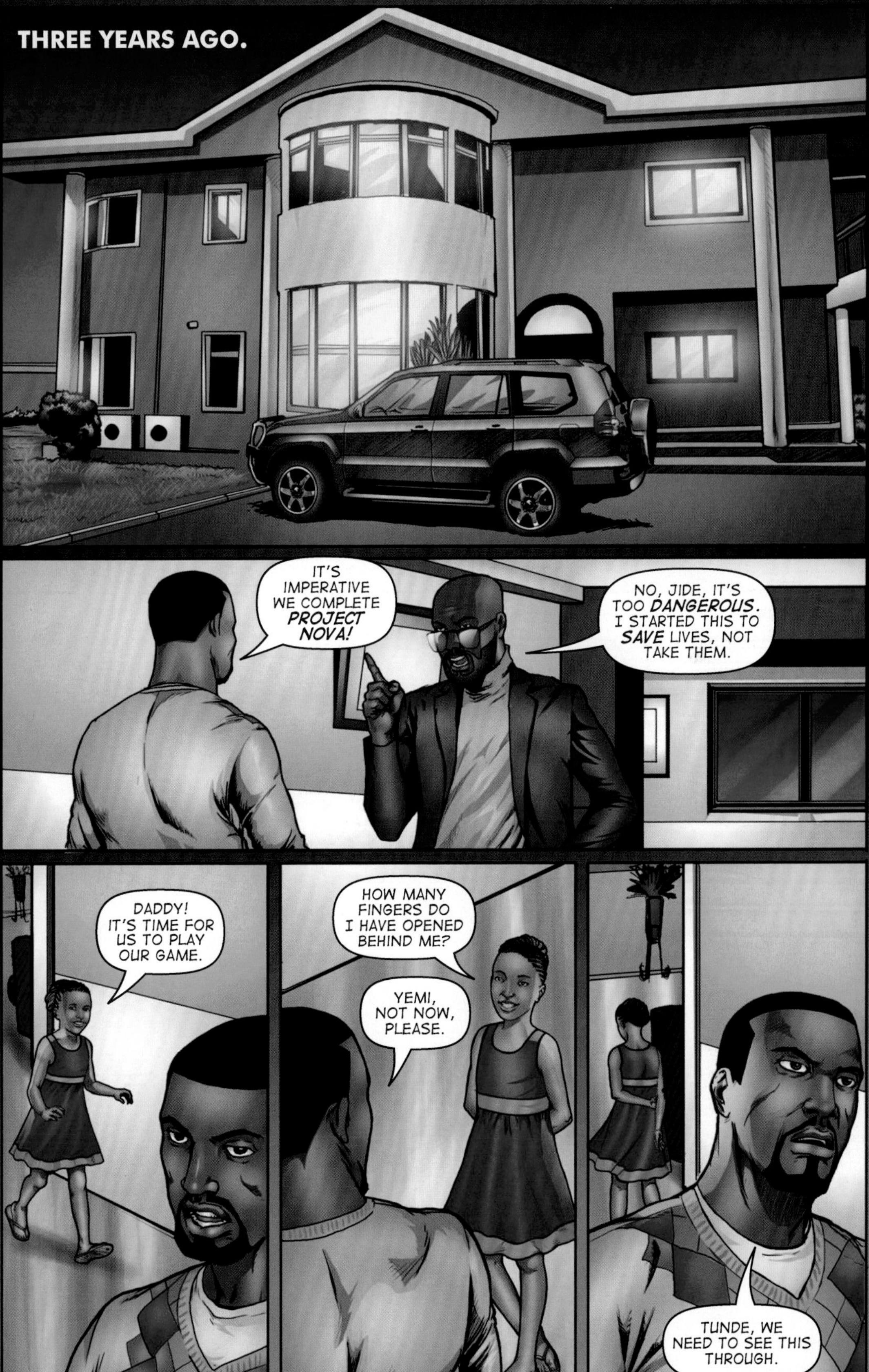
THREE YEARS AGO.
IT'S IMPERATIVE WE COMPLETE PROJECT NOVA!
NO, JIDE, IT'S TOO DANGEROUS. I STARTED THIS TO SAVE LIVES, NOT TAKE THEM.
DADDY! IT'S TIME FOR US TO PLAY OUR GAME.
HOW MANY FINGERS DO I HAVE OPENED BEHIND ME?
YEMI, NOT NOW, PLEASE.
TUNDE, WE NEED TO SEE THIS THROUGH.

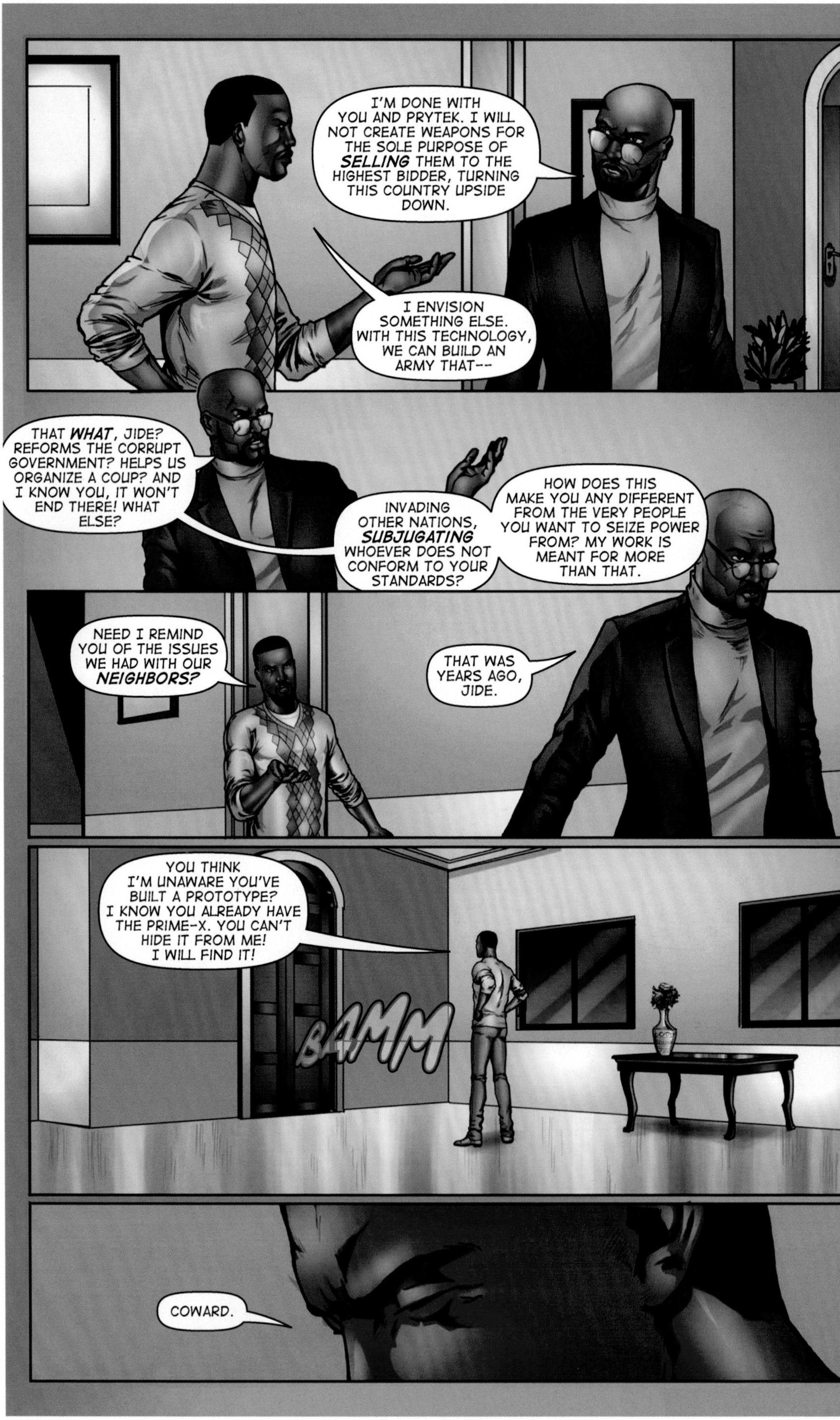
I'M DONE WITH YOU AND PRYTEK. I WILL NOT CREATE WEAPONS FOR THE SOLE PURPOSE OF SELLING THEM TO THE HIGHEST BIDDER, TURNING THIS COUNTRY UPSIDE DOWN.
I ENVISION SOMETHING ELSE. WITH THIS TECHNOLOGY, WE CAN BUILD AN ARMY THAT--
THAT WHAT, JIDE? REFORMS THE CORRUPT GOVERNMENT? HELPS US ORGANIZE A COUP? AND I KNOW YOU, IT WON'T END THERE! WHAT ELSE?
INVADING OTHER NATIONS, SUBJUGATING WHOEVER DOES NOT CONFORM TO YOUR STANDARDS?
HOW DOES THIS MAKE YOU ANY DIFFERENT FROM THE VERY PEOPLE YOU WANT TO SEIZE POWER FROM? MY WORK IS MEANT FOR MORE THAN THAT.
NEED I REMIND YOU OF THE ISSUES WE HAD WITH OUR NEIGHBORS?
THAT WAS YEARS AGO, JIDE.
YOU THINK I'M UNAWARE YOU'VE BUILT A PROTOTYPE? I KNOW YOU ALREADY HAVE THE PRIME-X. YOU CAN'T HIDE IT FROM ME! I WILL FIND IT!
BAMM
COWARD.

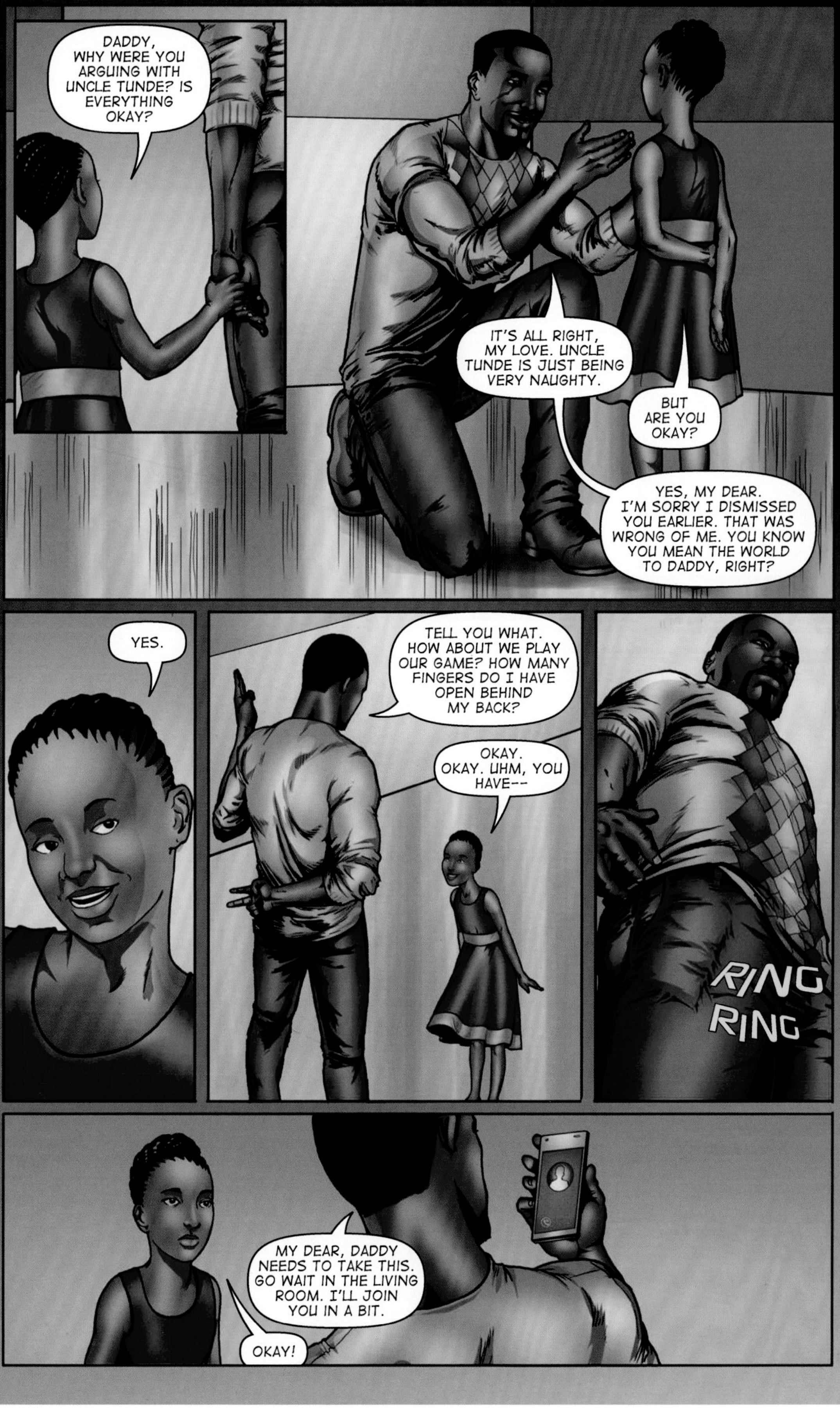
DADDY, WHY WERE YOU ARGUING WITH UNCLE TUNDE? IS EVERYTHING OKAY?
IT'S ALL RIGHT, MY LOVE. UNCLE TUNDE IS JUST BEING VERY NAUGHTY.
BUT ARE YOU OKAY?
YES, MY DEAR. I'M SORRY I DISMISSED YOU EARLIER. THAT WAS WRONG OF ME. YOU KNOW YOU MEAN THE WORLD TO DADDY, RIGHT?
YES.
TELL YOU WHAT. HOW ABOUT WE PLAY OUR GAME? HOW MANY FINGERS DO I HAVE OPEN BEHIND MY BACK?
OKAY. OKAY. UHM, YOU HAVE--
RING
RING
MY DEAR, DADDY NEEDS TO TAKE THIS. GO WAIT IN THE LIVING ROOM. I'LL JOIN YOU IN A BIT.
OKAY!

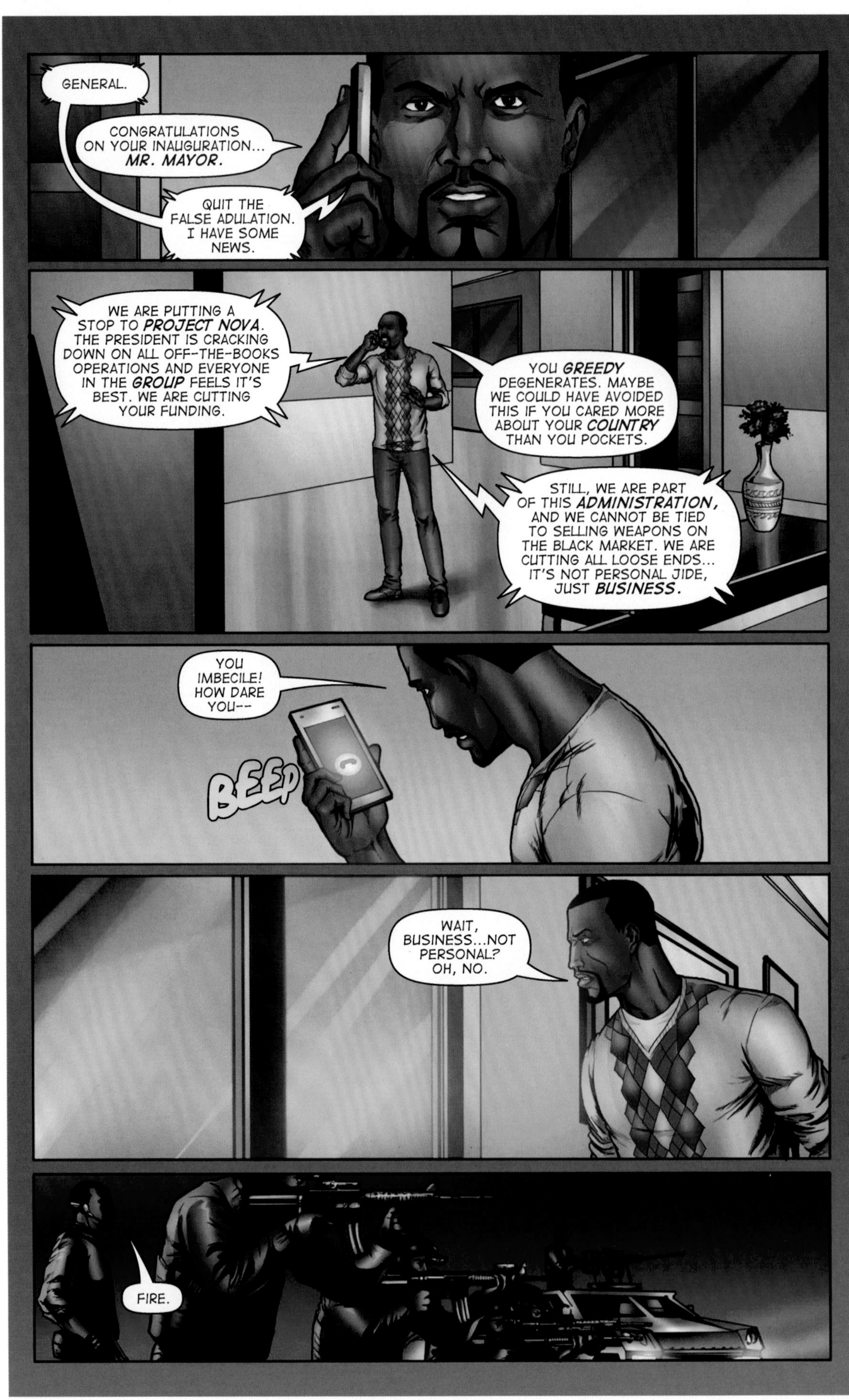

GENERAL.
CONGRATULATIONS ON YOUR INAUGURATION... MR. MAYOR.
QUIT THE FALSE ADULATION. I HAVE SOME NEWS.
WE ARE PUTTING A STOP TO PROJECT NOVA. THE PRESIDENT IS CRACKING DOWN ON ALL OFF-THE-BOOKS OPERATIONS AND EVERYONE IN THE GROUP FEELS IT'S BEST. WE ARE CUTTING YOUR FUNDING.
YOU GREEDY DEGENERATES. MAYBE WE COULD HAVE AVOIDED THIS IF YOU CARED MORE ABOUT YOUR COUNTRY THAN YOU POCKETS.
STILL, WE ARE PART OF THIS ADMINISTRATION, AND WE CANNOT BE TIED TO SELLING WEAPONS ON THE BLACK MARKET. WE ARE CUTTING ALL LOOSE ENDS... IT'S NOT PERSONAL JIDE, JUST BUSINESS.
YOU IMBECILE! HOW DARE YOU--
BEEP
WAIT, BUSINESS...NOT PERSONAL? OH, NO.
FIRE.

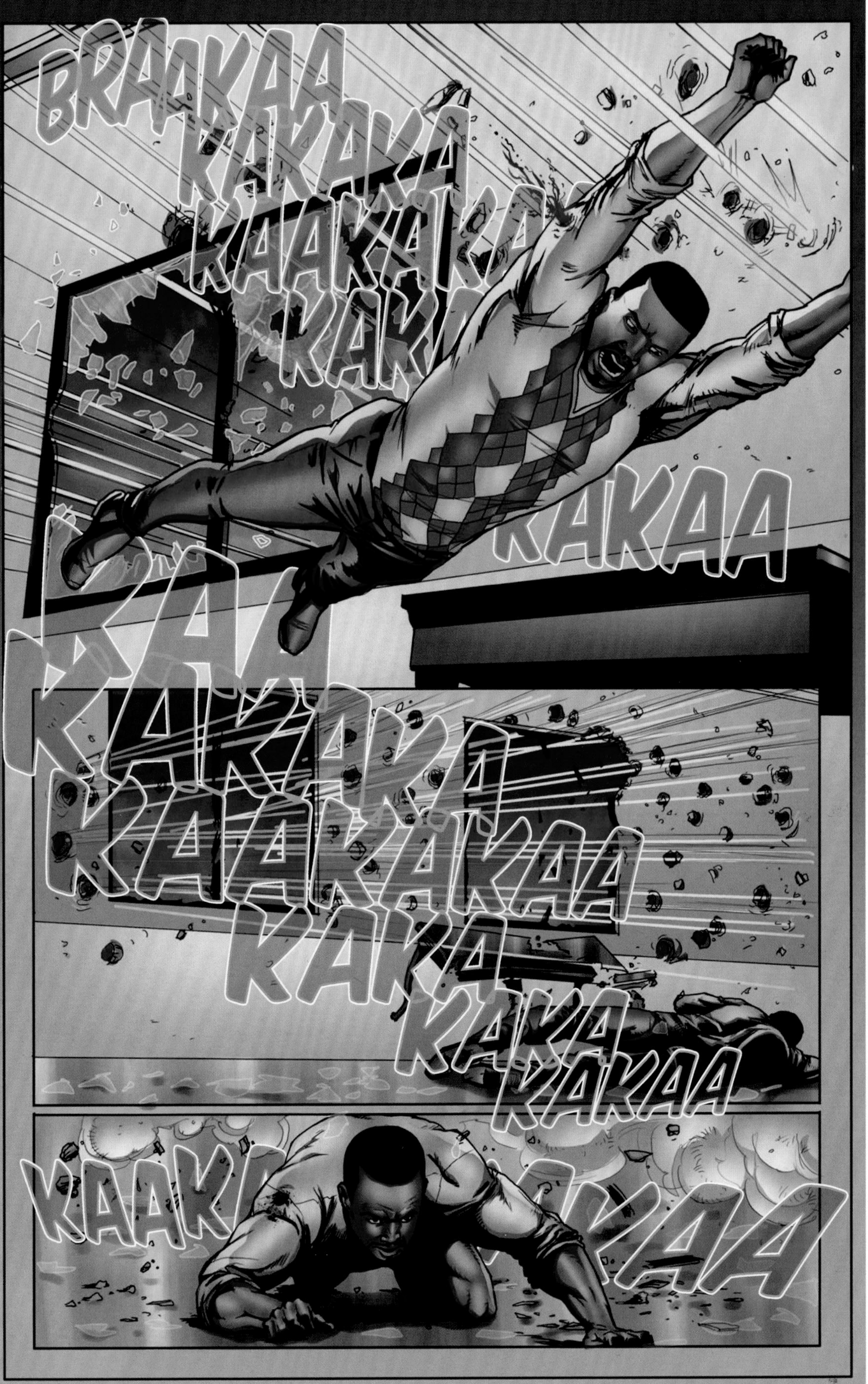
BRAAKAA
KAKAKA
KAKAKAKA
KAKA
KAKAA
KAKAKA
KAKAKAKAA
KAKA
KAKA
KAKAA
KAAKAKAKAA

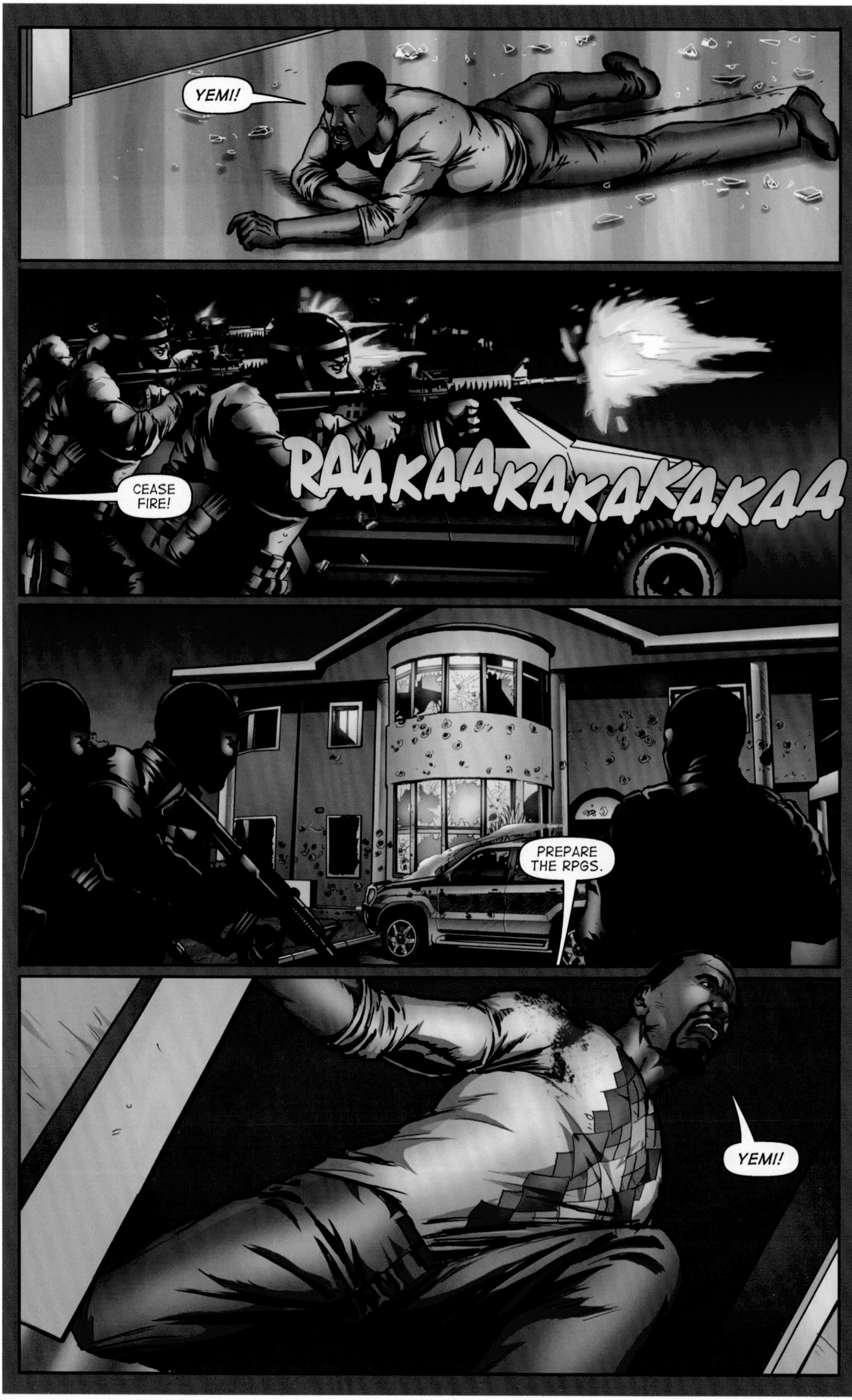
YEMI!
RAAKAAKAKAKAKAA
CEASE FIRE!
PREPARE THE RPGS.
YEMI!

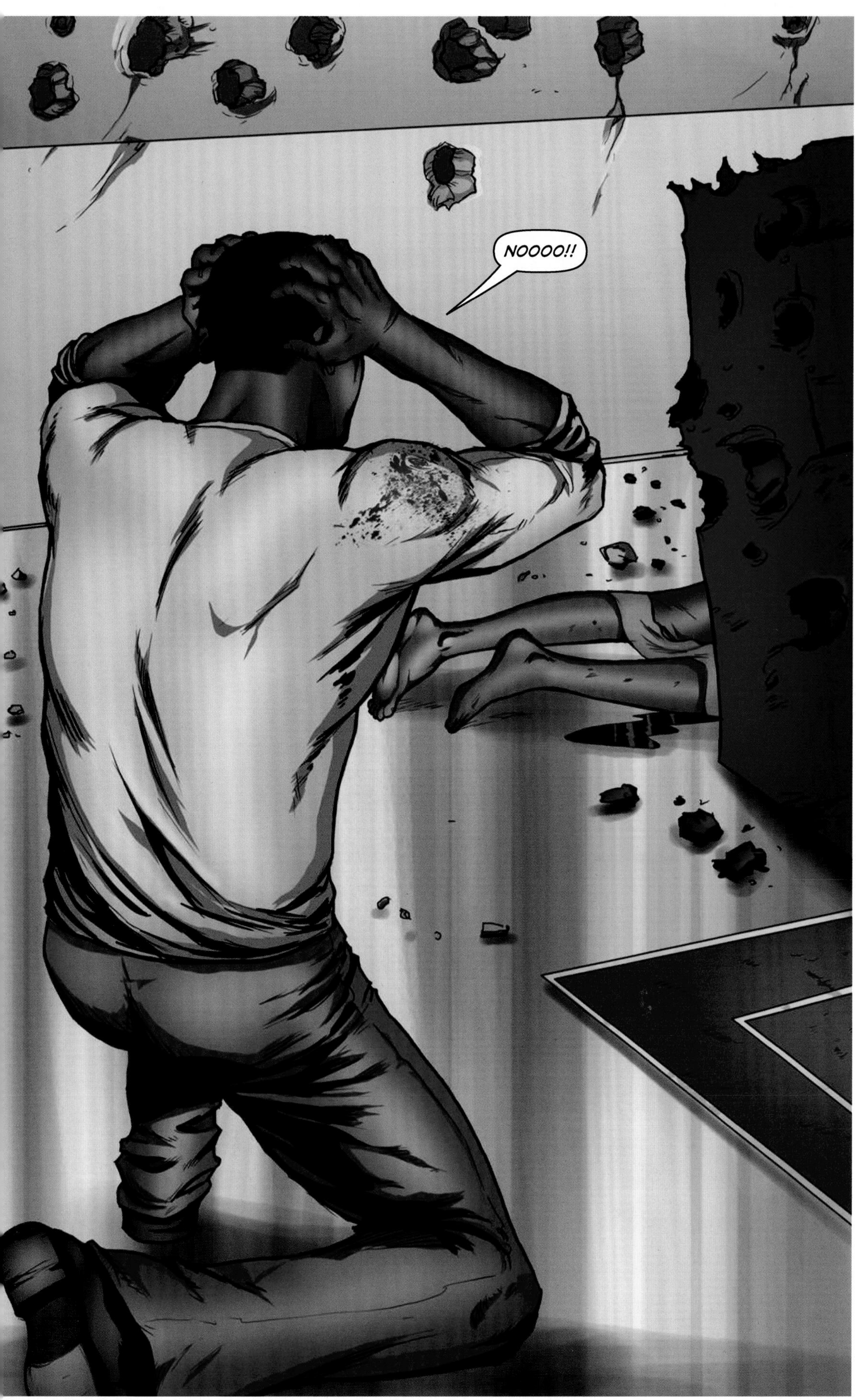
NOOOO!!

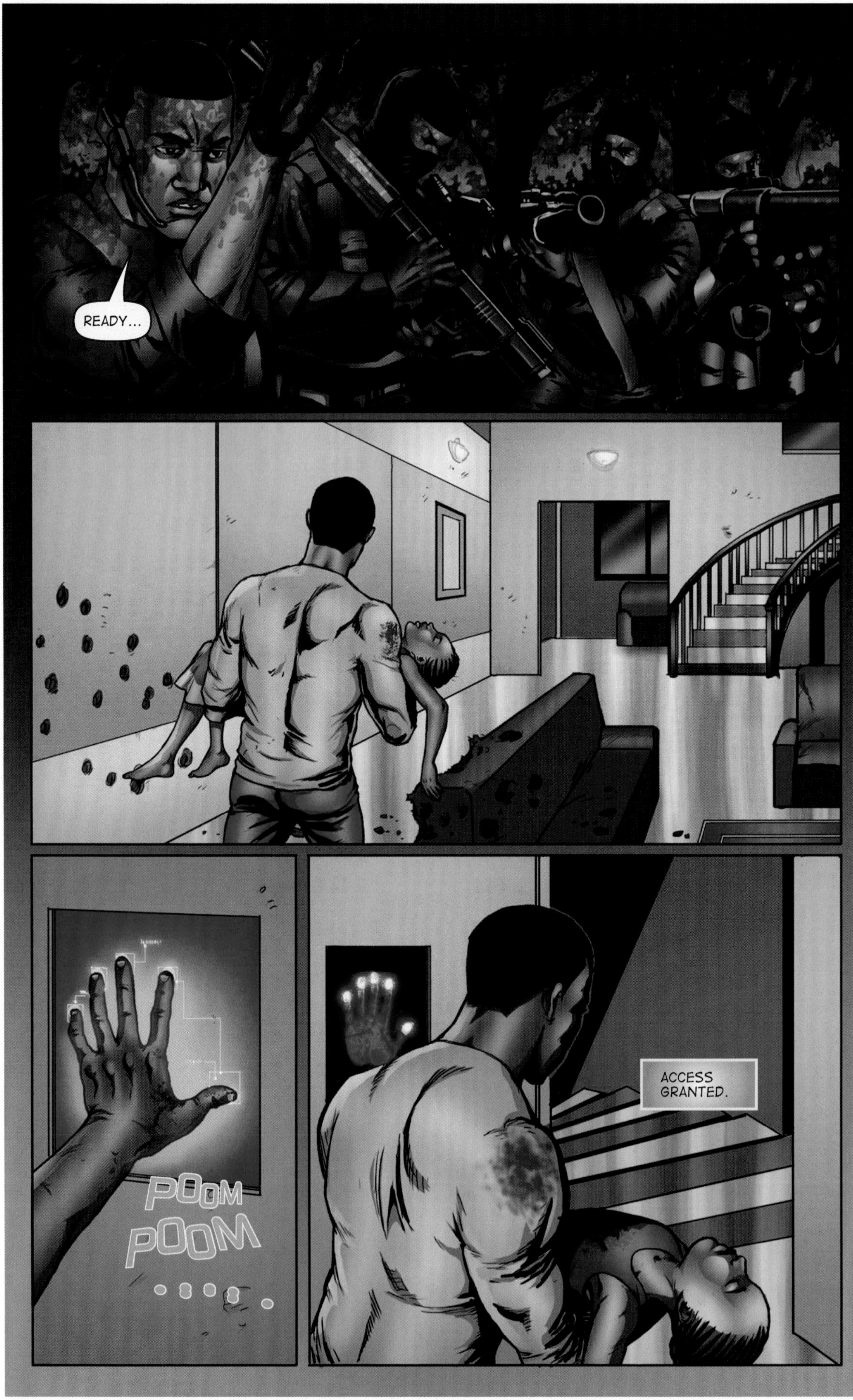
READY...
POOM
POOM
ACCESS GRANTED.

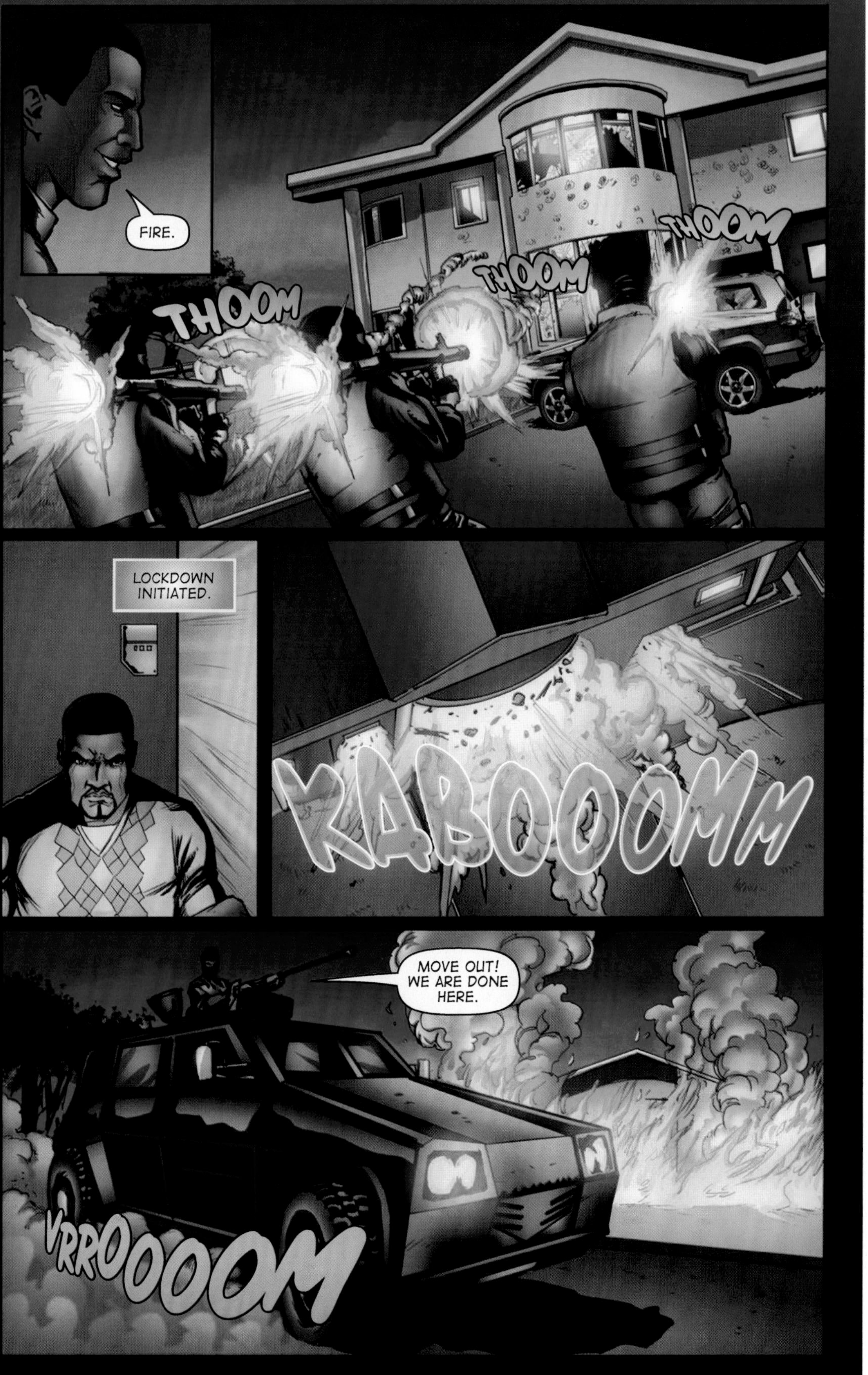
FIRE.
THOOM
THOOM
THOOM
LOCKDOWN INITIATED.
KABOOOMM
MOVE OUT! WE ARE DONE HERE.
VRROOOOM

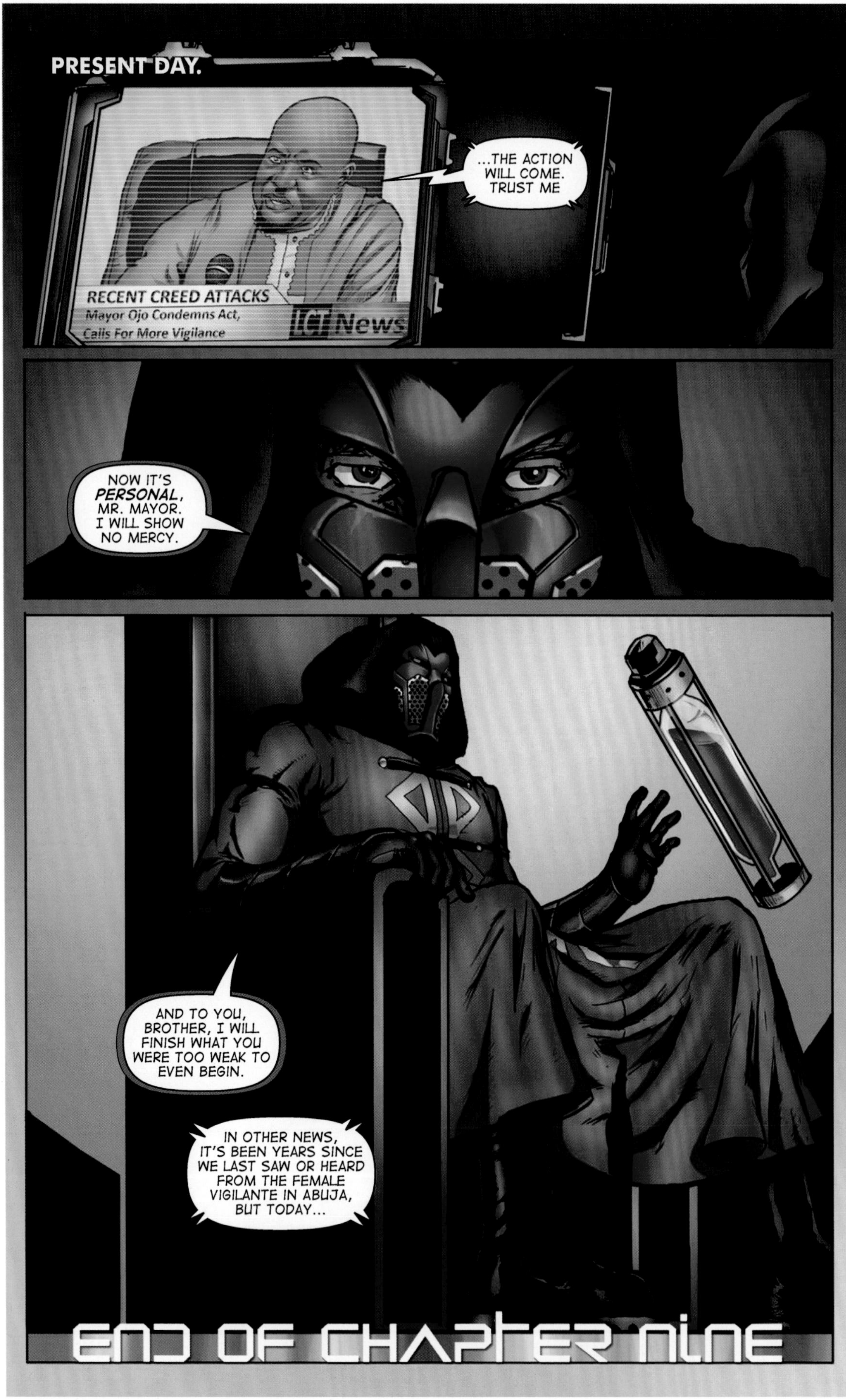
PRESENT DAY.
RECENT CREED ATTACKS
Mayor Ojo Condemns Act,
Calls For More Vigilance
LCT News
...THE ACTION WILL COME. TRUST ME
NOW IT'S *PERSONAL*, MR. MAYOR. I WILL SHOW NO MERCY.
AND TO YOU, BROTHER, I WILL FINISH WHAT YOU WERE TOO WEAK TO EVEN BEGIN.
IN OTHER NEWS, IT'S BEEN YEARS SINCE WE LAST SAW OR HEARD FROM THE FEMALE VIGILANTE IN ABUJA, BUT TODAY...
END OF CHAPTER NINE

FAN ART BY OZO MICHAEL EZEOGU

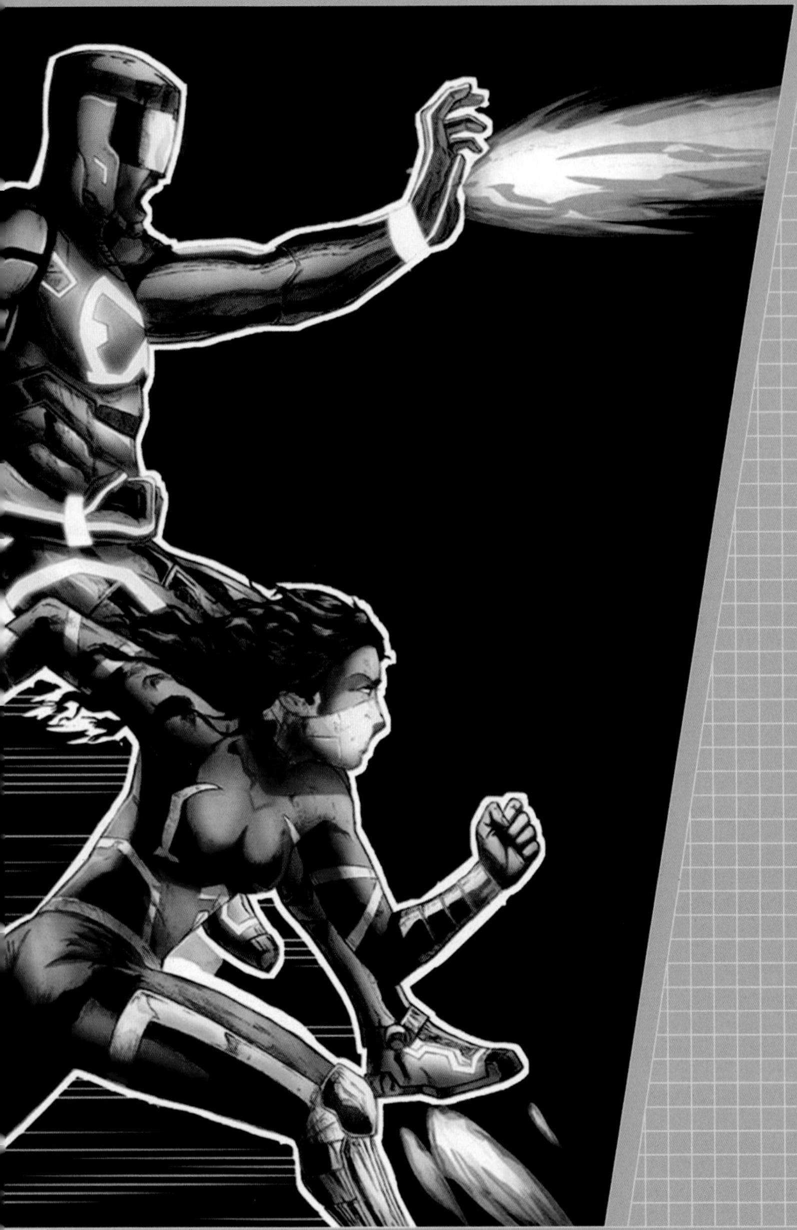

Wale Williams (EXO) and Zahra Martins (Fury) have known each other since they were kids. Both attended the same secondary school (high school) and karate classes where they constantly traded the number one and two spots over several years. They were high school sweethearts and stayed together until their relationship ended after Wale left Lagoon City.

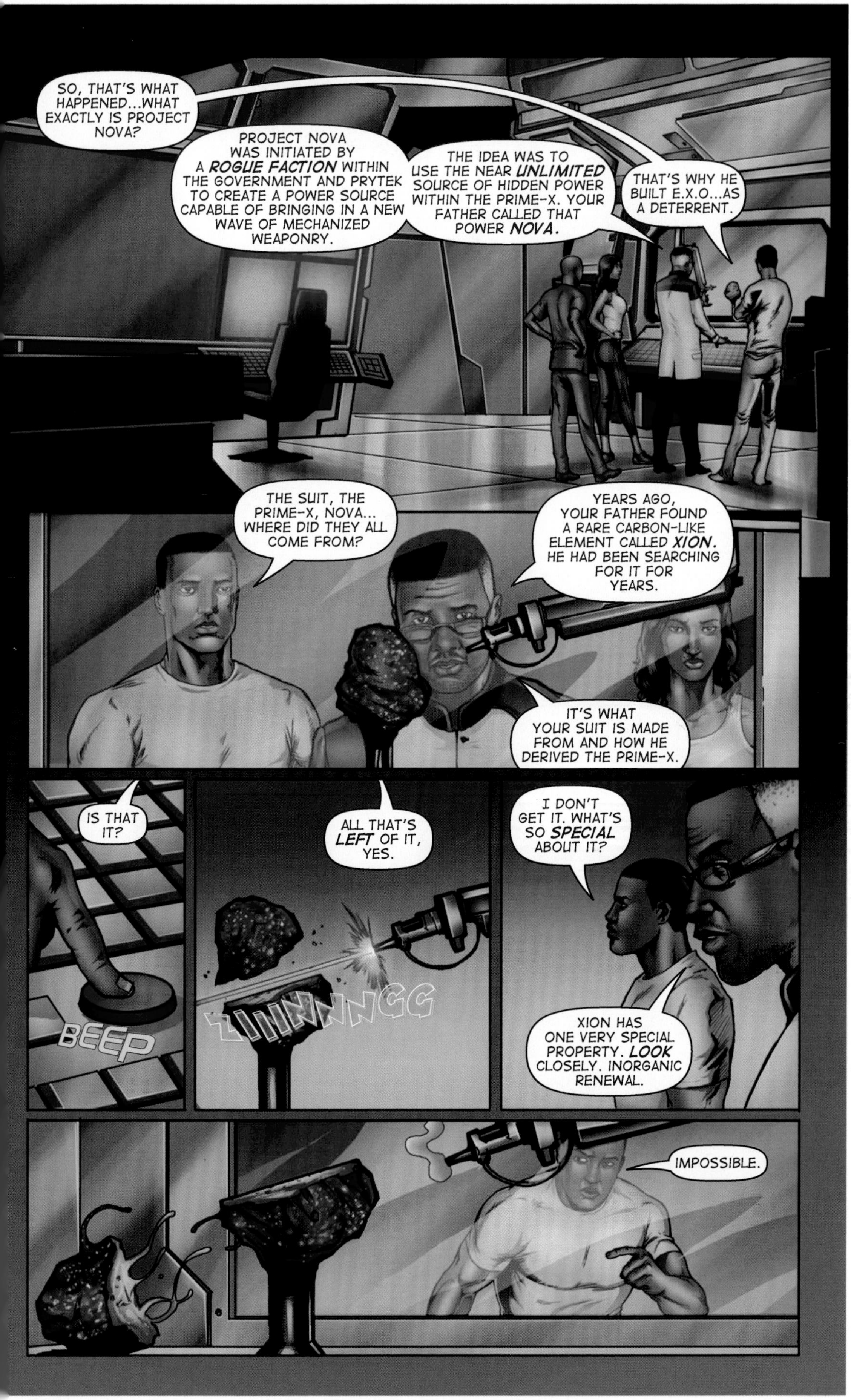
SO, THAT'S WHAT HAPPENED...WHAT EXACTLY IS PROJECT NOVA?
PROJECT NOVA WAS INITIATED BY A ROGUE FACTION WITHIN THE GOVERNMENT AND PRYTEK TO CREATE A POWER SOURCE CAPABLE OF BRINGING IN A NEW WAVE OF MECHANIZED WEAPONRY.
THE IDEA WAS TO USE THE NEAR UNLIMITED SOURCE OF HIDDEN POWER WITHIN THE PRIME-X. YOUR FATHER CALLED THAT POWER NOVA.
THAT'S WHY HE BUILT E.X.O...AS A DETERRENT.
THE SUIT, THE PRIME-X, NOVA... WHERE DID THEY ALL COME FROM?
YEARS AGO, YOUR FATHER FOUND A RARE CARBON-LIKE ELEMENT CALLED XION. HE HAD BEEN SEARCHING FOR IT FOR YEARS.
IT'S WHAT YOUR SUIT IS MADE FROM AND HOW HE DERIVED THE PRIME-X.
IS THAT IT?
BEEP
ALL THAT'S LEFT OF IT, YES.
ZIIINNNGG
I DON'T GET IT. WHAT'S SO SPECIAL ABOUT IT?
XION HAS ONE VERY SPECIAL PROPERTY. LOOK CLOSELY. INORGANIC RENEWAL.
IMPOSSIBLE.

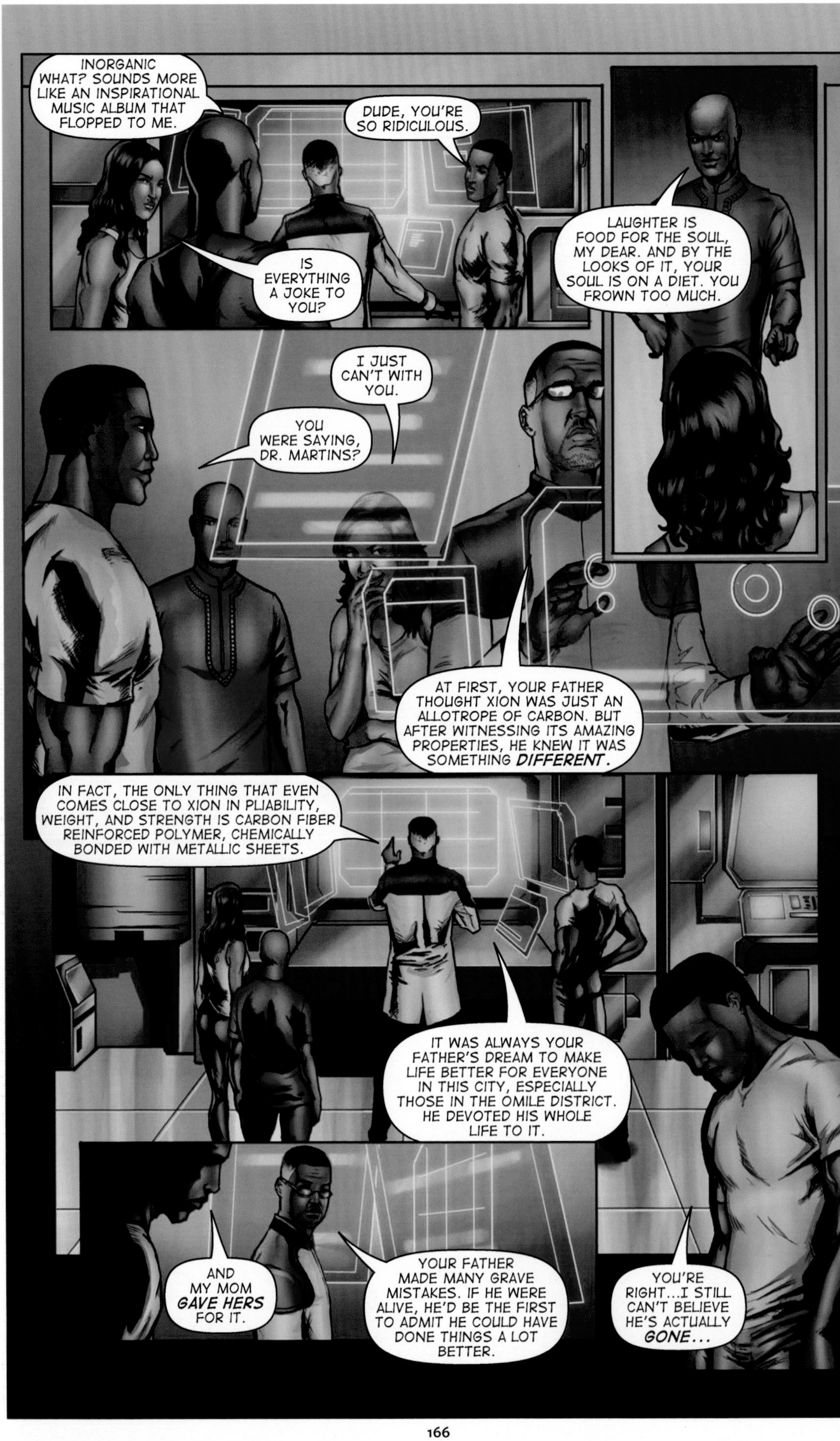
INORGANIC WHAT? SOUNDS MORE LIKE AN INSPIRATIONAL MUSIC ALBUM THAT FLOPPED TO ME.
DUDE, YOU'RE SO RIDICULOUS.
IS EVERYTHING A JOKE TO YOU?
LAUGHTER IS FOOD FOR THE SOUL, MY DEAR. AND BY THE LOOKS OF IT, YOUR SOUL IS ON A DIET. YOU FROWN TOO MUCH.
I JUST CAN'T WITH YOU.
YOU WERE SAYING, DR. MARTINS?
AT FIRST, YOUR FATHER THOUGHT XION WAS JUST AN ALLOTROPE OF CARBON. BUT AFTER WITNESSING ITS AMAZING PROPERTIES, HE KNEW IT WAS SOMETHING ***DIFFERENT***.
IN FACT, THE ONLY THING THAT EVEN COMES CLOSE TO XION IN PLIABILITY, WEIGHT, AND STRENGTH IS CARBON FIBER REINFORCED POLYMER, CHEMICALLY BONDED WITH METALLIC SHEETS.
IT WAS ALWAYS YOUR FATHER'S DREAM TO MAKE LIFE BETTER FOR EVERYONE IN THIS CITY, ESPECIALLY THOSE IN THE OMILE DISTRICT. HE DEVOTED HIS WHOLE LIFE TO IT.
AND MY MOM ***GAVE HERS*** FOR IT.
YOUR FATHER MADE MANY GRAVE MISTAKES. IF HE WERE ALIVE, HE'D BE THE FIRST TO ADMIT HE COULD HAVE DONE THINGS A LOT BETTER.
YOU'RE RIGHT...I STILL CAN'T BELIEVE HE'S ACTUALLY ***GONE...***

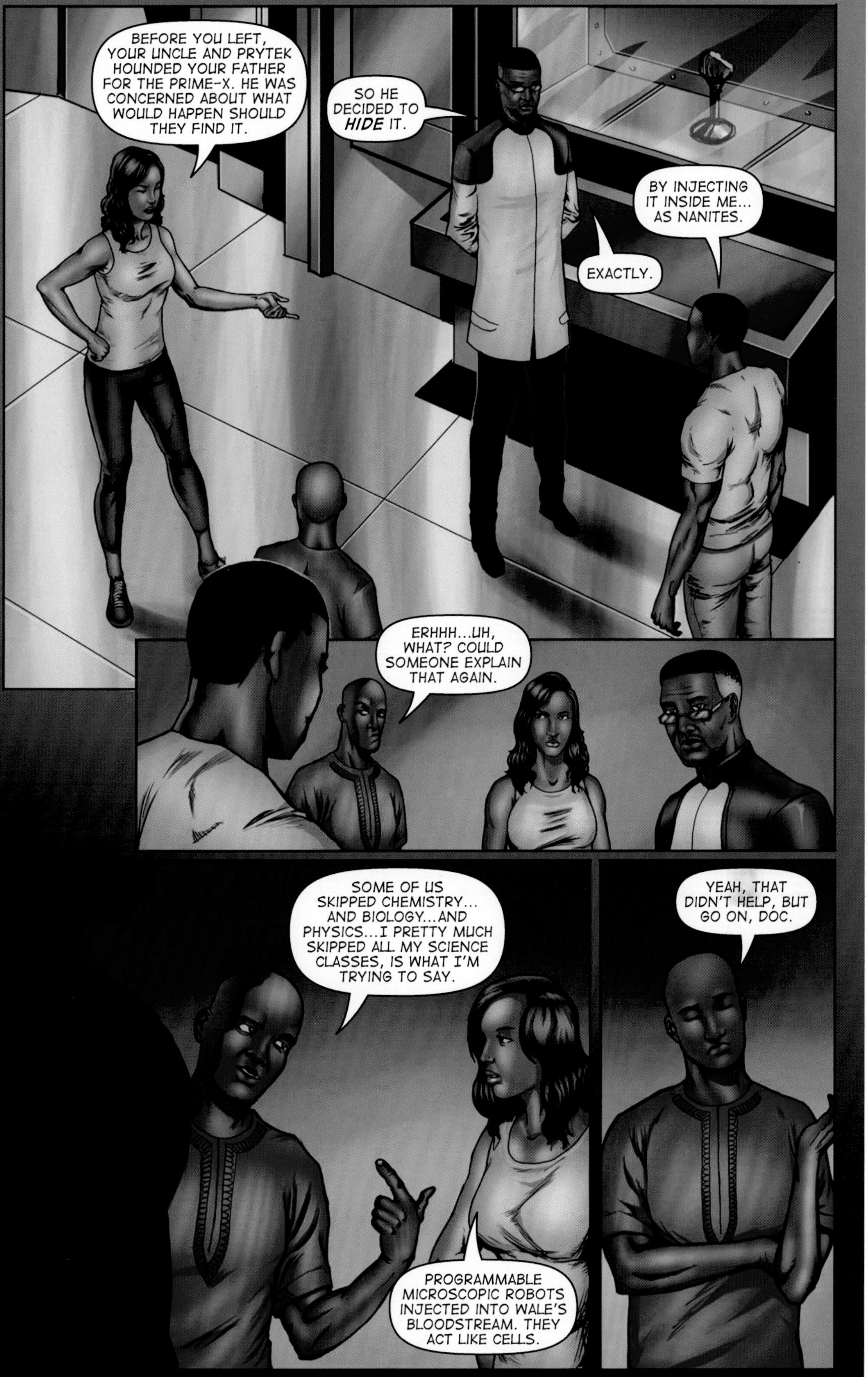
BEFORE YOU LEFT, YOUR UNCLE AND PRYTEK HOUNDED YOUR FATHER FOR THE PRIME-X. HE WAS CONCERNED ABOUT WHAT WOULD HAPPEN SHOULD THEY FIND IT.
SO HE DECIDED TO HIDE IT.
BY INJECTING IT INSIDE ME... AS NANITES.
EXACTLY.
ERHHH...UH, WHAT? COULD SOMEONE EXPLAIN THAT AGAIN.
SOME OF US SKIPPED CHEMISTRY... AND BIOLOGY...AND PHYSICS...I PRETTY MUCH SKIPPED ALL MY SCIENCE CLASSES, IS WHAT I'M TRYING TO SAY.
PROGRAMMABLE MICROSCOPIC ROBOTS INJECTED INTO WALE'S BLOODSTREAM. THEY ACT LIKE CELLS.
YEAH, THAT DIDN'T HELP, BUT GO ON, DOC.

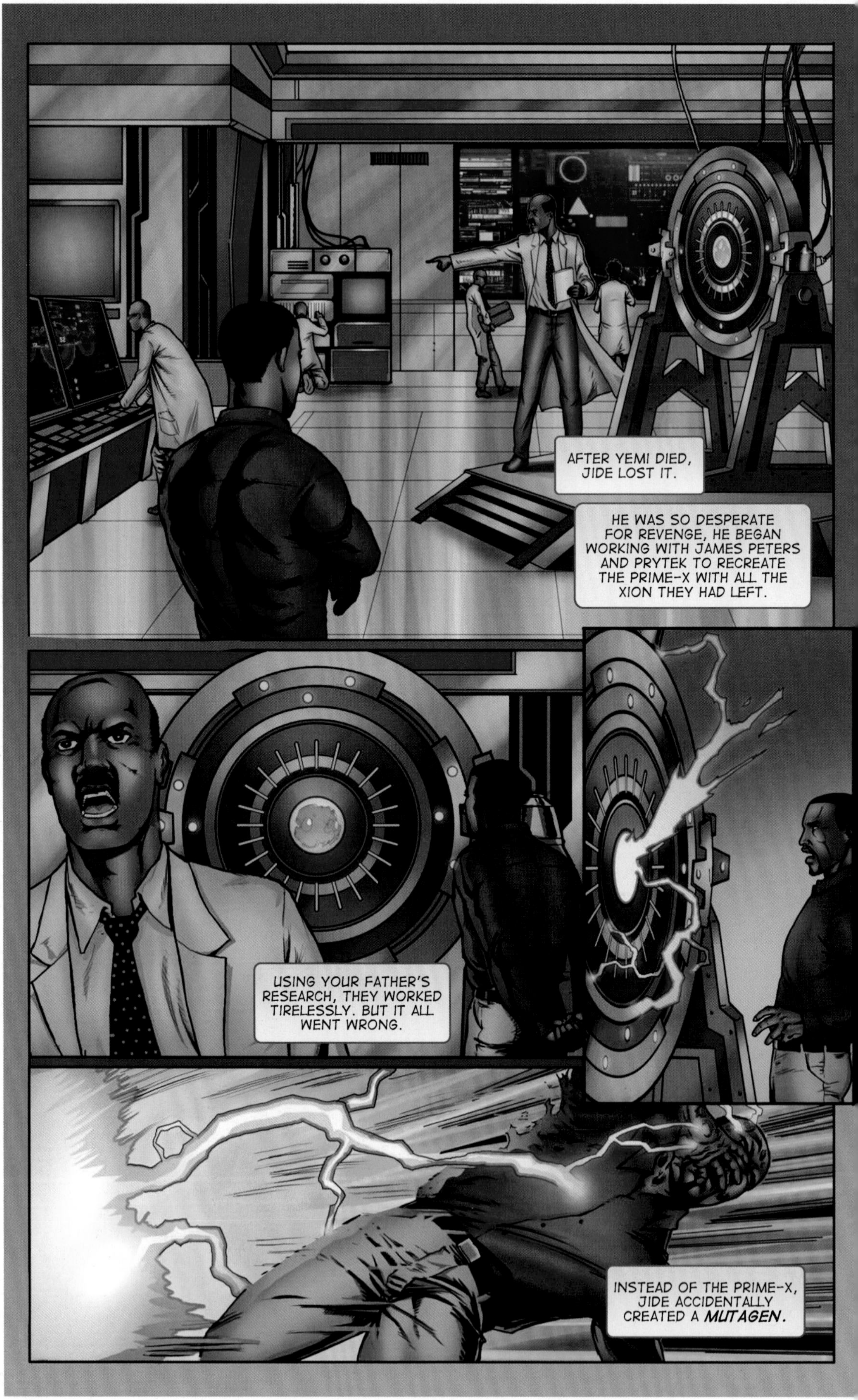
AFTER YEMI DIED, JIDE LOST IT.
HE WAS SO DESPERATE FOR REVENGE, HE BEGAN WORKING WITH JAMES PETERS AND PRYTEK TO RECREATE THE PRIME-X WITH ALL THE XION THEY HAD LEFT.
USING YOUR FATHER'S RESEARCH, THEY WORKED TIRELESSLY. BUT IT ALL WENT WRONG.
INSTEAD OF THE PRIME-X, JIDE ACCIDENTALLY CREATED A *MUTAGEN*.

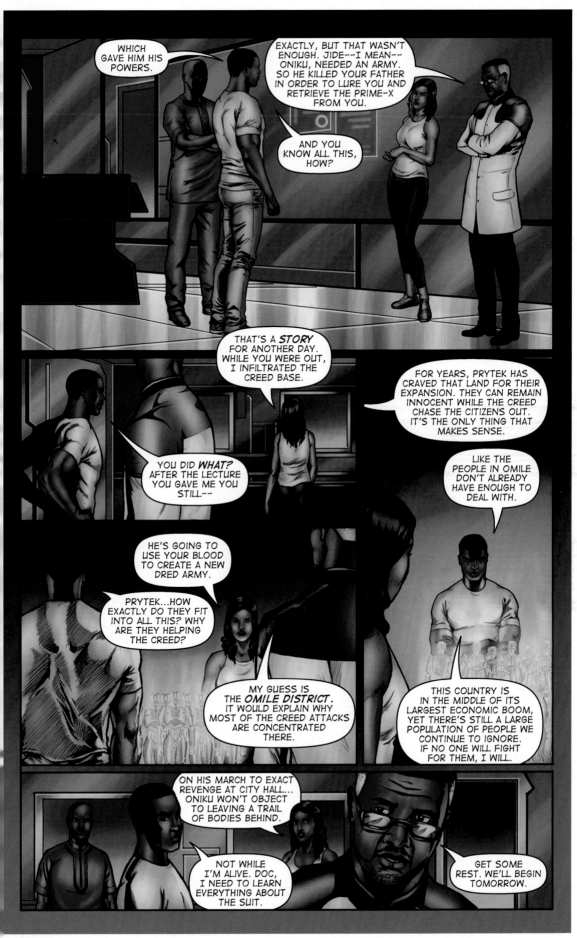

WHICH GAVE HIM HIS POWERS.

EXACTLY, BUT THAT WASN'T ENOUGH. JIDE--I MEAN-- ONIKU, NEEDED AN ARMY. SO HE KILLED YOUR FATHER IN ORDER TO LURE YOU AND RETRIEVE THE PRIME-X FROM YOU.

AND YOU KNOW ALL THIS, HOW?

THAT'S A *STORY* FOR ANOTHER DAY. WHILE YOU WERE OUT, I INFILTRATED THE CREED BASE.

FOR YEARS, PRYTEK HAS CRAVED THAT LAND FOR THEIR EXPANSION. THEY CAN REMAIN INNOCENT WHILE THE CREED CHASE THE CITIZENS OUT. IT'S THE ONLY THING THAT MAKES SENSE.

YOU DID *WHAT?* AFTER THE LECTURE YOU GAVE ME YOU STILL--

LIKE THE PEOPLE IN OMILE DON'T ALREADY HAVE ENOUGH TO DEAL WITH.

HE'S GOING TO USE YOUR BLOOD TO CREATE A NEW DRED ARMY.

PRYTEK...HOW EXACTLY DO THEY FIT INTO ALL THIS? WHY ARE THEY HELPING THE CREED?

MY GUESS IS THE *OMILE DISTRICT.* IT WOULD EXPLAIN WHY MOST OF THE CREED ATTACKS ARE CONCENTRATED THERE.

THIS COUNTRY IS IN THE MIDDLE OF ITS LARGEST ECONOMIC BOOM, YET THERE'S STILL A LARGE POPULATION OF PEOPLE WE CONTINUE TO IGNORE. IF NO ONE WILL FIGHT FOR THEM, I WILL.

ON HIS MARCH TO EXACT REVENGE AT CITY HALL.... ONIKU WON'T OBJECT TO LEAVING A TRAIL OF BODIES BEHIND.

NOT WHILE I'M ALIVE. DOC, I NEED TO LEARN EVERYTHING ABOUT THE SUIT.

GET SOME REST. WE'LL BEGIN TOMORROW.

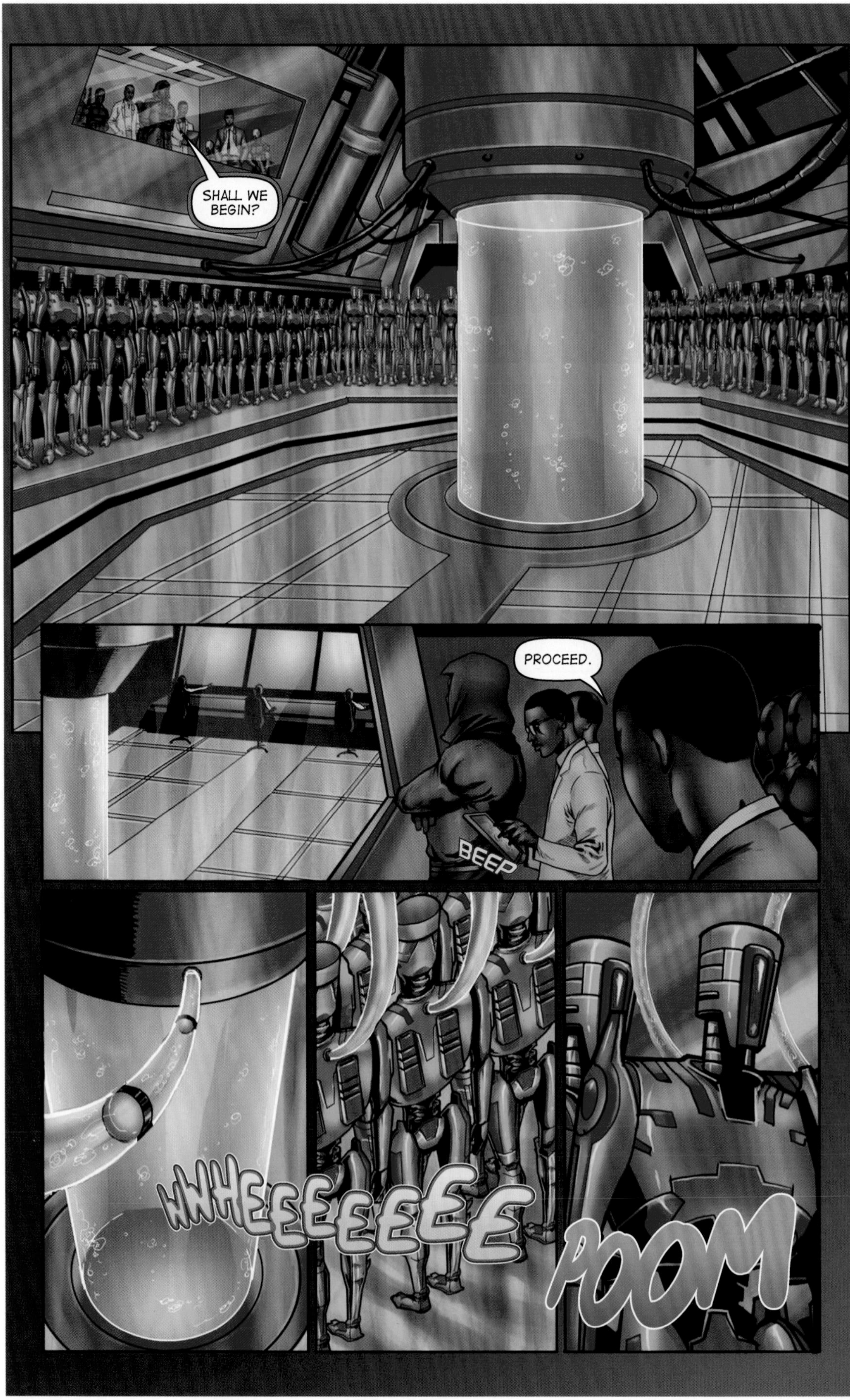
SHALL WE BEGIN?
PROCEED.
BEEP
WHEEEEEEE
POOM

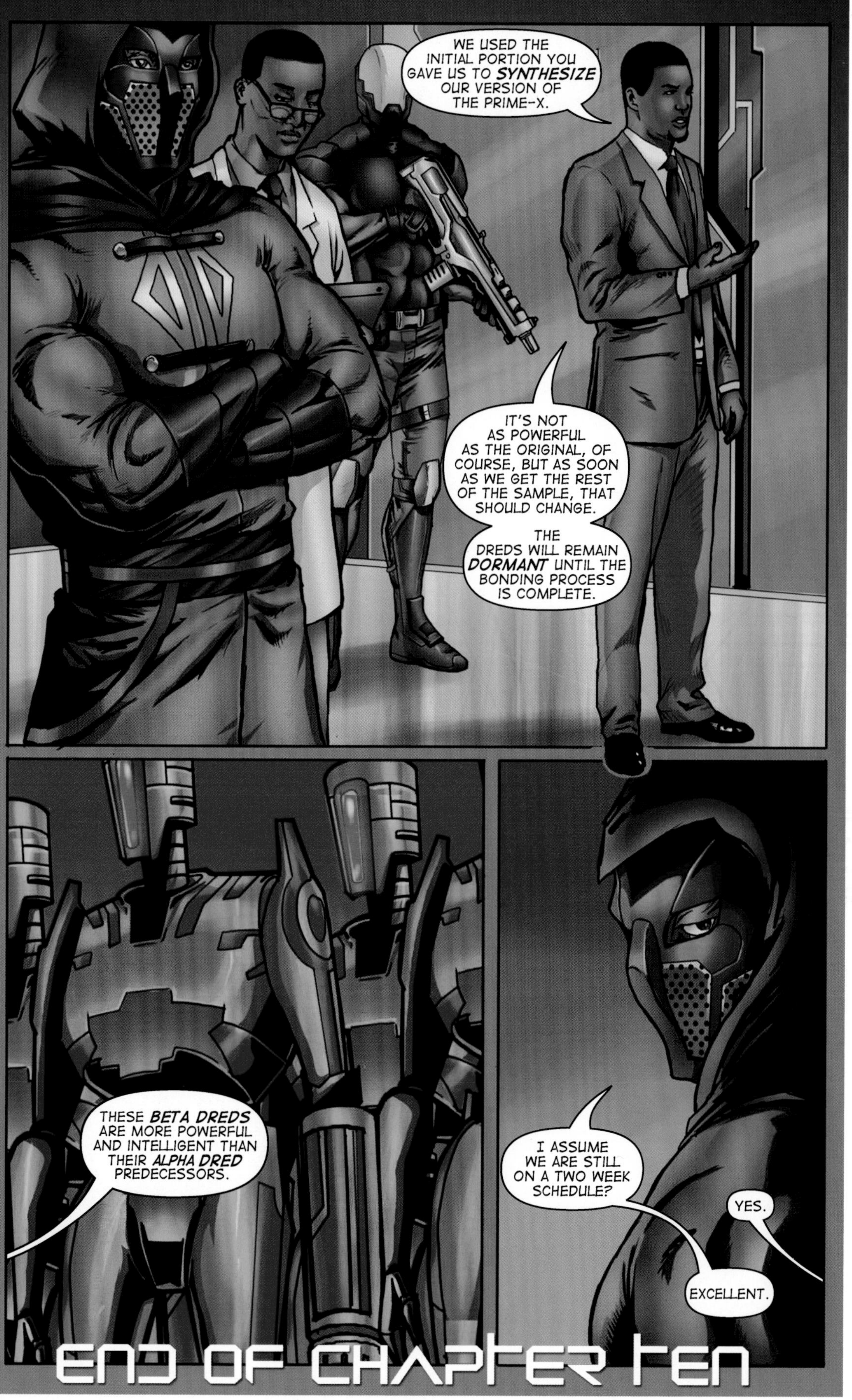
WE USED THE INITIAL PORTION YOU GAVE US TO SYNTHESIZE OUR VERSION OF THE PRIME-X.
IT'S NOT AS POWERFUL AS THE ORIGINAL, OF COURSE, BUT AS SOON AS WE GET THE REST OF THE SAMPLE, THAT SHOULD CHANGE.
THE DREDS WILL REMAIN DORMANT UNTIL THE BONDING PROCESS IS COMPLETE.
THESE BETA DREDS ARE MORE POWERFUL AND INTELLIGENT THAN THEIR ALPHA DRED PREDECESSORS.
I ASSUME WE ARE STILL ON A TWO WEEK SCHEDULE?
YES.
EXCELLENT.
END OF CHAPTER TEN

FAN ART BY CHIMA KALU

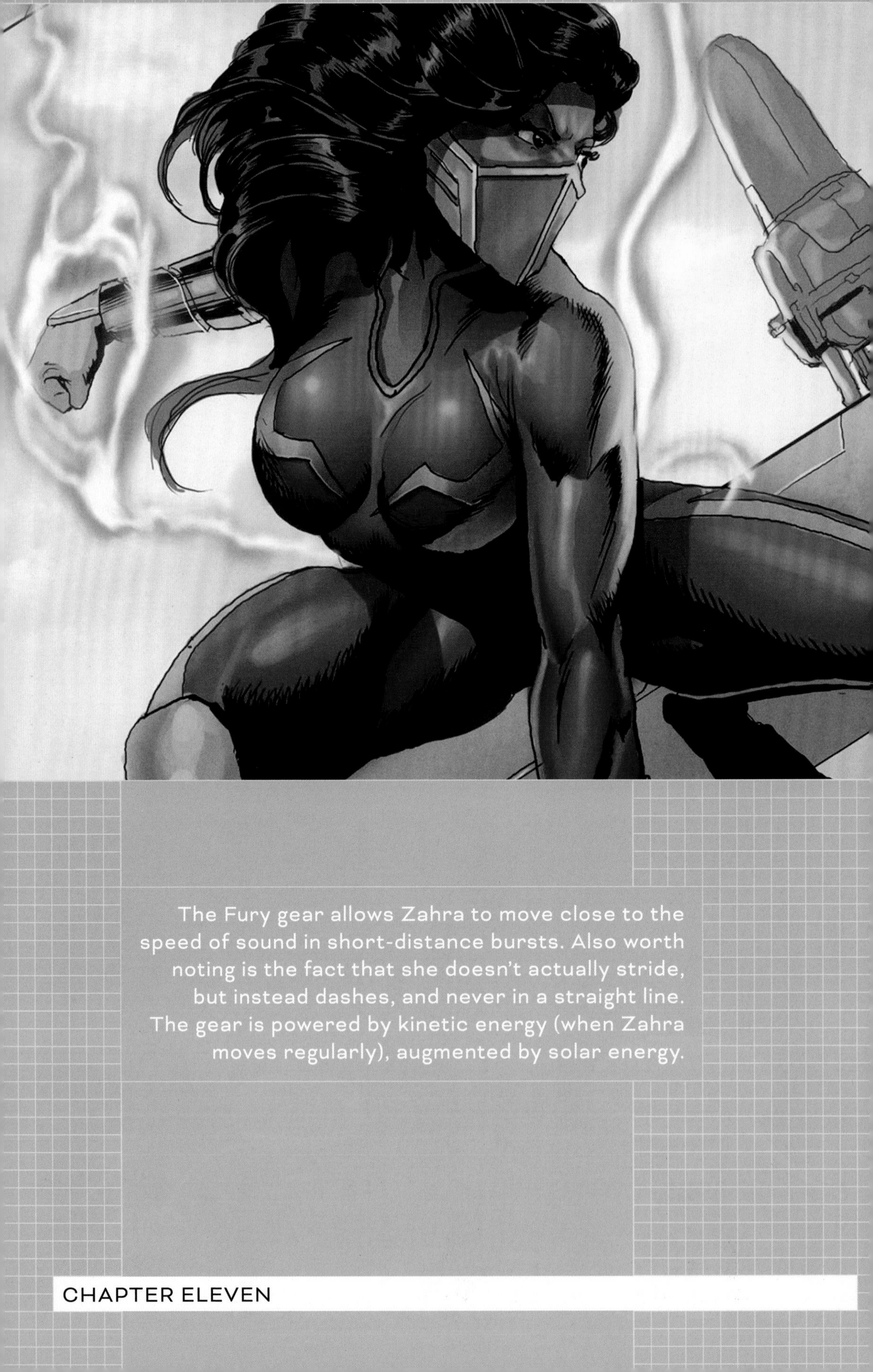

The Fury gear allows Zahra to move close to the speed of sound in short-distance bursts. Also worth noting is the fact that she doesn't actually stride, but instead dashes, and never in a straight line. The gear is powered by kinetic energy (when Zahra moves regularly), augmented by solar energy.

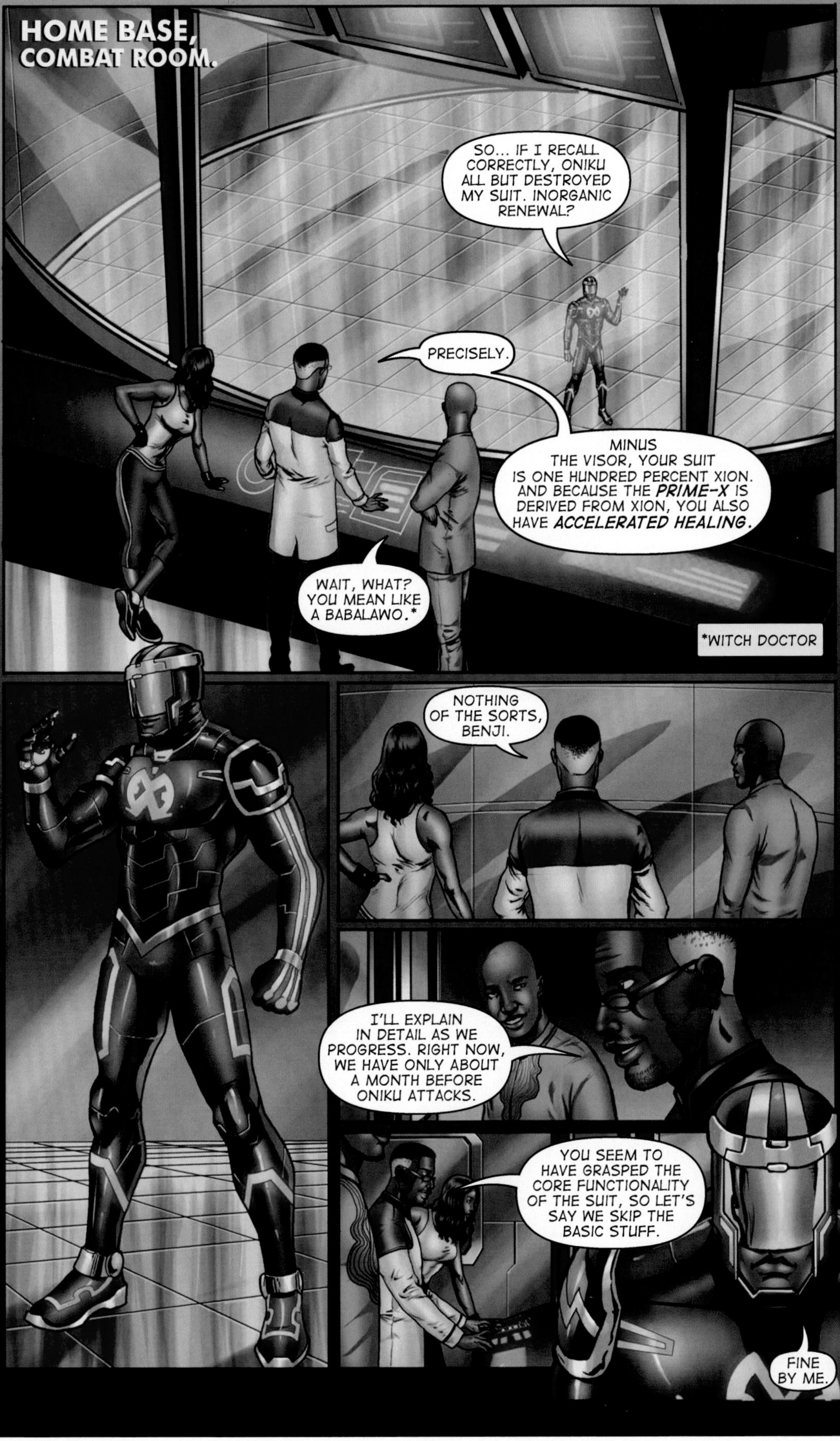
HOME BASE,
COMBAT ROOM.
SO... IF I RECALL CORRECTLY, ONIKU ALL BUT DESTROYED MY SUIT. INORGANIC RENEWAL?
PRECISELY.
MINUS THE VISOR, YOUR SUIT IS ONE HUNDRED PERCENT XION. AND BECAUSE THE PRIME-X IS DERIVED FROM XION, YOU ALSO HAVE ACCELERATED HEALING.
WAIT, WHAT? YOU MEAN LIKE A BABALAWO.*
*WITCH DOCTOR
NOTHING OF THE SORTS, BENJI.
I'LL EXPLAIN IN DETAIL AS WE PROGRESS. RIGHT NOW, WE HAVE ONLY ABOUT A MONTH BEFORE ONIKU ATTACKS.
YOU SEEM TO HAVE GRASPED THE CORE FUNCTIONALITY OF THE SUIT, SO LET'S SAY WE SKIP THE BASIC STUFF.
FINE BY ME.

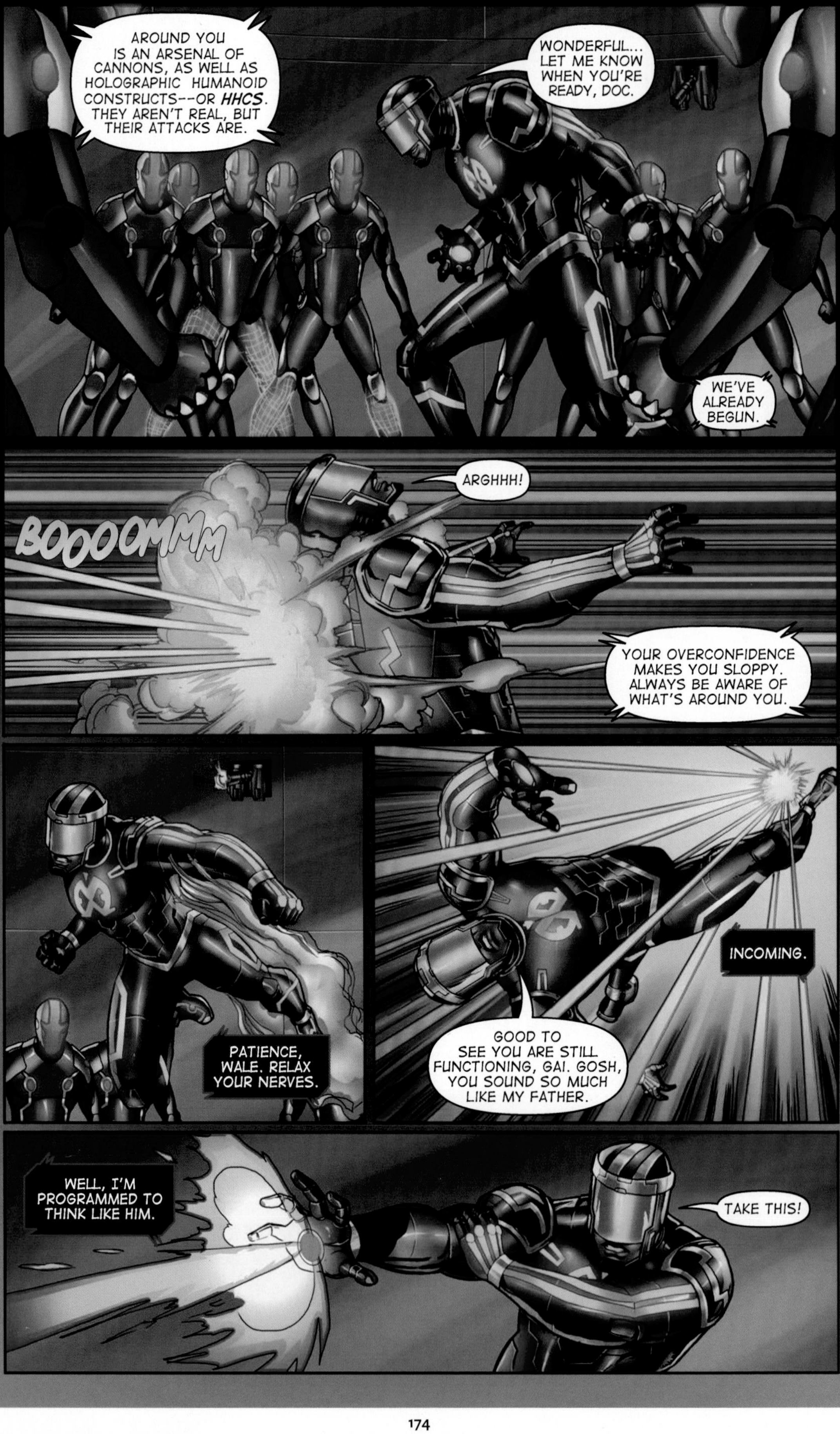
AROUND YOU IS AN ARSENAL OF CANNONS, AS WELL AS HOLOGRAPHIC HUMANOID CONSTRUCTS--OR HHCS. THEY AREN'T REAL, BUT THEIR ATTACKS ARE.
WONDERFUL... LET ME KNOW WHEN YOU'RE READY, DOC.
WE'VE ALREADY BEGUN.
ARGHHH!
BOOOOMMM
YOUR OVERCONFIDENCE MAKES YOU SLOPPY. ALWAYS BE AWARE OF WHAT'S AROUND YOU.
PATIENCE, WALE. RELAX YOUR NERVES.
INCOMING.
GOOD TO SEE YOU ARE STILL FUNCTIONING, GAI. GOSH, YOU SOUND SO MUCH LIKE MY FATHER.
WELL, I'M PROGRAMMED TO THINK LIKE HIM.
TAKE THIS!

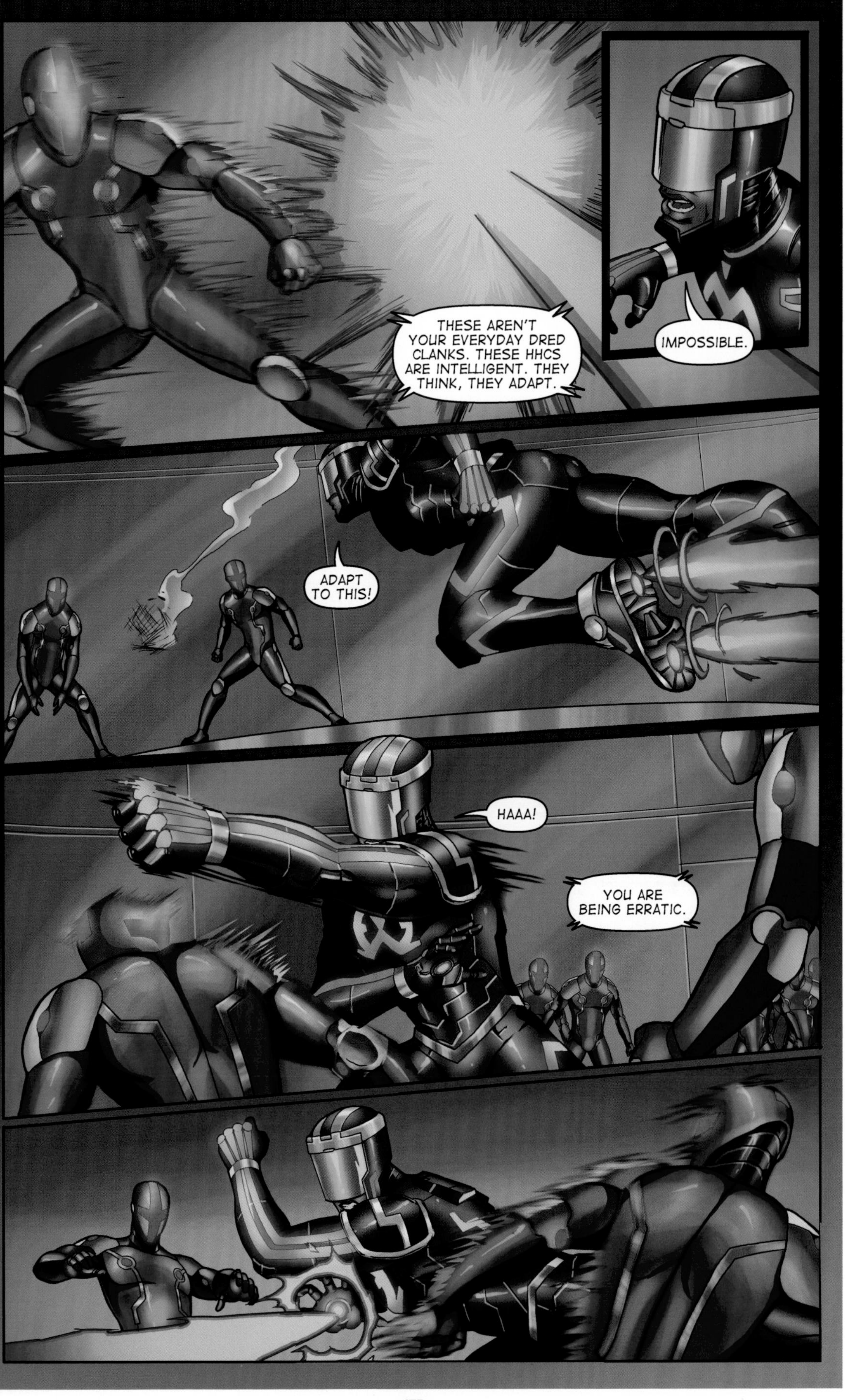
THESE AREN'T YOUR EVERYDAY DRED CLANKS. THESE HHCS ARE INTELLIGENT. THEY THINK, THEY ADAPT.
IMPOSSIBLE.
ADAPT TO THIS!
HAAA!
YOU ARE BEING ERRATIC.

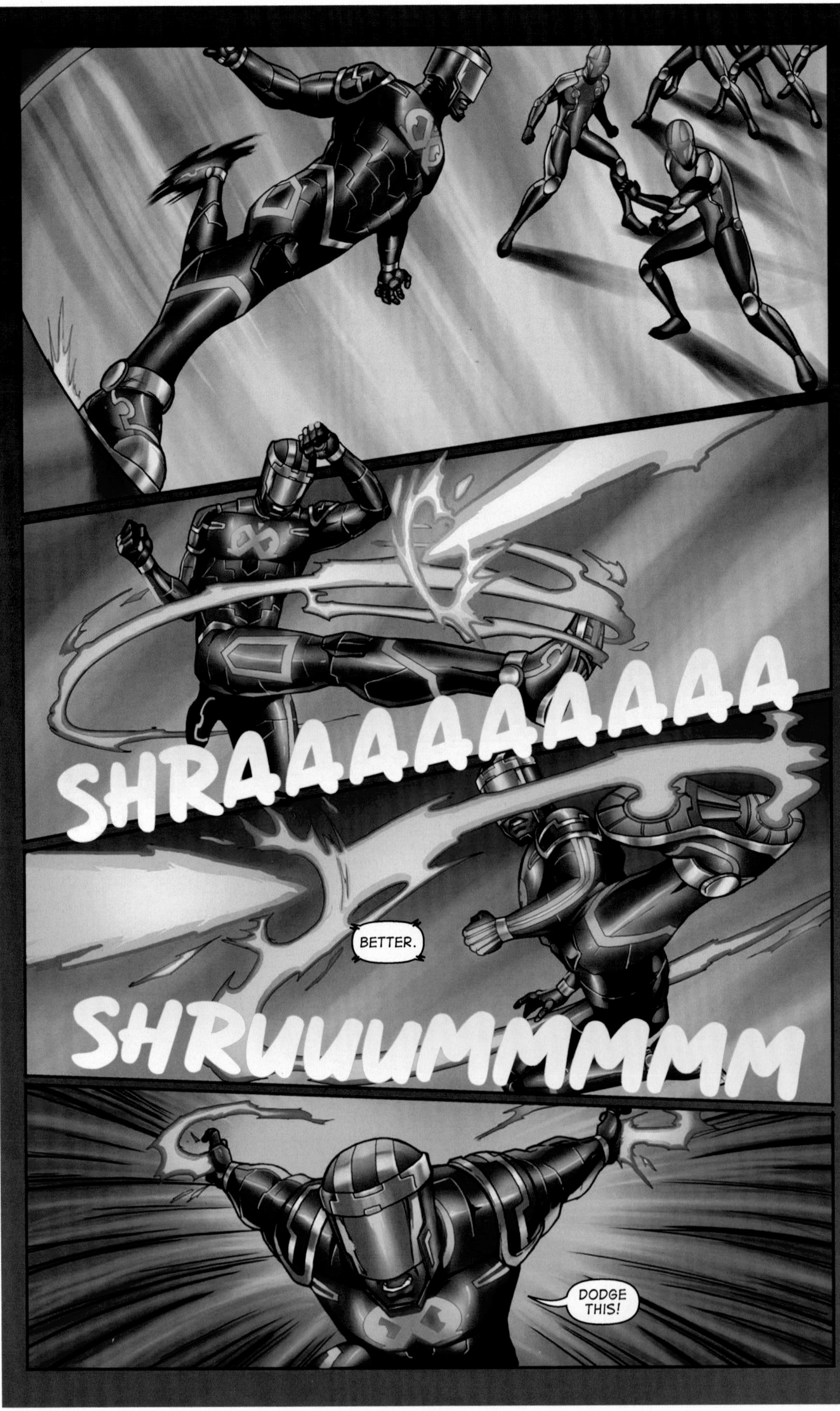
SHRAAAAAAAAAA
BETTER.
SHRUUUMMMMMM
DODGE THIS!

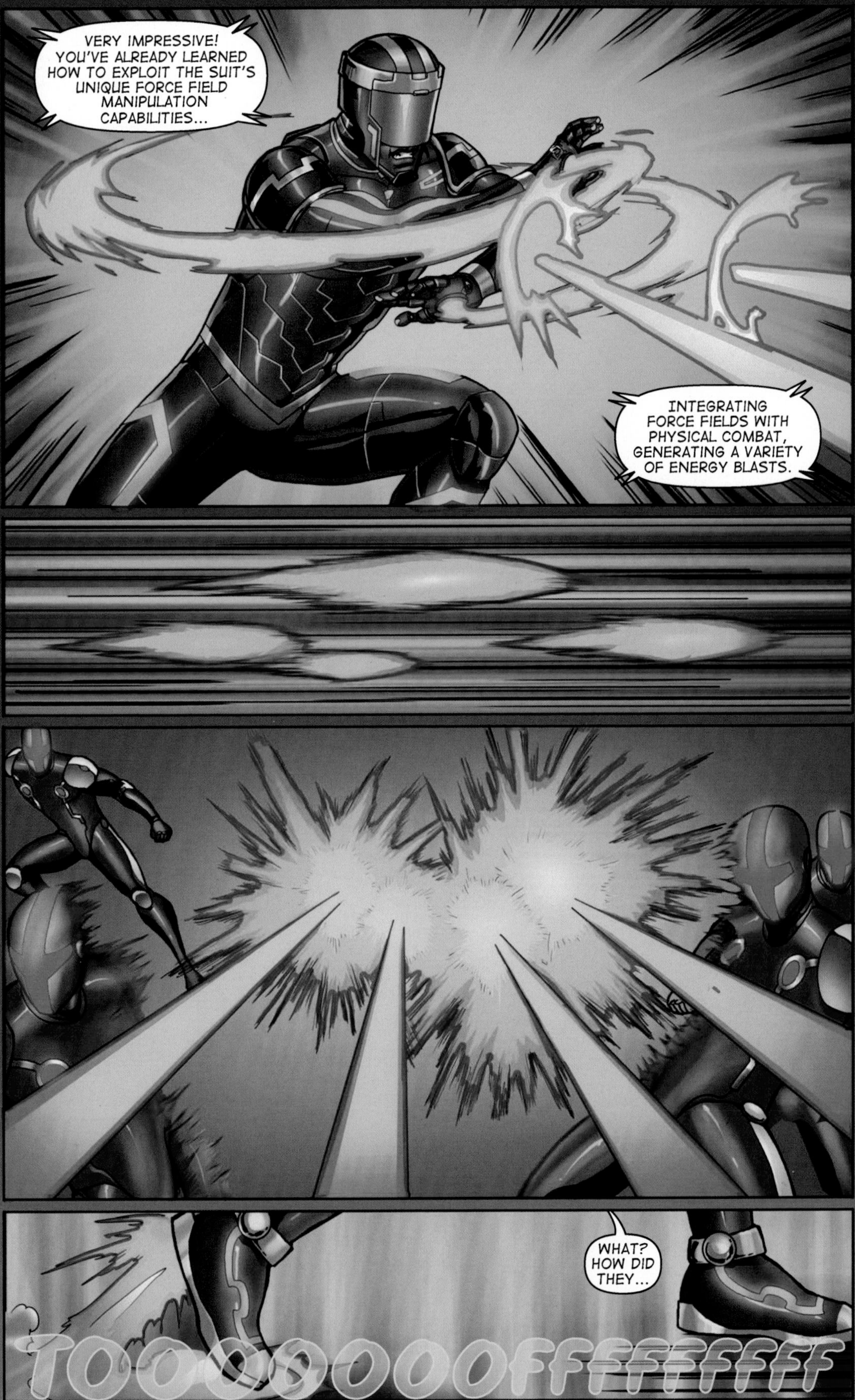
VERY IMPRESSIVE! YOU'VE ALREADY LEARNED HOW TO EXPLOIT THE SUIT'S UNIQUE FORCE FIELD MANIPULATION CAPABILITIES...
INTEGRATING FORCE FIELDS WITH PHYSICAL COMBAT, GENERATING A VARIETY OF ENERGY BLASTS.
WHAT? HOW DID THEY...
TOOOOOOOOOFFFFFFFFFF

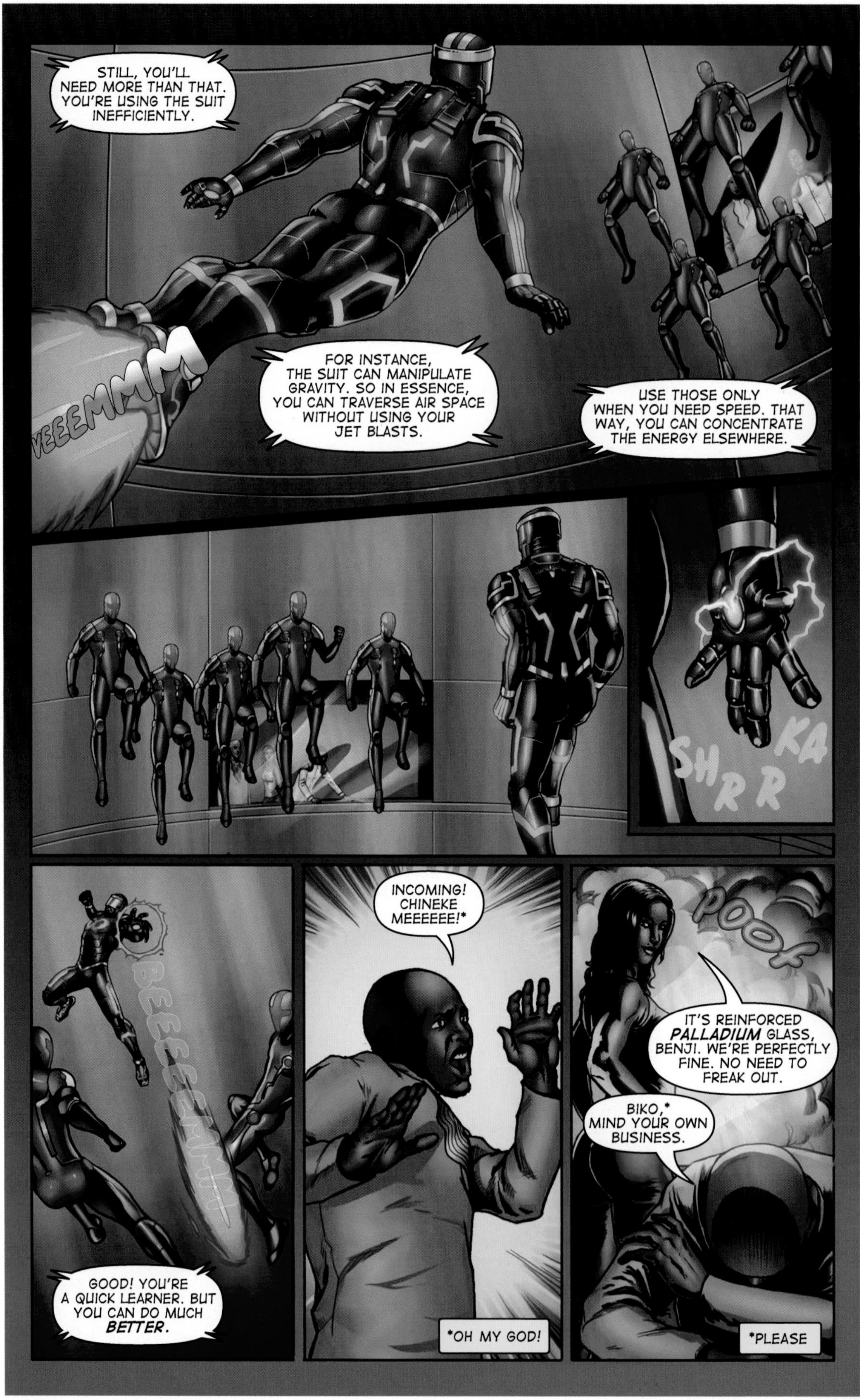
STILL, YOU'LL NEED MORE THAN THAT. YOU'RE USING THE SUIT INEFFICIENTLY.
VEEEMMMM
FOR INSTANCE, THE SUIT CAN MANIPULATE GRAVITY. SO IN ESSENCE, YOU CAN TRAVERSE AIR SPACE WITHOUT USING YOUR JET BLASTS.
USE THOSE ONLY WHEN YOU NEED SPEED. THAT WAY, YOU CAN CONCENTRATE THE ENERGY ELSEWHERE.
SHRR KA
BEEEEMMM
GOOD! YOU'RE A QUICK LEARNER. BUT YOU CAN DO MUCH **BETTER**.
INCOMING! CHINEKE MEEEEEE!*
*OH MY GOD!
POOF
IT'S REINFORCED ***PALLADIUM*** GLASS, BENJI. WE'RE PERFECTLY FINE. NO NEED TO FREAK OUT.
BIKO,* MIND YOUR OWN BUSINESS.
*PLEASE

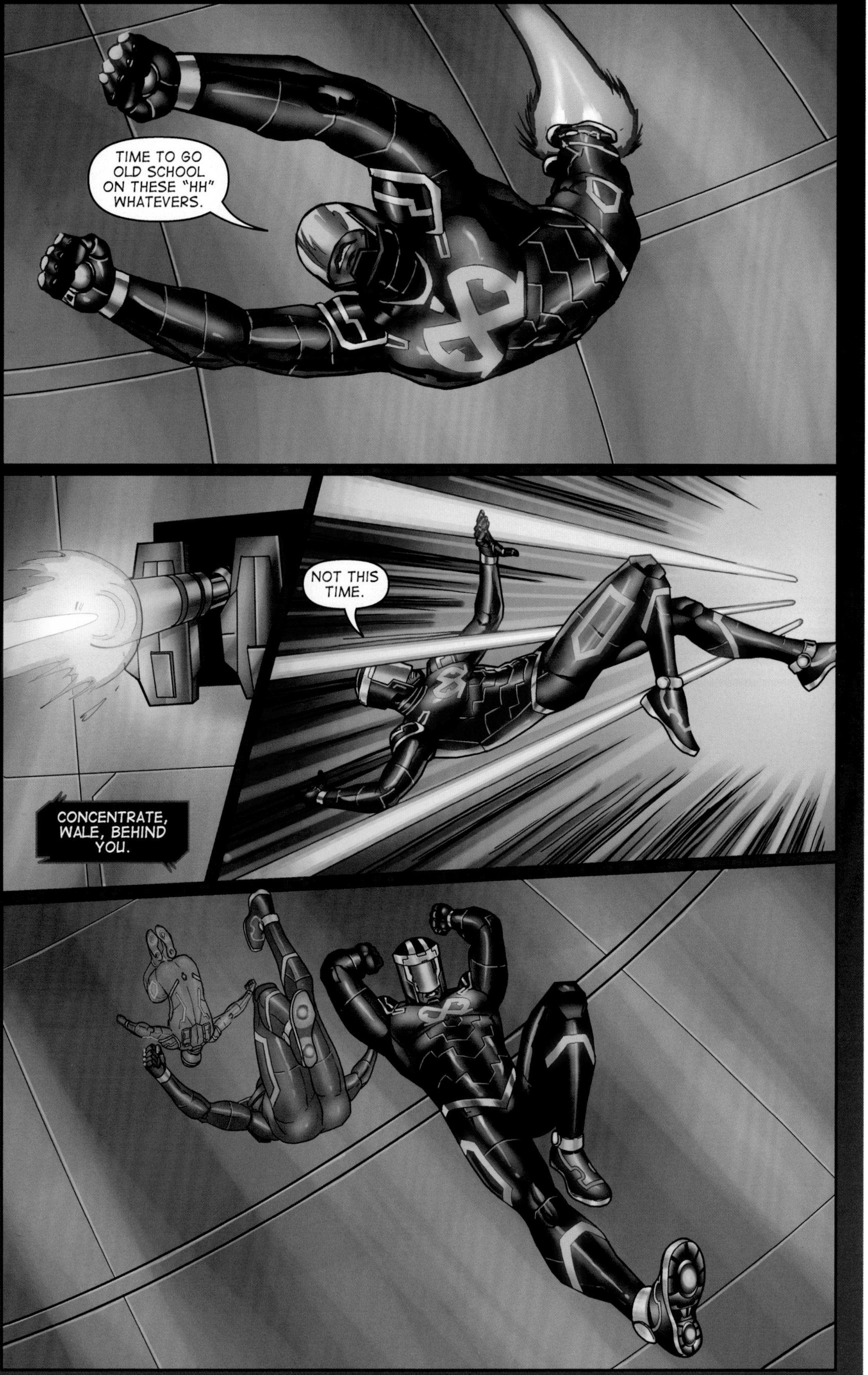
TIME TO GO OLD SCHOOL ON THESE "HH" WHATEVERS.
NOT THIS TIME.
CONCENTRATE, WALE, BEHIND YOU.

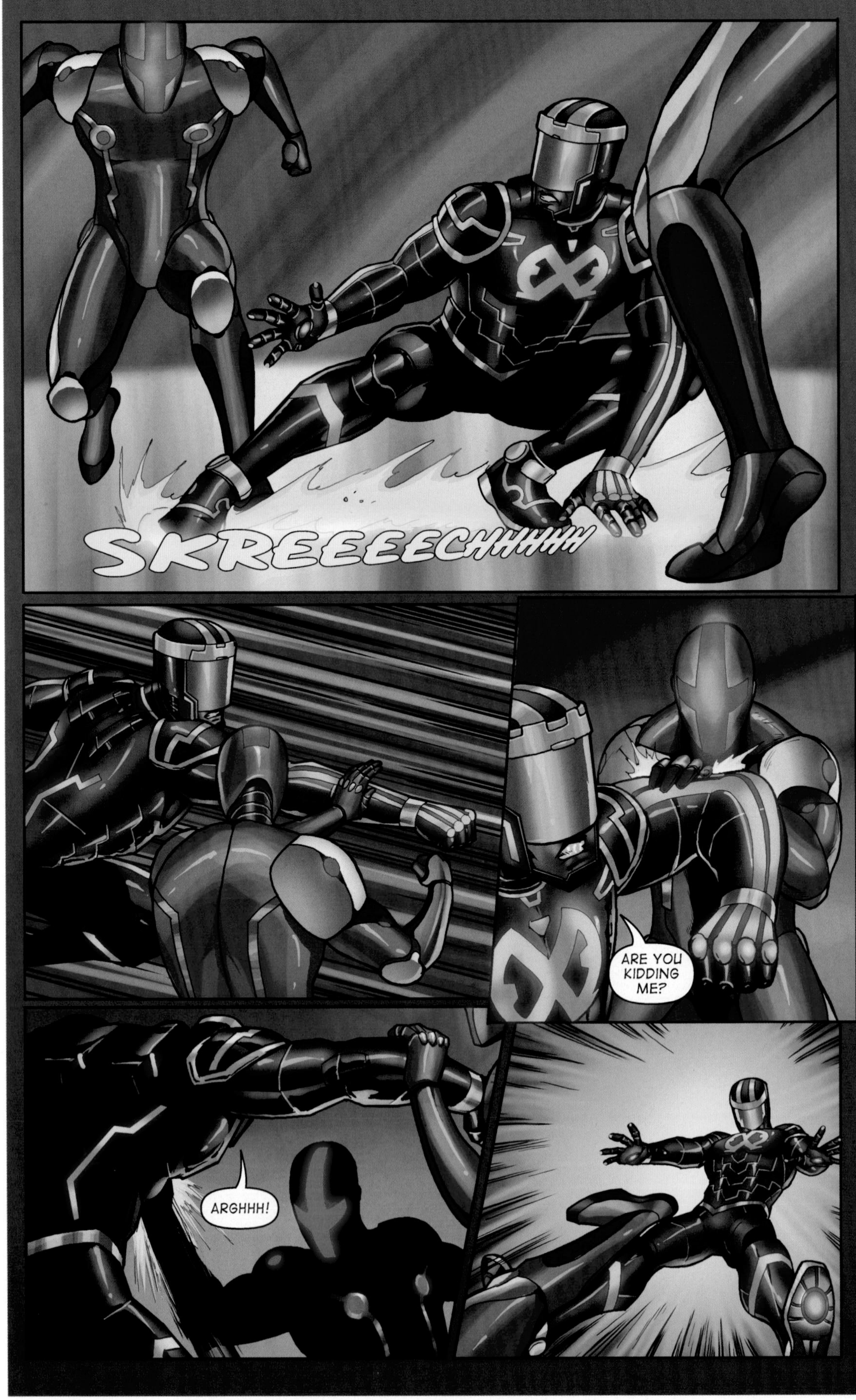
SKREEEEECHHHHHH
ARE YOU KIDDING ME?
ARGHHH!

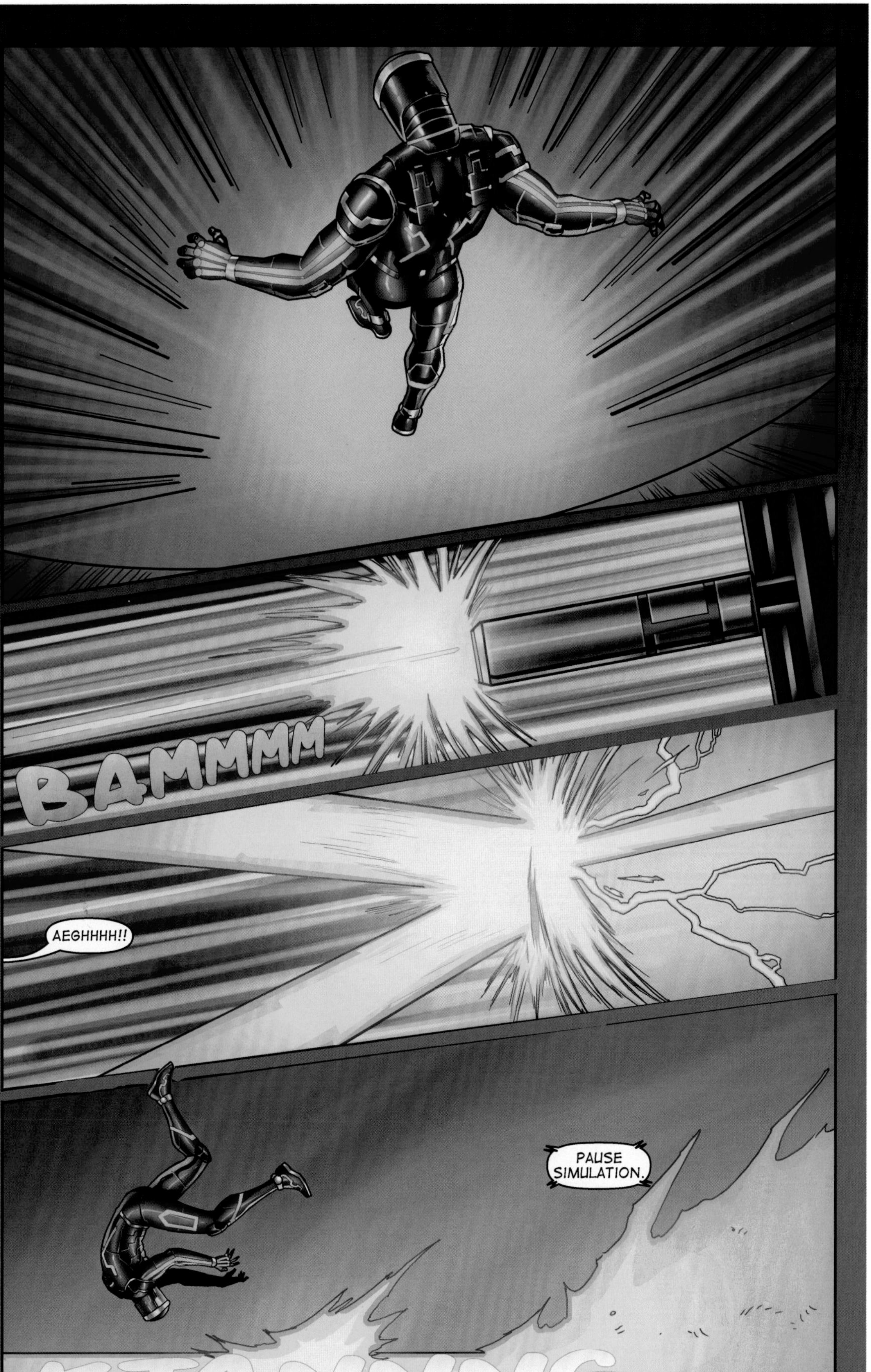
BAMMMM
AEGHHHH!!
PAUSE SIMULATION.
KTANNNG

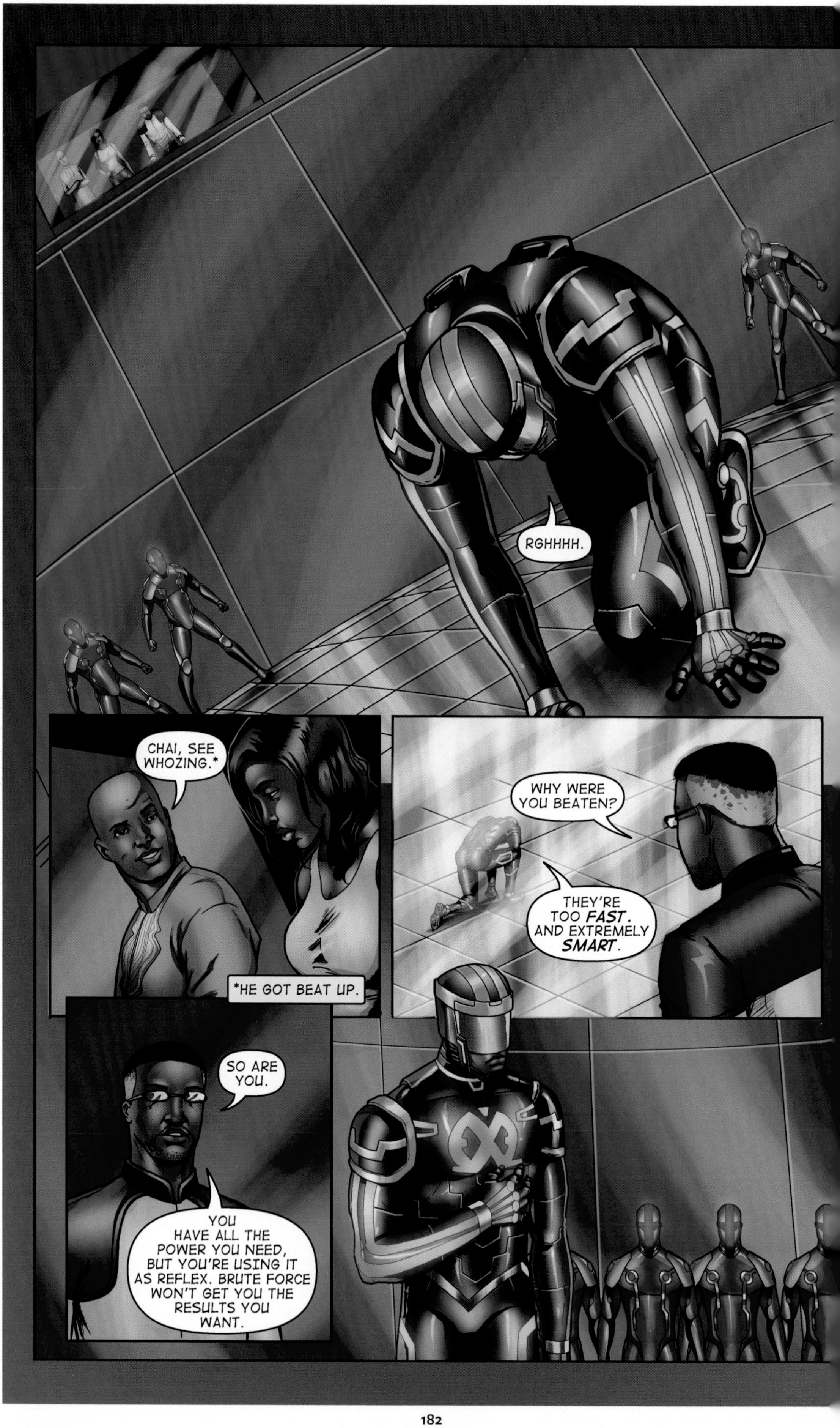
RGHHHH.
CHAI, SEE WHOZING.*
*HE GOT BEAT UP.
WHY WERE YOU BEATEN?
THEY'RE TOO FAST. AND EXTREMELY SMART.
SO ARE YOU.
YOU HAVE ALL THE POWER YOU NEED, BUT YOU'RE USING IT AS REFLEX. BRUTE FORCE WON'T GET YOU THE RESULTS YOU WANT.

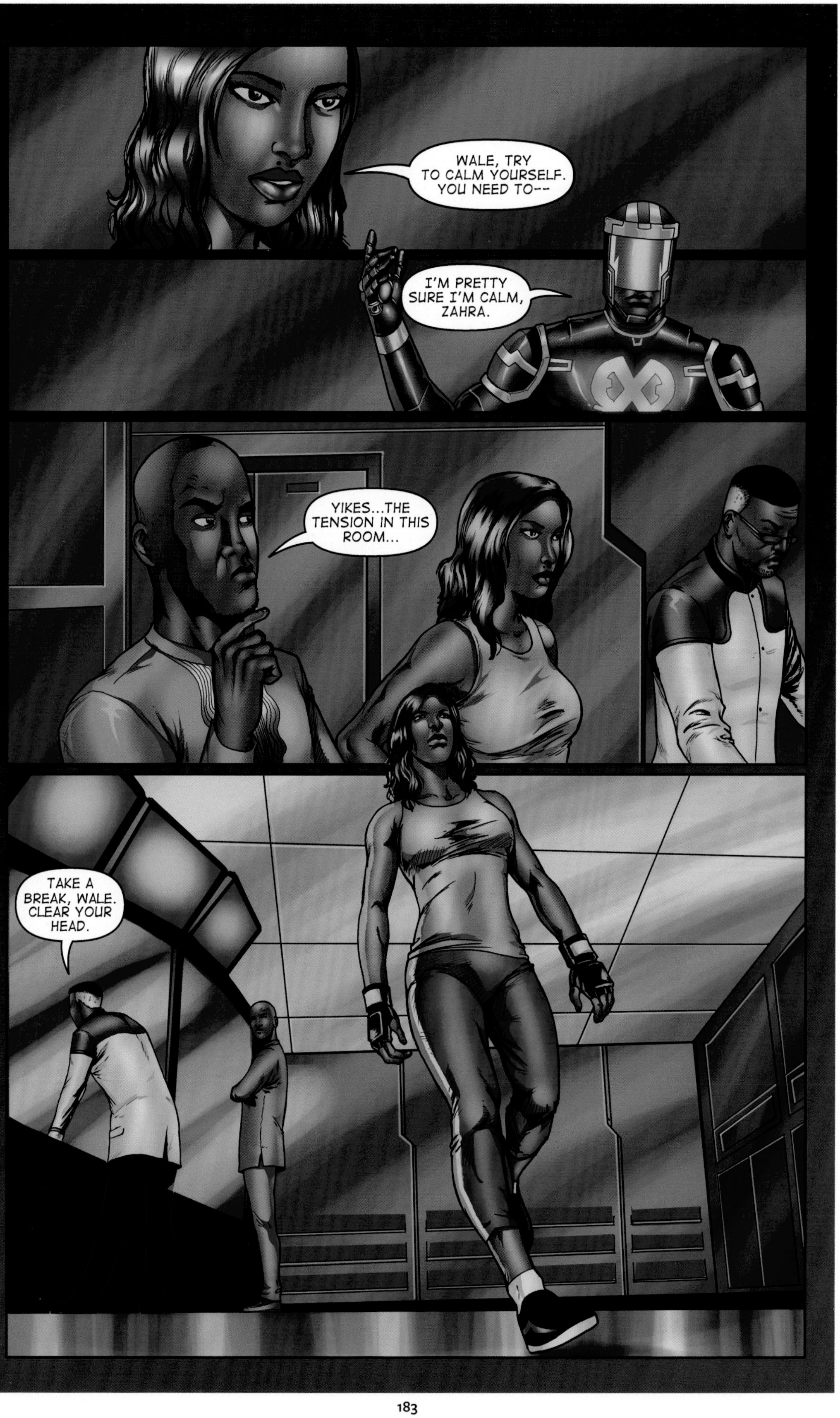
WALE, TRY TO CALM YOURSELF. YOU NEED TO--
I'M PRETTY SURE I'M CALM, ZAHRA.
YIKES...THE TENSION IN THIS ROOM...
TAKE A BREAK, WALE. CLEAR YOUR HEAD.

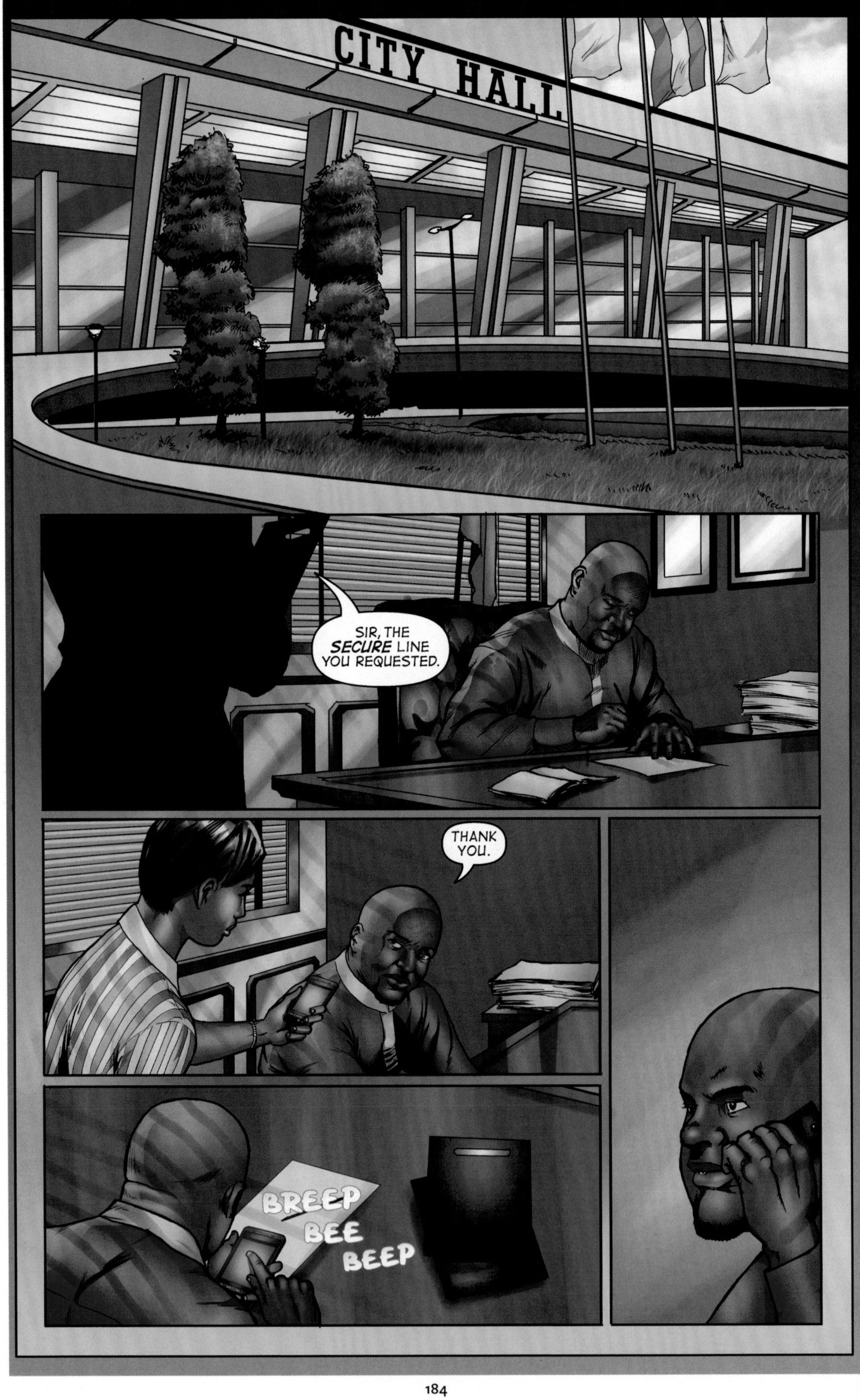
CITY HALL
SIR, THE SECURE LINE YOU REQUESTED.
THANK YOU.
BREEP
BEE
BEEP

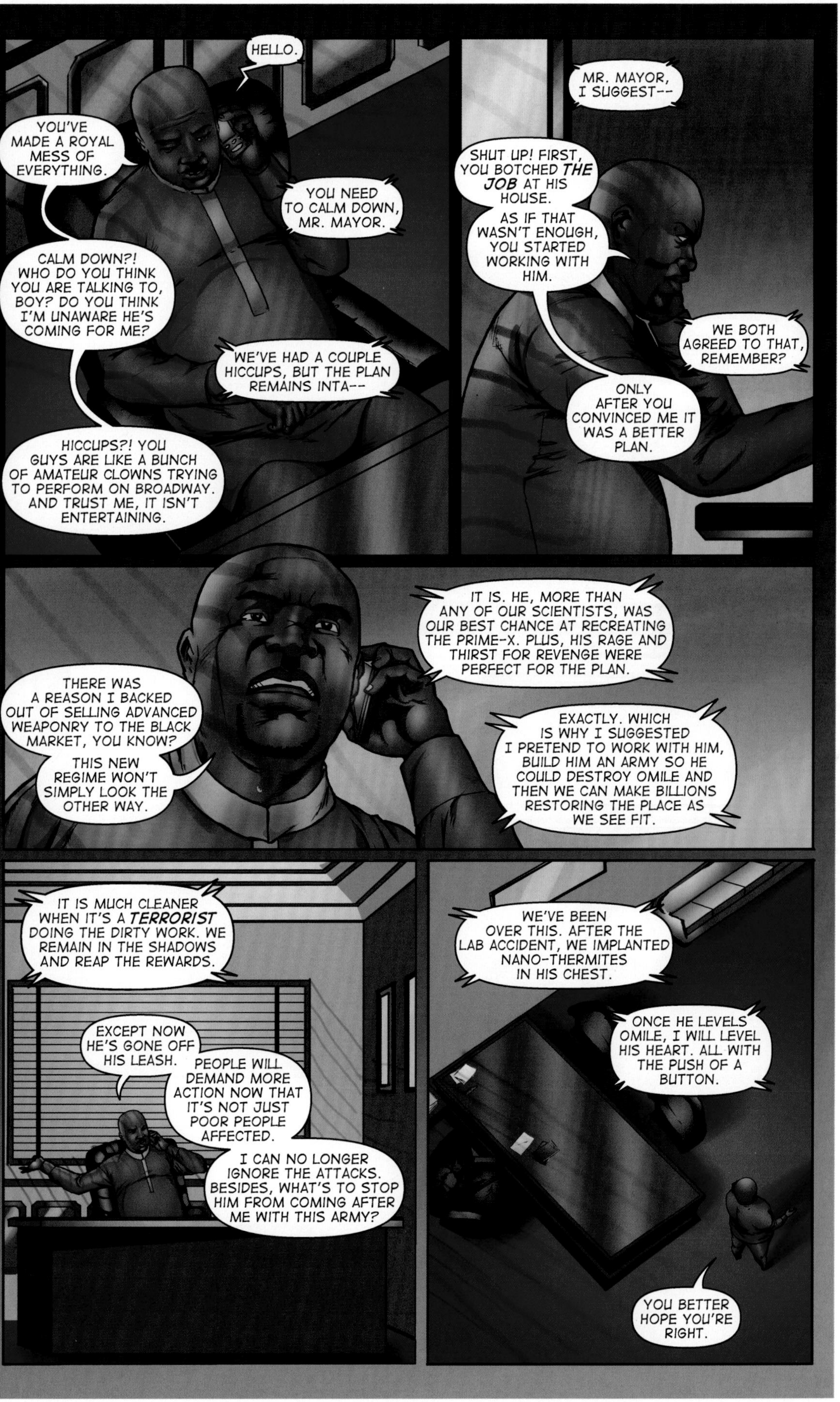
HELLO.
YOU'VE MADE A ROYAL MESS OF EVERYTHING.
YOU NEED TO CALM DOWN, MR. MAYOR.
CALM DOWN?! WHO DO YOU THINK YOU ARE TALKING TO, BOY? DO YOU THINK I'M UNAWARE HE'S COMING FOR ME?
WE'VE HAD A COUPLE HICCUPS, BUT THE PLAN REMAINS INTA--
HICCUPS?! YOU GUYS ARE LIKE A BUNCH OF AMATEUR CLOWNS TRYING TO PERFORM ON BROADWAY. AND TRUST ME, IT ISN'T ENTERTAINING.
MR. MAYOR, I SUGGEST--
SHUT UP! FIRST, YOU BOTCHED THE JOB AT HIS HOUSE.
AS IF THAT WASN'T ENOUGH, YOU STARTED WORKING WITH HIM.
WE BOTH AGREED TO THAT, REMEMBER?
ONLY AFTER YOU CONVINCED ME IT WAS A BETTER PLAN.
IT IS. HE, MORE THAN ANY OF OUR SCIENTISTS, WAS OUR BEST CHANCE AT RECREATING THE PRIME-X. PLUS, HIS RAGE AND THIRST FOR REVENGE WERE PERFECT FOR THE PLAN.
THERE WAS A REASON I BACKED OUT OF SELLING ADVANCED WEAPONRY TO THE BLACK MARKET, YOU KNOW?
THIS NEW REGIME WON'T SIMPLY LOOK THE OTHER WAY.
EXACTLY. WHICH IS WHY I SUGGESTED I PRETEND TO WORK WITH HIM, BUILD HIM AN ARMY SO HE COULD DESTROY OMILE AND THEN WE CAN MAKE BILLIONS RESTORING THE PLACE AS WE SEE FIT.
IT IS MUCH CLEANER WHEN IT'S A TERRORIST DOING THE DIRTY WORK. WE REMAIN IN THE SHADOWS AND REAP THE REWARDS.
EXCEPT NOW HE'S GONE OFF HIS LEASH.
PEOPLE WILL DEMAND MORE ACTION NOW THAT IT'S NOT JUST POOR PEOPLE AFFECTED.
I CAN NO LONGER IGNORE THE ATTACKS. BESIDES, WHAT'S TO STOP HIM FROM COMING AFTER ME WITH THIS ARMY?
WE'VE BEEN OVER THIS. AFTER THE LAB ACCIDENT, WE IMPLANTED NANO-THERMITES IN HIS CHEST.
ONCE HE LEVELS OMILE, I WILL LEVEL HIS HEART. ALL WITH THE PUSH OF A BUTTON.
YOU BETTER HOPE YOU'RE RIGHT.

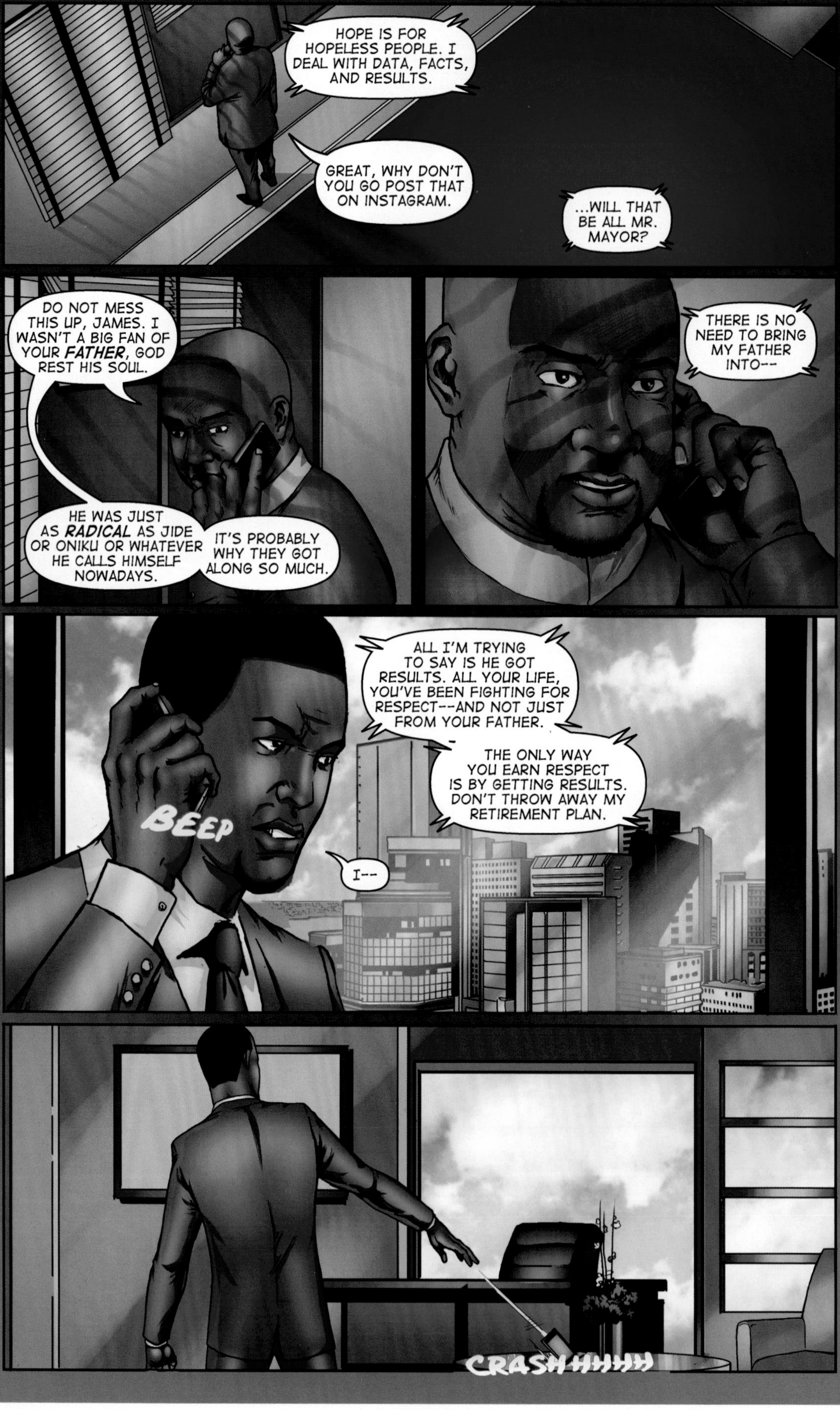
HOPE IS FOR HOPELESS PEOPLE. I DEAL WITH DATA, FACTS, AND RESULTS.
GREAT, WHY DON'T YOU GO POST THAT ON INSTAGRAM.
...WILL THAT BE ALL MR. MAYOR?
DO NOT MESS THIS UP, JAMES. I WASN'T A BIG FAN OF YOUR FATHER, GOD REST HIS SOUL.
HE WAS JUST AS RADICAL AS JIDE OR ONIKU OR WHATEVER HE CALLS HIMSELF NOWADAYS.
IT'S PROBABLY WHY THEY GOT ALONG SO MUCH.
THERE IS NO NEED TO BRING MY FATHER INTO--
ALL I'M TRYING TO SAY IS HE GOT RESULTS. ALL YOUR LIFE, YOU'VE BEEN FIGHTING FOR RESPECT--AND NOT JUST FROM YOUR FATHER.
THE ONLY WAY YOU EARN RESPECT IS BY GETTING RESULTS. DON'T THROW AWAY MY RETIREMENT PLAN.
BEEP
I--
CRASHHHHH

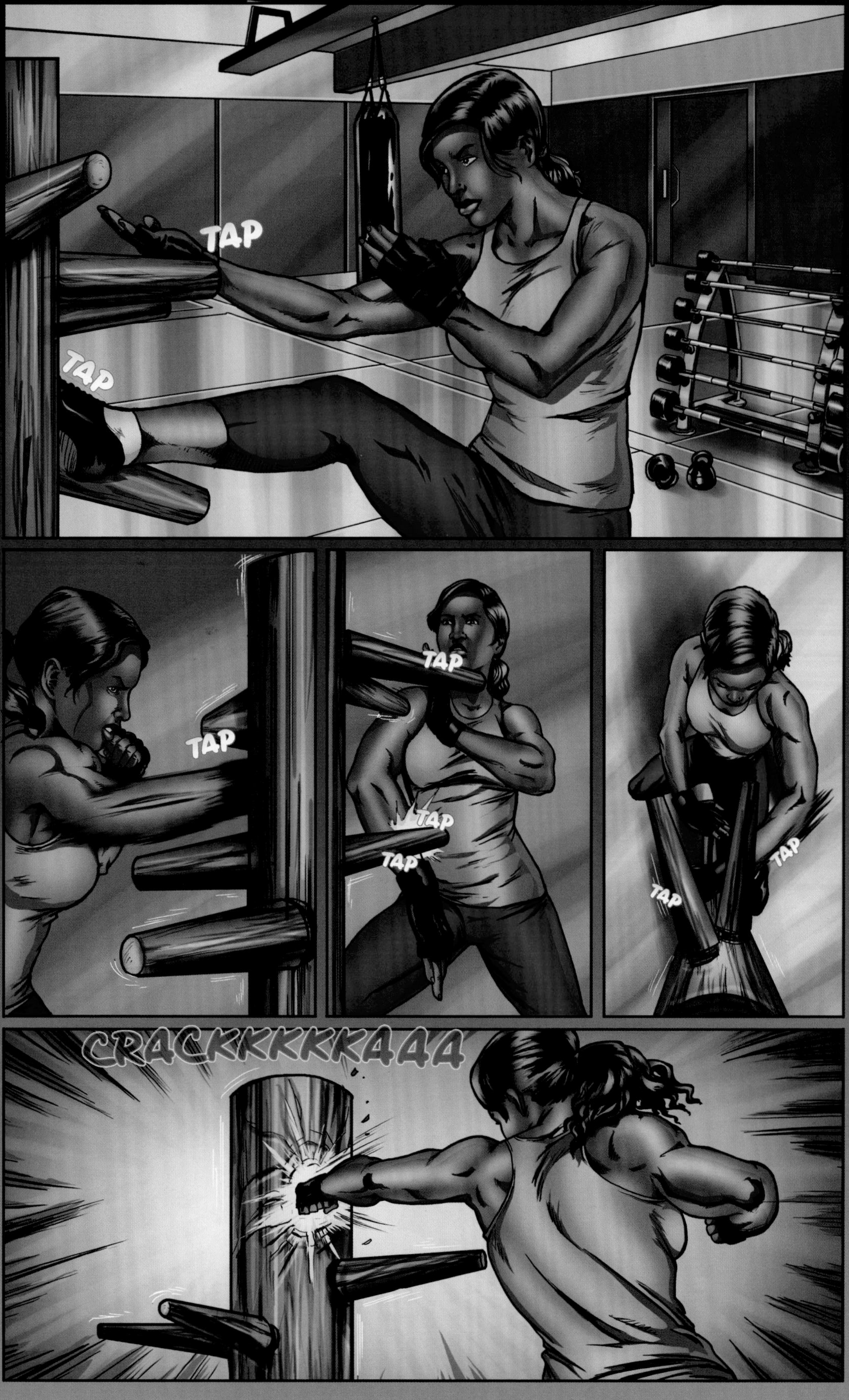
TAP
TAP
TAP
TAP
TAP
TAP
TAP
TAP
CRACKKKKKAAA

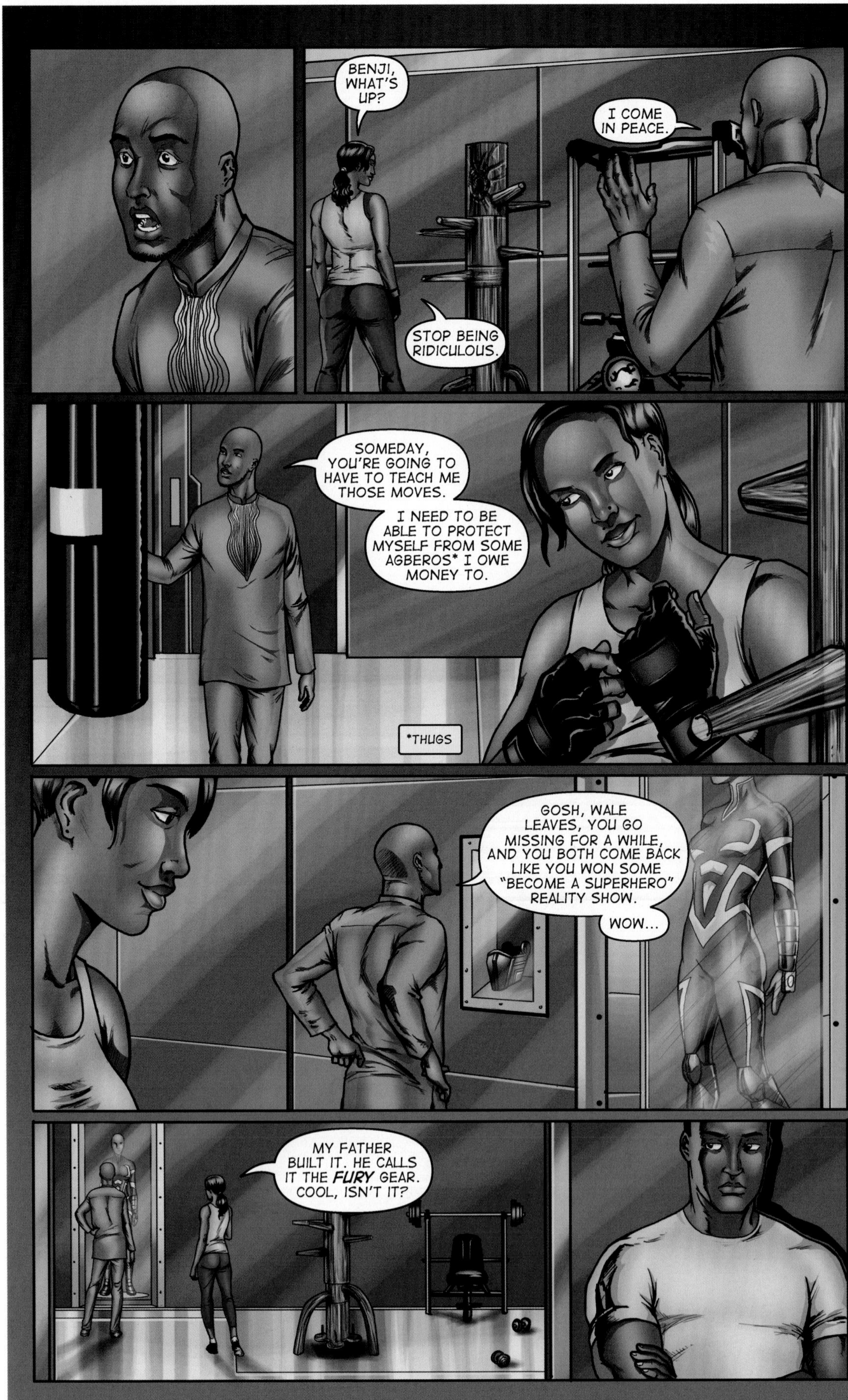
BENJI, WHAT'S UP?
I COME IN PEACE.
STOP BEING RIDICULOUS.
SOMEDAY, YOU'RE GOING TO HAVE TO TEACH ME THOSE MOVES.
I NEED TO BE ABLE TO PROTECT MYSELF FROM SOME AGBEROS* I OWE MONEY TO.
*THUGS
GOSH, WALE LEAVES, YOU GO MISSING FOR A WHILE, AND YOU BOTH COME BACK LIKE YOU WON SOME "BECOME A SUPERHERO" REALITY SHOW.
WOW...
MY FATHER BUILT IT. HE CALLS IT THE FURY GEAR. COOL, ISN'T IT?

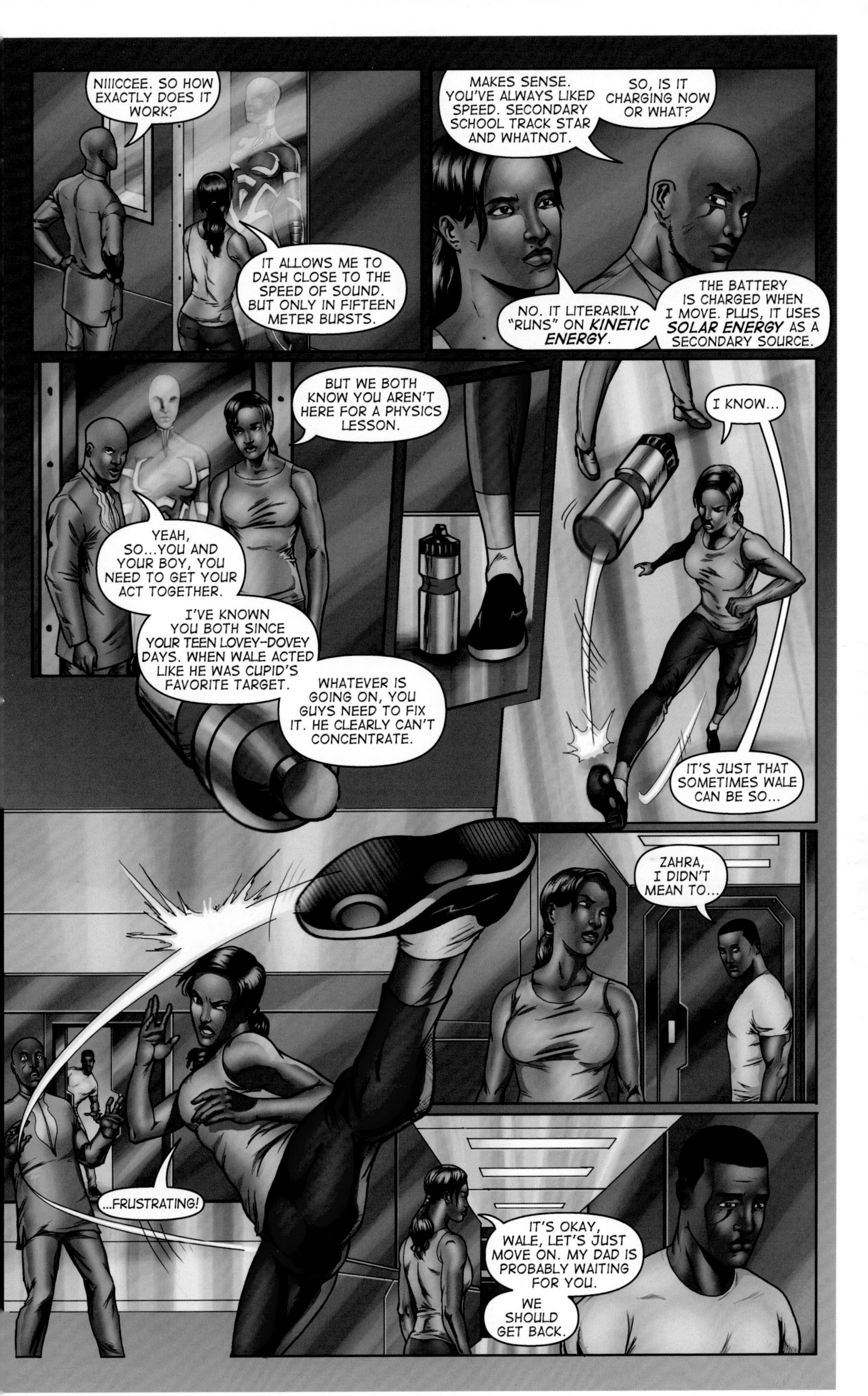
NIIICCEE. SO HOW EXACTLY DOES IT WORK?
IT ALLOWS ME TO DASH CLOSE TO THE SPEED OF SOUND. BUT ONLY IN FIFTEEN METER BURSTS.
MAKES SENSE. YOU'VE ALWAYS LIKED SPEED. SECONDARY SCHOOL TRACK STAR AND WHATNOT.
SO, IS IT CHARGING NOW OR WHAT?
NO. IT LITERARILY "RUNS" ON KINETIC ENERGY.
THE BATTERY IS CHARGED WHEN I MOVE. PLUS, IT USES SOLAR ENERGY AS A SECONDARY SOURCE.
BUT WE BOTH KNOW YOU AREN'T HERE FOR A PHYSICS LESSON.
YEAH, SO...YOU AND YOUR BOY, YOU NEED TO GET YOUR ACT TOGETHER.
I'VE KNOWN YOU BOTH SINCE YOUR TEEN LOVEY-DOVEY DAYS. WHEN WALE ACTED LIKE HE WAS CUPID'S FAVORITE TARGET.
WHATEVER IS GOING ON, YOU GUYS NEED TO FIX IT. HE CLEARLY CAN'T CONCENTRATE.
I KNOW...
IT'S JUST THAT SOMETIMES WALE CAN BE SO...
...FRUSTRATING!
ZAHRA, I DIDN'T MEAN TO...
IT'S OKAY, WALE, LET'S JUST MOVE ON. MY DAD IS PROBABLY WAITING FOR YOU.
WE SHOULD GET BACK.

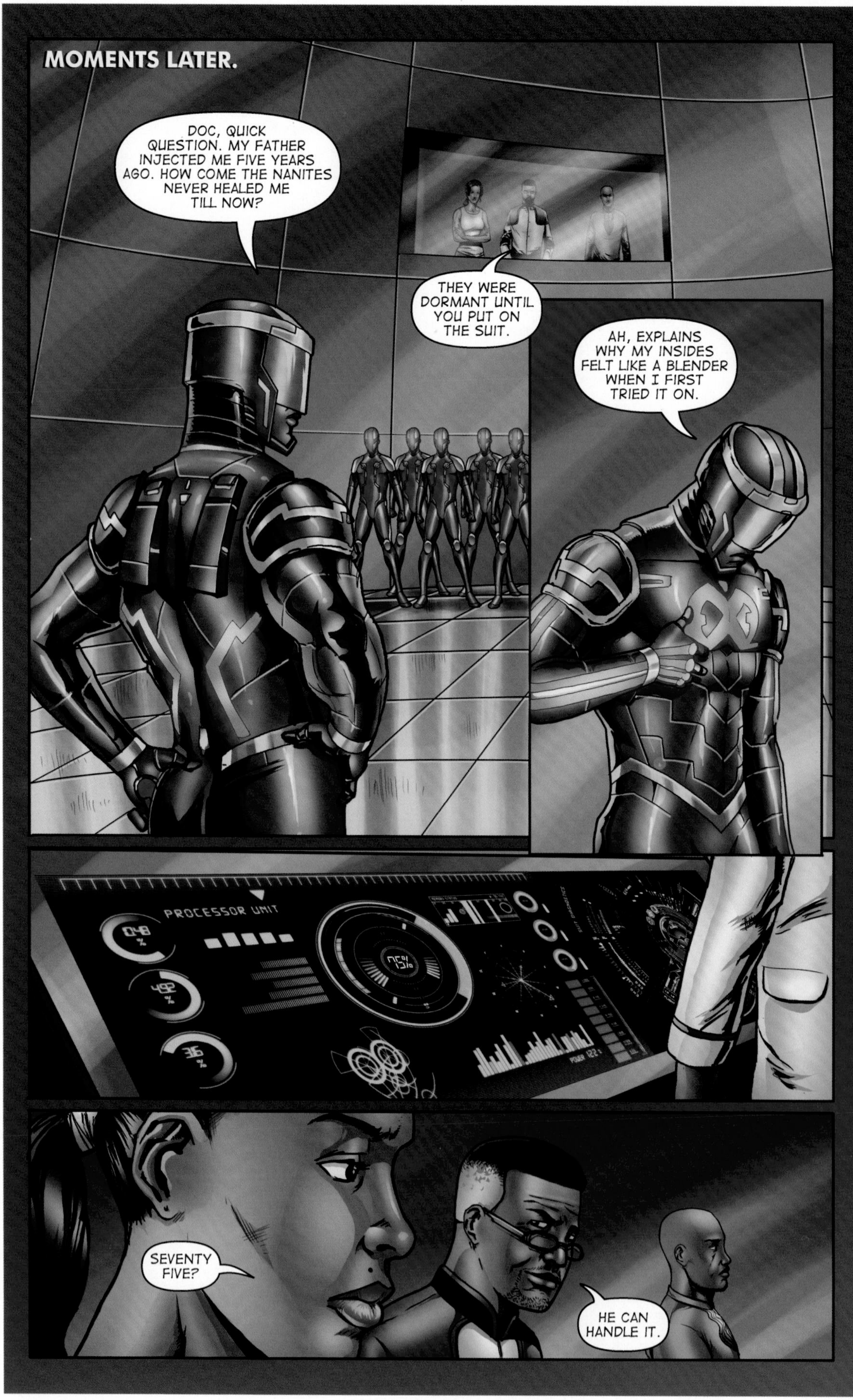
MOMENTS LATER.
DOC, QUICK QUESTION. MY FATHER INJECTED ME FIVE YEARS AGO. HOW COME THE NANITES NEVER HEALED ME TILL NOW?
THEY WERE DORMANT UNTIL YOU PUT ON THE SUIT.
AH, EXPLAINS WHY MY INSIDES FELT LIKE A BLENDER WHEN I FIRST TRIED IT ON.
PROCESSOR UNIT
SEVENTY FIVE?
HE CAN HANDLE IT.

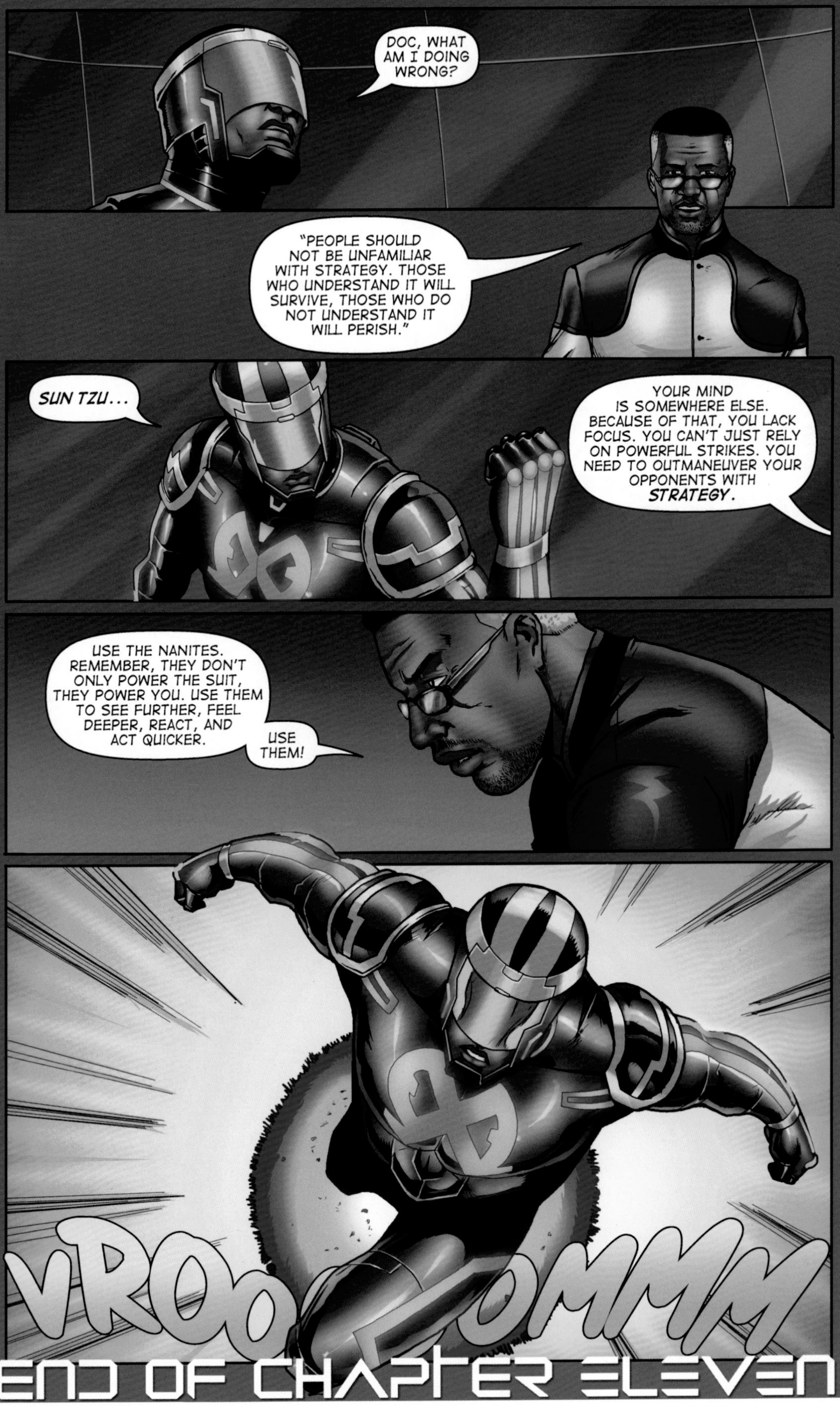

DOC, WHAT AM I DOING WRONG?
"PEOPLE SHOULD NOT BE UNFAMILIAR WITH STRATEGY. THOSE WHO UNDERSTAND IT WILL SURVIVE, THOSE WHO DO NOT UNDERSTAND IT WILL PERISH."
SUN TZU...
YOUR MIND IS SOMEWHERE ELSE. BECAUSE OF THAT, YOU LACK FOCUS. YOU CAN'T JUST RELY ON POWERFUL STRIKES. YOU NEED TO OUTMANEUVER YOUR OPPONENTS WITH STRATEGY.
USE THE NANITES. REMEMBER, THEY DON'T ONLY POWER THE SUIT, THEY POWER YOU. USE THEM TO SEE FURTHER, FEEL DEEPER, REACT, AND ACT QUICKER.
USE THEM!
VROOOOOMMM
END OF CHAPTER ELEVEN

The name "Oniku" is a play on two words from the Yoruba language. (The Yoruba are one of the three major tribes in Nigeria.) "Oni" roughly translates to mean "bringer," while the word "Iku" means "death." In essence, "Oni-Iku" would roughly translate to "Bringer of Death"—a grim reaper, so to speak.

CHAPTER TWELVE

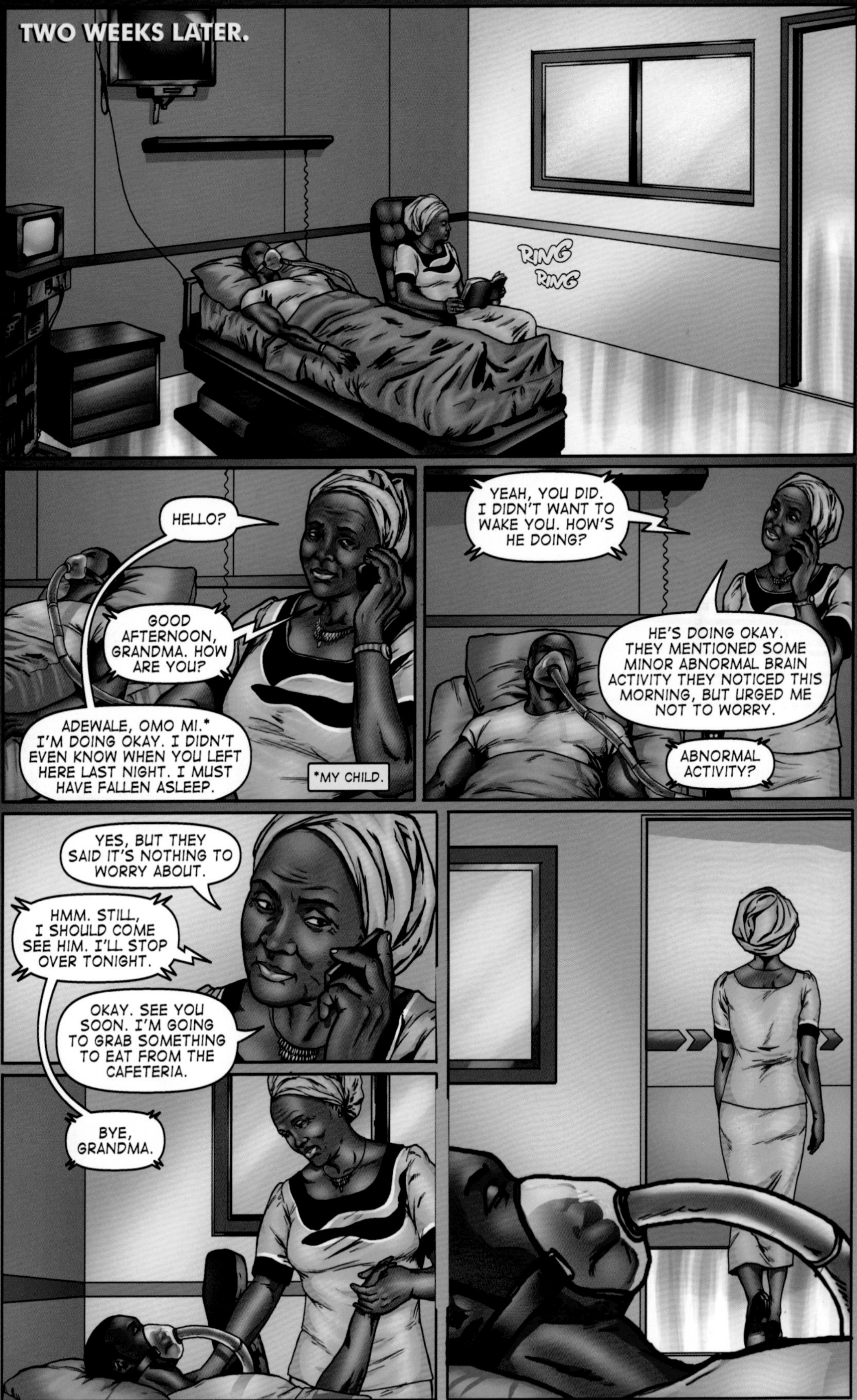

TWO WEEKS LATER.
RING RING
HELLO?
GOOD AFTERNOON, GRANDMA. HOW ARE YOU?
ADEWALE, OMO MI.* I'M DOING OKAY. I DIDN'T EVEN KNOW WHEN YOU LEFT HERE LAST NIGHT. I MUST HAVE FALLEN ASLEEP.
*MY CHILD.
YEAH, YOU DID. I DIDN'T WANT TO WAKE YOU. HOW'S HE DOING?
HE'S DOING OKAY. THEY MENTIONED SOME MINOR ABNORMAL BRAIN ACTIVITY THEY NOTICED THIS MORNING, BUT URGED ME NOT TO WORRY.
ABNORMAL ACTIVITY?
YES, BUT THEY SAID IT'S NOTHING TO WORRY ABOUT.
HMM. STILL, I SHOULD COME SEE HIM. I'LL STOP OVER TONIGHT.
OKAY. SEE YOU SOON. I'M GOING TO GRAB SOMETHING TO EAT FROM THE CAFETERIA.
BYE, GRANDMA.

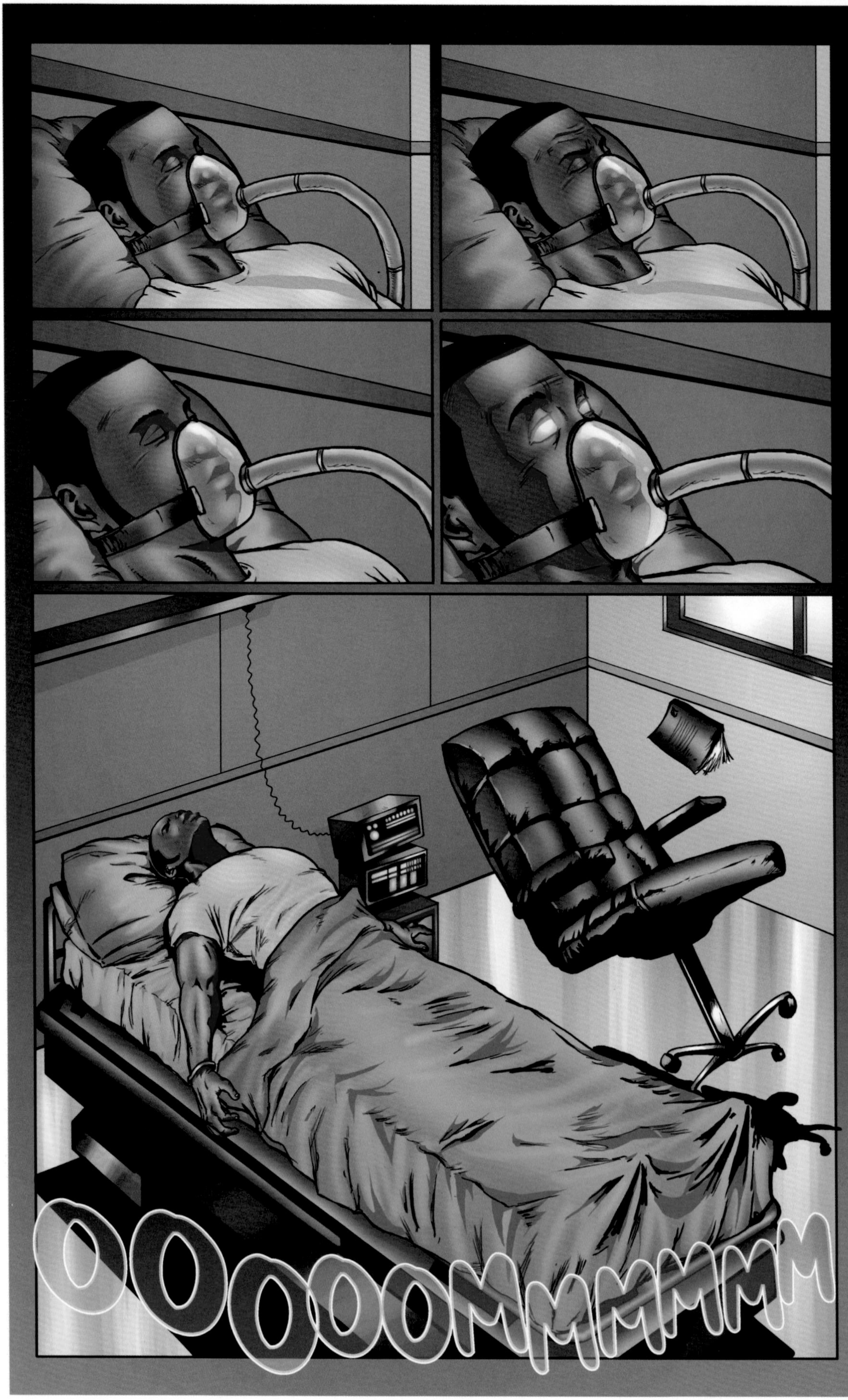
OOOOOMMMMMMM

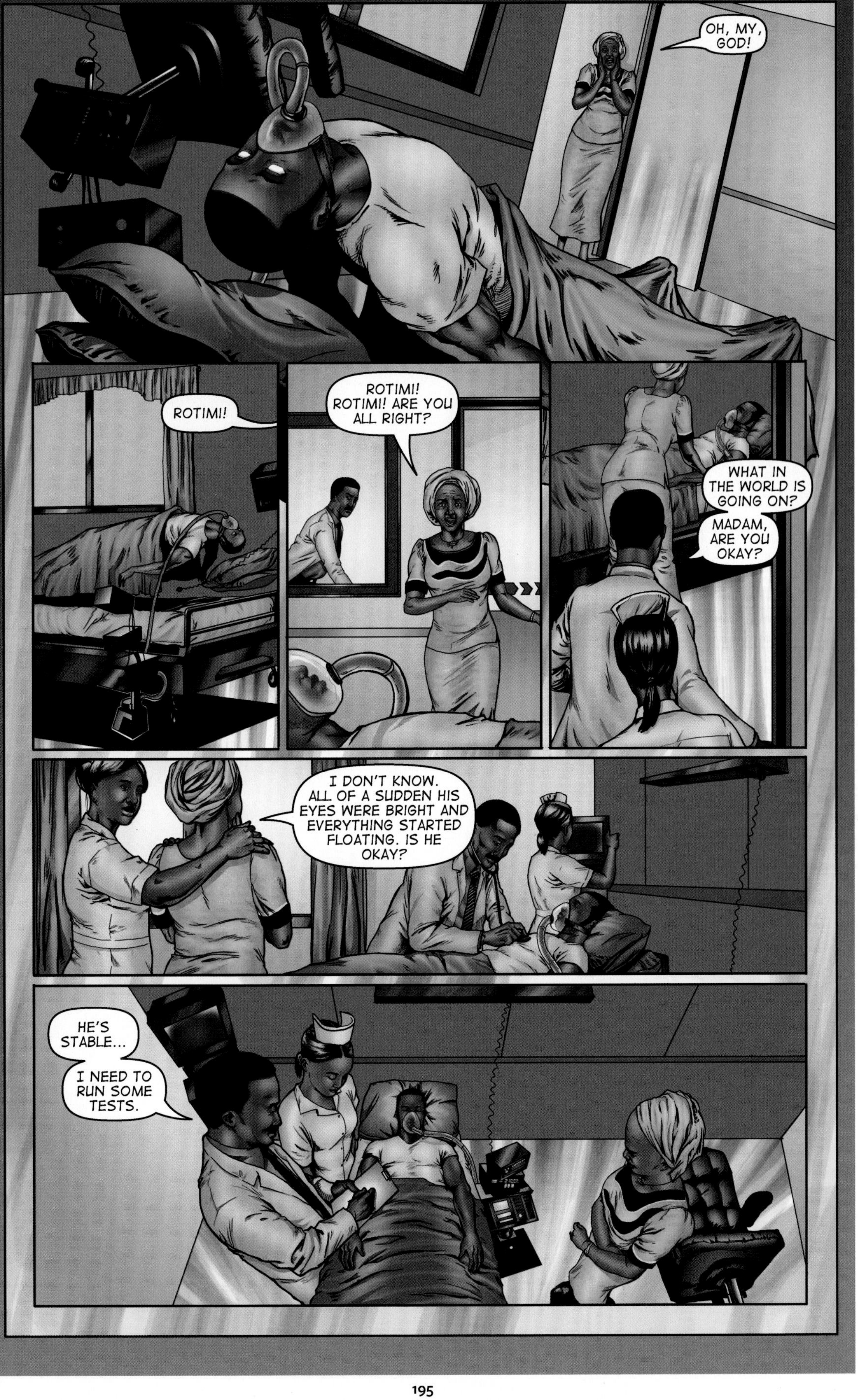
OH, MY, GOD!
ROTIMI!
ROTIMI! ROTIMI! ARE YOU ALL RIGHT?
WHAT IN THE WORLD IS GOING ON?
MADAM, ARE YOU OKAY?
I DON'T KNOW. ALL OF A SUDDEN HIS EYES WERE BRIGHT AND EVERYTHING STARTED FLOATING. IS HE OKAY?
HE'S STABLE...
I NEED TO RUN SOME TESTS.

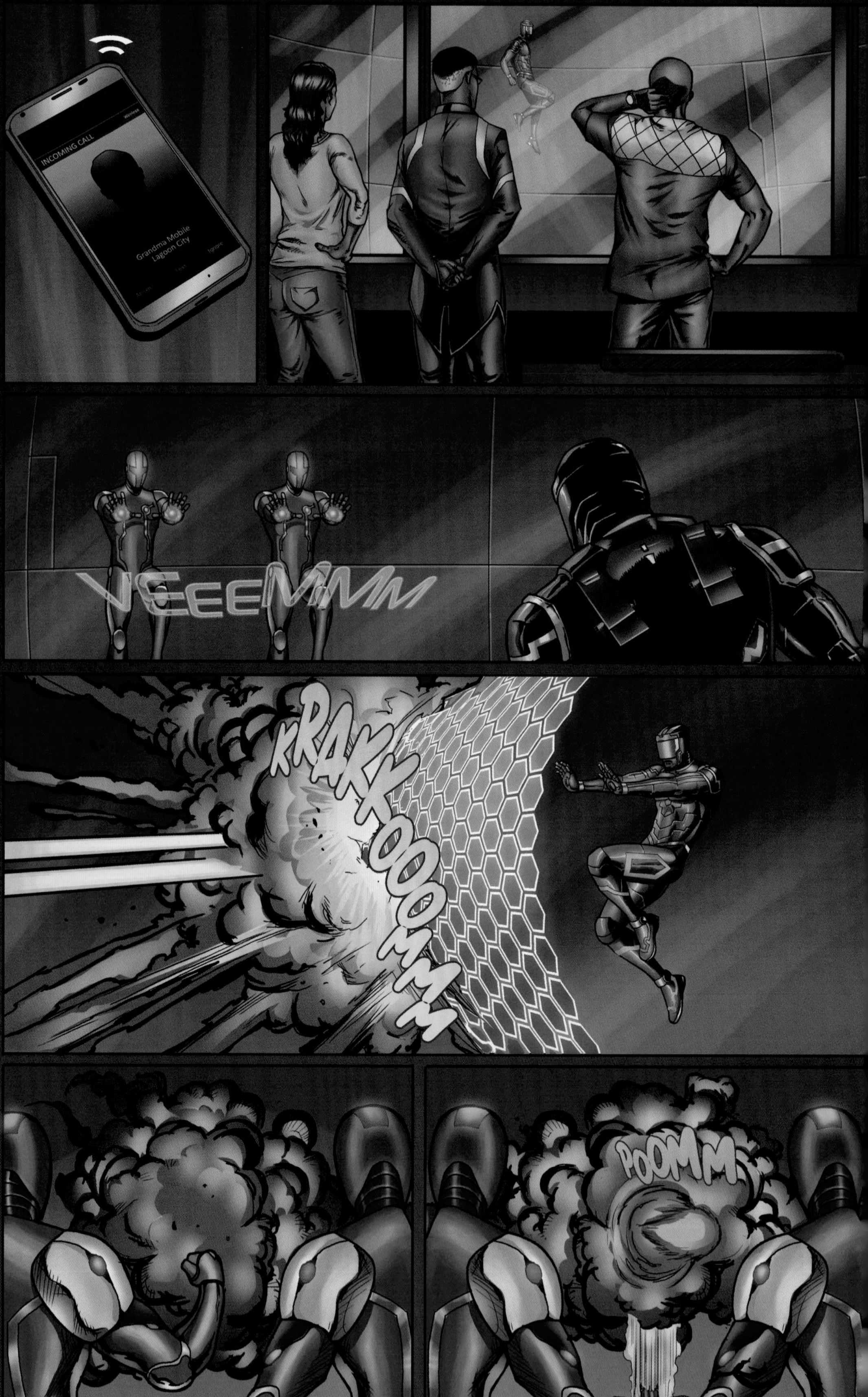
INCOMING CALL
Wireless
Grandma Mobile
Lagoon City
Ignore
VEEEMMM
KRAKKOOOMMM
POOMM

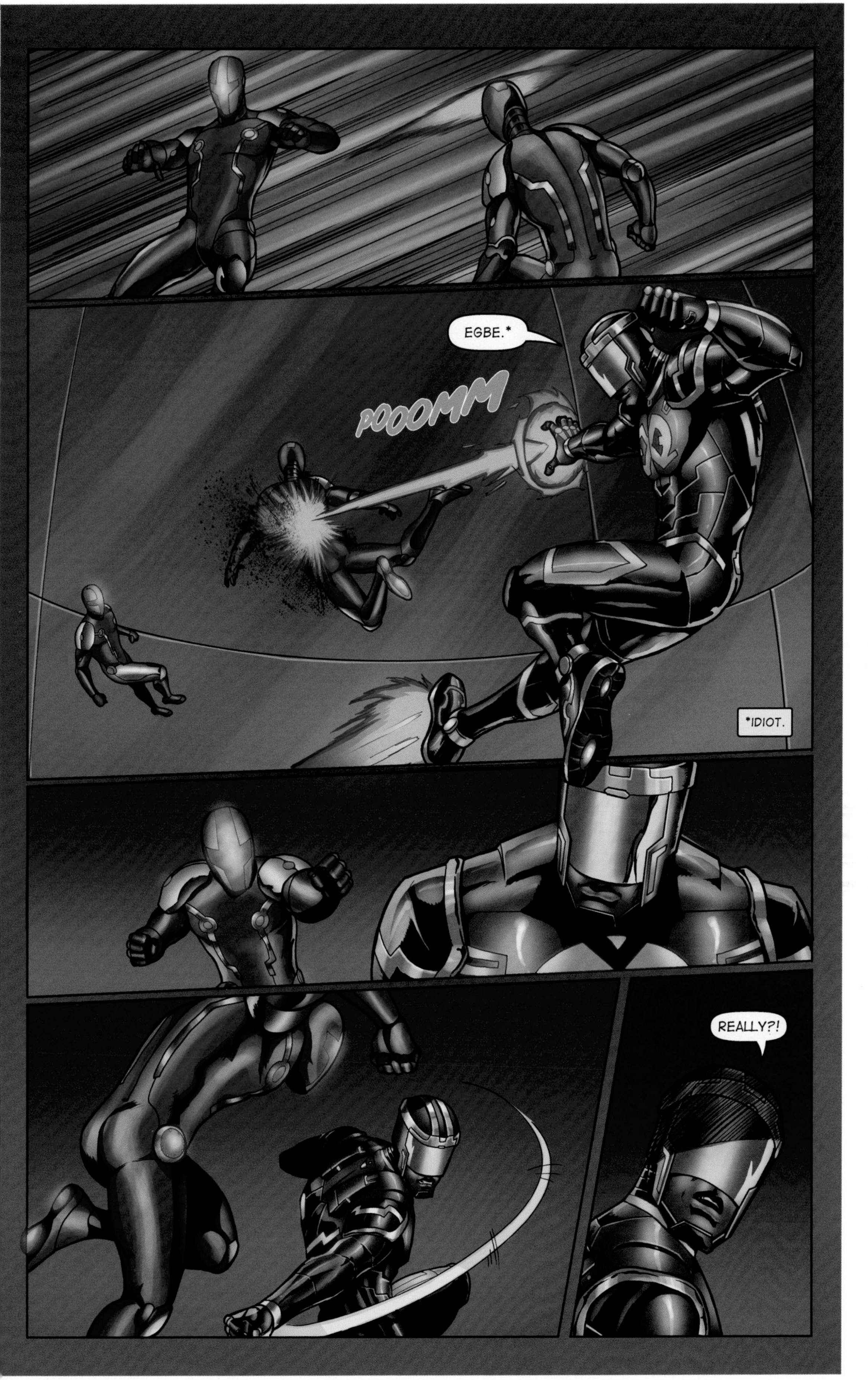
EGBE.*
POOOMM
*IDIOT.
REALLY?!

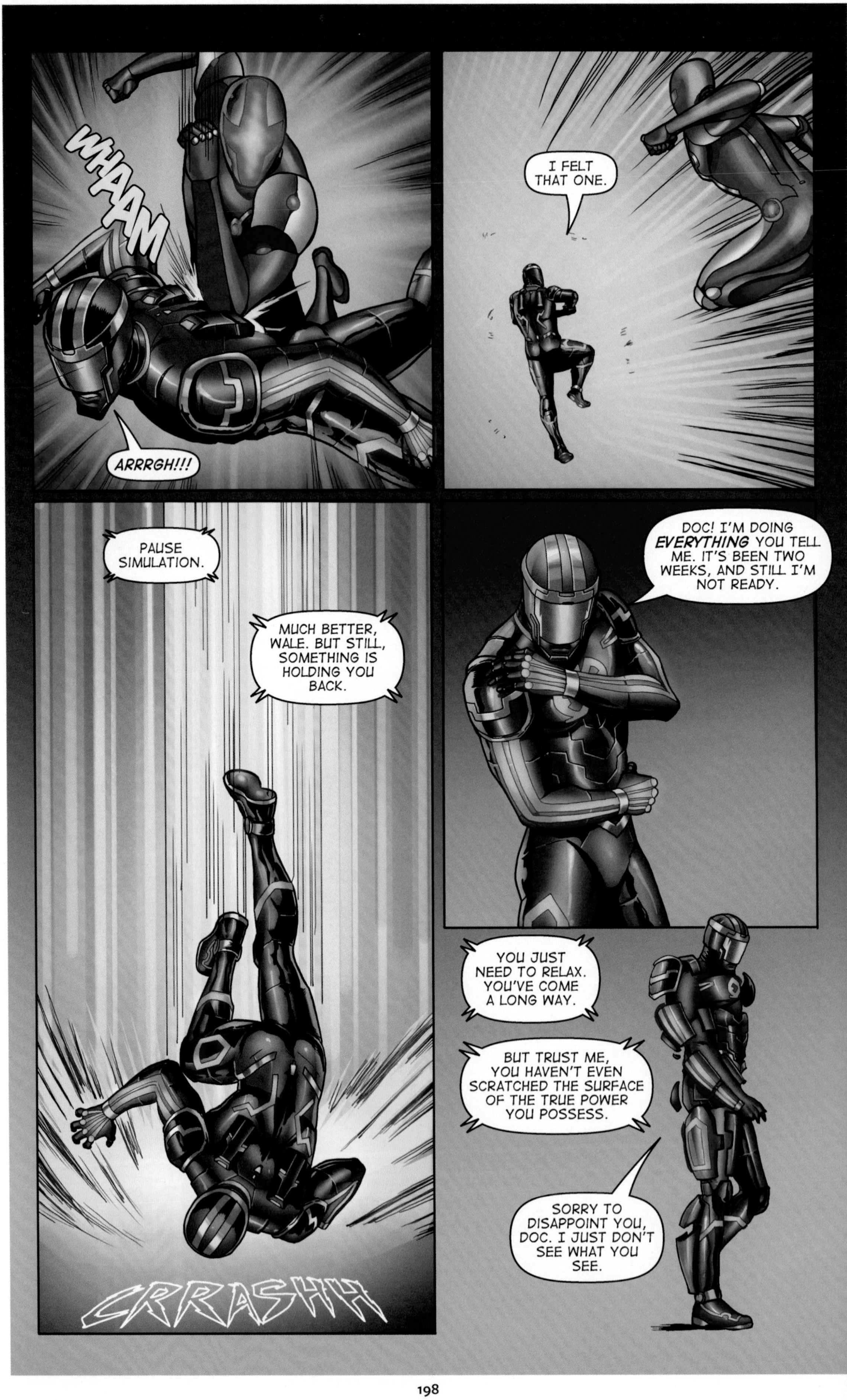
WHAAM
ARRRGH!!!
I FELT THAT ONE.
PAUSE SIMULATION.
MUCH BETTER, WALE. BUT STILL, SOMETHING IS HOLDING YOU BACK.
CRRASHH
DOC! I'M DOING *EVERYTHING* YOU TELL ME. IT'S BEEN TWO WEEKS, AND STILL I'M NOT READY.
YOU JUST NEED TO RELAX. YOU'VE COME A LONG WAY.
BUT TRUST ME, YOU HAVEN'T EVEN SCRATCHED THE SURFACE OF THE TRUE POWER YOU POSSESS.
SORRY TO DISAPPOINT YOU, DOC. I JUST DON'T SEE WHAT YOU SEE.

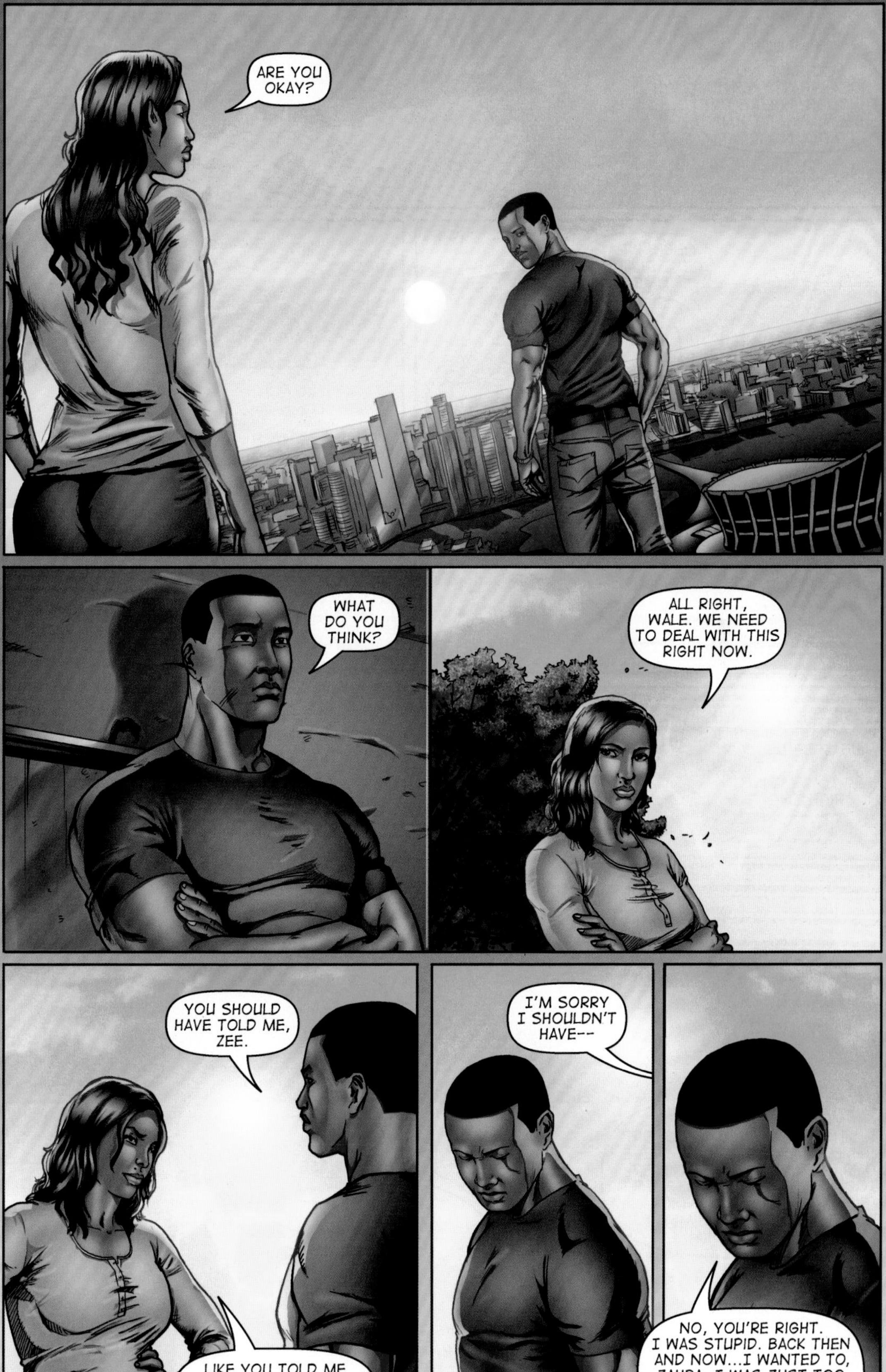
ARE YOU OKAY?
WHAT DO YOU THINK?
ALL RIGHT, WALE. WE NEED TO DEAL WITH THIS RIGHT NOW.
YOU SHOULD HAVE TOLD ME, ZEE.
LIKE YOU TOLD ME WHEN YOU VANISHED? AND ABANDONED ME? YOUR BROTHER, YOUR FRIENDS?
I'M SORRY I SHOULDN'T HAVE--
NO, YOU'RE RIGHT. I WAS STUPID. BACK THEN AND NOW...I WANTED TO, ZAHRA, I WAS JUST TOO SCARED. I COULDN'T FACE YOU. IT WAS TOO HARD.

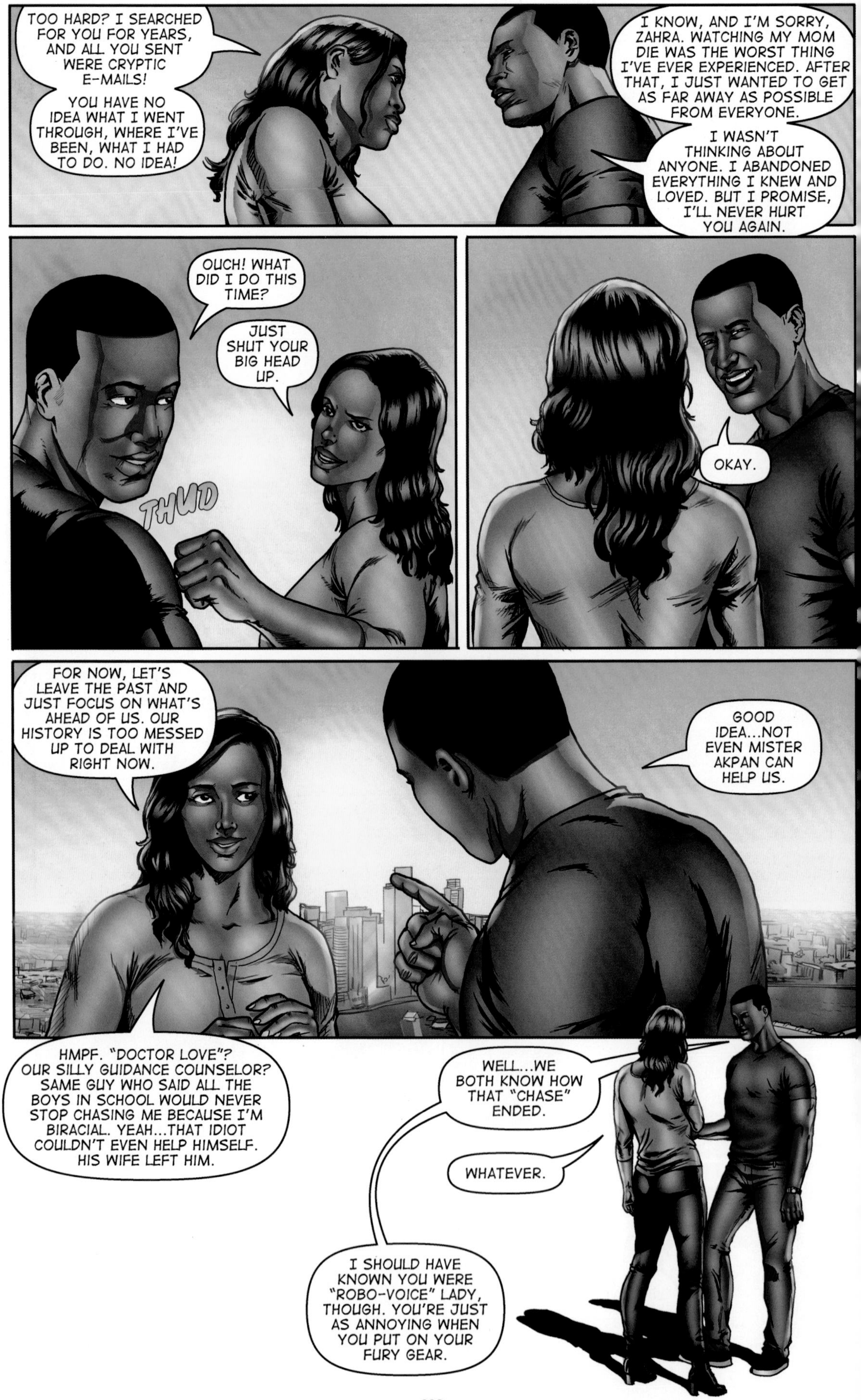
TOO HARD? I SEARCHED FOR YOU FOR YEARS, AND ALL YOU SENT WERE CRYPTIC E-MAILS!
YOU HAVE NO IDEA WHAT I WENT THROUGH, WHERE I'VE BEEN, WHAT I HAD TO DO. NO IDEA!
I KNOW, AND I'M SORRY, ZAHRA. WATCHING MY MOM DIE WAS THE WORST THING I'VE EVER EXPERIENCED. AFTER THAT, I JUST WANTED TO GET AS FAR AWAY AS POSSIBLE FROM EVERYONE.
I WASN'T THINKING ABOUT ANYONE. I ABANDONED EVERYTHING I KNEW AND LOVED. BUT I PROMISE, I'LL NEVER HURT YOU AGAIN.
THUD
OUCH! WHAT DID I DO THIS TIME?
JUST SHUT YOUR BIG HEAD UP.
OKAY.
FOR NOW, LET'S LEAVE THE PAST AND JUST FOCUS ON WHAT'S AHEAD OF US. OUR HISTORY IS TOO MESSED UP TO DEAL WITH RIGHT NOW.
GOOD IDEA...NOT EVEN MISTER AKPAN CAN HELP US.
HMPF. "DOCTOR LOVE"? OUR SILLY GUIDANCE COUNSELOR? SAME GUY WHO SAID ALL THE BOYS IN SCHOOL WOULD NEVER STOP CHASING ME BECAUSE I'M BIRACIAL. YEAH...THAT IDIOT COULDN'T EVEN HELP HIMSELF. HIS WIFE LEFT HIM.
WELL...WE BOTH KNOW HOW THAT "CHASE" ENDED.
WHATEVER.
I SHOULD HAVE KNOWN YOU WERE "ROBO-VOICE" LADY, THOUGH. YOU'RE JUST AS ANNOYING WHEN YOU PUT ON YOUR FURY GEAR.

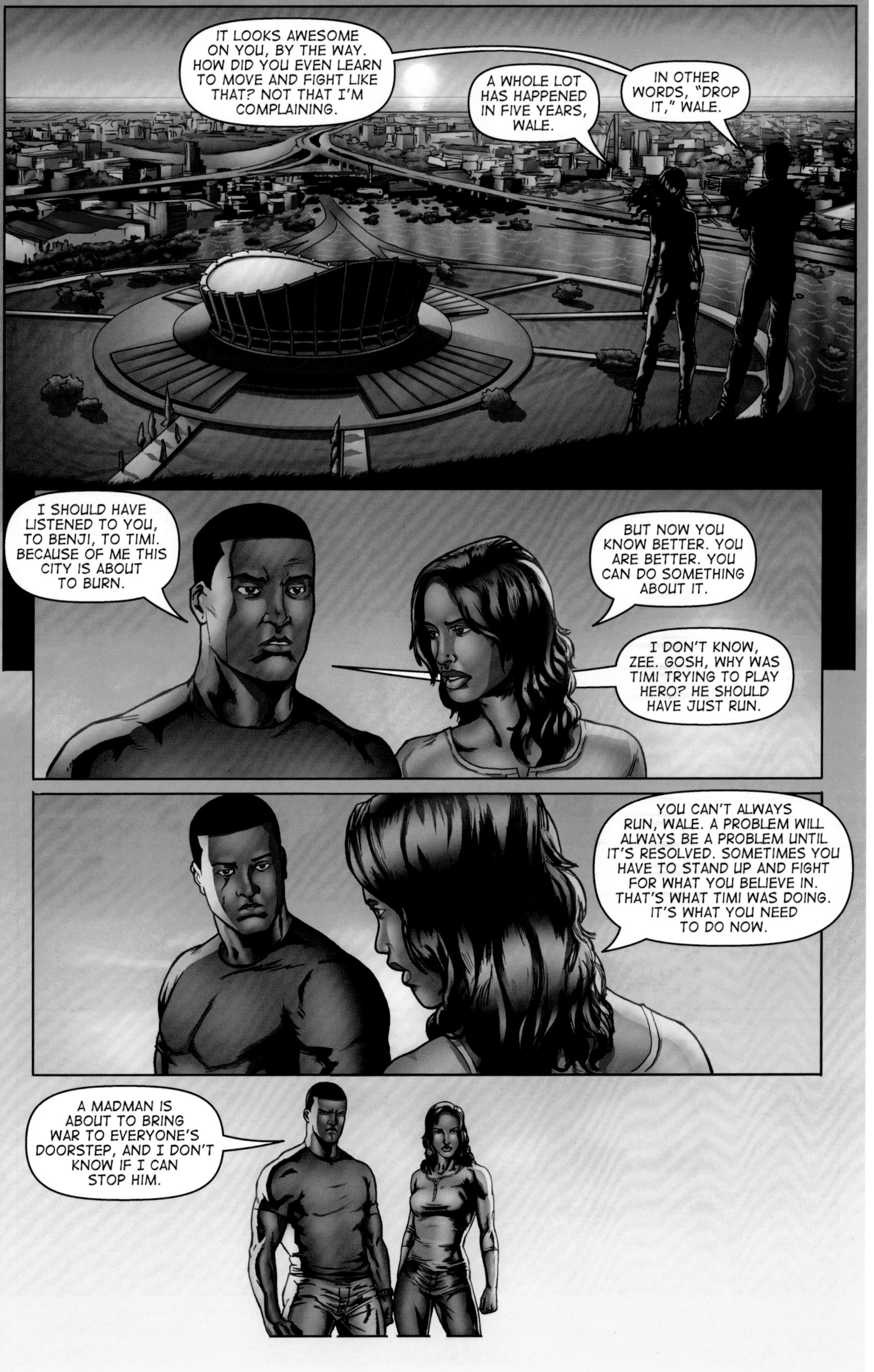
IT LOOKS AWESOME ON YOU, BY THE WAY. HOW DID YOU EVEN LEARN TO MOVE AND FIGHT LIKE THAT? NOT THAT I'M COMPLAINING.
A WHOLE LOT HAS HAPPENED IN FIVE YEARS, WALE.
IN OTHER WORDS, "DROP IT," WALE.
I SHOULD HAVE LISTENED TO YOU, TO BENJI, TO TIMI. BECAUSE OF ME THIS CITY IS ABOUT TO BURN.
BUT NOW YOU KNOW BETTER. YOU ARE BETTER. YOU CAN DO SOMETHING ABOUT IT.
I DON'T KNOW, ZEE. GOSH, WHY WAS TIMI TRYING TO PLAY HERO? HE SHOULD HAVE JUST RUN.
YOU CAN'T ALWAYS RUN, WALE. A PROBLEM WILL ALWAYS BE A PROBLEM UNTIL IT'S RESOLVED. SOMETIMES YOU HAVE TO STAND UP AND FIGHT FOR WHAT YOU BELIEVE IN. THAT'S WHAT TIMI WAS DOING. IT'S WHAT YOU NEED TO DO NOW.
A MADMAN IS ABOUT TO BRING WAR TO EVERYONE'S DOORSTEP, AND I DON'T KNOW IF I CAN STOP HIM.

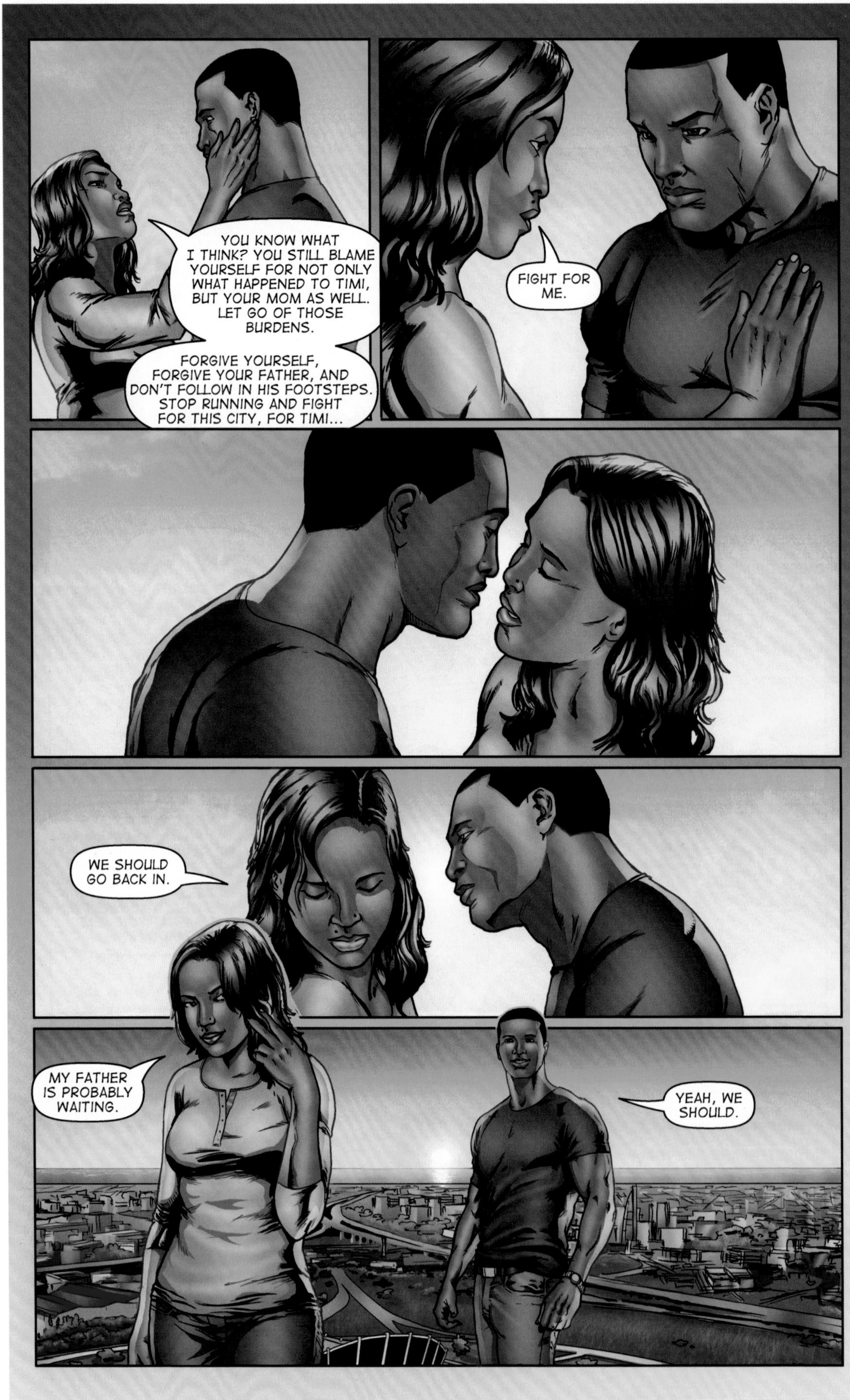
YOU KNOW WHAT I THINK? YOU STILL BLAME YOURSELF FOR NOT ONLY WHAT HAPPENED TO TIMI, BUT YOUR MOM AS WELL. LET GO OF THOSE BURDENS.
FORGIVE YOURSELF, FORGIVE YOUR FATHER, AND DON'T FOLLOW IN HIS FOOTSTEPS. STOP RUNNING AND FIGHT FOR THIS CITY, FOR TIMI...
FIGHT FOR ME.
WE SHOULD GO BACK IN.
YEAH, WE SHOULD.
MY FATHER IS PROBABLY WAITING.

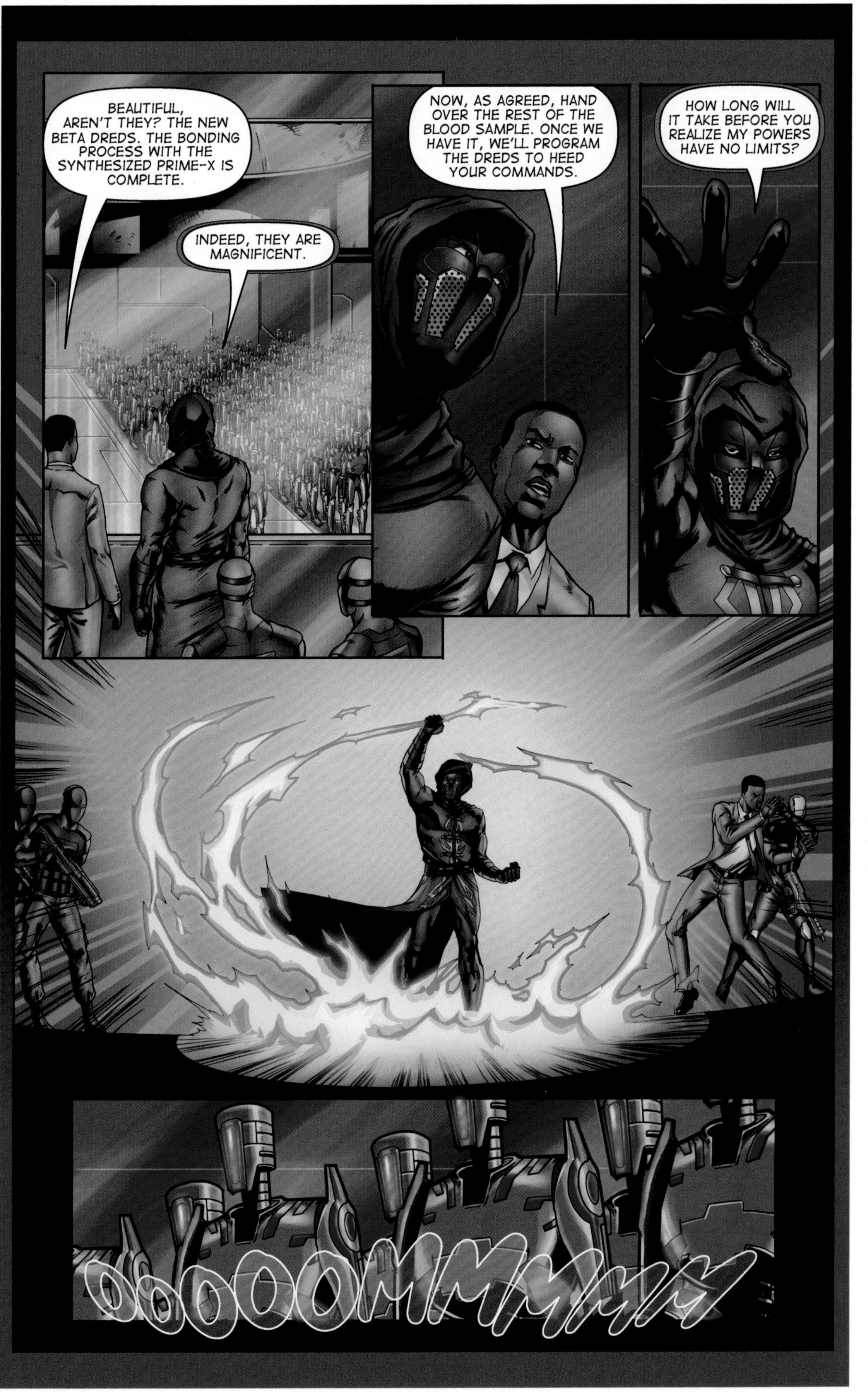
BEAUTIFUL, AREN'T THEY? THE NEW BETA DREDS. THE BONDING PROCESS WITH THE SYNTHESIZED PRIME-X IS COMPLETE.
INDEED, THEY ARE MAGNIFICENT.
NOW, AS AGREED, HAND OVER THE REST OF THE BLOOD SAMPLE. ONCE WE HAVE IT, WE'LL PROGRAM THE DREDS TO HEED YOUR COMMANDS.
HOW LONG WILL IT TAKE BEFORE YOU REALIZE MY POWERS HAVE NO LIMITS?
OoOOOOMMMMMM

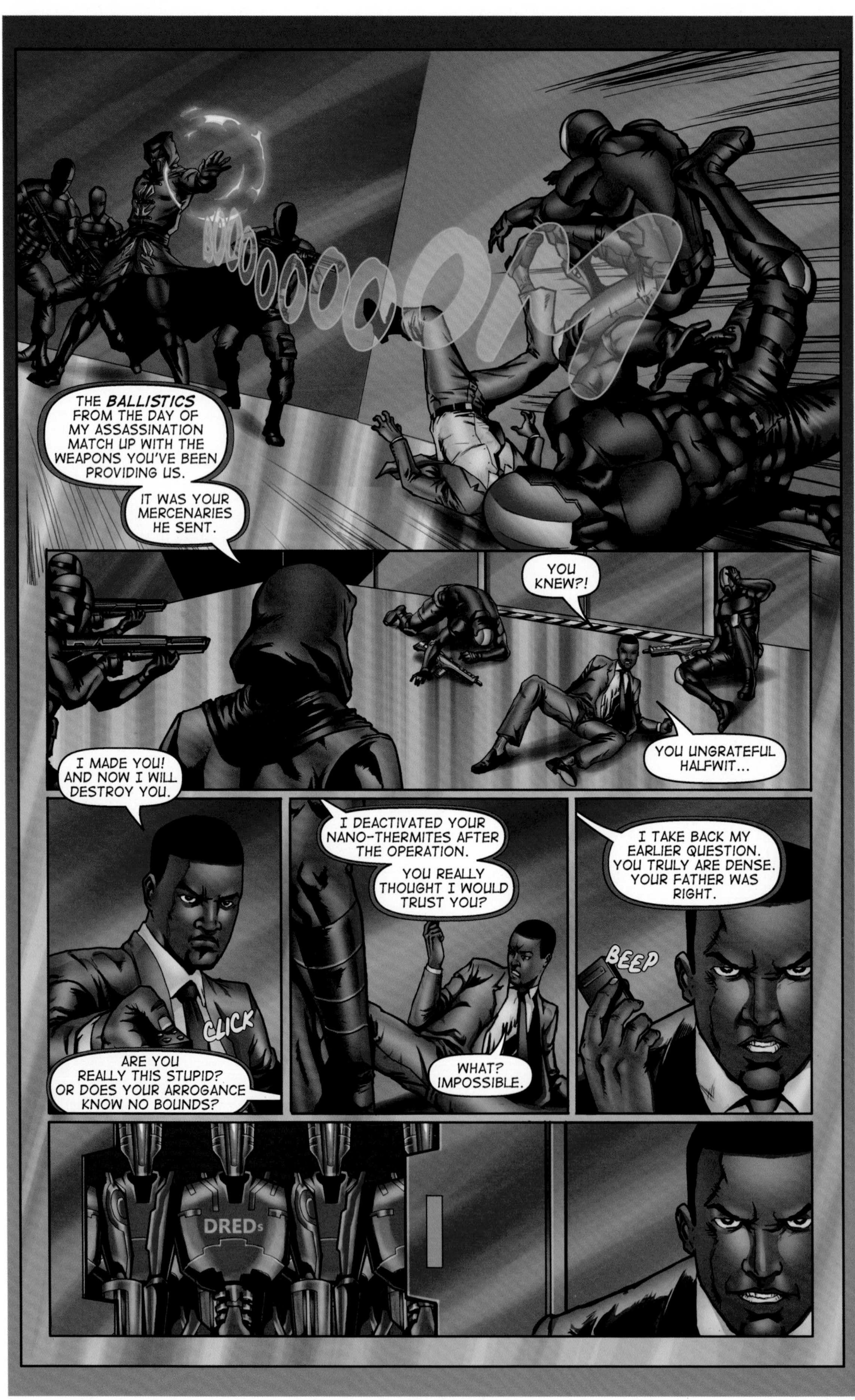
BOOOOOOOOOOM
THE BALLISTICS FROM THE DAY OF MY ASSASSINATION MATCH UP WITH THE WEAPONS YOU'VE BEEN PROVIDING US.
IT WAS YOUR MERCENARIES HE SENT.
YOU KNEW?!
YOU UNGRATEFUL HALFWIT...
I MADE YOU! AND NOW I WILL DESTROY YOU.
CLICK
ARE YOU REALLY THIS STUPID? OR DOES YOUR ARROGANCE KNOW NO BOUNDS?
I DEACTIVATED YOUR NANO-THERMITES AFTER THE OPERATION.
YOU REALLY THOUGHT I WOULD TRUST YOU?
WHAT? IMPOSSIBLE.
I TAKE BACK MY EARLIER QUESTION. YOU TRULY ARE DENSE. YOUR FATHER WAS RIGHT.
BEEP
DREDs

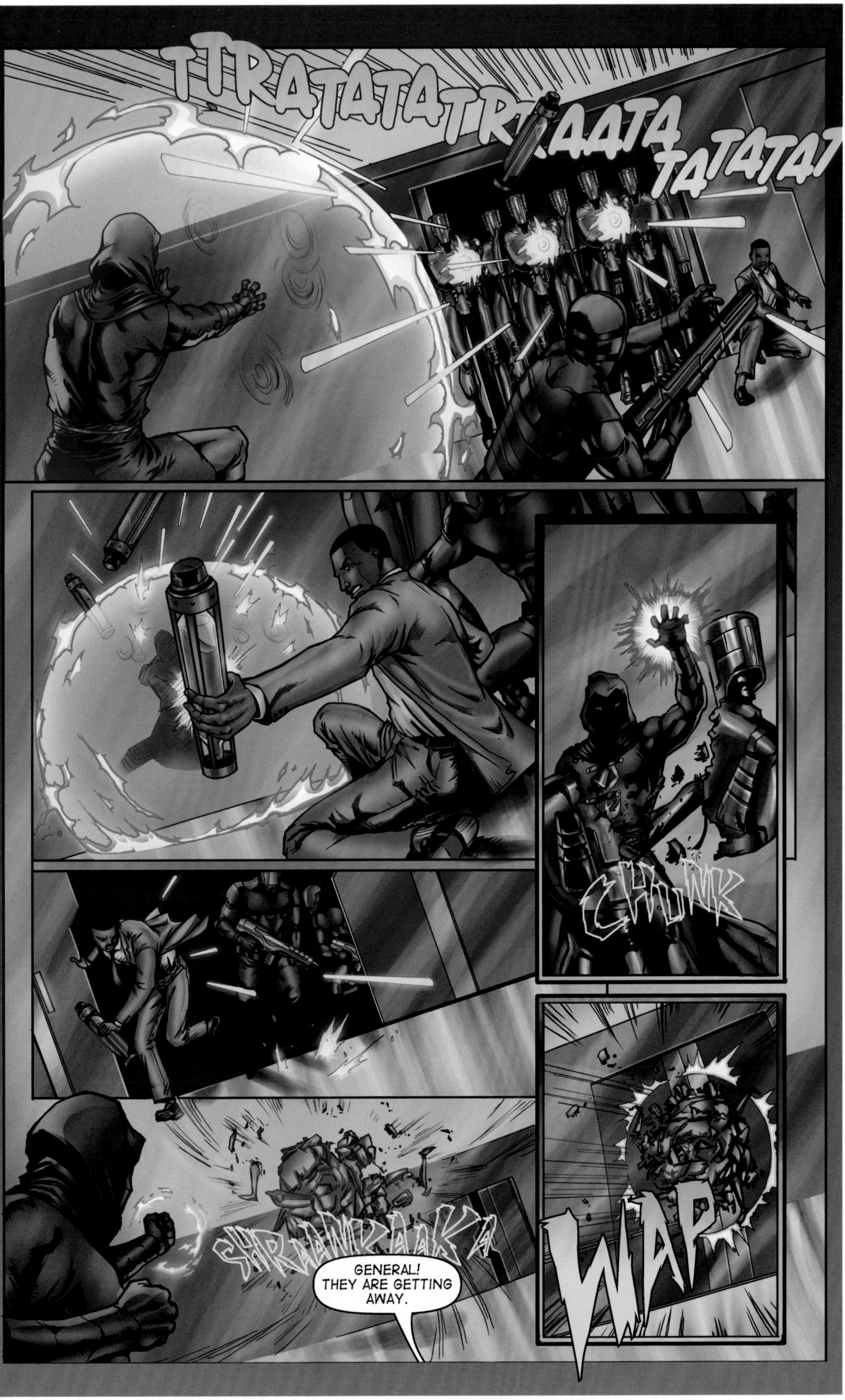
TTRATATATATR
AATA
TATATAT
CHUNK
GENERAL! THEY ARE GETTING AWAY.
WAP

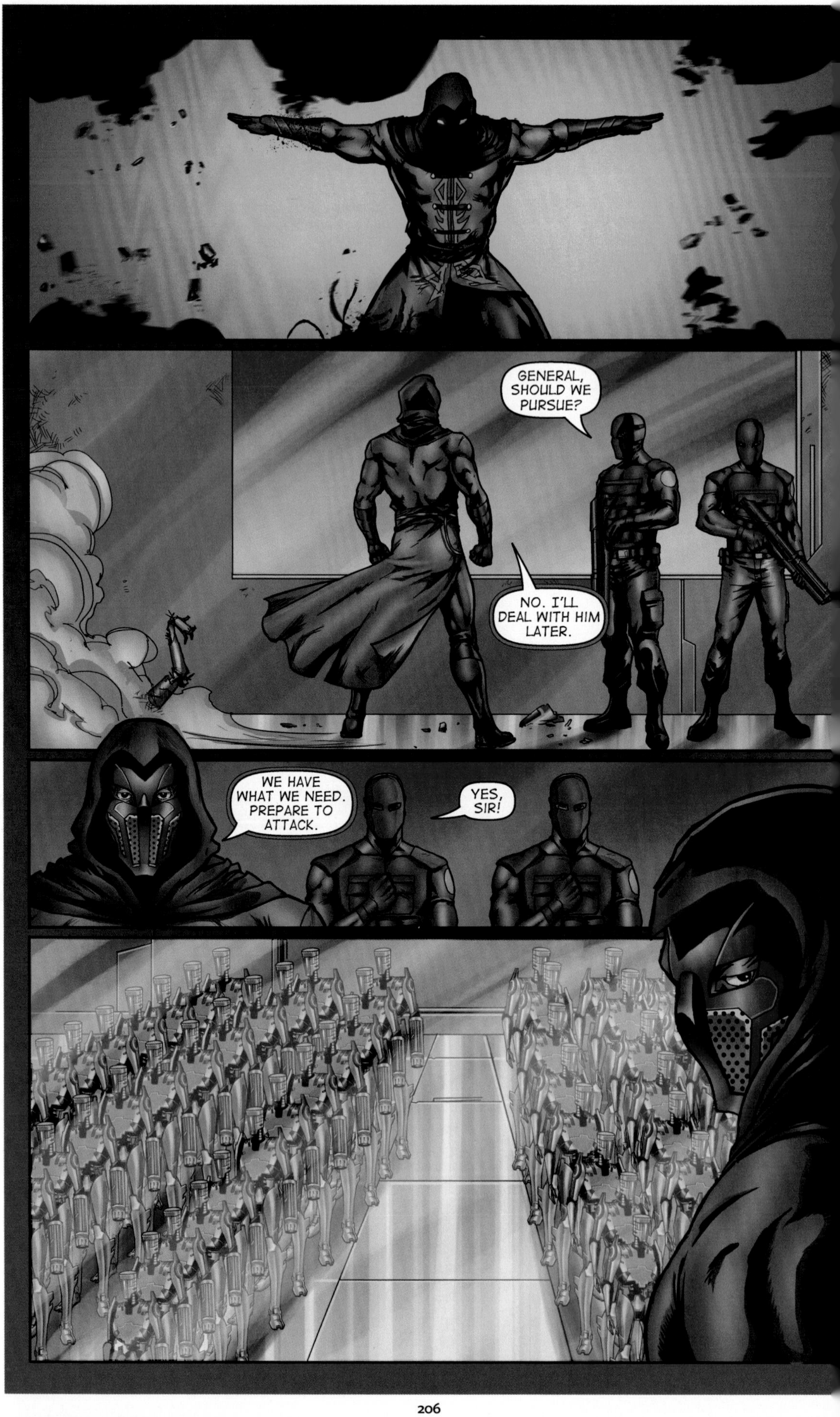
GENERAL, SHOULD WE PURSUE?
NO. I'LL DEAL WITH HIM LATER.
WE HAVE WHAT WE NEED. PREPARE TO ATTACK.
YES, SIR!

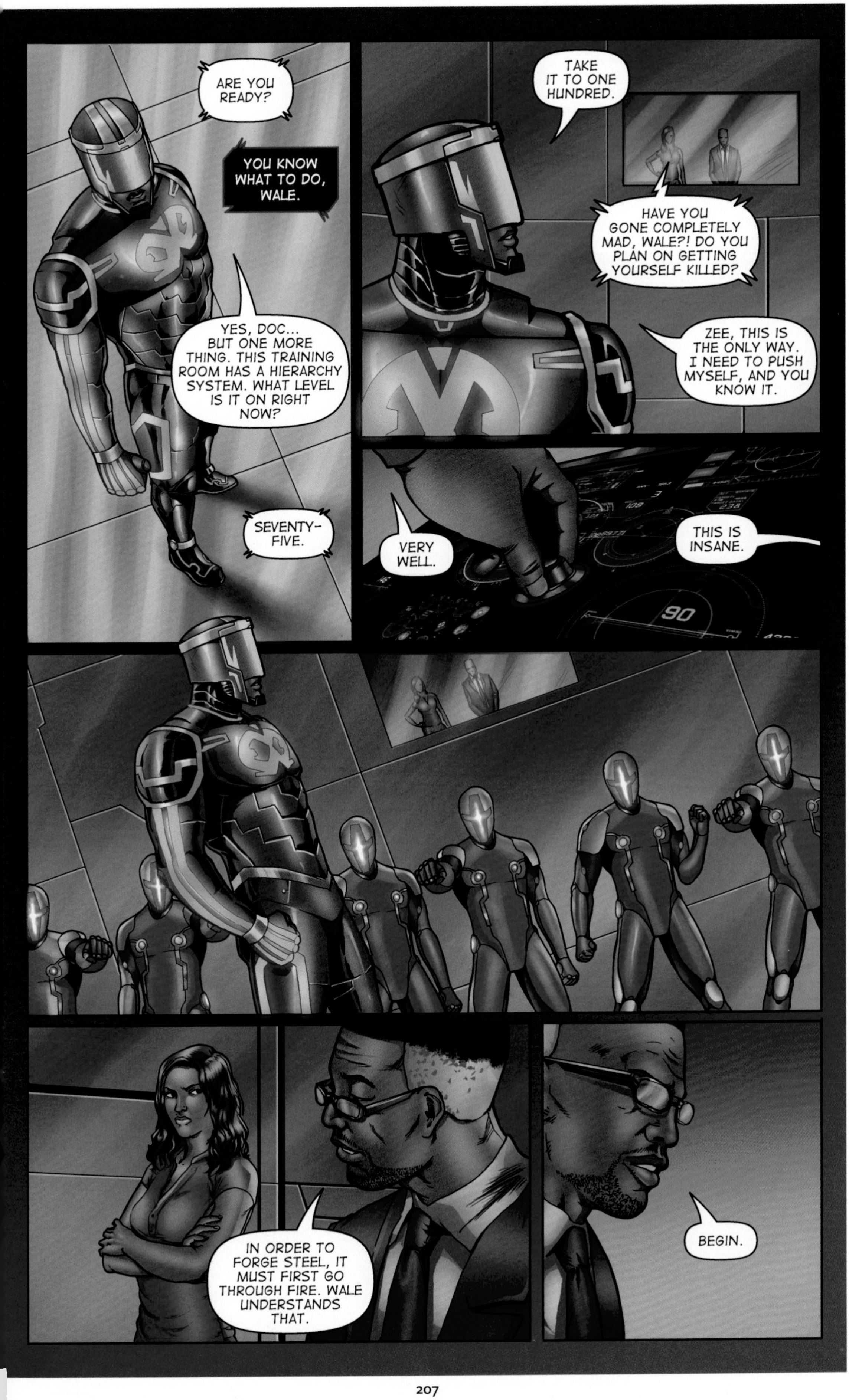
ARE YOU READY?
YOU KNOW WHAT TO DO, WALE.
YES, DOC... BUT ONE MORE THING. THIS TRAINING ROOM HAS A HIERARCHY SYSTEM. WHAT LEVEL IS IT ON RIGHT NOW?
SEVENTY-FIVE.
TAKE IT TO ONE HUNDRED.
HAVE YOU GONE COMPLETELY MAD, WALE?! DO YOU PLAN ON GETTING YOURSELF KILLED?
ZEE, THIS IS THE ONLY WAY. I NEED TO PUSH MYSELF, AND YOU KNOW IT.
VERY WELL.
THIS IS INSANE.
IN ORDER TO FORGE STEEL, IT MUST FIRST GO THROUGH FIRE. WALE UNDERSTANDS THAT.
BEGIN.

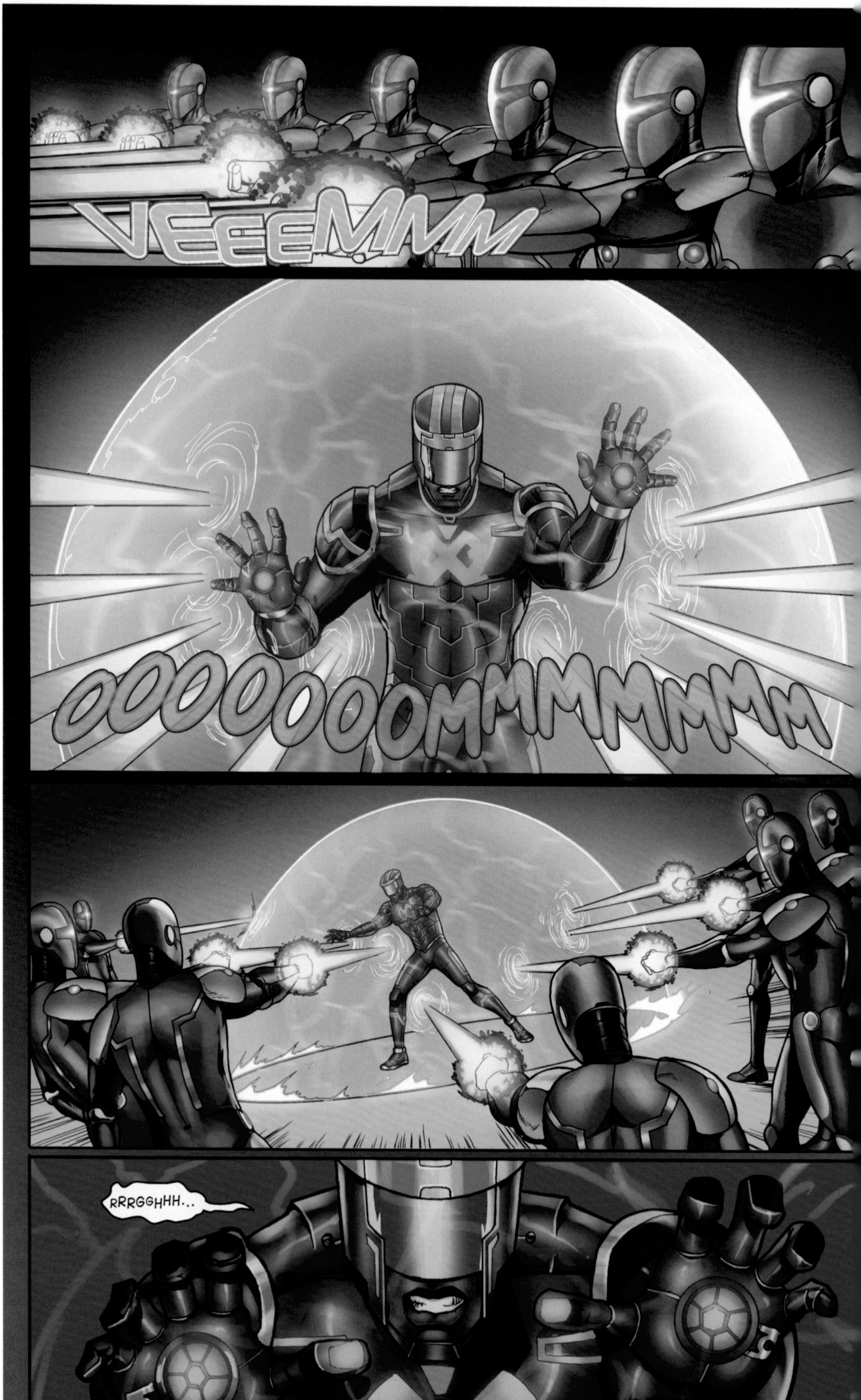
VEEEMMM
OOOOOOOMMMMMMM
RRRGGHHH...

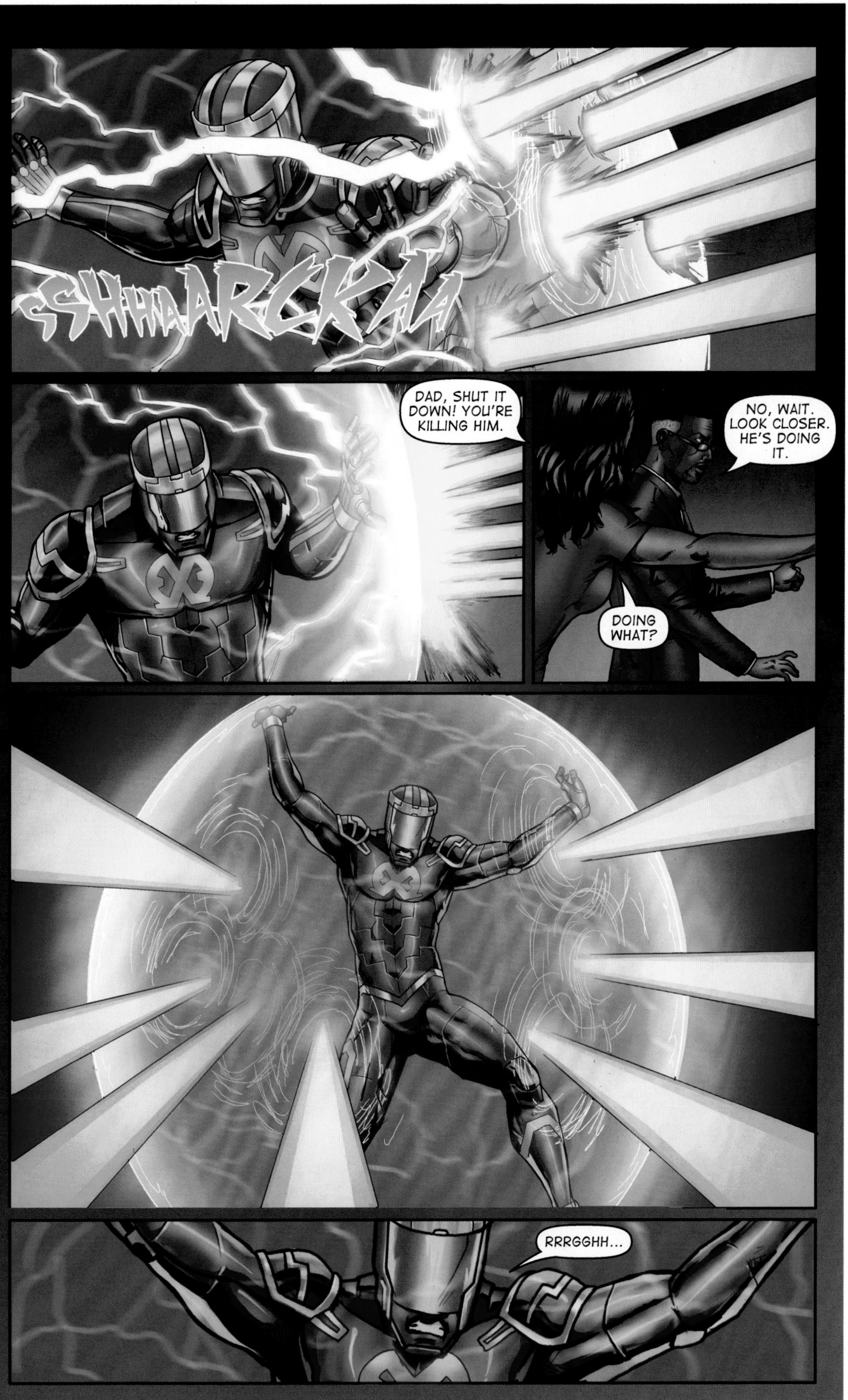
SSHHAARCKAA
DAD, SHUT IT DOWN! YOU'RE KILLING HIM.
NO, WAIT. LOOK CLOSER. HE'S DOING IT.
DOING WHAT?
RRRGGHH...

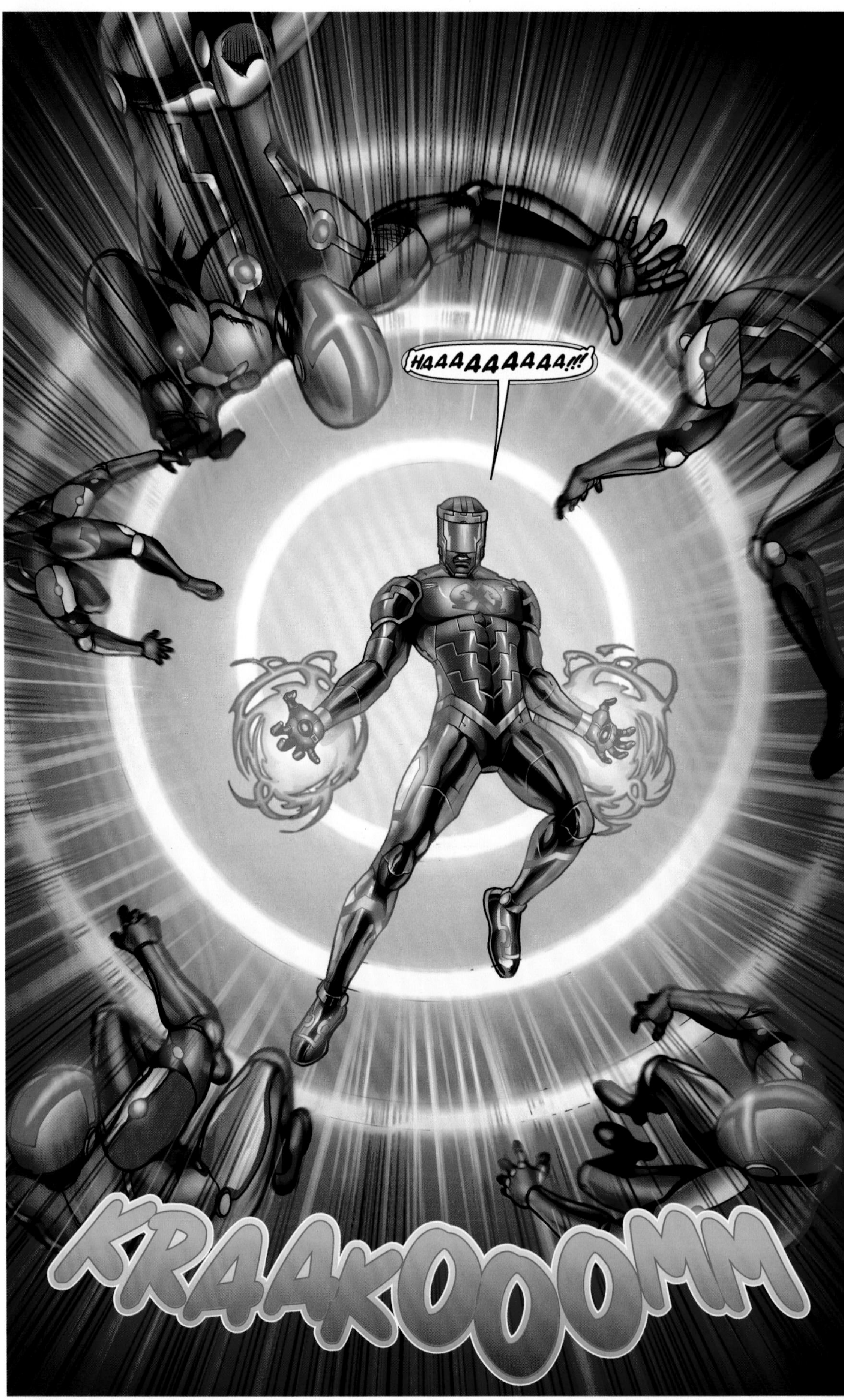
HAAAAAAAAA!!!
KRAAKOOOMM

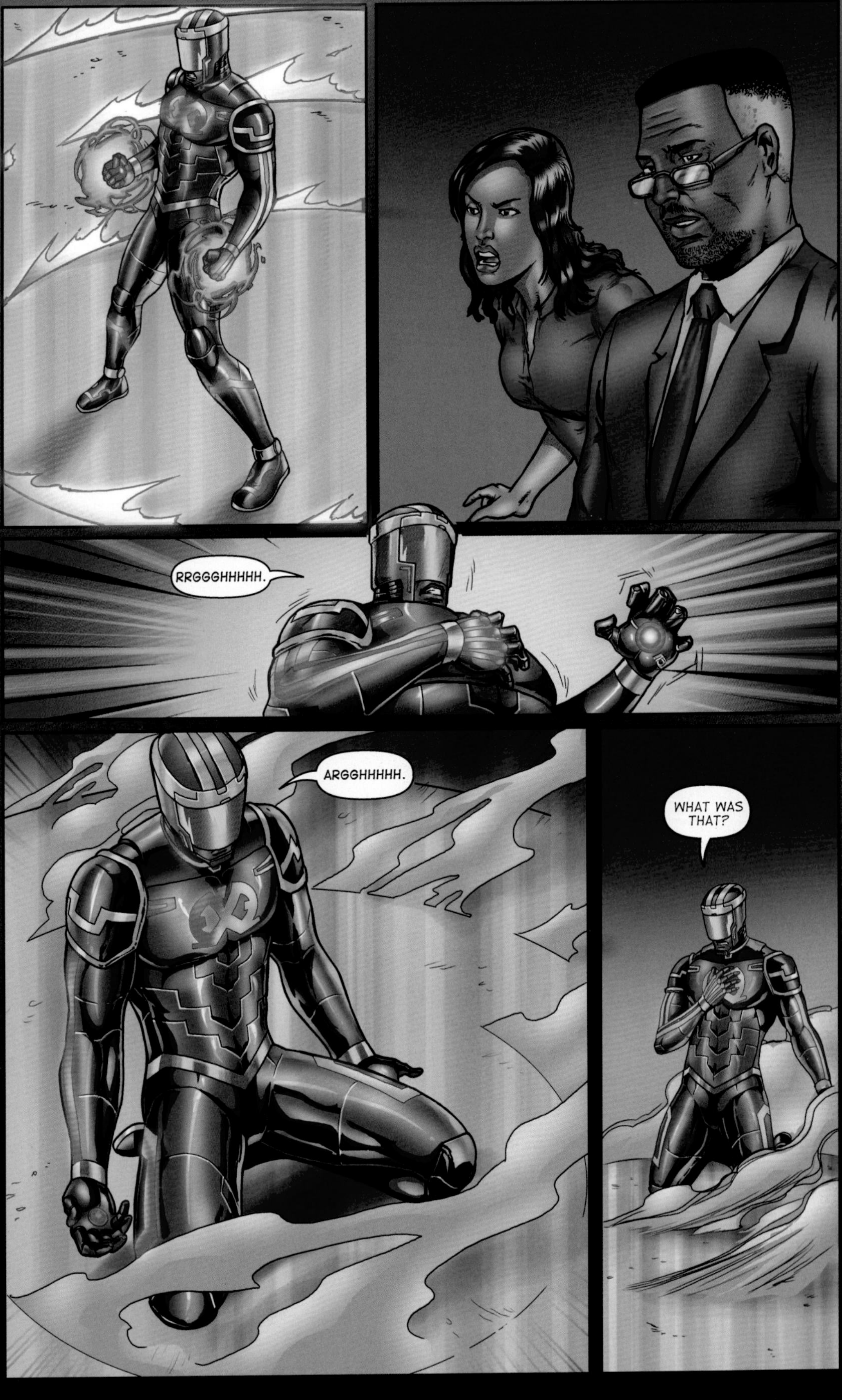
RRGGGHHHHH.
ARGGHHHHH.
WHAT WAS THAT?

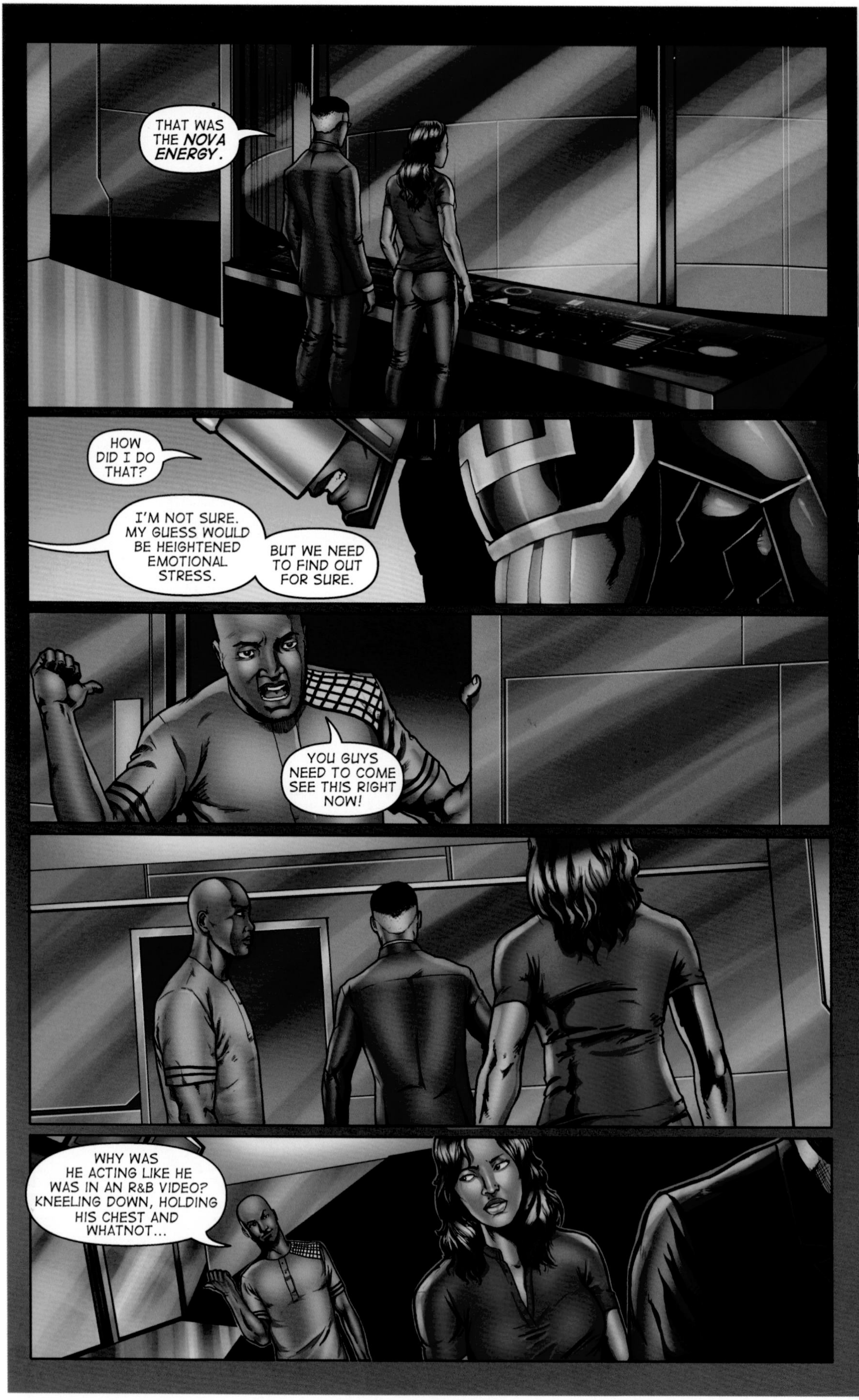
THAT WAS THE NOVA ENERGY.
HOW DID I DO THAT?
I'M NOT SURE. MY GUESS WOULD BE HEIGHTENED EMOTIONAL STRESS.
BUT WE NEED TO FIND OUT FOR SURE.
YOU GUYS NEED TO COME SEE THIS RIGHT NOW!
WHY WAS HE ACTING LIKE HE WAS IN AN R&B VIDEO? KNEELING DOWN, HOLDING HIS CHEST AND WHATNOT...

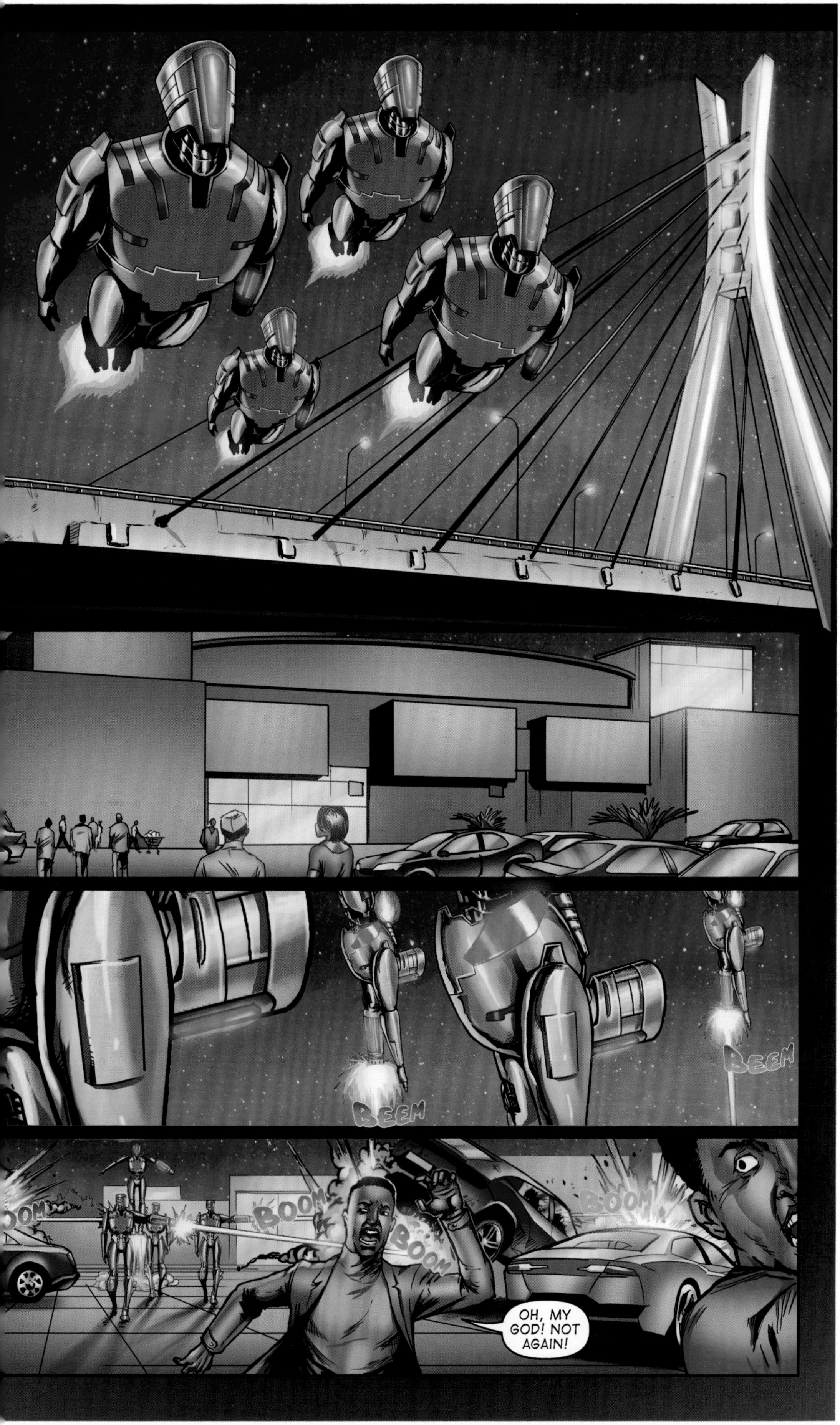
BEEM
BEEM
BOOM
BOOM
BOOM
BOOM
OH, MY GOD! NOT AGAIN!

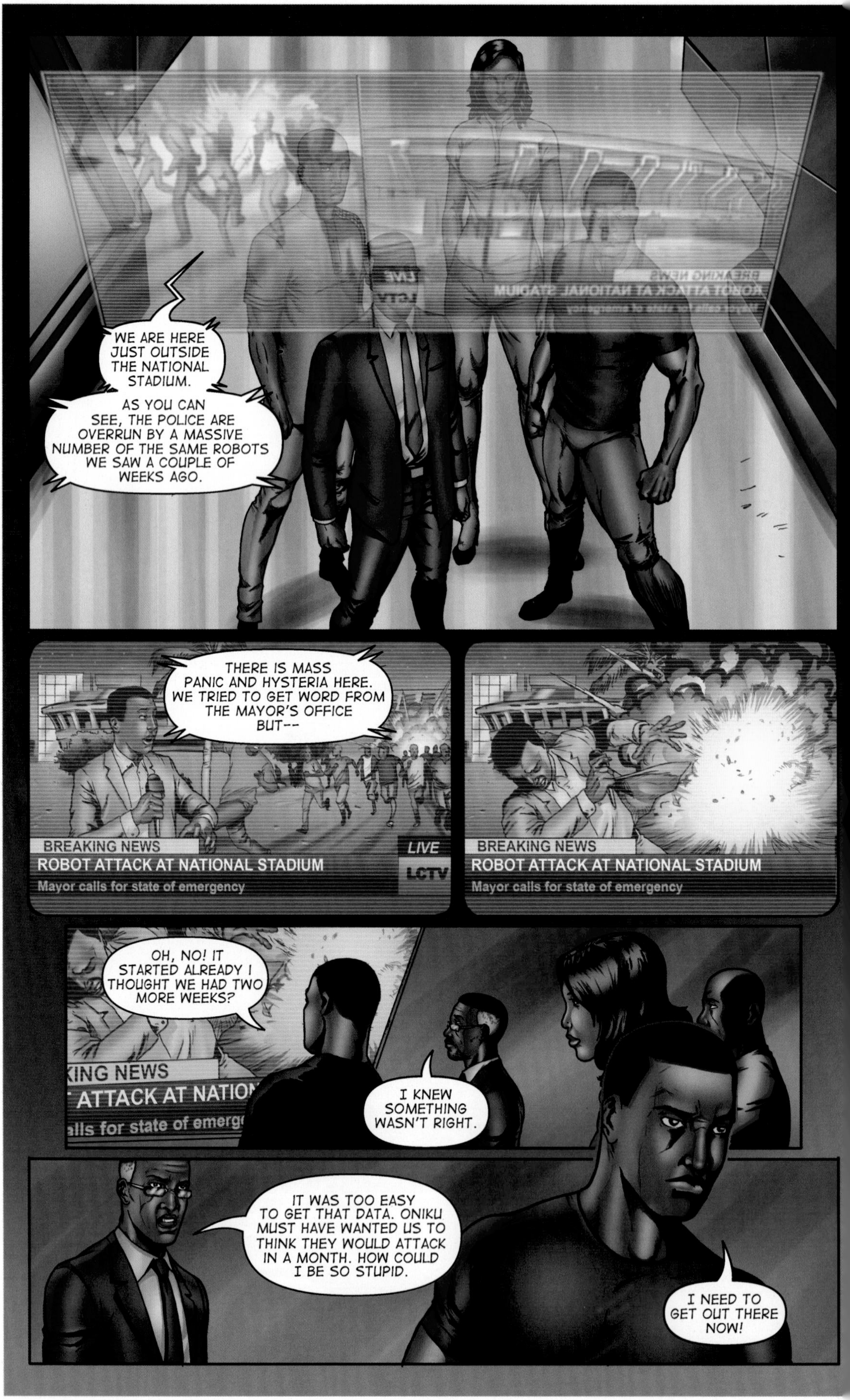
BREAKING NEWS
ROBOT ATTACK AT NATIONAL STADIUM
Mayor calls for state of emergency
LIVE
LCTV
WE ARE HERE JUST OUTSIDE THE NATIONAL STADIUM.
AS YOU CAN SEE, THE POLICE ARE OVERRUN BY A MASSIVE NUMBER OF THE SAME ROBOTS WE SAW A COUPLE OF WEEKS AGO.
THERE IS MASS PANIC AND HYSTERIA HERE. WE TRIED TO GET WORD FROM THE MAYOR'S OFFICE BUT--
BREAKING NEWS
ROBOT ATTACK AT NATIONAL STADIUM
Mayor calls for state of emergency
LIVE
LCTV
BREAKING NEWS
ROBOT ATTACK AT NATIONAL STADIUM
Mayor calls for state of emergency
OH, NO! IT STARTED ALREADY I THOUGHT WE HAD TWO MORE WEEKS?
KING NEWS
T ATTACK AT NATION
alls for state of emerg
I KNEW SOMETHING WASN'T RIGHT.
IT WAS TOO EASY TO GET THAT DATA. ONIKU MUST HAVE WANTED US TO THINK THEY WOULD ATTACK IN A MONTH. HOW COULD I BE SO STUPID.
I NEED TO GET OUT THERE NOW!

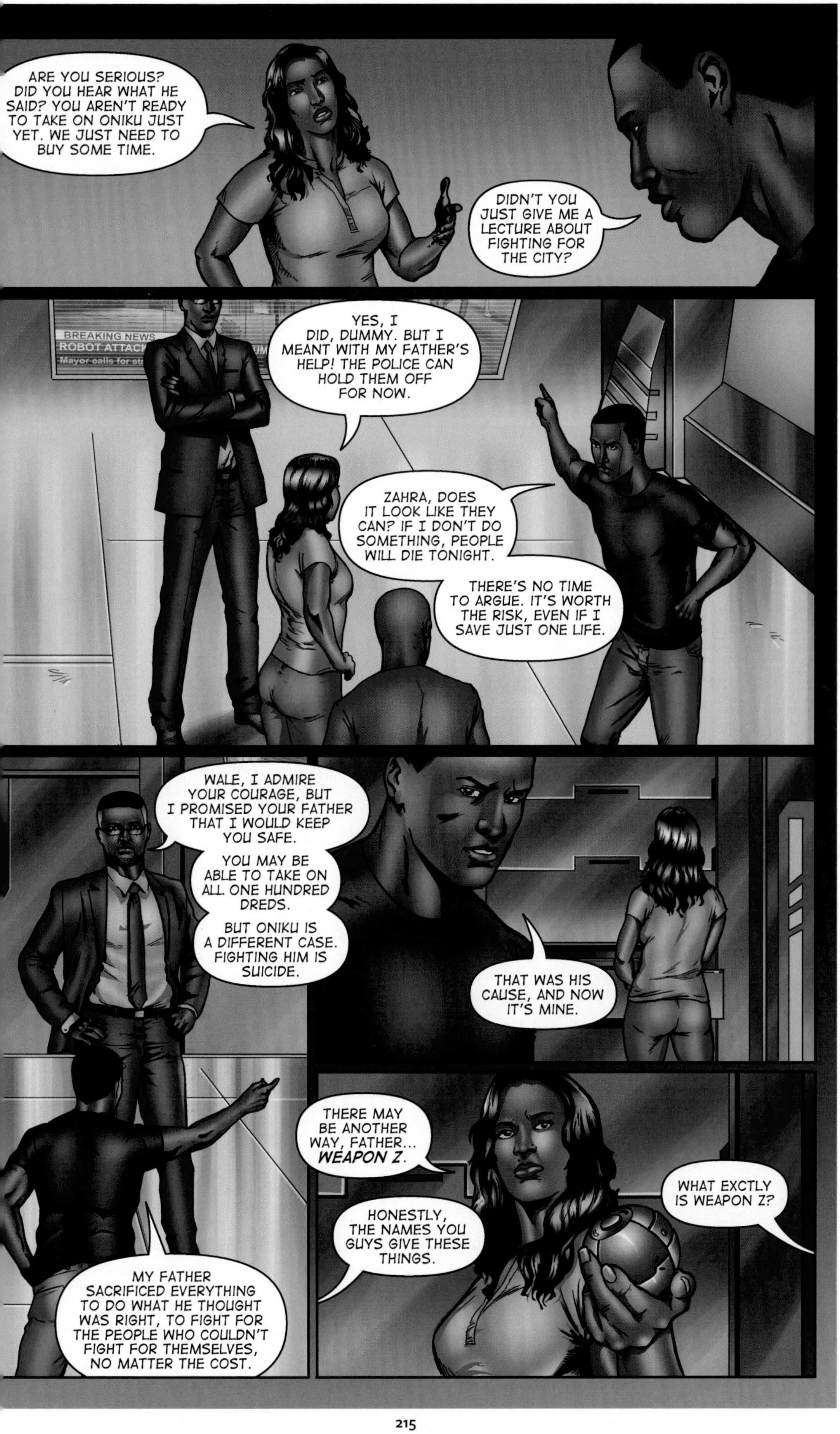
ARE YOU SERIOUS? DID YOU HEAR WHAT HE SAID? YOU AREN'T READY TO TAKE ON ONIKU JUST YET. WE JUST NEED TO BUY SOME TIME.
DIDN'T YOU JUST GIVE ME A LECTURE ABOUT FIGHTING FOR THE CITY?
BREAKING NEWS
ROBOT ATTACK
YES, I DID, DUMMY. BUT I MEANT WITH MY FATHER'S HELP! THE POLICE CAN HOLD THEM OFF FOR NOW.
ZAHRA, DOES IT LOOK LIKE THEY CAN? IF I DON'T DO SOMETHING, PEOPLE WILL DIE TONIGHT.
THERE'S NO TIME TO ARGUE. IT'S WORTH THE RISK, EVEN IF I SAVE JUST ONE LIFE.
WALE, I ADMIRE YOUR COURAGE, BUT I PROMISED YOUR FATHER THAT I WOULD KEEP YOU SAFE.
YOU MAY BE ABLE TO TAKE ON ALL ONE HUNDRED DREDS.
BUT ONIKU IS A DIFFERENT CASE. FIGHTING HIM IS SUICIDE.
THAT WAS HIS CAUSE, AND NOW IT'S MINE.
MY FATHER SACRIFICED EVERYTHING TO DO WHAT HE THOUGHT WAS RIGHT, TO FIGHT FOR THE PEOPLE WHO COULDN'T FIGHT FOR THEMSELVES, NO MATTER THE COST.
THERE MAY BE ANOTHER WAY, FATHER... ***WEAPON Z***.
HONESTLY, THE NAMES YOU GUYS GIVE THESE THINGS.
WHAT EXCTLY IS WEAPON Z?

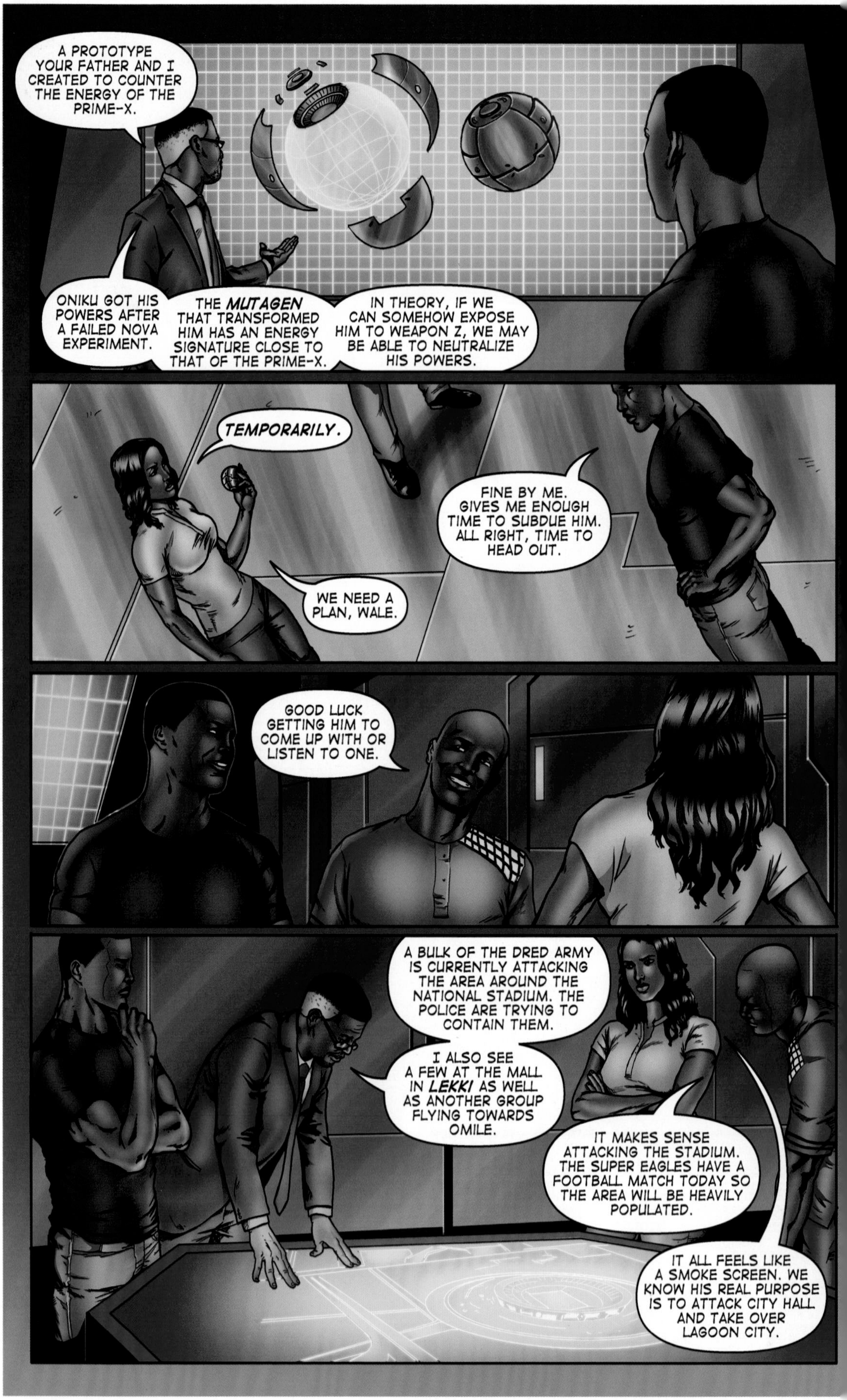
A PROTOTYPE YOUR FATHER AND I CREATED TO COUNTER THE ENERGY OF THE PRIME-X.
ONIKU GOT HIS POWERS AFTER A FAILED NOVA EXPERIMENT.
THE *MUTAGEN* THAT TRANSFORMED HIM HAS AN ENERGY SIGNATURE CLOSE TO THAT OF THE PRIME-X.
IN THEORY, IF WE CAN SOMEHOW EXPOSE HIM TO WEAPON Z, WE MAY BE ABLE TO NEUTRALIZE HIS POWERS.
TEMPORARILY.
FINE BY ME. GIVES ME ENOUGH TIME TO SUBDUE HIM. ALL RIGHT, TIME TO HEAD OUT.
WE NEED A PLAN, WALE.
GOOD LUCK GETTING HIM TO COME UP WITH OR LISTEN TO ONE.
A BULK OF THE DRED ARMY IS CURRENTLY ATTACKING THE AREA AROUND THE NATIONAL STADIUM. THE POLICE ARE TRYING TO CONTAIN THEM.
I ALSO SEE A FEW AT THE MALL IN *LEKKI* AS WELL AS ANOTHER GROUP FLYING TOWARDS OMILE.
IT MAKES SENSE ATTACKING THE STADIUM. THE SUPER EAGLES HAVE A FOOTBALL MATCH TODAY SO THE AREA WILL BE HEAVILY POPULATED.
IT ALL FEELS LIKE A SMOKE SCREEN. WE KNOW HIS REAL PURPOSE IS TO ATTACK CITY HALL AND TAKE OVER LAGOON CITY.

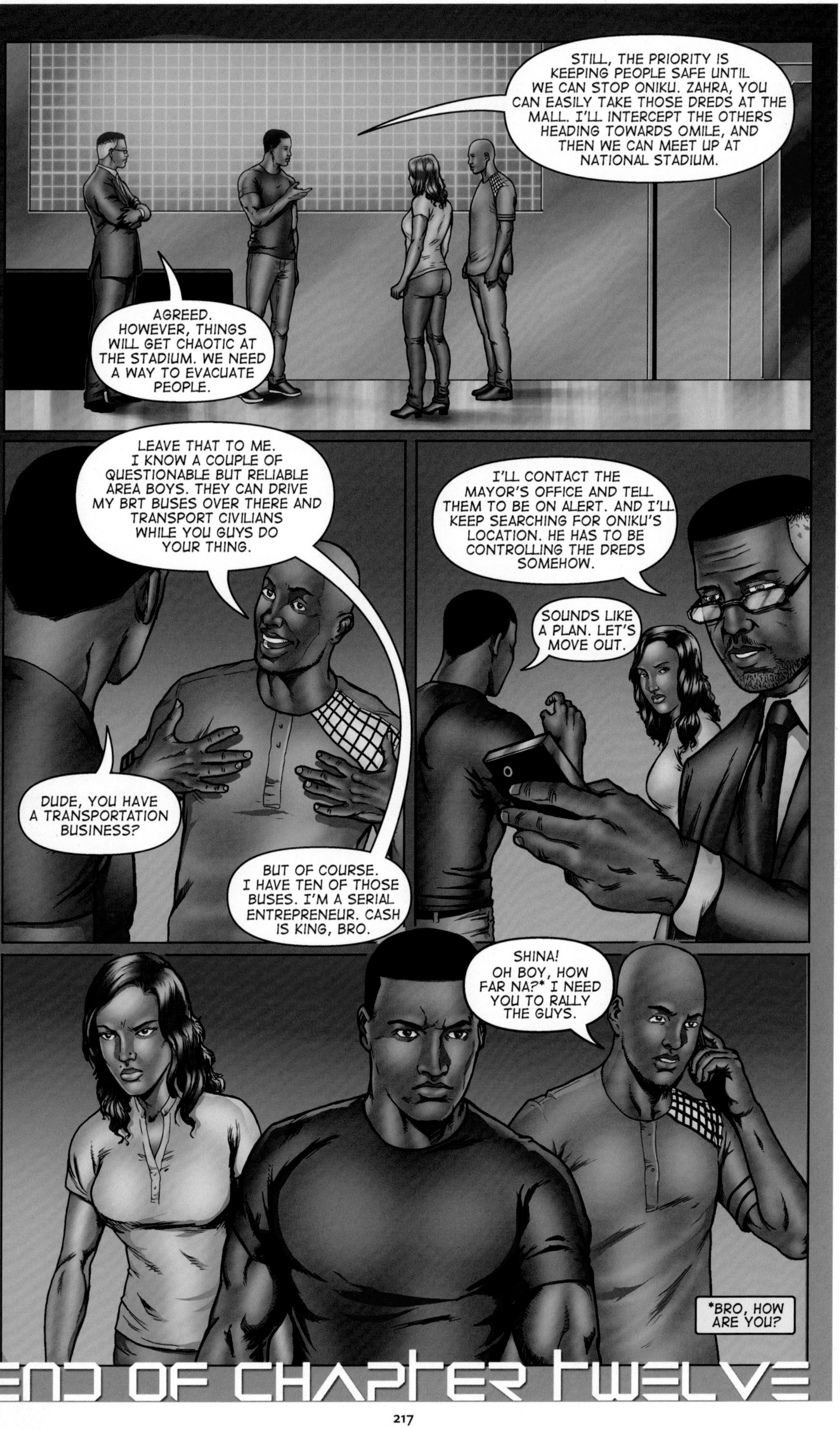
STILL, THE PRIORITY IS KEEPING PEOPLE SAFE UNTIL WE CAN STOP ONIKU. ZAHRA, YOU CAN EASILY TAKE THOSE DREDS AT THE MALL. I'LL INTERCEPT THE OTHERS HEADING TOWARDS OMILE, AND THEN WE CAN MEET UP AT NATIONAL STADIUM.
AGREED. HOWEVER, THINGS WILL GET CHAOTIC AT THE STADIUM. WE NEED A WAY TO EVACUATE PEOPLE.
LEAVE THAT TO ME. I KNOW A COUPLE OF QUESTIONABLE BUT RELIABLE AREA BOYS. THEY CAN DRIVE MY BRT BUSES OVER THERE AND TRANSPORT CIVILIANS WHILE YOU GUYS DO YOUR THING.
DUDE, YOU HAVE A TRANSPORTATION BUSINESS?
BUT OF COURSE. I HAVE TEN OF THOSE BUSES. I'M A SERIAL ENTREPRENEUR. CASH IS KING, BRO.
I'LL CONTACT THE MAYOR'S OFFICE AND TELL THEM TO BE ON ALERT. AND I'LL KEEP SEARCHING FOR ONIKU'S LOCATION. HE HAS TO BE CONTROLLING THE DREDS SOMEHOW.
SOUNDS LIKE A PLAN. LET'S MOVE OUT.
SHINA! OH BOY, HOW FAR NA?* I NEED YOU TO RALLY THE GUYS.
*BRO, HOW ARE YOU?
END OF CHAPTER TWELVE

FAN ART BY BABAJIDE BRIGGS ADEBIMPE

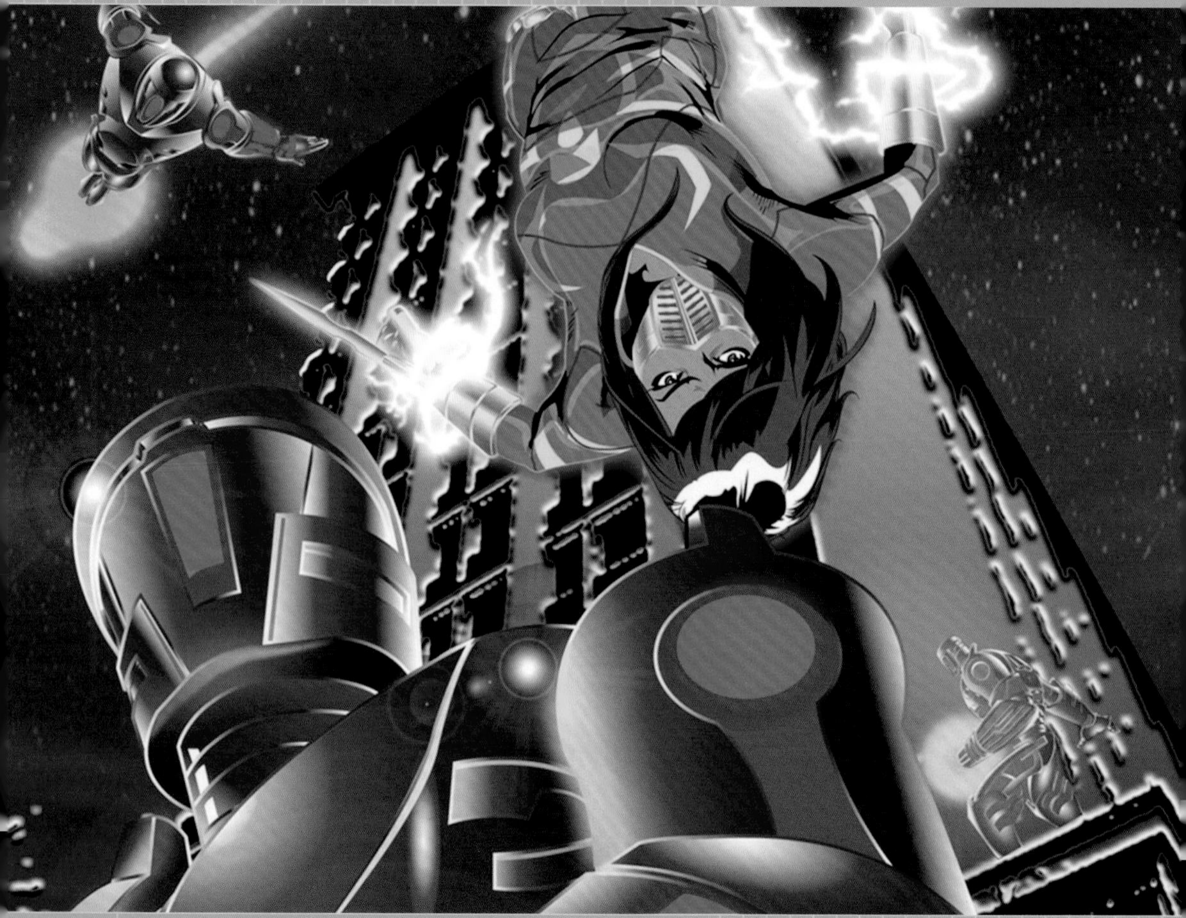

The DREDs (Dominant Robotic Exoskeletal Drones) were created by Prytek at the order of CEO James D. Peters. They come in two forms: the Alpha DREDs (silver in color) were created as prototypes using research left behind by Dr. Williams, and the DRED Ones (gold in color) were engineered using the data compiled by the Alphas, making them much smarter and stronger than their predecessors.

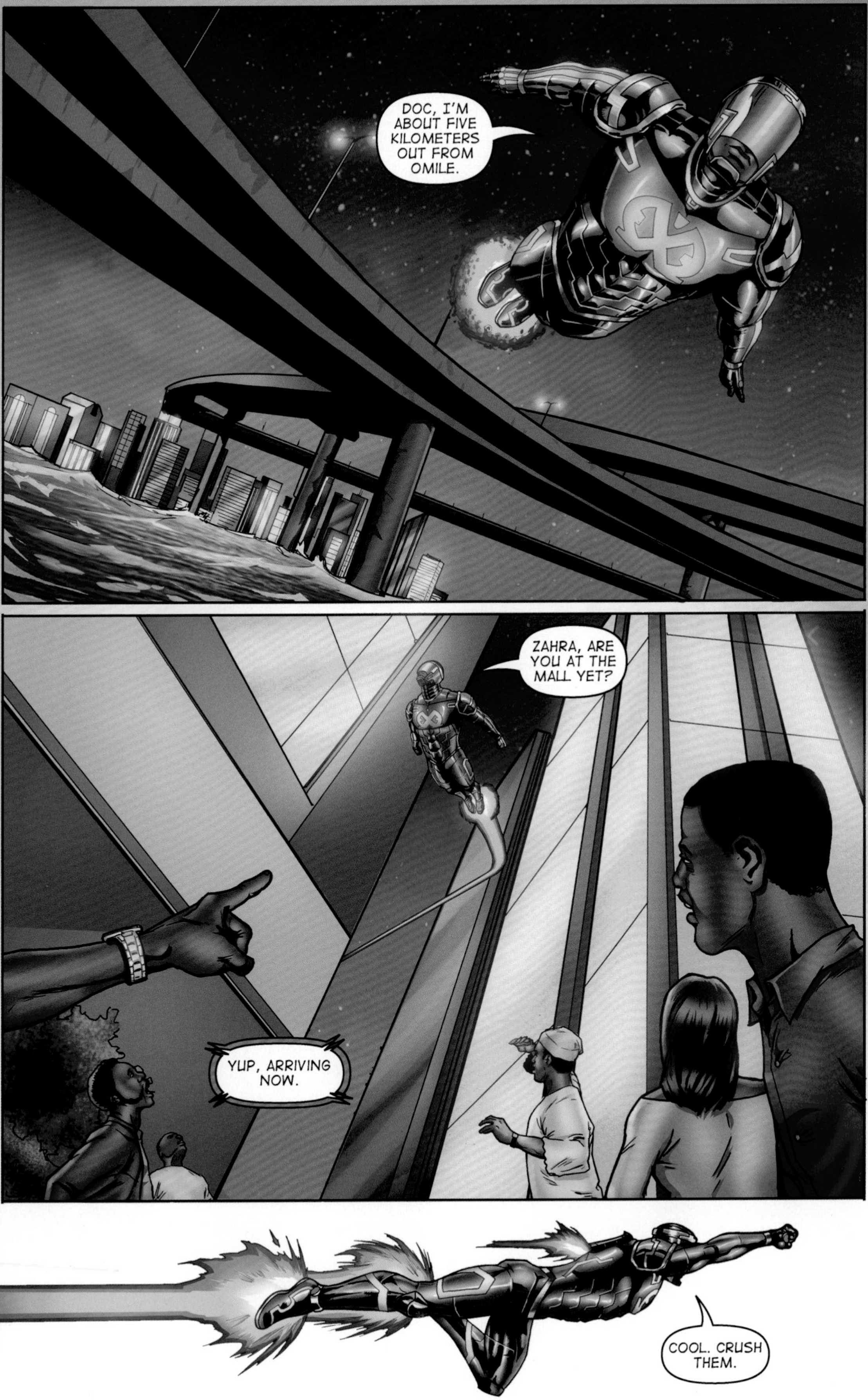
DOC, I'M ABOUT FIVE KILOMETERS OUT FROM OMILE.
ZAHRA, ARE YOU AT THE MALL YET?
YUP, ARRIVING NOW.
COOL. CRUSH THEM.

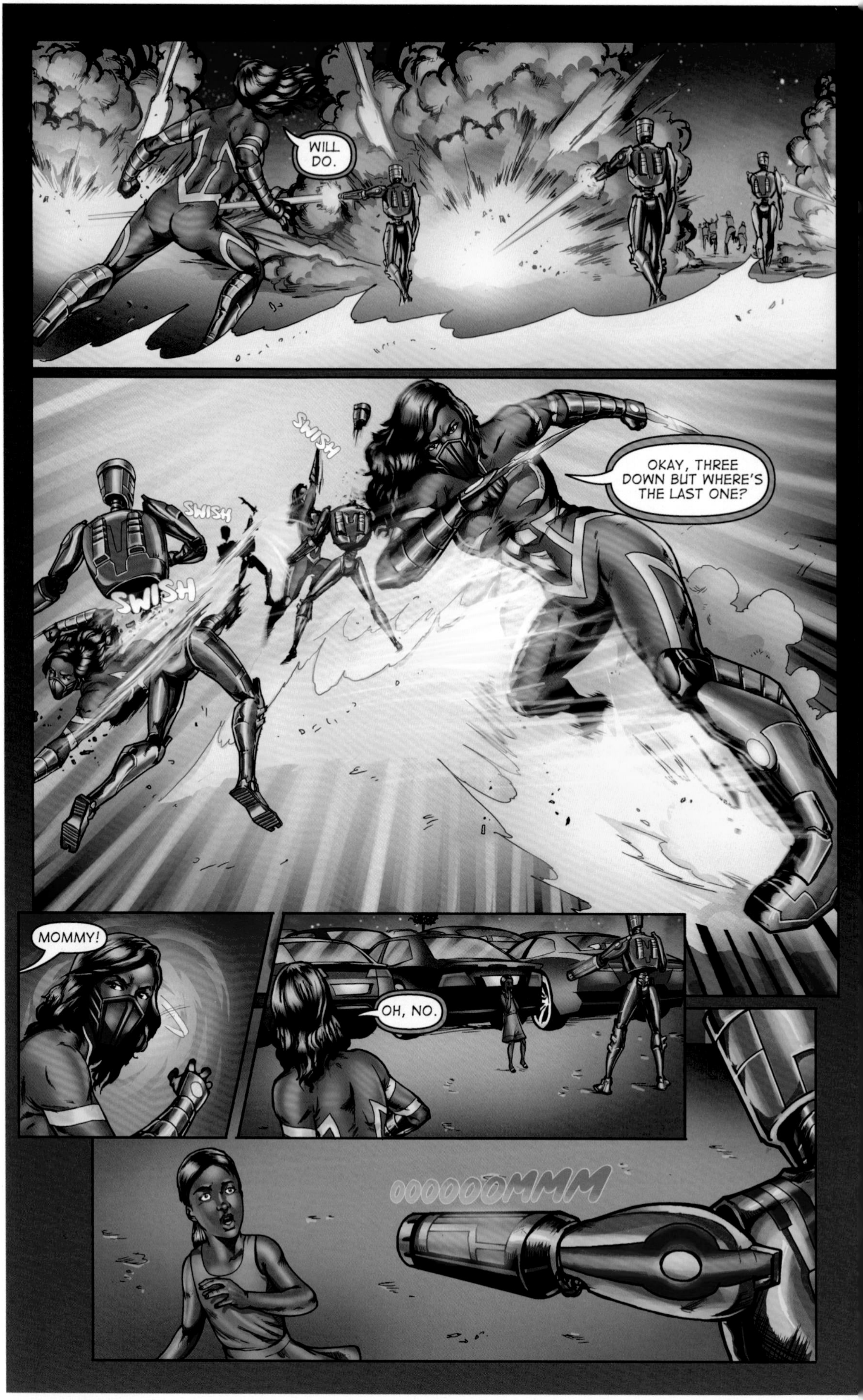
WILL DO.
SWISH
SWISH
SWISH
OKAY, THREE DOWN BUT WHERE'S THE LAST ONE?
MOMMY!
OH, NO.
OOOOOOMMM

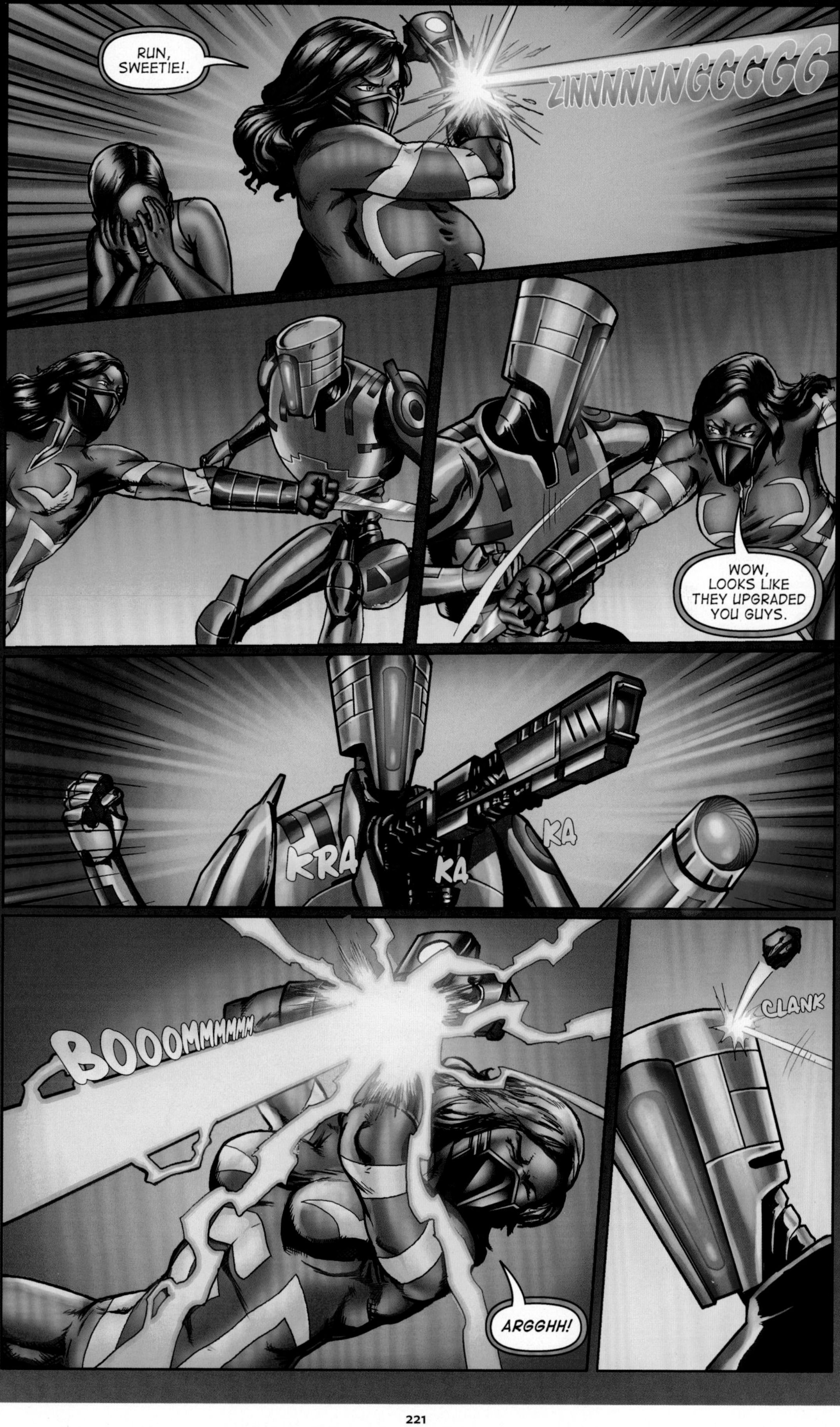
RUN, SWEETIE!.
ZINNNNNNGGGGG
WOW, LOOKS LIKE THEY UPGRADED YOU GUYS.
KRA
KA
KA
BOOOMMMMMM
ARGGHH!
CLANK

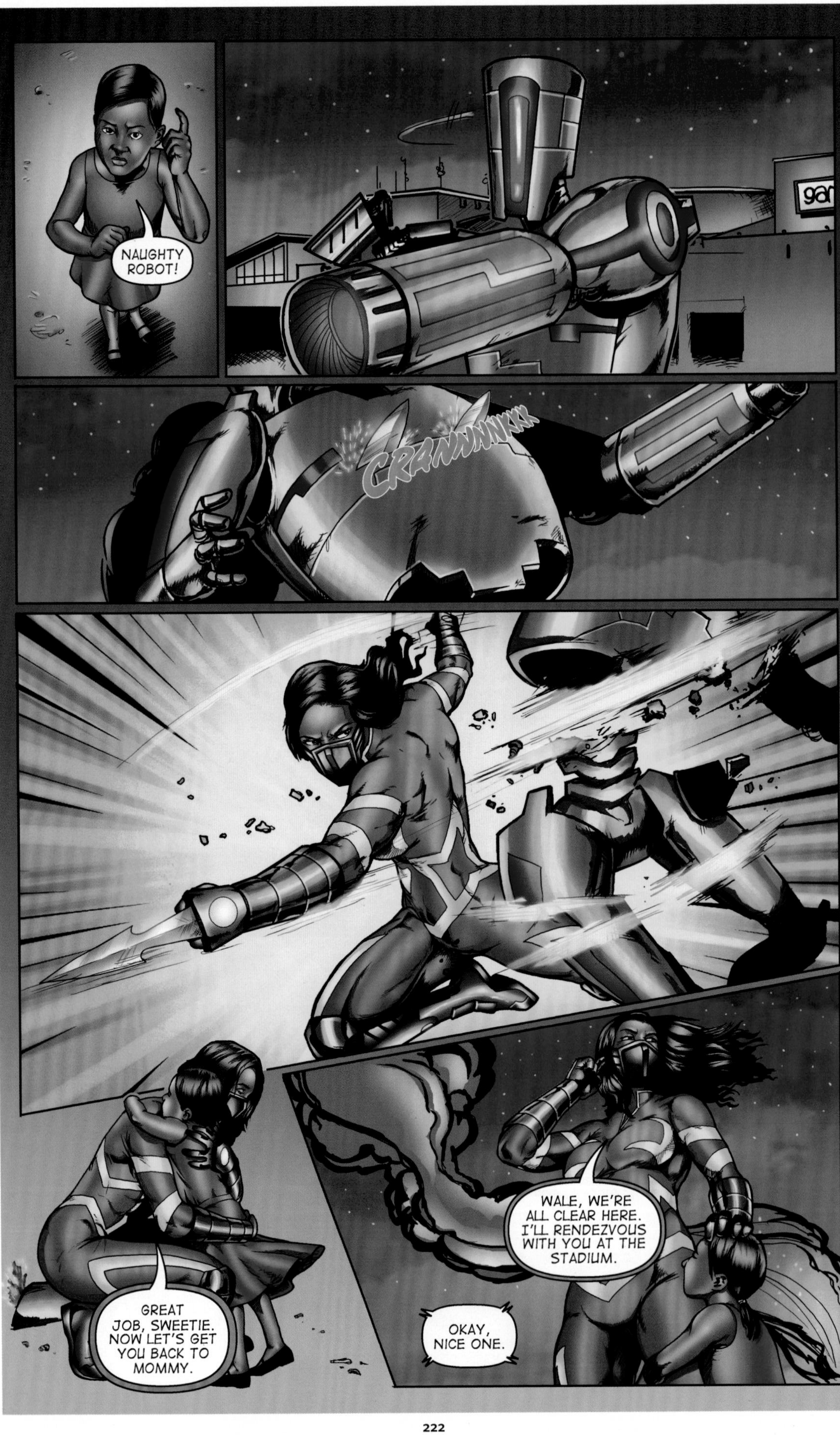
NAUGHTY ROBOT!
gar
CRANNNNKKK
GREAT JOB, SWEETIE. NOW LET'S GET YOU BACK TO MOMMY.
WALE, WE'RE ALL CLEAR HERE. I'LL RENDEZVOUS WITH YOU AT THE STADIUM.
OKAY, NICE ONE.

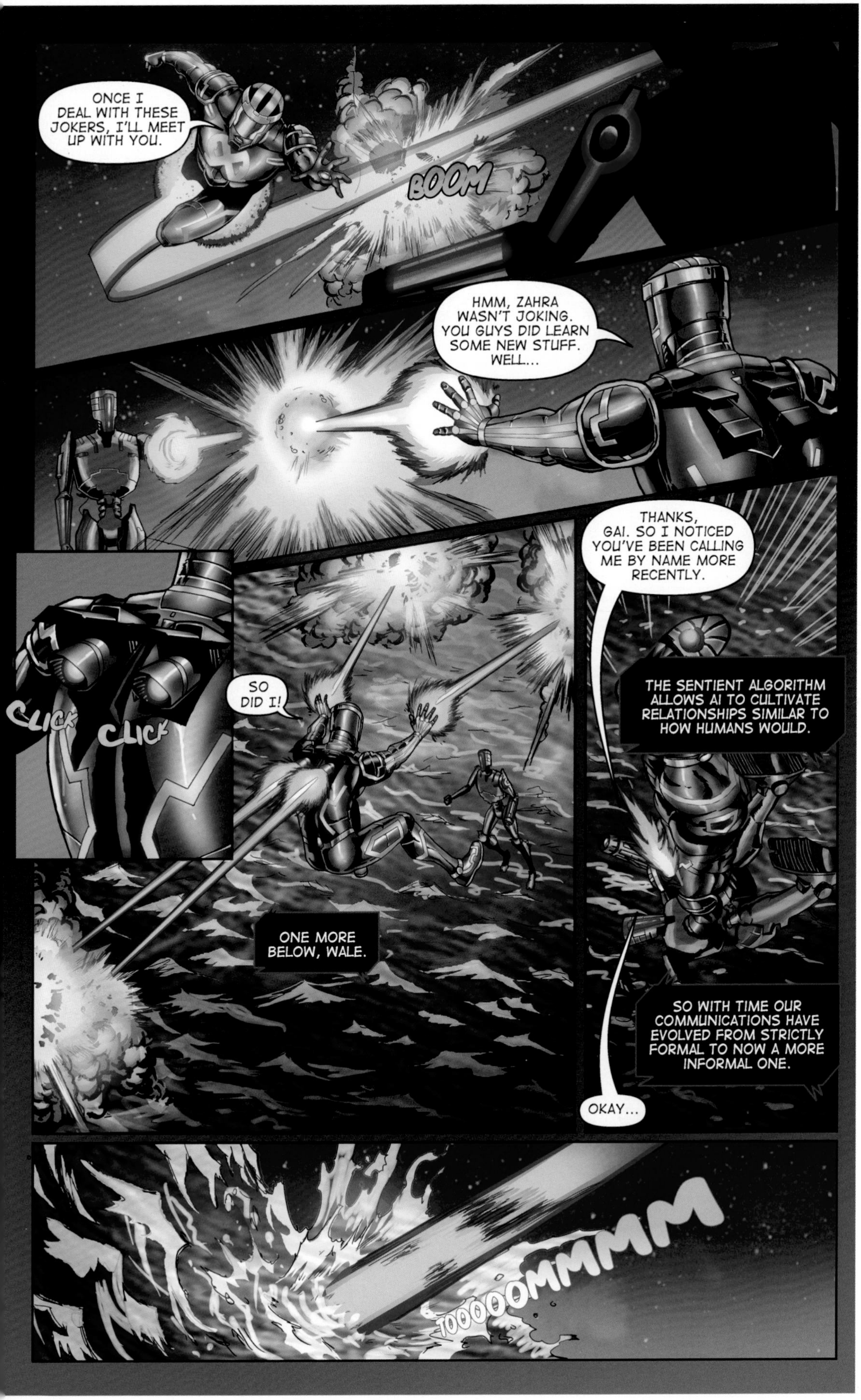

ONCE I DEAL WITH THESE JOKERS, I'LL MEET UP WITH YOU.
BOOM
HMM, ZAHRA WASN'T JOKING. YOU GUYS DID LEARN SOME NEW STUFF. WELL...
CLICK
CLICK
SO DID I!
ONE MORE BELOW, WALE.
THANKS, GAI. SO I NOTICED YOU'VE BEEN CALLING ME BY NAME MORE RECENTLY.
THE SENTIENT ALGORITHM ALLOWS AI TO CULTIVATE RELATIONSHIPS SIMILAR TO HOW HUMANS WOULD.
SO WITH TIME OUR COMMUNICATIONS HAVE EVOLVED FROM STRICTLY FORMAL TO NOW A MORE INFORMAL ONE.
OKAY...
TOOOOOOMMMMM

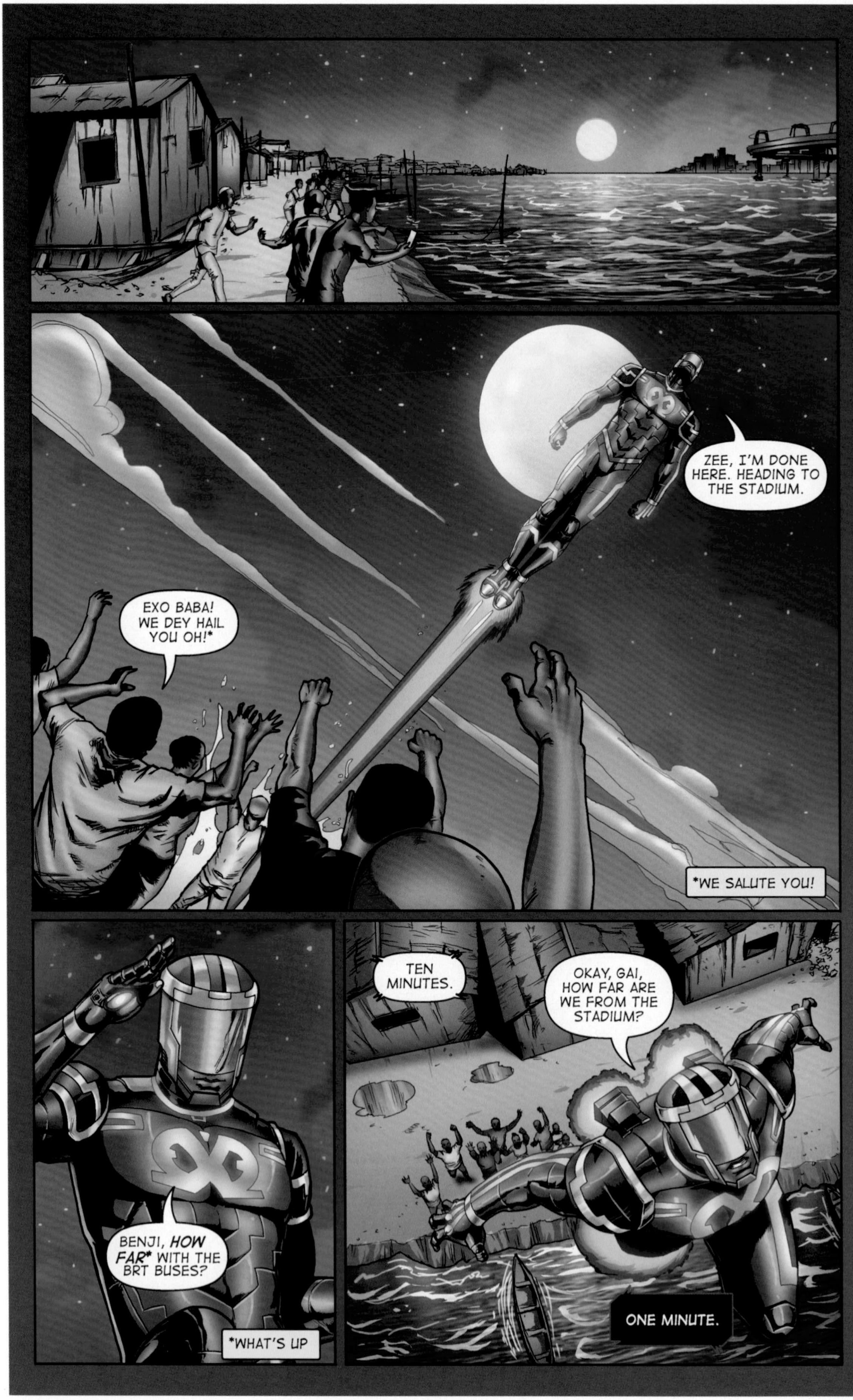
ZEE, I'M DONE HERE. HEADING TO THE STADIUM.
EXO BABA! WE DEY HAIL YOU OH!*
*WE SALUTE YOU!
BENJI, *HOW FAR** WITH THE BRT BUSES?
*WHAT'S UP
TEN MINUTES.
OKAY, GAI, HOW FAR ARE WE FROM THE STADIUM?
ONE MINUTE.

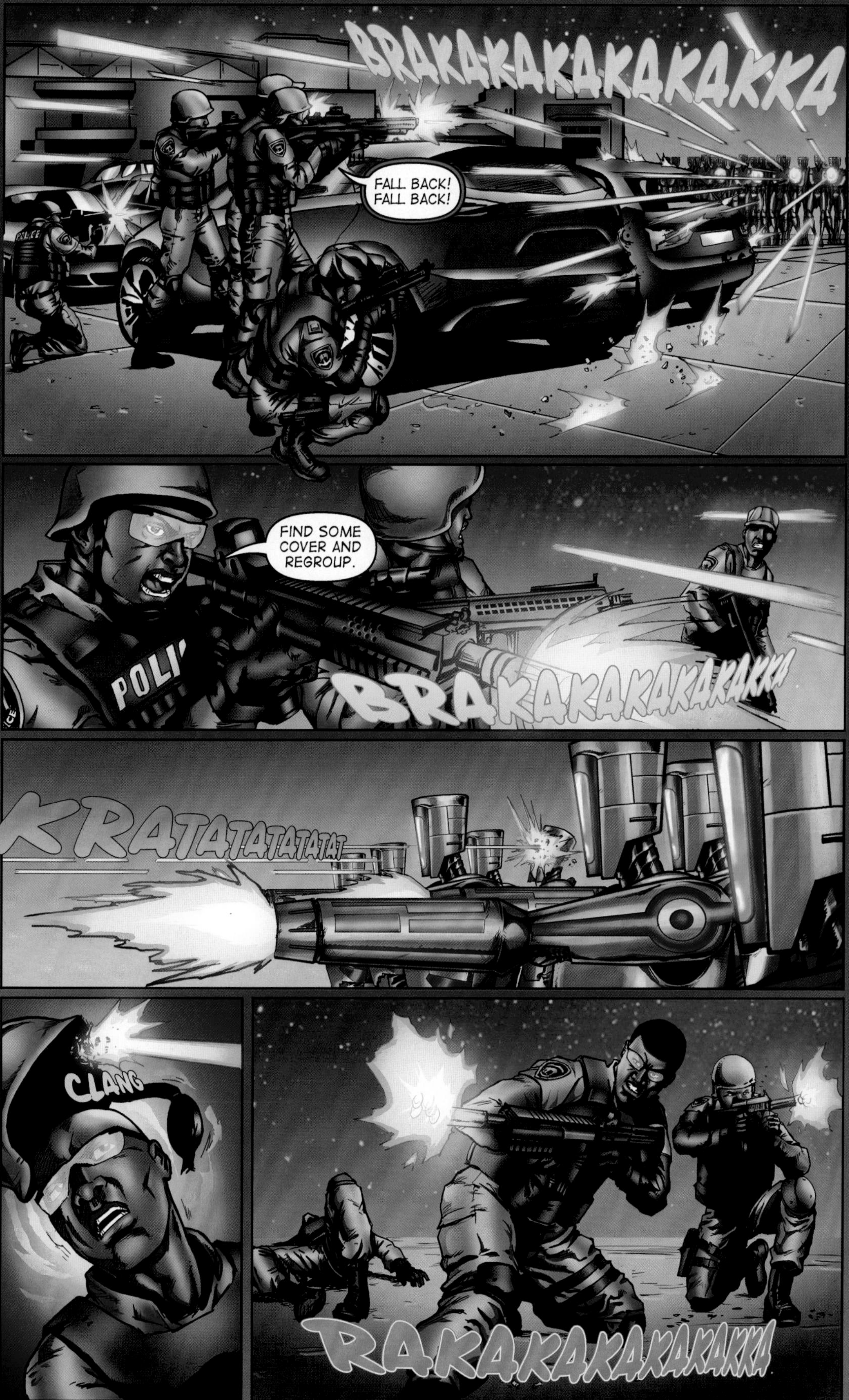
BRAKAKAKAKAKAKAKKA
POLICE
FALL BACK! FALL BACK!
FIND SOME COVER AND REGROUP.
POLI
BRAKAKAKAKAKAKKA
KRATATATATATAT
CLANG
RAKAKAKAKAKAKAKKA

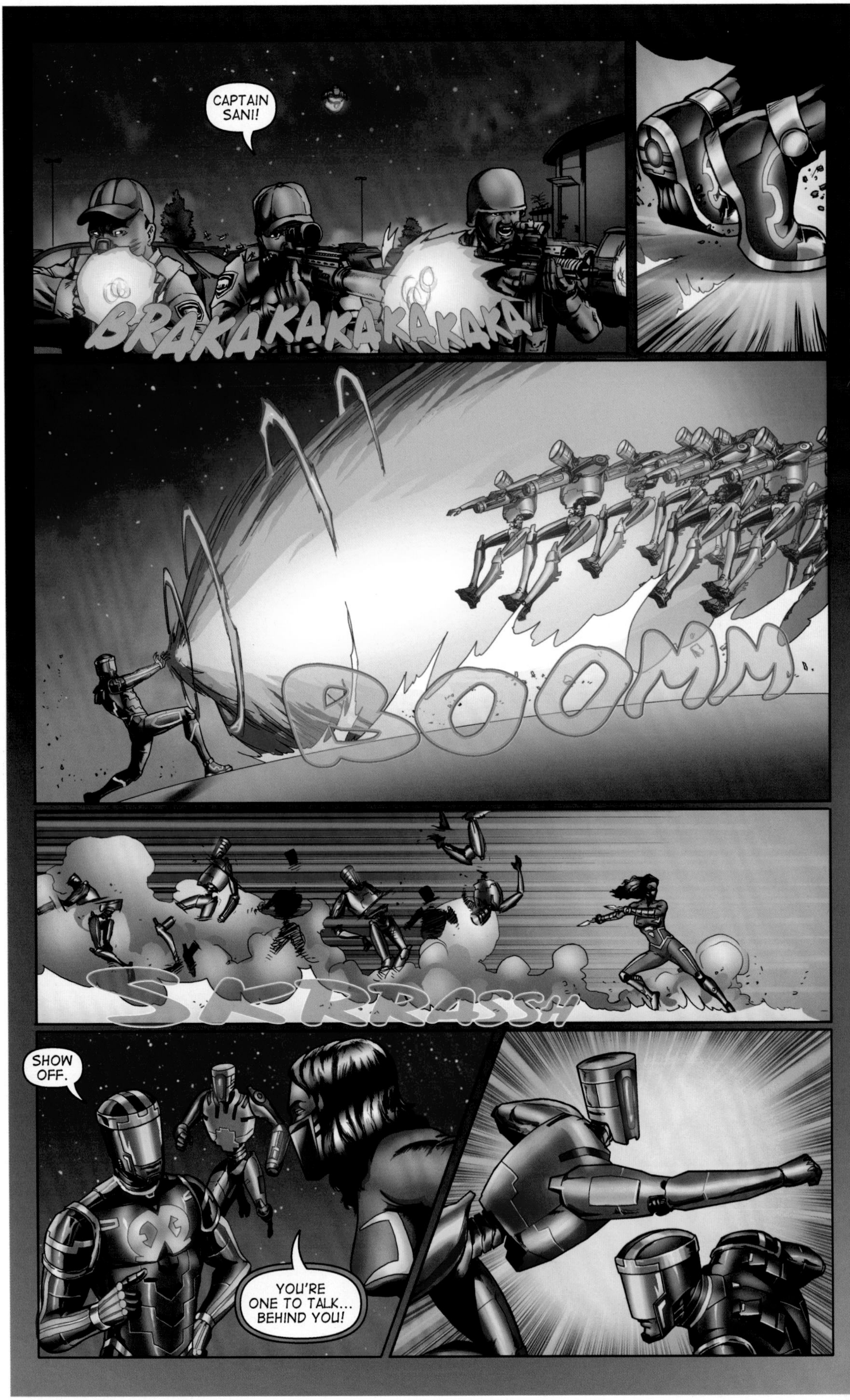
CAPTAIN SANI!
BRAKAKAKAKAKAKAKA
BOOMM
SKRRASSH
SHOW OFF.
YOU'RE ONE TO TALK... BEHIND YOU!

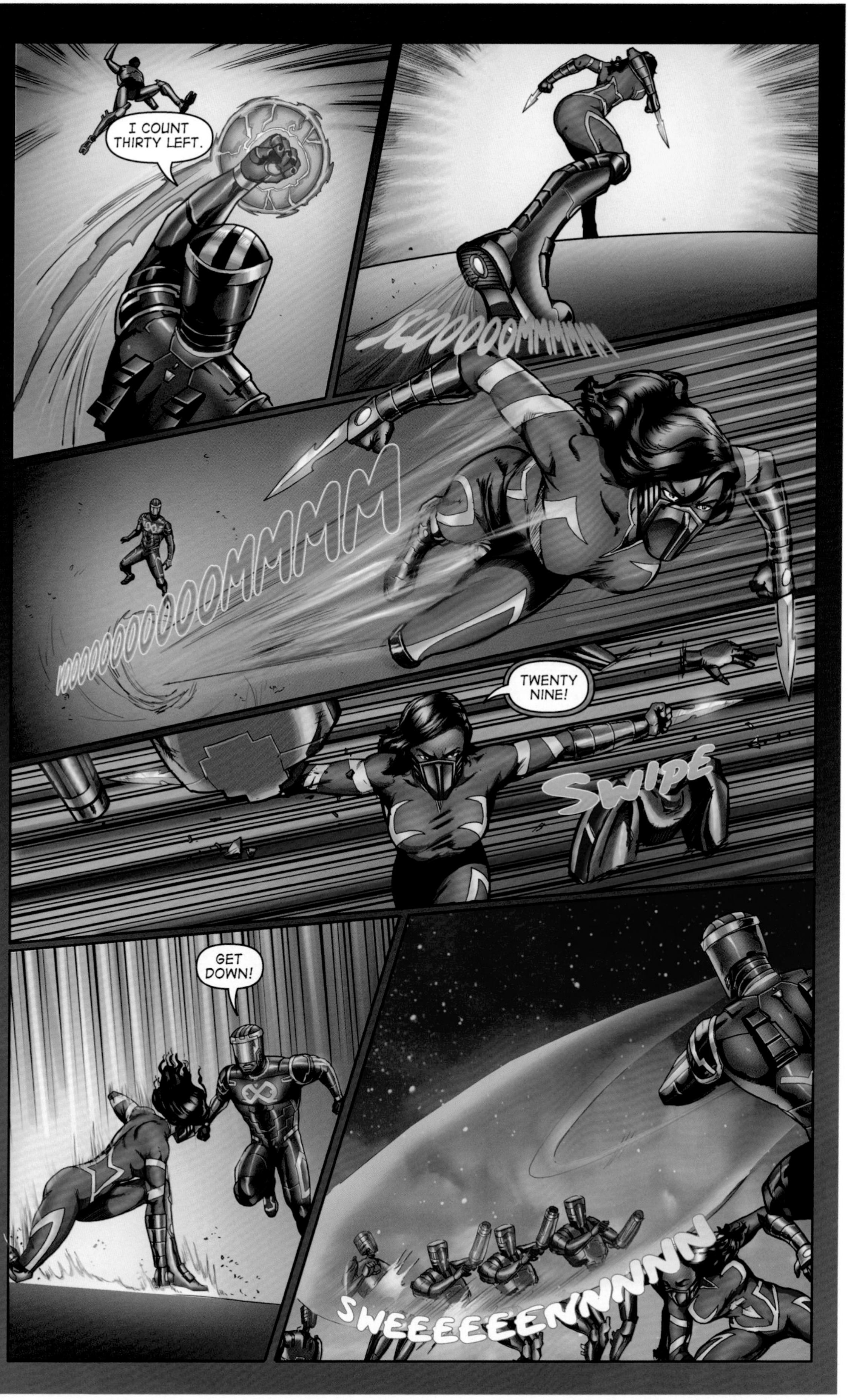
I COUNT THIRTY LEFT.
TWENTY NINE!
SWIPE
GET DOWN!

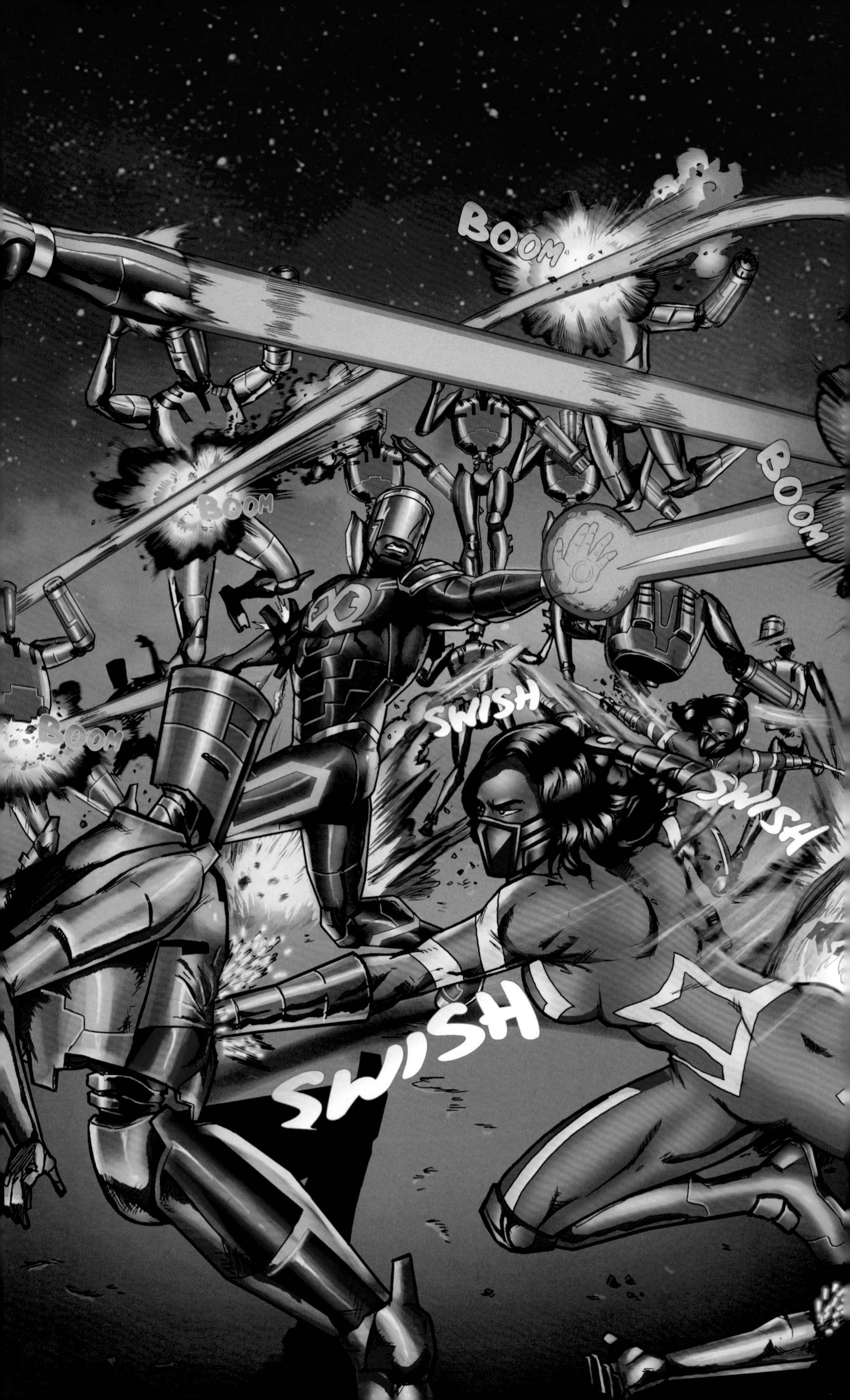
BOOM
BOOM
BOOM
BOOM
SWISH
SWISH
SWISH

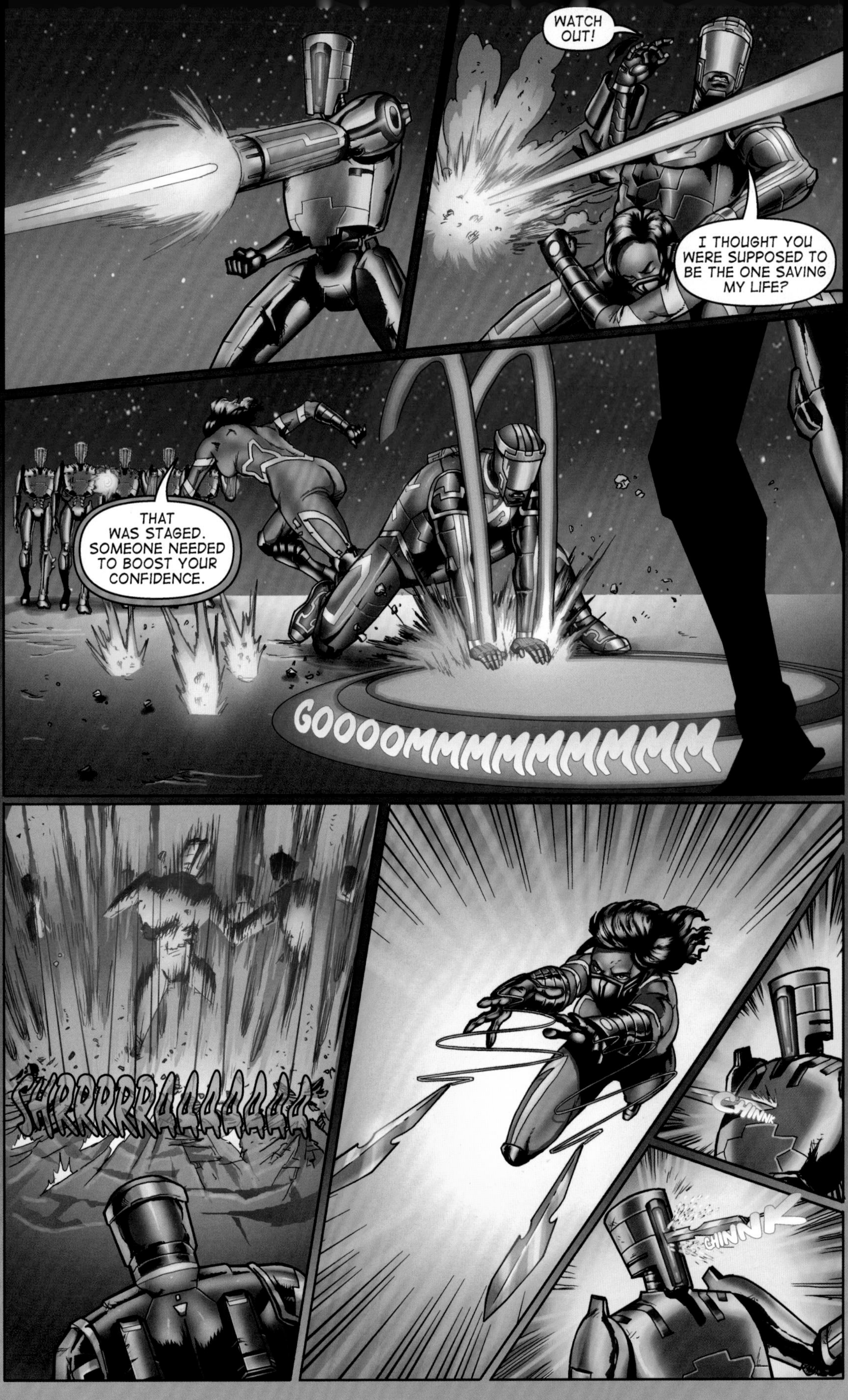
WATCH OUT!
I THOUGHT YOU WERE SUPPOSED TO BE THE ONE SAVING MY LIFE?
THAT WAS STAGED. SOMEONE NEEDED TO BOOST YOUR CONFIDENCE.
GOOOOMMMMMMMMMM
SHRRRRRAAAAAAAA
CHINNK
CHINNK

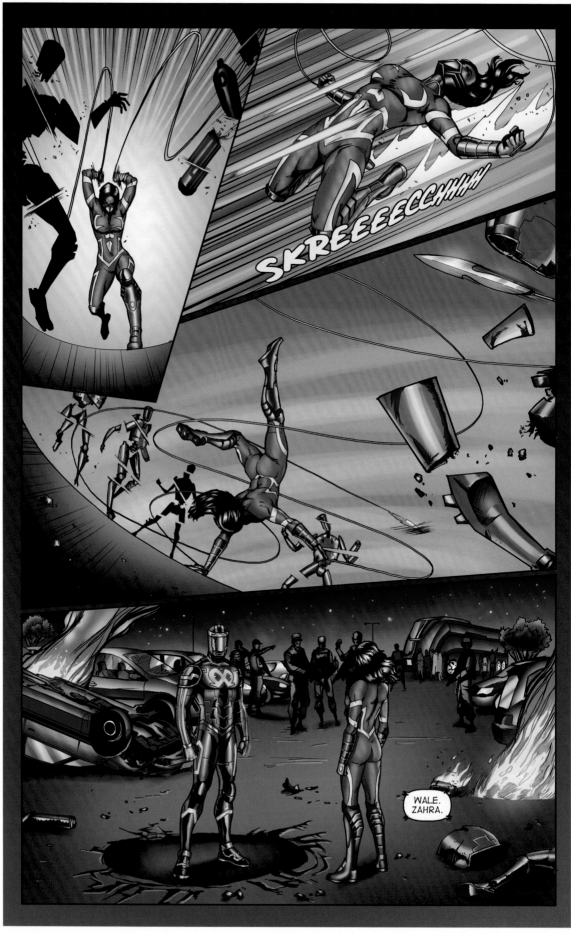

SKREEEEECCHHHH!

WALE.
ZAHRA.

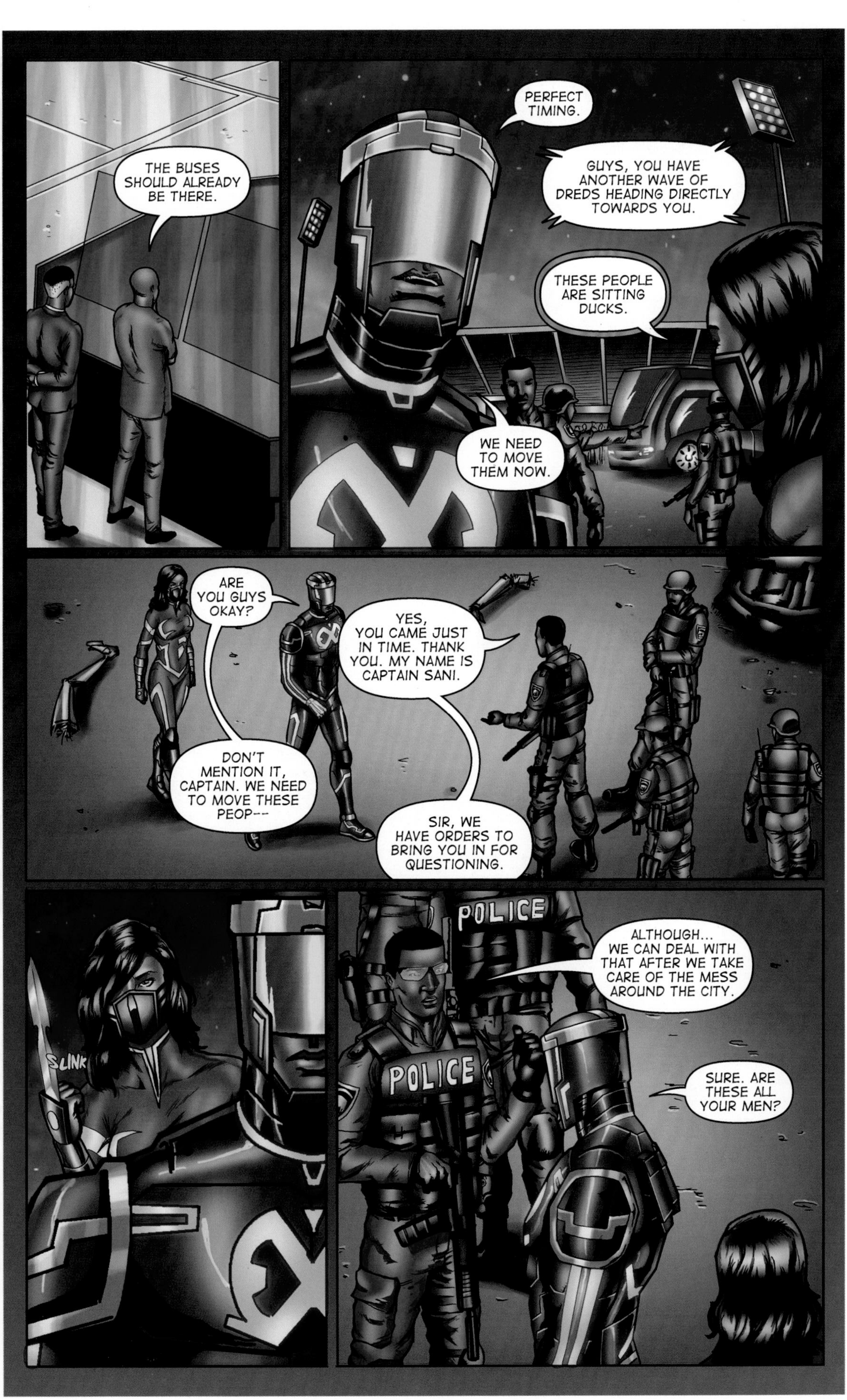
THE BUSES SHOULD ALREADY BE THERE.
PERFECT TIMING.
GUYS, YOU HAVE ANOTHER WAVE OF DREDS HEADING DIRECTLY TOWARDS YOU.
THESE PEOPLE ARE SITTING DUCKS.
WE NEED TO MOVE THEM NOW.
ARE YOU GUYS OKAY?
YES, YOU CAME JUST IN TIME. THANK YOU. MY NAME IS CAPTAIN SANI.
DON'T MENTION IT, CAPTAIN. WE NEED TO MOVE THESE PEOP---
SIR, WE HAVE ORDERS TO BRING YOU IN FOR QUESTIONING.
SLINK
POLICE
ALTHOUGH... WE CAN DEAL WITH THAT AFTER WE TAKE CARE OF THE MESS AROUND THE CITY.
POLICE
SURE. ARE THESE ALL YOUR MEN?

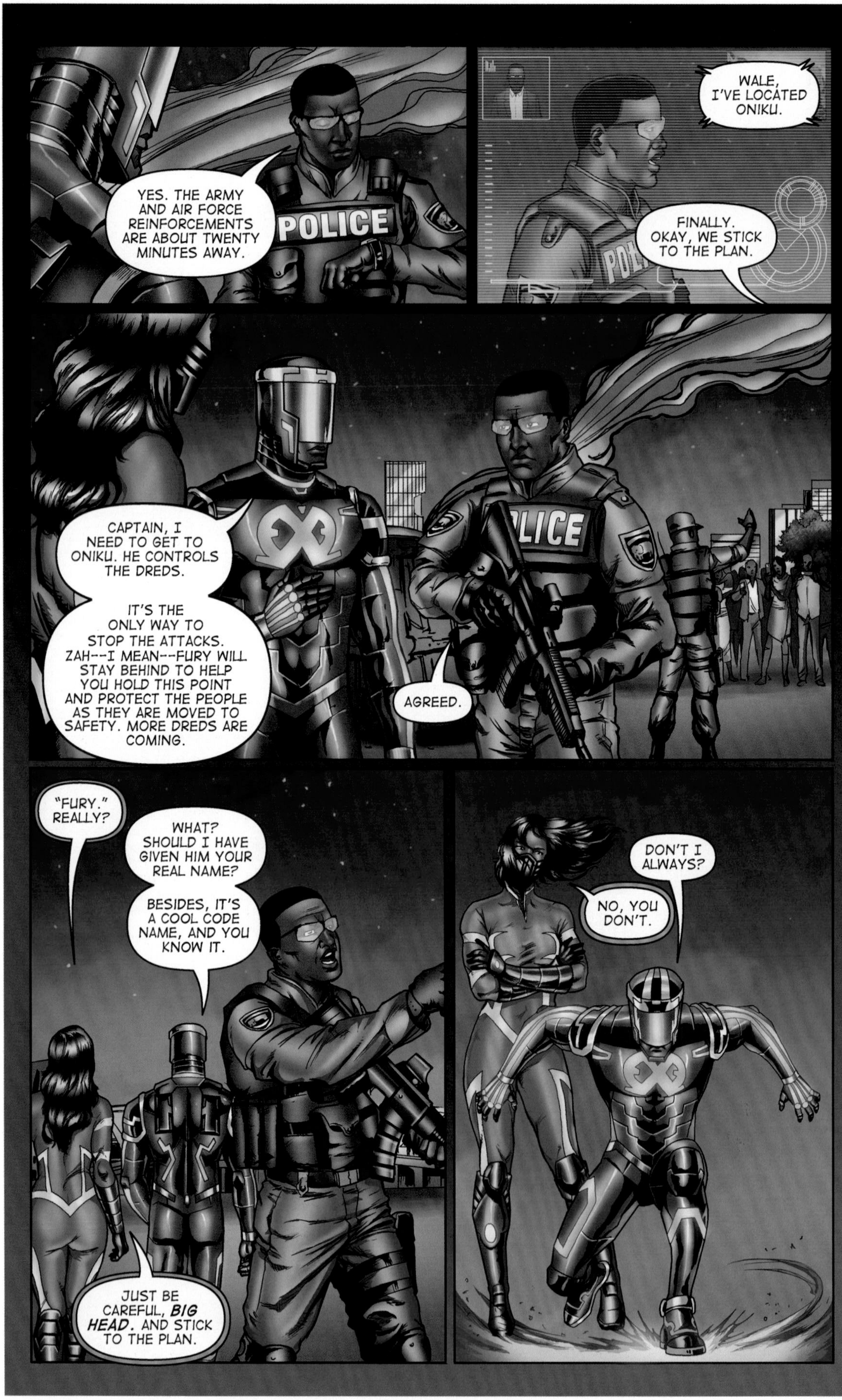

YES. THE ARMY AND AIR FORCE REINFORCEMENTS ARE ABOUT TWENTY MINUTES AWAY.
POLICE
WALE, I'VE LOCATED ONIKU.
FINALLY. OKAY, WE STICK TO THE PLAN.
CAPTAIN, I NEED TO GET TO ONIKU. HE CONTROLS THE DREDS.
IT'S THE ONLY WAY TO STOP THE ATTACKS. ZAH--I MEAN--FURY WILL STAY BEHIND TO HELP YOU HOLD THIS POINT AND PROTECT THE PEOPLE AS THEY ARE MOVED TO SAFETY. MORE DREDS ARE COMING.
AGREED.
"FURY." REALLY?
WHAT? SHOULD I HAVE GIVEN HIM YOUR REAL NAME?
BESIDES, IT'S A COOL CODE NAME, AND YOU KNOW IT.
JUST BE CAREFUL, ***BIG HEAD***. AND STICK TO THE PLAN.
DON'T I ALWAYS?
NO, YOU DON'T.

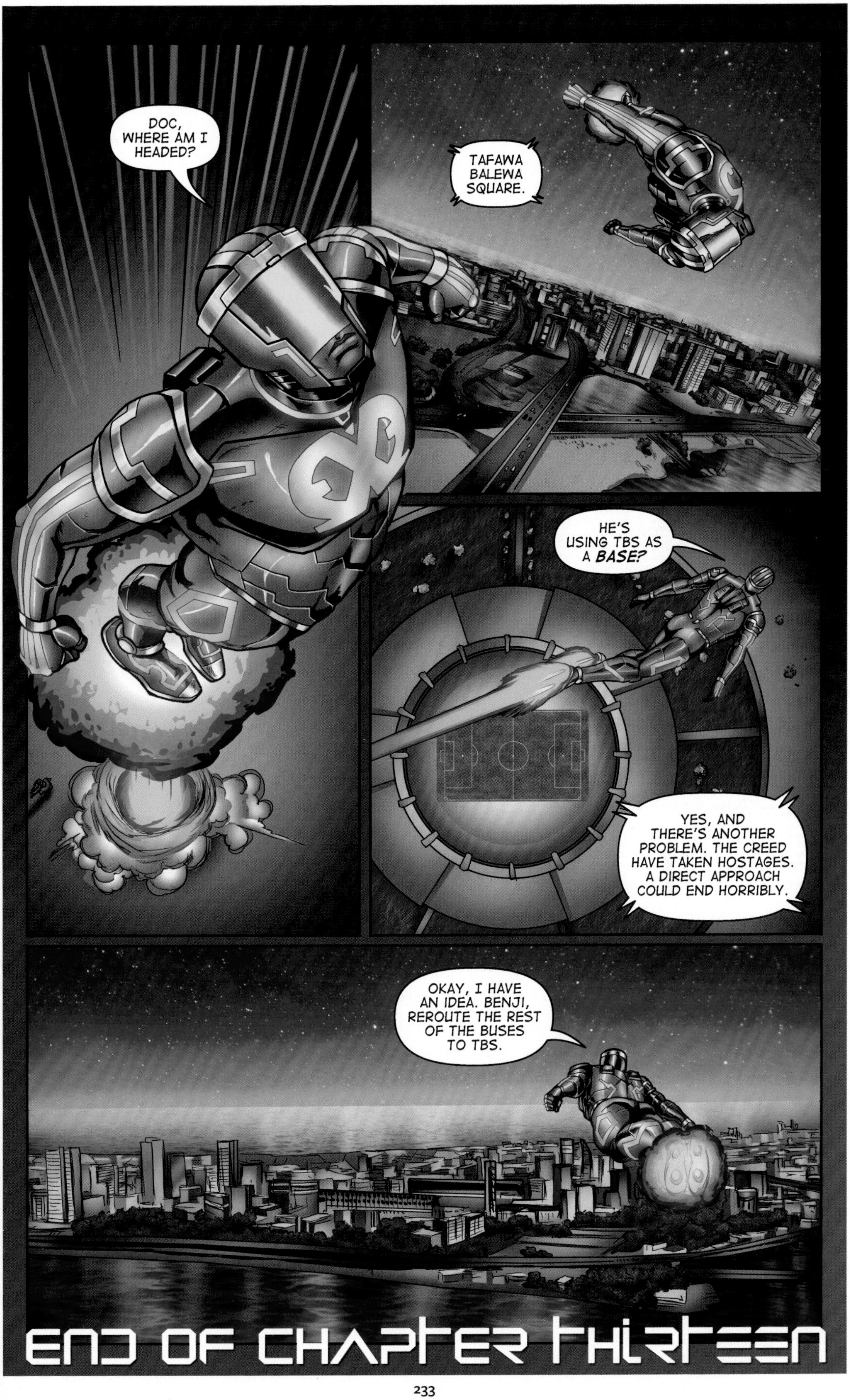
DOC, WHERE AM I HEADED?
TAFAWA BALEWA SQUARE.
HE'S USING TBS AS A *BASE?*
YES, AND THERE'S ANOTHER PROBLEM. THE CREED HAVE TAKEN HOSTAGES. A DIRECT APPROACH COULD END HORRIBLY.
OKAY, I HAVE AN IDEA. BENJI, REROUTE THE REST OF THE BUSES TO TBS.
END OF CHAPTER THIRTEEN

FAN ART BY EVERARD McBAIN

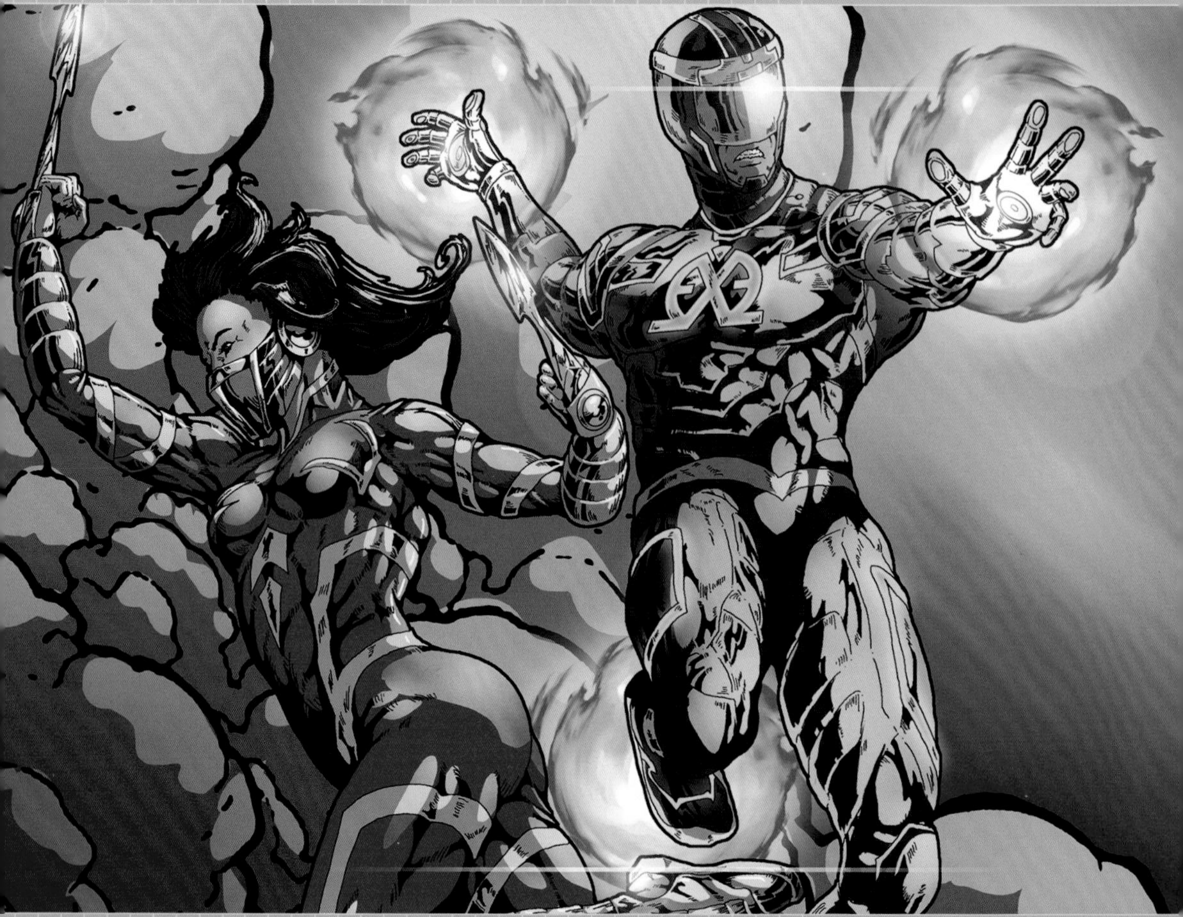

E.X.O.: The Legend of Wale Williams is an ongoing series of books broken into several sagas. You are currently reading the "Oniku Saga," and the next will be known as the "Avon Saga."

CHAPTER FOURTEEN

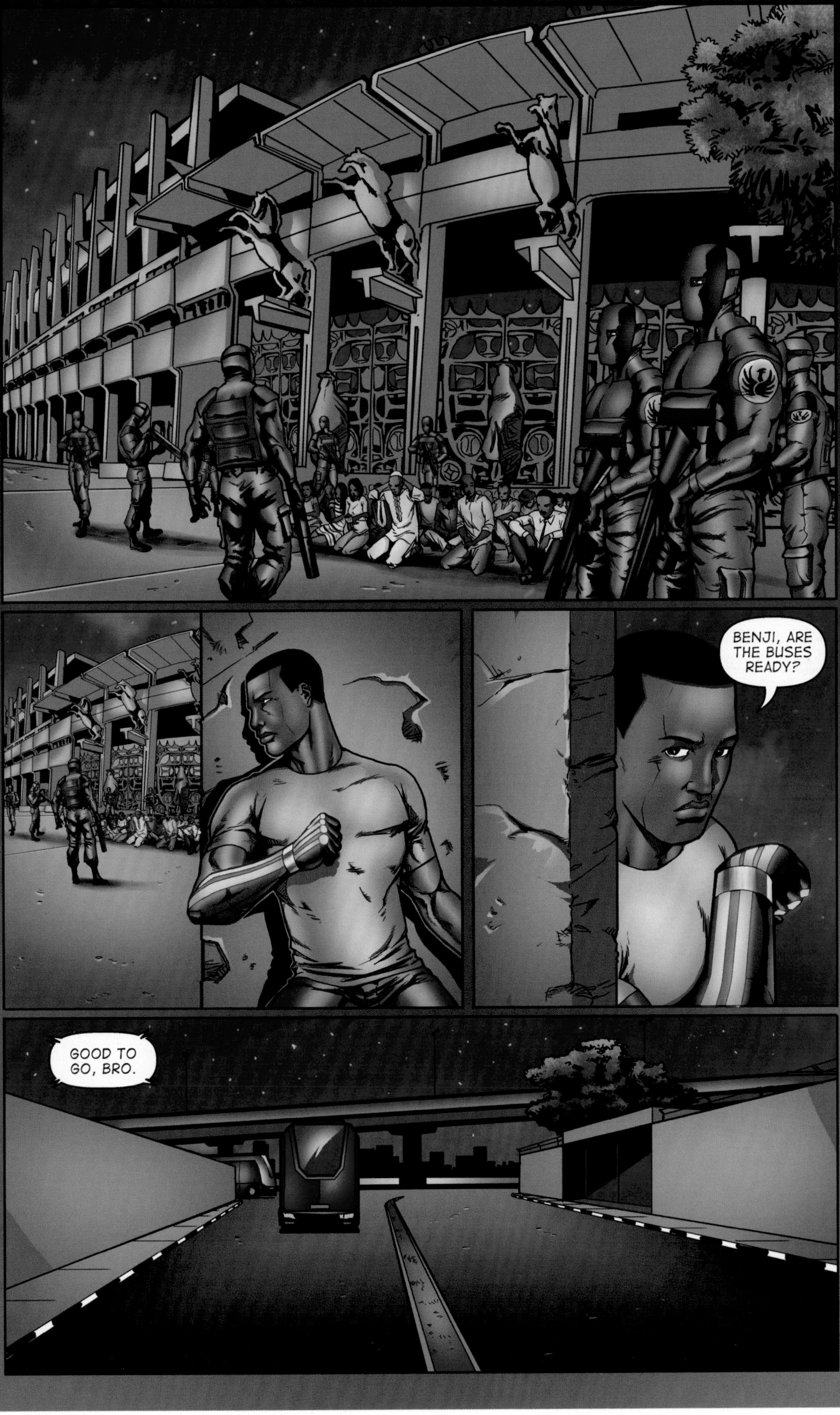
BENJI, ARE THE BUSES READY?
GOOD TO GO, BRO.

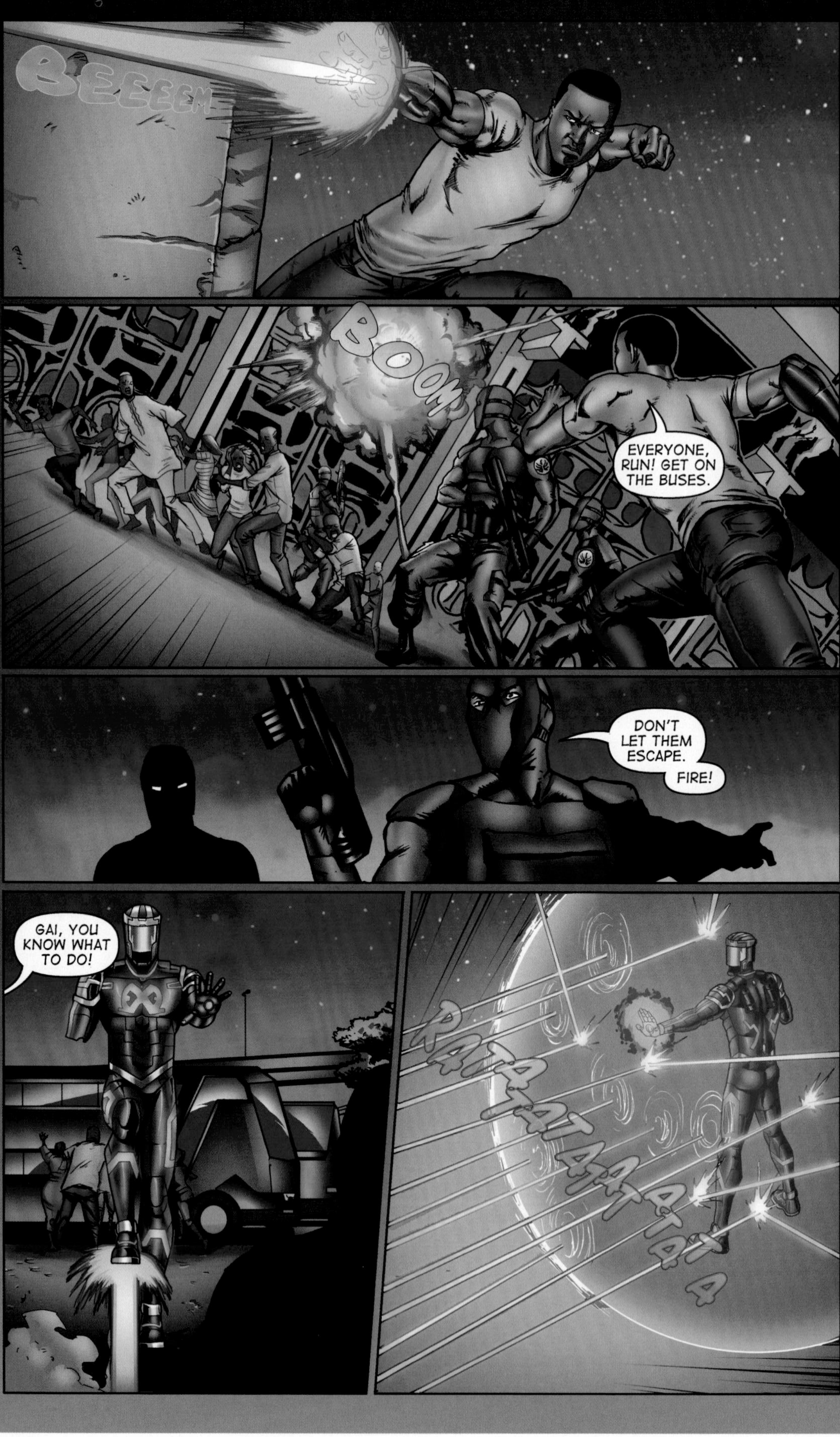
BEEEEEM
BOOM
EVERYONE, RUN! GET ON THE BUSES.
DON'T LET THEM ESCAPE.
FIRE!
GAI, YOU KNOW WHAT TO DO!
RATATATATATATATA

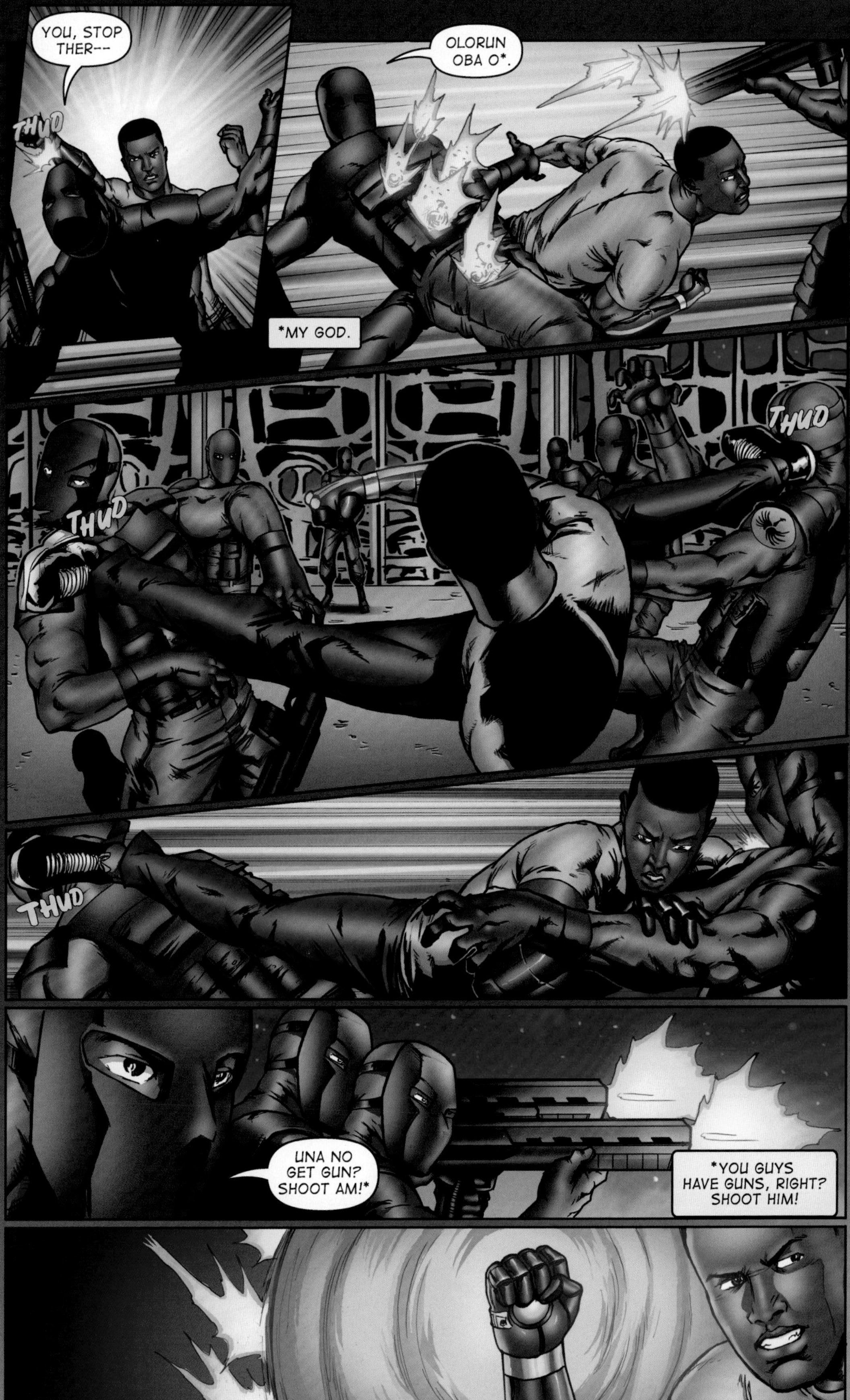

YOU, STOP THER--
THUD
OLORUN OBA O*.
*MY GOD.
THUD
THUD
THUD
UNA NO GET GUN? SHOOT AM!*
*YOU GUYS HAVE GUNS, RIGHT? SHOOT HIM!

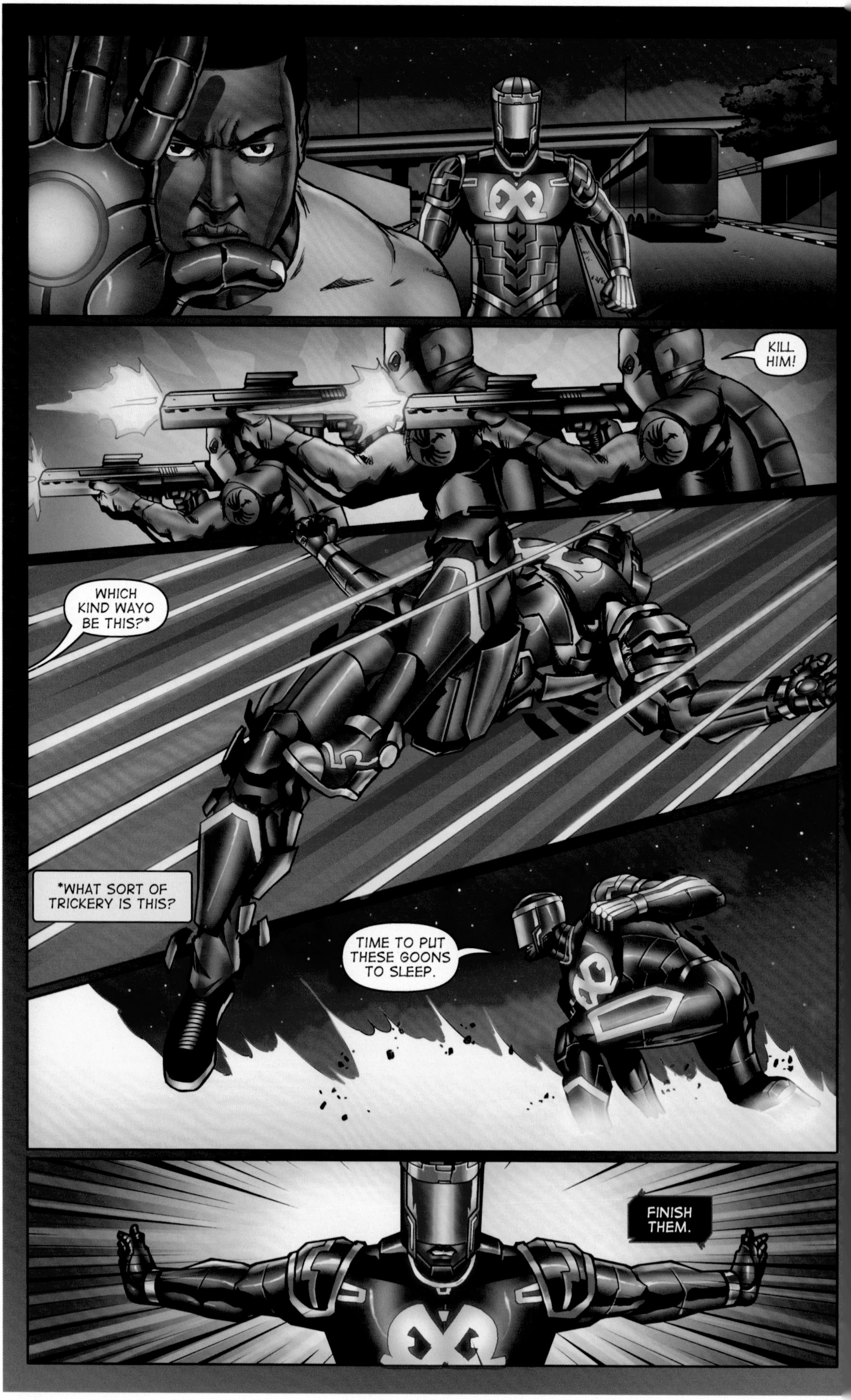
KILL HIM!
WHICH KIND WAYO BE THIS?*
*WHAT SORT OF TRICKERY IS THIS?
TIME TO PUT THESE GOONS TO SLEEP.
FINISH THEM.

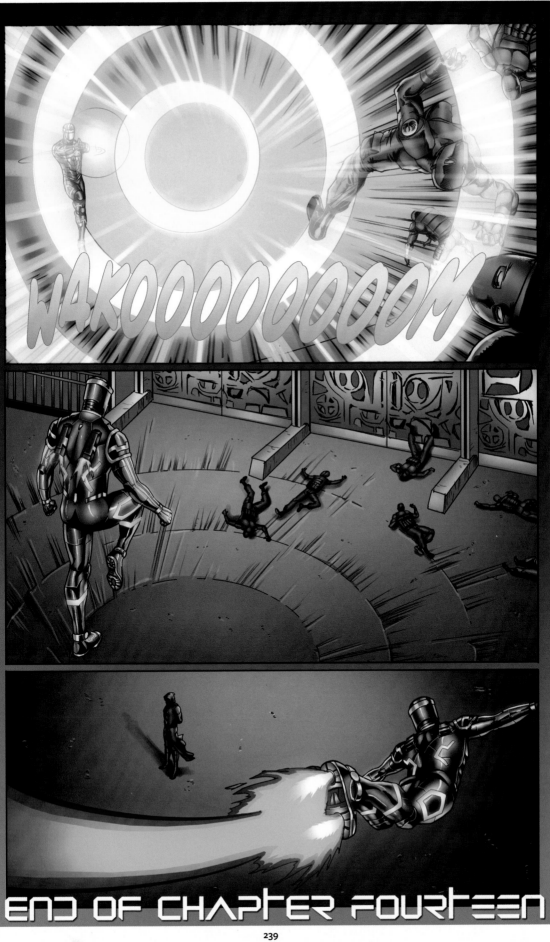

WAKOOOOOOOOOM

END OF CHAPTER FOURTEEN

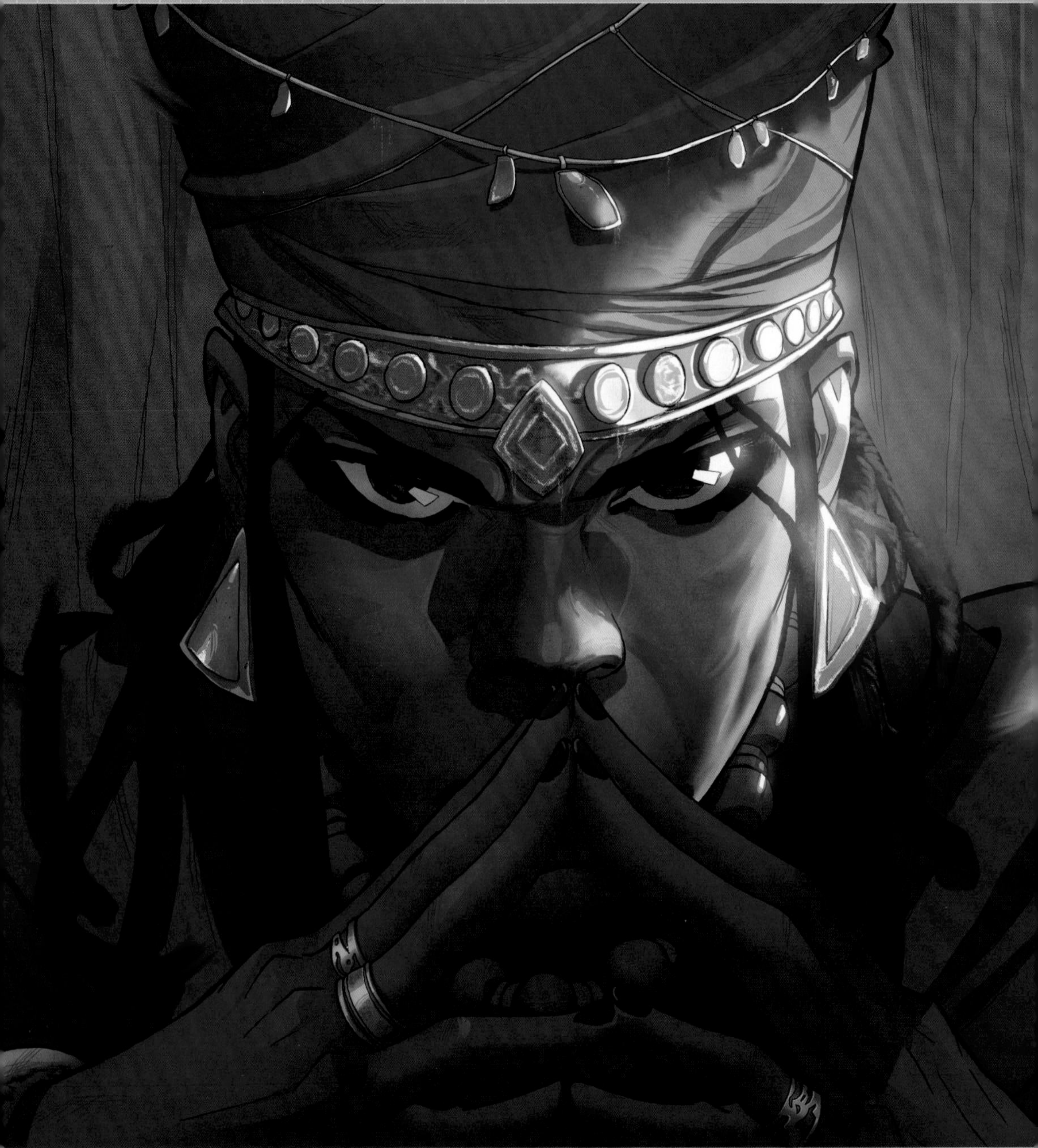

E.X.O.: The Legend of Wale Williams graphic novels and the character EXO exist within what is called the YouNeek YouNiverse, which was created by Roye Okupe to house a diverse roster of awesome heroes, villains, and locations with endless crossover possibilities from book to book. Other titles and characters in the YouNeek line of graphic novels include *Malika: Warrior Queen*, *Iyanu: Child of Wonder*, and *WindMaker*.

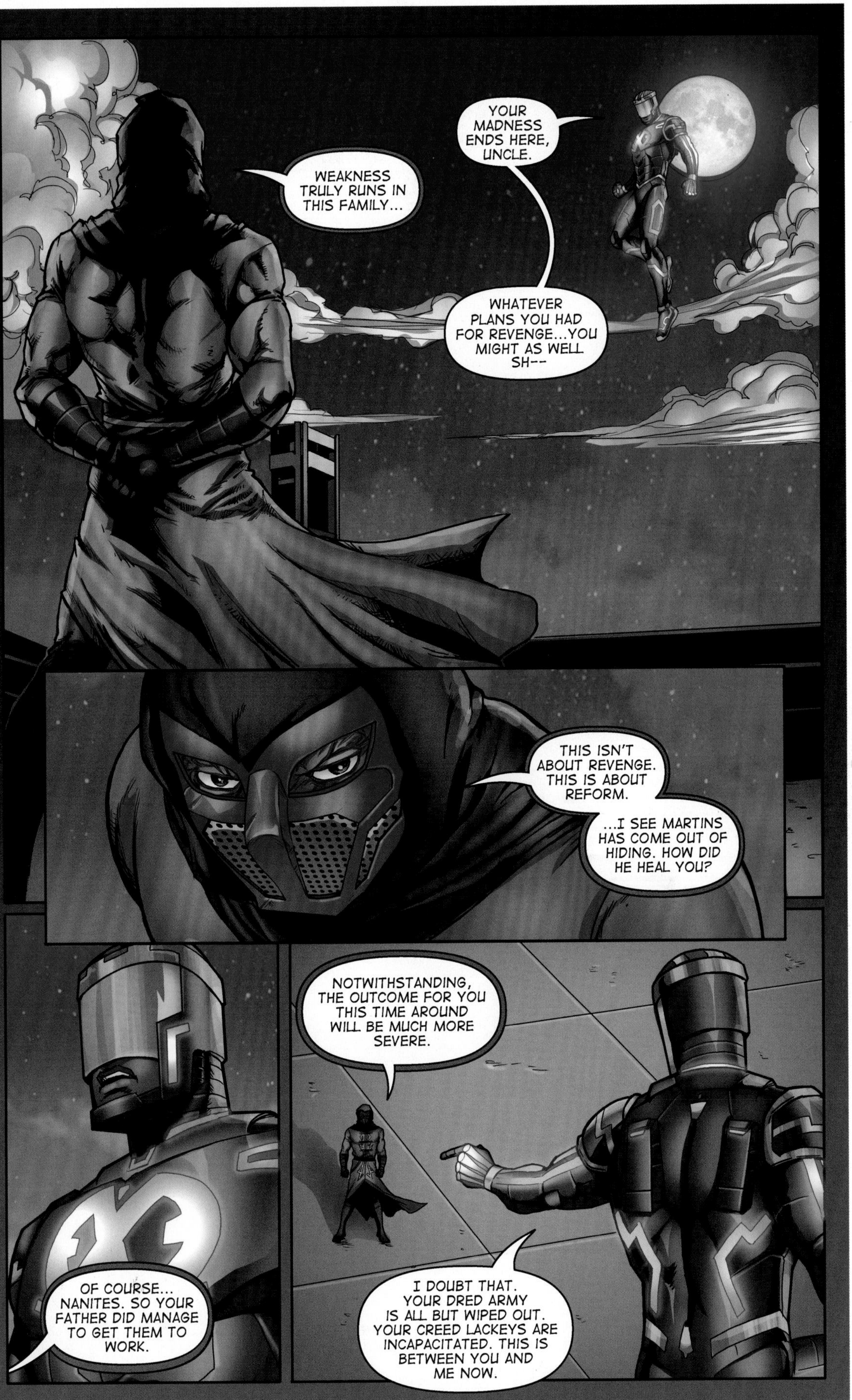
WEAKNESS TRULY RUNS IN THIS FAMILY...
YOUR MADNESS ENDS HERE, UNCLE.
WHATEVER PLANS YOU HAD FOR REVENGE...YOU MIGHT AS WELL SH--
THIS ISN'T ABOUT REVENGE. THIS IS ABOUT REFORM.
...I SEE MARTINS HAS COME OUT OF HIDING. HOW DID HE HEAL YOU?
OF COURSE... NANITES. SO YOUR FATHER DID MANAGE TO GET THEM TO WORK.
NOTWITHSTANDING, THE OUTCOME FOR YOU THIS TIME AROUND WILL BE MUCH MORE SEVERE.
I DOUBT THAT. YOUR DRED ARMY IS ALL BUT WIPED OUT. YOUR CREED LACKEYS ARE INCAPACITATED. THIS IS BETWEEN YOU AND ME NOW.

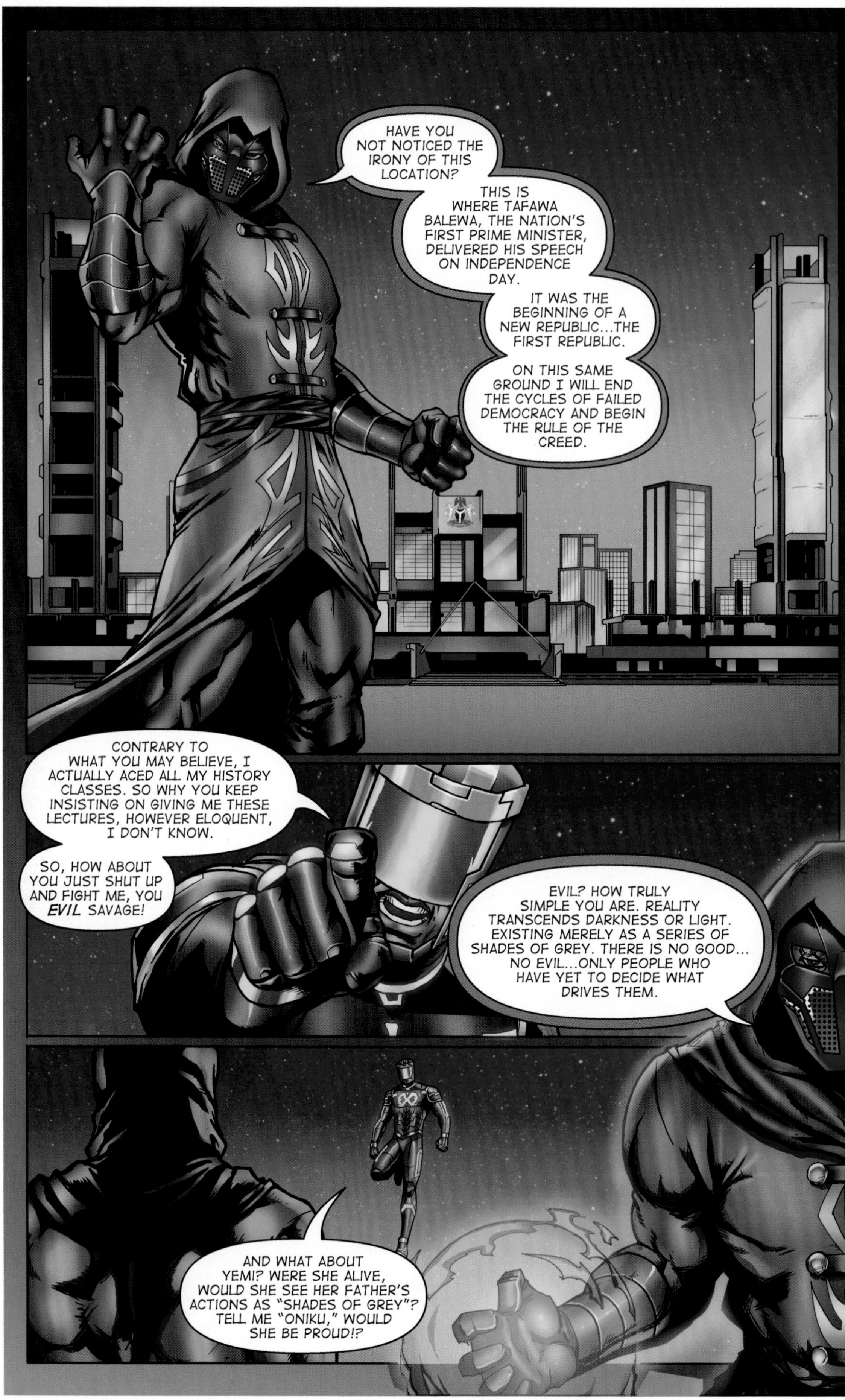

HAVE YOU NOT NOTICED THE IRONY OF THIS LOCATION?
THIS IS WHERE TAFAWA BALEWA, THE NATION'S FIRST PRIME MINISTER, DELIVERED HIS SPEECH ON INDEPENDENCE DAY.
IT WAS THE BEGINNING OF A NEW REPUBLIC...THE FIRST REPUBLIC.
ON THIS SAME GROUND I WILL END THE CYCLES OF FAILED DEMOCRACY AND BEGIN THE RULE OF THE CREED.
CONTRARY TO WHAT YOU MAY BELIEVE, I ACTUALLY ACED ALL MY HISTORY CLASSES. SO WHY YOU KEEP INSISTING ON GIVING ME THESE LECTURES, HOWEVER ELOQUENT, I DON'T KNOW.
SO, HOW ABOUT YOU JUST SHUT UP AND FIGHT ME, YOU ***EVIL*** SAVAGE!
EVIL? HOW TRULY SIMPLE YOU ARE. REALITY TRANSCENDS DARKNESS OR LIGHT. EXISTING MERELY AS A SERIES OF SHADES OF GREY. THERE IS NO GOOD... NO EVIL...ONLY PEOPLE WHO HAVE YET TO DECIDE WHAT DRIVES THEM.
AND WHAT ABOUT YEMI!? WERE SHE ALIVE, WOULD SHE SEE HER FATHER'S ACTIONS AS "SHADES OF GREY"? TELL ME "ONIKU," WOULD SHE BE PROUD!?

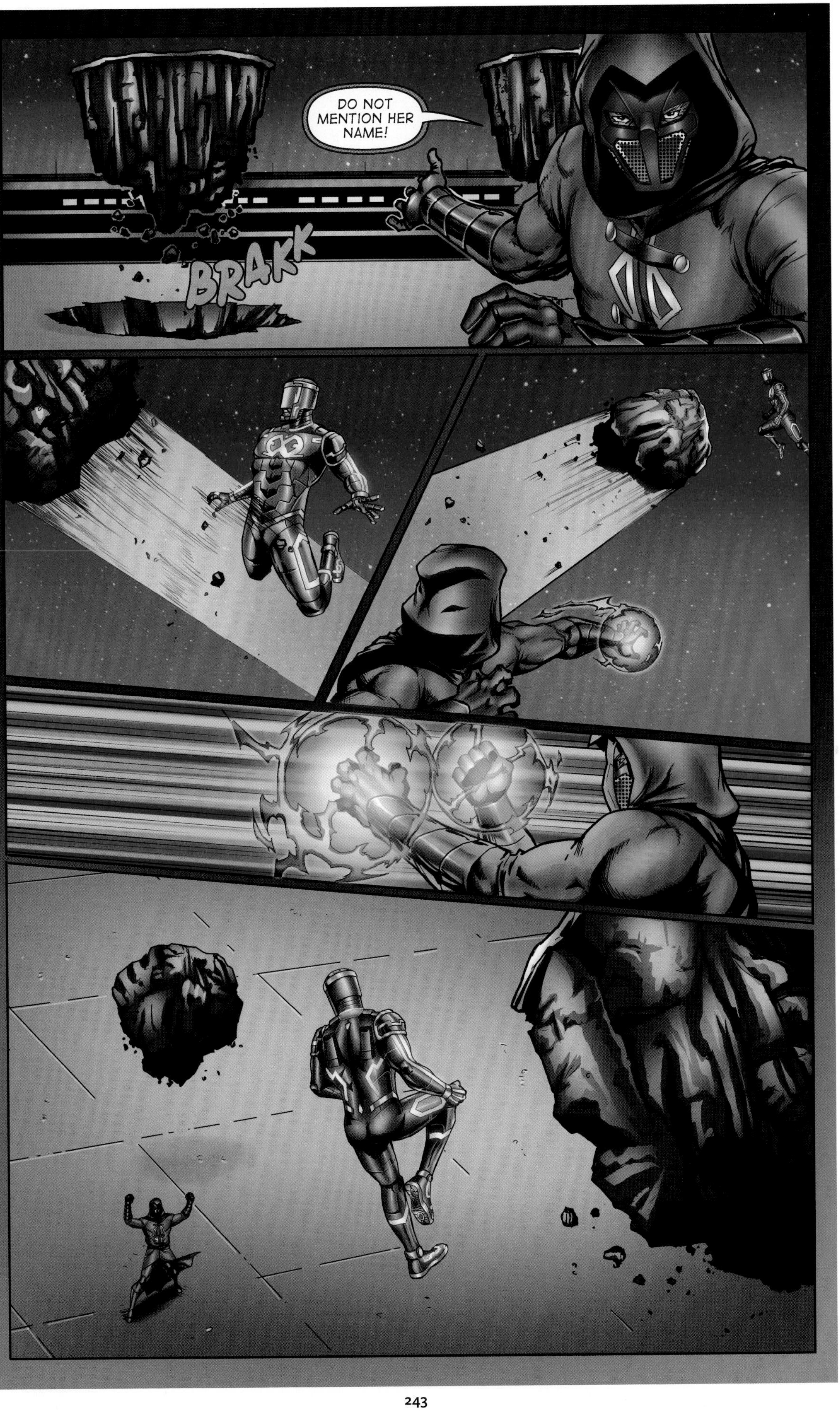
DO NOT MENTION HER NAME!
BRAKK

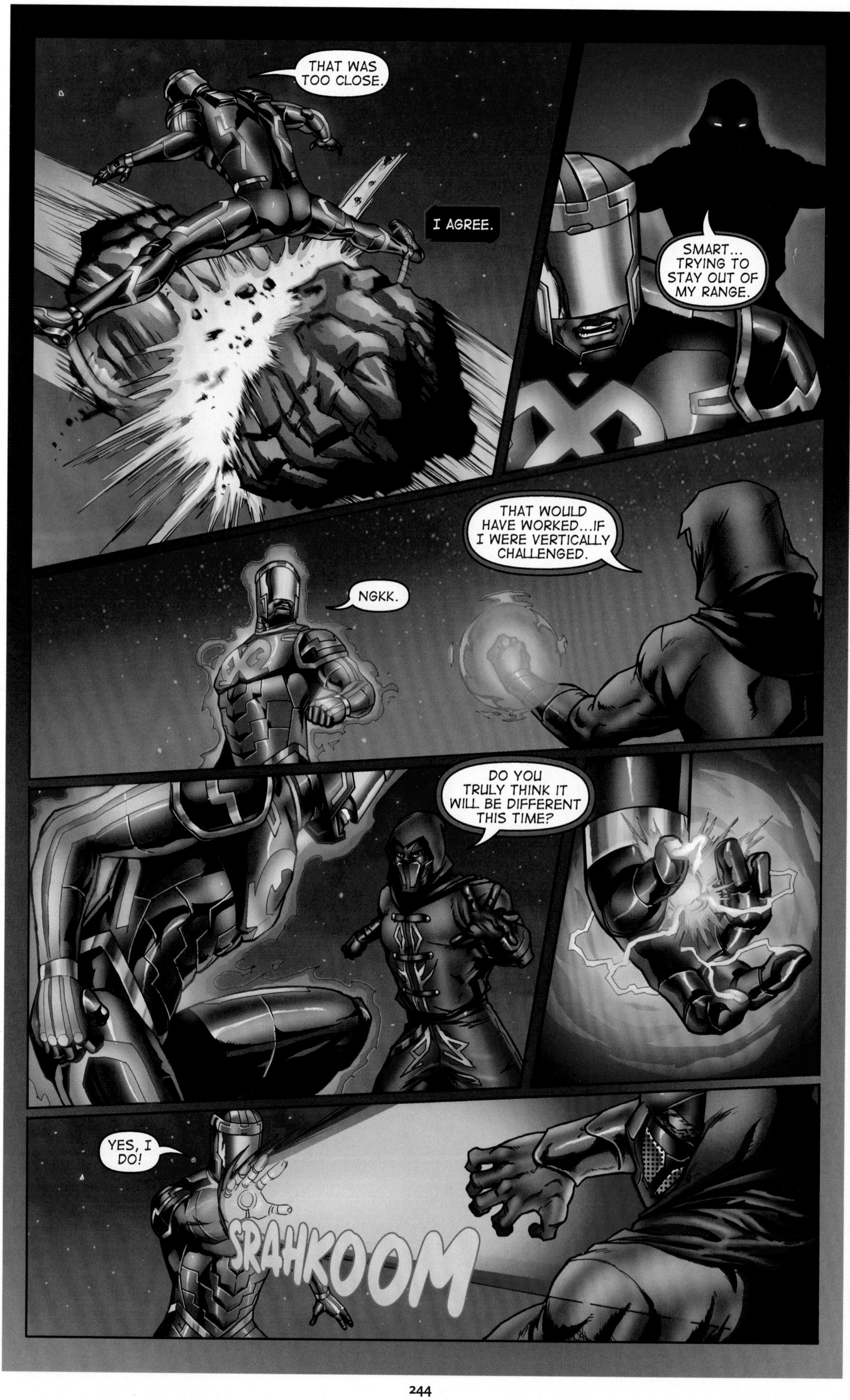
THAT WAS TOO CLOSE.
I AGREE.
SMART... TRYING TO STAY OUT OF MY RANGE.
THAT WOULD HAVE WORKED...IF I WERE VERTICALLY CHALLENGED.
NGKK.
DO YOU TRULY THINK IT WILL BE DIFFERENT THIS TIME?
YES, I DO!
SRAHKOOM

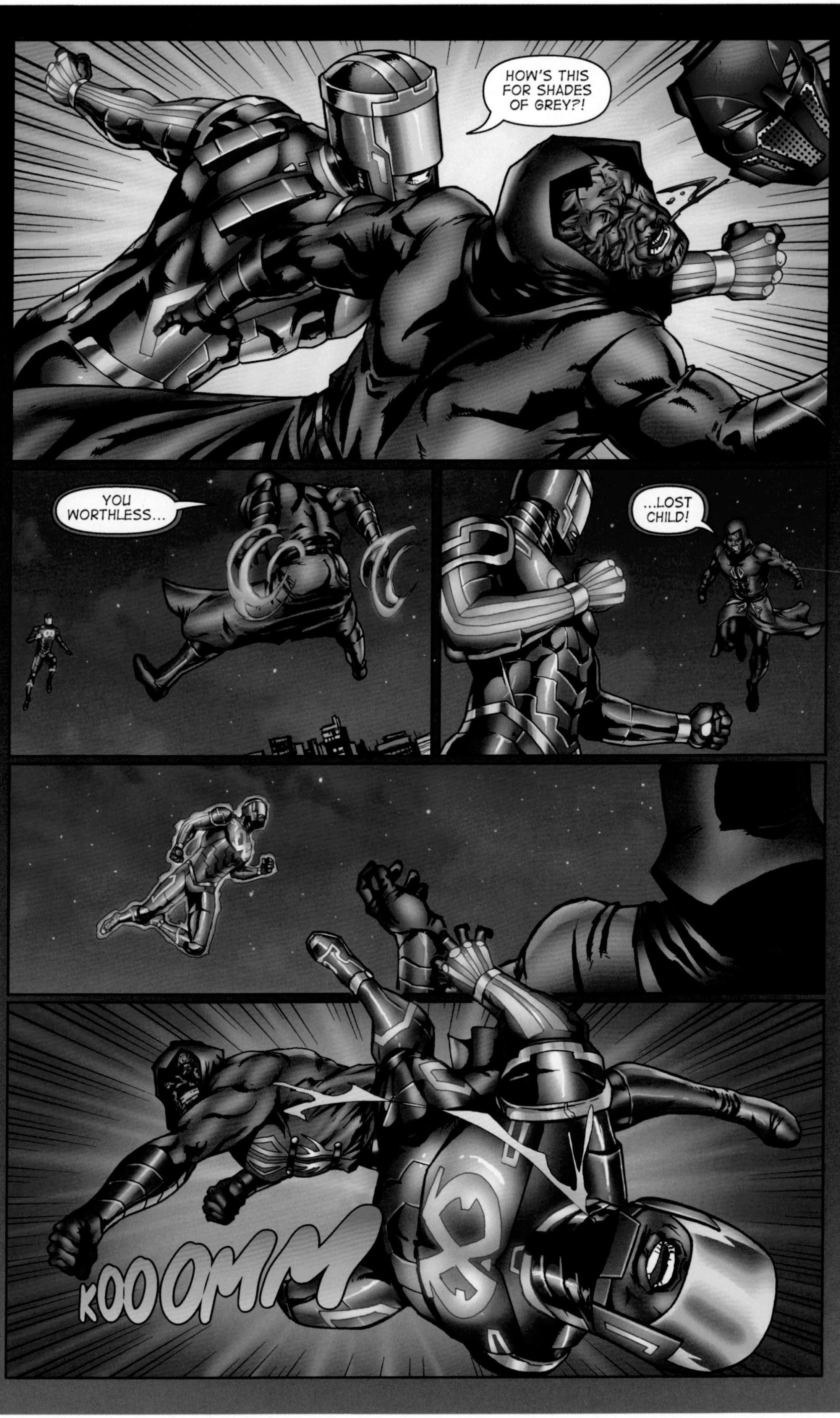
HOW'S THIS FOR SHADES OF GREY?!
YOU WORTHLESS...
...LOST CHILD!
KOOOMM

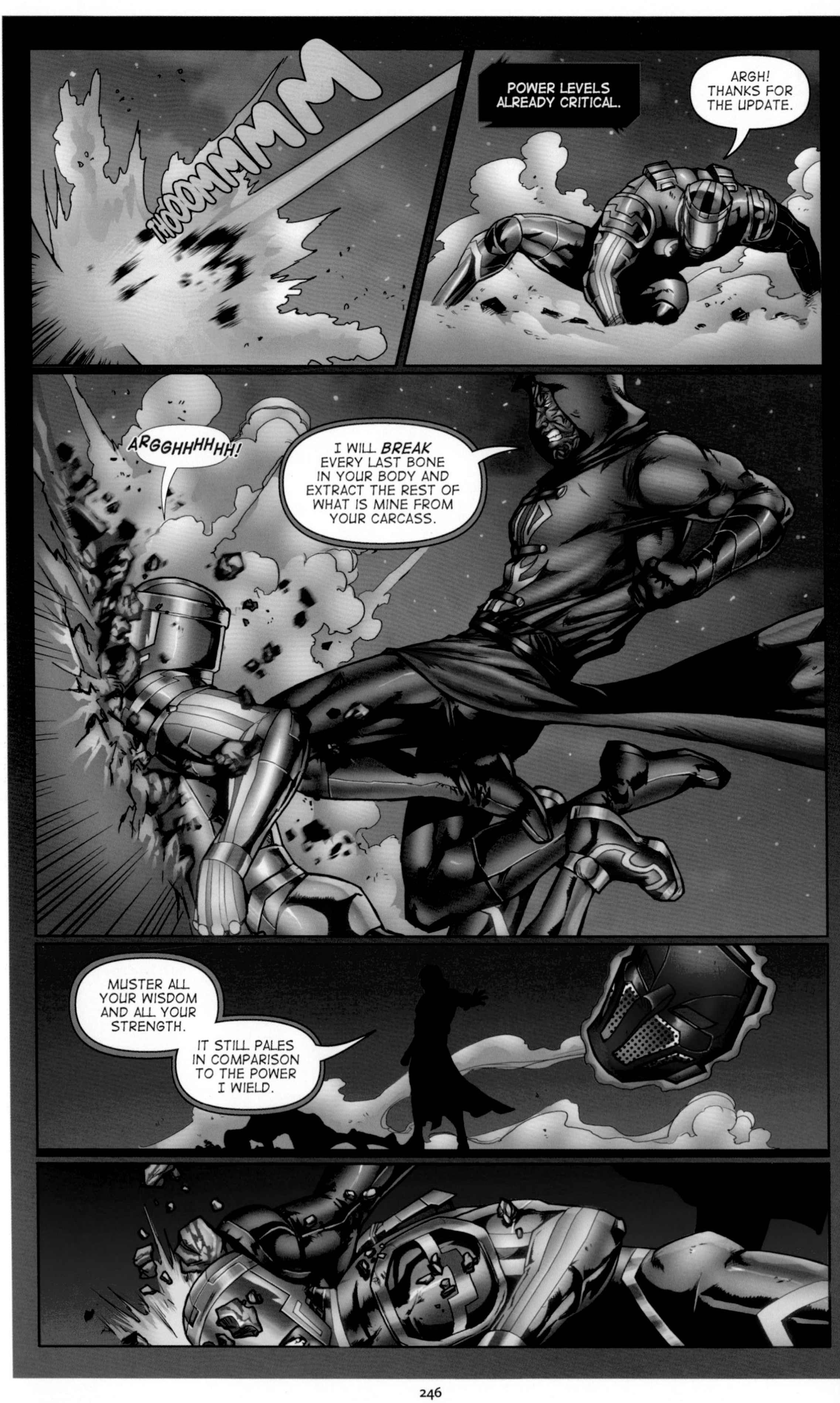
THOOOMMMMM
POWER LEVELS ALREADY CRITICAL.
ARGH! THANKS FOR THE UPDATE.
ARGGHHHHHH!
I WILL BREAK EVERY LAST BONE IN YOUR BODY AND EXTRACT THE REST OF WHAT IS MINE FROM YOUR CARCASS.
MUSTER ALL YOUR WISDOM AND ALL YOUR STRENGTH.
IT STILL PALES IN COMPARISON TO THE POWER I WIELD.

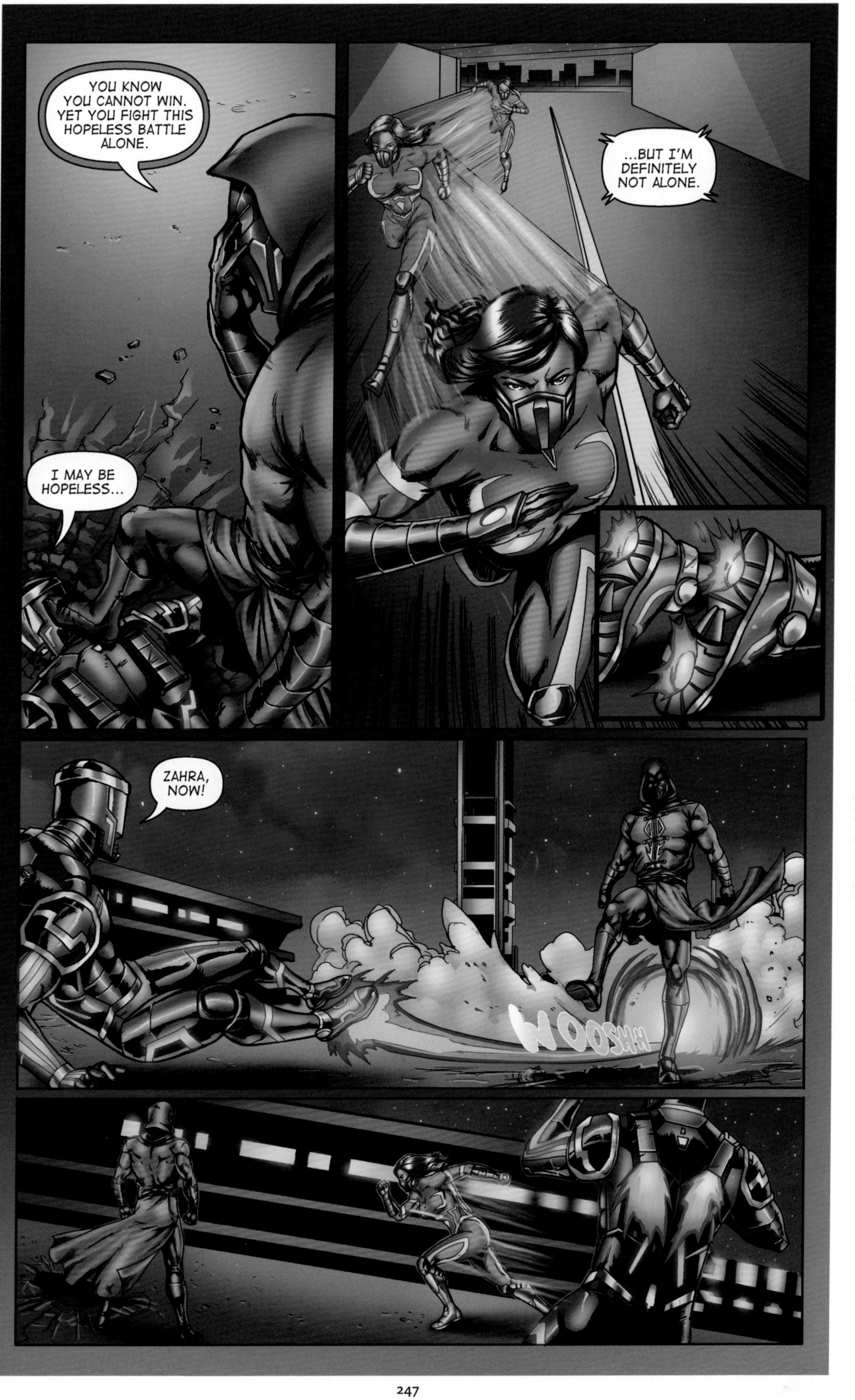
YOU KNOW YOU CANNOT WIN. YET YOU FIGHT THIS HOPELESS BATTLE ALONE.
I MAY BE HOPELESS...
...BUT I'M DEFINITELY NOT ALONE.
ZAHRA, NOW!
WOOSHH

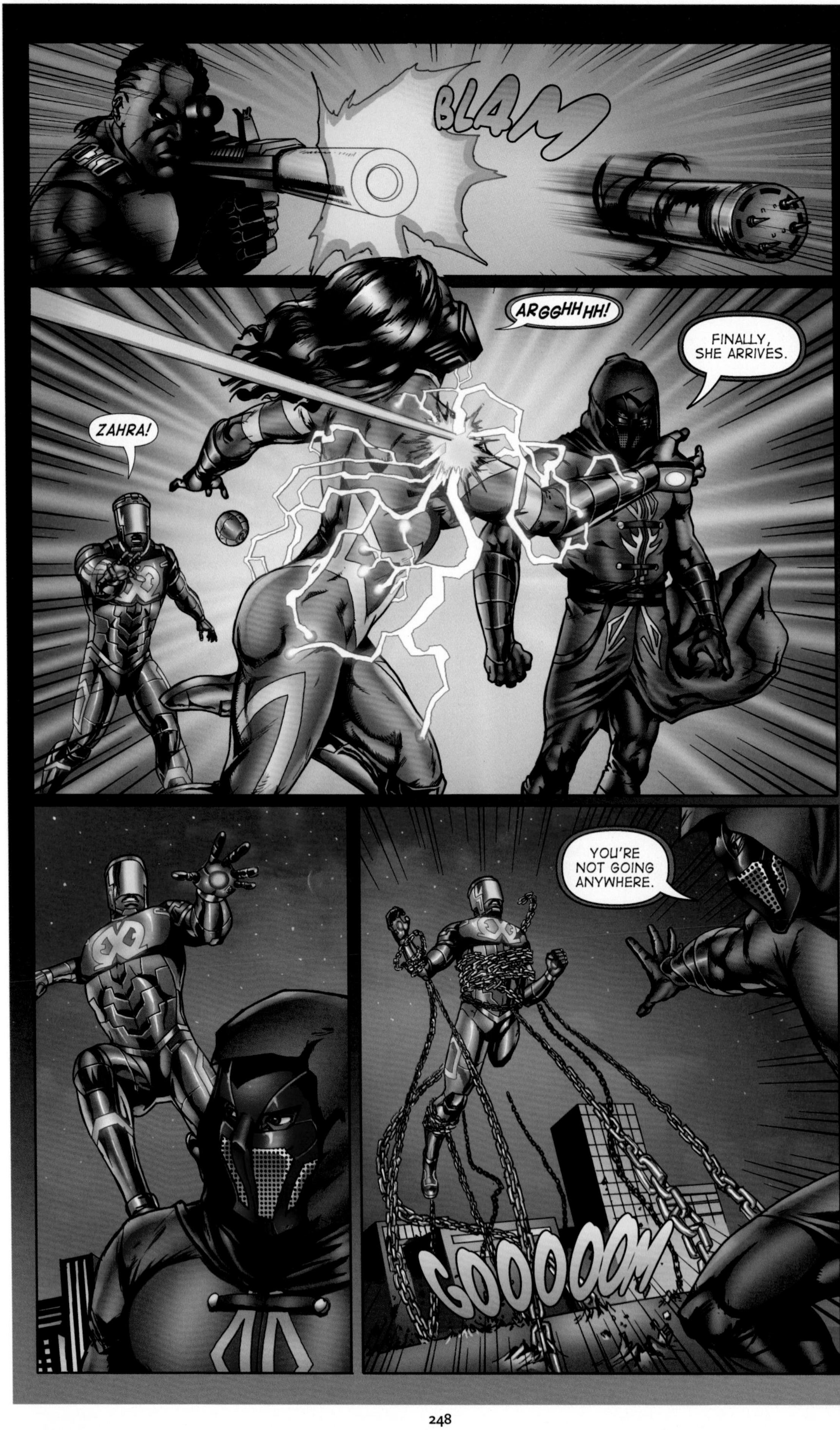
BLAM
ARGGHHHH!
FINALLY, SHE ARRIVES.
ZAHRA!
YOU'RE NOT GOING ANYWHERE.
GOOOOOM

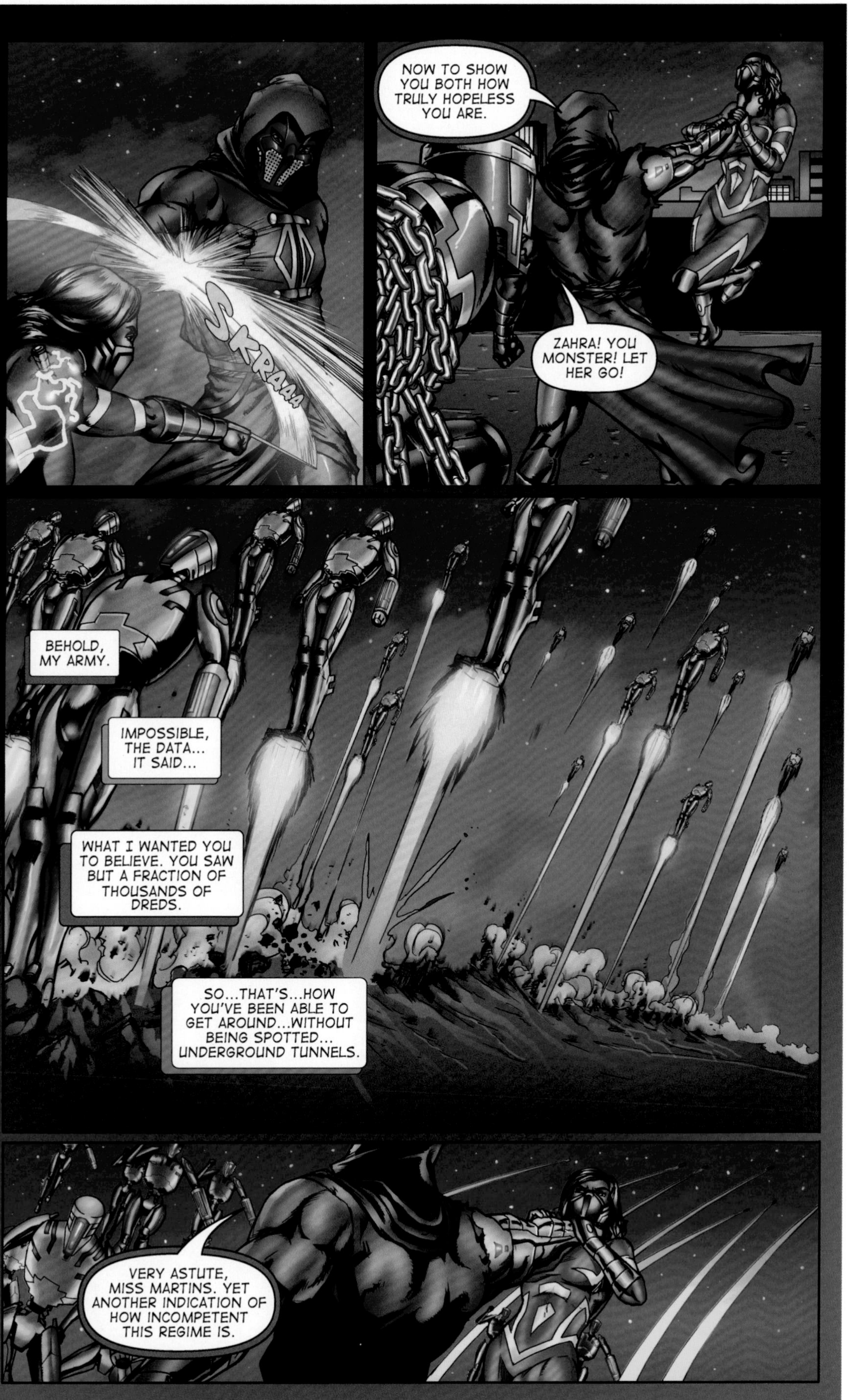
SKRAAA
NOW TO SHOW YOU BOTH HOW TRULY HOPELESS YOU ARE.
ZAHRA! YOU MONSTER! LET HER GO!
BEHOLD, MY ARMY.
IMPOSSIBLE, THE DATA... IT SAID...
WHAT I WANTED YOU TO BELIEVE. YOU SAW BUT A FRACTION OF THOUSANDS OF DREDS.
SO...THAT'S...HOW YOU'VE BEEN ABLE TO GET AROUND...WITHOUT BEING SPOTTED... UNDERGROUND TUNNELS.
VERY ASTUTE, MISS MARTINS. YET ANOTHER INDICATION OF HOW INCOMPETENT THIS REGIME IS.

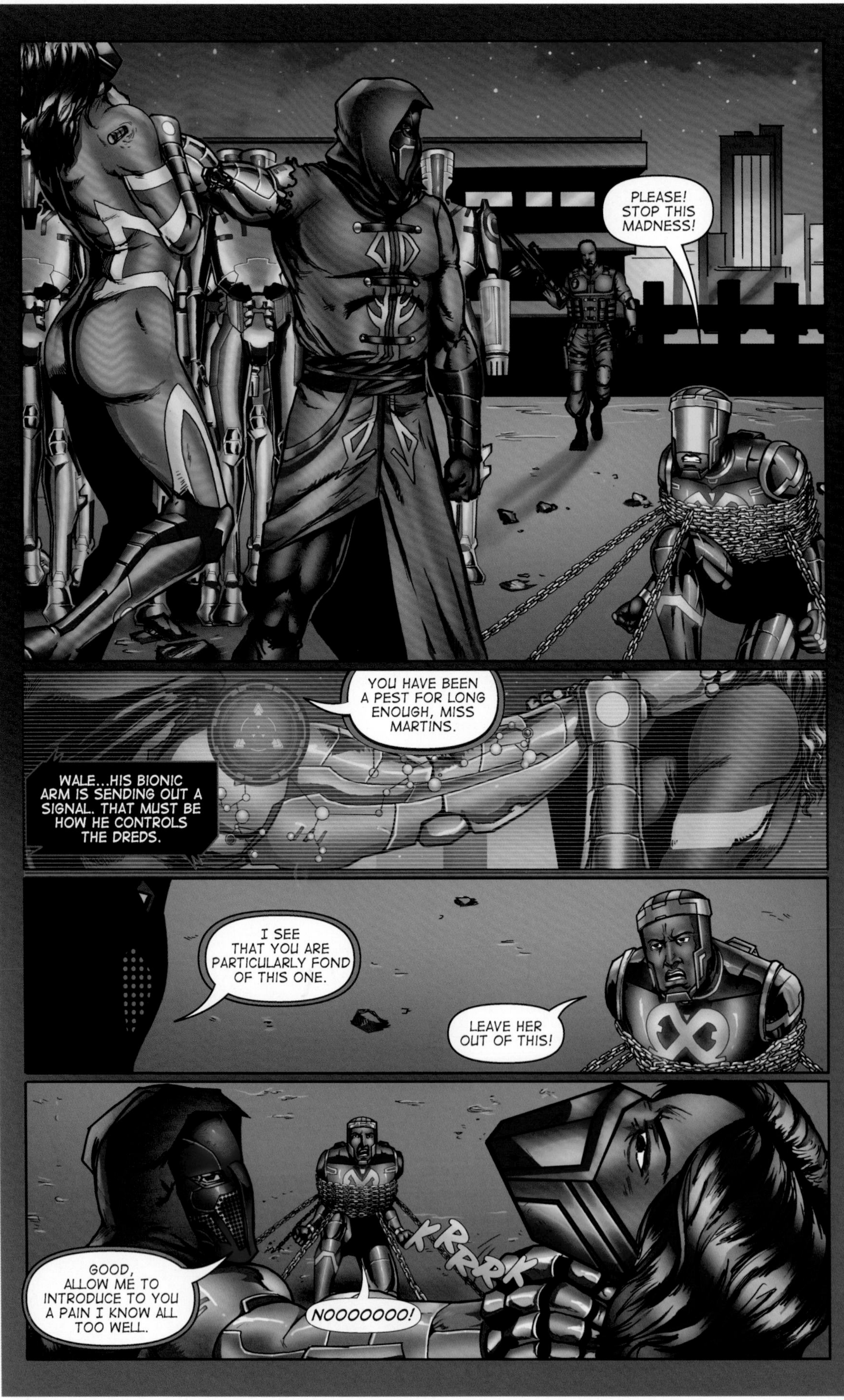
PLEASE! STOP THIS MADNESS!
YOU HAVE BEEN A PEST FOR LONG ENOUGH, MISS MARTINS.
WALE...HIS BIONIC ARM IS SENDING OUT A SIGNAL. THAT MUST BE HOW HE CONTROLS THE DREDS.
I SEE THAT YOU ARE PARTICULARLY FOND OF THIS ONE.
LEAVE HER OUT OF THIS!
KRRRK
GOOD, ALLOW ME TO INTRODUCE TO YOU A PAIN I KNOW ALL TOO WELL.
NOOOOOOO!

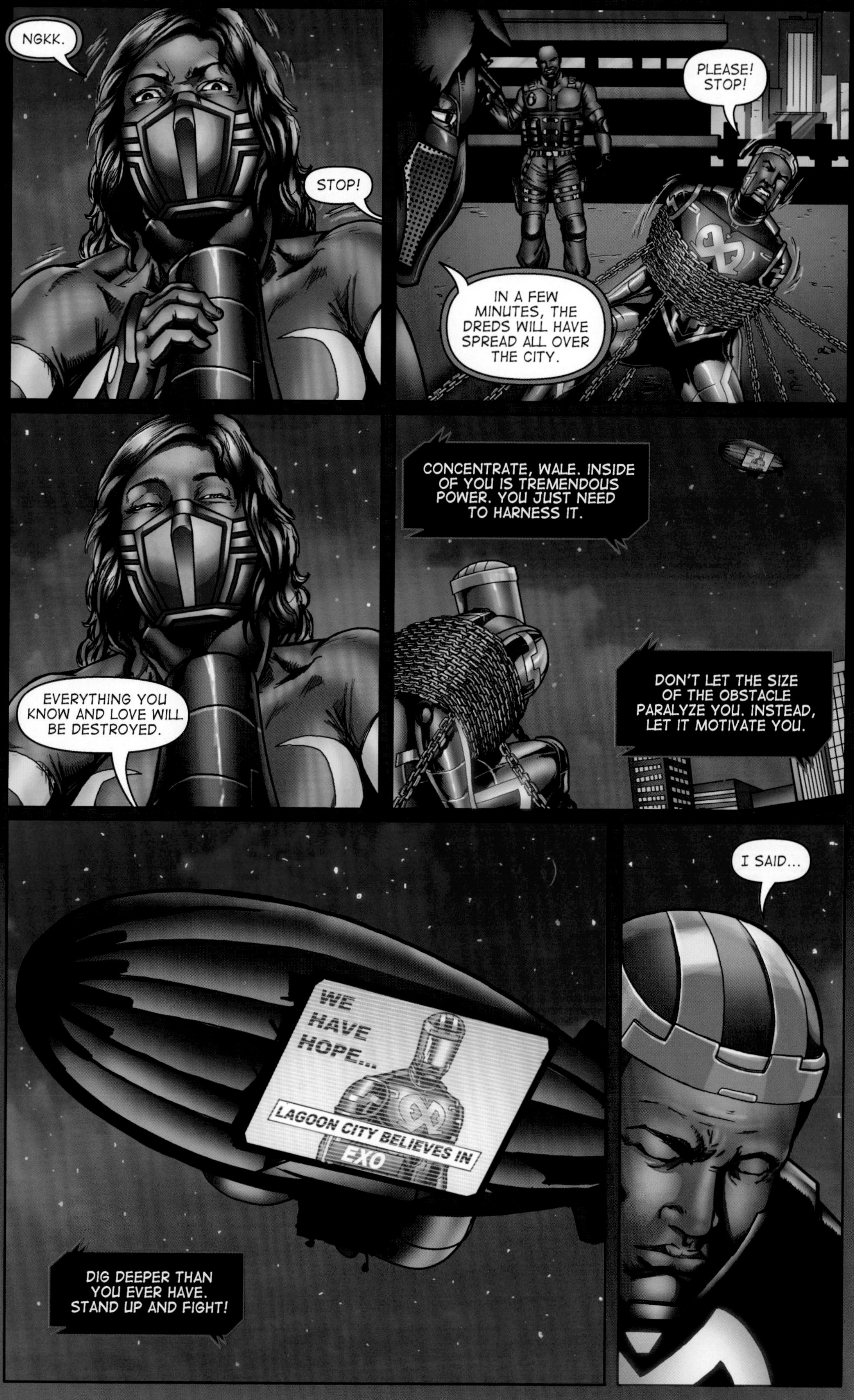
NGKK.
STOP!
PLEASE! STOP!
IN A FEW MINUTES, THE DREDS WILL HAVE SPREAD ALL OVER THE CITY.
EVERYTHING YOU KNOW AND LOVE WILL BE DESTROYED.
CONCENTRATE, WALE. INSIDE OF YOU IS TREMENDOUS POWER. YOU JUST NEED TO HARNESS IT.
DON'T LET THE SIZE OF THE OBSTACLE PARALYZE YOU. INSTEAD, LET IT MOTIVATE YOU.
WE HAVE HOPE...
LAGOON CITY BELIEVES IN
EXO
DIG DEEPER THAN YOU EVER HAVE. STAND UP AND FIGHT!
I SAID...

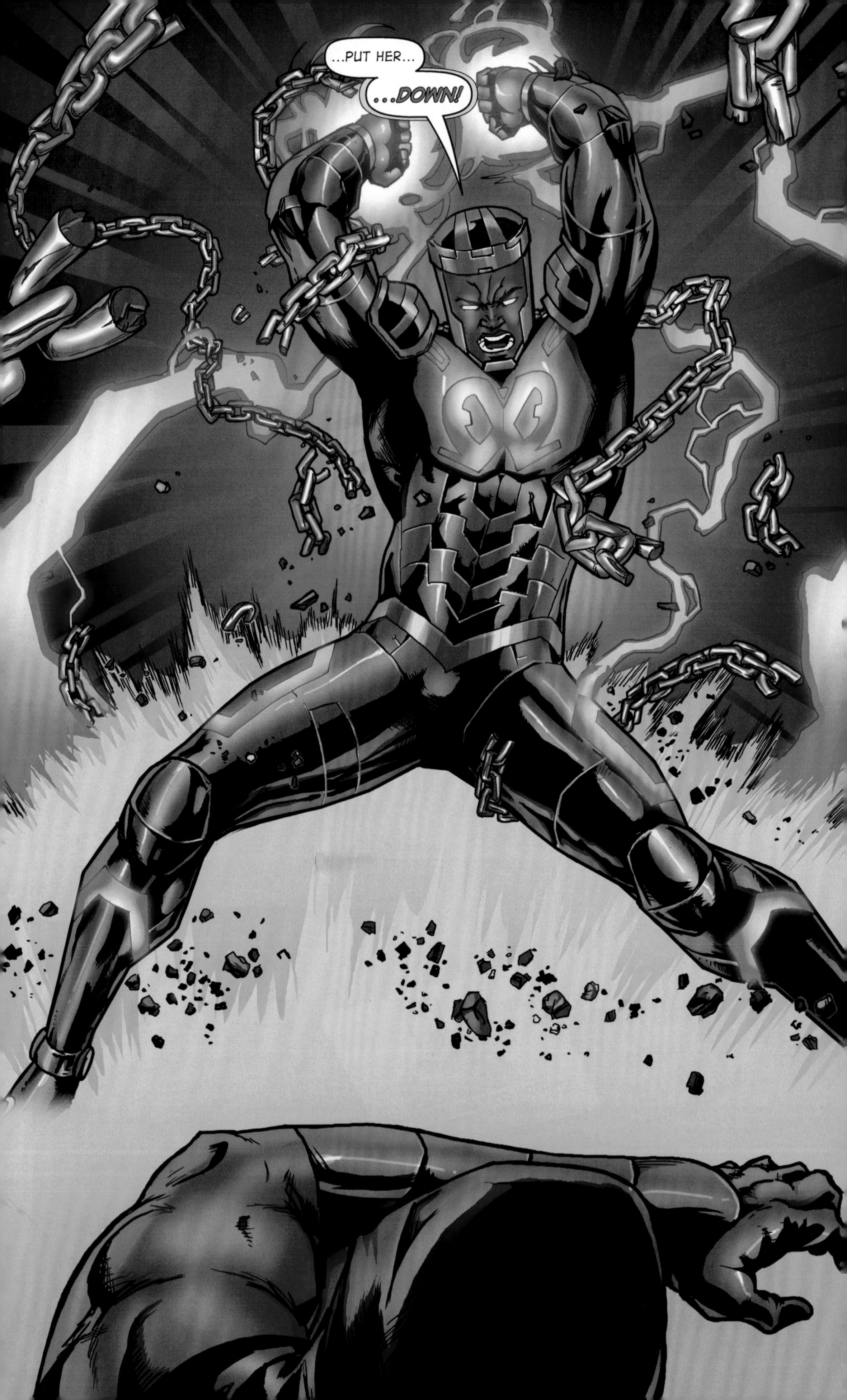
...PUT HER...
...DOWN!

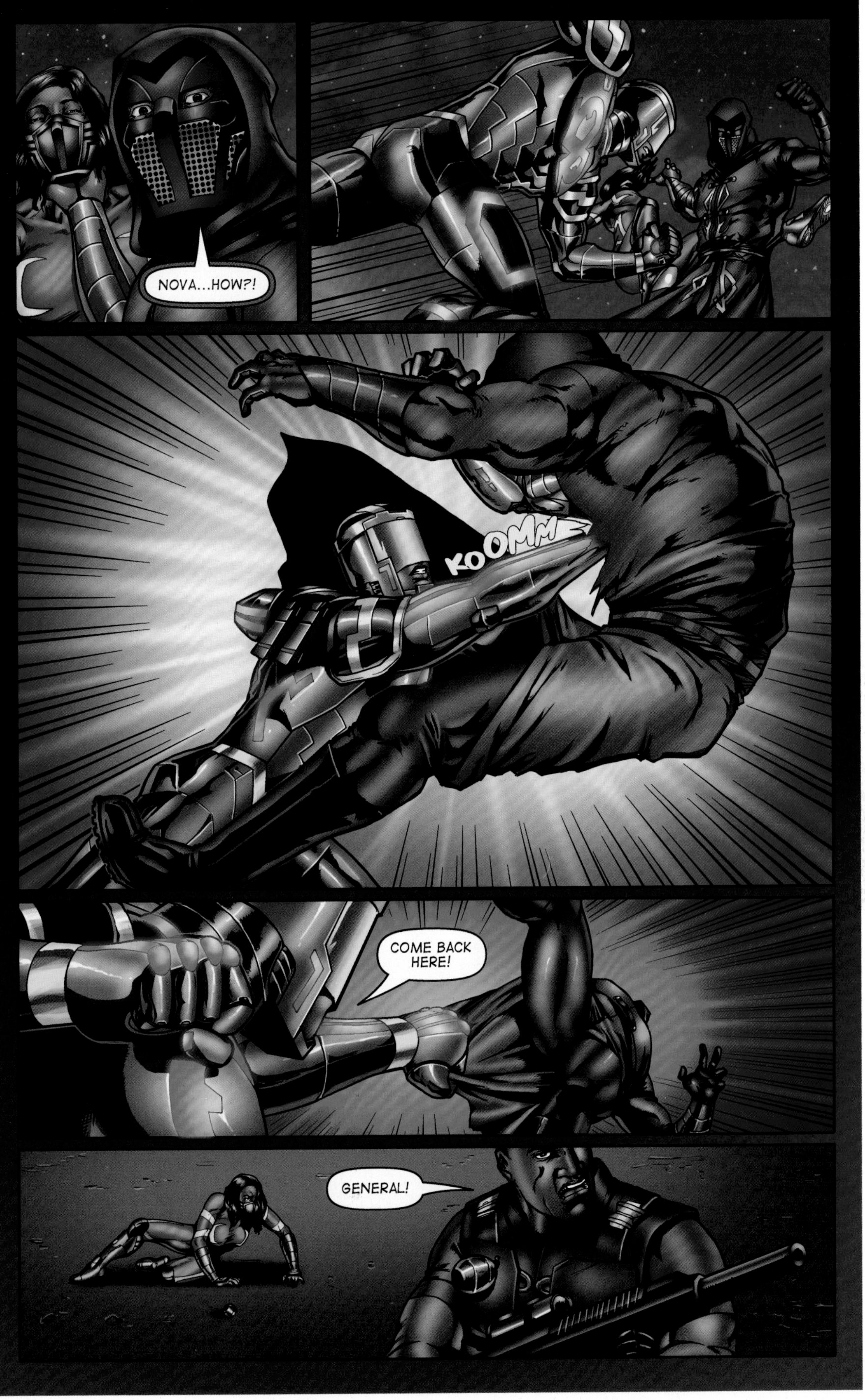
NOVA...HOW?!
KOOMM
COME BACK HERE!
GENERAL!

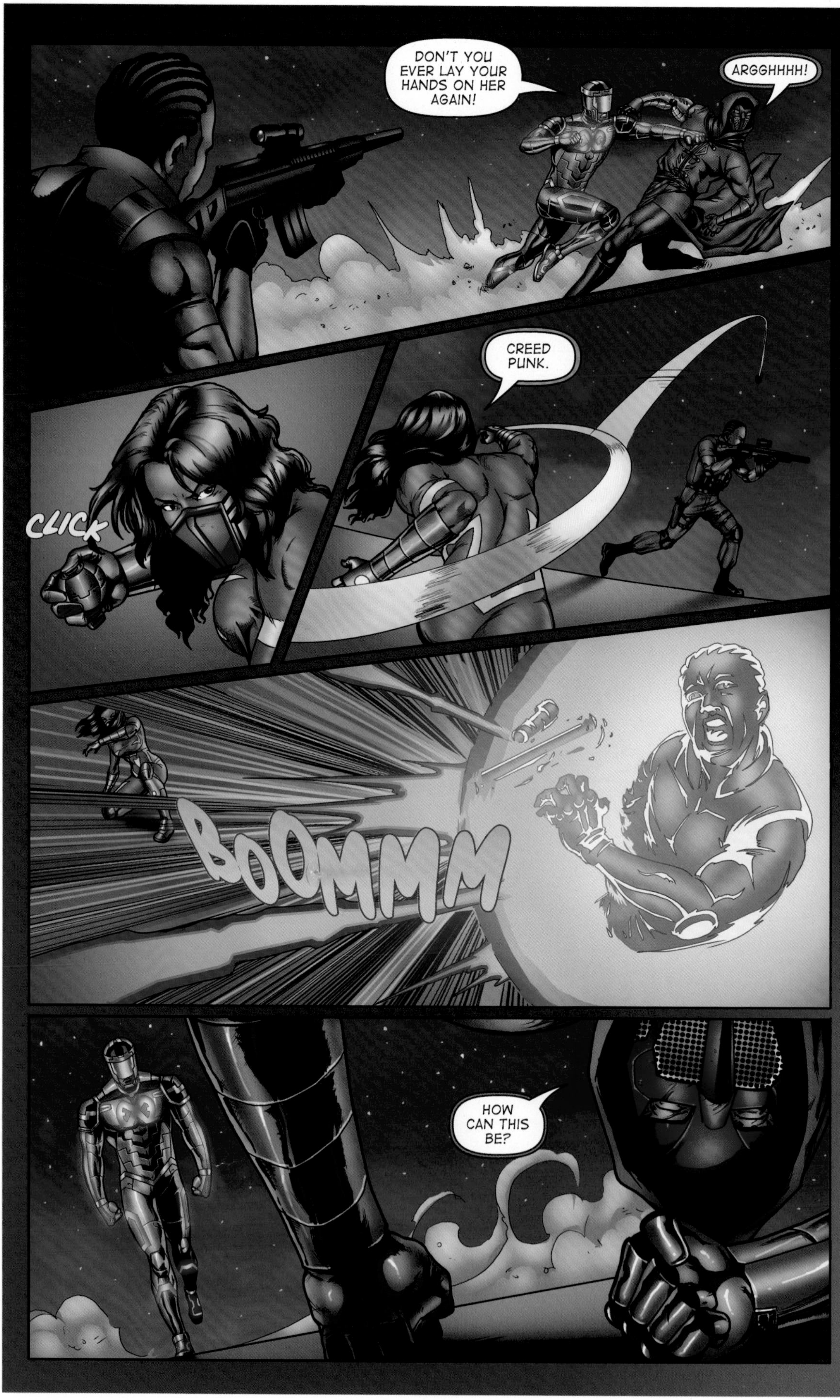
DON'T YOU EVER LAY YOUR HANDS ON HER AGAIN!
ARGGHHHH!
CLICK
CREED PUNK.
BOOMMM
HOW CAN THIS BE?

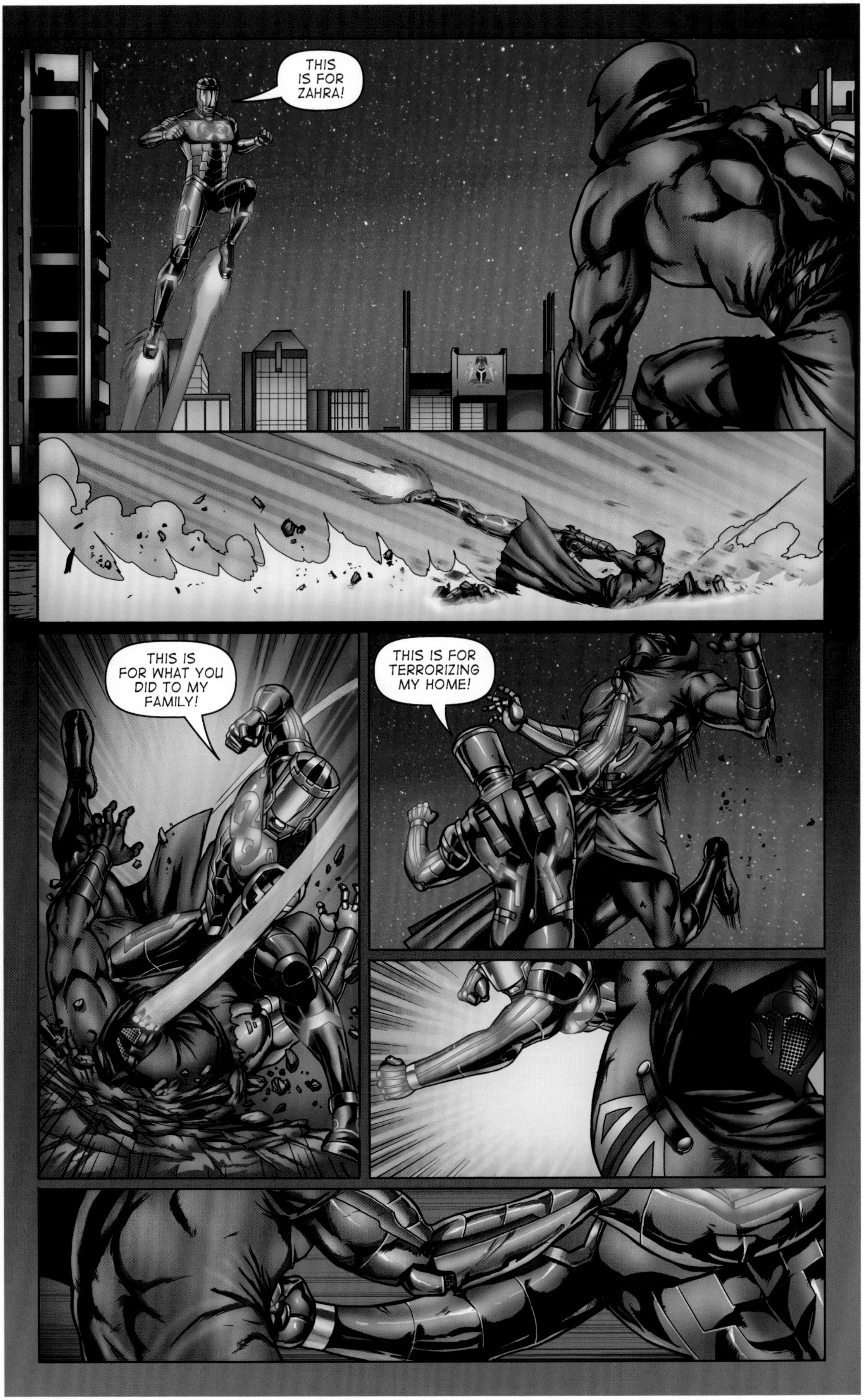
THIS IS FOR ZAHRA!
THIS IS FOR WHAT YOU DID TO MY FAMILY!
THIS IS FOR TERRORIZING MY HOME!

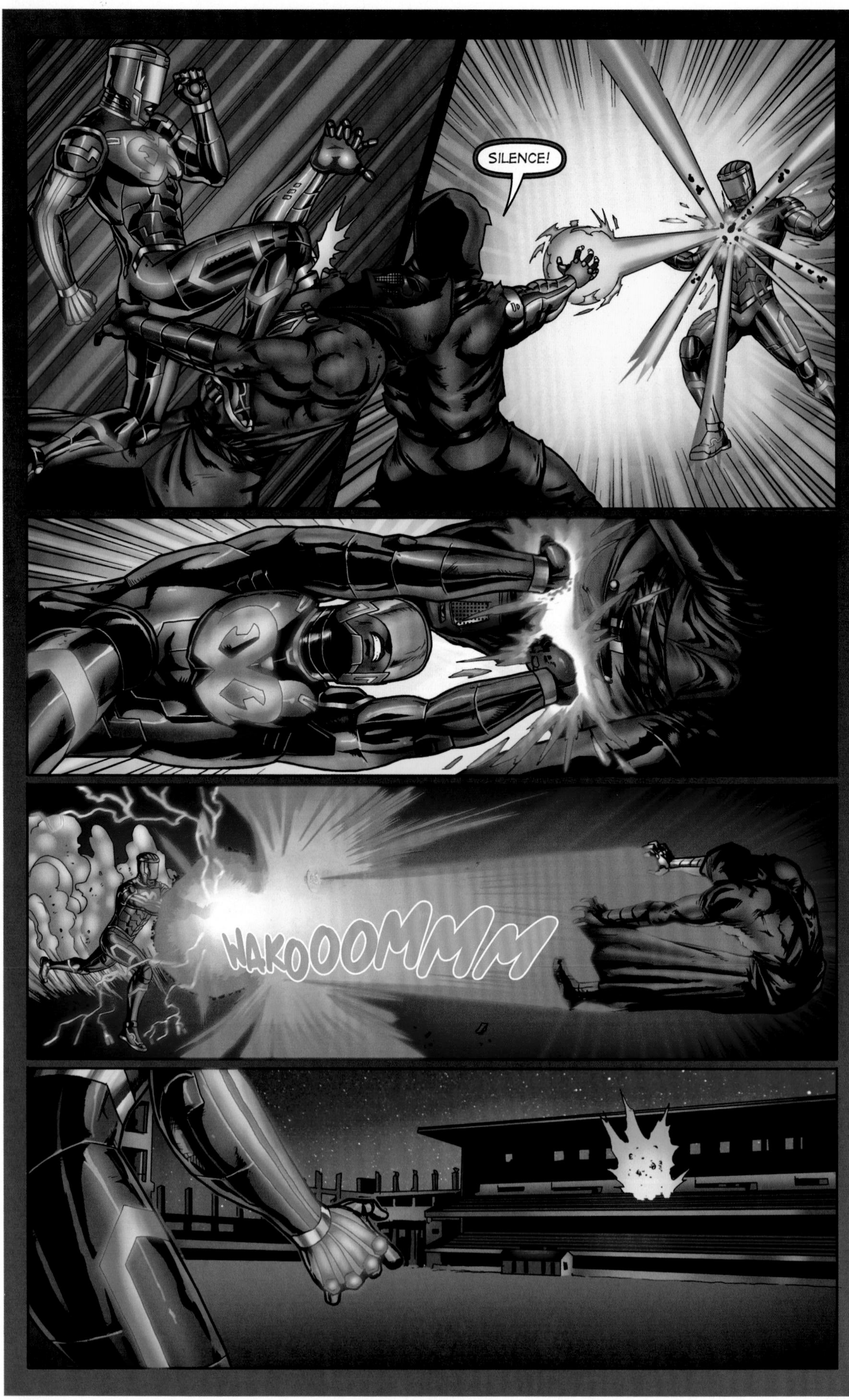
SILENCE!
WAKOOOMMMM

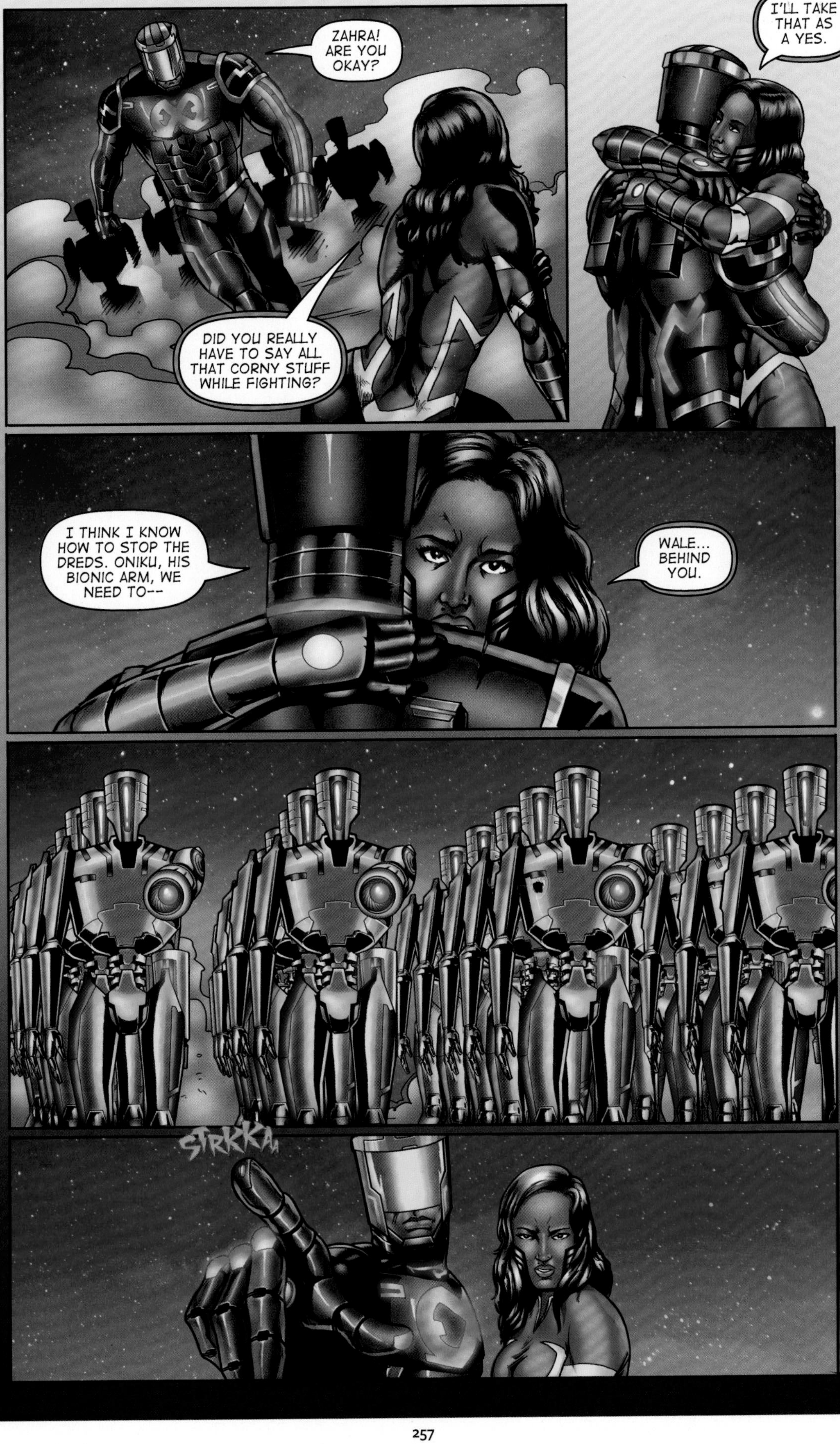
ZAHRA! ARE YOU OKAY?
DID YOU REALLY HAVE TO SAY ALL THAT CORNY STUFF WHILE FIGHTING?
I'LL TAKE THAT AS A YES.
I THINK I KNOW HOW TO STOP THE DREDS. ONIKU, HIS BIONIC ARM, WE NEED TO--
WALE... BEHIND YOU.
STRKKA

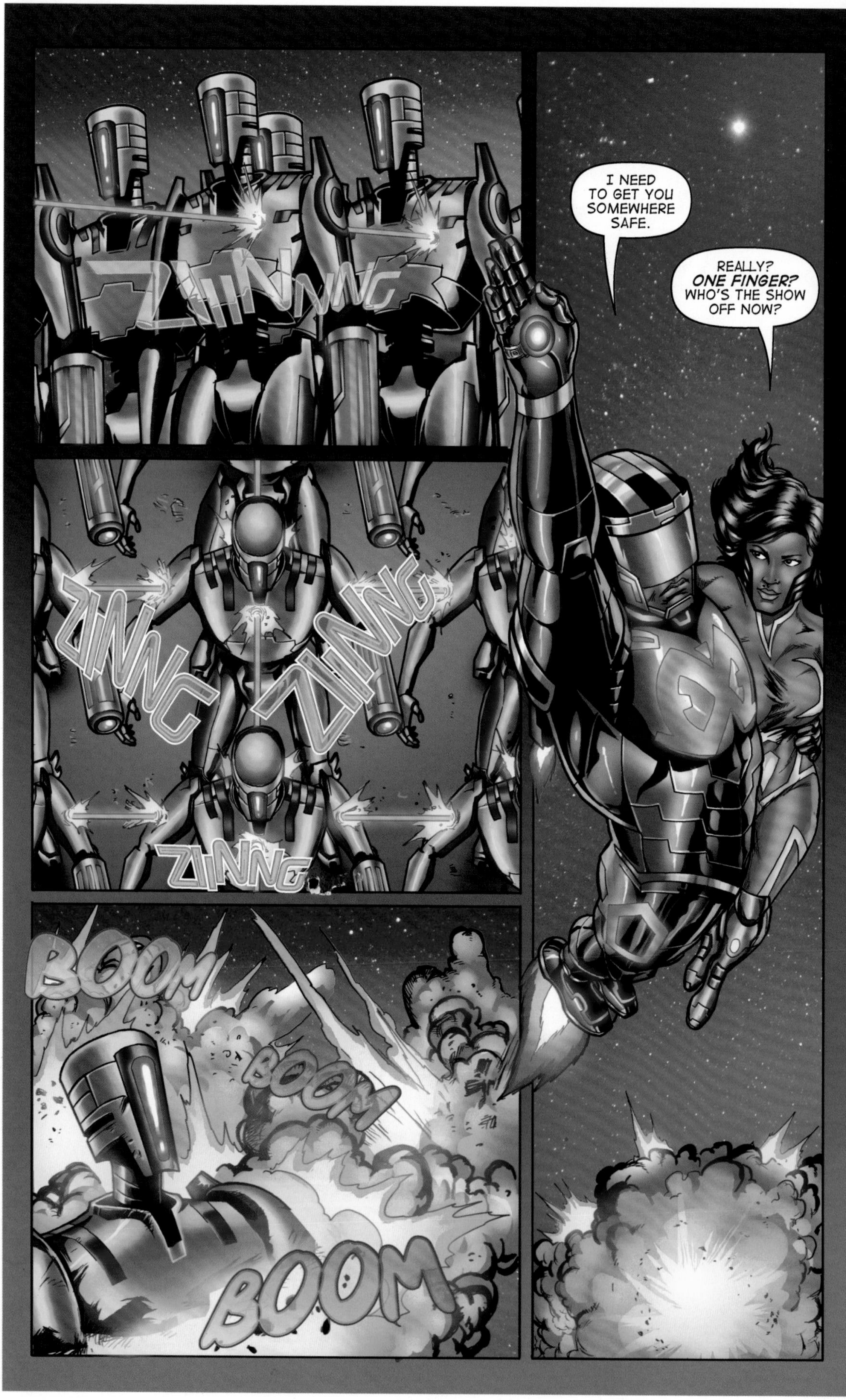
ZIIINNNG
ZIINNG
ZIINNG
ZIINNG
BOOM
BOOM
BOOM
I NEED TO GET YOU SOMEWHERE SAFE.
REALLY? ONE FINGER? WHO'S THE SHOW OFF NOW?

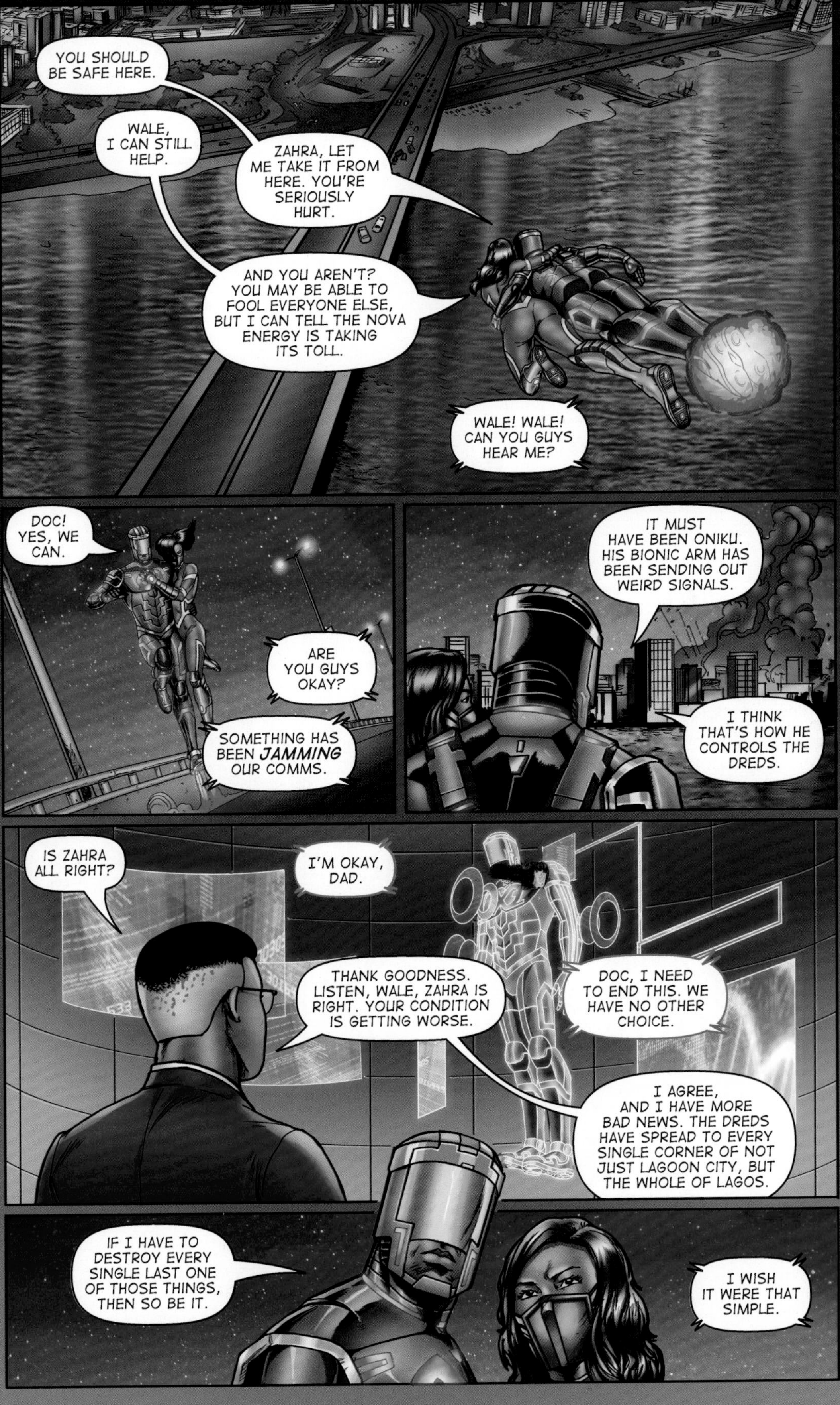
YOU SHOULD BE SAFE HERE.
WALE, I CAN STILL HELP.
ZAHRA, LET ME TAKE IT FROM HERE. YOU'RE SERIOUSLY HURT.
AND YOU AREN'T? YOU MAY BE ABLE TO FOOL EVERYONE ELSE, BUT I CAN TELL THE NOVA ENERGY IS TAKING ITS TOLL.
WALE! WALE! CAN YOU GUYS HEAR ME?
DOC! YES, WE CAN.
ARE YOU GUYS OKAY?
SOMETHING HAS BEEN *JAMMING* OUR COMMS.
IT MUST HAVE BEEN ONIKU. HIS BIONIC ARM HAS BEEN SENDING OUT WEIRD SIGNALS.
I THINK THAT'S HOW HE CONTROLS THE DREDS.
IS ZAHRA ALL RIGHT?
I'M OKAY, DAD.
THANK GOODNESS. LISTEN, WALE, ZAHRA IS RIGHT. YOUR CONDITION IS GETTING WORSE.
DOC, I NEED TO END THIS. WE HAVE NO OTHER CHOICE.
I AGREE, AND I HAVE MORE BAD NEWS. THE DREDS HAVE SPREAD TO EVERY SINGLE CORNER OF NOT JUST LAGOON CITY, BUT THE WHOLE OF LAGOS.
IF I HAVE TO DESTROY EVERY SINGLE LAST ONE OF THOSE THINGS, THEN SO BE IT.
I WISH IT WERE THAT SIMPLE.

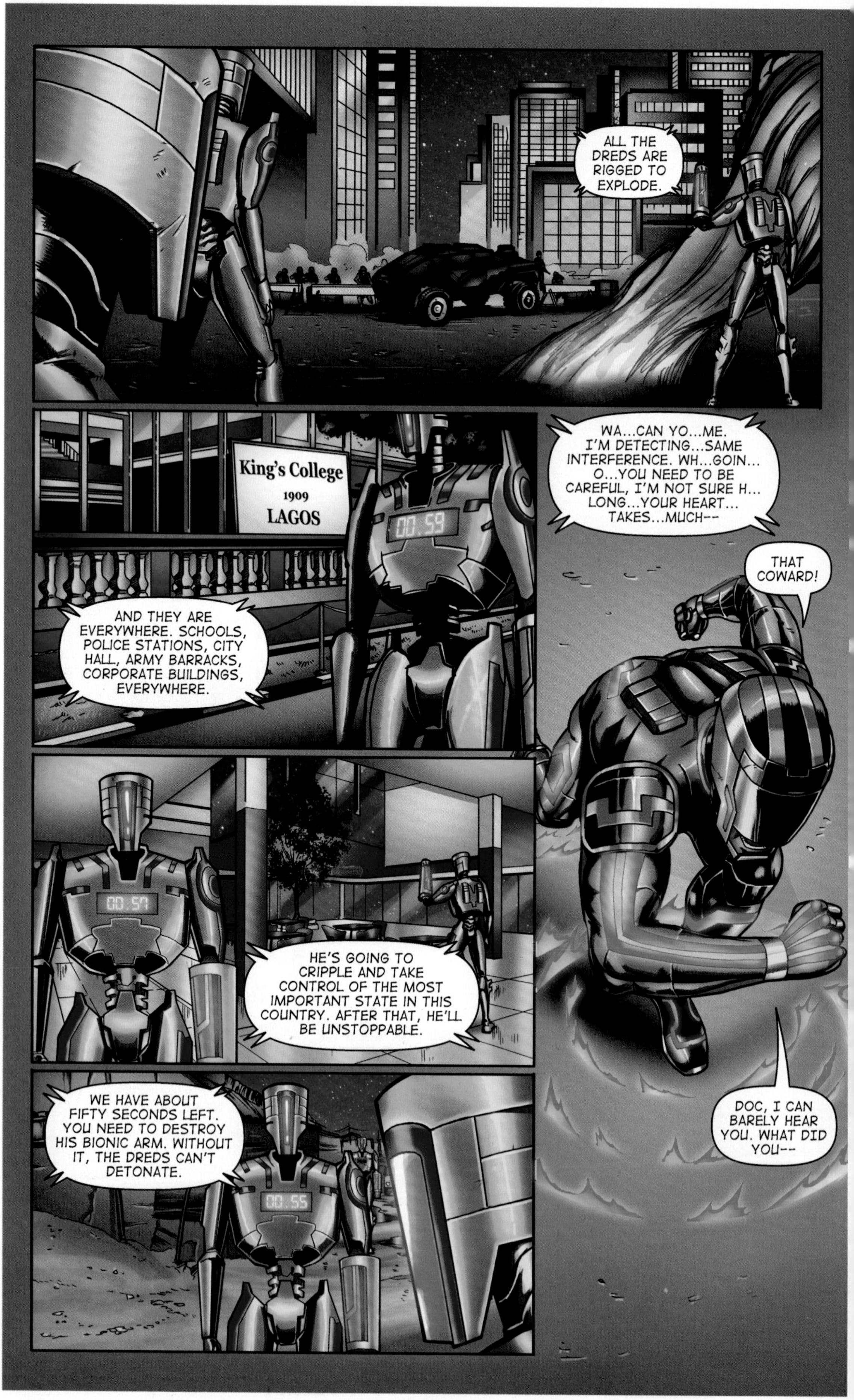
ALL THE DREDS ARE RIGGED TO EXPLODE.
King's College 1909 LAGOS
00.59
AND THEY ARE EVERYWHERE. SCHOOLS, POLICE STATIONS, CITY HALL, ARMY BARRACKS, CORPORATE BUILDINGS, EVERYWHERE.
WA...CAN YO...ME. I'M DETECTING...SAME INTERFERENCE. WH...GOIN... O...YOU NEED TO BE CAREFUL, I'M NOT SURE H... LONG...YOUR HEART... TAKES...MUCH--
THAT COWARD!
00.57
HE'S GOING TO CRIPPLE AND TAKE CONTROL OF THE MOST IMPORTANT STATE IN THIS COUNTRY. AFTER THAT, HE'LL BE UNSTOPPABLE.
WE HAVE ABOUT FIFTY SECONDS LEFT. YOU NEED TO DESTROY HIS BIONIC ARM. WITHOUT IT, THE DREDS CAN'T DETONATE.
00.55
DOC, I CAN BARELY HEAR YOU. WHAT DID YOU--

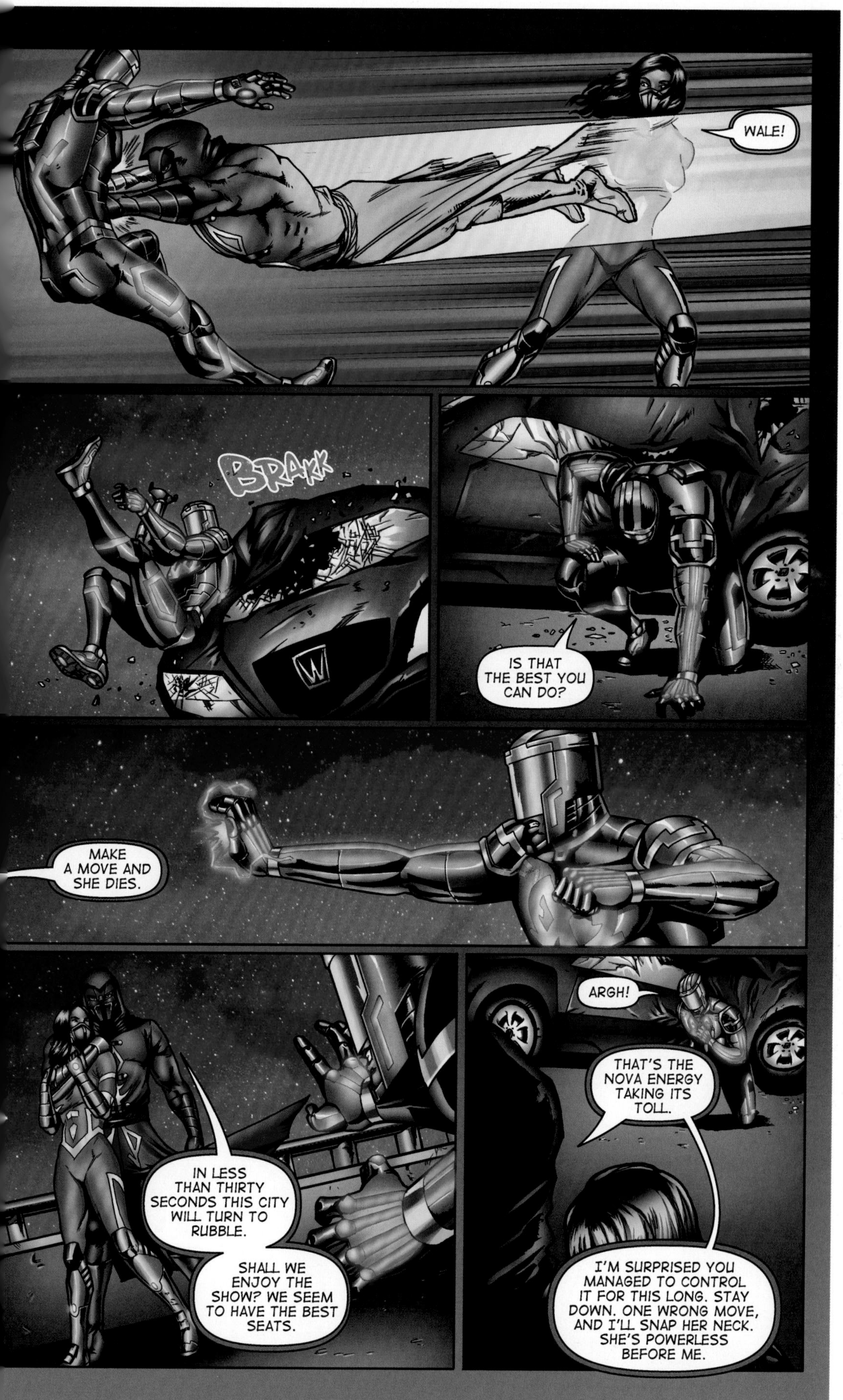
WALE!
BRAKK
IS THAT THE BEST YOU CAN DO?
MAKE A MOVE AND SHE DIES.
IN LESS THAN THIRTY SECONDS THIS CITY WILL TURN TO RUBBLE.
SHALL WE ENJOY THE SHOW? WE SEEM TO HAVE THE BEST SEATS.
ARGH!
THAT'S THE NOVA ENERGY TAKING ITS TOLL.
I'M SURPRISED YOU MANAGED TO CONTROL IT FOR THIS LONG. STAY DOWN. ONE WRONG MOVE, AND I'LL SNAP HER NECK. SHE'S POWERLESS BEFORE ME.

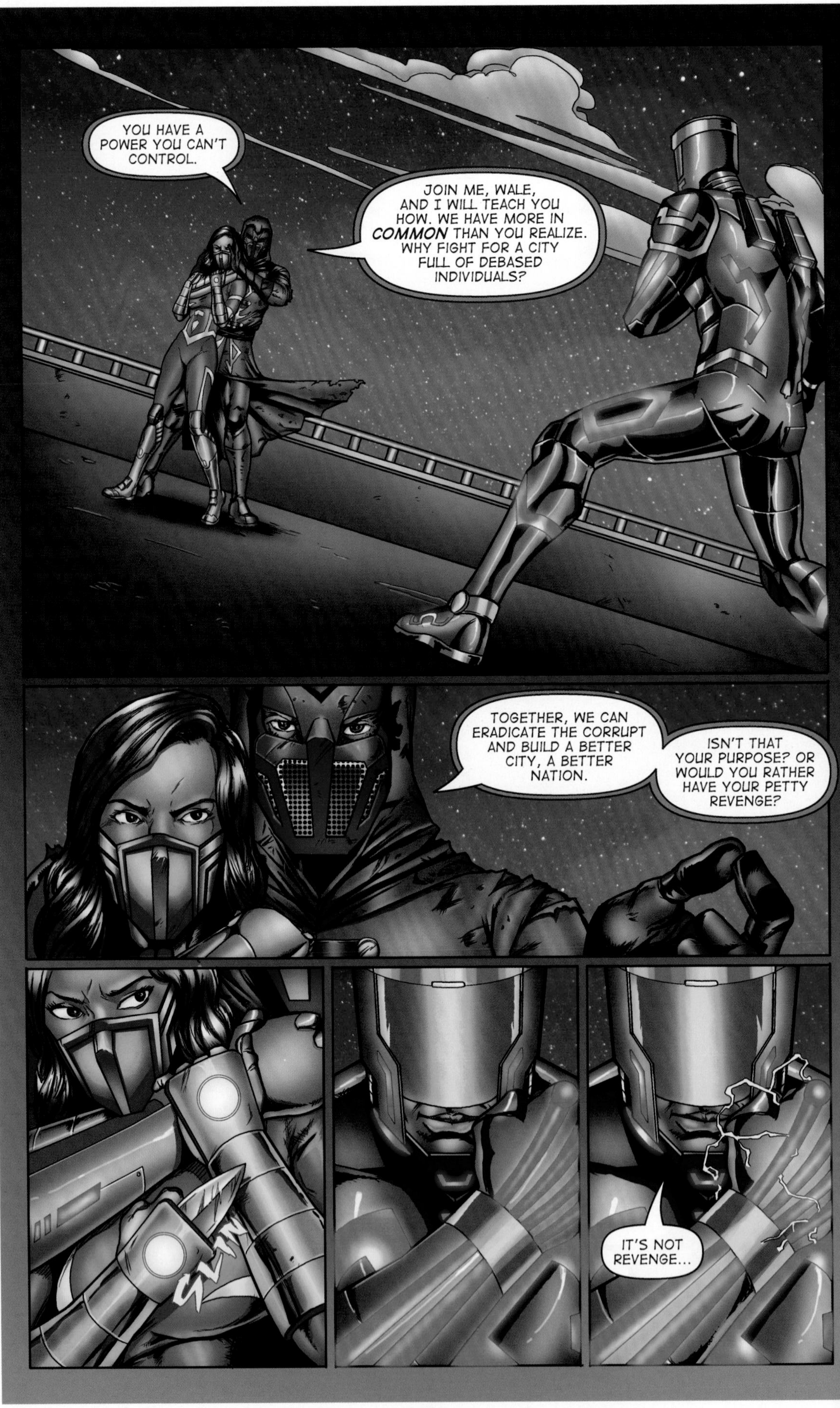
YOU HAVE A POWER YOU CAN'T CONTROL.
JOIN ME, WALE, AND I WILL TEACH YOU HOW. WE HAVE MORE IN *COMMON* THAN YOU REALIZE. WHY FIGHT FOR A CITY FULL OF DEBASED INDIVIDUALS?
TOGETHER, WE CAN ERADICATE THE CORRUPT AND BUILD A BETTER CITY, A BETTER NATION.
ISN'T THAT YOUR PURPOSE? OR WOULD YOU RATHER HAVE YOUR PETTY REVENGE?
IT'S NOT REVENGE...

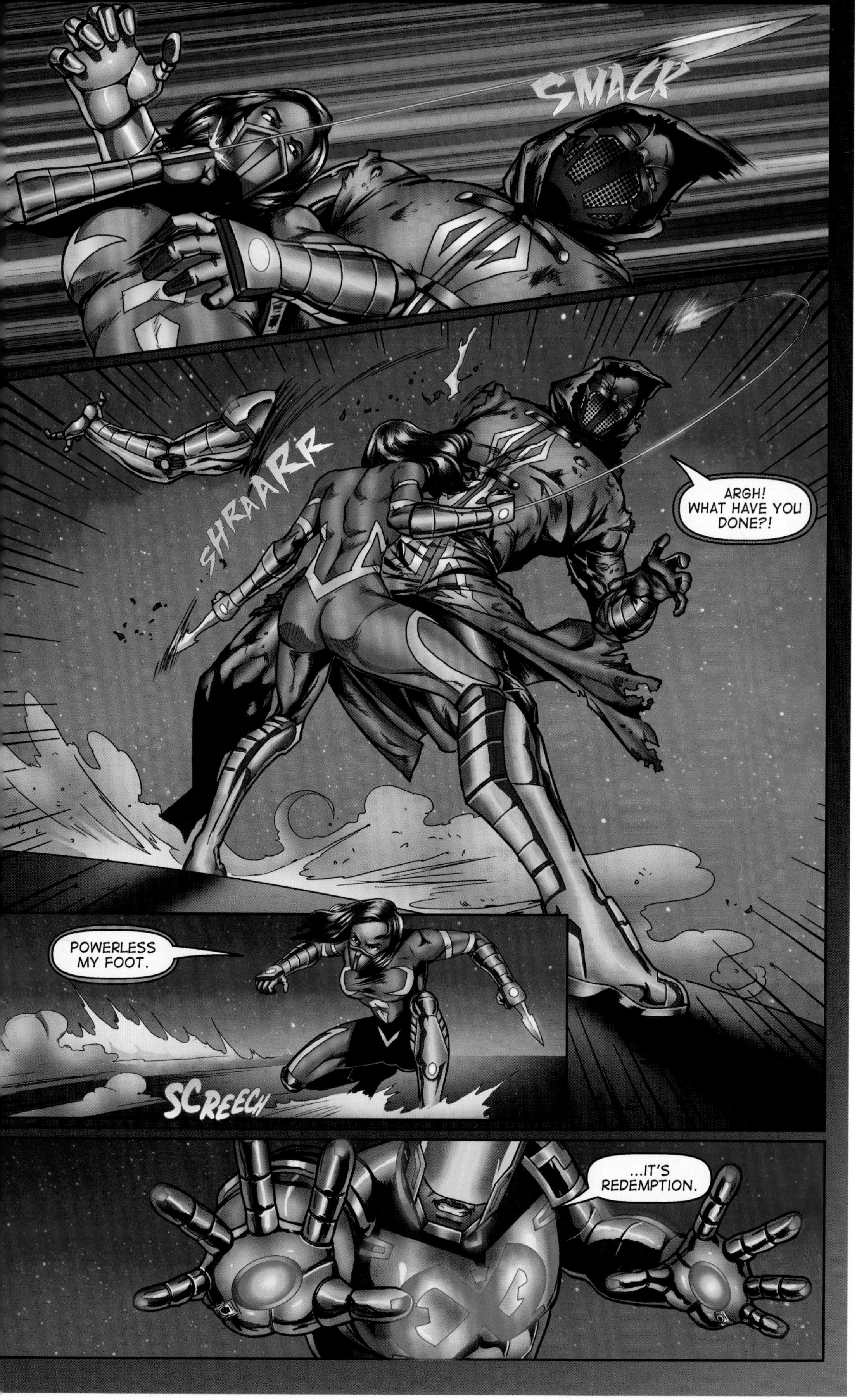
SMACK
SHRAARR
ARGH! WHAT HAVE YOU DONE?!
POWERLESS MY FOOT.
SCREECH
...IT'S REDEMPTION.

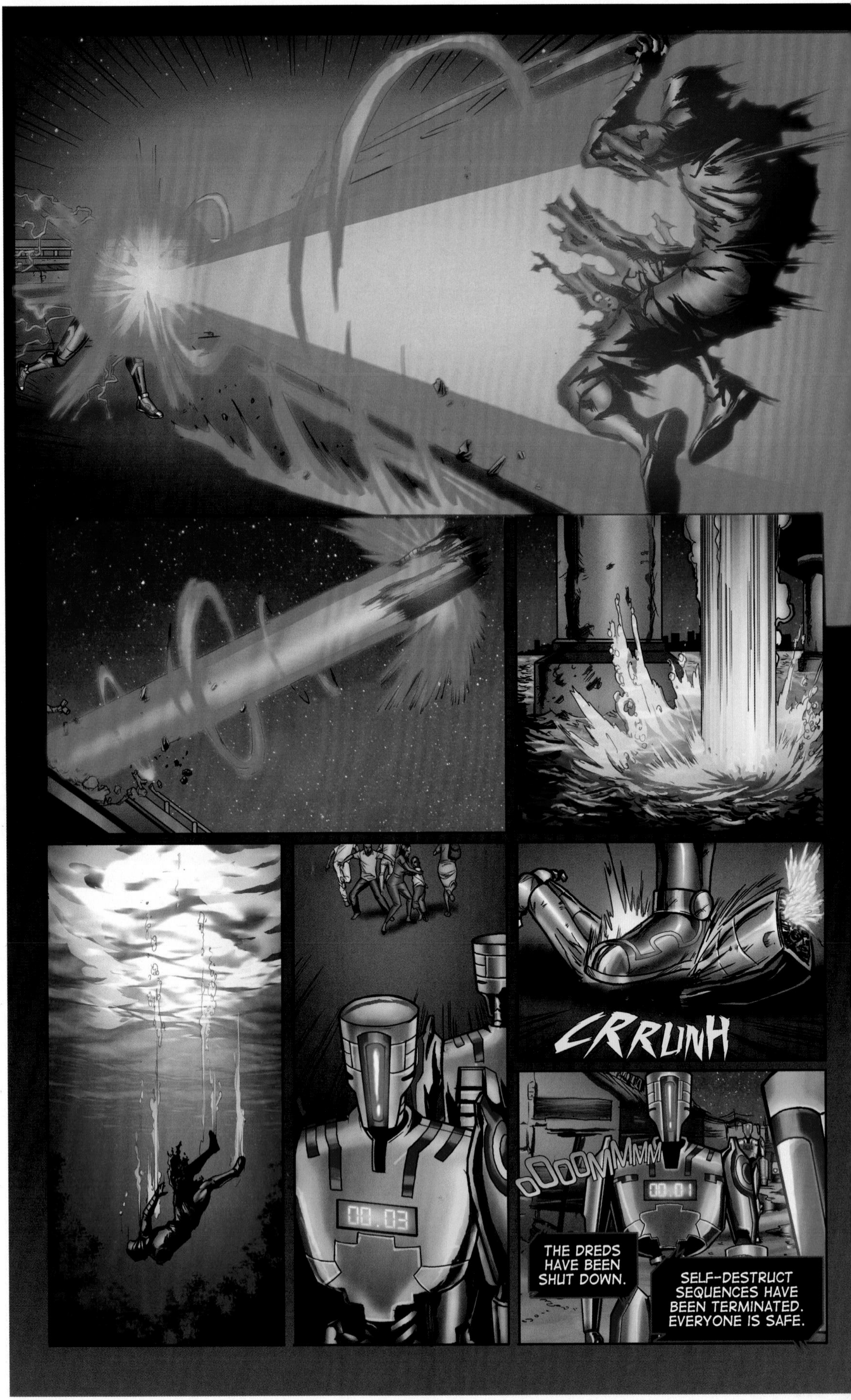
CRRUNH
OOOOMMMMM
00:03
00:01
THE DREDS HAVE BEEN SHUT DOWN.
SELF-DESTRUCT SEQUENCES HAVE BEEN TERMINATED. EVERYONE IS SAFE.

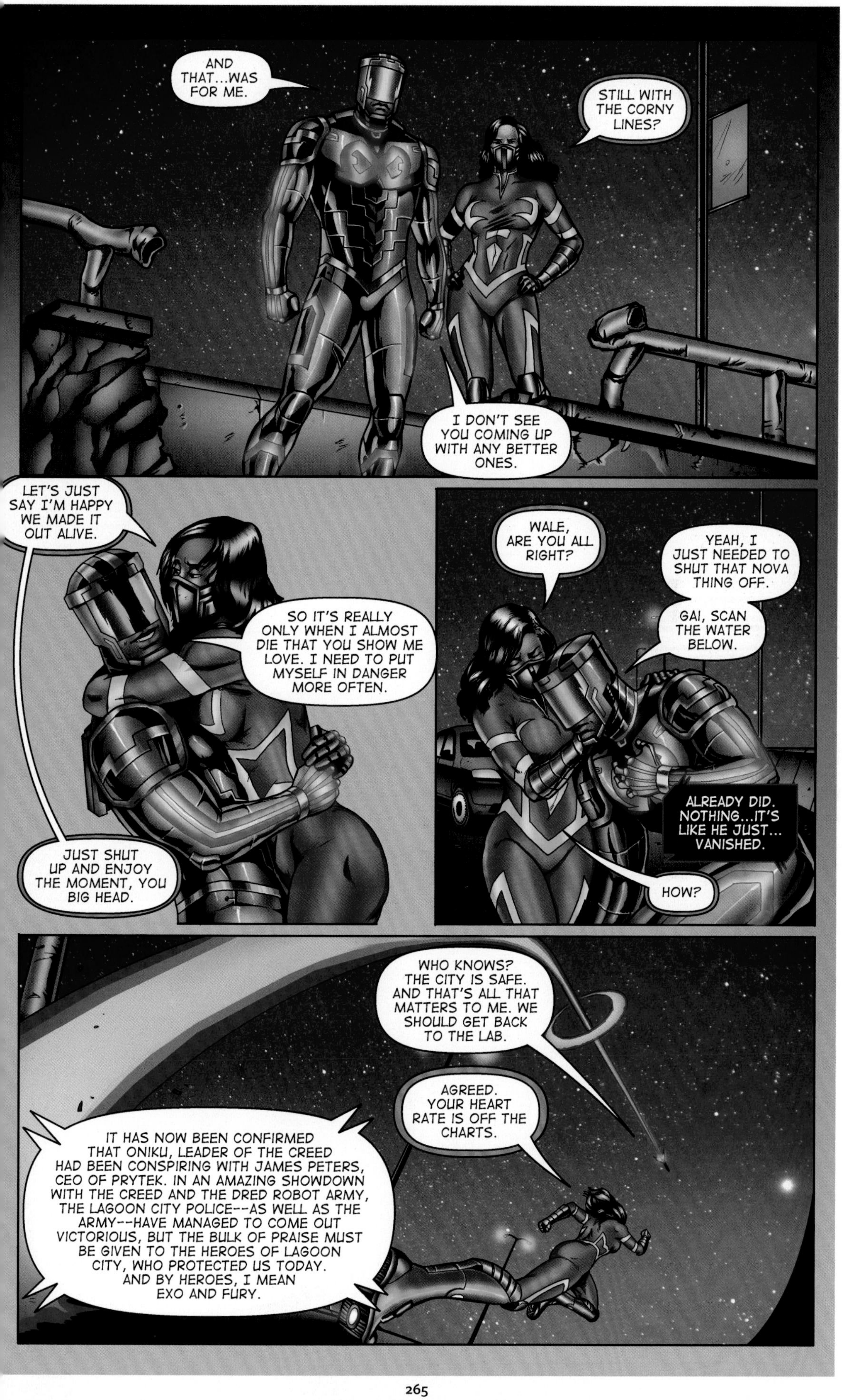
AND THAT...WAS FOR ME.
STILL WITH THE CORNY LINES?
I DON'T SEE YOU COMING UP WITH ANY BETTER ONES.
LET'S JUST SAY I'M HAPPY WE MADE IT OUT ALIVE.
SO IT'S REALLY ONLY WHEN I ALMOST DIE THAT YOU SHOW ME LOVE. I NEED TO PUT MYSELF IN DANGER MORE OFTEN.
JUST SHUT UP AND ENJOY THE MOMENT, YOU BIG HEAD.
WALE, ARE YOU ALL RIGHT?
YEAH, I JUST NEEDED TO SHUT THAT NOVA THING OFF.
GAI, SCAN THE WATER BELOW.
ALREADY DID. NOTHING...IT'S LIKE HE JUST... VANISHED.
HOW?
WHO KNOWS? THE CITY IS SAFE. AND THAT'S ALL THAT MATTERS TO ME. WE SHOULD GET BACK TO THE LAB.
AGREED. YOUR HEART RATE IS OFF THE CHARTS.
IT HAS NOW BEEN CONFIRMED THAT ONIKU, LEADER OF THE CREED HAD BEEN CONSPIRING WITH JAMES PETERS, CEO OF PRYTEK. IN AN AMAZING SHOWDOWN WITH THE CREED AND THE DRED ROBOT ARMY, THE LAGOON CITY POLICE--AS WELL AS THE ARMY--HAVE MANAGED TO COME OUT VICTORIOUS, BUT THE BULK OF PRAISE MUST BE GIVEN TO THE HEROES OF LAGOON CITY, WHO PROTECTED US TODAY. AND BY HEROES, I MEAN EXO AND FURY.

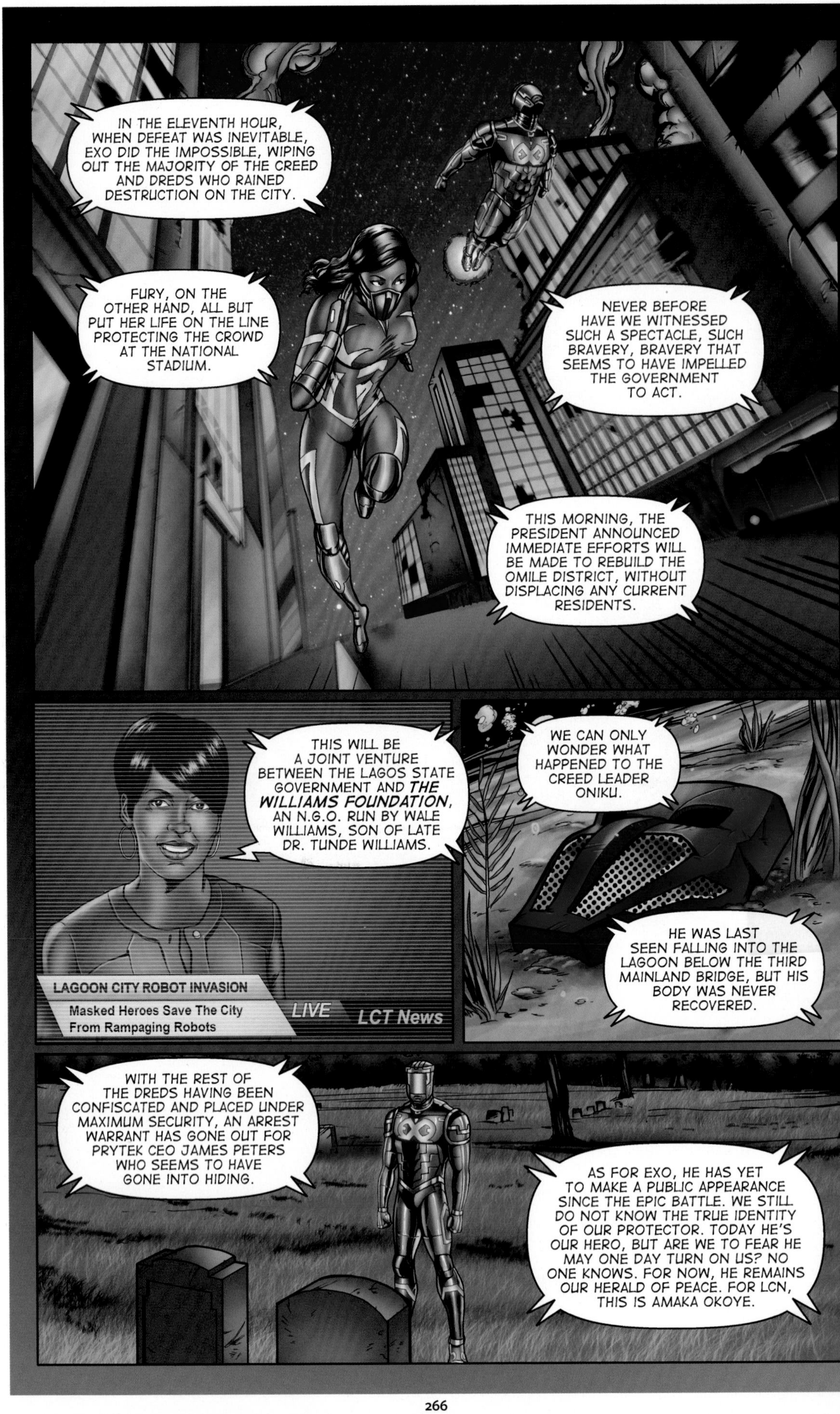
IN THE ELEVENTH HOUR, WHEN DEFEAT WAS INEVITABLE, EXO DID THE IMPOSSIBLE, WIPING OUT THE MAJORITY OF THE CREED AND DREDS WHO RAINED DESTRUCTION ON THE CITY.
FURY, ON THE OTHER HAND, ALL BUT PUT HER LIFE ON THE LINE PROTECTING THE CROWD AT THE NATIONAL STADIUM.
NEVER BEFORE HAVE WE WITNESSED SUCH A SPECTACLE, SUCH BRAVERY, BRAVERY THAT SEEMS TO HAVE IMPELLED THE GOVERNMENT TO ACT.
THIS MORNING, THE PRESIDENT ANNOUNCED IMMEDIATE EFFORTS WILL BE MADE TO REBUILD THE OMILE DISTRICT, WITHOUT DISPLACING ANY CURRENT RESIDENTS.
THIS WILL BE A JOINT VENTURE BETWEEN THE LAGOS STATE GOVERNMENT AND ***THE WILLIAMS FOUNDATION***, AN N.G.O. RUN BY WALE WILLIAMS, SON OF LATE DR. TUNDE WILLIAMS.
LAGOON CITY ROBOT INVASION
Masked Heroes Save The City From Rampaging Robots
LIVE
LCT News
WE CAN ONLY WONDER WHAT HAPPENED TO THE CREED LEADER ONIKU.
HE WAS LAST SEEN FALLING INTO THE LAGOON BELOW THE THIRD MAINLAND BRIDGE, BUT HIS BODY WAS NEVER RECOVERED.
WITH THE REST OF THE DREDS HAVING BEEN CONFISCATED AND PLACED UNDER MAXIMUM SECURITY, AN ARREST WARRANT HAS GONE OUT FOR PRYTEK CEO JAMES PETERS WHO SEEMS TO HAVE GONE INTO HIDING.
AS FOR EXO, HE HAS YET TO MAKE A PUBLIC APPEARANCE SINCE THE EPIC BATTLE. WE STILL DO NOT KNOW THE TRUE IDENTITY OF OUR PROTECTOR. TODAY HE'S OUR HERO, BUT ARE WE TO FEAR HE MAY ONE DAY TURN ON US? NO ONE KNOWS. FOR NOW, HE REMAINS OUR HERALD OF PEACE. FOR LCN, THIS IS AMAKA OKOYE.

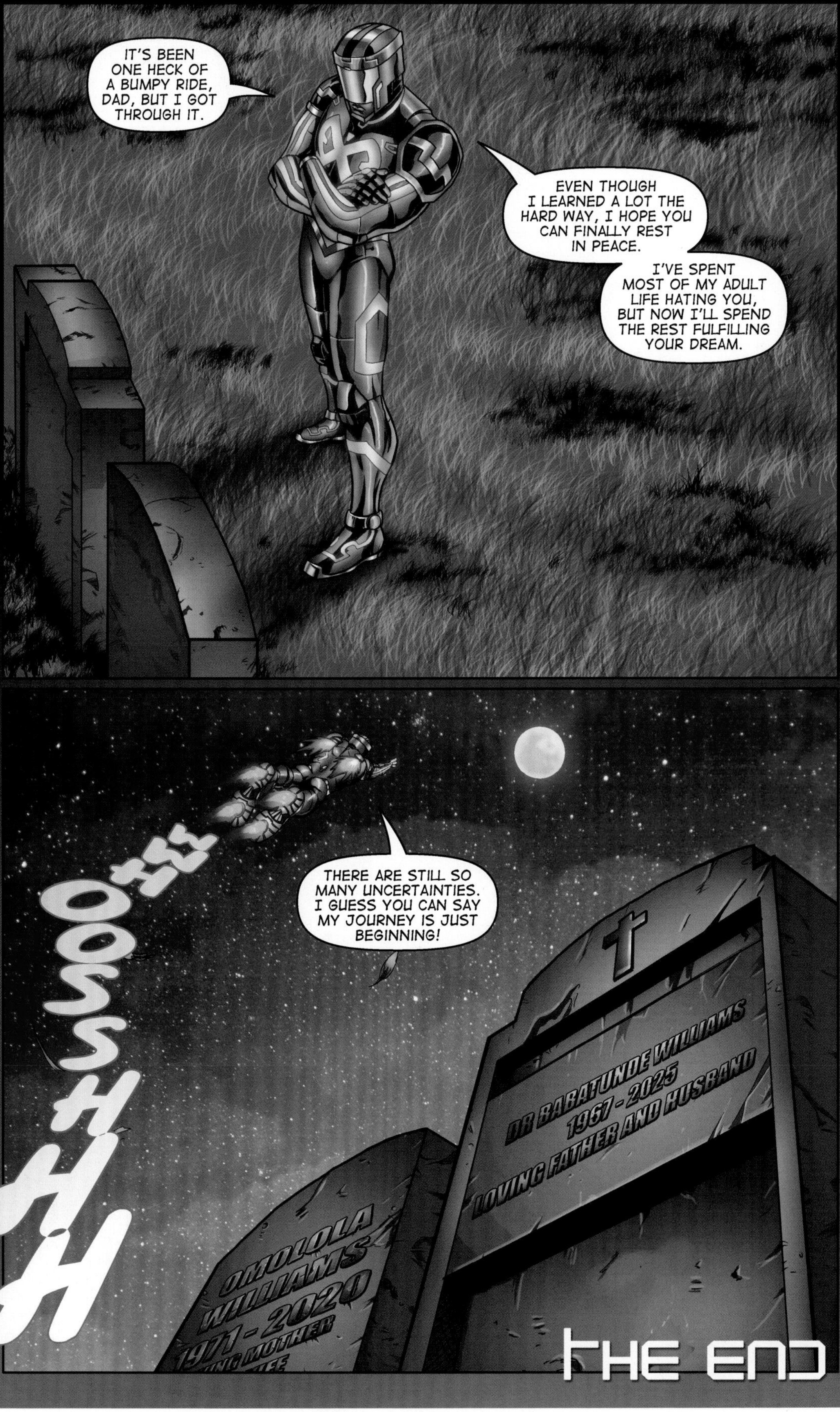

IT'S BEEN ONE HECK OF A BUMPY RIDE, DAD, BUT I GOT THROUGH IT.
EVEN THOUGH I LEARNED A LOT THE HARD WAY, I HOPE YOU CAN FINALLY REST IN PEACE.
I'VE SPENT MOST OF MY ADULT LIFE HATING YOU, BUT NOW I'LL SPEND THE REST FULFILLING YOUR DREAM.
WHOOSHHH
THERE ARE STILL SO MANY UNCERTAINTIES. I GUESS YOU CAN SAY MY JOURNEY IS JUST BEGINNING!
DR BABATUNDE WILLIAMS
1967 - 2025
LOVING FATHER AND HUSBAND
OMOLOLA WILLIAMS
1971 - 2020
THE END

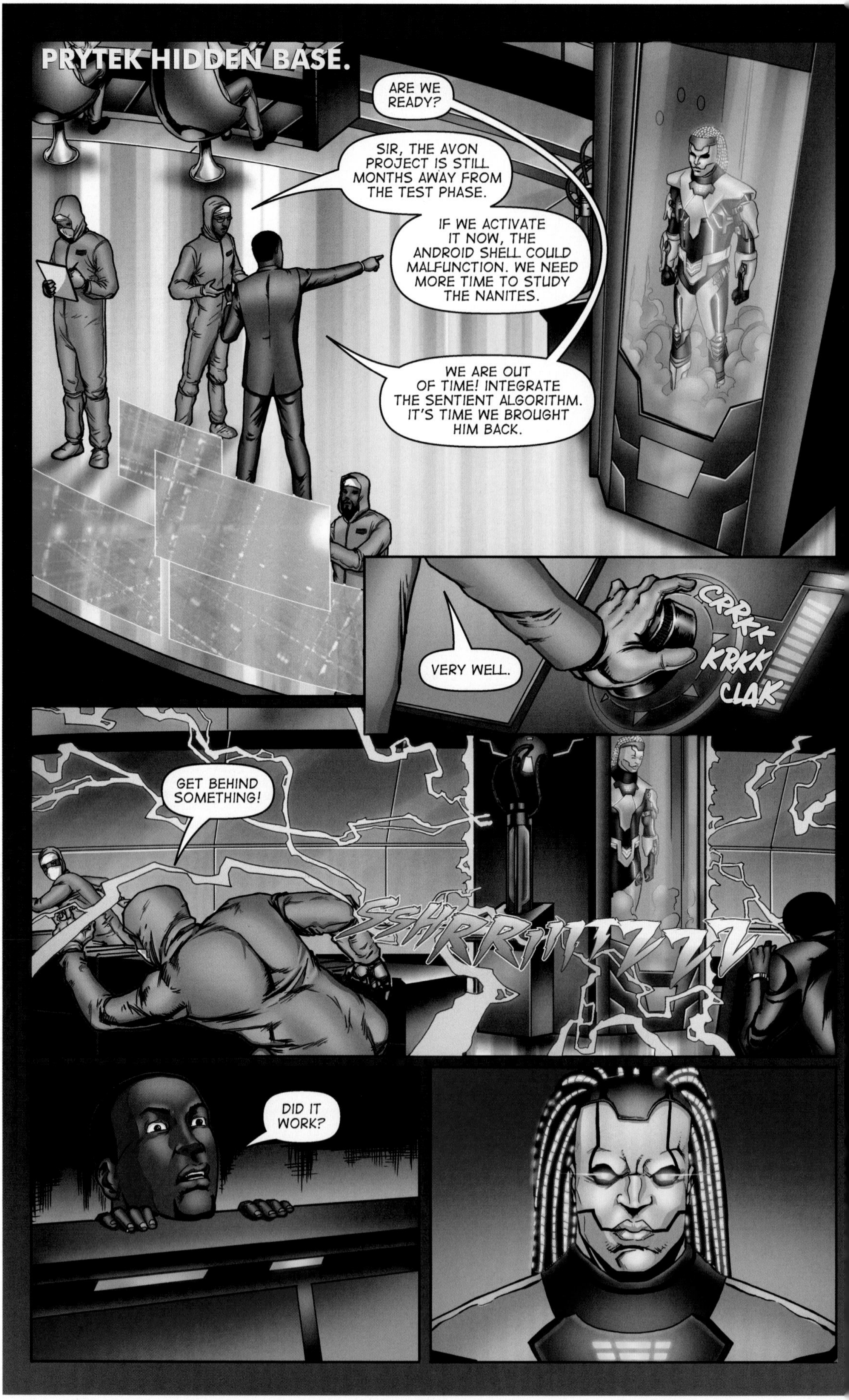
PRYTEK HIDDEN BASE.
ARE WE READY?
SIR, THE AVON PROJECT IS STILL MONTHS AWAY FROM THE TEST PHASE.
IF WE ACTIVATE IT NOW, THE ANDROID SHELL COULD MALFUNCTION. WE NEED MORE TIME TO STUDY THE NANITES.
WE ARE OUT OF TIME! INTEGRATE THE SENTIENT ALGORITHM. IT'S TIME WE BROUGHT HIM BACK.
VERY WELL.
CRRKK KRKK CLAK
GET BEHIND SOMETHING!
SSHRRIIITZZZZ
DID IT WORK?

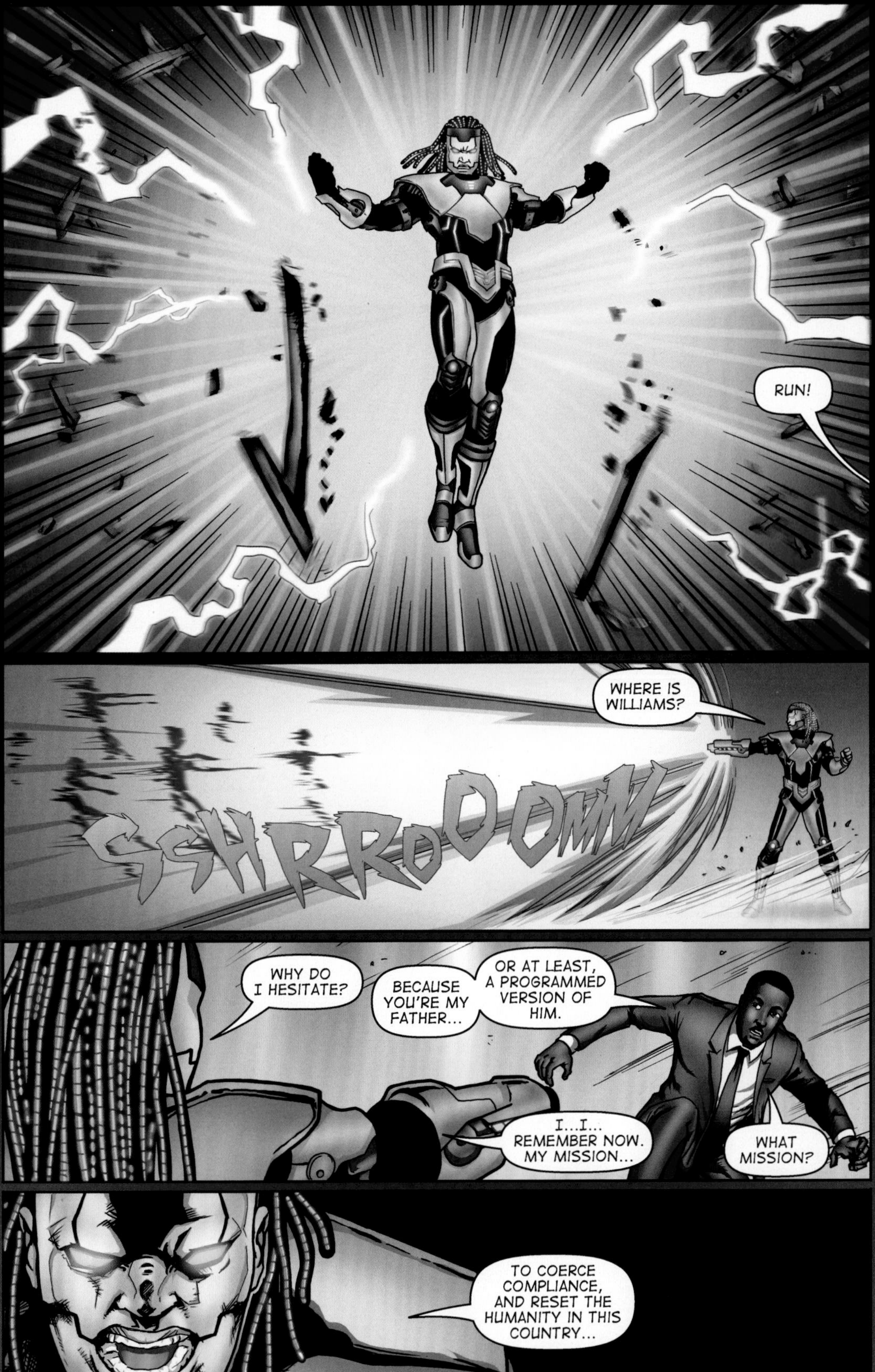
RUN!
WHERE IS WILLIAMS?
SSHRROOOMM
WHY DO I HESITATE?
BECAUSE YOU'RE MY FATHER...
OR AT LEAST, A PROGRAMMED VERSION OF HIM.
I...I... REMEMBER NOW. MY MISSION...
WHAT MISSION?
TO COERCE COMPLIANCE, AND RESET THE HUMANITY IN THIS COUNTRY...

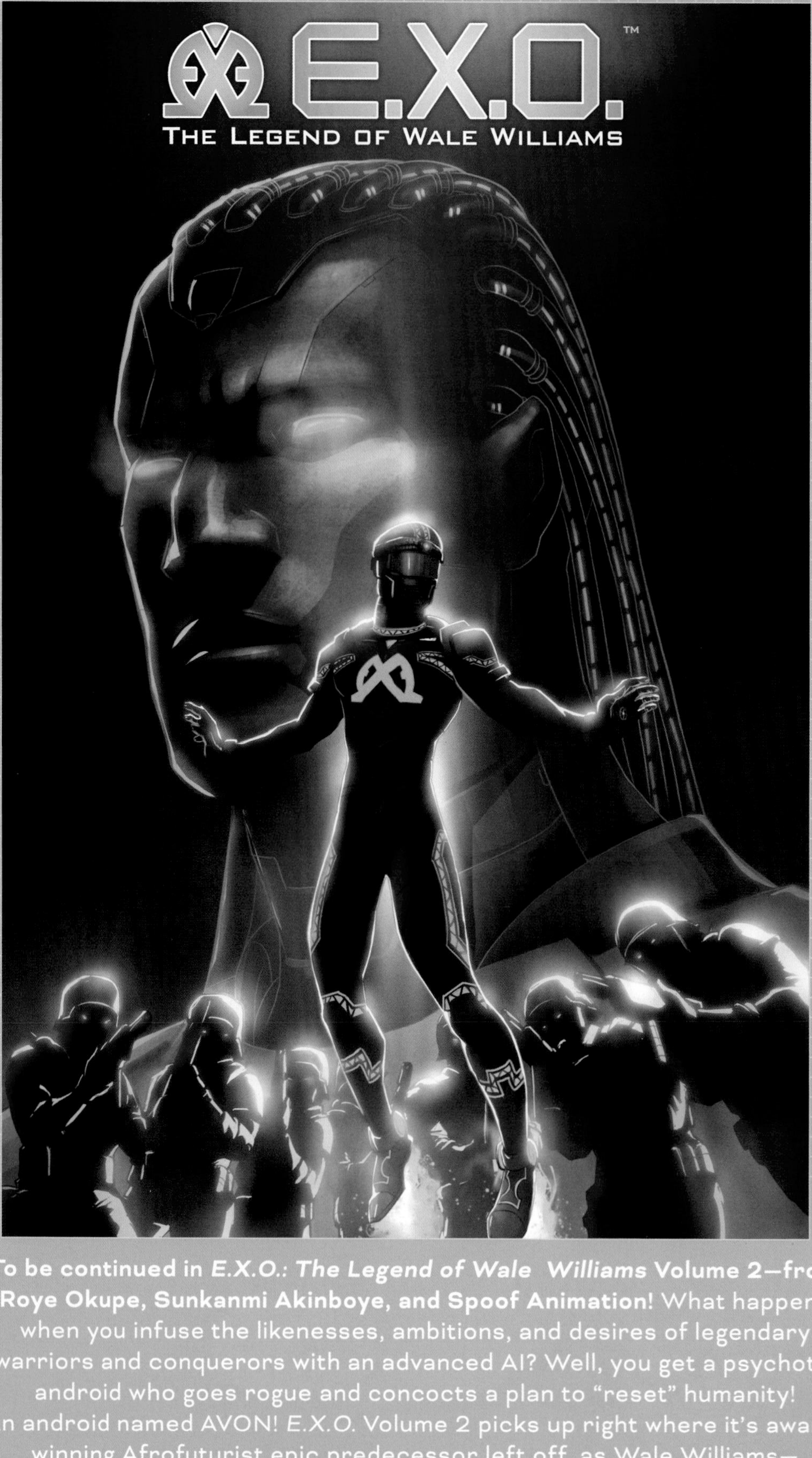
E.X.O.™
THE LEGEND OF WALE WILLIAMS

To be continued in *E.X.O.: The Legend of Wale Williams* Volume 2—from Roye Okupe, Sunkanmi Akinboye, and Spoof Animation! What happens when you infuse the likenesses, ambitions, and desires of legendary warriors and conquerors with an advanced AI? Well, you get a psychotic android who goes rogue and concocts a plan to "reset" humanity! An android named AVON! *E.X.O.* Volume 2 picks up right where it's award-winning Afrofuturist epic predecessor left off, as Wale Williams—aka tech-savvy superhero EXO—tries to save humanity!

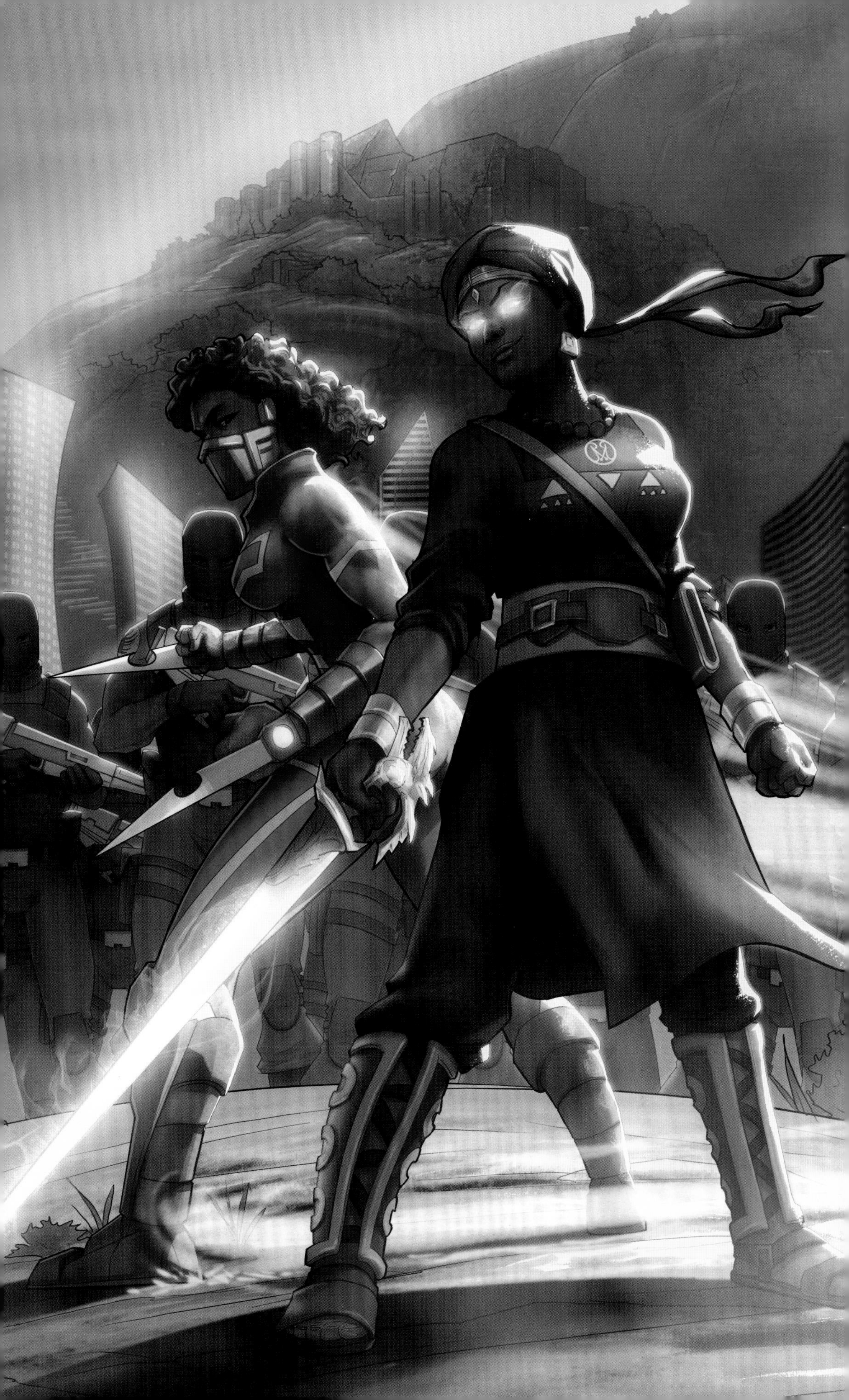

MALIKA
Warrior Queen

CREED & FURY

CREATOR AND WRITER
ROYE OKUPE

ART
SUNKANMI AKINBOYE

LETTERS
BODE JOSEPH

COLORS
ETUBI ONUCHEYO

COVER ART (PREVIOUS PAGE)
AND CONCEPT ART
GODWIN AKPAN

BONUS STORY—UNIQUE TO THIS EDITION!

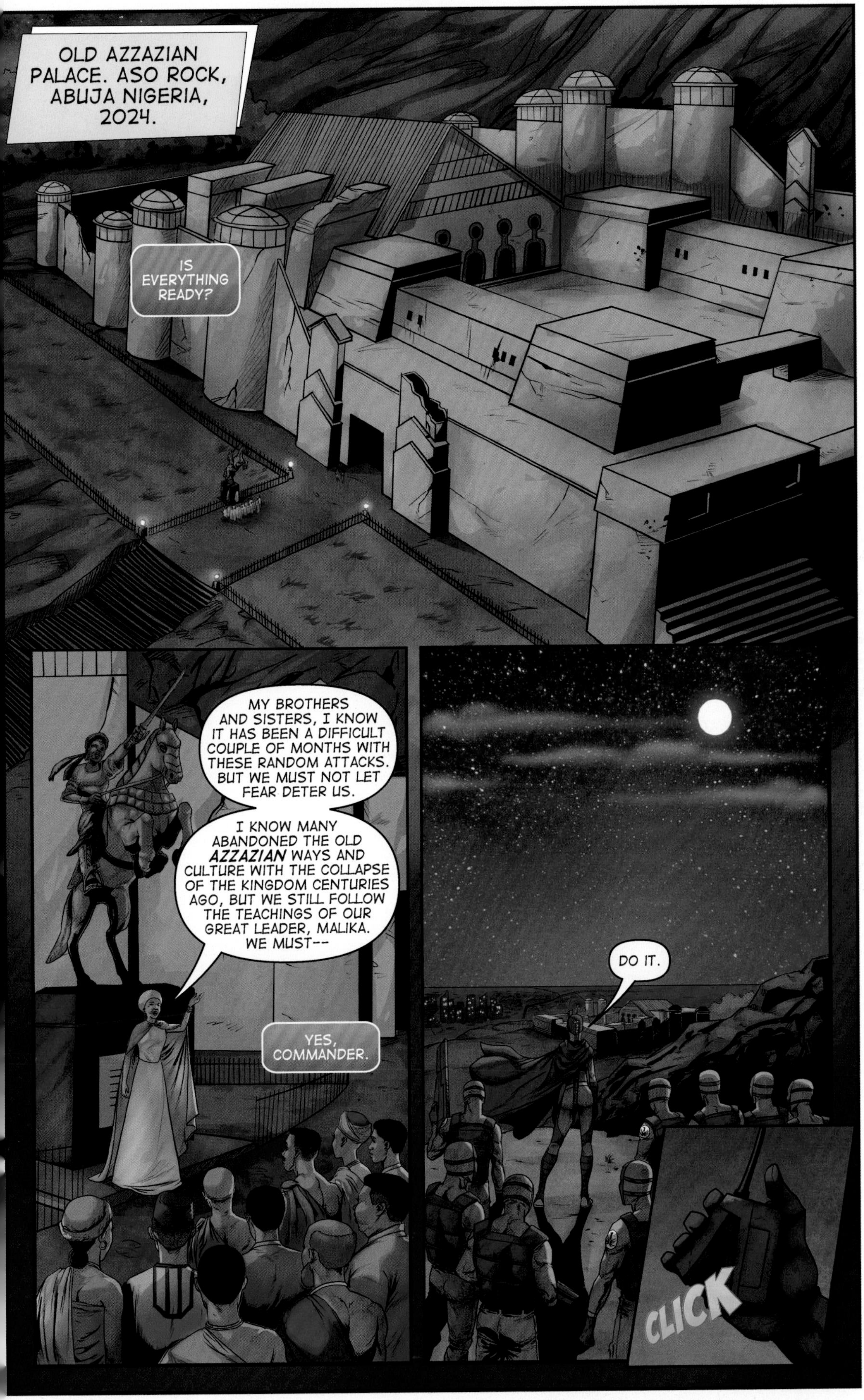
OLD AZZAZIAN PALACE. ASO ROCK, ABUJA NIGERIA, 2024.
IS EVERYTHING READY?
MY BROTHERS AND SISTERS, I KNOW IT HAS BEEN A DIFFICULT COUPLE OF MONTHS WITH THESE RANDOM ATTACKS. BUT WE MUST NOT LET FEAR DETER US.
I KNOW MANY ABANDONED THE OLD AZZAZIAN WAYS AND CULTURE WITH THE COLLAPSE OF THE KINGDOM CENTURIES AGO, BUT WE STILL FOLLOW THE TEACHINGS OF OUR GREAT LEADER, MALIKA. WE MUST--
YES, COMMANDER.
DO IT.
CLICK

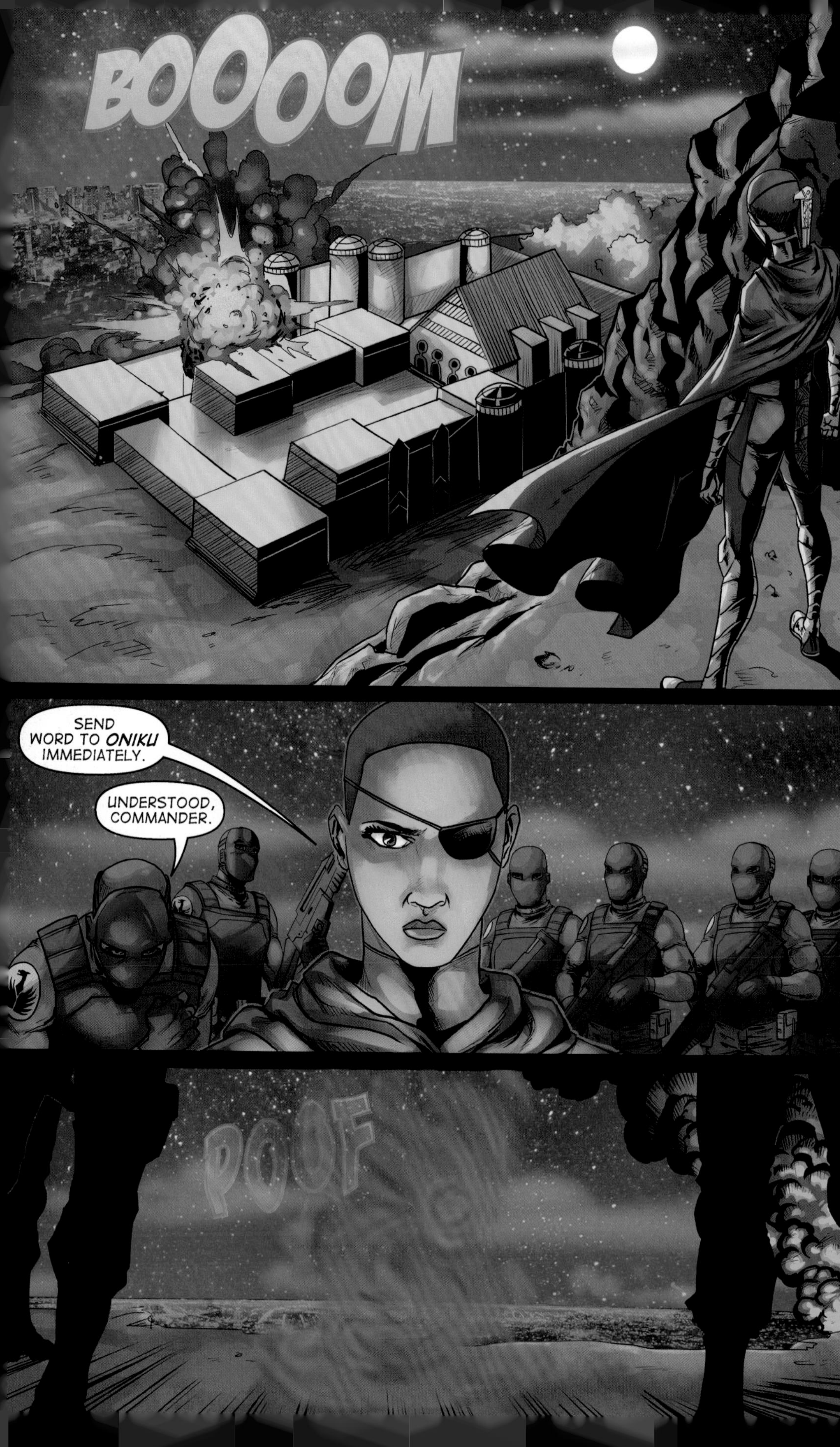
BOOOOOM
SEND WORD TO ONIKU IMMEDIATELY.
UNDERSTOOD, COMMANDER.
POOF

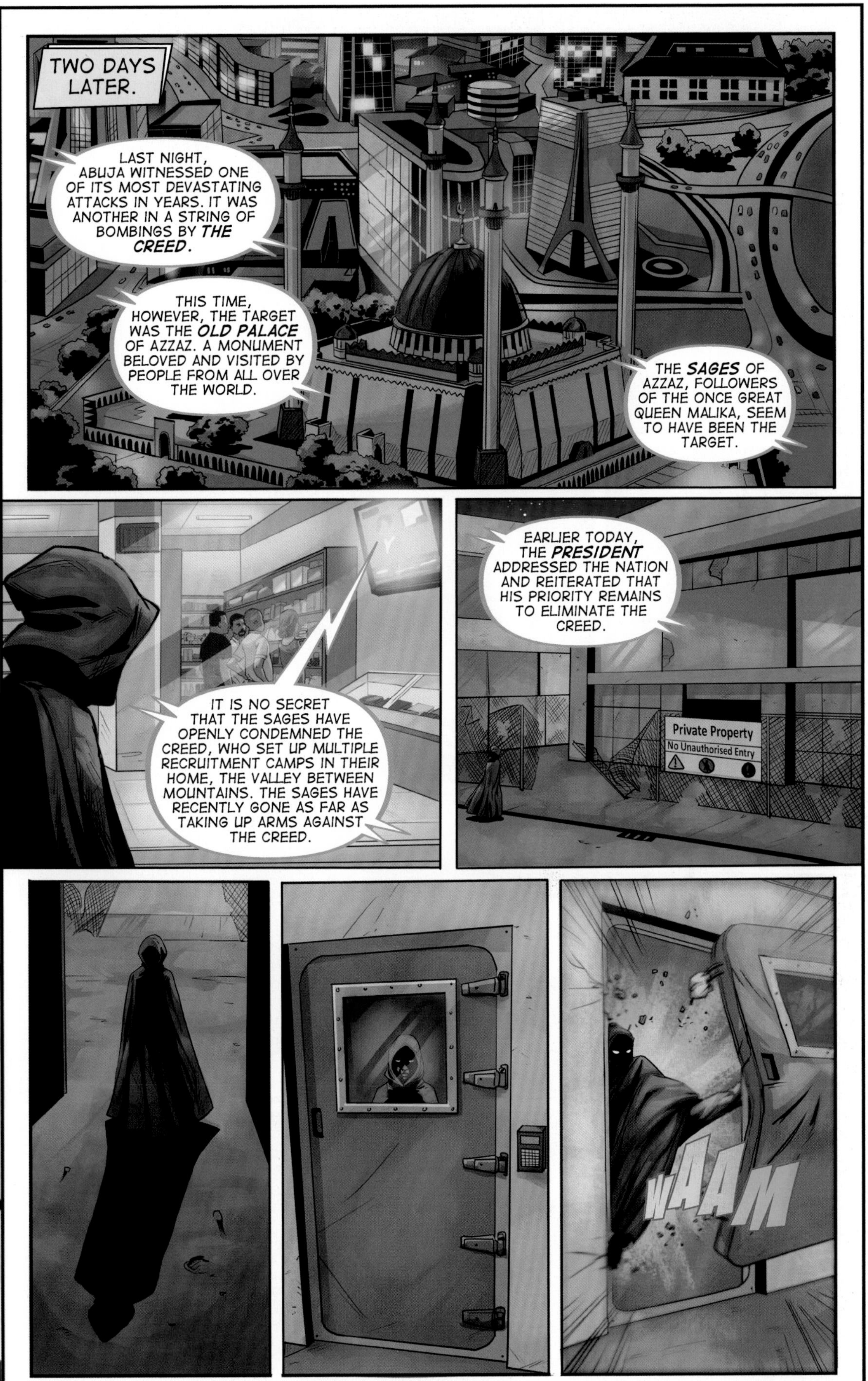
TWO DAYS LATER.
LAST NIGHT, ABUJA WITNESSED ONE OF ITS MOST DEVASTATING ATTACKS IN YEARS. IT WAS ANOTHER IN A STRING OF BOMBINGS BY THE CREED.
THIS TIME, HOWEVER, THE TARGET WAS THE OLD PALACE OF AZZAZ. A MONUMENT BELOVED AND VISITED BY PEOPLE FROM ALL OVER THE WORLD.
THE SAGES OF AZZAZ, FOLLOWERS OF THE ONCE GREAT QUEEN MALIKA, SEEM TO HAVE BEEN THE TARGET.
IT IS NO SECRET THAT THE SAGES HAVE OPENLY CONDEMNED THE CREED, WHO SET UP MULTIPLE RECRUITMENT CAMPS IN THEIR HOME, THE VALLEY BETWEEN MOUNTAINS. THE SAGES HAVE RECENTLY GONE AS FAR AS TAKING UP ARMS AGAINST THE CREED.
EARLIER TODAY, THE PRESIDENT ADDRESSED THE NATION AND REITERATED THAT HIS PRIORITY REMAINS TO ELIMINATE THE CREED.
Private Property
No Unauthorised Entry
WAAM

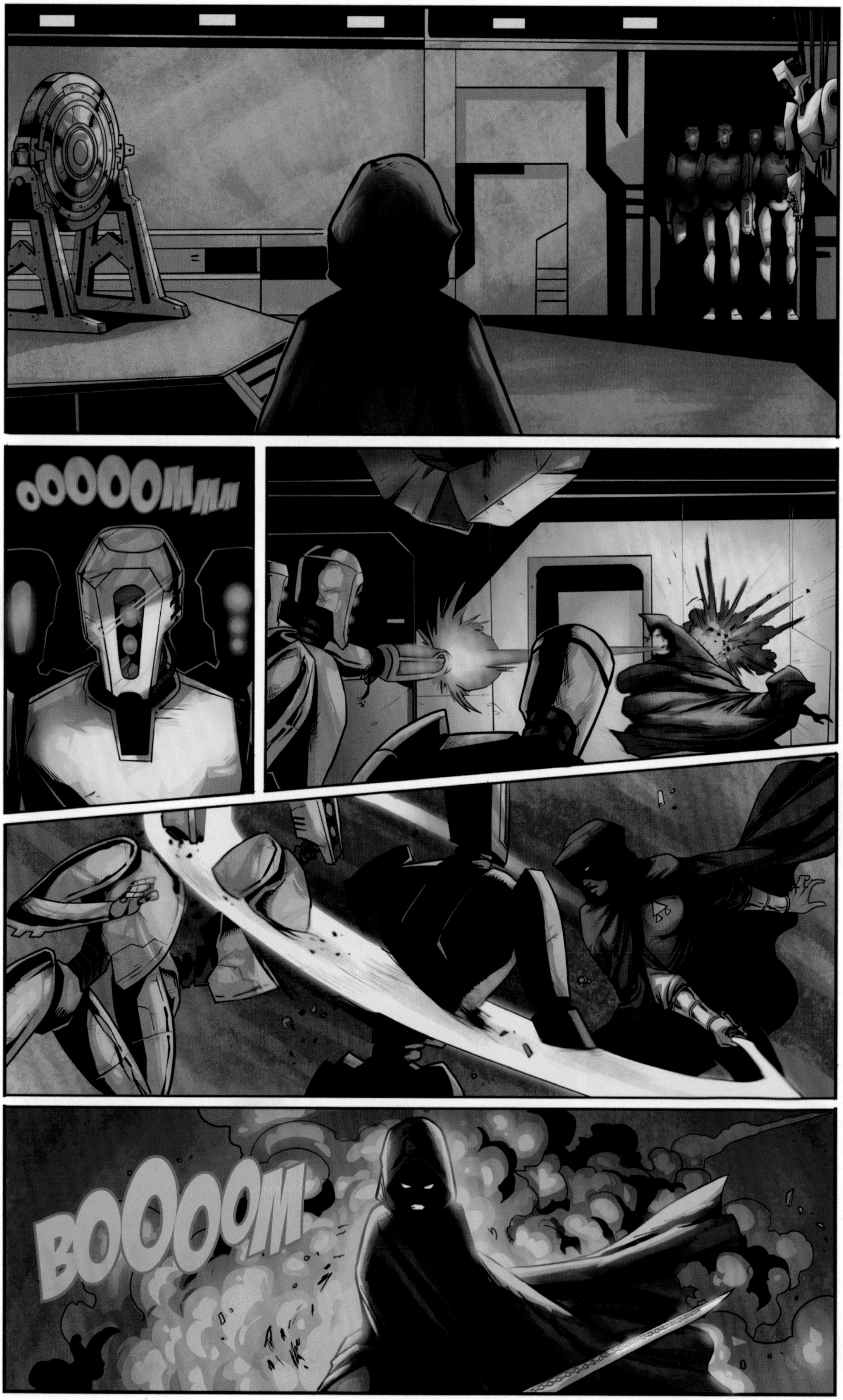
oOOOOMMM
BOOOOM

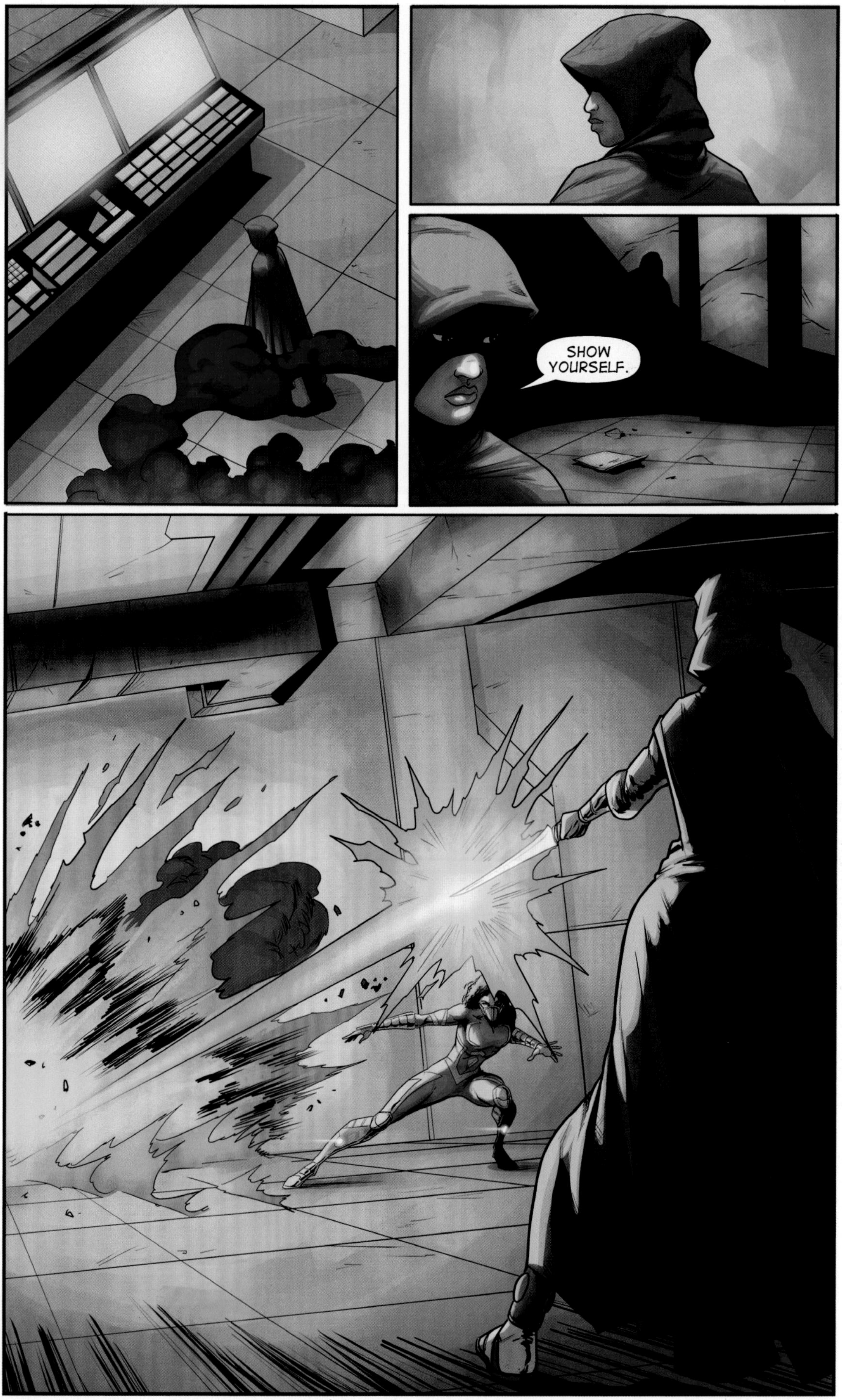
SHOW YOURSELF.

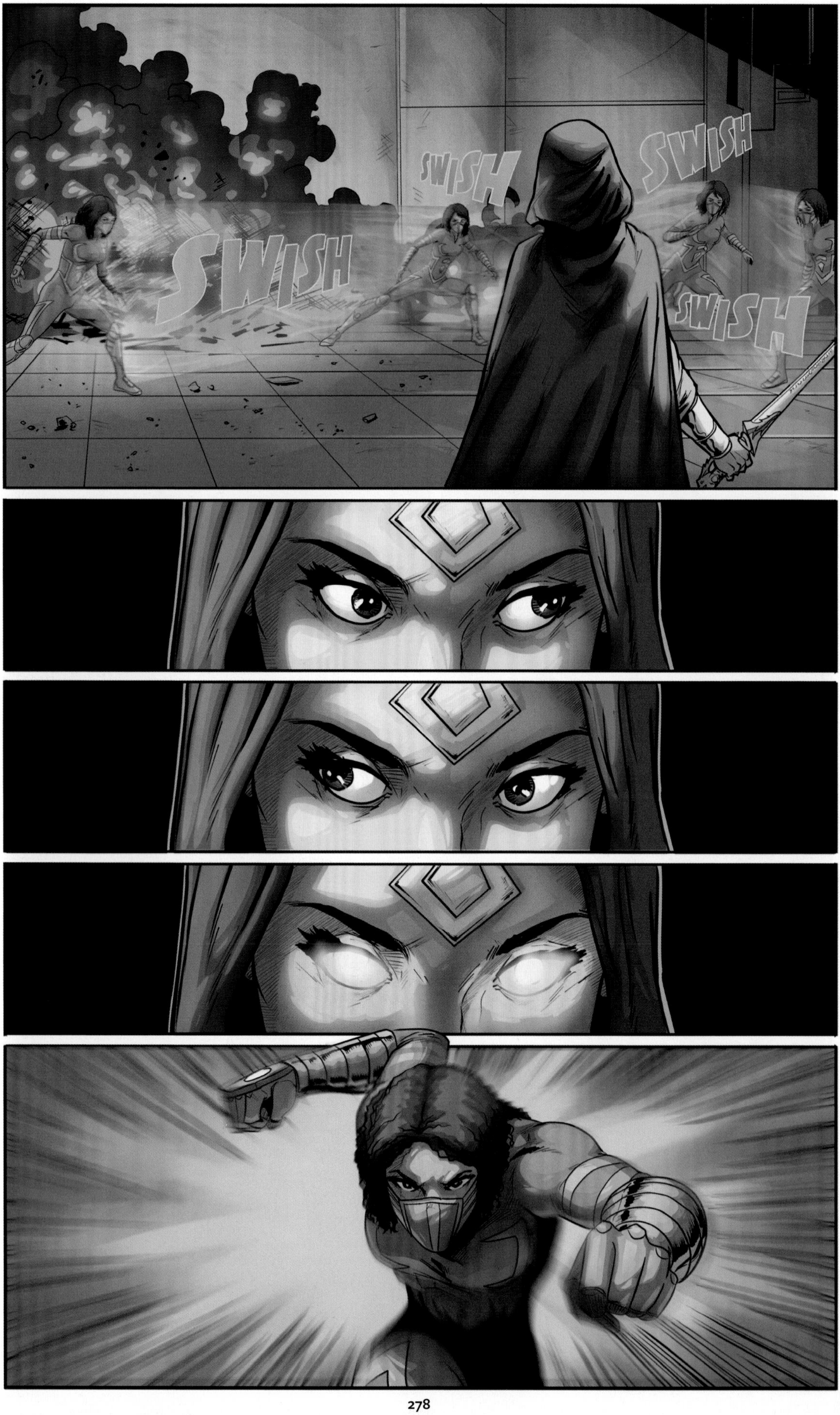
SWISH
SWISH
SWISH
SWISH

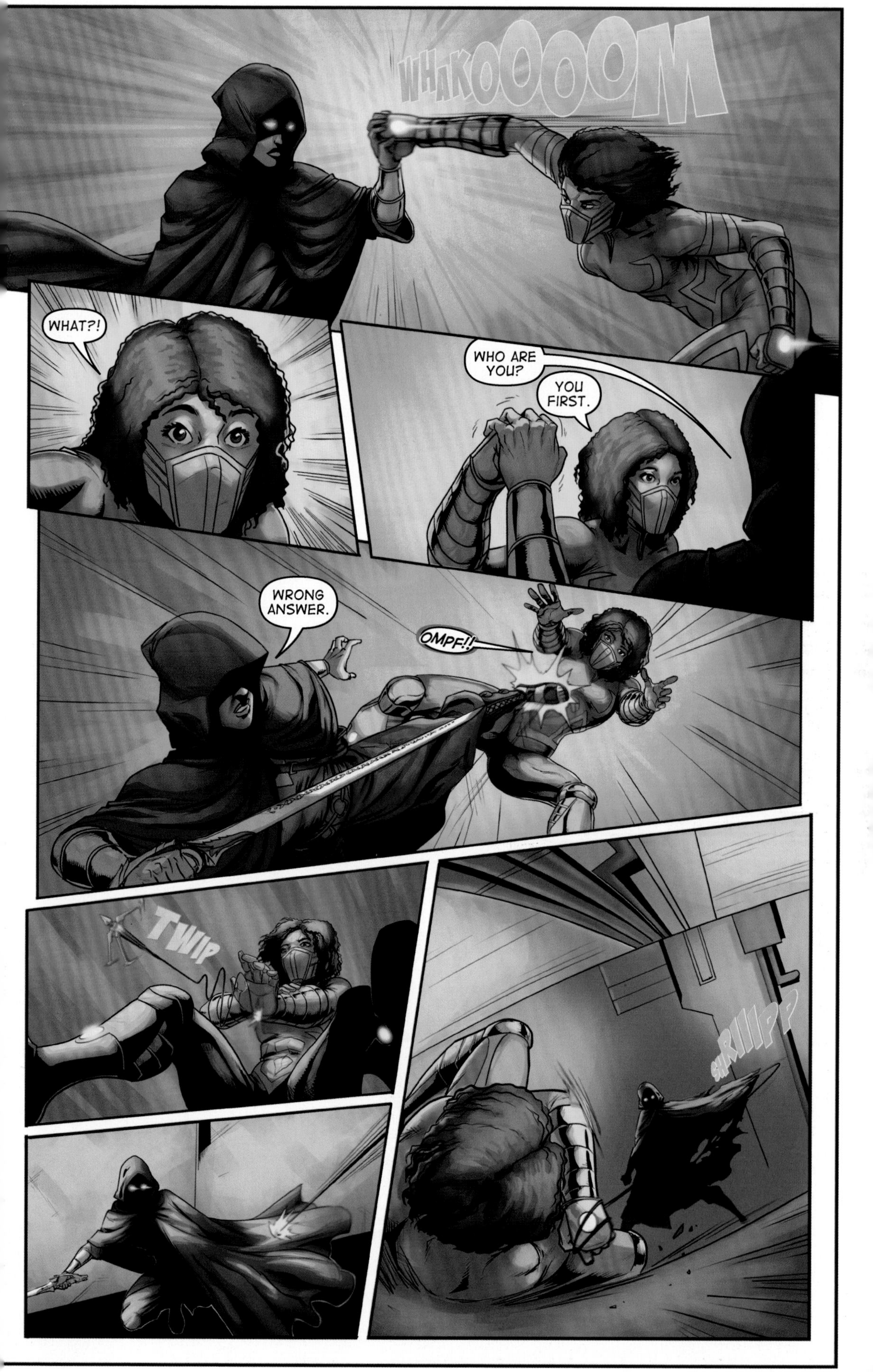
WHAKOOOOOM
WHAT?!
WHO ARE YOU?
YOU FIRST.
WRONG ANSWER.
OMPF!!
TWIP
SHRIIIPP

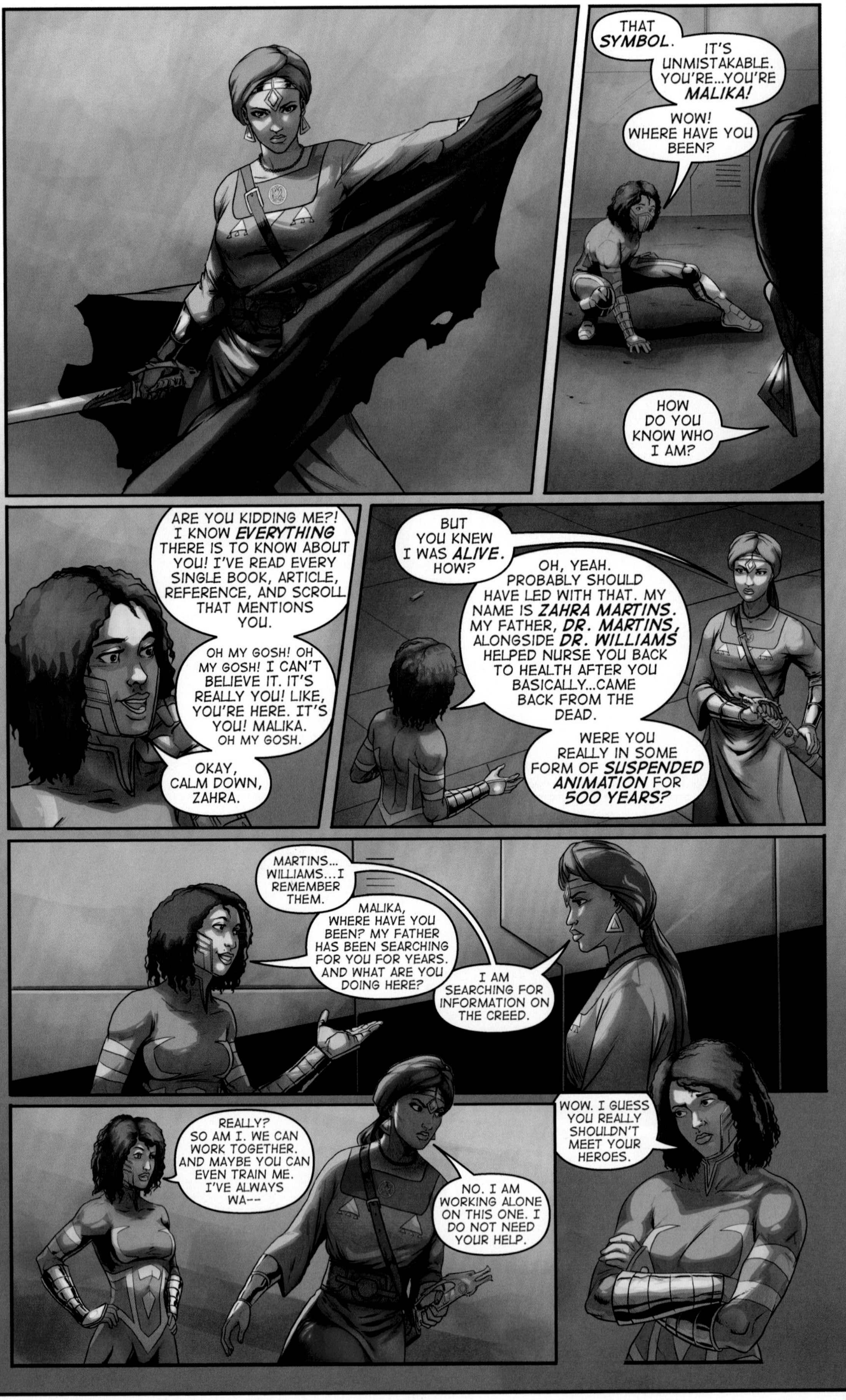
THAT SYMBOL.
IT'S UNMISTAKABLE. YOU'RE...YOU'RE MALIKA!
WOW! WHERE HAVE YOU BEEN?
HOW DO YOU KNOW WHO I AM?
ARE YOU KIDDING ME?! I KNOW EVERYTHING THERE IS TO KNOW ABOUT YOU! I'VE READ EVERY SINGLE BOOK, ARTICLE, REFERENCE, AND SCROLL THAT MENTIONS YOU.
OH MY GOSH! OH MY GOSH! I CAN'T BELIEVE IT. IT'S REALLY YOU! LIKE, YOU'RE HERE. IT'S YOU! MALIKA. OH MY GOSH.
OKAY, CALM DOWN, ZAHRA.
BUT YOU KNEW I WAS ALIVE. HOW?
OH, YEAH. PROBABLY SHOULD HAVE LED WITH THAT. MY NAME IS ZAHRA MARTINS. MY FATHER, DR. MARTINS, ALONGSIDE DR. WILLIAMS HELPED NURSE YOU BACK TO HEALTH AFTER YOU BASICALLY...CAME BACK FROM THE DEAD.
WERE YOU REALLY IN SOME FORM OF SUSPENDED ANIMATION FOR 500 YEARS?
MARTINS... WILLIAMS...I REMEMBER THEM.
MALIKA, WHERE HAVE YOU BEEN? MY FATHER HAS BEEN SEARCHING FOR YOU FOR YEARS. AND WHAT ARE YOU DOING HERE?
I AM SEARCHING FOR INFORMATION ON THE CREED.
REALLY? SO AM I. WE CAN WORK TOGETHER. AND MAYBE YOU CAN EVEN TRAIN ME. I'VE ALWAYS WA--
NO. I AM WORKING ALONE ON THIS ONE. I DO NOT NEED YOUR HELP.
WOW. I GUESS YOU REALLY SHOULDN'T MEET YOUR HEROES.

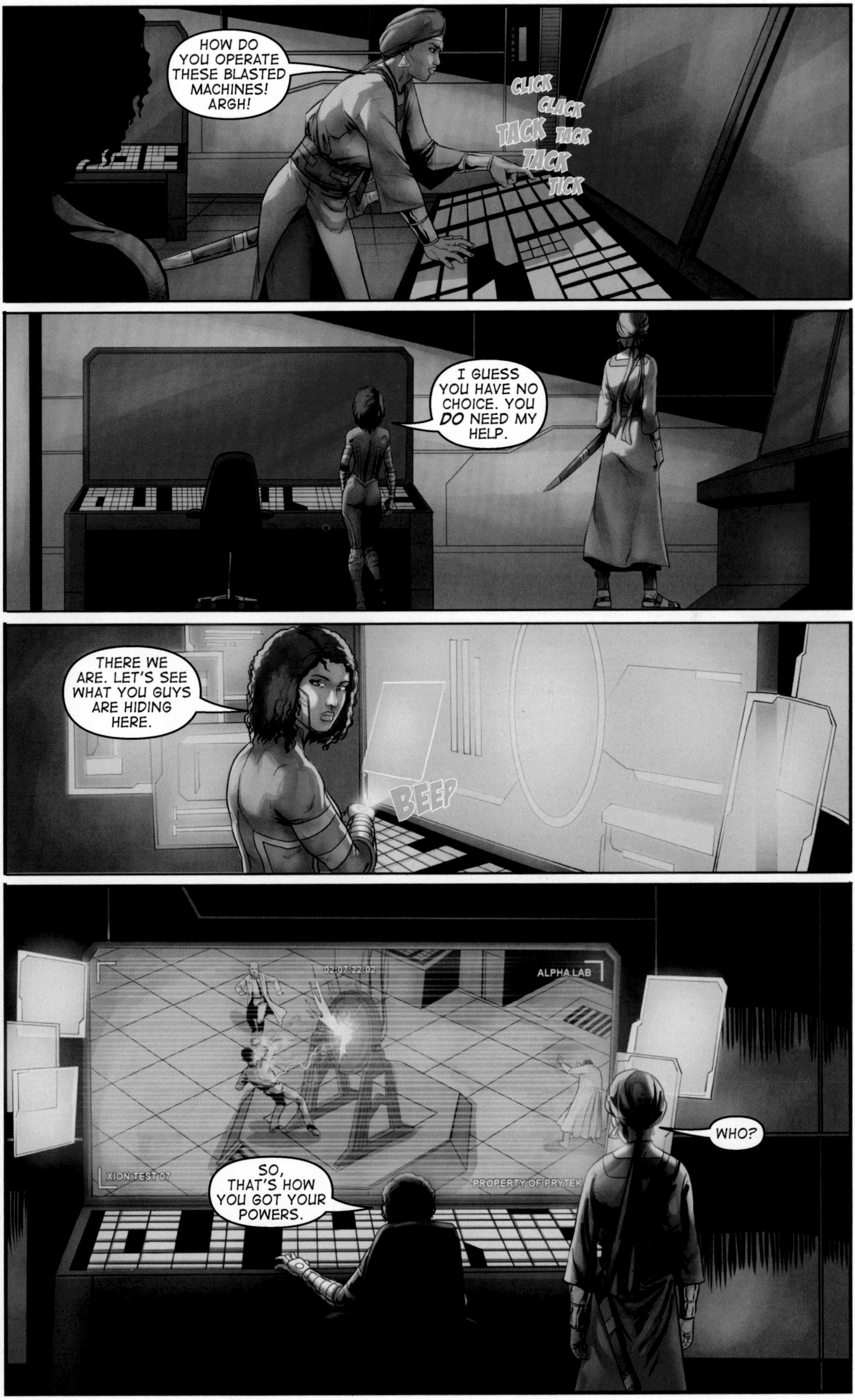
HOW DO YOU OPERATE THESE BLASTED MACHINES! ARGH!
CLICK
CLACK
TACK TACK
TACK
TICK
I GUESS YOU HAVE NO CHOICE. YOU *DO* NEED MY HELP.
THERE WE ARE. LET'S SEE WHAT YOU GUYS ARE HIDING HERE.
BEEP
02:07:22:02
ALPHA LAB
XION TEST 07
PROPERTY OF PRYTEK
WHO?
SO, THAT'S HOW YOU GOT YOUR POWERS.

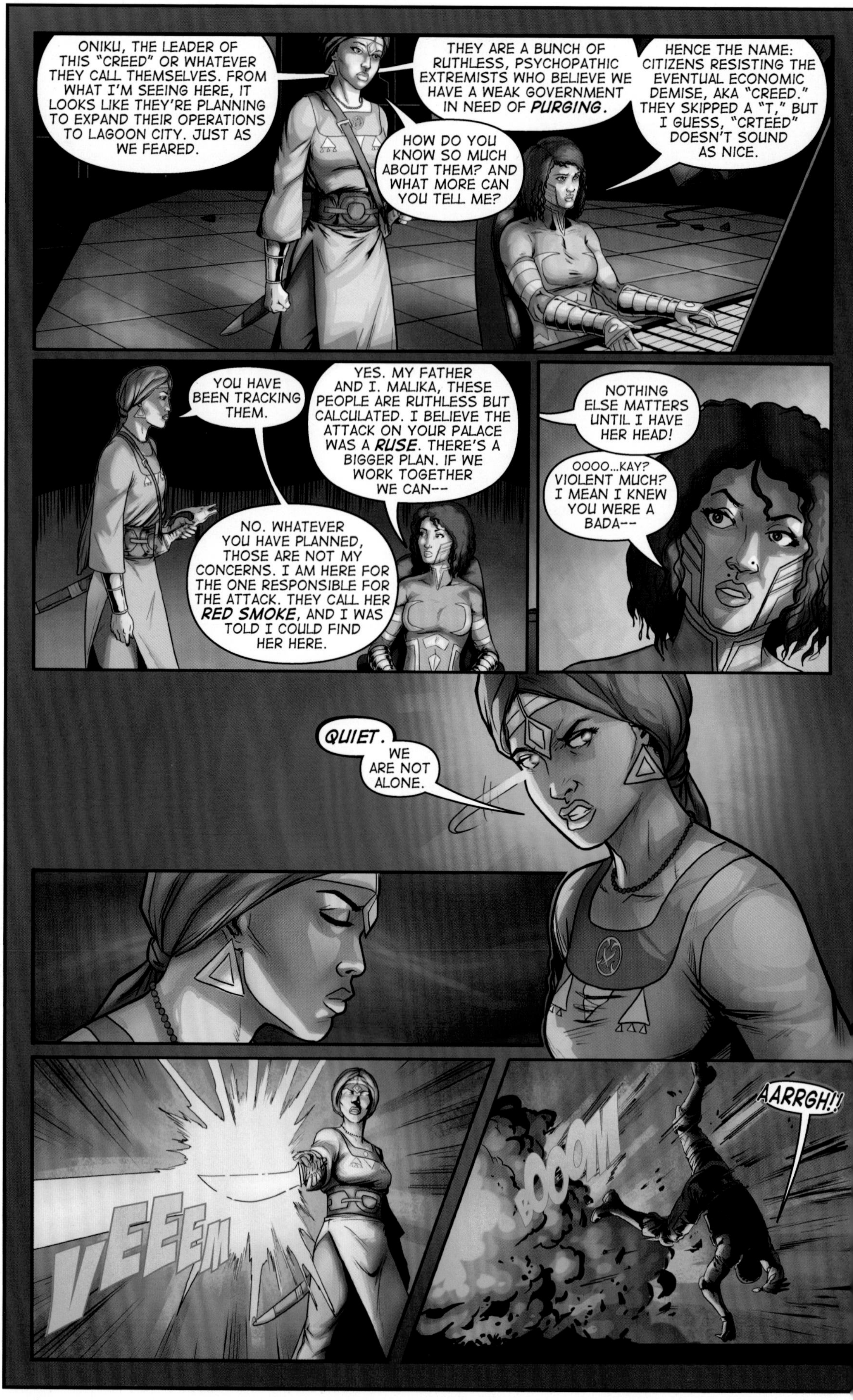
ONIKU, THE LEADER OF THIS "CREED" OR WHATEVER THEY CALL THEMSELVES. FROM WHAT I'M SEEING HERE, IT LOOKS LIKE THEY'RE PLANNING TO EXPAND THEIR OPERATIONS TO LAGOON CITY. JUST AS WE FEARED.
THEY ARE A BUNCH OF RUTHLESS, PSYCHOPATHIC EXTREMISTS WHO BELIEVE WE HAVE A WEAK GOVERNMENT IN NEED OF PURGING.
HOW DO YOU KNOW SO MUCH ABOUT THEM? AND WHAT MORE CAN YOU TELL ME?
HENCE THE NAME: CITIZENS RESISTING THE EVENTUAL ECONOMIC DEMISE, AKA "CREED." THEY SKIPPED A "T," BUT I GUESS, "CRTEED" DOESN'T SOUND AS NICE.
YOU HAVE BEEN TRACKING THEM.
YES. MY FATHER AND I. MALIKA, THESE PEOPLE ARE RUTHLESS BUT CALCULATED. I BELIEVE THE ATTACK ON YOUR PALACE WAS A RUSE. THERE'S A BIGGER PLAN. IF WE WORK TOGETHER WE CAN--
NO. WHATEVER YOU HAVE PLANNED, THOSE ARE NOT MY CONCERNS. I AM HERE FOR THE ONE RESPONSIBLE FOR THE ATTACK. THEY CALL HER RED SMOKE, AND I WAS TOLD I COULD FIND HER HERE.
NOTHING ELSE MATTERS UNTIL I HAVE HER HEAD!
OOOO...KAY? VIOLENT MUCH? I MEAN I KNEW YOU WERE A BADA--
QUIET. WE ARE NOT ALONE.
VEEEM
BOOOM
AARRGH!!

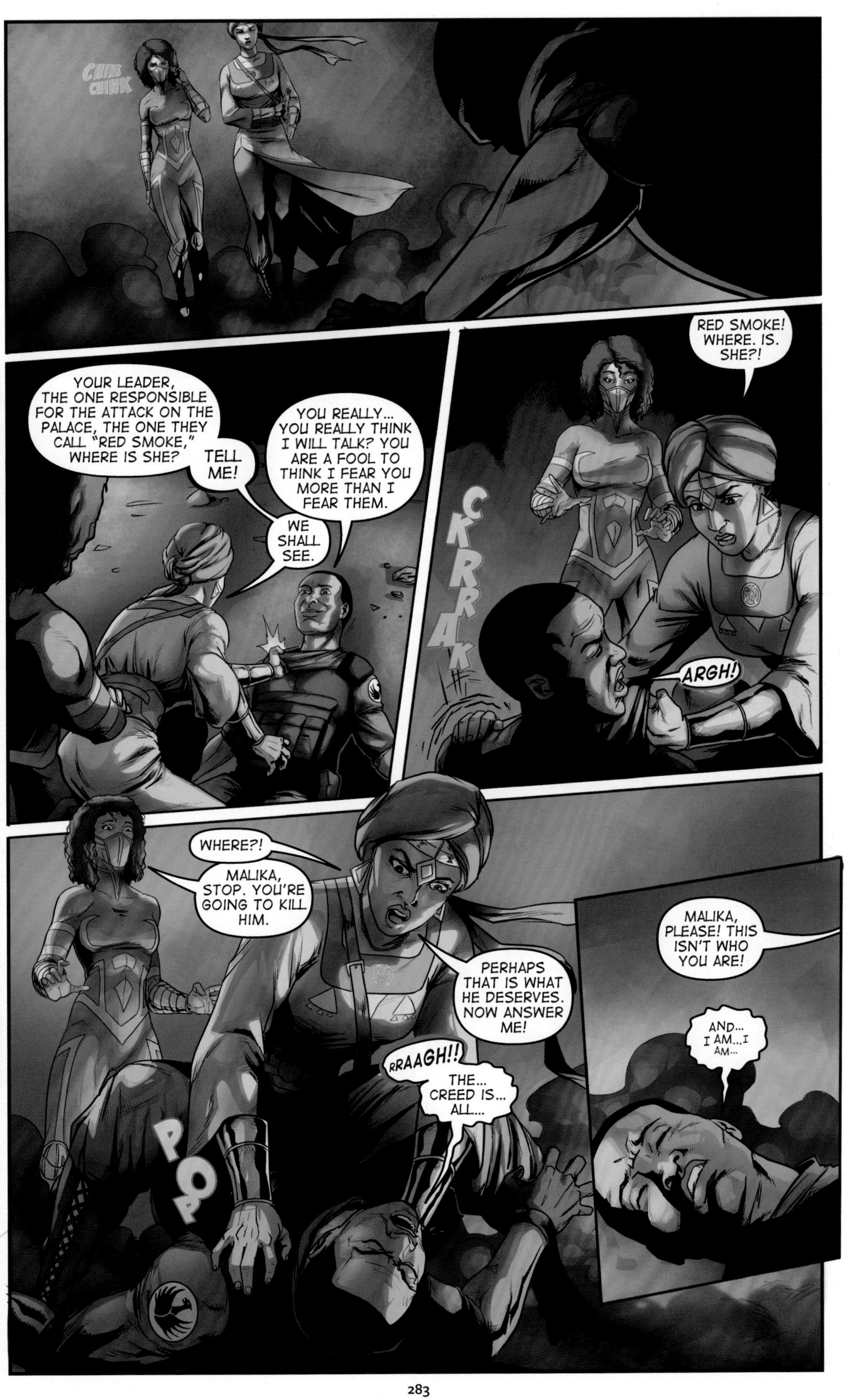
CHINK CHINK
YOUR LEADER, THE ONE RESPONSIBLE FOR THE ATTACK ON THE PALACE, THE ONE THEY CALL "RED SMOKE," WHERE IS SHE?
TELL ME!
YOU REALLY... YOU REALLY THINK I WILL TALK? YOU ARE A FOOL TO THINK I FEAR YOU MORE THAN I FEAR THEM.
WE SHALL SEE.
RED SMOKE! WHERE. IS. SHE?!
CKRRAK
ARGH!
WHERE?!
MALIKA, STOP. YOU'RE GOING TO KILL HIM.
PERHAPS THAT IS WHAT HE DESERVES. NOW ANSWER ME!
RRAAGH!!
THE... CREED IS... ALL...
POP
MALIKA, PLEASE! THIS ISN'T WHO YOU ARE!
AND... I AM... I AM...

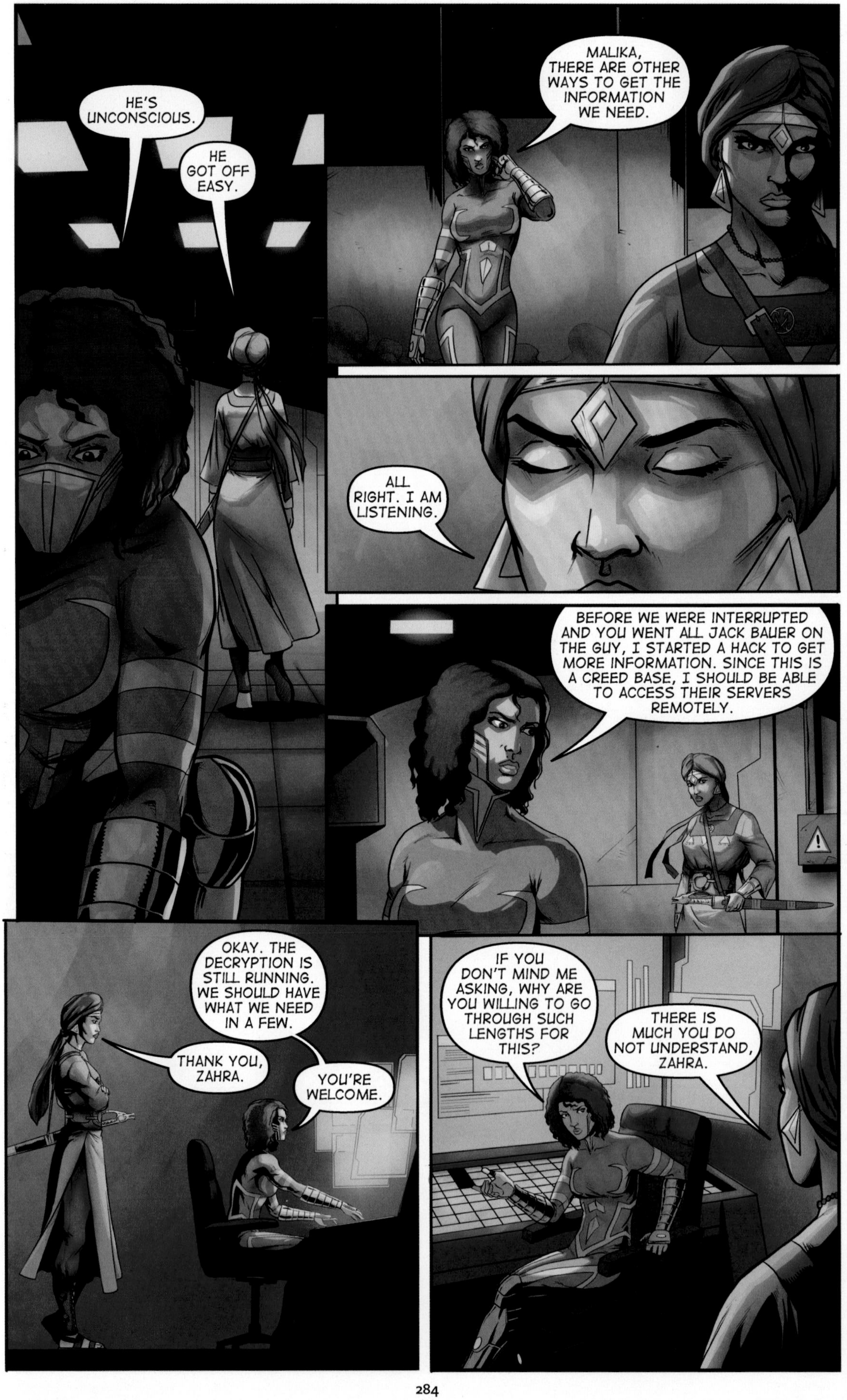
HE'S UNCONSCIOUS.
HE GOT OFF EASY.
MALIKA, THERE ARE OTHER WAYS TO GET THE INFORMATION WE NEED.
ALL RIGHT. I AM LISTENING.
BEFORE WE WERE INTERRUPTED AND YOU WENT ALL JACK BAUER ON THE GUY, I STARTED A HACK TO GET MORE INFORMATION. SINCE THIS IS A CREED BASE, I SHOULD BE ABLE TO ACCESS THEIR SERVERS REMOTELY.
OKAY. THE DECRYPTION IS STILL RUNNING. WE SHOULD HAVE WHAT WE NEED IN A FEW.
THANK YOU, ZAHRA.
YOU'RE WELCOME.
IF YOU DON'T MIND ME ASKING, WHY ARE YOU WILLING TO GO THROUGH SUCH LENGTHS FOR THIS?
THERE IS MUCH YOU DO NOT UNDERSTAND, ZAHRA.

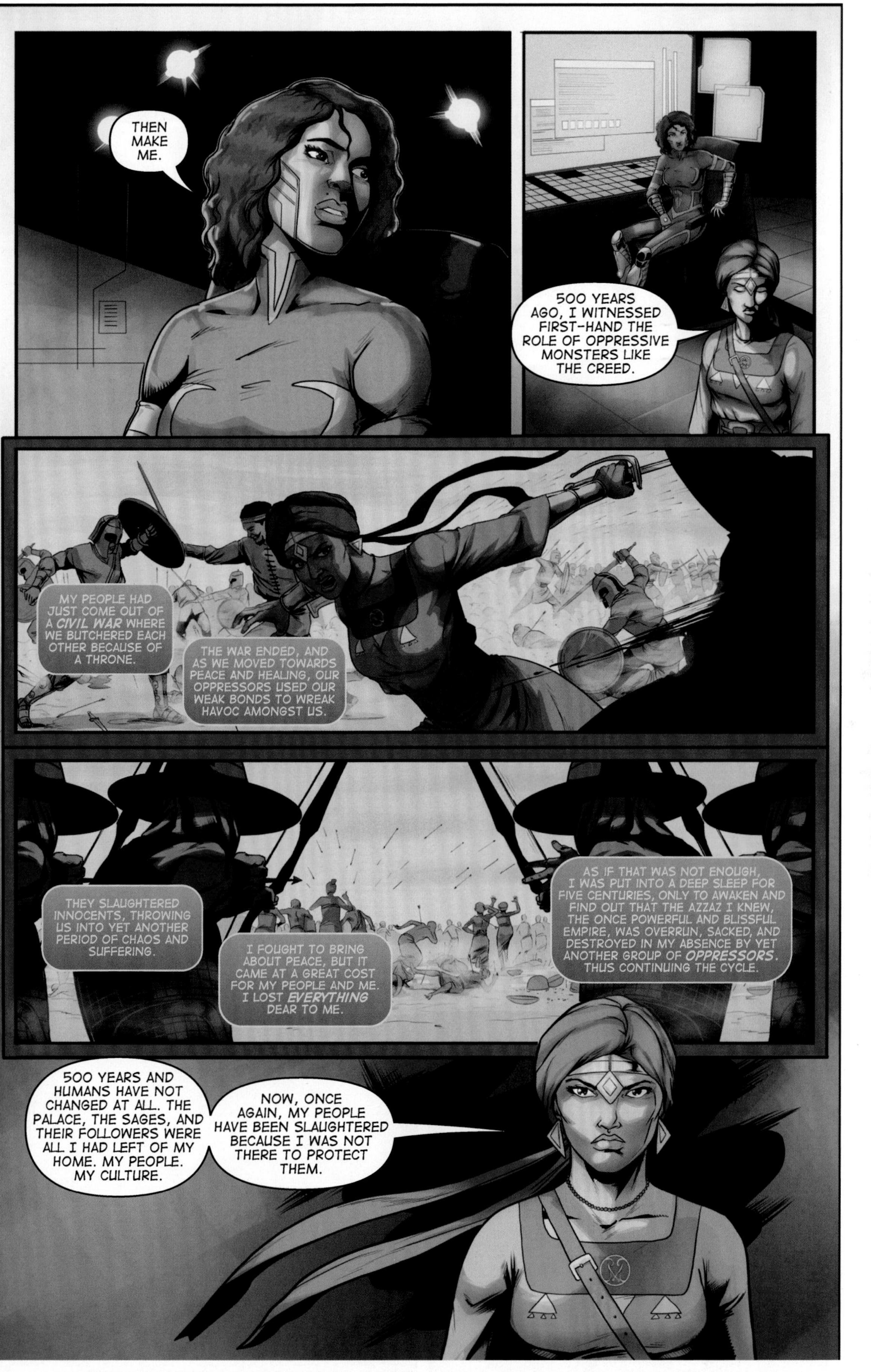
THEN MAKE ME.
500 YEARS AGO, I WITNESSED FIRST-HAND THE ROLE OF OPPRESSIVE MONSTERS LIKE THE CREED.
MY PEOPLE HAD JUST COME OUT OF A *CIVIL WAR* WHERE WE BUTCHERED EACH OTHER BECAUSE OF A THRONE.
THE WAR ENDED, AND AS WE MOVED TOWARDS PEACE AND HEALING, OUR OPPRESSORS USED OUR WEAK BONDS TO WREAK HAVOC AMONGST US.
THEY SLAUGHTERED INNOCENTS, THROWING US INTO YET ANOTHER PERIOD OF CHAOS AND SUFFERING.
I FOUGHT TO BRING ABOUT PEACE, BUT IT CAME AT A GREAT COST FOR MY PEOPLE AND ME. I LOST *EVERYTHING* DEAR TO ME.
AS IF THAT WAS NOT ENOUGH, I WAS PUT INTO A DEEP SLEEP FOR FIVE CENTURIES, ONLY TO AWAKEN AND FIND OUT THAT THE AZZAZ I KNEW, THE ONCE POWERFUL AND BLISSFUL EMPIRE, WAS OVERRUN, SACKED, AND DESTROYED IN MY ABSENCE BY YET ANOTHER GROUP OF *OPPRESSORS*. THUS CONTINUING THE CYCLE.
500 YEARS AND HUMANS HAVE NOT CHANGED AT ALL. THE PALACE, THE SAGES, AND THEIR FOLLOWERS WERE ALL I HAD LEFT OF MY HOME. MY PEOPLE. MY CULTURE.
NOW, ONCE AGAIN, MY PEOPLE HAVE BEEN SLAUGHTERED BECAUSE I WAS NOT THERE TO PROTECT THEM.

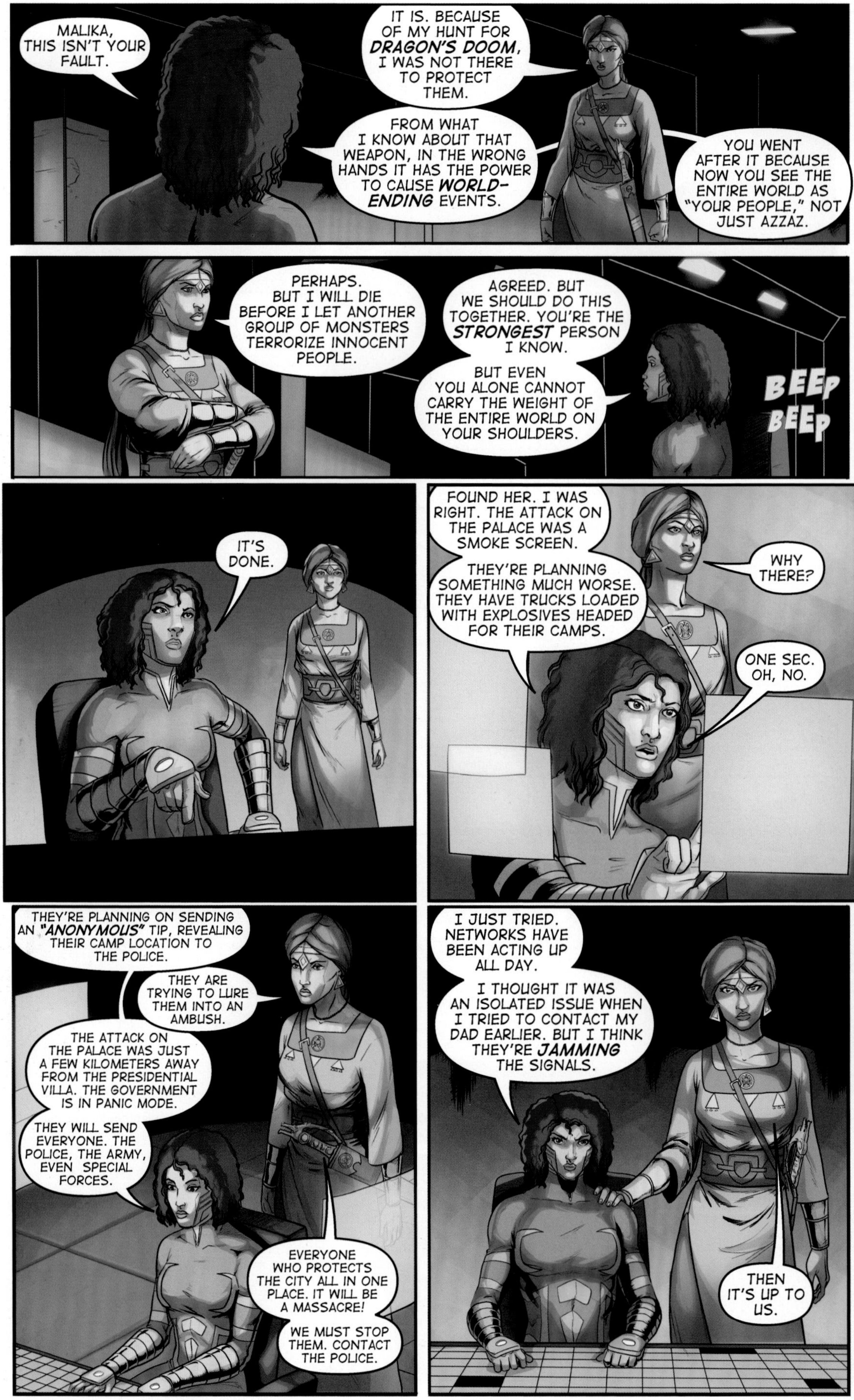
MALIKA, THIS ISN'T YOUR FAULT.
IT IS. BECAUSE OF MY HUNT FOR DRAGON'S DOOM, I WAS NOT THERE TO PROTECT THEM.
FROM WHAT I KNOW ABOUT THAT WEAPON, IN THE WRONG HANDS IT HAS THE POWER TO CAUSE WORLD-ENDING EVENTS.
YOU WENT AFTER IT BECAUSE NOW YOU SEE THE ENTIRE WORLD AS "YOUR PEOPLE," NOT JUST AZZAZ.
PERHAPS. BUT I WILL DIE BEFORE I LET ANOTHER GROUP OF MONSTERS TERRORIZE INNOCENT PEOPLE.
AGREED. BUT WE SHOULD DO THIS TOGETHER. YOU'RE THE STRONGEST PERSON I KNOW.
BUT EVEN YOU ALONE CANNOT CARRY THE WEIGHT OF THE ENTIRE WORLD ON YOUR SHOULDERS.
BEEP BEEP
IT'S DONE.
FOUND HER. I WAS RIGHT. THE ATTACK ON THE PALACE WAS A SMOKE SCREEN.
THEY'RE PLANNING SOMETHING MUCH WORSE. THEY HAVE TRUCKS LOADED WITH EXPLOSIVES HEADED FOR THEIR CAMPS.
WHY THERE?
ONE SEC. OH, NO.
THEY'RE PLANNING ON SENDING AN "ANONYMOUS" TIP, REVEALING THEIR CAMP LOCATION TO THE POLICE.
THEY ARE TRYING TO LURE THEM INTO AN AMBUSH.
THE ATTACK ON THE PALACE WAS JUST A FEW KILOMETERS AWAY FROM THE PRESIDENTIAL VILLA. THE GOVERNMENT IS IN PANIC MODE.
THEY WILL SEND EVERYONE. THE POLICE, THE ARMY, EVEN SPECIAL FORCES.
EVERYONE WHO PROTECTS THE CITY ALL IN ONE PLACE. IT WILL BE A MASSACRE!
WE MUST STOP THEM. CONTACT THE POLICE.
I JUST TRIED. NETWORKS HAVE BEEN ACTING UP ALL DAY.
I THOUGHT IT WAS AN ISOLATED ISSUE WHEN I TRIED TO CONTACT MY DAD EARLIER. BUT I THINK THEY'RE JAMMING THE SIGNALS.
THEN IT'S UP TO US.

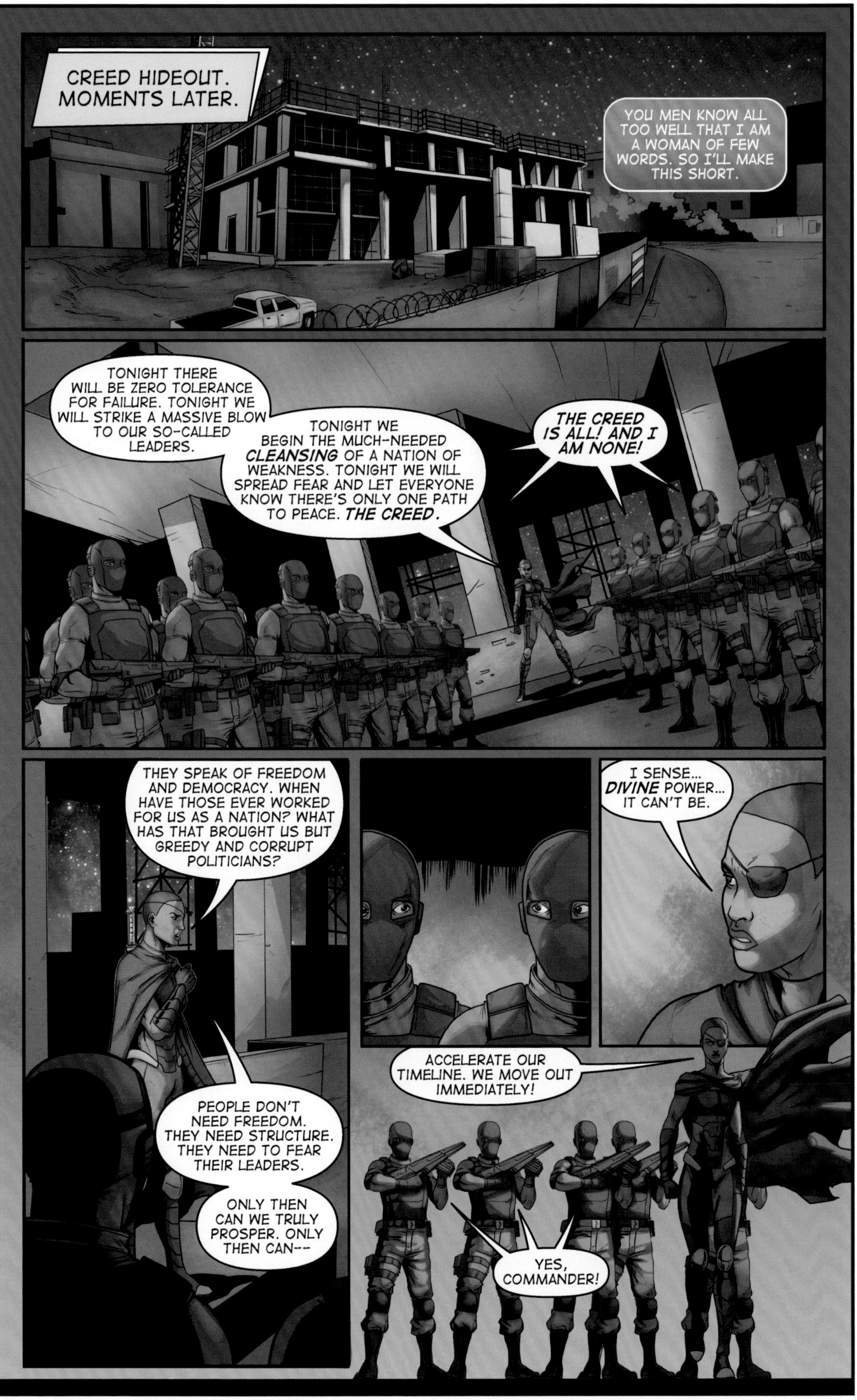
CREED HIDEOUT. MOMENTS LATER.
YOU MEN KNOW ALL TOO WELL THAT I AM A WOMAN OF FEW WORDS. SO I'LL MAKE THIS SHORT.
TONIGHT THERE WILL BE ZERO TOLERANCE FOR FAILURE. TONIGHT WE WILL STRIKE A MASSIVE BLOW TO OUR SO-CALLED LEADERS.
TONIGHT WE BEGIN THE MUCH-NEEDED CLEANSING OF A NATION OF WEAKNESS. TONIGHT WE WILL SPREAD FEAR AND LET EVERYONE KNOW THERE'S ONLY ONE PATH TO PEACE. THE CREED.
THE CREED IS ALL! AND I AM NONE!
THEY SPEAK OF FREEDOM AND DEMOCRACY. WHEN HAVE THOSE EVER WORKED FOR US AS A NATION? WHAT HAS THAT BROUGHT US BUT GREEDY AND CORRUPT POLITICIANS?
PEOPLE DON'T NEED FREEDOM. THEY NEED STRUCTURE. THEY NEED TO FEAR THEIR LEADERS.
ONLY THEN CAN WE TRULY PROSPER. ONLY THEN CAN--
I SENSE... DIVINE POWER... IT CAN'T BE.
ACCELERATE OUR TIMELINE. WE MOVE OUT IMMEDIATELY!
YES, COMMANDER!

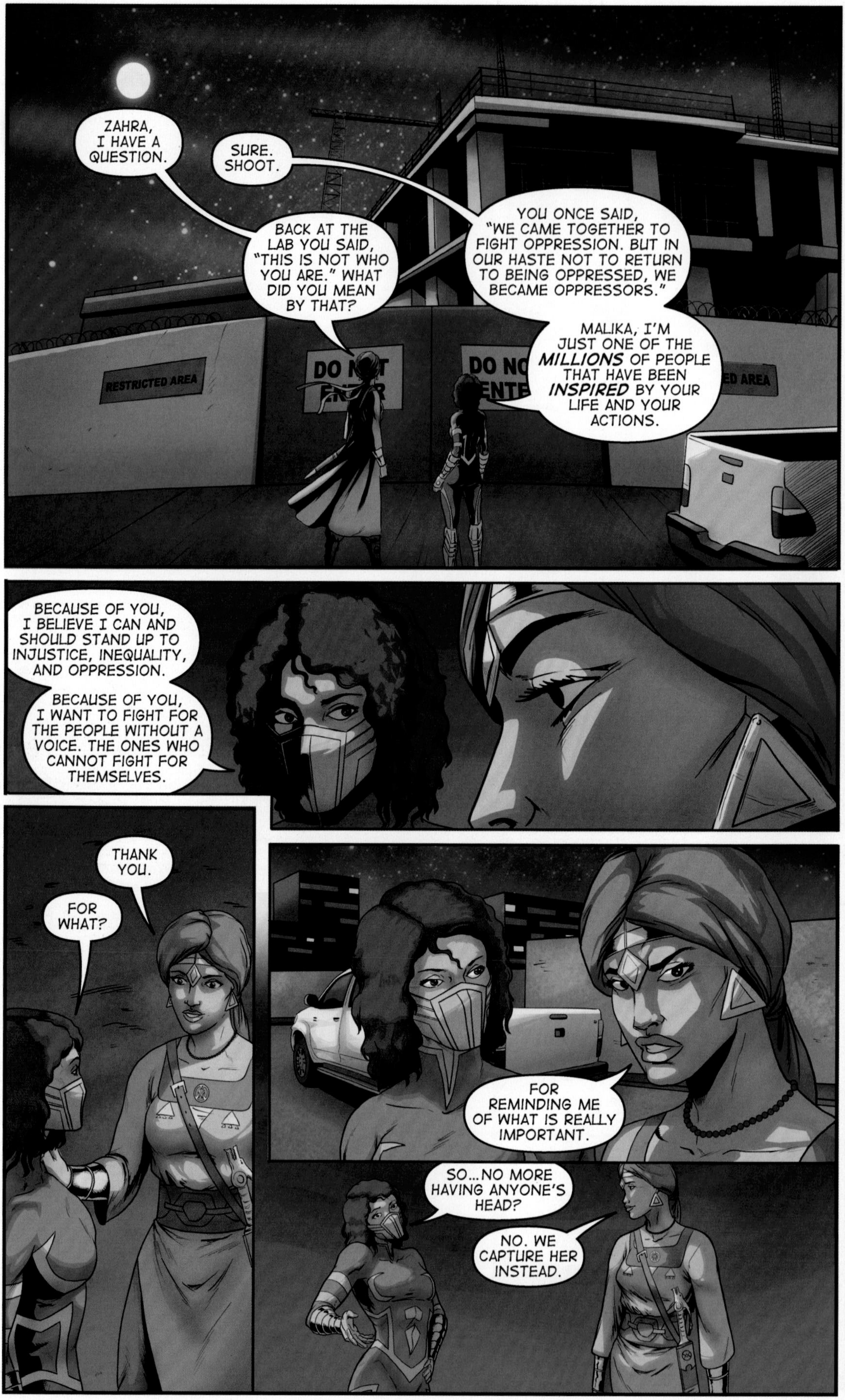
ZAHRA, I HAVE A QUESTION.
SURE. SHOOT.
BACK AT THE LAB YOU SAID, "THIS IS NOT WHO YOU ARE." WHAT DID YOU MEAN BY THAT?
YOU ONCE SAID, "WE CAME TOGETHER TO FIGHT OPPRESSION. BUT IN OUR HASTE NOT TO RETURN TO BEING OPPRESSED, WE BECAME OPPRESSORS."
MALIKA, I'M JUST ONE OF THE MILLIONS OF PEOPLE THAT HAVE BEEN INSPIRED BY YOUR LIFE AND YOUR ACTIONS.
RESTRICTED AREA
DO NOT ENTER
BECAUSE OF YOU, I BELIEVE I CAN AND SHOULD STAND UP TO INJUSTICE, INEQUALITY, AND OPPRESSION.
BECAUSE OF YOU, I WANT TO FIGHT FOR THE PEOPLE WITHOUT A VOICE. THE ONES WHO CANNOT FIGHT FOR THEMSELVES.
THANK YOU.
FOR WHAT?
FOR REMINDING ME OF WHAT IS REALLY IMPORTANT.
SO...NO MORE HAVING ANYONE'S HEAD?
NO. WE CAPTURE HER INSTEAD.

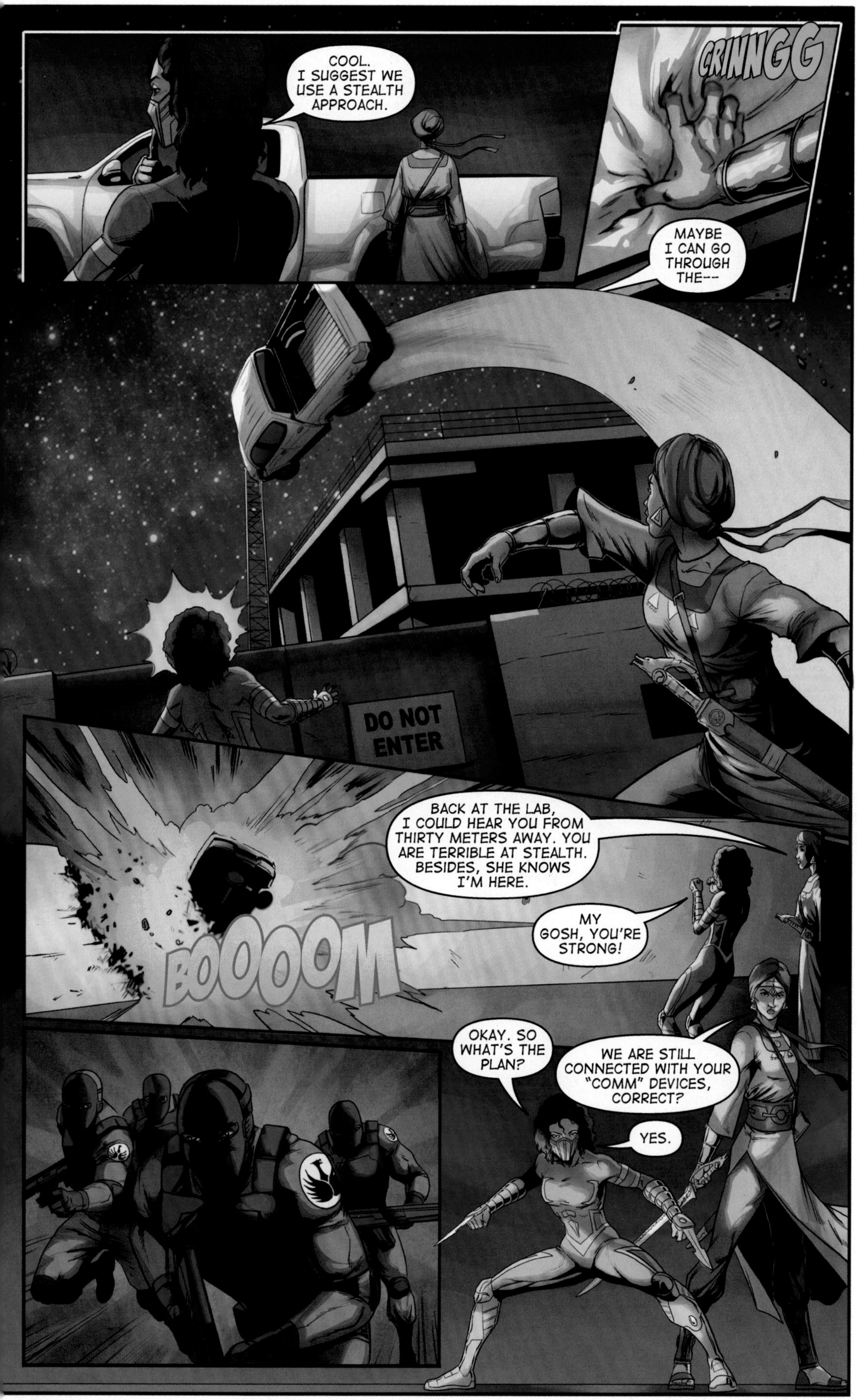
COOL. I SUGGEST WE USE A STEALTH APPROACH.
CRINNGG
MAYBE I CAN GO THROUGH THE--
DO NOT ENTER
BACK AT THE LAB, I COULD HEAR YOU FROM THIRTY METERS AWAY. YOU ARE TERRIBLE AT STEALTH. BESIDES, SHE KNOWS I'M HERE.
MY GOSH, YOU'RE STRONG!
BOOOOM
OKAY. SO WHAT'S THE PLAN?
WE ARE STILL CONNECTED WITH YOUR "COMM" DEVICES, CORRECT?
YES.

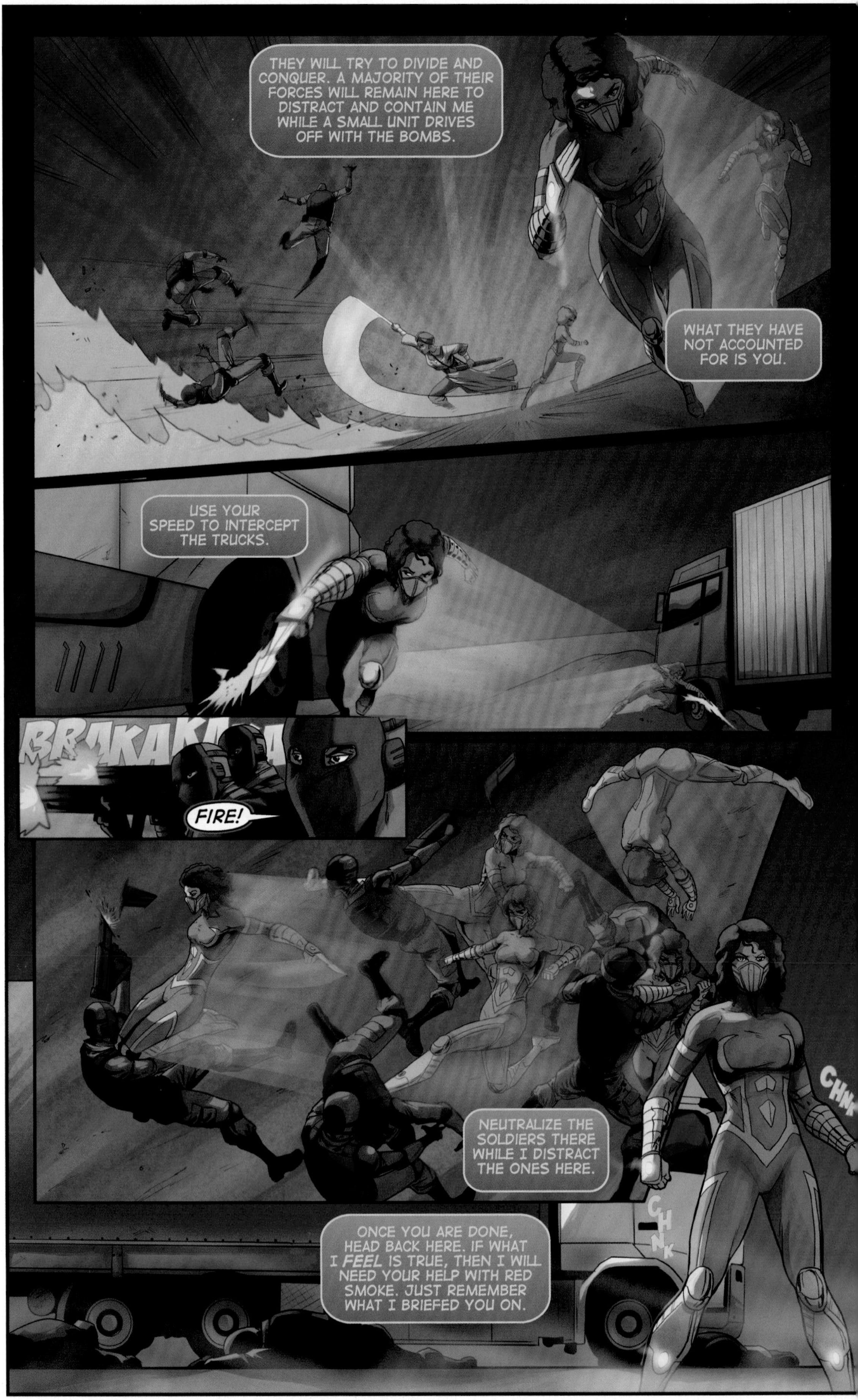
THEY WILL TRY TO DIVIDE AND CONQUER. A MAJORITY OF THEIR FORCES WILL REMAIN HERE TO DISTRACT AND CONTAIN ME WHILE A SMALL UNIT DRIVES OFF WITH THE BOMBS.
WHAT THEY HAVE NOT ACCOUNTED FOR IS YOU.
USE YOUR SPEED TO INTERCEPT THE TRUCKS.
BRAKAKA
FIRE!
NEUTRALIZE THE SOLDIERS THERE WHILE I DISTRACT THE ONES HERE.
CHNK
CHNK
ONCE YOU ARE DONE, HEAD BACK HERE. IF WHAT I *FEEL* IS TRUE, THEN I WILL NEED YOUR HELP WITH RED SMOKE. JUST REMEMBER WHAT I BRIEFED YOU ON.

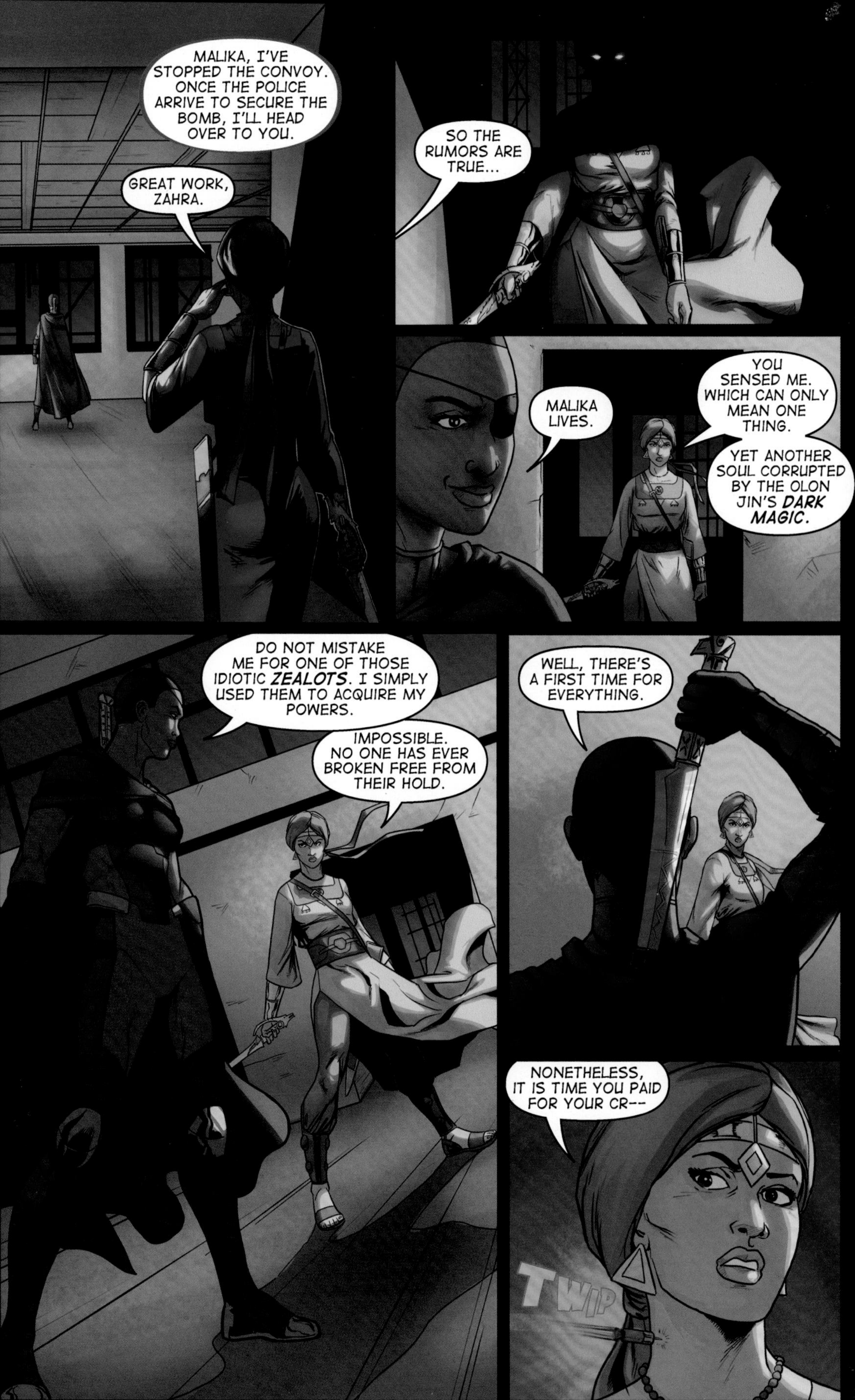

MALIKA, I'VE STOPPED THE CONVOY. ONCE THE POLICE ARRIVE TO SECURE THE BOMB, I'LL HEAD OVER TO YOU.
GREAT WORK, ZAHRA.
SO THE RUMORS ARE TRUE...
MALIKA LIVES.
YOU SENSED ME. WHICH CAN ONLY MEAN ONE THING.
YET ANOTHER SOUL CORRUPTED BY THE OLON JIN'S DARK MAGIC.
DO NOT MISTAKE ME FOR ONE OF THOSE IDIOTIC ZEALOTS. I SIMPLY USED THEM TO ACQUIRE MY POWERS.
IMPOSSIBLE. NO ONE HAS EVER BROKEN FREE FROM THEIR HOLD.
WELL, THERE'S A FIRST TIME FOR EVERYTHING.
NONETHELESS, IT IS TIME YOU PAID FOR YOUR CR--
TWIP

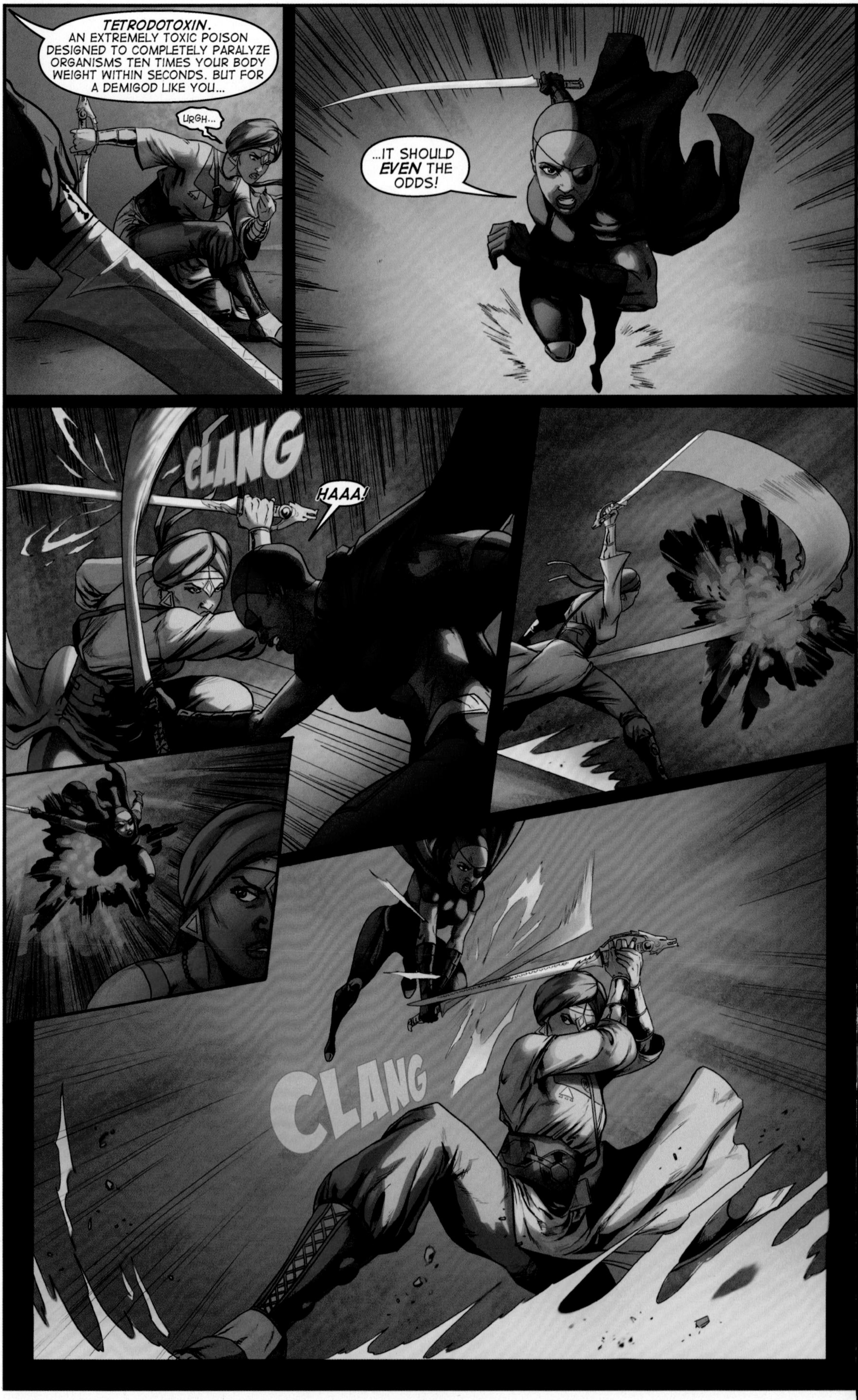
TETRODOTOXIN.
AN EXTREMELY TOXIC POISON DESIGNED TO COMPLETELY PARALYZE ORGANISMS TEN TIMES YOUR BODY WEIGHT WITHIN SECONDS. BUT FOR A DEMIGOD LIKE YOU...
URGH...
...IT SHOULD EVEN THE ODDS!
CLANG
HAAA!
CLANG

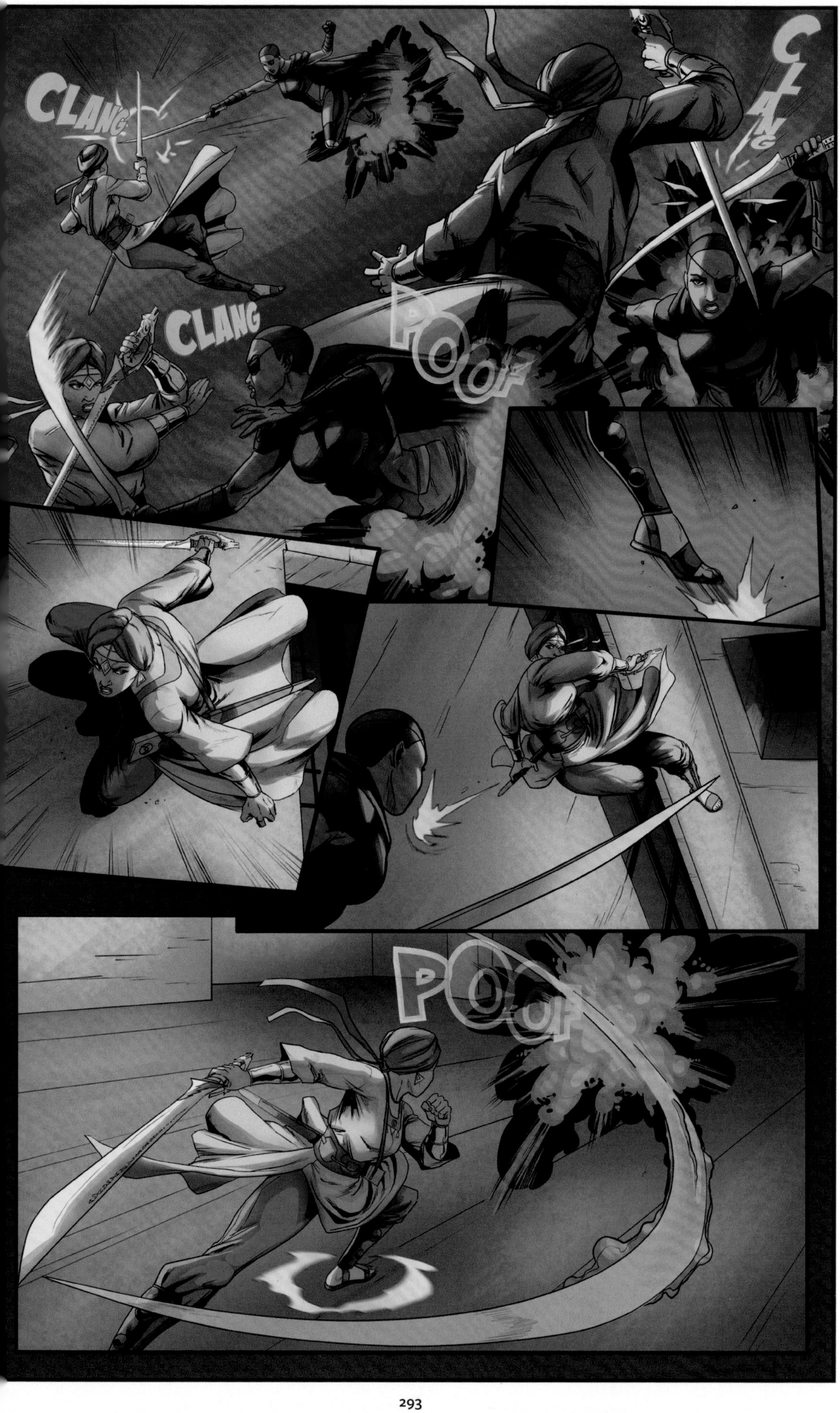
CLANG
CLANG
CLANG
POOF
POOF

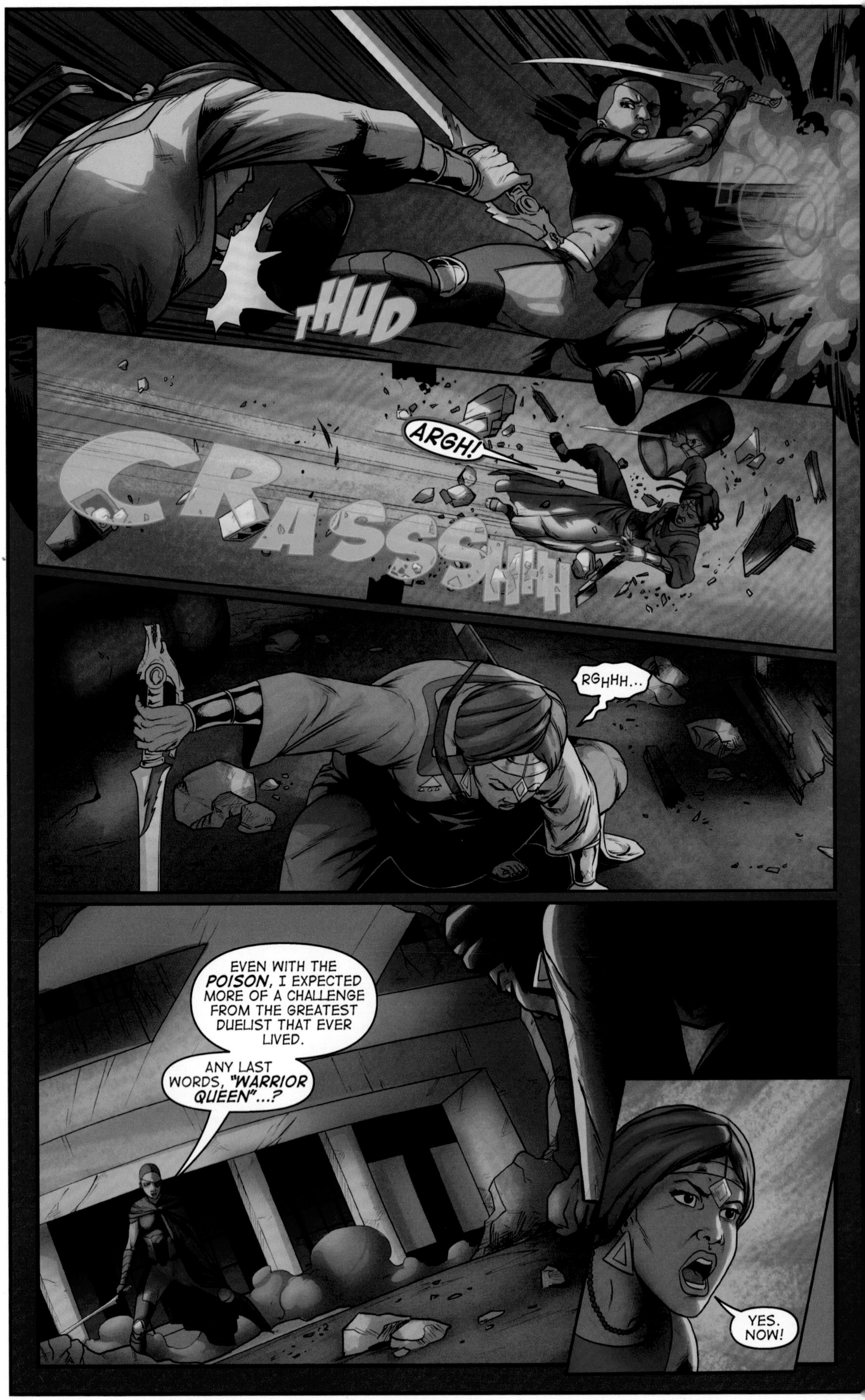
THUD
ARGH!
CRASSSHHH
RGHHH...
EVEN WITH THE POISON, I EXPECTED MORE OF A CHALLENGE FROM THE GREATEST DUELIST THAT EVER LIVED.
ANY LAST WORDS, "WARRIOR QUEEN"...?
YES. NOW!

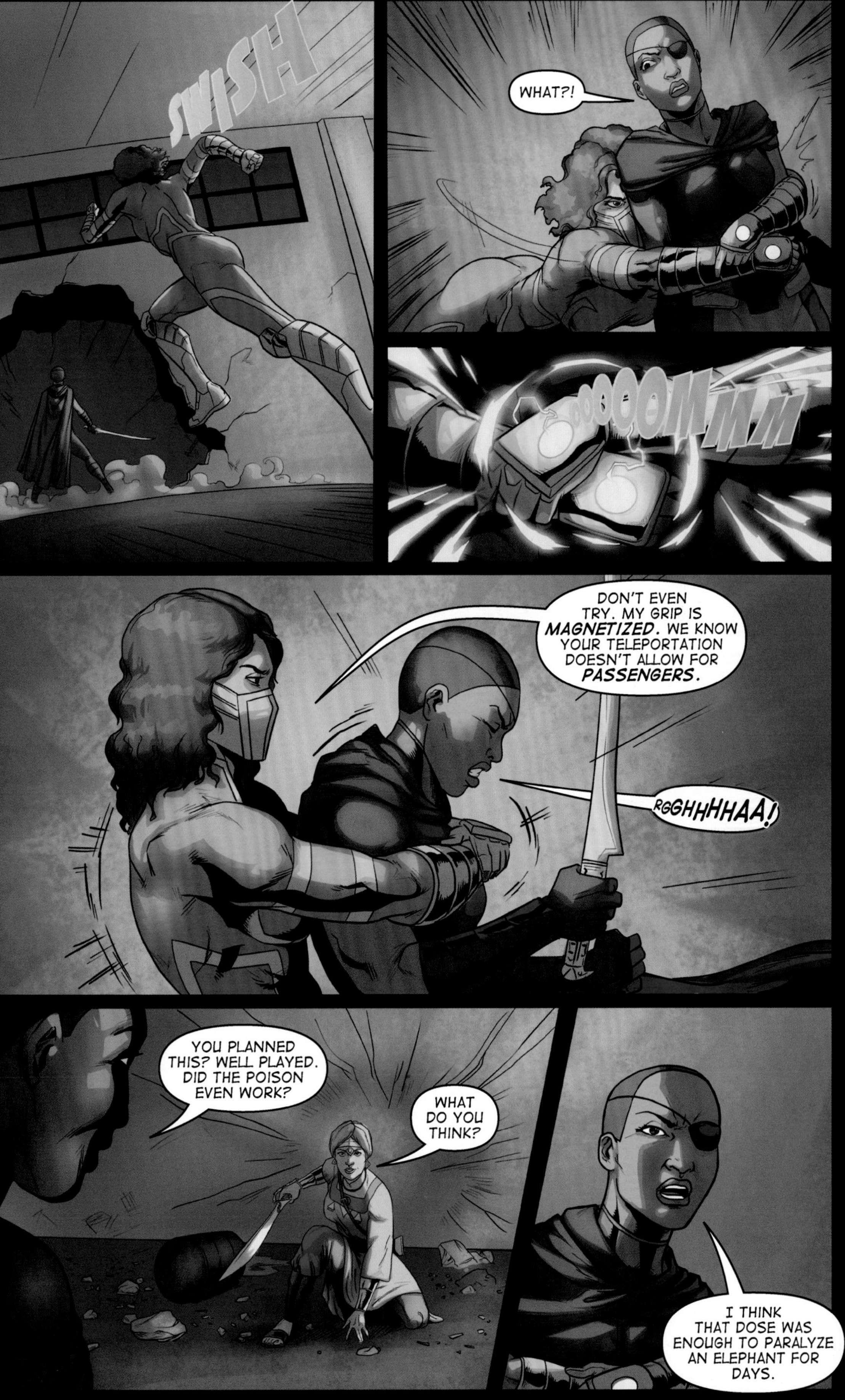
SWISH
WHAT?!
OOOOOOMMM
DON'T EVEN TRY. MY GRIP IS MAGNETIZED. WE KNOW YOUR TELEPORTATION DOESN'T ALLOW FOR PASSENGERS.
RGGHHHHAA!
YOU PLANNED THIS? WELL PLAYED. DID THE POISON EVEN WORK?
WHAT DO YOU THINK?
I THINK THAT DOSE WAS ENOUGH TO PARALYZE AN ELEPHANT FOR DAYS.

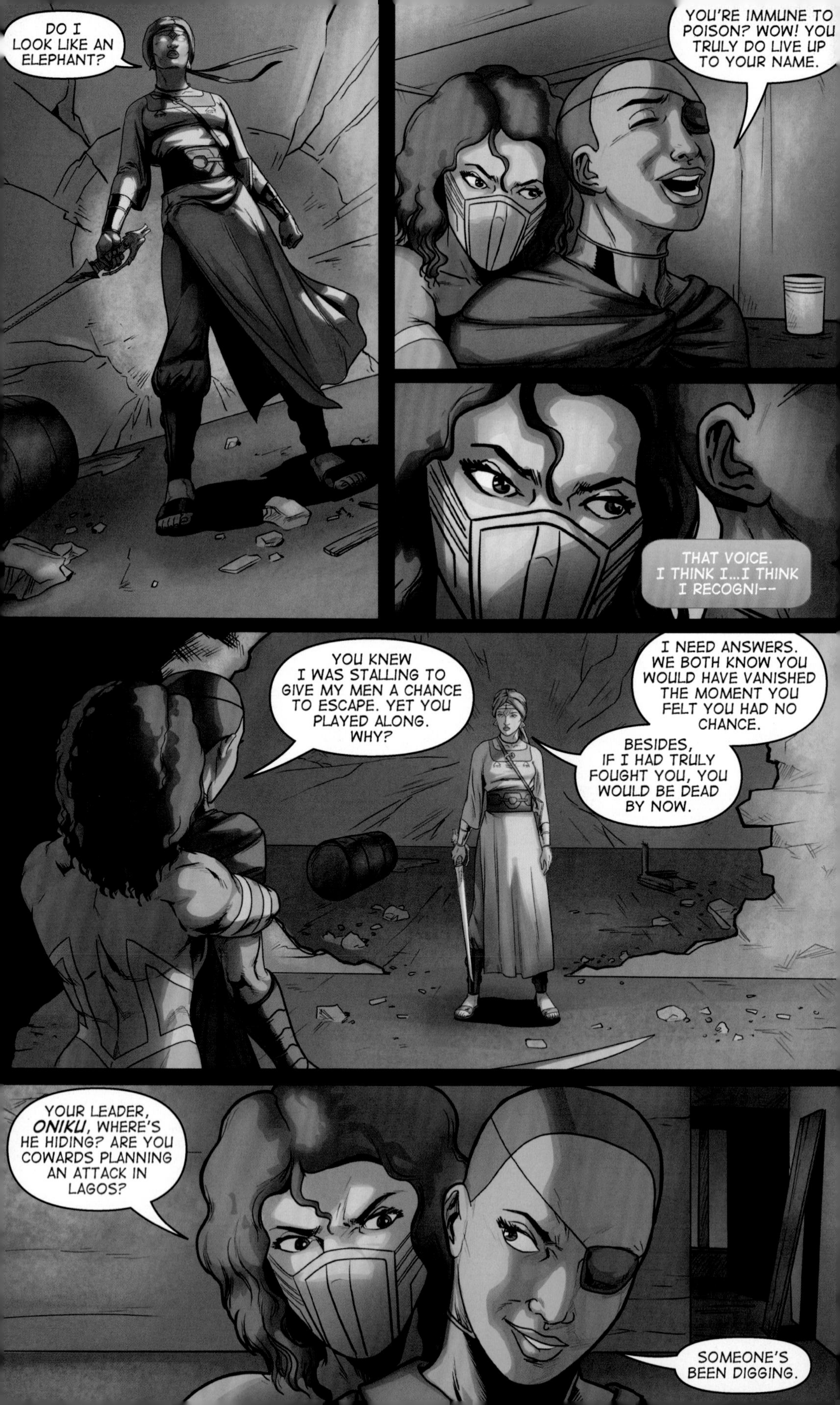
DO I LOOK LIKE AN ELEPHANT?
YOU'RE IMMUNE TO POISON? WOW! YOU TRULY DO LIVE UP TO YOUR NAME.
THAT VOICE. I THINK I...I THINK I RECOGNI--
YOU KNEW I WAS STALLING TO GIVE MY MEN A CHANCE TO ESCAPE. YET YOU PLAYED ALONG. WHY?
I NEED ANSWERS. WE BOTH KNOW YOU WOULD HAVE VANISHED THE MOMENT YOU FELT YOU HAD NO CHANCE.
BESIDES, IF I HAD TRULY FOUGHT YOU, YOU WOULD BE DEAD BY NOW.
YOUR LEADER, ONIKU, WHERE'S HE HIDING? ARE YOU COWARDS PLANNING AN ATTACK IN LAGOS?
SOMEONE'S BEEN DIGGING.

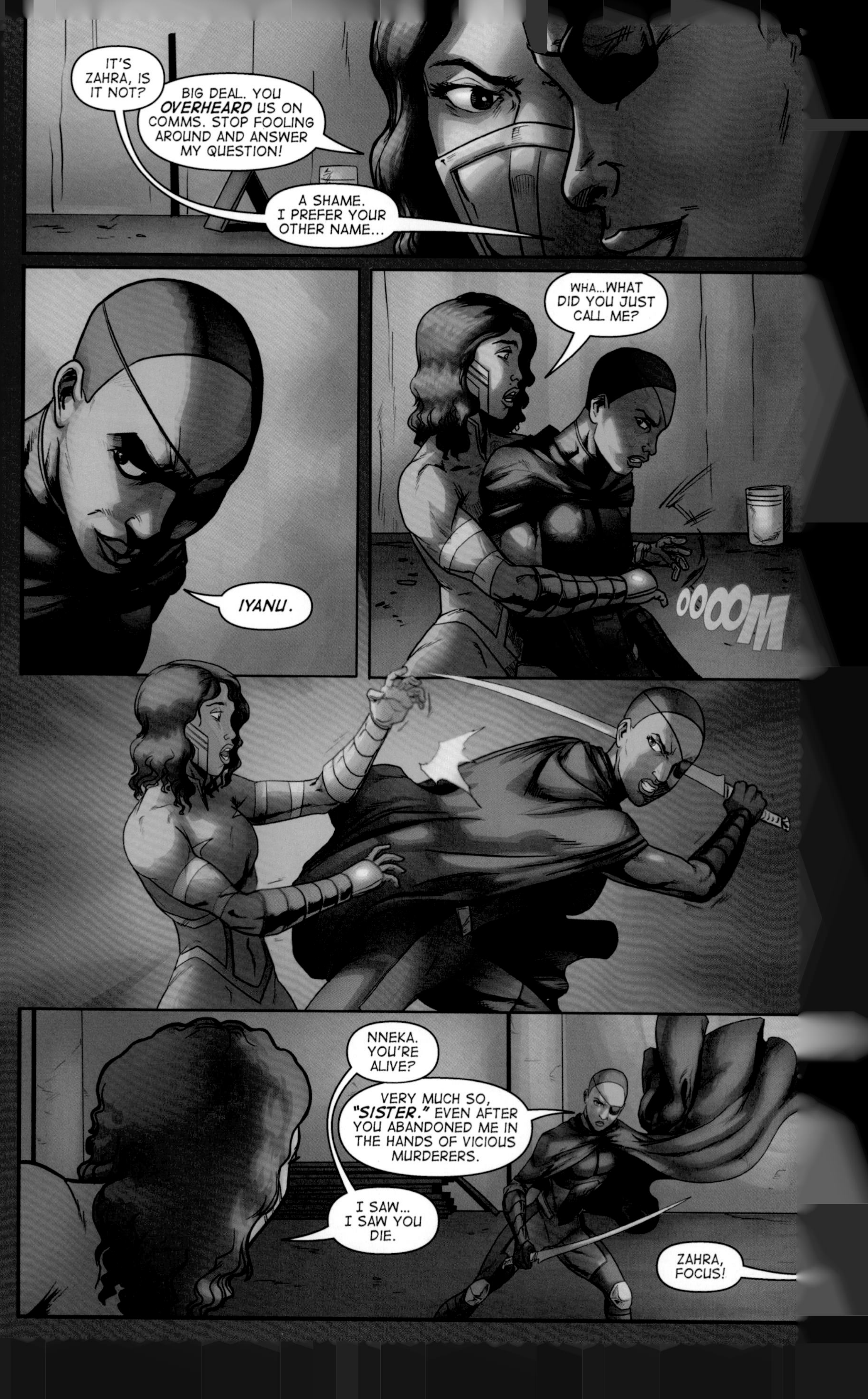
IT'S ZAHRA, IS IT NOT?
BIG DEAL. YOU OVERHEARD US ON COMMS. STOP FOOLING AROUND AND ANSWER MY QUESTION!
A SHAME. I PREFER YOUR OTHER NAME...
IYANU.
WHA...WHAT DID YOU JUST CALL ME?
OOOOM
NNEKA. YOU'RE ALIVE?
VERY MUCH SO, "SISTER." EVEN AFTER YOU ABANDONED ME IN THE HANDS OF VICIOUS MURDERERS.
I SAW... I SAW YOU DIE.
ZAHRA, FOCUS!

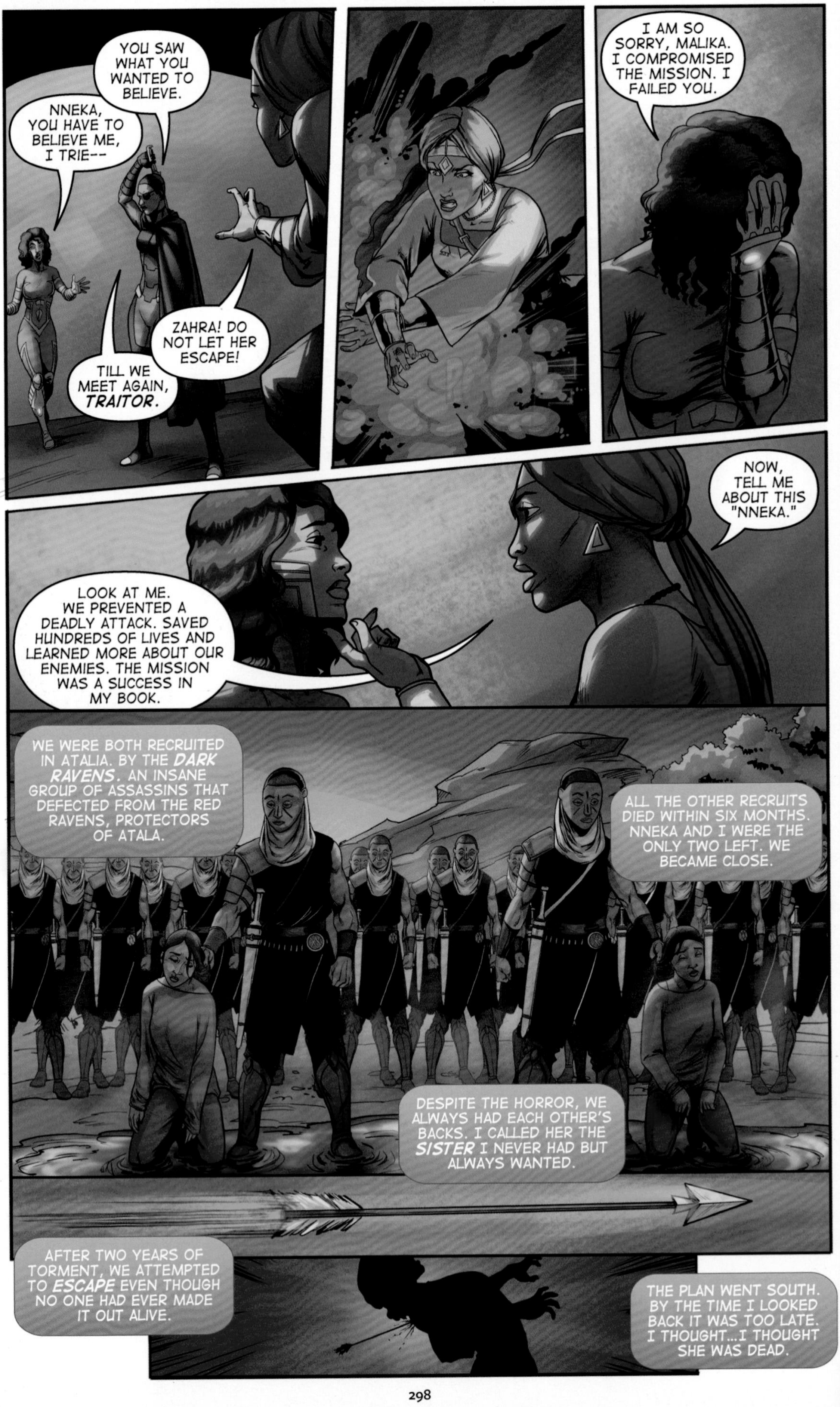
NNEKA, YOU HAVE TO BELIEVE ME, I TRIE--
YOU SAW WHAT YOU WANTED TO BELIEVE.
ZAHRA! DO NOT LET HER ESCAPE!
TILL WE MEET AGAIN, TRAITOR.
I AM SO SORRY, MALIKA. I COMPROMISED THE MISSION. I FAILED YOU.
LOOK AT ME. WE PREVENTED A DEADLY ATTACK. SAVED HUNDREDS OF LIVES AND LEARNED MORE ABOUT OUR ENEMIES. THE MISSION WAS A SUCCESS IN MY BOOK.
NOW, TELL ME ABOUT THIS "NNEKA."
WE WERE BOTH RECRUITED IN ATALIA. BY THE DARK RAVENS. AN INSANE GROUP OF ASSASSINS THAT DEFECTED FROM THE RED RAVENS, PROTECTORS OF ATALA.
ALL THE OTHER RECRUITS DIED WITHIN SIX MONTHS. NNEKA AND I WERE THE ONLY TWO LEFT. WE BECAME CLOSE.
DESPITE THE HORROR, WE ALWAYS HAD EACH OTHER'S BACKS. I CALLED HER THE SISTER I NEVER HAD BUT ALWAYS WANTED.
AFTER TWO YEARS OF TORMENT, WE ATTEMPTED TO ESCAPE EVEN THOUGH NO ONE HAD EVER MADE IT OUT ALIVE.
THE PLAN WENT SOUTH. BY THE TIME I LOOKED BACK IT WAS TOO LATE. I THOUGHT...I THOUGHT SHE WAS DEAD.

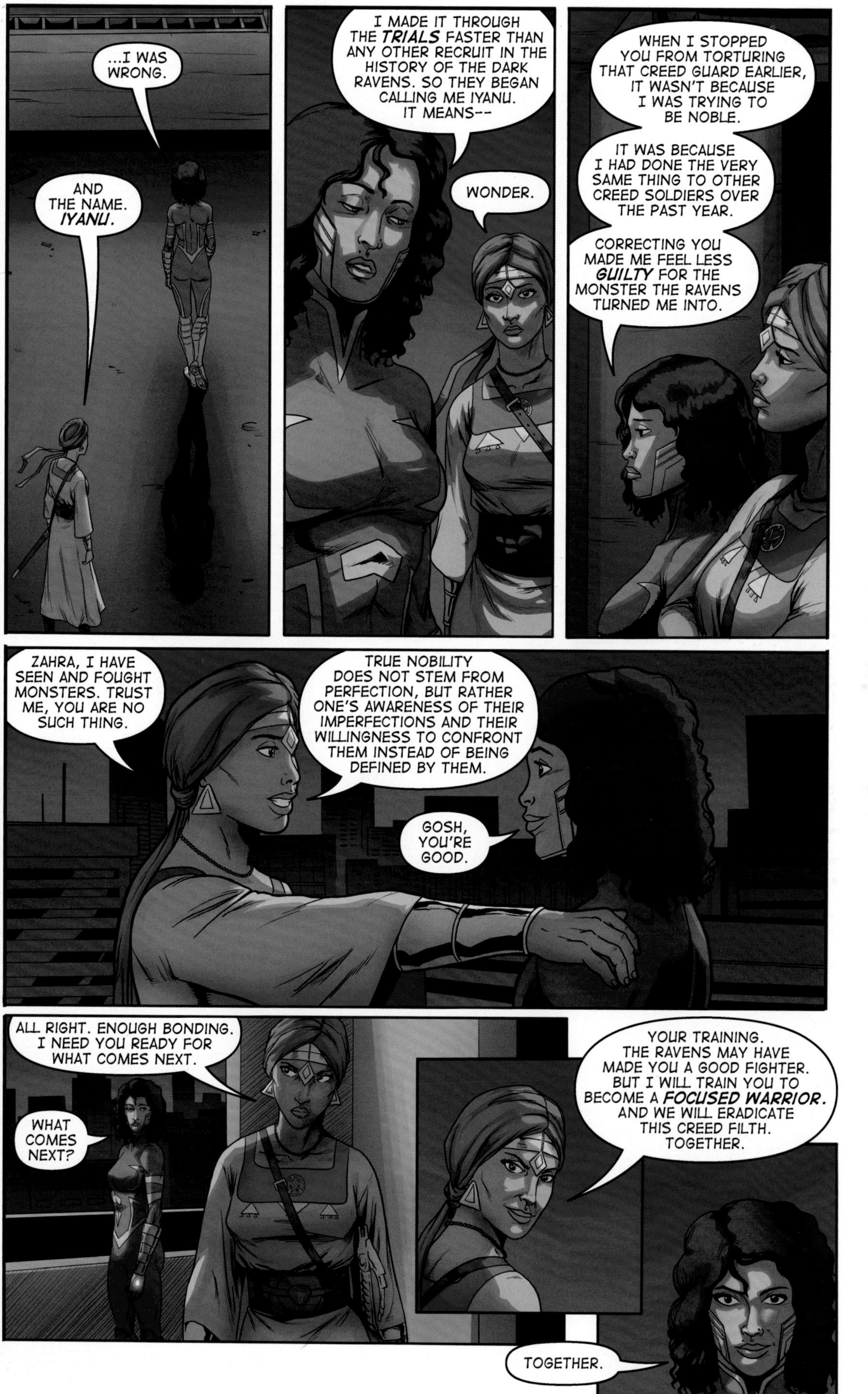
...I WAS WRONG.
AND THE NAME. *IYANU.*
I MADE IT THROUGH THE *TRIALS* FASTER THAN ANY OTHER RECRUIT IN THE HISTORY OF THE DARK RAVENS. SO THEY BEGAN CALLING ME IYANU. IT MEANS--
WONDER.
WHEN I STOPPED YOU FROM TORTURING THAT CREED GUARD EARLIER, IT WASN'T BECAUSE I WAS TRYING TO BE NOBLE.
IT WAS BECAUSE I HAD DONE THE VERY SAME THING TO OTHER CREED SOLDIERS OVER THE PAST YEAR.
CORRECTING YOU MADE ME FEEL LESS *GUILTY* FOR THE MONSTER THE RAVENS TURNED ME INTO.
ZAHRA, I HAVE SEEN AND FOUGHT MONSTERS. TRUST ME, YOU ARE NO SUCH THING.
TRUE NOBILITY DOES NOT STEM FROM PERFECTION, BUT RATHER ONE'S AWARENESS OF THEIR IMPERFECTIONS AND THEIR WILLINGNESS TO CONFRONT THEM INSTEAD OF BEING DEFINED BY THEM.
GOSH, YOU'RE GOOD.
ALL RIGHT. ENOUGH BONDING. I NEED YOU READY FOR WHAT COMES NEXT.
WHAT COMES NEXT?
YOUR TRAINING. THE RAVENS MAY HAVE MADE YOU A GOOD FIGHTER. BUT I WILL TRAIN YOU TO BECOME A *FOCUSED WARRIOR.* AND WE WILL ERADICATE THIS CREED FILTH. TOGETHER.
TOGETHER.

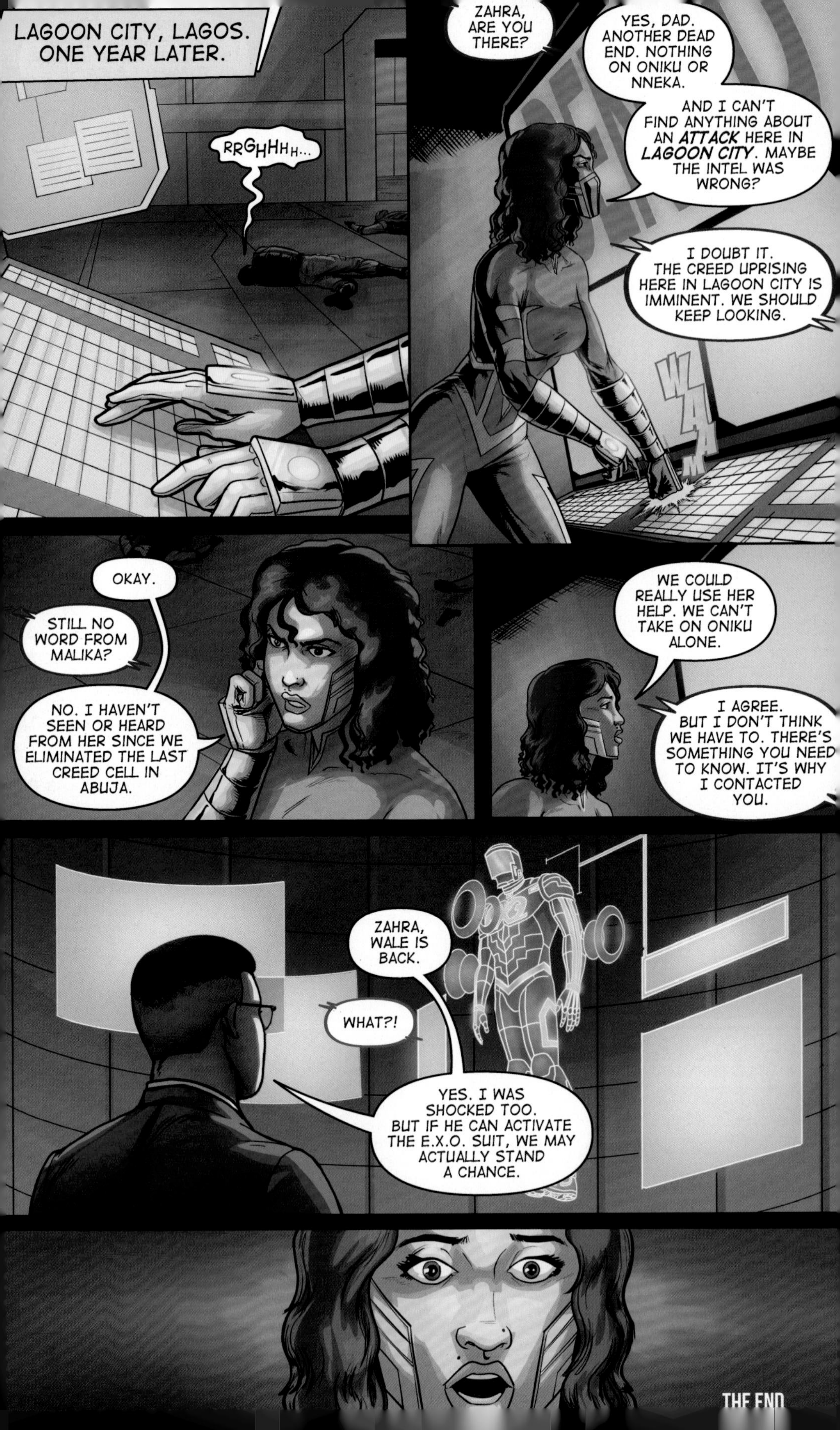
LAGOON CITY, LAGOS. ONE YEAR LATER.
RRGHHHH...
ZAHRA, ARE YOU THERE?
YES, DAD. ANOTHER DEAD END. NOTHING ON ONIKU OR NNEKA.
AND I CAN'T FIND ANYTHING ABOUT AN ATTACK HERE IN LAGOON CITY. MAYBE THE INTEL WAS WRONG?
I DOUBT IT. THE CREED UPRISING HERE IN LAGOON CITY IS IMMINENT. WE SHOULD KEEP LOOKING.
WAAM
OKAY.
STILL NO WORD FROM MALIKA?
NO. I HAVEN'T SEEN OR HEARD FROM HER SINCE WE ELIMINATED THE LAST CREED CELL IN ABUJA.
WE COULD REALLY USE HER HELP. WE CAN'T TAKE ON ONIKU ALONE.
I AGREE. BUT I DON'T THINK WE HAVE TO. THERE'S SOMETHING YOU NEED TO KNOW. IT'S WHY I CONTACTED YOU.
ZAHRA, WALE IS BACK.
WHAT?!
YES. I WAS SHOCKED TOO. BUT IF HE CAN ACTIVATE THE E.X.O. SUIT, WE MAY ACTUALLY STAND A CHANCE.
THE END

YouNeek YouNiverse Q&A with Creator Roye Okupe

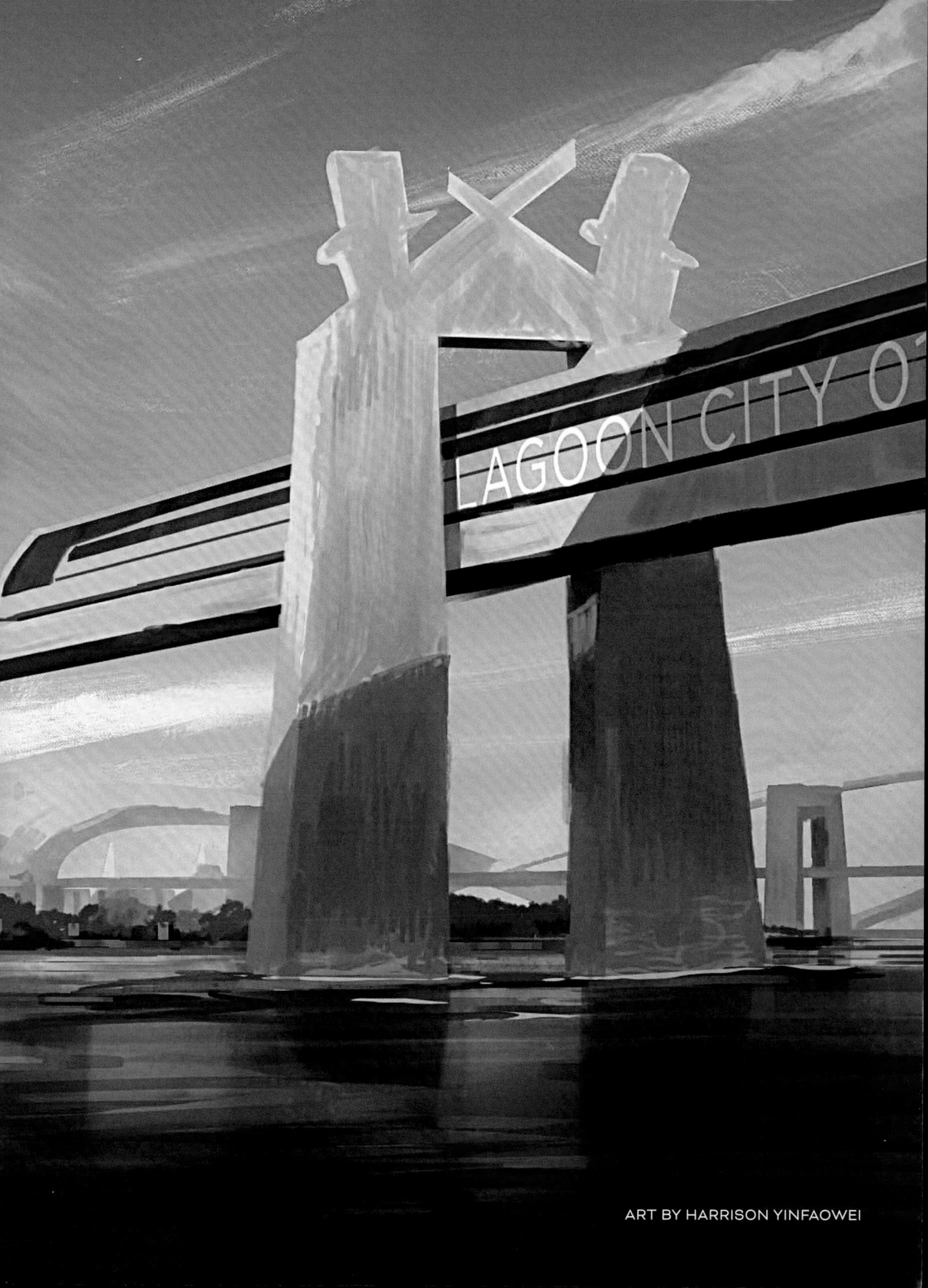
LAGOON CITY O

ART BY HARRISON YINFAOWEI

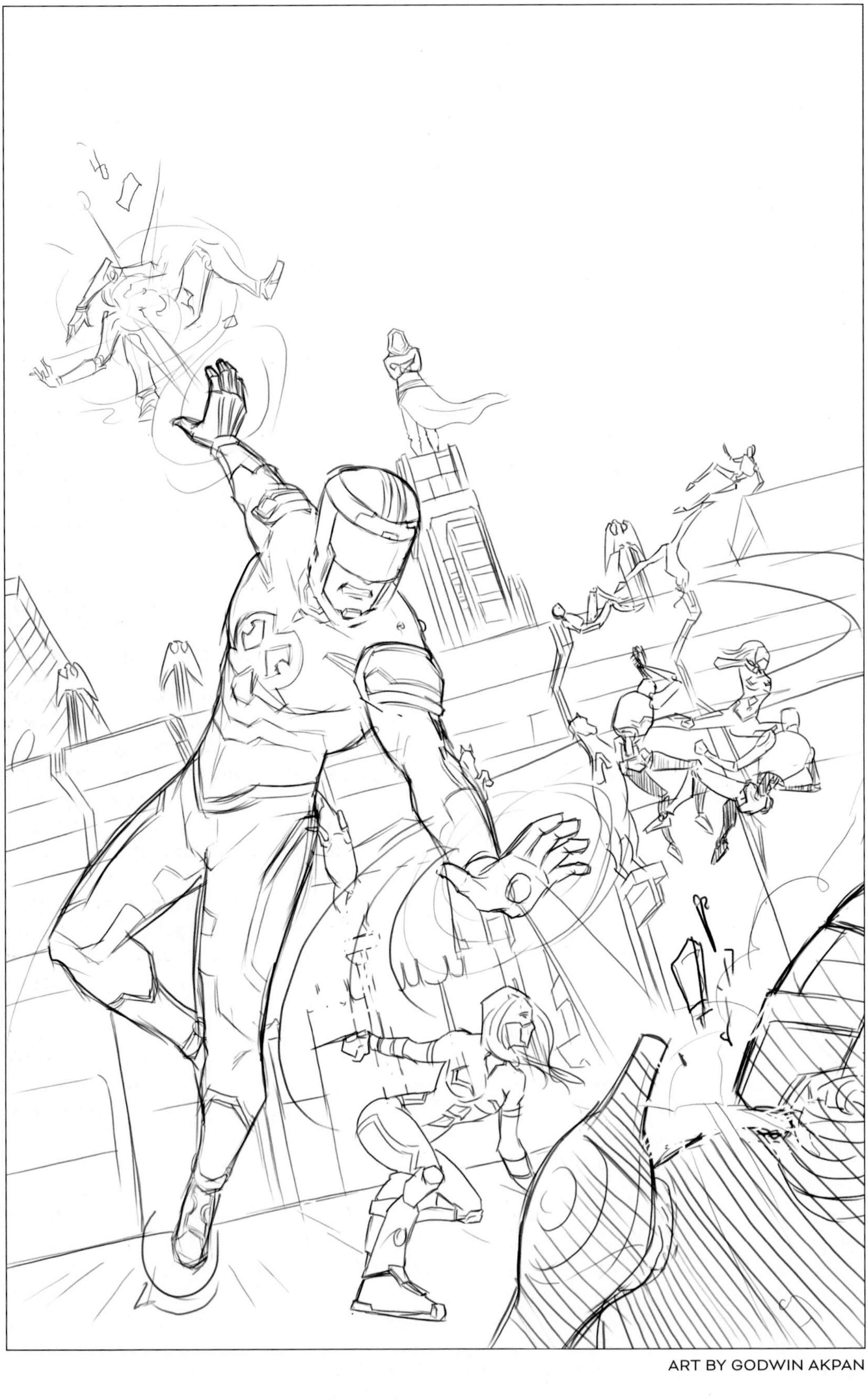

ART BY GODWIN AKPAN

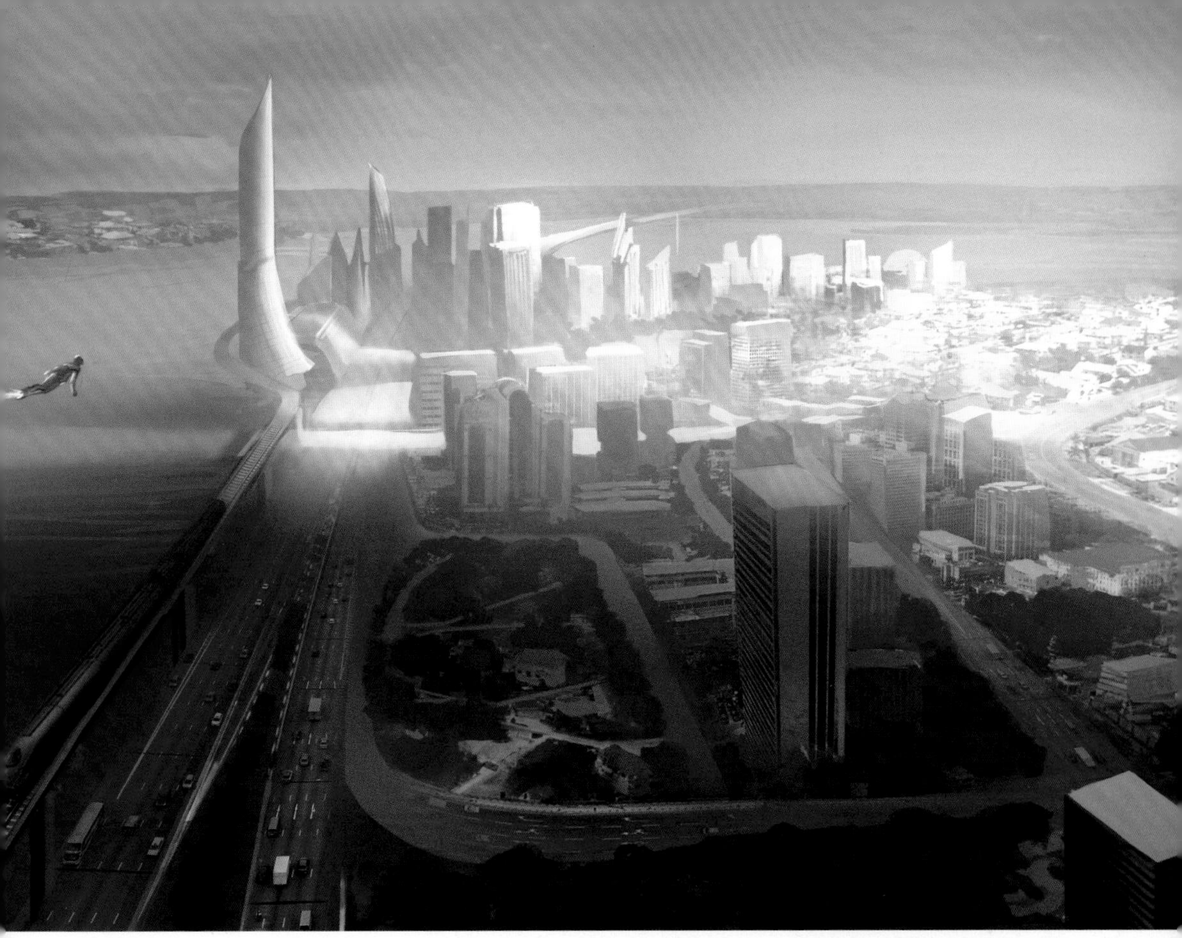

CITYSCAPE BY GODWIN AKPAN

Question: What was the inspiration behind creating the *E.X.O.* series?

As someone who was born and raised in Lagos, Nigeria, I always dreamt of putting my culture on display for a global audience. And what better way to do that than through an epic, sci-fi superhero tale!

Why set this story in Lagos, Nigeria? And why did you settle on the fictional name "Lagoon City" for the setting?

As of this writing, Lagos is the most populous city in Nigeria and the second-largest city in Africa, making it an amalgamation of many diverse cultures from all over the country and, at least in my opinion, one of the most exciting metropolises in the entire world. Architecture, food, fashion, nightlife, and culture are just a few of the amazing things that leave you in awe when you visit this beautiful city. And I am so proud that we were able to capture a decent amount of that spectacle in this volume.

As to the thinking behind the fictional name "Lagoon City," I wanted a term to describe the city as a whole. Like New York, the name Lagos can be used interchangeably for city and state. But unlike the term "New York City," you rarely hear people refer to the city of Lagos as "Lagos City." So, I decided to use the Lagos Lagoon—a body of water that touches most of the islands and the mainland that constitutes the city of Lagos—as a prefix. Hence the fictional term, Lagoon City. However, while the name "Lagoon City" is fictitious, the city's geography, look, and feel (ignoring my made-up districts and some other minor alterations) pays proper homage to the real Lagos.

You've spoken extensively about the difference between "E.X.O." and "EXO." Can you expand a bit on your reasoning behind using both?

Yes, so as I've explained, the term "E.X.O." which stands for Endogenic Xoskeletal Ordnance, is the suit our hero, Wale, wears. In contrast, the term "EXO" is the moniker the public gives Wale as their hero. The goal was to have something that simultaneously separated the two (hero and suit) and anchored them together, thereby highlighting their symbiotic relationship.

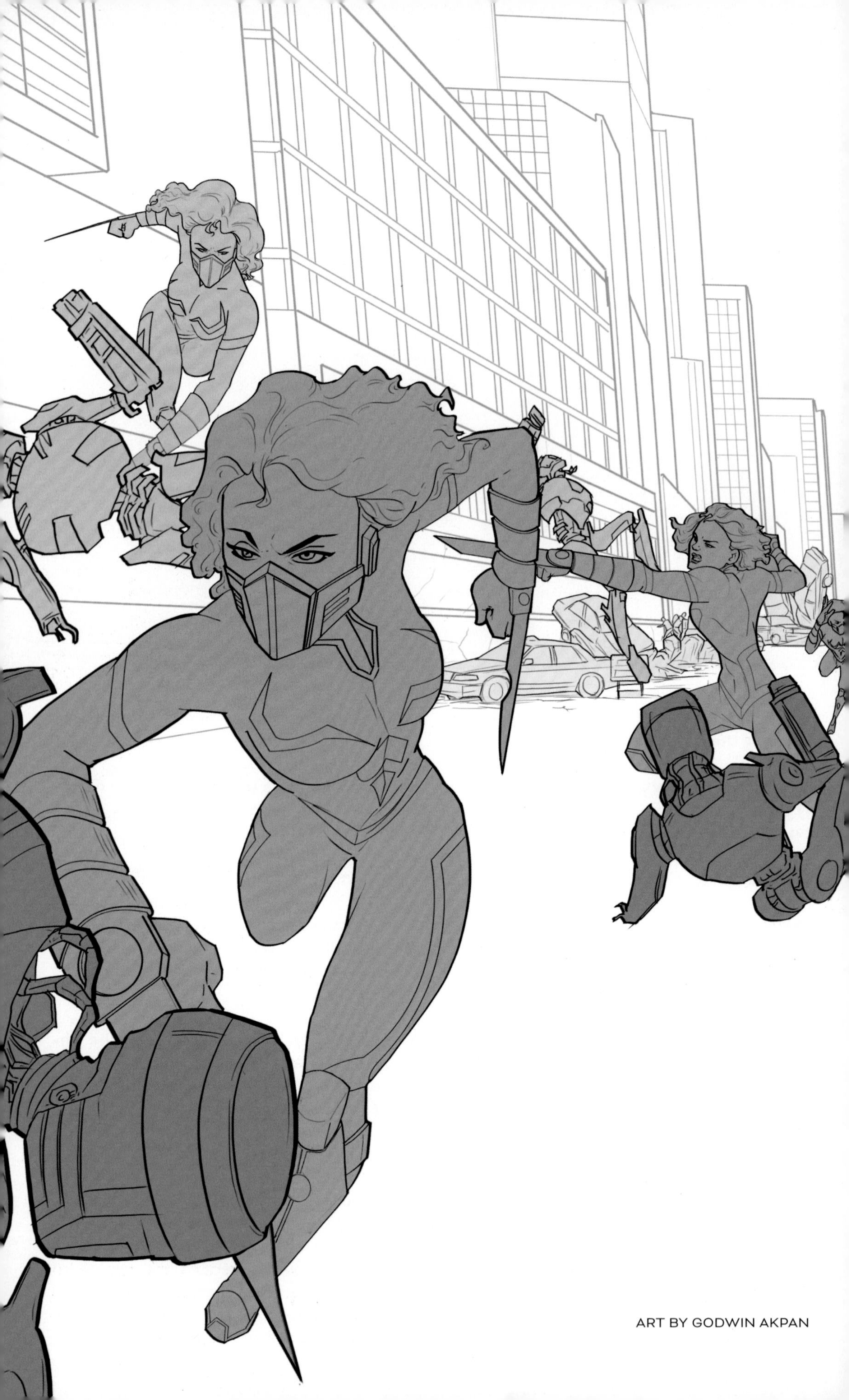

ART BY GODWIN AKPAN

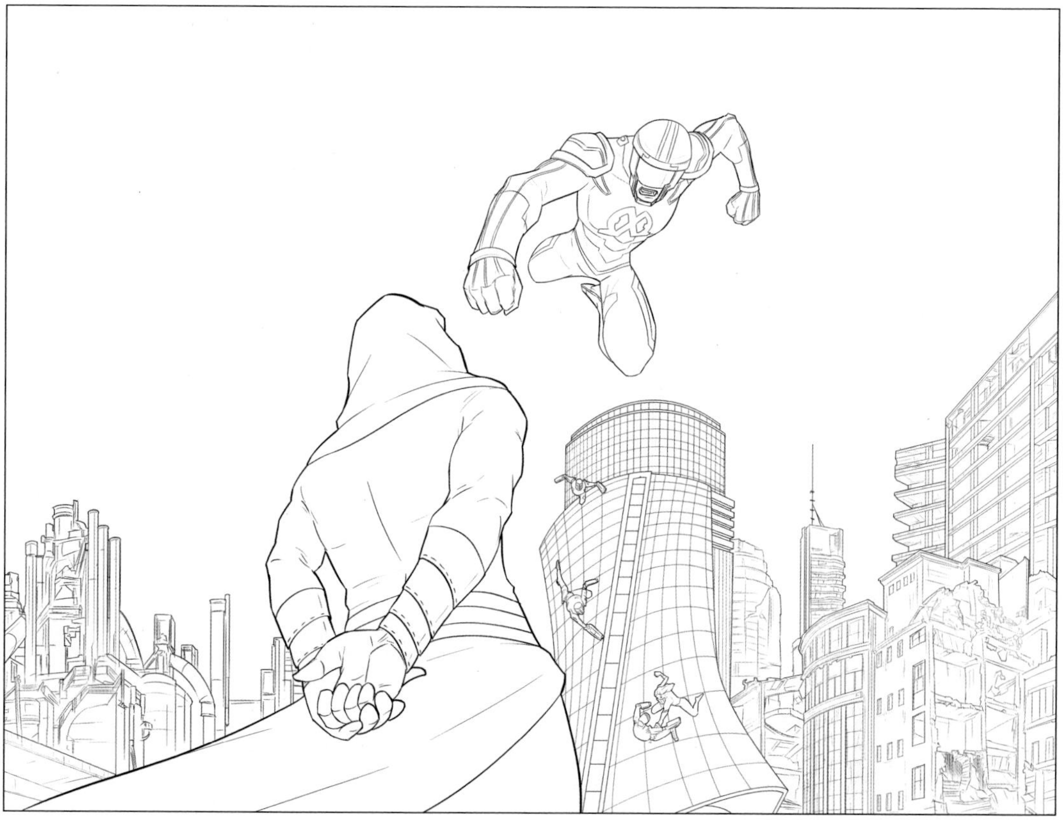

ABOVE: ART BY GODWIN AKPAN
BELOW: ZAHRA HEAD SHOTS BY SUNKANMI AKINBOYE

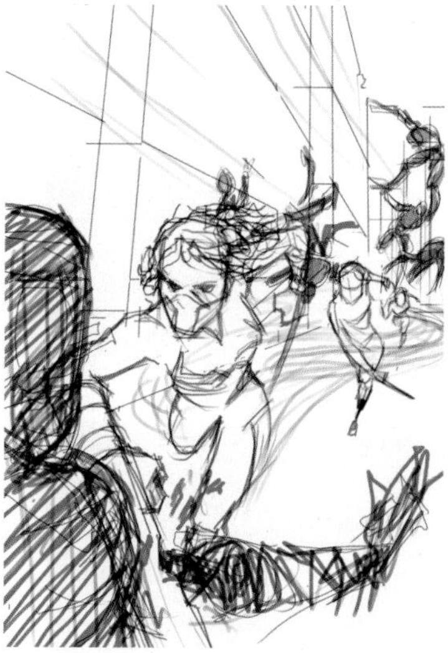

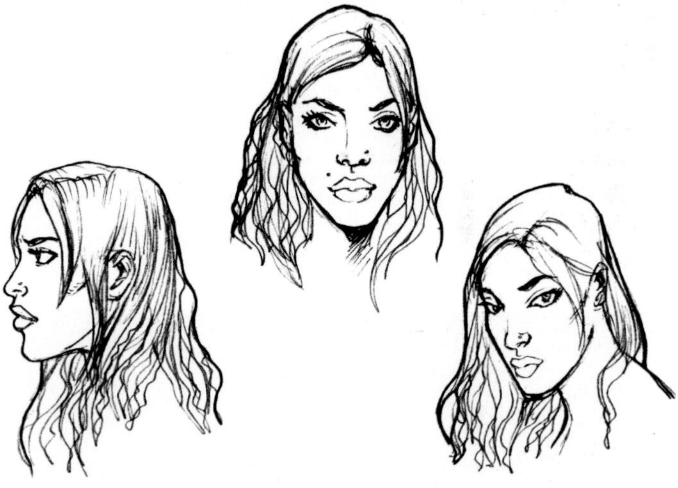

Can you tell us a little bit more about Zahra, AKA Fury, and your reasoning behind creating her as a character?

All my life, I've been surrounded by strong Black women, from my mom to my two older sisters and now my wife. So, for me, it was a no-brainer when I decided to write *E.X.O.* to include a female superhero. And not merely as a sidekick or romantic interest, but someone who had their own arc, backstory, and unique motivations, as well as strengths and weaknesses.

Zahra is someone who steals the scene every single time she appears in a panel, and I absolutely love it. In fact, ever since I released the first *E.X.O.* volume, she is the one character that fans and readers consistently clamor to see in her own book. To me, all that this means is that I've succeeded with what I set out to do with the character in the first place. I can't wait till you guys see more of Zahra as the YouNiverse progresses.

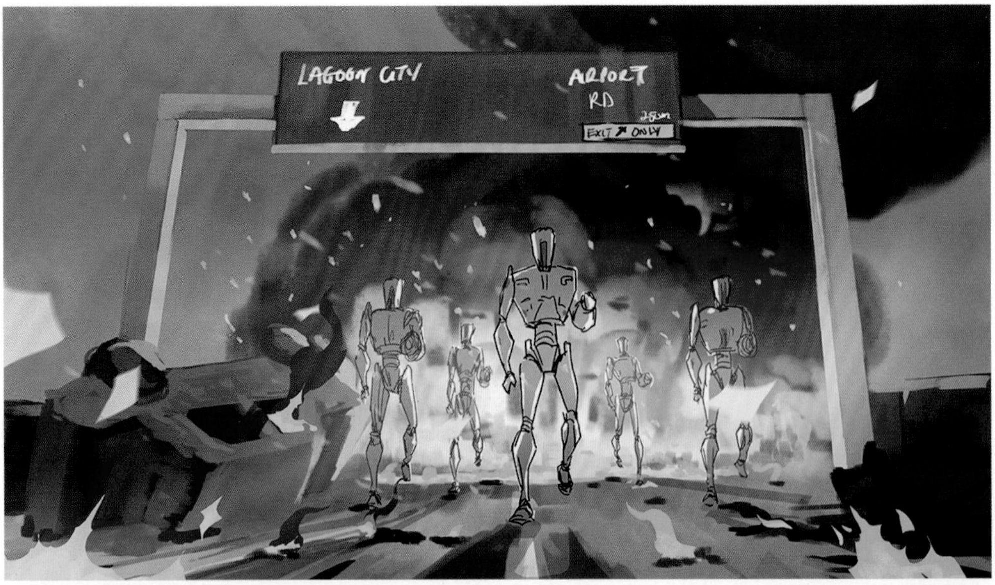
LAGOON CITY
AIRPORT
RD
EXIT ONLY

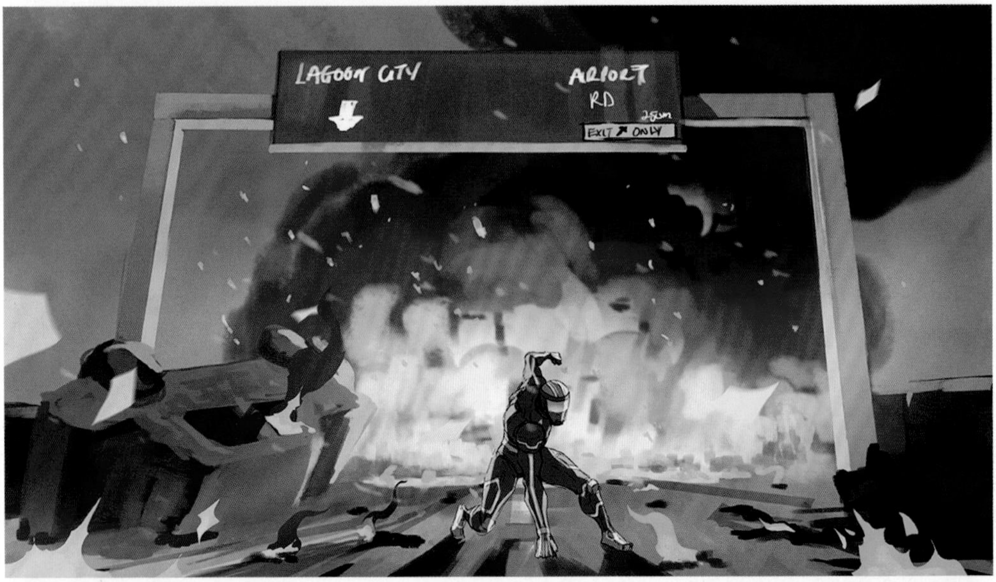
LAGOON CITY
AIRPORT
RD
EXIT ONLY

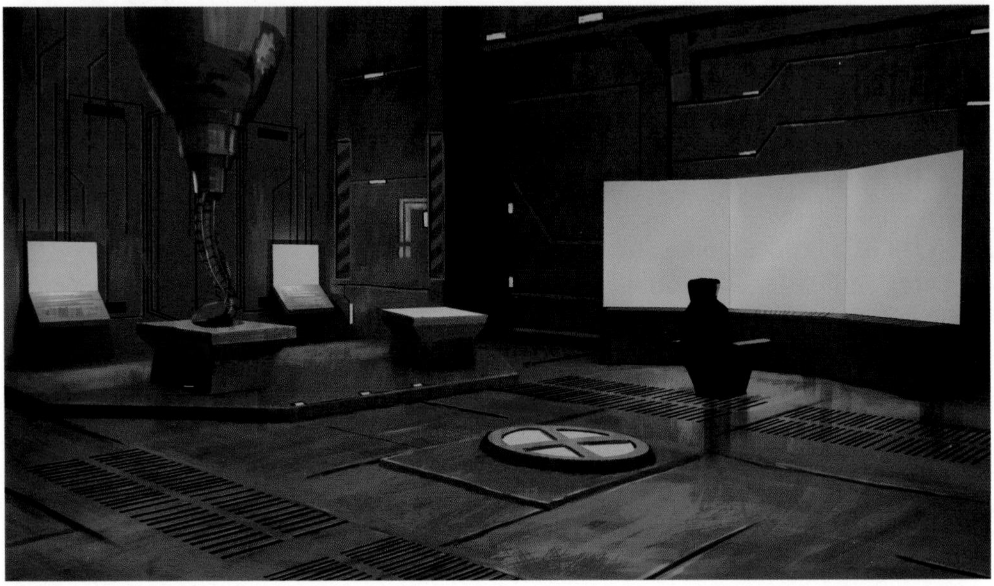

THIS PAGE AND FACING PAGE: IMAGES BY HARRISON YINFAOWEI

What is the most important thing you would like people to take away from after reading this first volume?

The importance of forgiveness. I sometimes think that we as human beings forget how much of a weight unforgiveness can be in our lives, how it can hamper our growth and prevent us from becoming the best versions of ourselves. This is especially true when the party we harbor unforgiveness towards is a close family member, which is essentially what Wale struggles with throughout his journey to become the hero he was always meant to be in *E.X.O.* Volume 1. It is not until Wale forgives his father that he can truly become EXO and save the entire Lagoon City from the menacing Oniku. Without the weight of unforgiveness, Wale is able to channel all the internal power within to defeat his external foe.

Now don't get me wrong, I'm not here to say that forgiveness is easy. Sometimes it can be very difficult and painful, as I've experienced in my own life. However, it doesn't take away from the fact that it is necessary.

How does the *E.X.O.* series fit into the overall YouNeek YouNiverse?

I can't wait for you to find out yourself when you read the rest of the books in the YouNiverse!

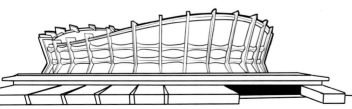

LINE ART BY SUNKANMI AKINBOYE

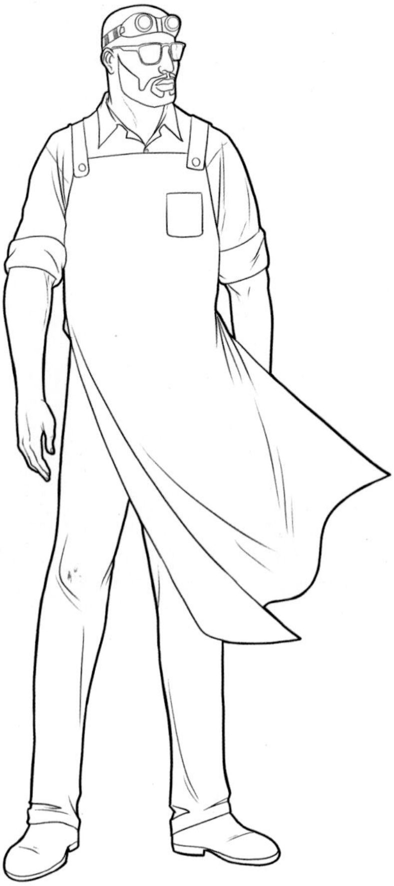

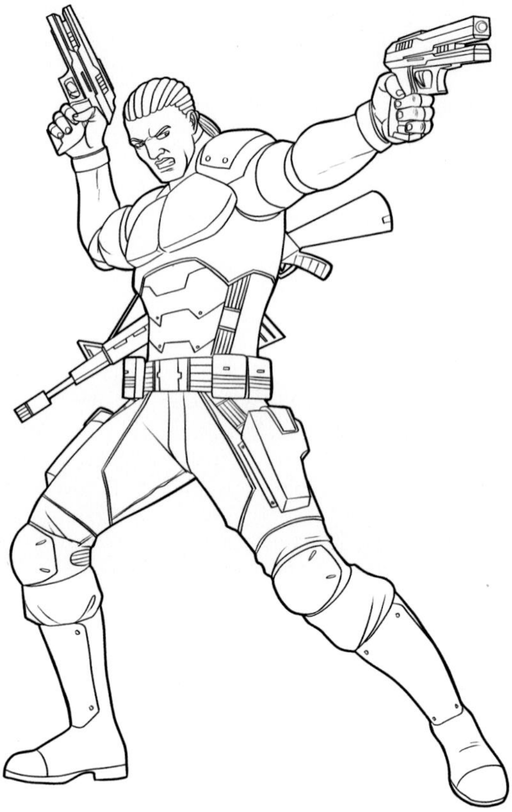

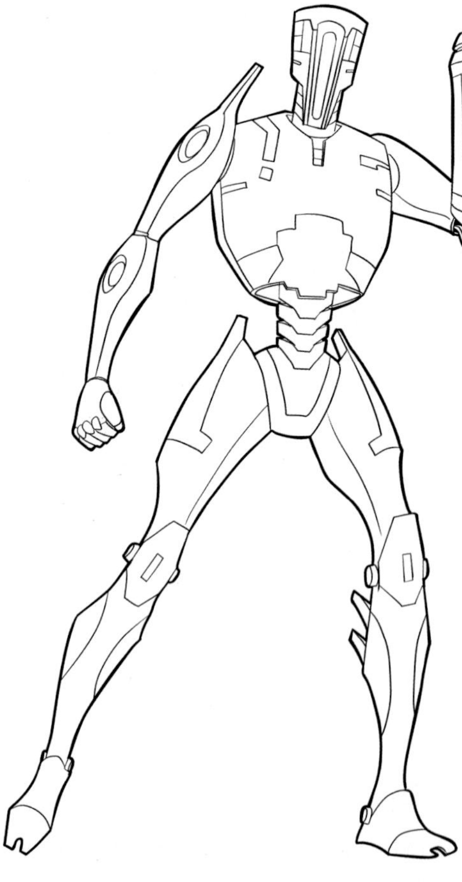

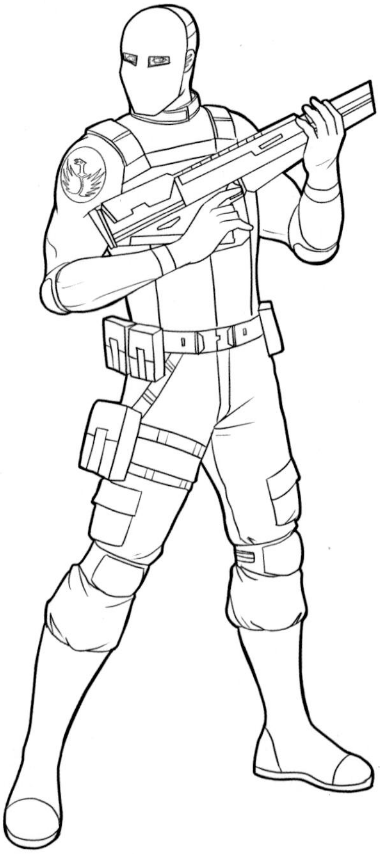

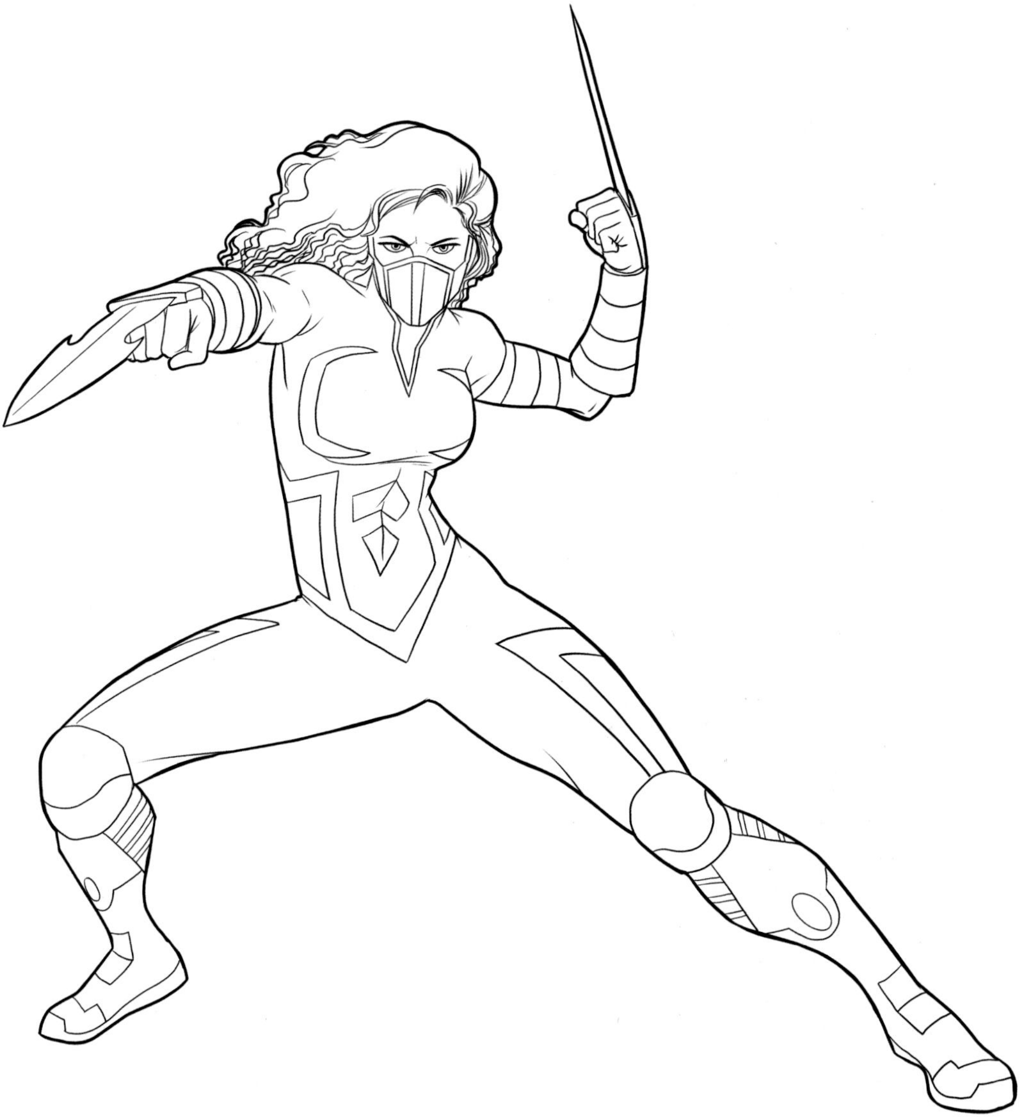

CHARACTER ART BY SUNKANMI AKINBOYE

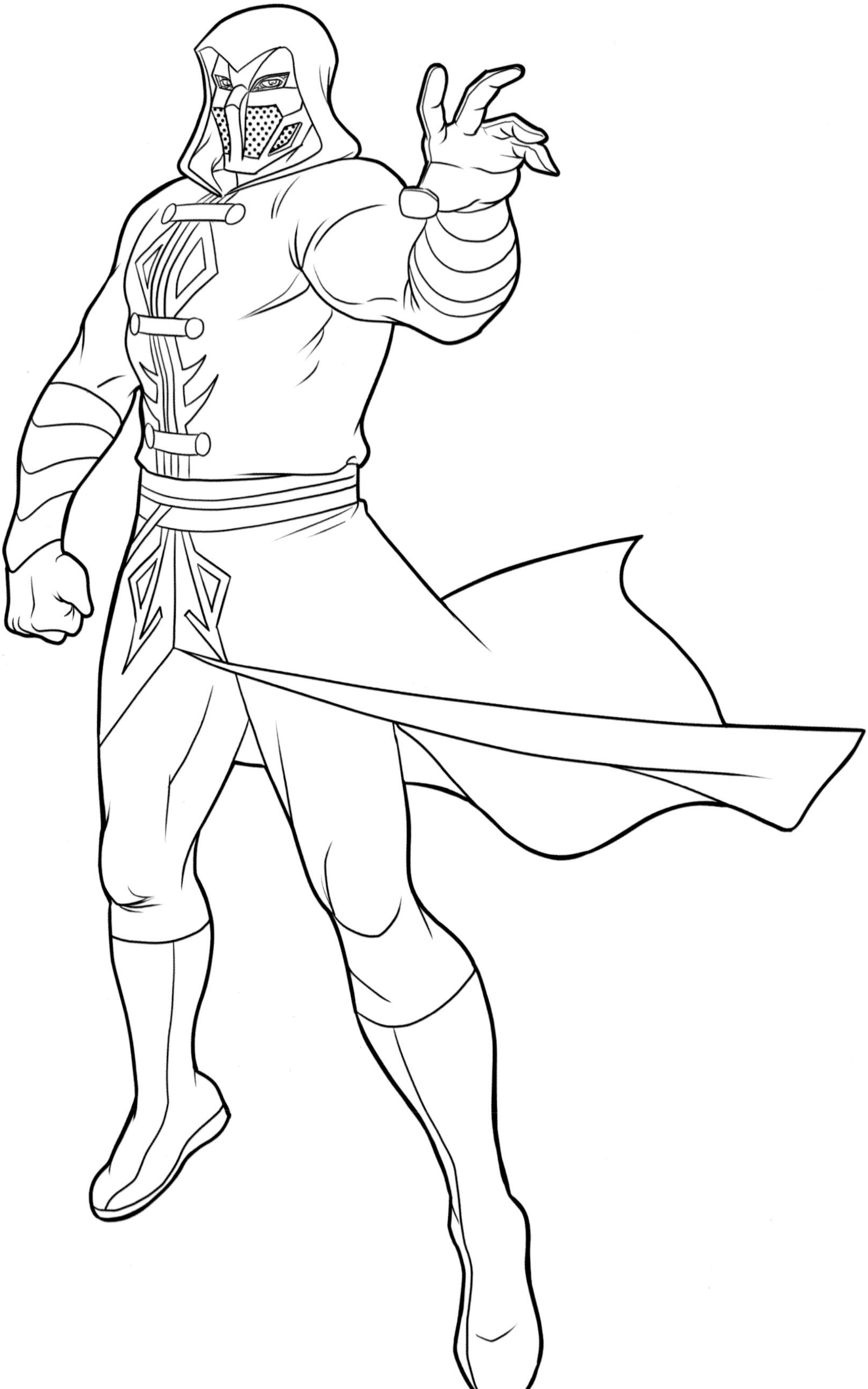

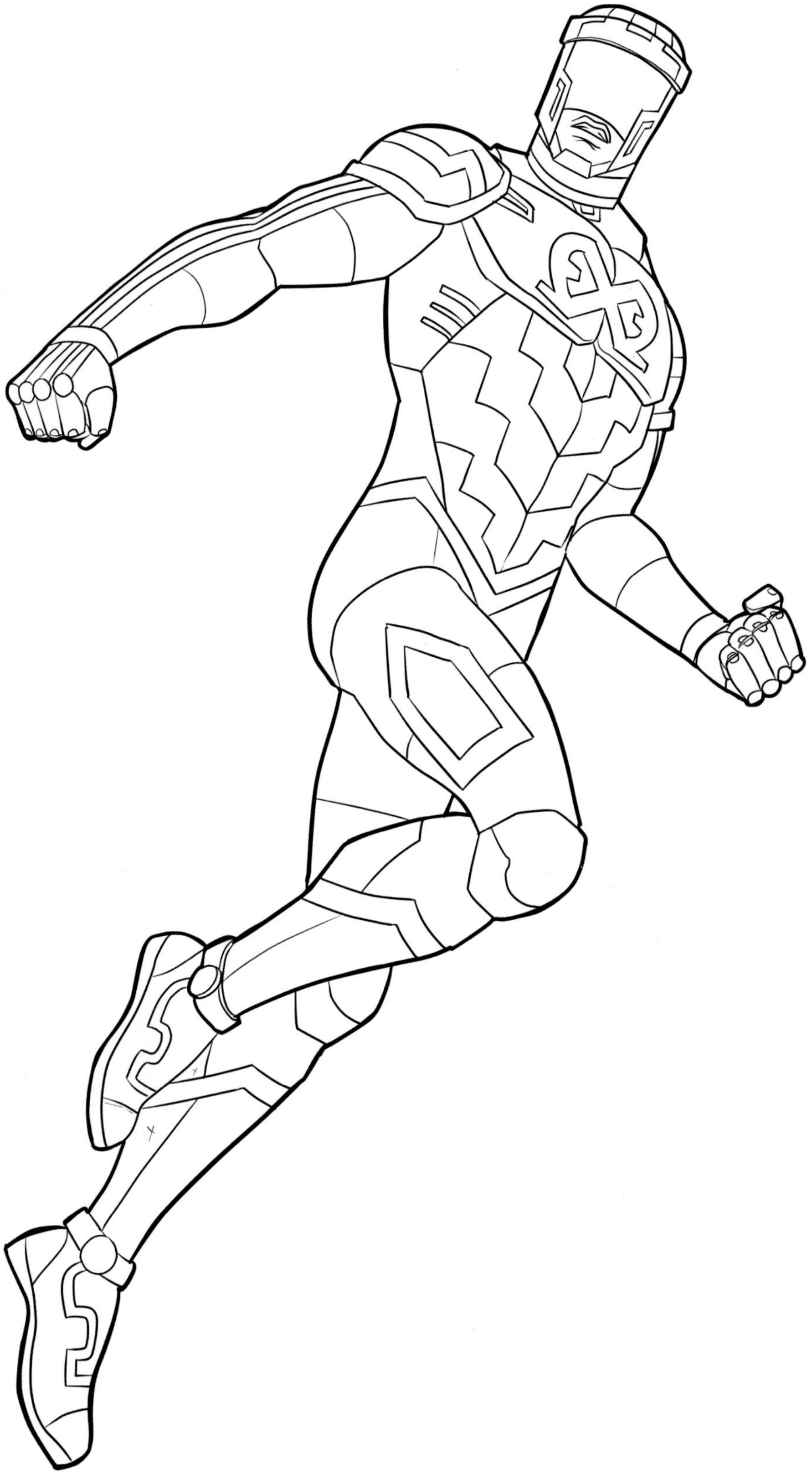

ONIKU AND EXO CHARACTER ART BY SUNKANMI AKINBOYE

MALIKA
Warrior Queen
VOLUME ONE
ROYE OKUPE
WITH
CHIMA KALU
AND
RAPHAEL KAZEEM

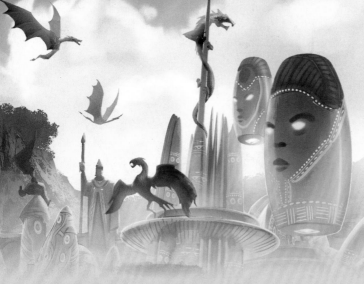

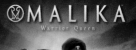

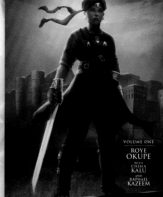

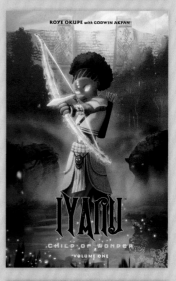

Dark Horse Books and YouNeek Studios are proud to present a shared universe of fantasy and superhero stories inspired by African history, culture, and mythology—created by the best Nigerian comics talent!

ROYE OKUPE with GODWIN AKPAN
IYANU
CHILD OF WONDER
VOLUME ONE

Malika: Warrior Queen Volume 1

(pronounced: "Ma-Lie-Kah")
Written by Roye Okupe.
Illustrated by Chima Kalu.
Colors by Raphael Kazeem.
Letters by Spoof Animation.

Begins the tale of the exploits of queen and military commander Malika, who struggles to keep the peace in her ever-expanding empire, Azzaz.

Sept. 2021 Trade Paperback 336 Pages
$24.99 US $33.99 CA • 9781506723082

Malika: Warrior Queen Volume 2

Written by Roye Okupe.
Illustrated by Sunkanmi Akinboye.
Colors by Etubi Onucheyo and Toyin Ajetunmobi.
Letters by Spoof Animation.

Dec. 2021 Trade Paperback 280 Pages
$24.99 US $33.99 CA • 9781506723075

Iyanu: Child of Wonder Volume 1

(pronounced: "Ee-Yah-Nu")
Written by Roye Okupe.
Illustrated by Godwin Akpan.
Letters by Spoof Animation.

A teenage orphan with no recollection of her past discovers that she has abilities that rival the ancient deities told of in folklore. These abilities are the key to bringing back an "age of wonders," to save a world on the brink of destruction!

Sept. 2021 Trade Paperback 120 Pages
$19.99 US $25.99 CA • 9781506723044

WindMaker Volume 1

Written by Roye Okupe.
Illustrated by Sunkanmi Akinboye and Toyin Ajetunmobi.
Letters by Spoof Animation.

The West African nation of Atala is thrust into an era of unrest and dysfunction after their beloved president turns vicious dictator.

April 2022 Trade Paperback 144 Pages
$19.99 US $25.99 CA • 9781506723112

E.X.O.: The Legend of Wale Williams Volume 1

Written by Roye Okupe.
Illustrated by Sunkanmi Akinboye.
Colors by Raphael Kazeem.
Letters by Spoof Animation.

The oldest son of a world-renowned scientist, Wale Williams—aka tech-savvy superhero EXO—tries to save Lagoon City from a deadly group of extremists. But before this "pending" superhero can do any good for his city, there is one person he must save first—himself!

Oct. 2021 Trade Paperback 280 Pages
$24.99 US $33.99 CA • 9781506723020

E.X.O.: The Legend of Wale Williams Volume 2

Written by Roye Okupe.
Illustrated by Sunkanmi Akinboye.
Colors by Etubi Onucheyo and Tarella Pablo.
Letters by Spoof Animation.

Feb. 2022 Trade Paperback 280 Pages
$24.99 US $33.99 CA • 9781506723037

E.X.O.
THE LEGEND OF WALE WILLIAMS
VOLUME ONE
ROYE OKUPE • SUNKANMI AKINBOYE • RAPHAEL KAZEEM

DARK HORSE BOOKS

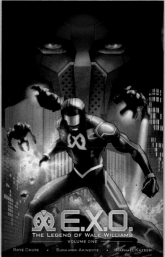

YOUNEEK STUDIOS

DarkHorse.com

Press Inquiries:
pr@darkhorse.com

Sales Inquiries:
tradesales@darkhorse.com